off.
white

Readings on Power, Privilege, and Resistance
Second Edition

Michelle Fine, Lois Weis, Linda Powell Pruitt, April Burns

ROUTLEDGE
NEW YORK AND LONDON

Routledge
New York and London
Published in 2004 by
Routledge
270 Madison Avenue
New York, New York 10016
www.routledge-ny.com

Published in Great Britain by
Routledge
2 Park Square
Milton Park, Abingdon
Oxon OX14 4RN U.K.
www.routledge.co.uk

10 9 8 7 6 5 4 3 2 1

Off white : readings on power, privilege, and resistance / Michelle Fine ... [et al.],
editiors. — 2nd ed.
        p.   cm.
   Includes bibliographical references.
   ISBN 0-415-94964-5 (alk. paper) — ISBN 0-415-94965-3 (pbk. : alk. paper)
  1. Whites — Race identity — United States. 2. Racism — United States. 3. Social classes —
United States. 4. United States — Race relations. 5. Race awareness — United States.
6. Discrimination in education — United States. 7. Education — Social aspects — United States.
I. Fine, Michelle.
   E184.A1O338 2004
   305.8'00973 — dc22
                                                           2004004889

Contents

Preface

Michelle Fine, Lois Weis, Linda Powell Pruitt, and April Burns

High in the tower, where I sit above the loud complaining of the human sea, I know many souls that toss and whirl and pass, but none that intrigue me more than the Souls of White Folk.

Of them, I am singularly clairvoyant. I see in and through them. I view them from unusual points of vantage. Not as a foreigner do I come, for I am native, not foreign, bone of their thought and flesh of their language. Mine is not the knowledge of the traveler or the colonial composite of dear memories, words and wonder. Nor yet is my knowledge that which servants have of masters, or mass of class, or capitalist of artisan. Rather I see these souls undressed and from the back and side. I see the working of their entrails. I know their thoughts, and they know I know. This knowledge makes them now embarrassed, now furious! They deny me my right to live and be and call me misbirth! My word to them mere bitterness and my soul, pessimism. And yet as they preach and strut and shout and threaten, crouching as they clutch at rags and facts and fancies to hide their nakedness, they go twisting, flying by my tired eyes and I see them every stripped — ugly, human.

—W. E. B. Du Bois

Our 1997 edition of *Off White* sought to pierce the silence Du Bois so tellingly described more than 80 years ago on the question of peering into the "souls of white folk," then an awesome and daunting task. In retrospect, it is now hard to believe that the topic managed to avoid scholarly study for so long. Although theorists and researchers as varied as Nancy Hartsock, Dorothy Smith, Judith Rollins, Patricia Hill Collins, Gloria Anzaldua, Audre Lorde, Clayton Alderfer, bell hooks, and Toni Morrison argued persuasively for research on privilege from "unusual points of vantage," few studies took up this challenge. White standpoints, privileged standpoints, were generally taken as a "benign norm" or, in some cases, the oppressive standard — either way escaping serious scrutiny.

The first edition of *Off White* cartwheeled into this protected silence, placing whiteness front and center of analysis to subject it to the kind of examination that rouses it out of unmarked space. Du Bois spoke of his "high tower" as a place of perspective, a place to stand to see beyond individuals and events to individual patterns and processes. This perspective came from the multidisciplinary and varied work of colleagues throughout and beyond the academy.

In the first edition of *Off White*, we selected our contributors primarily from the fields of psychology and education. Both fields have generated vexing and debilitating internal contradictions within race studies. Each has a long history of scholarship on topics of race, ethnicity, and racism, and each has contributed to what Sandra Harding calls the "racial ordering of society."

Psychology, the home of IQ testing, special education, multicultural studies, cross-cultural psychology, intergroup relations, and stereotyping research, has spawned studies of personality, intelligence, motivation, achievement, and other measures of "merit" and competence that have camouflaged the ever-raced biases for ordering the world. So, too, education, lauded as a site of democratic inquiry, heterogeneity, and exposure to and celebration of "difference," has become instead a foundational space within which children of differing races, ethnicities, social class, language backgrounds, and genders "learn their place" in the more broad culture. A great deal of research, particularly within the past 30 years, has shown explicitly how schools, despite intentions to the contrary, serve to sort children along social class, race, and gender lines, contributing to massive inequalities in educational and, later, health, income, housing, and criminal justice outcomes. Indeed, the school has been shown to be a primary site for such sorting, in spite of the goodwill of large numbers of teachers, administrators, and associated professionals. The preferred and acceptable frameworks and methods of psychological research have been complicit in encouraging this ordering.

Through these two fields, whiteness has come to be more than itself, embodying objectivity, normality, truth, knowledge, merit, motivation, achievement, and trustworthiness; it accumulates invisible and unrecognized supports that contribute to the already accumulated and bolstered capital of whiteness. Rarely, however, is it acknowledged that whiteness demands and constitutes hierarchy, exclusion, and deprivation. The production and maintenance of white privilege is a difficult task. The very academic frameworks and practices of education and psychology have worked hard to prop up racial hierarchies, securing the place of select groups within these hierarchies for many years now. A trenchant analysis of the "propping up" function of these fields is long overdue.

As profoundly as psychology and education are implicated in the production of whiteness, however, and its rigid emergence as norm, it is also the case that within both disciplines there is a bubbling and emergent set of scholars who have pushed beyond an analysis of categories to critically investigate the very structuring of racial hierarchies. By interweaving race and ethnicity with gender, colonialism, nation, social class, and sexuality, and by analyzing the ways in which social institutions carry and voice multiple discourses of race, these researchers have begun to unravel the ways in which race operates through and with gender, social class, and sexuality. The authors in the first volume sought to understand the ways in which race and racial hierarchies work with and through other forms of lived identity and institutional life to produce and sustain power inequities.

These scholars spent considerable energy centering the voices of those historically excluded and marginalized. Voices of those positioned at the "margins" or "on the edge" are being heard within and across all disciplines, contributing to a reformation of what constitutes "knowledge." Although we do not mean to overstate the transformative success, we do state that it is indeed the case that significant challenge has taken place in academic canons and that these challenges at least partially reflect the social movements of women and men of color as well as white women, gays, lesbians and bisexuals, persons with disabilities, and the working class and poor. The singular coherent white and male, heterosexual, and elite narrative no longer survives with comfort and security within any of our fields. Indeed, the study of whiteness tilts and exposes, not only by adding previously silenced and alienated voices but also by studying the very rules that have covertly governed the conversation.

This volume also could be described as "*Off White*, Enhanced." We organized this book into five sections, each named with active verbs, which symbolize our understanding that whiteness is created, constructed, and protected in active ways. We included a set of essays that demonstrates with specificity and explicitness how whiteness as privilege operates in the overall distribution and accumulation of global and national wealth and political power (Apple; De Jesus and Lykes; Winant), in the differential impact of federal policies (Brodkin), in the production and maintenance of advantage in fundamental social institutions such as schools (Burns; Fine; Rosenberg; Revilla, Wells, and Holme), in university life (Gilmore, Smith, and Kairaiuak; Pruitt), in housing (Low), in the law and the courts (Carney; Crosby and Blake-Beard; Guinier and Torres), at work (Weis, Proweller, and Centrie), in medicine (David), and in research methods (Duneier; Morawski; Hurtado and Stewart).

Finally, this edition of *Off White* can be distinguished from the first volume as it struggles to theorize whiteness as a representation in popular culture (Carlson; Macpherson; McCarthy et al.) and embodiment (Carter; Jones; Kimmel and Mahler; Walkerdine, Lucey, and Melody), and to complicate how the "living" of whiteness can resist, rather than simply benefit from, racialized domination. To address this latter point, we included a fully new section of essays designed to reveal the ways in which whiteness is resisted, transformed, troubled, and converted into social responsibility in international and national social movements (Guinier and Torres), in schools (Burns; Lawrence and Tatum), in transnational homes (Twine), and in everyday social interactions (Iyer, Leach, and Pedersen). Compared with the first edition, this edition is more explicit about the material embeddedness of racialized stratifications in the United States and more insistent about how whiteness as privilege has been transformed through the practice of critique and activism. With the range, breadth, and contrast of our authors we seek to demonstrate the dialectics of oppression and resistance, in contexts in which privilege has been challenged and contested.

ON BEING SINGULARLY CLAIRVOYANT

Du Bois used this concept in two senses. First, as in the root definition of "seeing clearly" — apprehending new possibilities beyond what whiteness has always sought to obscure — and second, as the "ability to discern things which are not necessarily present to the senses." We too learn to listen, see, and feel differently as we move whiteness from its perceived centrality. We sense that the world has been altered dramatically, in the global and the everyday micropractices, in the years since the first edition of *Off White*. Perhaps never has it been more necessary or important to see beyond the information most readily available to more clearly discern the signs of the times. The stakes are higher for our questions about macrostructural arrangements and realignments of wealth, whiteness, and privilege; about identity and social transformations; and about bifurcations, inequities, and the world splitting at the seams. We cannot imagine a more intellectually invigorating and politically energized set of readings, which are designed to educate, provoke, and mobilize, than the ones we gathered here.

And so we continue to delight in midwifing this colorful, quilted text from which learners of all ages can draw smart theory, vivid research, and powerful pedagogies. We are thrilled to have been fortunate enough to gather such an array of writers, diverse by discipline, theoretical spin, political orientation, race, ethnicity, language, and sexuality, in one conversational site. We hope that these studies provide more tools to struggle with whiteness as a pivotal feature of what Winant and Omi have called the "racial formation."

ON KNOWING WHAT WE KNOW

We said we would not publish another volume of *Off White*; in fact, in the 1997 preface we were so bold as to suggest that books on whiteness should stop being published. We imagined that this volume would be sufficient to provoke and establish a new discourse on privilege and race. We wanted only a cautionary tale, and simultaneously we worried that it would provoke a fetish of whiteness studies.

But, like Du Bois, we had to face the consequences of what we learned following the publication of the first edition. Simply put, we were wrong about the future of whiteness. As expected, whiteness studies have proliferated through many disciplines and with a rippling effect. Whiteness has come to be studied as representation, ideology, performance, hegemony, science, media, consumption, a trope for colonialism and the new empire. Writings have swelled on the material bases of whiteness, discursive analyses of whiteness, and psychoanalytic treatment of whiteness in the imaginations of us all. These profitable works have not "ended" whiteness studies; more accurately, they have demonstrated the power and impact of excavating and highlighting that which had previously been unnamed.

Since 1997, *Off White* has been taught heavily in psychology, sociology, and education courses. Colleagues tell us that the book is particularly valuable in college and university settings where white students are engaged with, but somewhat resistant to, multi-cultural studies. Students of color have been electrified to discover a set of notions that has always been common sense or "mother wit" in their homes and communities described, analyzed, and measured by (white) scholars. In these academic contexts, especially in schools of education, professors are looking for a volume that speaks with, to, and against the grain of whiteness as a stance of untroubled privilege, naturalized merit, or simply "exemption" from conversations about race. And so, we are delighted to bring to you a newly titled volume: *Off White: Readings on Power, Privilege, and Resistance.*

This new edition can be thought of as "*Off White*, Revisited." Our fundamental task in this edition remains the same: to provide colorful conversation about whiteness, prying it open and wedging it off its unexamined center. Yet to honor the developments in our understanding of whiteness, we began the process of revision by polling colleagues who assign *Off White*. We asked which chapters they more routinely teach and what topics they wish were better represented in the volume. To the latter question, we heard a desire for more pieces that focus on the materiality of whiteness as privilege, and chapters that can help students understand the need for subversion of white privilege in activism, responsibility, and social justice work. These educators seek materials that can reveal to students how whiteness manifests as financial, academic, housing, and health care "quality" and "deficit." They also wanted concrete examples of the ways (white) individuals and (multiracial) collectives assert their positions to insist on social change in schools, communities, and society at large. We also heard a desire for pieces that more explicitly speak to the theory of research methods for studying whiteness, racial formations, and privilege in nonessentialized ways.

And so, we focus this volume more deliberately on the material conditions of whiteness as privilege and on the turns of whiteness produced when individuals and collectives challenge contemporary racial formations. For this reason, some favorites from the first volume have been replaced with a series of new pieces that broaden the analysis of whiteness. Many of the studies that remain have been updated. In this volume we more intentionally set out to document the rhythms and movements of white domination through the state, private, and major public institutions, and to recognize the self-conscious departures from and resistances toward racialized (in)justice enacted through white bodies and allies.

Constructing

ONE

Behind Blue Eyes: Whiteness and Contemporary U.S. Racial Politics

Howard Winant

INTRODUCTION

At an urban college campus in California, whites and blacks, Latinos and Asians, sit side-by-side in the overcrowded classroom, and in their own separate groups in the cafeteria. As they drive home to their segregated neighborhoods, they pump the same high-volume hip-hop sounds through their car speakers. A few miles up the interstate, neo-Nazis train at a private ranch. A few miles the other way, a multiracial garment workers' union is being organized; a majority of the workers in the bargaining unit are Asians and Latinos, but there are some whites. Among the organizers, one of the most effective is a young white woman who speaks good Spanish.

Clearly, there are many varieties of "whiteness." This essay examines racial politics and culture as they shape the status of whites. I begin from the premise that it is no longer possible to assume a "normalized" whiteness, whose invisibility and relatively monolithic character signify immunity from political or cultural challenge. An alternative perspective is demanded, one that begins from a recognition of *white racial dualism.* The discussion of this theme, in the next section of this essay, is an extension to whites of the Du Boisian idea that in a racist society the "color line" fractures the self, that it imposes a sort of schizophrenia on the bearers of racialized identities, which forces them to see themselves simultaneously from within and without. Du Bois of course intended this analysis to explain problems of black politics and culture at the turn of the 20th century; it was a time when few publicly questioned the normalization of whiteness. His idea can be extrapolated to whites at the end of the 20th century; today, I suggest, whiteness has been deeply fissured by the racial conflicts of the post-civil rights period. Since the 1960s contemporary racial discourse has been unable to function as a logic of racial superiority and justified exclusion. Therefore it has been forced into *re*articulations, *re*presentations, *re*interpretations of the meaning of race and, perforce, of whiteness.

In the following section of this paper I analyze the *new politicization of whiteness* that has taken shape particularly in the post-civil rights era — the period since the ambiguous victory of the civil rights movement in the mid-1960s. Here I discuss the reasons why, contrary to the racially egalitarian thrust of the civil rights "revolution," the significance of white identity was reinterpreted and repoliticized — largely in a reactionary direction — in the wake of the 1960s.

Next, I analyze the range of *white racial projects* that the contemporary politics of racial dualism generates. How do interpretations of the meaning of whiteness link to political positions, policies, and programs? I discuss a series of racial projects that span the political continuum, and develop some critical perspectives on the "left" or "progressive" projects.

In the final section, I focus on *the future of whiteness* in the United States and sketch out some elements of what potential antiracist politics for whites might look like.

WHITENESS AS RACIAL DUALISM

Once, U.S. society was a nearly monolithic racial hierarchy, in which everyone knew "his" place. Today, nobody knows where he or she fits in the U.S. racial order.

Thirty years after the enactment of civil rights legislation, agreement about the continuing existence of racial subordination has vanished. The meaning of race has been deeply problematized. Why? Because the legacy of centuries of white supremacy lives on in the present, despite the partial victories of the 1960s. Because the idea of "equality," it turned out, could be reinterpreted, rearticulated, reinserted in the business-as-usual framework of U.S. politics and culture. Because that framework is extremely resilient and able to absorb political challenges, even fundamental and radical ones. Because the outlawing of formal discrimination, which was a crucial and immediate objective of the 1960s movements, did not mean that informal racist practices would be eradicated, or indeed even that anti-discrimination laws would be seriously enforced.

And yet it would be inaccurate to say that the movement failed. In virtually every area of social life, the impact of the postwar racial mobilizations is plain to see (Jaynes & Williams, 1989). Although in some sectors, like housing desegregation, massive efforts to transform an entrenched and complex pattern of racial discrimination were largely (though not entirely) defeated (Massey & Denton, 1993), in other areas — for example, the desegregation of the armed forces (Butler, 1980; Moskos, 1988) — really remarkable change occurred.

Therefore, not only blacks (and other racially identified minorities) but also whites, now experience a division in their racial identities. On the one hand, whites inherit the legacy of white supremacy, from which they continue to benefit. But on the other hand, they are subject to the moral and political challenges posed to that inheritance by the partial but real successes of the black movement (and affiliated movements). These movements advanced a countertradition to white supremacy, one that envisioned a radicalized, inclusive, participatory democracy; a substantively egalitarian economy; and a nonracial state. They deeply affected whites as well as blacks, exposing and denouncing often unconscious beliefs in white supremacy, and demanding new and more respectful forms of behavior in relation to nonwhites. Just as the movements partially reformed white supremacist institutions, so they partially transformed white racial consciousness. Obviously, they did not destroy the deep structures of white privilege, but they did make counterclaims on behalf of the racially excluded and subordinated. As a result, white identities have been displaced and refigured: They are now contradictory, as well as confused and anxiety-ridden, to an unprecedented extent. It is this situation that I describe as white racial dualism.[1]

THE NEW POLITICIZATION OF WHITENESS

What are the implications of post-civil rights era racial dualism for contemporary politics? There seems little doubt that the new politicization of whiteness plays a crucial role in determining the direction of U.S. politics today. Many analysts have pointed to the significance of race as a "wedge issue" that divides the Democratic Party, inducing large numbers of working-class (or middle-class) whites to vote Republican (Edsall, 1992; Greenberg, 1985). Of course, this "wedge" has been there for a long time: it operated under slavery, flourished in the late 19th-century populist era, and problematized the New Deal Coalition. It threatened to split the Democratic Party in 1948. It did in fact split the party after the 1960s.

Since that time the meaning of whiteness has been cast into doubt: Does it signify privilege or is it merely one identity — one form of "difference" — among others? To what extent is race still a salient marker of social position and status, and to what extent is it a relic of the past in a society now determined to be "color blind?" In some respects, the crisis of "whiteness" does reflect the greater racial egalitarianism of the post-civil rights period. In other ways this crisis is merely the latest defense of white supremacy, which now covers itself with the fig leaf of a formal egalitarianism. The contemporary crisis of whiteness — its dualistic allegiances to privilege and equality, to color consciousness and color blindness, to formally equal justice and to substantive social justice — can be discerned in the contradictory character of white identity today.

There were three new developments that set the stage for the new politicization of whiteness. First, the *erosion of white ethnicity* in the post-WWII period meant that a more uniform racial identity, that of "Euro-American," became available to whites. Second, *class politics lost much of its resonance* in a postindustrial economy characterized by capital flight and downsizing; as a result standards of living stagnated and opportunities for political mobilization along class lines faded. Third, the limited reforms achieved by the black movement and its allies in the 1960s were susceptible to reinterpretation by the right, making a *de facto racial reaction* ideologically palatable to the political center.

Thus from the late 1960s on, white identity has been reinterpreted, rearticulated in a dualistic fashion: on the one hand egalitarian, on the other hand privileged; on the one hand individualistic and "color blind," on the other hand "normalized" and white.

Nowhere is this new framework of the white "politics of difference" more clearly on display than in the reaction to affirmative action policies of all sorts (in hiring, university admissions, federal contracting, etc.). Assaults on these policies, which have been developing since their introduction as tentative and quite limited efforts at racial redistribution (Johnson, 1967, but see also Steinberg, 1995), are currently at hysterical levels. These attacks are clearly designed to effect ideological shifts, rather than to shift resources in any meaningful way. They represent whiteness as *disadvantage*, something that has few precedents in U.S. racial history (Gallagher, 1995). This imaginary white disadvantage — for which there is almost no evidence at the empirical level — has achieved widespread popular credence, and provides the cultural and political "glue" that holds together a wide variety of reactionary racial politics.

White Racial Projects

Both the onset of white racial dualism and the new politicization of whiteness in the post-civil rights era reflect the fragmentation of earlier concepts of white racial identity and of white supremacy more generally. In their place, a variety of concepts of the meaning of whiteness have emerged. How can we analyze and evaluate in a systematic fashion this range of white racial projects?

As I have argued elsewhere (Omi & Winant, 1994; Winant, 1994), the concept of racial projects is crucial to understanding the dynamics of racial formation in contemporary society.

Existing racial projects can be classified along a political spectrum, according to explicit criteria drawn from the meaning each project attaches to "whiteness." Such a classification will necessarily be somewhat schematic, since in the real world of politics and culture ideas and meanings, as well as social practices, tend to overlap in unpredictable ways. Nevertheless, I think it would be beneficial to attempt to sort out alternative conceptions of whiteness, along with the politics that both flow from and inform these conceptions. This is what I attempt here, focusing on five key racial projects, which I term *far right, new right, neoconservative, neoliberal,* and *new abolitionist.*

The Far Right Racial Project

On the far right the cornerstone of white identity is belief in an ineluctable, unalterable racialized difference between whites and nonwhites. Traditionally, this belief has been biologically grounded, and in many respects it remains so today. But a distinct modernizing tendency exists on the far right as well. It is thus necessary to distinguish between explicitly fascist and "neofascist" currents within the far right racial project.

Explicitly fascist elements on the far right can be identified by two features: their frank belief in the biological superiority of whites over nonwhites (and Jews), and their insurrectionary posture vis-à-vis the state. Although their accounts of the nature and sources of racial difference vary, often relying on religious doctrine, as in the case of the so-called Christian Identity movement, which identifies blacks and Jews as "mud people" whose origins are different from those of "Aryans," a biologistic element is always present. Explicitly fascist groups on the far right openly admire Nazi race-thinking, fantasize about racial genocide, and dream of establishing an all-white North American nation, or, failing that, seceding from the United States to establish such a nation, possibly in the Northwest (Diamond, 1995; Novick, 1995; Ridgeway, 1990; Southern Poverty Law Center, 1995).

Although acts of racial and anti-Semitic terror continue and even increase, and the elaboration of fascist doctrine continues as well, significant modernizing currents have appeared on the far right in the past decade, leading me to assert that the "neofascist" dimension of the far right's racial project has gained considerable ground. These tendencies occupy an intermediate position between the explicit fascism I have discussed and the more mainstream *new right* racial project that I address in the following section.

"Neofascists" generally have an ultraright provenance — a history of association with the KKK or Nazi groups — but they now actively seek to renovate the far right's traditions of white racial nationalism (Walters, 1987) and open advocacy of white supremacy. Largely as a result of the challenges posed by the 1960s, the far right, no less than other U.S. political currents, has been forced to rearticulate racial meanings, to reinterpret the content of "whiteness" and the politics that flows from it.

"Neofascism's" response has been political mobilization on racial grounds: If blacks have their organizations and movements, why shouldn't whites? The various activities of David Duke exemplify the new trend: his electoral campaigns, his attempts at student organization (for example, his effort to create white student unions on college campuses), and his emblematic National Association for the Advancement of White People.[2]

In the far right's view, the state has been captured by "race mixers" and will have to be recaptured by white racial nationalists in order to end the betrayal of "traditional values" that a racially egalitarian and pluralistic national politics and culture would portend. Whether this reactionary objective could happen by peaceful means, or whether an armed insurrection would be required to achieve it, remains a matter of dispute. Whether a rhetoric of absolute racial difference (à la the explicitly fascist currents on the far right) will be most effective in accomplishing this or whether a rhetoric of white victimization and white rights (à la the renovated neofascist currents on the far right) will work better in the post-civil rights era is also in question. But on one objective both currents of the far right project are united: The United States must remain a white man's country.

The New Right Racial Project

The contemporary new right has its origins in resistance to the black movement of the 1950s and 60s — with the Wallace campaign of 1968 (Edsall, 1992), this resistance crystallized as a national electorally oriented, reactionary social movement. The Wallace campaign drew large numbers of far right activists, Klansmen, and neo-Nazis into electoral politics for the first time in the postwar period (Diamond, 1995; Novick, 1995; Ridgeway, 1990). Although his initial 1964 run for the presidency had emphasized southern intransigence, states' rights, and explicit resistance to racial reform in general, by 1968 Wallace had formulated a right-wing populism, which went well beyond mere resistance to racial integration.

Like the far right, the new right seeks to present itself as the tribune of disenfranchised whites. But the new right is distinguished — if not always sharply — from the far right by several factors. First, rather than espouse racism and white supremacy, it prefers to present these themes subtextually with the familiar "code-word" phenomenon. Second, it wholeheartedly embraces mainstream political activity, rather than abjuring it or looking at it suspiciously. Third, it can accept a measure of nonwhite social and political participation, and even membership (think of Alan Keyes, for instance), so long as this is pursued on a "color-blind" basis and adheres to the rest of the authoritarian nationalist formula. For the far right in general, "color blindness" is race mixing and therefore *verboten*. For the new right, suitably authoritarian versions of "color blindness" are fine.

The new right diverges from neoconservatism (discussed below) in its willingness to practice racial politics subtextually, through coding, manipulation of racial fears, and so forth. *De facto* it recognizes the persistence of racial difference in U.S. society. The new right understands perfectly well that its mass base is white, and that its political success depends on its ability to interpret white identity in positive political terms. Precisely because of its willingness to exploit racial fears and employ racially manipulative practices, the new right has been effective in achieving much of its agenda for political and cultural reaction and social structural recomposition. These were crucial to the new right's ability to provide a solid base of electoral and financial support for the Republican Party and the Reagan "revolution." The demagoguery employed by George Bush in the1988 Willie Horton campaign ads, or by Pete Wilson or Phil Gramm in their contemporary attacks on immigrants and affirmative action, shows this strategy is far from exhausted. Neoconservatism has not, and could not, deliver such tangible political benefits, and in fact lacks an equivalent mass political base.

The Neoconservative Racial Project

Neoconservative discourse seeks to *preserve* white advantages through denial of racial difference. For neoconservatism, racial difference is something to be overcome, a blight on the core United States values — both politically and culturally speaking — of universalism and individualism.

The doctrine of natural rights frames the liberal view of citizenship that in turn informs the neoconservative vision of race. It is visible in the dissent of Justice Harlan from the *Plessy* decision in 1896. It is visible in "the American creed" which Myrdal claimed as a universalizing and individuating tendency that would ultimately sweep away irrational race prejudice and bigotry in the United States (Myrdal, 1962 [1944]). It is visible in the founding documents of U.S. neoconservatism, such as Glazer's essay on "the American ethnic pattern" (Glazer, 1975). And it is visible in the basic antistatism and laissez-faire attitude of neoconservatives, in regard to racial matters.

Besides its fundamental suspicion of racial difference, which it also seeks to equate (or reduce) to ethnicity (Omi & Winant, 1994, pp. 14–23), the neoconservative project has cast doubt on the tractability of issues of racial equality, tending to argue that the state cannot ameliorate poverty through social policy, but in fact only exacerbates it (Williams, 1982). These positions indicate the substantial distance the neoconservative project has traveled from the liberal statism, and indeed the racial pluralism, with which its chief spokespeople once identified; for example, in Glazer and Moynihan's *Beyond the Melting Pot* (1970, but see also Steinberg, 1995).[3]

The appeal to universalism — for example, in terms of social policy or critical educational or literary standards — is far more subtle than open or coded appeals to white racial fears since it has far greater capacity to represent race in apparently egalitarian and democratic terms. Indeed the very hallmark of the neoconservative argument has been that, beyond the proscription of explicit racial discrimination, every invocation of racial significance manifests "race-thinking," and is thus suspect:

> In the phrase reiterated again and again in the Civil Rights Act of 1964, no distinction was to be made in the right to vote, in the provision of public services, the right to public education, on the ground of "race, color, religion, or national origin." Paradoxically, we then began an extensive effort to record the race, color and (some) national origins of just about every student and employee and recipient of government benefits or services in the nation.... This monumental restructuring of public policy, ... it is argued by Federal administrators and courts, is required to enforce the laws against discrimination. It is a transitional period, they say, to that condition called for in the Constitution and the laws, when no account at all is to be taken of race, color and national origin. But others see it as a direct contradiction of the Constitution and the laws, and of the consensus that emerged after long struggle in the middle 1960s. (Glazer, 1975, p. 4)

Yet a refusal to engage in "race-thinking" amounts to a defense of the racial status quo, in which systematic racial inequality and, yes, discrimination as well, are omnipresent.[4]

Thus the neoconservative perspective is not as inclusionary as it superficially appears. Indeed, neoconservatism suffers from *bad faith*. It may serve for some as a rationalizing formula, a lament about the complexities of a social world in which the traditional verities, and indeed the traditional speakers, writers, and political actors, have come under challenge from a host of "others," but as soon as it advances beyond critique to proposals for action its pious professions of universality and liberality are quickly replaced by advocacy of laissez-faire social policies, and hence of the *status quo*.

The Neoliberal Racial Project

Neoliberal discourse seeks to *limit* white advantages through denial of racial difference. The overlap with neoconservatism is, of course, hardly accidental. Yet there are significant differences in political orientation between the two projects.

Neoliberalism recognizes the cross-cutting and competitive dynamics of race- and class-based forms of subordination in the postindustrial, post-civil rights era. It seeks systematically to narrow the differences that divide working- and middle-class people as a strategy for improving the "life-chances" of minorities, who are disproportionately poor. It thus attempts to appeal to whites with arguments about the medium- and long-term consequences upon their living standards of downward mobility and greater impoverishment of nonwhites. The neoliberal racial project can thus be described as social democratic, focused on social structure (as opposed to cultural representation à la the various right-wing racial projects), and somewhat class reductionist in its approach to race.

The most effective, as well as controversial, spokesperson for the neoliberal racial project has undoubtedly been William Julius Wilson. In a series of prominent scholarly works and political interventions, Wilson argued for the use of class-based criteria (and consequently, against the use of racial logics) in formulating social policy aimed at achieving greater substantive equality in U.S. society. He has contended that this reorientation of social policy priorities is both better suited to the contemporary dynamics of capitalist development, and more politically strategic in ways that explicit, racially oriented policies are not.

A similar argument has been proposed by Michael Lind, who argues, "The American elites that subsidize and staff both the Republican and the Democratic parties have steadfastly waged a generation-long class war against the middle and working classes" (Lind, 1995a, p. 35) using race, as well as other divisions, to achieve unprecedented levels of power and concentrated wealth.

Both Wilson and Lind call for a nationalism of the left, a populist alliance of the have-nots, regardless of race, against the haves. Lind's version is perhaps more radical and certainly more explicitly nationalist: He proposed specific measures to tax corporate flight, restrict immigration, and establish a "common high-wage trading bloc." Like Wilson, he proposed to eliminate affirmative action, which he would replace with a

transracial America, ... [where] a color-blind, gender neutral regime of individual rights would be combined with government activism promoting a high degree of substantive social and economic equality. (Lind, 1995b, p. 15)

The neoliberal project actively promotes a pragmatic vision of greater substantive equality, linking class and race, and arguing for the necessity of transracial coalition politics. These themes seem to me worthy of support, and receive more discussion below in this essay's concluding section.

For the present I wish simply to register some of my unease with the neoliberal project in respect to its treatment of race. Most specifically, I question the argument that race-specific policies should receive less attention in a progressive political agenda (Wilson, 1987, pp. 10–12). Despite protestations that the neoliberal approach is more hardheaded, more willing to face up to the difficult questions of the supposed "rise of social pathologies in the ghetto," it is also noteworthy that the neoliberal project tends to deny, sometimes explicitly and sometimes implicitly, the ongoing relevance of white supremacy to ghetto and barrio poverty. It tends to deemphasize the "dirty little secret" of continued racial hostility, segregation, and discrimination of all sorts.

Powerful as some of Wilson's, Lind's, and others' arguments are, they do not succeed in demonstrating the demise of racism or white privilege. They largely fail to recognize the ongoing racial dualism that prevails in the contemporary period, perceiving post-civil rights era conflicts between whites and racially defined minorities merely as strategic problems, and paying less attention to the deep-seated *structural* racial conflicts endemic to U.S. society.

This weakness is more noticeable in some areas than others, for example, in respect to residential segregation or criminal justice issues, which simply cannot be understood as outcomes of "color-blind" capitalist development imperatives or deindustrialization, and are certainly not the product of affirmative action. Rather, the imperviousness of these problems to political reform testifies to the continuing viability of old-fashioned white supremacy, and to the competitive advantages whiteness still has to offer.

What drops out of the neoliberal project, then, is precisely the cultural and moral dimensions of white supremacy. The neoliberal project does not challenge whites on their willingness to receive a "psychological wage," which amounts to a tangible benefit acquired at the expense of nonwhites (Du Bois, 1935/1977; Harris, 1993; Roediger, 1991). Indeed, the neoliberal project does not challenge whites to abjure the *real* wage subsidies, the artificially low unemployment rates, or the host of other material benefits they receive by virtue of their whiteness (Lipsitz, 1995).

Nevertheless, the neoliberal project does undertake a crucial task: the construction of a transracial political agenda and the articulation of white and minority interests in a viable strategic perspective. This is something that has been missing from the U.S. political scene since the enactment of civil rights legislation 30 years ago.

The New Abolitionist Racial Project

The new abolitionist project stresses the "invention of whiteness" as a pivotal development in the rise of U.S. capitalism. Advocates of this view have begun a process of historical reinterpretation that aims to set race — or more properly, the gestation and evolution of white supremacy — at the center of U.S. politics and culture. Thus far, they have focused attention on a series of formative events and processes: the precedent of British colonial treatment of the Irish (Allen, 1994); the early, multiracial resistance to indentured servitude and quasi slavery, which culminated in the defeat of Bacon's Rebellion in late 17th-century Virginia; the self-identification of "free" workers as white in the antebellum North (Ignatiev, 1995; Roediger, 1991); and the construction of a "white republic" in the late 19th century (Saxton, 1990).

These studies, in some cases quite prodigious intellectual efforts, have had a significant impact on how we understand not only racial formation but also class formation and the developing forms of popular culture in U.S. history. What they reveal above all is how crucial the construction of whiteness was, and remains, for the development and maintenance of capitalist class rule in the United States. Furthermore, these analyses also show how the meaning of whiteness, like that of race in general, has time and again proved flexible enough to adapt to shifts in the capitalist division of labor, to reform initiatives which extended democratic rights, and to changes in ideology and cultural representation.

The core message of the new abolitionist project is the imperative of repudiation of white identity and white privilege. But how is this rejection of whiteness to be accomplished? Both analytical and practical measures are envisioned. On the intellectual level, the new abolitionist project invites us to contemplate the emptiness, indeed vacuity, of the white category:

> It is not merely that whiteness is oppressive and false; it is that whiteness is *nothing but* oppressive and false.... It is the empty and terrifying attempt to build an identity based on what one isn't and on whom one can hold back. (Roediger, 1991, p. 13; emphasis in original)

On the practical level, the argument goes, whites can become "race traitors" by rejecting their privilege, by refusing to collude with white supremacy. When you hear that racist joke, confront its teller. When you see the police harassing a nonwhite youth, try to intervene or at least bear witness.

It is easy to sympathize with this analysis, at least up to a point. The postwar black movement, which in the U.S. context at least served as the point of origin for all the "new social movements" and the much-reviled "politics of identity," taught the valuable lesson that politics went "all the way down." That is, meaningful efforts to achieve greater social justice could not tolerate a public-private or a collective-individual distinction. Trying to change society meant trying to change one's own life. The formula "the personal is political," commonly associated with feminism, had its early origins among the militants of the civil rights movement (Evans, 1980).

The problems come when deeper theoretical and practical problems are raised. Despite their explicit adherence to a "social construction" model of race (one that bears a significant resemblance to my own work with Michael Omi), theorists of the new abolitionist project do not take that insight as seriously as they should. They employ it chiefly to argue against biologistic conceptions of race, which is fine; but they fail to consider the complexities and rootedness of social construction, or as I would term it, racial formation. Is the social construction of whiteness so flimsy that it can be repudiated by a mere act of political will, or even by widespread and repeated acts aimed at rejecting white privilege? I think not; whiteness may not be a legitimate cultural identity in the sense of having a discrete, "positive" content, but it is certainly an overdetermined political and cultural identity nevertheless, having to do with socioeconomic status; religious affiliation; ideologies of individualism, opportunity, and citizenship; nationalism, and so forth. Like any other complex of beliefs and practices, "whiteness" is imbedded in a highly articulated social structure and system of significations; rather than trying to repudiate it, we shall have to rearticulate it.

That sounds like a daunting task, and of course it is, but it is not nearly as impossible as erasing whiteness altogether, as the new abolitionist project seeks to do. Furthermore, because whiteness is a relational concept, unintelligible without reference to nonwhiteness — note how this is true even of Roediger's formulation about "build[ing] an identity based on what one isn't" — that rearticulation (or reinterpretation, or deconstruction) of whiteness can begin relatively easily, in the messy present, with the recognition that whiteness *already* contains substantial nonwhite elements. Of course, that recognition is only the beginning of a large and arduous process of political labor, to which I return in the concluding section of this essay.

Notwithstanding these criticisms of the new abolitionist project, many of its insights remain vital to the process of reformulating, or synthesizing, a progressive approach to whiteness. Its attention is directed toward precisely the place where the neoliberal racial project is weak: the point at which white identity constitutes a crucial support to white supremacy, and a central obstacle to the achievement of substantive social equality and racial justice.

CONCLUDING NOTES: WHITENESS AND CONTEMPORARY U.S. POLITICS

In a situation of racial dualism, as Du Bois observed more than 90 years ago, race operates both to assign us and to deny us our identity. It both makes the social world intelligible, and simultaneously renders it opaque and mysterious. Not only does it allocate resources, power, and privilege; it also provides means for challenging that allocation. The contradictory character of race provides the context in which racial dualism — or the "color-line," as Du Bois designated it, has developed as "the problem of the 20th century."

So what's new? Only that, as a result of incalculable human effort, suffering, and sacrifice, we now realize that these truths apply across the board. *Whites and whiteness can no longer be exempted* from the comprehensive racialization process that is the hallmark of U.S. history and social structure.

This is the present-day context for racial conflict and thus for U.S. politics in general, because race continues to play its designated role of crystallizing all the fundamental issues in U.S. society. As always, we articulate our anxieties in racial terms: wealth and poverty, crime and punishment, gender and sexuality, nationality and citizenship, culture and power, are all articulated in the United States primarily through race.

So, once again, what's new? It's the problematic of *whiteness* that has emerged as the principal source of anxiety and conflict in the postwar United States. Although this situation was anticipated or prefigured at earlier moments in the nation's past — for example, in the "hour of eugenics" (Barkan, 1992; Gould, 1981; Kevles, 1985) — it is far more complicated now than ever before, largely because of the present unavailability of biologistic forms of racism as a convenient rationale for white supremacy.[5]

Whiteness — visible whiteness, resurgent whiteness, whiteness as a color, whiteness as *difference* — this is what's new, and newly problematic, in contemporary U.S. politics. The reasons for this have already emerged in my discussion of the spectrum of racial projects and the particular representations these projects assign to whiteness. Most centrally, the problem of the meaning of whiteness appears as a direct consequence of the movement challenge posed in the 1960s to white supremacy. The battles of that period have not been resolved; they have not been won or lost; however battered and bruised, the demand for substantive racial equality and general social justice still lives. And although it lives, the strength of white supremacy is in doubt.

The racial projects of the right are clear efforts to resist the challenge to white supremacy posed by the movements of the 1960s and their contemporary inheritors. Each of these projects has a particular relationship to the white supremacist legacy, ranging from the far right's efforts to justify and solidify white entitlements, through the new right's attempts to utilize the white supremacist tradition for more immediate and expedient political ends, to the neoconservative project's quixotic quest to surgically separate the liberal democratic tradition from the racism that traditionally underwrote it. The biologistic racism of the far right, the expedient and subtextual racism of the new right, and the bad-faith antiracism of the neoconservatives have many differences from each other, but they have at least one thing in common. They all seek to maintain the long-standing associations between whiteness and U.S. political traditions, between whiteness and U.S. nationalism, between whiteness and universalism. They all seek in different ways to preserve white identity from the particularity, the difference, which the 1960s movement challenge assigned to it.

The racial projects of the left are the movements' successors (as is neoconservatism, in a somewhat perverse sense). Both the neoliberal racial project and the new abolitionist project seek to fulfill the movement's thwarted dreams of a genuinely (i.e., substantively) egalitarian society, one in which significant redistribution of wealth and power has taken place, and race no longer serves as the most significant marker between winners and losers, haves and have-nots, powerful and powerless. Although they diverge significantly — because the neoliberals seek to accomplish their ends through a conscious diminution of the significance of race, and the new abolitionists hope to achieve similar ends through a conscious reemphasizing of the importance of race — they also have one very important thing in common. They both seek to rupture the barrier between whites and racially defined minorities, the obstacle that prevents joint political action. They both seek to associate whites and nonwhites, to reinterpret the meaning of whiteness in such a way that it no longer has the power to impede class alliances.

Although the differences and indeed the hostility — between the neoliberal and new abolitionist projects, between the reform-oriented and radical conceptions of whiteness — are quite severe it is vital that adherents of these two progressive racial projects recognize that they each hold part of the key to challenging white supremacy in the contemporary United States, and that their counterpart project holds the other part of the key. Neoliberals rightfully argue that a pragmatic approach to transracial politics is vital if the momentum of racial reaction is to be halted or reversed. New abolitionists properly emphasize challenging the ongoing commitment to white supremacy on the part of many whites.

Both of these positions need to draw on each other, not only in strategic terms but in theoretical ones as well. The recognition that racial identities — all racial identities, including whiteness — have become implacably dualistic, could be far more liberating on the left than it has thus far been. For neoliberals, it could permit and indeed justify an acceptance of race consciousness and even nationalism among racially defined minorities as a necessary but partial response to disenfranchisement, disempowerment, and super-exploitation. There is no inherent reason why such a political position could not coexist with a strategic awareness of the need for strong, class-conscious, transracial coalitions. We have seen many such examples in the past: in the antislavery movement, in the communist movement of the 1930s (Kelley, 1994), and in the 1988 presidential bid of Jesse Jackson, to name but a few. This is not to say that all would be peace and harmony if such alliances could come more permanently into being. But there is no excuse for not attempting to find the pragmatic "common ground" necessary to create them.

New abolitionists could also benefit from a recognition that on a pragmatic basis, whites can ally with racially defined minorities without renouncing their whiteness. If they truly agree that race is a socially constructed concept, as they claim, new abolitionists should also be able to recognize that racial identities are not either-or matters, not closed concepts that must be upheld in a reactionary fashion or disavowed in a comprehensive act of renunciation. The following exemplifies postmodern language I dislike: Racial identities are deeply "hybridized"; they are not "sutured, but remain open to rearticulation . . . To be white in America is to be very black. If you don't know how black you are, you don't know how American you are." (Thompson, 1995, p. 429).

REFERENCES

Allen, T. W. (1994). *The invention of the white race: Racial oppression and social control* (Vol. 1). New York: Verso.

Barkan, E. (1992). *The retreat of scientific racism: Changing concepts of race in Britain and the U.S. between the World Wars*. New York: Cambridge University Press.

Butler, J. S. (1980). *Inequality in the military: The black experience*. Saratoga, CA: Century Twenty One.

Butterfield, F. (1995, October 5). More blacks in their 20's have trouble with the law. *New York Times*.

Chalmers, D. A. (1981). *Hooded Americanism: The history of the Ku Klux Klan*. New York: Franklin Watts.

Diamond, S. (1995). *Roads to dominion: Right-wing movements and political power in the United States*. New York: Guilford.

D'Souza, D. (1995). *The end of racism*. New York: Free Press.

Du Bois, W. E. B. (1977). *Black reconstruction in America: An essay toward a history of the part which black folk played in the attempt to reconstruct democracy in America, 1860–1880*. New York: Atheneum. (Original work published in 1935)

Duster, T. (1990). *Backdoor to Eugenics*. New York: Routledge.

Edsall, T. B. (with Edsall, M.). (1992). *Chain reaction: The impact of race, rights, and Taxes on American politics* (Rev. ed.). New York: Norton.

Evans, S. (1980). *Personal politics*. New York: Random House.

Gallagher, C. (1995). White reconstruction in the university. *Socialist Review, 94*, 1–2.

Glazer, N. (1975). *Affirmative discrimination: Ethnic inequality and public policy*. New York: Basic Books.

Glazer, N., & Moynihan, D. P. (1970). *Beyond the melting pot* (2nd ed.). Cambridge: MIT Press.

Gordon, D. (1987). 6% unemployment ain't natural. *Social Research, 54*(2).

Gould, S. J. (1981). *The mismeasure of man*. New York: W. W. Norton.

Greenberg, S. B. (1985). *Report on Democratic defection: Report prepared for the Michigan House Democratic Campaign Committee*. Washington, DC: The Analysis Group.

Harris, C. (1993). Whiteness as property. *Harvard Law Review, 106*.

Herrnstein, R., & Murray, C. (1994). *The bell curve: Intelligence and class structure in American life*. New York: Free Press.

Ignatiev, N. (1995). *How the Irish became white: Irish-Americans and African-Americans in nineteenth century Philadelphia*. New York: Verso.

Jaynes, G. D., & Williams, R. M., Jr. (1989). *A common destiny: Blacks and American society*. Washington, DC: National Academy Press.

Johnson, L. B. (1967). To secure these rights. In L. Rainwater & W. Yancey (Eds.), *The Moynihan report and the politics of controversy*. Cambridge: MIT Press.

Kelley, R. D. G. (1994). *Race rebels: Culture, politics, and the black working class*. New York: Free Press.

Kevles, D. J. (1985). *In the name of Eugenics: Genetics and the uses of human heredity*. New York: Knopf.

Langer, E. (1990, July 16–23). The American Neo-Nazi movement today. *The Nation*.

Lind, M. (1995a, June). To have and have not: Notes on the progress of the American class war. *Harper's*.

Lind, M. (1995b). *The next American nation: The new nationalism and the fourth American Revolution*. New York: Free Press.

Lipsitz, G. (1995, September). The possessive investment in whiteness. *American Quarterly, 47*(3).

Massey, D. S., & Denton, N. A. (1993). *American apartheid*. Cambridge: Harvard University Press.

Moskos, C. (1988). *Soldiers and sociology*. Alexandria: U.S. Army Research Institute for the Behavioral and Social Sciences.

Myrdal, G. (1962). *An American dilemma: The Negro problem and modern democracy, twentieth anniversary edition*. New York: Harper & Row.

Neckerman, K., & Kirschenman, J. (1991, November). Hiring strategies, racial bias, and inner-city workers. *Social Problems, 38*(4).

Novick, M. (1995). *White lies, white power: The fight against white supremacy and reactionary violence*. Monroe, ME: Common Courage.

Omi, M., & Winant, H. (1993). On the theoretical concept of race. In C. McCarthy & W. Critchlow (Eds.), *Race, identity, and representation in education*. New York: Routledge.

Omi, M., & Winant, H. (1994). *Racial formation in the United States: From the 1960s to the 1990s* (2nd ed.). New York: Routledge.

Quadagno, J. (1994). *The color of welfare: How racism undermined the war on poverty*. New York: Oxford University Press.

Ridgeway, J. (1990). *Blood in the face: The Ku Klux Klan, Aryan nations, skinheads, and the rise of a new white culture*. New York: Thunder's Mouth.

Roediger, D. R. (1991). *The wages of whiteness: Race and the making of the American working class*. New York: Verso.

Saxton, A. (1990). *The rise and fall of the white republic: Class politics and mass culture in nineteenth century America*. New York: Verso.

Southern Poverty Law Center. (1995, August). *Aryan world Congress focuses on militias and an expected revolution* (Klanwatch Intelligence Report 79). Montgomery, AL: Author.

Steinberg, S. (1995). *Turning back: The retreat from racial justice in American thought and policy*. Boston: Beacon.

Thompson, R. F. (1995). "The Kongo Atlantic tradition," cited in Shelley Fisher Fishkin, "Interrogating 'whiteness,' complicating 'blackness,' remapping American culture." *American Quarterly*, 47(3).

Walters, R. (1987, Fall). White racial nationalism in the United States. *Without Prejudice I*, 1.

Williams, W. (1982). *The state against blacks*. New York: McGraw-Hill.

Wilson, W. J. (1987). *The truly disadvantaged: The inner city, the underclass, and public policy*. Chicago: University of Chicago Press.

Winant, H. (1994). *Racial conditions: politics, theory, comparisons*. Minneapolis: University of Minnesota Press.

NOTES

Michael Omi and I conceived this paper together. Thanks, brother, as always. Comments from Chip Gallagher, Magali Larson, David Roediger, and Mun Wong are also gratefully acknowledged.

1. The obvious reference in these remarks is to Myrdal's framework (1962 [1944]). Without endorsing his entire perspective, which I think proceeds in an idealistic fashion, it is possible to affirm the vitality of Myrdal's central premise: that democratic principles remain incompatible with racial subordination.

2. A thoughtful discussion of Duke may be found in Langer (1990, pp. 94–98). Already in the 1970s Duke had begun the renovation of his Klan ideology:

   > We see [the Ku Klux Klan] as a social movement in the traditional sense. The same way that the Sons of Liberty were. The same way the Communist Party was.... In other words, a movement for social change and not just a fraternity for people to get together and have fun or salute the past. (quoted in Chalmers, 1981, p. 10)

3. Even in the later *Affirmative Discrimination*, Glazer affirms as one of the three formative principles of "the American ethnic pattern" the idea that "no group .... would be required to give up its group character and distinctiveness as the price of full entry into the American society and polity" (Glazer, 1978, p. 5). Yet it is questionable how much this pluralism can be sustained without a recognition of racial difference, since race is at a minimum an important dimension of political mobilization and cultural distinctiveness.

4. Without entering too far into the question of what constitutes "objective" racial inequality it must be recognized that on such issues as housing (Massey & Denton, 1993), employment discrimination (Neckerman & Kirschenman, 1991), criminal justice (Butterfield, 1995), welfare (Quadagno, 1994), or unemployment, the evidence is rather unambiguous. If anything the data minimize inequality. Take unemployment: Here official statistics

neglect the informal economy, which is a primary source of employment and locus of discrimination against racially defined minority workers. Unemployment data measure only "active" job seekers, not those who have been without (formal) jobs for a long time or those who have become discouraged in their job search. These constructions of the data on unemployment have a political subtext: the reduction of the numerator on the monthly BLS report obviously improves the image of the party in power (Gordon, 1987). There are also ample grounds on which to question the racial logic of unemployment figures, which rely on census categories (Omi & Winant, 1994, pp. 3–4, 82).

5. Professor Troy Duster has raised important questions about my argument (with Michael Omi) that biologistic racism has been discredited, or at least relegated, to a secondary status in contemporary debates about race. In his *Backdoor to Eugenics* (Duster, 1990) he suggested that biologism is as susceptible to rearticulation as any other ideological dimension of racism. Additional evidence for this argument is provided by the appearance of *The Bell Curve* (Herrnstein & Murray, 1994). Omi and I take the view that, although scientific grounds for racism are no more dead than religious ones, the biologistic argument cannot regain the cachet it possessed in the 19th and early 20th centuries; the political dimensions of race will persevere as its predominant determinants (Omi & Winant, 1993, 1994).

TWO

How Did Jews Become White Folks?

Karen Brodkin

The American nation was founded and developed by the Nordic race, but if a few more million members of the Alpine, Mediterranean and Semitic races are poured among us, the result must inevitably be a hybrid race of people as worthless and futile as the good-for-nothing mongrels of Central America and Southeastern Europe.

—Kenneth Roberts, "Why Europe Leaves Home"

It is clear that Kenneth Roberts did not think of my ancestors as white, like him. The late 19th century and early decades of the 20th saw a steady stream of warnings by scientists, policymakers, and the popular press that "mongrelization" of the Nordic or Anglo-Saxon race — the real Americans — by inferior European races (as well as by inferior non-European ones) was destroying the fabric of the nation.

I continue to be surprised when I read books that indicate that America once regarded its immigrant European workers as something other than white, as biologically different. My parents are not surprised; they expect anti-Semitism to be part of the fabric of daily life, much as I expect racism to be a part of it. They came of age in the Jewish world of the 1920s and 1930s, at the peak of anti-Semitism in America.[1] They are rightly proud of their upward mobility and think of themselves as pulling themselves up by their own bootstraps. I grew up during the 1950s in the Euro-ethnic New York suburb of Valley Stream, where Jews were simply one kind of white folks and where ethnicity meant little more to my generation than food and family heritage. Part of my ethnic heritage was the belief that Jews were smart and that our success was due to our own efforts and abilities, reinforced by a culture that valued sticking together, hard work, education, and deferred gratification.

I am willing to affirm all those abilities and ideals and their contribution to Jews' upward mobility, but I also argue that they were still far from sufficient to account for Jewish success. I say this because the belief in a Jewish version of Horatio Alger has become a point of entry for some mainstream Jewish organizations to adopt a racist attitude against African Americans especially and to oppose affirmative action for people of color.[2] Instead I want to suggest that Jewish success is a product not only of ability but also of the removal of powerful social barriers to its realization.

It is certainly true that the United States has a history of anti-Semitism and of beliefs that Jews are members of an inferior race. But Jews were hardly alone. American anti-Semitism was part of a broader pattern of late 19th-century racism against all southern and eastern European immigrants, as well as against Asian immigrants, not to mention African Americans, Native Americans, and Mexicans. These views justified all sorts of discriminatory treatment, including closing the doors, between 1882 and 1927, to immigration from Europe and Asia. This picture changed radically after World War II. Suddenly, the same folks who had promoted nativism and xenophobia were eager to believe that the Euro-origin people whom they had deported, reviled as members of inferior races, and prevented from immigrating only a few years earlier, were now middle-class white suburban citizens.[3]

It was not an educational epiphany that made those in power change their hearts, their minds, and our race. Instead, it was the biggest and best affirmative action program in the history of our nation, and it was for Euromales. That is not how it was billed, but it is the way it worked out in practice. I tell this story to show the institutional nature of racism and the centrality of state policies to creating and changing races. Here, those policies reconfigured the category of whiteness to include European immigrants. There are similarities and differences in the ways each of the European immigrant groups became "whitened." I tell the story in a way that links anti-Semitism to other varieties of anti-European racism because this highlights what Jews shared with Euro-immigrants.

EURORACES

The U.S. "discovery" that Europe was divided into inferior and superior races began with the racialization of the Irish in the mid-19th century and flowered in response to the great waves of immigration from southern and eastern Europe that began in the late 19th century. Before that time, European immigrants — including Jews — had been largely assimilated into the white population. However, the 23 million European immigrants who came to work in U.S. cities in the waves of migration after 1880 were too many and too concentrated to absorb. Since immigrants and their children made up more than 70% of the population of most of the country's largest cities, by the 1890s urban America had taken on a distinctly southern and eastern European immigrant flavor. Like the Irish in Boston and New York, their urban concentrations in dilapidated neighborhoods put them cheek by jowl next to the rising elites and the middle class with whom they shared public space and to whom their working-class ethnic communities were particularly visible.

The Red Scare of 1919 clearly linked anti-immigrant with anti-working-class sentiment — to the extent that the Seattle general strike by largely native-born workers was blamed on foreign agitators. The Red Scare was fueled by an economic depression, a massive postwar wave of strikes, the Russian Revolution, and another influx of postwar immigration. Strikers in the steel and garment industries in New York and New England were mainly new immigrants. "As part of a fierce counteroffensive, employers inflamed the historic identification of class conflict with immigrant radicalism." Anticommunism and anti-immigrant sentiment came together in the Palmer raids and deportation of immigrant working-class activists. There was real fear of revolution. One of President Wilson's aides feared it was "the first appearance of the soviet in this country."[4]

Not surprisingly, the belief in European races took root most deeply among the wealthy, U.S.-born Protestant elite, who feared a hostile and seemingly inassimilable working class. By the end of the 19th century, Senator Henry Cabot Lodge pressed Congress to cut off immigration to the United States; Theodore Roosevelt raised the alarm of "race suicide" and took Anglo-Saxon women to task for allowing "native" stock to be outbred by inferior immigrants. In the early 20th century, these fears gained a great deal of social legitimacy thanks to the efforts of an influential network of aristocrats and scientists who developed theories of eugenics — breeding for a "better" humanity — and scientific racism.

Key to these efforts was Madison Grant's influential *The Passing of the Great Race*, published in 1916. Grant popularized notions developed by William Z. Ripley and Daniel Brinton that there existed three or four major European races, ranging from the superior Nordics of northwestern Europe to the inferior southern and eastern races of the Alpines, Mediterraneans, and worst of all, Jews, who seemed to be everywhere in his native New York City. Grant's nightmare was race-mixing among Europeans. For him, "the cross between any of the diree European races and a Jew is a Jew." He didn't have good things to say about Alpine or Mediterranean "races" either. For Grant, race and class were interwoven: The upper class was racially pure Nordic; the lower classes came from the lower races.[5]

Far from being on the fringe, Grant's views were well within the popular mainstream. Here is the *New York Times* describing the Jewish Lower East Side of a century ago:

> The neighborhood where these people live is absolutely impassable for wheeled vehicles other than their pushcarts. If a truck driver tries to get through where their pushcarts are standing they apply to him all kinds of vile and indecent epithets. The driver is fortunate if he gets out of the street without being hit with a stone or having a putrid fish or piece of meat thrown in his face. This neighborhood, peopled almost entirely by the people who claim to have been driven from Poland and Russia, is the eyesore of New York and perhaps the filthiest place on the western continent. It is impossible for a Christian to live there because he will be driven out, either by blows or the dirt and stench. Cleanliness is an unknown quantity to these people. They cannot be lifted up to a higher plane because they do not want to be. If the cholera should ever get among these people, they would scatter its germs as a sower does grain.[6]

Such views were well within the mainstream of the early 20th-century scientific community.[7] Madison Grant and eugenicist Charles B. Davenport organized the Galton Society in 1918 in order to foster research, promote eugenics, and restrict immigration.[8] Lewis Terman, Henry Goddard, and Robert Yerkes, developers of the "intelligence" test, believed firmly that southeastern European immigrants, African Americans, American Indians, and Mexicans were "feebleminded." And indeed, more than 80% of the immigrants whom Goddard tested at Ellis Island in 1912 turned out to be just that, as measured by his test. Racism fused with eugenics in scientific circles, and the eugenics circles overlapped with the nativism of white Protestant elites. During World War I, racism shaped the army's development of a mass intelligence test. Psychologist Robert Yerkes, who developed the test, became an even stronger advocate of eugenics after the war. Writing in the *Atlantic Monthly* in 1923, he noted,

> If we may safely judge by the army measurements of intelligence, races are quite as significantly different as individuals.... [A]lmost as great as the intellectual difference between negro [*sic*] and white in the army are the differences between white racial groups.... For the past ten years or so the intellectual status of immigrants has been disquietingly low. Perhaps this is because of the dominance of the Mediterranean races, as contrasted with the Nordic and Alpine.[9]

By the 1920s, scientific racism sanctified the notion that real Americans were white and that real whites came from northwest Europe. Racism by white workers in the West fueled laws excluding and expelling the Chinese in 1882. Widespread racism led to closing the immigration door to virtually all Asians and most Europeans between 1924 and 1927, and to deportation of Mexicans during the Great Depression.

Racism in general, and anti-Semitism in particular, flourished in higher education. Jews were the first of the Euro-immigrant groups to enter college in significant numbers, so it was not surprising that they faced the brunt of discrimination there. The Protestant elite complained that Jews were unwashed, uncouth, unrefined, loud, and pushy. Harvard University president A. Lawrence Lowell, who was also a vice president of the Immigration Restriction League, was open about his opposition to Jews at Harvard. The Seven Sister schools had a reputation for "flagrant discrimination." M. Carey Thomas, Bryn Mawr president, may have been some kind of feminist, but she was also an admirer of scientific racism and an advocate of immigration restriction. She "blocked both the admission of black students and the promotion of Jewish instructors."[10]

Jews are justifiably proud of the academic skills that gained them access to the most elite schools of the nation despite the prejudices of their gatekeepers. However, it is well to remember that they had no serious competition from their Protestant classmates. This is because college was not about academic pursuits. It was about social connection—through its clubs, sports, and other activities, as well as in the friendships one was expected to forge with other children of elites. From this, the real purpose of the college experience, Jews remained largely excluded.

This elite social mission had begun to come under fire and was challenged by a newer professional training mission at about the time Jews began entering college. Pressures for change were beginning to transform the curriculum and to reorient college from a gentleman's bastion to a training ground for the middle-class professionals needed by an industrial economy. "The curriculum was overhauled to prepare students for careers in business, engineering, scientific farming, and the arts, and a variety of new professions such as accounting and pharmacy that were making their appearance in American colleges for the first time."[11] Occupational training was precisely what had drawn Jews to college. In a setting where disparagement of intellectual pursuits and the gentleman's C were badges of distinction, it certainly wasn't hard for Jews to excel. Jews took seriously what their affluent Protestant classmates disparaged, and, from the perspective of nativist elites, took unfair advantage of a loophole to get where they were not wanted.

Patterns set by these elite schools to close those "loopholes" influenced the standards of other schools, made anti-Semitism acceptable, and "made the aura of exclusivity a desirable commodity for the college-seeking clientele."[12] Fears that colleges "might soon be overrun by Jews" were publicly expressed at a 1918 meeting of the Association of New England Deans. In 1919 Columbia University took steps to decrease the number of its Jewish students by a set of practices that soon came to be widely adopted. They developed a psychological test based on the World War I army intelligence tests to measure "innate ability—and middle-class home environment;" and they redesigned the admission application to ask for religion, father's name and birthplace, a photo, and personal interview. Other techniques for excluding Jews, like a fixed class size, a chapel requirement, and preference for children of alumni, were less obvious.[13]

Sociologist Jerome Karabel has argued that current criteria for college admission—which mix grades and test scores with well-roundedness and character, as well as a preference (or affirmative action) for athletes and children of alumni, which allowed schools to select more affluent Protestants—had their origins in these exclusionary efforts. Their proliferation in the 1920s caused the intended drop in the numbers of Jewish law, dental, and medical students as well as the imposition of quotas in engineering, pharmacy, and veterinary schools.[14]

Columbia's quota against Jews was well known in my parents' community. My father is very proud of having beaten it and been admitted to Columbia Dental School on the basis of his skill at carving a soap ball. Although he became a teacher instead because the tuition was too high, he took me to the dentist every week of my childhood and prolonged the agony by discussing the finer points of tooth-filling and dental care. My father also almost failed the speech test required for his teaching license because he didn't speak "standard," that is, nonimmigrant, nonaccented English. For my parents and most of their friends, English was the language they had learned when they went to school, because their home and neighborhood language was Yiddish. They saw the speech test as designed to keep all ethnics, not just Jews, out of teaching.

There is an ironic twist to this story. My mother always urged me to speak well, like her friend Ruth Saronson, who was a speech teacher. Ruth remained my model for perfect diction until I went away to college. When I talked to her on one of my visits home, I heard the New York accent of my version of "standard English," compared with the Boston academic version.

My parents believe that Jewish success, like their own, was due to hard work and a high value placed on education. They attended Brooklyn College during the Depression. My mother worked days and went to school at night; my father went during the day. Both their families encouraged them. More accurately, their families expected it. Everyone they knew was in the same boat, and their world was made up of Jews who were advancing just as they were. The picture for New York — where most Jews lived — seems to back them up. In 1920, Jews made up 80% of the students at New York's City College, 90% of Hunter College, and before World War I, 40% of private Columbia University. By 1934, Jews made up almost 24% of all law students nationally and 56% of those in New York City. Still, more Jews became public school teachers, like my parents and their friends, than doctors or lawyers. Indeed, Ruth Jacknow Markowitz has shown that "my daughter, the teacher" was, for parents, an aspiration equivalent to "my son, the doctor."[15]

How we interpret Jewish social mobility in this milieu depends on with whom we compare them. Compared with other immigrants, Jews were upwardly mobile. But compared with nonimmigrant whites, that mobility was very limited and circumscribed. The existence of anti-immigrant, racist, and anti-Semitic barriers kept the Jewish middle class confined to a small number of occupations. Jews were excluded from mainstream corporate management and corporately employed professions, except in the garment and movie industries, in which they were pioneers. Jews were almost totally excluded from university faculties (the few who made it had powerful patrons). Eastern European Jews were concentrated in small businesses, and in professions where they served a largely Jewish clientele. We shouldn't forget Jewish success in organized crime in the 1920s and 1930s as an aspect of upward mobility. Arnold Rothstein "transformed crime from a haphazard, small-scale activity into a well-organized and well-financed business operation." There were also Detroit's Purple Gang, Murder Incorporated in New York, a whole host of other big-city Jewish gangs in organized crime, and of course Meyer Lansky.[16]

Although Jews, as the Euro-ethnic vanguard in college, became well established in public school teaching — as well as visible in law, medicine, pharmacy, and librarianship before the postwar boom — these professions should be understood in the context of their times. In the 1930s they lacked the corporate context they have today, and Jews in these professions were certainly not corporation based. Most lawyers, doctors, dentists, and pharmacists were solo practitioners, depended upon other Jews for their clientele, and were considerably less affluent than their counterparts today.[17]

Compared to Jewish progress after World War II, Jews' prewar mobility was also very limited. It was the children of Jewish businessmen, but not those of Jewish workers, who flocked to college. Indeed, in 1905 New York, the children of Jewish workers had as little schooling as the children of other immigrant workers.[18] My family was quite the model in this respect. My grandparents did not go to college, but they did have a modicum of small business success. My father's family owned a pharmacy. Although my mother's father was a skilled garment worker, her mother's family was large and always had one or another grocery or deli in which my grand-mother participated. It was the relatively privileged children of upwardly mobile Jewish immigrants like my grandparents who began to push on the doors to higher education even before my parents were born.

Especially in New York City — which had almost one and a quarter million Jews by 1910 and retained the highest concentration of the nation's 4 million Jews in 1924 — Jews built a small-business-based middle class and began to develop a second-generation professional class in the interwar years. Still, despite the high percentages of Jews in eastern colleges, most Jews were not middle class, and fewer than 3% were professionals — compared with somewhere between two thirds and three quarters in the postwar generation.[19]

My parents' generation believed that Jews overcame anti-Semitic barriers because Jews are special. My answer is that the Jews who were upwardly mobile were special among Jews (and were also well placed to write the story). My generation might well respond to our parents' story of pulling themselves up by their own bootstraps with "But think what you might have been without the racism and with some affirmative action!" And that is precisely what the post–World War II boom; the decline of systematic, public, anti-Euro racism and anti-Semitism; and govern-mental affirmative action extended to white males.

WHITENING EURO-ETHNICS

By the time I was an adolescent, Jews were just as white as the next white person. Until I was eight, I was a Jew in a world of Jews. Everyone on Avenue Z in Sheepshead Bay was Jewish. I spent my days playing and going to school on three blocks of Avenue Z, and visiting my grand-parents in the nearby Jewish neighborhoods of Brighton Beach and Coney Island. There were plenty of Italians in my neighborhood, but they lived around the corner. They were a kind of Jew, but on the margins of my social horizons. Portuguese were even more distant, at the end of the bus ride, at Sheepshead Bay. The shul, or temple, was on Avenue Z, and I begged my father to take me like all the other fathers took their kids, but religion wasn't part of my family's Judaism. Just how Jewish my neighborhood was hit me in first grade, when I was one of two kids to go to school on Rosh Hashanah. My teacher was shocked — she was Jewish, too, and I was embarrassed to tears when she sent me home. I was never again sent to school on Jewish holidays. We left that world in 1949 when we moved to Valley Stream, Long Island, which was Protestant and Republican and even had farms until Irish, Italian, and Jewish ex-urbanites like us gave it a more suburban and Democratic flavor.

Neither religion nor ethnicity separated us at school or in the neighborhood — except temporarily. During my elementary school years, I remember a fair number of dirt-bomb (a good suburban weapon) wars on the block. Periodically, one of the Catholic boys would accuse me or my brother of killing his god, to which we'd reply, "Did not," and start lobbing dirt bombs. Sometimes he'd get his friends from Catholic school and I'd get mine from public school kids on the block, some of whom were Catholic. Hostilities didn't last for more than a couple of hours and punctuated an otherwise friendly relationship. They ended by our junior high years, when other things became more important. Jews, Catholics and Protestants, Italians, Irish, Poles, "English" (I don't remember hearing WASP as a kid) were mixed up on the block and in school. We thought of ourselves as middle class and very enlightened because our ethnic backgrounds seemed so irrelevant to high school culture. We didn't see race (we thought), and racism was not part of our peer consciousness. Nor were the immigrant or working-class histories of our families.

As with most chicken-and-egg problems, it is hard to know which came first. Did Jews and other Euro-ethnics become white because they became middle class? That is, did money whiten? Or did being incorporated into an expanded version of whiteness open up the economic doors to middle-class status? Clearly, both tendencies were at work.

Some of the changes set in motion during the war against fascism led to a more inclusive version of whiteness. Anti-Semitism and anti-European racism lost respectability. The 1940 census no longer distinguished native whites of native parentage from those, like my parents, of immigrant parentage, so Euro-immigrants and their children were more securely white by submersion in an expanded notion of whiteness.[20]

Theories of nurture and nature replaced theories of nature and biology. Instead of dirty and dangerous races that would destroy American democracy, immigrants became ethnic groups whose children had successfully assimilated into the mainstream and risen to the middle class. In this new myth, Euro-ethnic suburbs like mine became the measure of American democracy's victory over racism. Jewish mobility became a new Horatio Alger story. In time and with hard work, every ethnic group would get a piece of the pie, and the United States would be a nation with equal opportunity for all its people to become part of a prosperous middle-class majority. And it seemed that Euro-ethnic immigrants and their children were delighted to join middle America.

This is not to say that anti-Semitism disappeared after World War II, only that it fell from fashion and was driven underground. In the last few years it has begun to surface among some parts of the right-wing militia movement, skinheads, and parts of the religious Right. Micah Sifry's revelation of Richard Nixon's and George Bush's personal anti-Semitism and its prevalence in both their administrations indicates its persistence in the Protestant elite.[21] Although elites do not have a monopoly on anti-Semitism, they do have the ability to restrict Jews' access to the top echelons of corporate America. Since the war, however, glass ceilings on Jewish mobility have become fewer and higher. Although they may still suppress the number of Jews and other Euro-ethnics in the upper class, it has been a long time since they could keep them out of even the highest reaches of the middle class. Indeed, the presence of Jews among the finance capitalists and corporate criminals of the 1980s may have fueled a resurgence in right-wing circles of the other anti-Semitic stereotype, of Jews as Shylocks.

Although changing views on who was white made it easier for Euro-ethnics to become middle class, economic prosperity also played a very powerful role in the whitening process. The economic mobility of Jews and other Euro-ethnics derived ultimately from America's postwar economic prosperity and its enormously expanded need for professional, technical, and managerial labor, as well as on government assistance in providing it.

The United States emerged from the war with the strongest economy in the world. Real wages rose between 1946 and 1960, increasing buying power a hefty 22% and giving most Americans some discretionary income. American manufacturing, banking, and business services were increasingly dominated by large corporations, and these grew into multinational corporations. Their organizational centers lay in big, new urban headquarters that demanded growing numbers of clerical, technical, and managerial workers. The postwar period was a historic moment for real class mobility and for the affluence we have erroneously come to believe was the American norm. It was a time when the old white and the newly white masses became middle class.[22]

The GI Bill of Rights, as the 1944 Serviceman's Readjustment Act was known, is arguably the most massive affirmative action program in American history. It was created to develop needed labor force skills and to provide those who had them with a lifestyle that reflected their value to the economy. The GI benefits that were ultimately extended to 16 million GIs (of the Korean War as well) included priority in jobs — that is, preferential hiring, but no one objected to it then — financial support during the job search, small loans for starting up businesses, and, most important, low-interest home loans and educational benefits, which included tuition and living expenses. This legislation was rightly regarded as one of the most revolutionary postwar programs. I call it affirmative action because it was aimed at and disproportionately helped male, Euro-origin GIs.[23] GI benefits, like the New Deal affirmative action programs before them and the 1960s affirmative action programs after them, were responses to protest. Business executives and the general public believed that the war economy had only temporarily halted the Great Depression. Many feared its return and a return to the labor strife and radicalism of the 1930s. "Memories of the Depression remained vivid, and many people suffered from what Davis Ross has aptly called 'depression psychosis' — the fear that the war would inevitably be followed by layoffs and mass unemployment."[24]

It was a reasonable fear. The 11 million military personnel who had been demobilized in the 1940s represented a quarter of the U.S. labor force. In addition, ending war production brought a huge number of layoffs, growing unemployment, and a high rate of inflation. To recoup wartime losses in real wages that had been caused by inflation as well as by the unions' no-strike pledge in support of the war effort, workers staged a massive wave of strikes in 1946. More workers went out on strike that year than ever before. There were strikes in all the heavy industries: railroad, coal mining, auto, steel, and electrical. For a brief moment it looked like class struggle all over again. But government and business leaders had learned from the experience of bitter labor struggles after World War I just how important it was to assist demobilized soldiers. The GI Bill resulted from their determination to avoid those mistakes this time. The biggest benefits of this legislation were college and technical school educations, and very cheap home mortgages.[25]

EDUCATION AND OCCUPATION

It is important to remember that, prior to the war, a college degree was still very much a "mark of the upper class," that colleges were largely finishing schools for Protestant elites. Before the postwar boom, schools could not begin to accommodate the American masses. Even in New York City before the 1930s, neither the public schools nor City College had room for more than a tiny fraction of potential immigrant students.[26]

Not so after the war. The almost 8 million GIs who took advantage of their educational benefits under the GI Bill caused "the greatest wave of college building in American history." White male GIs were able to take advantage of their educational benefits for college and technical training, so they were particularly well positioned to seize the opportunities provided by the new demands for professional, managerial, and technical labor.

It has been well documented that the GI educational benefits transformed American higher education and raised the educational level of that generation and generations to come. With many provisions for assistance in upgrading their educational attainments, veterans pulled ahead of nonveterans in earning capacity. In the long run it was the nonveterans who had fewer opportunities.[27]

Postwar expansion made college accessible to Euromales in general and to Jews in particular. My generation's "Think what you could have been!" answer to our parents became our reality as quotas and old occupational barriers fell and new fields opened up to Jews. The most striking result was a sharp decline in Jewish small businesses and a skyrocketing increase in Jewish professionals. For example, as quotas in medical schools fell, the numbers of Jewish M.D.s shot up. If Boston is any indication, just over 1% of all Jewish men before the war were doctors, but 16% of the postwar generation became M.D.s. A similar Jewish mass movement took place in college and university faculties, especially in "new and expanding fields in the social and natural sciences."[28]

Although these Jewish college professors tended to be sons of businessmen and professionals, the postwar boom saw the first large-scale class mobility among Jewish men. Sons of working-class Jews now went to college and became professionals themselves—according to the Boston survey, almost two thirds of them. This compared favorably with three quarters of the sons of professional fathers.[29]

But if Jews' upward mobility was due to a lowering of racial barriers, then how have the children of other southern and eastern European immigrants fared? Stephen Steinberg provides one comparison—that of college faculties. Although Jews were the first group to go to college in any great numbers, the proportions of faculty comprising southern and eastern European Catholics has grown rapidly since World War II. Thus Catholic faculty and graduate students have steadily increased, Protestants have decreased, and Jews have reached a plateau, such that Protestants are underrepresented on college faculties while Catholics were approaching parity by 1974.

Steinberg argued that the lag had less to do with values about education than with difficulties that largely rural Catholic immigrants had in translating rural skills into financial success in an urban industrial setting. Once the opportunities were provided by the GI Bill and associated programs, they too took full advantage of education as a route to upward mobility. Whereas the first cohorts of Jewish faculty came from small-business backgrounds, Catholic faculty came from working-class families who benefited from postwar programs.[30] Steinberg argued that class backgrounds, more specifically the occupational resources of different immigrant streams, are important for shaping their relative mobility. But we need to place his argument in the broader racial perspective of institutional whiteness. That is, Irish, Jews and southern and eastern European Catholics were all held back until they were granted—willingly or unwillingly—the institutional privileges of socially sanctioned whiteness. This happened most dramatically after World War II.

Even more significantly, the postwar boom transformed America's class structure—or at least its status structure—so that the middle class expanded to encompass most of the population. Before the war, most Jews, like most other Americans, were part of the working class, defined in terms of occupation, education, and income. Already upwardly mobile before the war relative to other immigrants, Jews floated high on this rising economic tide, and most of them entered the middle class. The children of other immigrants did too. Still, even the high tide missed some Jews. As late as 1973, some 15% of New York's Jews were poor or near poor, and in the 1960s, almost 25% of employed Jewish men remained manual workers.[31]

The reason I refer to educational and occupational GI benefits as affirmative action programs for white males is because they were decidedly not extended to African Americans or to women of any race. Theoretically they were available to all veterans; in practice women and black veterans did not get anywhere near their share. Women's Army and Air Force units were initially organized as auxiliaries, hence not part of the military. When that status was changed, in July 1943, only those who reenlisted in the armed forces were eligible for veterans' benefits. Many women thought they were simply being demobilized and returned home. The majority remained and were ultimately eligible for veterans' benefits. But there was little counseling, and a social climate that discouraged women's careers and independence cut down on women's knowledge and sense of entitlement. The Veterans Administration kept no statistics on the number of women who used their GI benefits.[32]

The barriers that almost completely shut African American GIs out of their benefits were even more formidable. In Neil Wynn's portrait, black GIs anticipated starting new lives, just like their white counterparts. More than 43% hoped to return to school, and most expected to relocate, to find better jobs in new lines of work. The exodus from the South toward the North and West was particularly large. So it was not a question of any lack of ambition on the part of African American GIs. White male privilege was shaped against the backdrop of wartime racism and postwar sexism. African Americans were also less likely than whites, regardless of GI status, to gain new jobs commensurate with their wartime jobs. For example, in San Francisco, by 1948, black Americans "had dropped back halfway to their prewar employment status."[33]

Black GIs faced discrimination in the educational system as well. Despite the end of restrictions on Jews and other Euro-ethnics, African Americans were not welcome in white colleges. Black colleges were overcrowded, but the combination of segregation and prejudice made for few alternatives. About 20,000 black veterans attended college by 1947, most in black colleges, but almost as many, 15,000, could not gain entry. Predictably, the disproportionately few African Americans who did gain access to their educational benefits were able, like their white counterparts, to become doctors and engineers, and to enter the black middle class.[34]

SUBURBANIZATION

In 1949, ensconced in Valley Stream, I watched potato farms turn into Levittown and Idlewild (later Kennedy) airport. This was the major spectator sport in our first years on Long Island. A typical weekend would bring various aunts, uncles, and cousins out from the city. After a huge meal, we'd pile into the car — itself a novelty — to look at the bulldozed acres and comment on the matchbox construction. During the week, my mother and I would look at the houses going up within walking distance.

Bill Levitt built a basic, 900–1,000 square foot, somewhat expandable house for a lower-middle-class and working-class market on Long Island, and later in Pennsylvania and New Jersey. Levittown started out as 2,000 units of rental housing at $60 a month, designed to meet the low-income housing needs of a returning war vets, many of whom, like my Aunt Evie and Uncle Julie, were living in Quonset huts. By May 1947, Levitt and Sons had acquired enough land in Hempstead Township on Long Island to build 4,000 houses, and by the next February, he had built 6,000 units and named the development after himself. After 1948, federal financing for the construction of rental housing tightened, and Levitt switched to building houses for sale. By 1951, Levittown was a development of some 15,000 families.[35]

At the beginning of World War II, about one third of all American families owned their houses. That percentage doubled in 20 years. Most Levittowners looked just like my family. They came from New York City or Long Island; about 17% were military, from nearby Mitchell Field; Levittown was their first house, and almost everyone was married. Three quarters of the 1947 inhabitants were white collar, but by 1950 more blue-collar families had moved in, so that by 1951, "barely half" of the new residents were white collar, and by 1960 their occupational profile was somewhat more working class than for Nassau County as a whole. By this time too, almost one third of Levittown's people were either foreign-born or, like my parents, first-generation U.S.-born.[36]

The Federal Housing Administration (FHA) was key to buyers and builders alike. Thanks to the FHA, suburbia was open to more than GIs. People like us would never have been in the market for houses without FHA and Veterans Administration (VA) low-down-payment, low-interest, long-term loans to young buyers. Most suburbs were built by "merchant builders," large-scale entrepreneurs like Levitt, who obtained their own direct FHA and VA loans. In the view of one major builder, "without FHA and VA loans merchant building would not have happened." A great deal was at stake. FHA and VA had to approve subdivision plans and make the appraisals upon which house buyers' loans were calculated. FHA appraisals effectively set the price a house could sell for, since it established the amount of the mortgage it would insure. The VA was created after the war, and it followed FHA policies. Most of the benefits in both programs went to the suburbs, and half of all suburban housing in the 1950s and 1960s was financed by FHA or VA loans. Federal highway funding was also important to suburbanization. The National Defense Highway Act of 1941 put the government in the business of funding 90% of a national highway system (the other 10% came from the states), which developed a network of freeways between and around the nation's metropolitan areas, making suburbs and automobile commuting a way of life. State zoning laws and services were also key. "A significant and often crucial portion of the required infrastructure — typically water sewer, roads, parks, schools — was provided by the existing community, which was in effect subsidizing the builder and indirectly the new buyer or renter."[37]

In residential life, as in jobs and education, federal programs and GI benefits were crucial for mass entry into a middle-class, home-owning suburban lifestyle. Together they raised the American standard of living to a middle-class one. It was in housing policy that the federal government's racism reached its high point. Begun in 1934, the FHA was a New Deal program whose original intent was to stimulate the construction industry by insuring private loans to buy or build houses. Even before the war, it had stimulated a building boom. The FHA was "largely run by representatives of the real estate and banking industries."[38] As early as 1955, Charles Abrams blasted it:

> A government offering such bounty to builders and lenders could have required compliance with a nondiscrimination policy. Or the agency could at least have pursued a course of evasion, or hidden behind the screen of local autonomy. Instead, FHA adopted a racial policy that could well have been culled from the Nuremberg laws. From its inception FHA set itself up as the protector of the all white neighborhood. It sent its agents into the field to keep Negroes and other minorities from buying houses in white neighborhoods.[39]

The FHA believed in racial segregation. Throughout its history, it publicly and actively promoted restrictive covenants. Before the war, these forbade sales to Jews and Catholics as well as to African Americans. The deed to my house in Detroit had such a covenant, which theoretically prevented it from being sold to Jews or African Americans. Even after the Supreme Court outlawed restrictive covenants in 1948, the FHA continued to encourage builders to write them in against African Americans. FHA underwriting manuals openly insisted on racially homogeneous neighborhoods, and their loans were made only in white neighborhoods. I bought my Detroit house in 1972, from Jews who were leaving a largely African American neighborhood. By that time, restrictive covenants were a dead letter, but block busting by realtors was replacing it.

With the federal government behind them, virtually all developers refused to sell to African Americans. Palo Alto and Levittown, like most suburbs as late as 1960, were virtually all white. Out of 15,741 houses and 65,276 people, averaging 4.2 people per house, only 220 Levittowners, or 52 households, were "nonwhite." In 1958, Levitt announced publicly, at a press conference held to open his New Jersey development, that he would not sell to black buyers. This caused a furor because the state of New Jersey (but not the U.S. government) prohibited discrimination in federally subsidized housing. Levitt was sued and fought it. There had been a white riot in his Pennsylvania development when a black family moved in a few years earlier. In New Jersey, he was ultimately persuaded by township ministers to integrate. West Coast builder Joe Eichler had a policy of selling to any African American who could afford to buy. But his son pointed out that his father's clientele in more affluent Palo Alto was less likely to feel threatened. They liked to think of themselves as liberal, which was relatively easy to do because there were relatively few African Americans in the Bay area, and fewer still could afford homes in Palo Alto.[40]

The result of these policies was that African Americans were totally shut out of the suburban boom. An article in *Harper's* described the housing available to black GIs.

> On his way to the base each morning, Sergeant Smith passes attractive air-conditioned, FHA-financed housing project. It was built for service families. Its rents are little more than the Smiths pay for their shack. And there are half-a-dozen vacancies, but not for Negroes.[41]

Urban renewal made postwar cities into bad places to live. At a physical level, urban renewal reshaped them, and federal programs brought private developers and public officials together to create downtown central business districts where there had formerly been a mix of manufacturing, commerce, and working-class neighborhoods. Manufacturing was scattered to the peripheries of the city, which were ringed and bisected by a national system of highways. Some working-class neighborhoods were bulldozed, but others remained. In Los Angeles, as in New York's Bronx, the postwar period saw massive freeway construction right through the heart of old working-class neighborhoods. In East Los Angeles and Santa Monica, Chicana and Chicano and African American communities were divided in half or blasted to smithereens by the highways bringing Angelenos to the new white suburb or to make way for civic monuments like Dodger Stadium.[42]

Urban renewal was the other side of the process by which Jewish and other working-class Euro-immigrants became middle class. It was the push to suburbia's seductive pull. The fortunate white survivors of urban renewal headed disproportionately for suburbia, where they could partake of prosperity and the good life. There was a reason for its attraction. It was often cheaper to buy in the suburbs than to rent in the city. Even Euro-ethnics and families who would be considered working class, based on their occupations, were able to buy into the emerging white suburban lifestyle. And as Levittown indicates, they did so in increasing numbers, so that by 1966 half of all workers and 75% of those under 40 nationwide lived in suburbs. They too were considered middle class.[43]

If the federal stick of urban renewal joined the FHA carrot of cheap mortgages to send masses of Euro-Americans to the suburbs, the FHA had a different kind of one-two punch for African Americans. Segregation kept them out of the suburbs, and redlining made sure they could not buy or repair their homes in the neighborhoods in which they were allowed to live. The FHA practiced systematic redlining. This was a practice developed by its predecessor, the Home Owners Loan Corporation (HOLC), which in the 1930s developed an elaborate neighborhood rating system that placed the highest (green) value on all-white, middle-class neighborhoods, and the lowest (red) on racially nonwhite or mixed and working-class neighborhoods. High ratings meant high property values. The idea was that low property values in redlined neighborhoods made them bad investments. The FHA was, after all, created by and for banks and the housing industry. Redlining warned banks not to lend there, and the FHA would not insure mortgages in such neighborhoods. Redlining created a self-fulfilling prophesy.

The FHAs and VAs refusal to guarantee loans in redlined neighborhoods made it virtually impossible for African Americans to borrow money for home improvement or purchase. It took the civil rights movement to make these practices and their devastating consequences public. As a result, those who fought urban renewal, or who sought to make a home in the urban ruins, found themselves locked out of the middle class. They also faced an ideological assault that labeled their neighborhoods slums and called them slum-dwellers.[44]

CONCLUSION

The record is very clear. Instead of seizing the opportunity to end institutionalized racism, the federal government did its level best to shut and double-seal the postwar window of opportunity in African Americans' faces. It consistently refused to combat segregation in the social institutions that were key to upward mobility in education, housing, and employment. Moreover, federal programs that were themselves designed to assist demobilized GIs and young families systematically discriminated against African Americans. Such programs reinforced white and nonwhite racial distinctions, even as intrawhite racialization was falling out of fashion. This other side of the coin, that white men of northwest European ancestry and white men of southeastern European ancestry were treated equally in theory and in practice with regard to the benefits they received, was part of the larger postwar whitening of Jews and other eastern and southern Europeans.

The myth that Jews pulled themselves up by their own bootstraps ignores the fact that it took federal programs to create the conditions whereby the abilities of Jews and other European immigrants could be recognized and rewarded rather than denigrated and denied. The GI Bill and FHA and VA mortgages, even though they were advertised as open to all, functioned as a set of racial privileges. They were privileges because they were extended to white GIs but not to black GIs. Such privileges were forms of affirmative action that allowed Jews and other Euro-American men to become suburban homeowners and to get the training that allowed them—but much less so women vets or war workers—to become professionals, technicians, salesmen, and managers in a growing economy. Jews' and other white ethnics' upward mobility was due to programs that allowed us to float on a rising economic tide. To African Americans, the government offered the cement boots of segregation, redlining, urban renewal, and discrimination.

Those racially skewed gains have been passed across the generations, so that racial inequality seems to maintain itself naturally even after legal segregation ended. Today, I own a house in Venice, California, like the one in which I grew up in Valley Stream, and my brother until recently owned a house in Palo Alto much like an Eichler house. Both of us are where we are thanks largely to the postwar benefits our parents received and passed on to us, and to the educational benefits we received in the 1960s as a result of affluence and the social agitation that developed from the black Freedom Movement. I have white, African American, and Asian American colleagues whose parents received fewer or none of America's postwar benefits and who expect never to own a house despite their considerable academic achievements. Some of these colleagues who are a few years younger than I also carry staggering debts for their education, which they expect to have to repay for the rest of their lives.

Conventional wisdom has it that the United States has always been an affluent land of opportunity. But the truth is that affluence has been the exception and that real upward mobility has required massive affirmative action programs. The myth of affluence persists today long after the industrial boom, and the public policies that supported good union contracts and real employment opportunities for (almost) all are gone. It is increasingly clear that the affluent period between 1940 and 1970 or 1975 was an aberrant one for America's white working class. The Jewish ethnic wisdom I grew up with, that we pulled ourselves up by our own bootstraps, by sticking together, by being damned smart, leaves out an important part of the truth: that not all Jews made it and that those who did had a great deal of help from the federal government.

Today, in a shrinking economy, where downward mobility is the norm, the children and grandchildren of the postwar beneficiaries of the economic boom have some precious advantages. For example, having parents who own their own homes or who have decent retirement benefits can make a real difference in a young person's ability to take on huge college loans or to come up with a down payment for a house. Even this simple inheritance helps perpetuate the gap between whites and people of color. Sure, Jews needed ability, but that was never enough for more than a few to make it. The same applies today. Whatever advantages I bequeath them, my sons will never have their parents' or grandparents' experience of life on a rising economic tide.

Public policies such as the anti-immigrant Proposition 187 and anti-affirmative action Proposition 209 in California, the abolition of affirmative action policies at the University of California, and media demonization of African Americans and Central American immigrants as lazy welfare cheats encourage feelings of white entitlement to middle-class privilege. But our children's and grandchildren's realities are that they are downwardly mobile relative to their grandparents, not because people of color are getting the good jobs by affirmative action but because the good jobs and prosperity in general are ceasing to exist.

References

Abrams, C. (1955). *Forbidden neighbors: A study of prejudice in housing*. New York: Harper & Brothers.

Barkan, E. (1992). *The retreat of scientific racism: Changing concepts of race in Britain and the United States between the World Wars*. New York: Cambridge University Press.

Berger, B. (1960). *Working class suburb: A study of auto workers in suburbia*. Berkeley: University of California Press.

Binkin, M., & Eitelberg, M. J. (1982). *Blacks and the military*. Washington, DC: Brookings Institution.

Brody, D. (1980). *Workers in industrial America: Essays on the twentieth century struggle*. New York: Oxford University Press.

Brown, F. J. (1946). *Educational opportunities for veterans*. Washington, DC: Public Affairs Press, American Council on Public Affairs.

Cockcroft, E. (1990). *Signs from the heart: California chicane murals*. Venice, CA: Social and Public Art Resource Center.

Dalfiume, R. M. (1969). *Desegregation of the U.S. Armed Forces: Fighting on two fronts 1939–1953*. Columbia: University of Missouri Press.

Davis, M. (1990). *City of quartz*. London: Verso.

Dinnerstein, L. (1987). *Uneasy at home: Anti-Semitism and the American Jewish experience*. New York: Columbia University Press.

Dobriner, W. M. (1963). *Class in suburbia*. Englewood Cliffs, NJ: Prentice Hall.

"East side vendors." (1893, July 30). *New York Times*. (Reprinted in *Portal to America: The lower east side 1870–1925*, by A. Schoener, 1967, New York: Holt, Rinehart and Winston. Quoted in *In their place: White America defines her minorities, 1850–1950*, by L. H. Carlson & G. A. Colburn, 1972, New York: Wiley)

Eichler, N. (1982). *The merchant builders*. Cambridge, MA: MIT Press.

Foner, J. (1974). *Blacks and the military in American history: A new perspective*. New York: Praeger Publishers.

Gans, H. (1962). *The urban villagers*. New York: Free Press of Glencoe.

Gelfand, M. (1975). *A nation of cities: The federal government and urban America, 1933–1965*. New York: Oxford University Press.

Gerber, D. (Ed.). (1986). *Anti-Semitism in American history*. Urbana: University of Illinois Press.

Gilman, S. (1996). *Smart Jews: The construction of the image of Jewish superior intelligence*. Lincoln: University of Nebraska Press.

Gordon, M. (1964). *Assimilation in American life: The role of race, religion and national origins*. New York: Oxford University Press.

Gould, S. J. (1981). *The mismeasure of man*. New York: Norton.

Grant, M. (1916). *The passing of the great race: Or the racial basis of European history*. New York: Charles Scribner.

Greer, S. (1965). *Urban renewal and American cities*. Indianapolis: Bobbs-Merrill.

Hartman, C. (1975). *Housing and social policy*. Englewood Cliffs, NJ: Prentice Hall.

Higham, J. (1955). *Strangers in the land*. New Brunswick, NJ: Rutgers University Press.

Hurd, C. (1946). *The Veterans' Program: A complete guide to its benefits, rights, and options*. New York: McGraw-Hill.

Jackson, K. T. (1985). *Crabgrass frontier: The suburbanization of the United States*. New York: Oxford University Press.

Johnson, J. J. (1967). *Ebony brass: An autobiography of Negro frustration amid aspiration*. New York: William Frederick Press.

Karabel, J. (1984). Status-group struggle, organizational interests, and the limits of institutional autonomy. *Theory and Society, 13*, 1–40.

Lief, B. J., & Goering, S. (1987). The implementation of the federal mandate for fair housing. In G. A. Tobin (Ed.), *Divided neighborhoods: Changing patterns of racial segregation* (pp. 227–267). Beverly Hills, CA: Sage Publications.

Markowitz, R. J. (1993). *My daughter, the teacher: Jewish teachers in the New York City schools*. New Brunswick, NJ: Rutgers University Press.

Monkkonen, E. H. (1988). *America becomes urban*. Berkeley: University of California Press.

Moore, D. D. (1992). On the fringes of the city: Jewish neighborhoods in three boroughs. In D. Ward & O. Zunz (Eds.), *The landscape of modernity: Essays on New York City, 1900–1940*. New York: Russell Sage Foundation.

Mosch, T. R. (1975). *The GI Bill: A breakthrough in educational and social policy in the United States*. Hicksville, NY: Exposition Press.

Nalty, B. C., & MacGregor, M. J. (Eds.). (1981). *Blacks in the military: Essential documents*. Wilmington, DE: Scholarly Resources.

Nash, G. B., Jeffrey, J. R., Howe, J. R., Davis, A. F., Frederick, P. J., & Winkler, A. M. (1986). *The American people: Creating a nation and a society*. New York: Harper & Row.

Pardo, M. (1990). Mexican-American women grassroots community activists: "Mothers of East Los Angeles." *Frontiers, 11*(1), 1–7.

Patterson, T. C. (1997). *Inventing Western civilization*. New York: Monthly Review Press.

Ripley, W. Z. (1923). *The races of Europe: A sociological study*. New York: Appleton.

Rodriguez, S. (1997, May 2). *Tourism, whiteness, and the vanishing Anglo*. Paper presented at the conference "Seeing and Being Seen: Tourism in the American West," Center for the American West, Boulder, CO.

Sansbury, G. (1997). "Dear Senator Capehart": Letters sent to the U.S. Senate's 1954 FHA investigation. *Planning History Studies, 11*(2), 19–46.

Sifry, M. (1993, January 25). Anti-Semitism in America. *The Nation*, 92–99.

Silberman, C. E. (1985). *A certain people: American Jews and their lives today*. New York: Summit Books.

Sklare, M. (1971). *America's Jews*. New York: Random House.

Sowell, T. (1981). *Ethnic America: A history*. New York: Basic Books.

Squires, G. D. (Ed.). (1989). *Unequal partnerships: The political economy of urban redevelopment in postwar America*. New Brunswick, NJ: Rutgers University Press.

Steinberg, S. (1974). *The academic melting pot: Catholics and Jews in American higher education*. New York: McGraw-Hill.

Steinberg, S. (1989). *The ethnic myth: Race, ethnicity and class in America* (2nd ed.). Boston: Beacon Press.

Synott, M. G. (1986). Anti-Semitism and American universities: Did quotas follow the Jews? In D. A. Gerber (Ed.), *Anti-Semitism in American history* (pp. 233–274). Urbana: University of Illinois Press.

Thomas, L. M. (1996). The soul of identity: Jews and Blacks. In S. F. Fishkin & J. Rubin-Dorsky (Eds.), *People of the book* (pp. 169–186). Madison: University of Wisconsin Press.

Tobin, G. A. (Ed.). (1987). *Divided neighborhoods: Changing patterns of racial segregation*. Beverly Hills, CA: Sage Publications.

U.S. Bureau of the Census. (1940). *Sixteenth census of the United States* (Vol. 2). Washington, DC: U.S. Government Printing Office.

Walker, O. (1970). The Windsor Hills School story. *Integrated Education: Race and Schools, 8*(3), 4–9.

Weiss, M. A. (1987). *The rise of the community builders: The American real estate industry and urban land planning*. New York: Columbia University Press.

Willenz, J. A. (1983). *Women veterans: America's forgotten heroines*. New York: Continuum.

Wynn, N. A. (1976). *The Afro-American and the Second World War*. London: Paul Elek.

NOTES

1. Gerber 1986; Dinnerstein 1987, 1994.
2. On the belief in Jewish and Asian versions of Horatio Alger, see Steinberg 1989, chap. 3; Gilman 1996. On Jewish culture, see Gordon 1964; see Sowell 1981 for an updated version.
3. Not all Jews are white or unambiguously white. It has been suggested, for example, that Hasidim lack the privileges of whiteness. Rodriguez (1997, 12, 15) began to unpack the claims of white Jewish "amenity migrants" and the different racial meanings of Chicano

claims to a crypto-Jewish identity in New Mexico. See also Thomas 1996 on African American Jews.

4. Higham 1955, 226.

5. M. Grant 1916; Ripley 1923; see also Patterson 1997; M. Grant, quoted in Higham 1955, 156.

6. *New York Times*, 30 July 1893, "East Side Street Vendors," reprinted in Schoener 1967, 57–58.

7. Gould 1981; Higham 1955; Patterson 1997, 108–115.

8. It was intended, as Davenport wrote to the president of the American Museum of Natural History, Henry Fairfield Osborne, as "an anthropological society ... with a central governing body, self-elected and self-perpetuating, and very limited in members, and also confined to native Americans [sic] who are anthropologically, socially and politically sound, no Bolsheviki need apply" (Barkan 1992, 67–68).

9. Quoted in Carlson and Colburn 1972, 333–334.

10. Synott 1986, 249–250, 233–274. For why Jews entered college earlier than other immigrants, and for a challenge to views that attribute it to Jewish culture, see Steinberg 1989.

11. Ibid., 229.

12. Synott 1986, 250. On anti-Semitism in higher education, see also Steinberg 1989, chaps. 5 and 9; Karabel 1984; Silberman 1985.

13. Synott 1986, 239–240.

14. Although quotas on Jews persisted into the 1950s at some of the elite schools, they were much attenuated, as the postwar college-building boom gave the coup de grace to the gentleman's finishing school.

15. Steinberg 1989, 137, 227; Markowitz 1993.

16. Silberman 1985, 88–117. On Jewish mobility, see Sklare 1971, 63–67; see M. Davis 1990, 146, n. 25, for exclusion of Jewish lawyers from corporate law in Los Angeles. Silberman 1985, 127–130.

17. Gerber 1986, 26.

18. Steinberg 1989, chap. 5.

19. Ibid., 225. Between 1900 and 1930, New York City's population grew from 3.4 million to 6.9 million, and at both times immigrants and children of immigrants were 80% of all white heads of household (Moore 1992, 270, n. 28).

20. This census also explicitly changed the Mexican race to white (U.S. Bureau of the Census 1940, 2:4).

21. Sifry 1993, 92–99.

22. Nash et al. 1986, 885–886.

23. On planning for veterans, see F. J. Brown 1946; Hurd 1946; Mosch 1975; "Post-war Jobs for Veterans" 1945; Willenz 1983.

24. Wynn 1976, 15.

25. G. B. Nash et al. 1986, 885; Eichler 1982, 4; Wynn 1976, 15; Mosch 1975, 20.

26. Willenz 1983, 165.

27. J. Nash et al. 1986, 885; Willenz 1983, 165. On mobility among veterans and nonveterans, see Havighurst et al. 1951.

28. Silberman 1985, 124, 121–122; Steinberg 1989, 137.

29. Silberman 1985, 121–122. None of the Jewish surveys asked what women were doing. Silberman claimed that Jewish women stayed out of the labor force prior to the 1970s, but the preponderance of women among public school teachers calls this into question.

30. Steinberg 1974, 1989, chap. 5.
31. Steinberg 1989, 89–90.
32. Willenz 1983, 20–28, 94–97. I thank Nancy G. Cattell for calling my attention to the fact that women GIs were ultimately eligible for benefits.
33. Wynn 1976, 114, 116.
34. On African Americans in the U.S. military, see Foner 1974; Dalfiume 1969; Johnson 1967; Binkin and Eitelberg 1982; Nalty and MacGregor 1981. On schooling, see Walker 1970, 4–9.
35. Hartman (1975, 141–142) cited massive abuses in the 1940s and 1950s by builders under the Section 608 program in which "the FHA granted extraordinarily liberal concessions to lackadaisically supervised private developers to induce them to produce rental housing rapidly in the postwar period." Eichler (1982) indicated that things were not that different in the subsequent FHA-funded home-building industry.
36. Dobriner 1963, 91, 100.
37. For home-owning percentages and the role of merchant builders, see Eichler 1982, 5, 9, 13. Jackson (1985, 205, 215) gave an increase in families living in owner-occupied buildings, rising from 44% in 1934 to 63% in 1972. See Monkkonen (1988, 184–185) on the scarcity of mortgages. See Gelfand (1975, chap. 6) on federal programs. On the location of highway interchanges, as in the appraisal and inspection process, Eichler (1982, 13) claimed that large-scale builders also often bribed and otherwise influenced the outcomes in their favor.
38. Weiss 1987, 146; Jackson 1985, 203–205.
39. Jackson 1985, 213; Abrams 1955, 22. See also Gelfand 1975; Tobin 1987; Lief and Goering 1987, 227–267; Sansbury 1997, 30–31.
40. Eichler 1982. See also Race and Housing 1964.
41. Quoted in Foner 1974, 195.
42. On urban renewal and housing policies, see Greer 1965; Hartman 1975; Squires 1989. On Los Angeles, see Pardo 1990; Cockroft 1990.
43. Jackson 1985, 206; D. Brody 1980, 192. Not only did suburbs proliferate, they also differentiated themselves into working and middle class based on the income disparities of occupations; see Berger 1960 for a case study.
44. See Gans 1962.

THREE

Behind the Gates:
Social Splitting and the "Other"

Setha Low

VISITING MY SISTER IN SAN ANTONIO

On our first visit to my sister's new home in San Antonio, Texas, my husband, Joel, and I are amazed to find two corral gates blocking the entrance to her development. I push an intercom button on the visitors' side. Getting no response, I hit the button repeatedly, finally rousing a disembodied voice that asks who we want to see. I shout Anna and Bob's last name. The entrance gate swings open, and we accelerate through onto a divided drive enclosed by a six-foot wall covered with bougainvillea and heavenly bamboo.

Once inside, large homes loom beside small vacant lots with "for sale" signs. The houses are mostly southwestern stucco painted Santa Fe colors with terra-cotta tile roofs and a sprinkling of brick colonials with slate shingles and wood trim. Uniformly attractive, with neat lawns and matching foundation plantings, the street looks like a set from the movie *Pleasantville*. It is not just peaceful, wealthy, and secure, but unreal, like a doll's house or a planned development in Sim City.[1] Everything looks perfect.

Desire for safety, security, community, and "niceness," as well as wanting to live near people like themselves because of a fear of "others" and of crime, is not unique to this family, but expressed by most residents living in gated communities. How they make sense of their new lives behind gates and walls, as well as the social consequences of their residential choices, is the subject of this reading. The emergence of a fortress mentality and its phenomenal success is surprising in the United States, where the majority of people live in open and unguarded neighborhoods. Thus, the rapid increase in the numbers of Americans moving to secured residential enclaves invites a more complex account of their motives and values. Like other middle-class Americans, residents of gated communities are looking for a place where they feel comfortable and secure, but this seemingly self-evident explanation reflects different underlying meanings and intentions. And collectively, their individual decisions are transforming the American dream of owning a suburban home in a close-knit community with easy access to nature into a vision that includes gates, walls, and guards.[2]

On the basis of eight years of ethnographic research in gated communities in New York City, suburban Long Island, New York, and San Antonio, Texas, I present the stories of residents' search for security, safety, and community in a globalizing world. Parents with children, young married couples, empty nesters, singles, widows, and retirees recount the details of living in recently constructed gated developments. Their residential histories and daily experiences highlight the significance of this growing middle- and upper-middle-class lifestyle and the conflicting values embodied in its architecture.

One explanation for the gated community's popularity is that it materially and metaphorically incorporates otherwise conflicting, and in some cases polarized, social values that make up the moral terrain of middle-class life. For example, it reflects urban and suburban tensions in the United States regarding social class, race, and ethnicity and at the same time represents the perennial concern with creating community. The gated community's symbolic power rests on its ability to order personal and social experience.

Architectural symbols such as gates and walls also provide a rationale for the moral inconsistencies of everyday life. For instance, many residents want to feel safe in their homes and argue that walls and gates help keep out criminals, but gated communities are not safer than nongated suburban neighborhoods, where crime rates are already low.[3] Instead, the logic of the symbolism satisfies conventional middle-class understandings of the nature of criminal activity — "it makes it harder for them to get in" — and justifies the choice to live in a gated community in terms of its moral and physical consequences — "look at my friends who were randomly robbed living in a nongated development."

Living in a gated community represents a new version of the middle-class American dream precisely because it temporarily suppresses and masks, even denies and fuses, the inherent anxieties and conflicting social values of modern urban and suburban life. It transforms Americans' dilemma of how to protect themselves and their children from danger, crime, and unknown others while still perpetuating open, friendly neighborhoods and comfortable, safe homes. It reinforces the norms of a middle-class lifestyle in a historical period in which everyday events and news media exacerbate fears of violence and terrorism. Thus, residents cite their "need" for gated communities to provide a safe and secure home in the face of a lack of other societal alternatives.

Gated residential communities, however, intensify social segregation, racism, and exclusionary land use practices already in place in most of the United States and raise a number of values conflicts for residents. For instance, residents acknowledge their misgivings about the possible false security provided by the gates and guards, but at the same time, even that false security satisfies their desire for emotional security associated with childhood and the neighborhoods where they grew up. Living in a gated development contributes to residents' sense of well-being but comes at the price of maintaining private guards and gates as well as conforming to extensive homeowners' association rules and regulations. Individual freedom and ease of access for residents must be limited in order to achieve greater privacy and social control for the community as a whole. These contradictions — which residents are aware of and talk about — provide an opportunity to understand the psychological and social meaning-making processes Americans use to order their lives.

Defining the Gated Community

A gated community is a residential development surrounded by walls, fences, or earth banks covered with bushes and shrubs, with a secured entrance. In some cases, protection is provided by inaccessible land such as a nature reserve and, in a few cases, by a guarded bridge.[4] The houses, streets, sidewalks, and other amenities are physically enclosed by these barriers, and entrance gates are operated by a guard or are opened with a key or electronic identity card. Inside the development there is often a neighborhood watch organization or professional security personnel who patrol on foot or by automobile.

Gated communities restrict access not just to residents' homes but also to the use of public spaces and services — roads, parks, facilities, and open space — contained within the enclosure. Communities vary in size from a few homes in very wealthy areas to as many as 21,000 homes in Leisure World in Orange County, California — with the number of residents indexed to the level of amenities and services. Many include golf courses, tennis courts, fitness centers, swimming pools, lakes, or unspoiled landscape as part of their appeal; commercial and public facilities are rare. Gated communities are different from other exclusive suburban developments, condominiums, cooperatives, and doorman apartment buildings found throughout the United States. At the level of the built environment, the walls and gates are visible barriers that have social and psychological as well as physical effects. In practical terms, gated communities restrict access to streets and thoroughfares that would otherwise be available for public as well as for private transportation. And in some cases, gated communities limit access to open space and park land donated by the developer to the municipality or town in exchange for building higher density housing than allowed by local zoning. Such land is designated as in the public domain but is available only to people who live within the development.

The number of people estimated to be living in gated communities in the United States increased from 4 million in 1995, to 8 million in 1997 and to 16 million in 1998. By 1997, it was estimated that there were in excess of 20,000 gated communities with more than 3 million housing units. A recently released census note by Tom Sanchez and Robert E. Lang, however, provided more accurate demographic statistics based on two new questions on gating and controlled access that were added to the 2001 American Housing Survey.[5] They found that 7,058,427, or 5.9% of households reporting that they live in communities, live in those surrounded by walls or fences, and 4,013,665 households, or 3.4%, live in communities where the access is controlled by some means such as entry codes, key cards, or security guard approval. The percentages varied by region with the West having the highest number of households living in walled or gated communities (11.1%), followed by the South (6.8%), the Northeast (3.1%), and the Midwest (2.1%). The metropolitan areas of Los Angeles, Houston, and Dallas have more than 1 million walled residential units.[6] These figures correspond to the original estimates that approximately 16 million people live in gated communities (16,234,384 based on the census, assuming 2.3 persons per average household) and that most are located in the Sun Belt.[7] Sanchez and Lang also found two distinct kinds of gated communities: those composed of mostly white, affluent homeowners, and those composed of minority renters with moderate incomes. They also found that African Americans were less likely to live in a gated community than Hispanics or whites.

But it is not just a U.S. phenomenon — gated communities are proliferating in Latin America, China, the Philippines, New Zealand, Australia, postapartheid South Africa, Indonesia, Germany, France, the former communist countries of Eastern Europe, urbanizing nations of the Arab world such as Egypt, Lebanon, and Saudi Arabia, and tourist centers along the Spanish coastline and the Côte d'Azur. In each context, gated communities serve different purposes and express distinct cultural meanings. For example, they house expatriate workers in Saudi Arabia, replicate socialist *datcha* housing in Moscow, provide a secure lifestyle in the face of extreme poverty in Southeast Asia, protect residents from urban violence in South Africa, create exclusive compounds for emerging elites in Bulgaria and China, and offer exclusive second homes or industry-sponsored housing in Western Europe. Gated communities are found at every income level throughout Latin America and take various forms, including upgraded housing complexes, retrofitted older neighborhoods, upscale center-city condominiums, small suburban developments, and large-scale master planned communities. Gating is a global trend drawing on U.S. models but also evolving from local architecture and sociohistorical circumstances, and is always embedded within specific cultural traditions.[8]

Fear of Others

Against whom was the Great Wall to serve as a protection? Against the people from the north. Now, I come from the southeast of China. No northern people can menace us there. We read of them in the books of the ancients; the cruelties they commit in accordance with their nature make us sigh in our peaceful arbors. The faithful representations of the artist show us the faces of the damned, their gaping mouths, their jaws furnished with great pointed teeth, their half-shut eyes that already seem to be seeking out the victim which their jaws will rend and devour. When our children are unruly, we show them these pictures, and at once they fly weeping into our arms. But nothing more than that do we know about these northerners. We have not seen them, and if we remain in our villages we shall never see them, even if on their wild horses they should ride as hard as they can straight towards us — the land is too vast and would not let them reach us; they would end their course in the empty air.

—Franz Kafka, "The Great Wall of China"[9]

My husband and I have reservations about going to a Fourth of July party, but my sister coaxes us with the promise of margaritas and sinful desserts, finally winning us over. Dressed in New York chic, we cross the street to enter an imposing Santa Fe-style house decorated with Mexican furniture and colorful textiles, full of people talking, children racing about, and our hosts serving drinks and dishing out enormous quantities of food. My husband wanders out to the pool, while I stay inside where it is air-conditioned. My choices are watching television with the older men or sitting with our hosts' teenage son and his friends. I sit down with the teenagers, and I am soon involved in a spirited discussion.

"Should we go downtown after dinner to see the fireworks along Riverwalk?" the host's son asks. Riverwalk is the commercially successful development that revitalized the center of San Antonio.

"Will there be many Mexicans there?" a tall, gangly boy in a Nike T-shirt and nylon running shorts asks.

"It'll be mobbed with Mexicans; I'm not sure I want to go," a girl with heavy blond bangs responds.

I am struck by how they used the word *Mexican*. Yesterday I toured the local missions where the complex history of Spanish conquest and resettlement of indigenous peoples is inscribed in the protective walls of the church compounds. Surely, these young people learn about Texas history in school.

I interrupt the flow of conversation and ask them what they mean by "Mexican." A young man in baggy khakis and a baseball hat worn backward looks at me curiously. "Why, the Mexicans who live downtown, on the south side of the city."

"What makes you think they are Mexican?" I ask, frowning a bit. "Because they speak Spanish?"

"They are dangerous," a young woman in a tennis skirt asserts, "packing knives and guns. Our parents don't allow us to go downtown at night."

They decide to stay and watch the fireworks from the golf course — at least they would not be with their parents — and wander off to find their other friends.

I remain at the table, my mind racing to bring together scattered bits of the history and culture of the region. Texas was originally part of Mexico, colonized by the Spanish. The majority of people who live in Texas identify themselves as descendants of the Spanish or Mexicans, or both, who settled the area. "Mexicans" can refer to the founding families of San Antonio, hacienda owners and other landholders, who make up a significant part of the political elite and upper class. "Mexicans" also can mean visiting Mexican nationals who maintain summer houses in the region and this neighborhood. There are people who legally immigrated to Texas but retain strong ties to their birthplace and call themselves "Mexicans." Finally, there are the "Mexicans" who the teenagers mentioned, a stereotyped group of what some locals think of as poor, undocumented workers who speak Spanish but who in fact come from all over Latin America.

The teenagers' discussion of "Mexicans" reminds me of T. C. Boyle's novel about a gated community in southern California. In one passage the protagonist is arguing with the president of the homeowners association about a decision to add gates to their walled suburban housing development.

"The gate thing is important — probably the single most important agendum we've taken up in my two years as president."

"You really think so? To me, I say it's unnecessary — and, I don't know, irresponsible somehow.... I lean more to the position that we live in a democracy.... I mean, we all have a stake in things, and locking yourself away from the rest of society, how can you justify that?"

"Safety. Self-protection. Prudence. You lock your car, don't you? Your front door? ... I know how you feel ... but this society isn't what it was — and it won't be until we get control of the borders."

"That's racist, Jack, and you know it."

"Not in the least — it's a question of national sovereignty. Did you know that the U.S. accepted more immigrants last year than all the other countries of the world combined and that half of them settled in California? And that's legal immigrants people with skills, money, education."[10]

Does Boyle capture what these teenagers are feeling? Are they reflecting local attitudes about immigration and the permeable boundary between Mexico and Texas that lies just a 2-and-a-half-hour car ride away?

But it is not just in Texas and California that residents of gated communities regard immigrants as a source of fear. In New York as well residents identify "ethnic changes" and a changing socioeconomic environment as potentially threatening.

CAROL AND TED — IT'S ETHNIC CHANGES

Elena, one of my graduate students, and I arrive at Manor House earlier than expected, so we stop and talk with the guard at the gate. He is a young African American man with short hair, wearing a conservative uniform — blue shirt and navy slacks. He is quite cordial, and invites us into his small room. This is his second job in a gated community. He likes working here, but feels that the residents sometimes expect too much: "After all, we are not police." He had worked at the Homestead where the residents complained that the guards were not doing their jobs. At Manor Place it's better, but residents still do not want their rights infringed on. Elena asks him if he feels that living in a secure environment affects the residents in any way. He responds that it makes them more demanding and not very responsible. They expect the guards to relieve them of all obligations and problems, and to "jump to the rescue" even though the guards have no real power.

As Elena continues to converse with him, I reflect on how nice it is to have her with me on this interview. Elena was born in Romania, and has never been inside an American suburban home. In contrast to my experience, she is amazed that a couple with only one child would choose to live in such a large house. She provides her own cultural perspective and compares everything she sees to her life to Eastern Europe.

"Did you ask everything you wanted to?"

"It's great," she replies enthusiastically. "He feels that residents are too dependent on him, which will ultimately lead to problems. I'm not sure what kind of problems, but I can talk to him again later."

He waves us on, and we pass through the visitors' gate. It is a beautiful day, sunny and breezy. We drive along the winding road, passing a number of just-completed houses, all painted in pole colors, with shutters, porches, and landscape planting. There is subtle variation in style and design, but nonetheless the houses look remarkably similar to one another. Each is placed back from the curb with shrubs, grass, and flowers arranged in neat beds between the house and the street. The interviewee's Vineyard model has a garage and driveway tucked away on the side of the house, allowing ample room for a wraparound porch in front. We arrive on time, park the car, and walk up the driveway.

Carol and Ted Corral are waiting for us at the door. They are both in their early 50s, casually dressed in tan slacks and matching polo shirts. Ted is a large, red-faced man with a loud voice, whereas Carol has blond-gray hair, more soft-spoken and gentle. When they learn that we drove out from the city, they invite us to sit outside to enjoy the sunshine on the patio. We decline because the noise from airplanes overhead and the ongoing construction would interfere with tape-recording.

They have been living at Manor House for eight months, and had previously lived in Great Neck for 28 years. Ted admits that it was "traumatic" to move, but they "made it," and he is now trying to minimize the impact of the move on their lives.

Carol tells me that they were attached to their previous home because they brought up their children there and because it had been built for them. Prior to Great Neck, they had lived in Brooklyn. "A long time ago," Ted adds, implying that he couldn't really remember.

Elena asks about their life in Great Neck. Ted replies that it's a great community socially, and that the children had a good school. It's an affluent community and offers lots of benefits. Carol adds that most of her friends were made there when her children were small. Great Neck had everything, so they did not have to leave for entertainment, restaurants, or even adult education courses. "It's almost like living in the city," Carol says, "but better."

Ted describes the community as "very, very educated.... You know, so everyone goes on to college, and it stressed the role of family, and you know, it's just a wonderful community. But it's changing, it's undergoing internal transformations."

Carol says, "It's ethnic changes."

And Ted repeats, "It's ethnic changes; that's a very good way of putting it."

Carol agrees and adds that it started to happen "in the last, probably, seven to eight years." The changing composition of the neighborhood made them so uncomfortable they decided to move.

I ask about their prior residence in Brooklyn. Ted shrugs his shoulders. I say that I would like to know about why they left for comparison purposes, and finally Carol answers. She tells me they had moved from Brooklyn to bring up their children in a better environment. The school system was changing, and they did not want their children to go to school with children from lower socioeconomic backgrounds who were being bused into their Brooklyn neighborhood.

"Those kids were wild," she says, "and had a different upbringing." She wanted to protect her children from exposure to the kinds of problems these kids might cause. The neighborhood was still comfortable, but the school system was not "desirable," as she tactfully put it. They had both grown up in Brooklyn, but the neighborhood changed, so they decided to build their own home in the suburbs.

Elena asks how they found Manor House. Ted answers, "driving by." Carol says there had been an announcement in the newspaper, and people were discussing that it had gone bankrupt and then had reopened under new ownership. I ask how they decided to move here, and Ted answers that they were looking for something that would suit their lifestyle better. He adds that they chose a gated community because they wanted a secure lifestyle with no hassles and no responsibilities.

I ask whether they would consider living in the city again and they both agree that moving back to the city would be out of the question. They had lived there for 25 years, but when they moved to the suburbs they had done so for a reason. They would never go back. Carol says the city was so different now compared with when she was growing up. "You're always on guard when you're walking." She still loves the city, but does not want to live there. She wants to come home to tranquility.

Dualistic thinking is a form of social splitting used to cope with anxiety and fear. It oversimplifies and dichotomizes cultural definitions and social expectations to differentiate the self from the other Anglos from "Mexicans," whites from illegal immigrants, or whites from "ethnic others." The concept of splitting draws on psychoanalytic relational theory, particularly Melanie Klein's work on the development of object relations. According to Klein, psychological splitting is the process of disassociation between "good" and "bad" representations beginning when the infant differentiates external and internal relationships by splitting the mother into good and bad, incorporating the good mother who can be identified with, and rejecting the bad. It is a psychological means of dealing with contradictory and often conflicting feelings.[11]

Psychological splitting can be used as a form of denial and resistance, providing a means of distancing oneself from an undesirable self-image and projecting it onto another. Social splitting is often used to project social fears onto a more vulnerable group, such as the Jews during World War II, or the homeless on the streets of present-day New York City. It also helps to explain the kind of us-versus-them thinking employed by the gated community residents to rationalize their fears of those outside the gates.

During periods of economic decline and social stress, middle-class people become anxious about maintaining their social status — what is referred to in these interviews as "the good life" — and seek to identify the reasons that their environment and social world is deteriorating. Social splitting offers a strategy that is reinforced by cultural stereotypes and media distortions, allowing people to psychologically separate themselves from people who they perceive as threatening their tranquility and neighborhood stability. The walls and gates of the community reflect this splitting physically as well as metaphorically, with "good" people (the good part of us) inside, and the "bad" remaining outside.

Advertisements for gated communities evoke this social splitting and even go a step further in envisaging what is being defended against. For example, the developer of Sanctuary Cove, Australia's first gated community, told reporters, "The streets these days are full of cockroaches and most of them are human. Every man has a right to protect his family, himself and his possessions, to live in peace and safety." On the basis of his study of gated communities in Australia, Matthew Burke found that the solidifying of perimeter barriers led to a greater sense of residents being "insiders," and reinforced the reverse process that "designates those beyond the walls as 'outsiders' [as] inevitable."[12]

Gating also involves the "racialization" of space in which the representation and definition of "other" is based on human biological characteristics, particularly racial categories. In the past, overt racial categorization provided the ideological context for restrictive immigration laws and discriminatory deed restrictions and mortgage programs. More recently, phenotypical characteristics are used to justify social prejudice and unfounded fears.[13] The thinking of one gated community resident in Sun Meadow, Texas, highlights how race still plays a dominant role in eliciting fear of the other in contemporary society.

Helen—Seeking Privacy from Someone at the Door

Helen answers the doorbell after two rings, as I wait outside admiring her elaborately carved door with cut-glass panels. Through the glass I can see an atrium, two stories high, and an adjoining living room. It is a tan Scottsdale house with a red tile roof, similar in style to others on the street, but set at an angle on a corner lot to give it a distinctive flair. As Helen opens the door her fox terrier jumps out and runs down the driveway, barking at the children Rollerblading by. She waves to her son as he catches the dog by the collar, and then invites me inside.

Helen is in her mid-40s, plump, with brown hair and hazel eyes. She is dressed for golf in yellow shorts and matching shirt. Helen and her husband, Ralph, are avid golfers and active members of the Sun Meadow Club. They purchased their home from the original developer before he went bankrupt and have lived there for over 10 years. They were one of the first families to move in. Helen, her husband, and son lived in a number of different cities before moving to Sun Meadow because of her husband's varied businesses. She is a stay-at-home mother and is considering starting a business when her son finishes high school.

They originally moved to Sun Meadow for the golf course but now would only consider living in a gated community. When I ask her why, she replies, "Because after seeing that there are so many beautiful neighborhoods that are not [in] a secure area, [and] that's where burglaries and murders take place. It's an open door [saying] to people, come on in. Why should they try anything here when they can go somewhere else first? It's a strong deterrent, needless to say."

She feels that there is less crime in gated developments than in San Antonio in general. She knows people living in equally nice nongated neighborhoods who have experienced break-ins and who have been assaulted with weapons. The worst that has happened in Sun Meadow is that a few cars have come through and "messed things up." She thinks that it was probably kids. Only a few families have been robbed or burglarized.

Helen feels that her community is different because it is secured. Without the gates, she thinks, anybody could come knocking on your door and put you in a compromising situation. She illustrates her point by telling me what happened to friend who lives "in a lovely community" outside of Washington, DC: "She said this fellow came to the door and she was very intimidated because she was white, and he was black, and you didn't get many blacks in her neighborhood. She only bought it [what he was selling] just to hurry and quick get him away from the door, because she was scared as hell. That's terrible to be put in that situation. I like the idea of having security."

Helen and Ralph put on their burglar alarm every time they leave, although she thinks they may be overly cautious. She also keeps her doors locked, because she has had people walk in her front door thinking her house was for sale.

I ask her if she is concerned about crime in Sun Meadow. She answers, "No, not here, but in San Antonio." She goes on to explain that San Antonio, like any major city, has problems:

There are gangs. People are overworked, they have families, they are underpaid, the stress is out of control, and they abuse their children. The children go out because they don't like their home life. There's too much violence everywhere. It starts in the city, but then the kids get smart enough and say, "Oh, gee, I need money for x, y, or z, but it's really hot in the city, let's go out and get it someplace else." We're the natural target for it. So being in a secure area, I don't have to worry as much as another neighborhood that doesn't have security.

She cannot imagine any city in the United States that does not have to worry, because so many people in the city live in poverty. She tells me about her friends living in a wealthy suburb who had their car stolen at gunpoint. They were going to move out of the neighborhood, which did not have gates or security, to a small town outside of San Antonio. When they investigated further, however, they learned that the small town had just as much crime as San Antonio. Helen concludes that it does not matter whether it is the city or the suburbs, you have to live in a gated community, or at least have enough property to have a dog, a security system on your house, and warning signs on your door.

Ironically, Helen's concern with crime developed after she moved into Sun Meadow, but living there reinforces the importance of having gates and guards for personal security. She is more concerned about someone walking into her house than with crime in general. Yet she is one of the few residents who specifically cites an example in which racial difference triggered a sense of fear. Like Ted and Carol Corral, who moved because of "ethnic changes," Helen alludes to her friend's experience as the kind of thing that she is frightened of. "She was scared as hell," Helen comments. Her story—although displaced on her friend—suggests how Helen would feel if a black person came to her door. It is also unclear in the first vignette whether the Corrals are referring to racial or cultural differences in Great Neck. They could be referring to the large influx of Iranian Jews into their suburban neighborhood or the increasing number of Latino immigrants on Long Island. In both cases, however, these interviews conflate racial and ethnic differences with an increased potential for crime.

Racist fears about the "threat" of a visible minority, whether it is blacks, Latinos, "Orientals," or Koreans, are remarkably similar. This is because many neighborhoods in the United States are racially homogeneous. Thus, the physical space of the neighborhood and its racial composition become synonymous. This "racialized" spatial ordering and the identification of a space with a group of people is a fundamental aspect of how suburban landscapes reinforce racial prejudice and discrimination.[14]

Why should Helen's friend feel fearful just because a stranger comes to her door selling things? In Brooklyn and any urban neighborhood or integrated suburb, this would happen all the time. Think of how many times religious groups distributing pamphlets and recruiting converts knock on doors in all but the most isolated settings. Except for gated communities and other kinds of communities with secured, restricted entrances, such as military bases, prisons, boarding schools, doorman apartment buildings, or special hospitals, contact with people soliciting, selling, proselytizing, and campaigning is commonplace. In most neighborhoods the streets and the sidewalks are still public, and cross-cultural and cross-racial contact is still possible and even encouraged.

Another aspect of "fear of other" to consider is how the talk about the "other," the "discourse of fear," is used by residents to explain why gates are important. One example from Long Island (post-9/11) illustrates this point.

LINDA—SEPARATING OURSELVES FROM THE GREAT UNWASHED

Linda is a young mother of two boys, 10 and 12 years old, in her early 30s. She is trim and keeps fit by running daily. She is a little nervous at being interviewed, but she is able to think about her surroundings and reflect on what her experiences have been there. Divorced, she lives in her recently deceased mother's house. It is a three-bedroom house, well furnished, although it is showing some signs of age. The entrance to the house is up a winding path, and the entry porch is set parallel to the road, making it feel very private even though it is an attached townhouse. Linda moved to Pine Hills two years ago, but her mother bought the house more than 15 years ago, when it was first built.

Her mother had moved to Pine Hills because she wanted to be in a setting where there would be neighbors close by, and to have the safety of the gate. Linda laughs and says,

> The security of the gate. Five dollars an hour, when they're asleep. I don't know how much security the gate is worth. Some of the guards just let you fly right in. The others have to strip-search you. It really depends. I guess that has been my experience with coming in. Some of them ore okay, others want your fingerprints.
>
> [For her mother] it was just basically being less isolated on a big piece of property, and a couple of years before that we had something [happen]. There were helicopters flying over this area. I mean, this may be going back 10 years. I don't remember specifically when, but some inmate, they were looking for someone who had escaped who had a murder record. That was quite freaky. You would look out in the backyard and there'd be woods out there, and you'd wonder who is out there.

Linda goes on to say that she tries not to get a false sense of security.

> Because, you know . . . people can come in here on foot. There's a golf course right behind us, and anyone could be wandering around on there, and decide to traipse through here.
>
> Honestly I don't know how useful the gate is. The gate is useful in preventing vehicles from getting in; that is, if the person at the gate is alert and competent. Most of the time I do get a call if somebody's coming. What can I say about the gate? We did have same robberies here some years ago. I'll try to summarize this: [it's] good in preventing robberies whereby, you know, somebody would need a vehicle to load a whole lot of loot into a car or a van or whatever. But as far as preventing people on foot, it's ridiculous. You know, if anyone would have an interest in coming into this community and causing some kind of havoc or whatever, I think there are many ways they could get in.

Linda tells the following story to illustrate her point:

One time, one of my neighbor's boys, the little one, was missing. And this woman, I mean, she was white as a sheet, and she was really going to have a nervous breakdown. And we couldn't find him. He was actually in another neighbor's house with his friend, playing. I had called that house to find out, not realizing they were away, and there was a workman in the house. And these boys didn't know the workman. The workman just walked in there, went into the kid's room, and started working. So she wasn't at ease [because it was so easy for the workman to walk in without any adults being home, and that her boy was there with a strange workman].

You know, we are not living in very secure times now . . . I can tell you that after a couple of robberies some of the older residents here felt comfortable with hiring a security car for patrolling the grounds. So they did try to do that.

To get in there is a password. I generally don't give mine out, unless it's a close friend or somebody that I know, or somebody who has my key and needs to get in. Usually, the people at the gate, they know you and they just let you in. A lot of people have automatic openers for the gate. Actually, I don't have one of those, I have a cord that I can just slip in, and get in.

But Linda thinks that it is more than just security:

This is my theory: Long Island is very prestige minded. And I think the very fact of having a guard at the gate is akin to living in Manhattan in a doorman building versus a three-flight walk-up type of thing. There's a certain "pass through the gate" of it. You know, other than the safety issue, just a kind of separating ourselves from the great unwashed, shall we say.

And I think with the gate thing, there is an increasing sense of insecurity all over the place. I think people are beginning to realize they are not really safe anywhere in middle America. We have had so much violence occurring, the school shootings, you know. That could be part of it.

In this interview Linda tells a story about a workman who walks into a house, without anyone even noticing. This occurs in conjunction with a mother's fear that her youngest child is missing. Again an outsider is feared, even when he had nothing to do with the incident. Just his presence evokes comment.

Whether it is Mexicans, black salesmen, workers, or "ethnic changes," the message is the same: Residents are using the walls, entry gates, and guards in an effort to keep perceived dangers outside of their homes, neighborhoods, and social world. Contact incites fear and concern, and in response they are moving to exclusive, private, residential developments where they can keep other people out with guards and gates. The walls are making visible the systems of exclusion that are already there; now the walls are constructed in concrete.

Social splitting, purified spaces, and racialization help to explain how this kind of dualistic thinking develops and becomes embedded in local culture. Residents talk about their fear of the poor, the workers, the "Mexicans," and the "newcomers," as well as their retreat behind walls, where they think they will be safe. But there is fear even behind the walls. There are workers who enter the community every day, and residents must go out in order to buy groceries, shop, or see a movie. The gates provide some protection, but residents would like more. Even though the gates and guards exclude the feared "others" from living with them, "they" can slip by the gate, follow your car in, crawl over the wall, or, worse, the guard can fall asleep. Informal conversations about the screening of guards and how they are hired, as well as discussions about increasing the height and length of the protective walls as new threats appear, are frequent in the locker room of the health club, on the tennis court, and during strolls in the community in the evening.

The discourse of fear encompasses many social concerns about class, race, and ethnic exclusivity and gender.[15] It provides a verbal component that complements — and even reinforces — the visual landscape of fear created by the walls, gates, and guards. By matching the discourse of the inhabitants with the ideological thrust of the material setting, we enrich our understanding of the social construction and social production of places where the well-to-do live.

Gated community residents use gates to create the community they are searching for. But their personal housing decisions have had unintended societal consequences. Most important, they are disruptive of other people's ability to experience "community": community in the sense of an integration of the suburb and the city, community in terms of access to public open space, and community within the American tradition of racial and ethnic integration and social justice.

Architecture and the layout of towns and suburbs provide concrete, anchoring points of people's everyday life. These anchoring points reinforce our ideas about society at large. Gated communities and the social segregation and exclusion they materially represent make sense of and even rationalize problems Americans have with race, class, and gender inequality and social discrimination. The gated community contributes to a geography of social relations that produces fear and anxiety simply by locating a person's home and places identity in a secured enclave, gated, guarded, and locked.[16]

One of the striking features of the world today is that large numbers of people feel increasingly insecure. Whether attributed to globalization and economic restructuring, or the breakdown of the traditional institutions of social control, it has become imperative that governments and neighborhoods respond.[17] The threat of terrorism in the United States following the attack on the World Trade Center deepened Americans' fears. Yet to date the only solutions offered are increased policing in the public sector, and walling and gating, surveillance technologies, and armed guards in the private. These are inadequate solutions for what is actually a complex set of issues ranging from profound concerns about one's continued existence and emotional stability to everyday problems with economic survival and maintaining a particular way of life. Gated community residents then, like many Americans, are also searching for security.

The reasons people give for their decision to move to a gated community vary widely, and the closer you get to the person and his or her individual psychology, the more complex the answer. At a societal level, people say they move because of their fear of crime and others. They move to secure a neighborhood that is stable and a home that will retain its resale value. They move to have control of their environment and of the environment of those who live nearby. Residents in rapidly growing areas want to live in a private community for the services. And retirees particularly want the low maintenance and lack of responsibility that come with living in a private condominium development.

At a personal level, though, residents are searching for the sense of security and safety that they associate with their childhood. When they talk about their concern with "others," they are splitting — socially and psychologically — the good and bad aspects of (and good and bad people in) American society. The gates are used symbolically to ward off many of life's unknowns, including unemployment, loss of loved ones, and downward mobility. Of course, gates cannot deliver all that is promised, but they are one attempt to resurrect aspects of the American dream that many people feel they have lost.

My sister and her family are visiting us as I complete this reading. Anna complains about the length of time it takes her to drive out of her gated community in the morning to take Alexandra to high school. Dust, ditches, and a never-ending string of angry drivers snake slowly past the main artery outside their gate. All other available routes also detour around impassable gates and feed onto this single road that is limited to two lanes by endless construction projects. She has to wait for a stranger to wave and let her into the line of traffic.

"The irony is that we are trapped behind our own gates," Anna says, "unable to exit. Instead of keeping people out, we have shut ourselves in."

REFERENCES

Atlas, R. (1999). Designing safe communities and neighborhood. *Proceedings of the American Planning Association*.

Blakely, E. J., & Snyder, M. G. (1997). *Fortress America: Gated communities in the United States*. Washington, DC: Brookings Institution.

Burke, M. (2001, February 20–22). *The pedestrian behavior of residents in gated communities*. Paper presented at Walking the 21st Century, Perth, Western Australia.

Cabrales Baragas, L. F. (2002, July 17–20). *Latinamérica: Paises abiertos, ciudades cerradas*. Coloquio, Guadalajara, Jalisco, Mexico.

Cabrales Baragas, L. F., & Zamora, E. C. (2001). Segregacion residencial y fragmentacion urbana. *Espirdl, Estudios sabre Estado y Sociedod*, 7(20), 223–253.

Caldeira, T. P. R. (1996). Fortified enclaves: The new urban segregation. *Public Culture*, 8, 303–328.

Carvalho, M., George, R. V., & Anthony, K. H. (1997). Residential satisfaction in *condominios exclusivos* in Brazil. *Environment and Behavior*, 29(6), 734–768.

Connell, J. (1999). Beyond manilla: Walls, malls, and private spaces. *Environment and Planning A*, 31, 417–439.

Dixon, J., Dupuis, A., Lysnar, P., & Mouat, C. (2002, June 5–9). *Body corporate: Prospects for private urban governance in New Zealand*. Paper presented at the International Conference on Private Urban Governance, Institute of Geography, Johannes Gutenberg Universität, Mainz.

Dixon, J. A., & Reicher, S. (1997). Intergroup contact and desegregation in the new South Africa. *British Journal of Social Psychology*, 36, 361–381.

Fine, M. (2000). "Whiting out" social justice. In R. T. Carter (Ed.), *Addressing cultural issues in organizations* (pp. 35–50). Thousand Oaks, CA: Sage.

Frantz, K. (2000–2001). Gated communities in the USA: A new trend in urban development. *Espace, Populations, Societes*, 101–113.

Glasze, G., & Alkhayyal, A. (2002). Gated housing estates in the Arab world: Case studies in Lebanon and Riyadh, Saudi Arabia. *Environment and Planning B: Planning and Design*, 29, 321–336.

Hayden, D. (2003). *Building American suburbia: Green fields and urban growth, 1820–2000*. New York: Pantheon Books.

Jaillet, M. -C. (1999). Pent-on parler de secession urbaine a propos des villes européenes? *Revue Esprit*, 258, 145–167.

Janoschka, M. (2002a, June 5–9). *Nordelta: A private new town in competition with local author-*

ities. Paper presented at the International Conference on Private Urban Governance, Institute of Geography, Johannes Gutenberg Universität, Mainz.

Lentz, S., & Lindner, P. (2002, June 5–9). *Social differentiation and privatization of space in post-socialist Moscow*. Paper presented at the International Conference on Private Urban Governance, Institute of Geography, Johannes Gutenberg Universität, Mainz.

Martin, B., & Talpade, C. (1986). Feminist politics: What's home got to do with it? In T. de Lauretis (Ed.), *Feminist studies/critical studies* (pp. 191–212). Bloomington: Indiana University Press.

Massey, D. (1994). *Space, place, and gender*. Minneapolis: University of Minnesota Press.

Massey, D. S., & Denton, N. (1988). Suburbanization and segregation. *American Journal of Sociology, 94*(3), 592–626.

Ngin, C. (1993). A new look at the old "race" language. *Explorations in Ethnic Studies, 16*(1), 5–18.

Paquot, T. (2000, May/June). Villas privées. *Urbanisme, 312*, 60–85.

Ray, B. K., Halseth, G., & Johnson, B. (1997). The changing "face" of the suburbs. *International Journal of Urban and Regional Research, 21*(1), 75–99.

Sanchez, T., & Lang, R. L. (2002). *Security versus status. The two worlds of gated communities*. Census Note 02: 02. Alexandria: Metropolitan Institute at Virginia Tech.

Silver, C. (2002). Construction at deconstruction des identités de-genre. *Cahier du Genre, 31*, 185–201. (Paris: Caisse National d'Assurance Vieillesse)

Tulchin, J. S., & Golding, H. A. (2003) Citizen security in regional perspective. In H. Frühling, J. S. Tulchin, & H. Golding (Eds.), *Crime and violence in Latin America*. Washington, DC: Woodrow Wilson Center.

Waldrop, A. (2002, November 20–24). *Fortification and class relations: The case of a New Delhi colony*. Paper presented at the American Anthropological Association Annual Meeting, New Orleans.

Webster, C. (2002a, June 5–9). *Private communities and China's dual land market*. Paper presented at the International Conference on Private Urban Governance, Institute of Geography, Johannes Gutenberg Universität, Mainz.

Webster, C. (2002b). Property rights and the public realm: Gates, green-belts, and gemeinshaft. *Environment and Planning B: Planning and Design, 29*(3), 397–412.

Webster, C., Glasze, G., & Frantz, K. (2002). Guest editorial. *Environment and Planning B: Planning and Design, 29*(3), 315–320.

ADDITIONAL READINGS

Angotti, T. (1997). A metropolis of enclaves: Image and reality in North America. *Urbana, 22*, 13–24.

Barnett, J. (1986). *The elusive city*. New York: Harper & Row.

Baxandall, R., & Ewan, E. (2000). *Picture windows: How the suburbs happened*. New York: Basic Books.

Beito, D. T. (2002). The private places of St. Louis: Urban infrastructure through private planning. In D. T. Beito, P. Gordon, & A. Tabarrok (Eds.), *The voluntary city: Choice, community, and civil society* (pp. 47–75). Ann Arbor: University of Michigan Press.

Beito, D. T., Gordon, P., & Tabarrok, A. (Eds.). (2002). *The voluntary city: Choice, community, and civil society*. Ann Arbor: University of Michigan Press.

Benson, B. (1998). *To serve and protect*. New York: New York University Press.

Boyle, T. C. (1995). *The tortilla curtain* (pp. 100–103). New York: Viking.

Brennan, D., & Zelinka, A. (1997, August). Safe and sound. *Planning*, 4–10.

Bullard, R., & Lee, C. (1994). Racism and American apartheid. In R. D. Bullard, J. E. Grigsby, & C. Lee (Eds.), *Residential apartheid* (pp. 1–16). Los Angeles: Center of Afro-American Studies.

Caldeira, T. P. R. (2000). *City of walls: Crime, segregation, and citizenship in São Paulo*. Berkeley: University of California Press.

Colvard, K. (1997). Crime is down? Don't confuse us with the facts. *HFG Review*, 2(1), 19–26.

Crowe, T. (1991). *Crime prevention through environmental design*. Stoneham, MA: Butterworth-Heinerflalm.

Davis, M. (1990). *City of quartz: Excavating the future in Los Angeles*. London: Verso.

Davis, M. (1992). Fortress Los Angeles: The militarization of urban space. In M. Sorkin (Ed.), *Variations on a theme park* (pp. 154–180). New York: Noonday.

Denton, N. (1994). Are African-Americans still hypersegregated? In R. B. Bullard, J. E. Grigsby III, & C. Lee (Eds.), *Residential apartheid* (pp. 49–81). Los Angeles: Center for Afro-American Studies.

Devine, J. (1996). *Maximum security*. Chicago: University of Chicago Press.

Dillon, D. (1994). Fortress America: More and more of us are living behind locked gates. *Planning*, 60(6), 8–13.

Donahue, P. (1993, December 2). Town builds fence to keep people out. Transcript of television show *Donahue*.

Fine, M. (1990). "The public" in public schools: The social construction/constriction of moral communities. *Journal of Social Issues*, 46(1), 107–119.

Fischler, M. S. (1998, August 16). Security the draw at gated communities. *New York Times*, pp. 14L1: 6.

Flusty, S. (1997). Building paranoia. In N. Ellin (Ed.), *Architecture of fear* (pp. 47–60). New York: Princeton Architectural Press.

Foucault, M. (1977). Discipline and punish. In Alan Sheridan (Trans.), *The birth of the prison*. New York: Random House.

Foucault, M. (1984, October). Des espaces autres. *Architecture, Movement, Continuité*, 46–49.

Frug, G. E. C. (1999). *City making: Building communities without building walls*. Princeton, NJ: Princeton University Press.

Guterson, D. (1992, November). No place like home. *Harper's Magazine*, 35–64.

Hannigan, J. (1998). *Fantasy city*. New York: Routledge.

Harvey, D. (1990). *The condition of postmodernity*. New York: Blackwell.

Jackson, K. T. (1985). *Crabgrass frontier*. Oxford: Oxford University Press.

Jacobs, J. (1961). *The death and life of great American cities*. New York: Random House.

Janoschka, M. (2002b, July 17–20). *Latinaménica: Paises abiertos, ciudades cerradas*. Paper presented at Urbanizaciones Privadas in Buenos Aires. Hacia un nuevo modelo de la ciudad latinamenicana? Guadalajara, Jalisco.

Judd, D. (2002, June 5–9). *Policy communities and the reconstruction of the local state*. Paper presented at the International Conference on Private Urban Governance, Institute of Geography, Johannes Gutenberg Universität, Mainz.

Kenny, L. D. (2000). *Daughters of suburbia*. New Brunswick, NJ: Rutgers University Press.

King, A. (1990). *Urbanism, colonialism, and the world economy*. New York: Routledge.

Klein, M. (1975). On the sense of loneliness. In *Envy and gratitude and other works, 1946–1963* (pp. 300–313). New York: Delta.

Lang, R. E., & Danielson, K. A. (1997). Gated communities in America. *Housing Policy Debate, 8*(4), 867–899.

Langdon, P. (1994). *A better place to live.* Amherst: University of Massachusetts Press.

Lis, C., & Soly, H. (1979). *Poverty and capitalism in pre-industrial Europe.* New York: Humanities Press.

Low, S. M. (1992). Symbolic ties that bind. In I. Altman & S. Low (Eds.), *Place attachment* (pp. 165–184). New York: Plenum.

Low, S. M. (1996). A response to Castells: An anthropology of the city. *Critique of Anthropology, 16,* 57–62.

Low, S. M. (1997). Urban fear: Building fortress America [Annual review]. *City and Society,* 52–72.

Low, S. M. (2000). *On the plaza: The politics of public space and culture.* Austin: University of Texas Press.

Low, S. M. (2001). The edge and the center: Gated communities and the discourse of urban fear. *American Anthropologist, 103*(1), 45–58.

Marcuse, P. (1997). The enclave, the citadel, and the ghetto. *Urban Affairs Review, 33*(2), 228–264.

McKenzie, E. (2002, June 5–9). *Private residential governance in the U.S.* Paper presented at the International Conference on Private Urban Governance, Institute of Geography, Johannes Gutenberg Universität, Mainz.

Merry, S. (1993). Mending walls and building fences: Constructing the private neighborhood. *Journal of Legal Pluralism, 33,* 71–90.

Merry, S. (2001). Spatial governmentality and the new urban social order: Controlling gender violence through law. *American Anthropologist, 103*(1), 36–45.

Mollenkopf, J., & Castells, M. (1991). *The dual city.* New York: Russell Sage.

Mumford, L. (1961). *The city in history.* New York: Harcourt, Brace, and World.

Newman, K. S. (1993). *Declining fortunes: The withering of the American dream.* New York: Basic Books.

Newman, O. (1972). *Defensible space.* New York: Macmillian.

Newman, O. (1980). *Community of interest.* Garden City, NY: Anchor Press.

Ortner, S. (1998). Generation X: Anthropology in a media-saturated world. *Cultural Anthropology, 13*(3), 414–440.

Phillips, K. (1991). *The politics of rich and poor.* New York: HarperCollins.

Schlosser, E. (1998, December). The prison-industrial complex. *Atlantic Monthly,* 51–77.

Sennett, R. (1970). *The uses of disorder.* Harmondsworth: Penguin.

Sennett, R. (1977). *The fall of public man.* New York: Knopf.

Sibley, D. (1995). *Geographies of exclusion.* London: Routledge.

Smith, N. (1984). *Uneven development.* Oxford: Basil Blackwell.

South, S., & Crowder, K. D. (1997). Residential mobility between cities and suburbs: Race, suburbanization, and back-to-the-city moves. *Demography, 34*(4), 525–538.

Stephenson, N. (2000). *Snow crash.* New York: Bantam Doubleday Dell.

Stone, C. (1996). Crime and the city. In *Breaking away: The future of cities* (pp. 98–103). New York: Twentieth Century Fund Press.

Susser, I. (1996). The construction of poverty and homelessness in U.S. cities. *Annual Review of Anthropology, 25,* 411–435.

Turner, E. S. (1999, June 10). Gilded drainpipes. *London Review of Books*, 31–32.

Webster, C. (2001). Gated cities of tomorrow. *Town Planning Review*, 72(2), 149–170.

Wilson-Doenges, G. (2000). An exploration of sense of community and fear of crime in gated communities. *Environment and Behavior*, 32(5), 597–611.

Zucker, P. (1959). *Town and square: From agora to the village green*. Cambridge, MA: MIT Press.

NOTES

1. A computer game that allows players to create simulated houses, neighborhoods, and cities.
2. Hayden 2003.
3. Atlas 1999.
4. Frantz 2000–2001.
5. Sanchez and Lang 2002. My sincere thanks to Haya El Massar who alerted me to the release of these figures and to Robert Lang and Tom Sanchez for allowing me to use their census note for this reading.
6. Sanchez and Lang 2002, based on their text and Table 2. On the top 10 metropolitan regions.
7. Blakely and Snyder 1997 for original estimate and Sanchez and Lang 2002 for census totals.
8. Carvalho, George, and Anthony 1997; Dixon and Reicher 1997; Jaillet 1999; Paquot 2000; Caldeira 2000; Frantz 2000–2001; Connell 1999; Burke 2001; Lentz and Lindner 2002; Glasze and Alkhayyal 2002; Janoschka 2002a and b; Dixon et al. 2002; Webster 2002; Webster, Glasze, and Frantz 2002; Waldrop 2002; see also Cabrales Barajas 2002 for the recent Latin American work.
9. From Franz Kafka's story "The Great Wall of China," in which he asserts through the voice of a Chinese narrator that the real purpose of the wall was not to serve as protection from ravaging hordes but to give people a sense of unity in their separate and isolated villages.
10. See T. C. Boyle *The Tortilla Curtain* (New York: Viking, 1995), 100–103.
11. Silver 2002.
12. Burke 2001, 147.
13. Ngin 1993.
14. Ray, Halseth, and Johnson 1997.
15. Kevin Birth also suggested that age may play a role in structuring these communities, especially the age of those who are feared (personal communication).
16. Massey 1994; Fine 2000; Martin and Talpede 1986.
17. Tulchin and Golding forthcoming.

FOUR

Black Infants and White Men:
Tied into a Single Garment of Destiny

Ronald David

I write as a pediatrician with an abiding concern for infant mortality rates and what they signify. As well, I write as a male with concern for the premature deaths of men. I approach both concerns with an unwavering conviction: Relationships are primary. All else is derivative. The resolution of these public health dilemmas will be found in and through relationships primarily. Advances in and greater access to medical technology and care will reduce mortality rates nominally.

I am supported in the foregoing convictions and inspired by at least one psychologist, James Lynch (1977, p. xv). Author of *The Broken Heart*, Lynch asserted, "Loneliness can break the human heart." The focus of Lynch's book is clear: "To document the fact that reflected in our hearts there is a biological basis for our need to form loving human relationships. If we fail to fulfill that need, our health is in peril."

I am emboldened further by the wisdom of Martin Luther King Jr. (1968, p. 68), who asserted, "We are caught in an inescapable network of mutuality, tied in to a single garment of destiny. Whatever affects one directly affects all indirectly. We are made to live together because of the inter-related structure of reality."

Motivated by these psychological and theological perspectives, my objective is to examine threads of evidence — some sturdy, others more delicate — which, when woven together, reveal a part of the garment binding the fate of black infants born prematurely to the fate of white men at risk for coronary artery disease in midlife. Indeed, my objective is even more ambitious than that. I hope to catalyze a dialogue or study that seeks to transcend the all-too-typical focus on race, gender, and social class as the primary causal or confounding variables affecting population health outcomes.

So deeply do I hold to the previously stated conviction that we are "tied into a single garment of destiny" that it will be treated as a given, a foundational claim for which I offer no proof and upon which I build my argument. The question for me is not whether there is a connection between these apparently disparate morbid experiences, infant mortality, and coronary artery disease. Rather, the question is, what is the nature of the connection?

Although I focus this essay explicitly on black infants and white men, I wish to make clear that my concern is for children, men, and women of every race and class. In my clinical experience as a neonatologist I have witnessed and grieved the deaths of a greater number of white infants than black. Statistical averaging cannot obscure the image of their individual tender faces; no ranking of relative rates can console my grief for them or their families. I believe that we are mistaken if we imagine that it is possible to be truly concerned about the health and well-being of infants without having compassion for their mothers, and their fathers..

I shall make one additional prefatory remark before moving to the core of this essay. As a former health policy analyst and administrator, I am hopeful that the broader implications of this perspective for public policy and civic discourse will be obvious. I do not believe that we can diligently and persistently strive to adopt fair, just, and compassionate public policy as it affects others unless we experience "them" as being meaningfully related to "us." As a corollary, to the extent that we deny our relationship to the other we will continue to articulate and implement selfish and mean-spirited public policy and, thereby, hamper our efforts to promote community health.

It is against this background that I serve as tailor for a "garment of destiny." I will begin sewing this garment with the thread and material I am most familiar with — a variety of data and hypotheses regarding infant mortality. I will then turn to a consideration of coronary artery disease in men.

INFANT MORTALITY AS A BAROMETER OF THE HEALTH OF COMMUNITIES

What does it mean when the children of a community die before they celebrate their first birthday? To judge from the headlines appearing in four major northeastern newspapers, the answer seems simple.

In August 1990 the chairman of the Department of Pediatrics at a University Health Center was quoted in the *Pittsburgh Post Gazette* as having said, "The biggest factor [leading to low birth weight and infant mortality] is lack of adequate medical care during pregnancy." (Mark A. Sperling, August 15, 1990, p. C-3.)

In August 1990 the editor of the *Philadelphia Inquirer* wrote, "Infants ... are dying because their mothers couldn't — or wouldn't — get proper prenatal care." (August 20, 1990, p. A-12.)

Again, in August 1990 a headline in the *New York Times* read, "The hard thing about cutting infant mortality is educating mothers." (Robert Pear, August 12, 1990, p. E-5.)

Subsequently, in February 1995 an editorial headline in the *Wall Street Journal* read, "Infant mortality, Mother's morality." In this editorial a physician argued, "Sexually promiscuous mothers or those who abuse drugs or have psychosocial pathology are in part responsible for these unflattering [infant mortality] statistics." (Kenneth Prager, February 1, 1995, p. A-13.)

More than a decade later, these headlines still illustrate the prevailing wisdom that poor pregnancy outcomes are a function of mothers' behaving irresponsibly, immorally, or failing to receive adequate medical prenatal care. However, according to Mark Twain, "There are always simple solutions to complex problems; and they are always wrong."

My experiences as an African American in clinical and academic medicine, public health administration, public policy deliberation, and theological reflection lead me to conclude that infant mortality rates are a sign of spiritual crisis in our American community. In elaborating this assertion, I will briefly review the history of infant mortality rate analysis and explore the key elements of an alternative hypothesis to explain those data.

A Brief History of Infant Mortality Rate Analysis

In the middle of the 19th century the first counts of infant deaths were crude but were thought to be a consequence of the unsafe and unsanitary physical environment of cities. The focus shifted in the late 1800s to a concern that infant diets and feeding practices were inadequate or unhealthy and, hence, were a cause of death equal in importance to "foul and vitiated air." In the early 1900s the focus shifted again. This time attention was being paid to the ability of mothers to bear, give birth to, and rear children (Meckel, 1990).

This last shift was reinforced — indeed, catalyzed — by the emergence of pediatrics and obstetrics and gynecology as medical specialties. Obstetricians, in particular, were quick to define pregnancy as a pathologic condition requiring medical supervision. They also denounced and demeaned midwives as superstitious, dangerous, and dirty.

There were physicians and public health professionals who espoused a more comprehensive, alternative perspective. For example, Dr. Josephine Baker, the first director of the New York City Bureau of Child Hygiene, observed in 1908, "The infant mortality rate is the most sensitive index of municipal housekeeping of a community. It is more than that; it is an index of civic interest, cooperation, consciousness and worth." I turn to a consideration of the potential validity of this prescient perspective now.

Infant Mortality as a Sign of Spiritual Crisis

In her reference to "municipal housekeeping," Dr. Baker acknowledged the importance of safe and sanitary physical environments, and adequate and healthy nutrition, in reducing the rate of infant deaths. "Civic interest, cooperation, consciousness and worth," I contend, are references to the spiritual vitality of a community. Specifically, a community that is spiritually alive and integrative is one in which all members are valued participants in a creative dialogue. In such a community, autonomy and interdependence are balanced, mutually enhancing forces of survival, evolution, and transformation.

In contrast, a spiritually disintegrative community is one in which civic interests are superseded by self-interest. People engage in debate more than they do dialogue. Competition is the rule and cooperation the exception. And an individual's value hinges (primarily) on race, gender, and social class. To appreciate the potential effect of such a vacuous spiritual experience on the well-being of women and infants, it is important to define health.

Health is the realized potential for adaptation and transformation in and through relationships. We are relational beings inescapably. We are complex and creative whole/parts. Ken Wilber argued cogently, "Reality is not composed of things or processes.... Rather it is composed of whole/parts, or *holons*" (Wilber, 1995, p. 33). Holons maintain integrity (autonomy) as "wholes" while simultaneously engaging as "parts." The whole/part realizes emergent or creative properties that are more than the sum of its constituents. Holons that adapt and transform become more complex (both differentiated and integrated), survive, and create. Holons that fail to adapt, dissipate, disintegrate, and die.

We have come to know from the study of cosmology and physics that this adaptive, transformative evolution has been operative in the physical universe from the time of the big bang (Swimme & Berry, 1992). Evidence from the biological sciences strongly suggests that this holds true for living organisms. Data from the fields of anthropology, history, and sociology reveal that this is no less true for human societies (Wilber, 1995, pp. 32–78).

For humans, this potential for adaptation and transformation (and healing) can only be realized in and through mutually supportive and challenging relationships. This relational imperative is the heart of the Hebraic scriptural concept of *shalom* (J. Wilkinson, 1998). The evidence is compelling if not incontrovertible — everywhere there is a tear in the fabric of human relationships, people are ill at ease, afflicted with disease, or suffer premature death — biological, psychological, social, and spiritual (for examples, see Josselson, 1992; Pilisuk & Hillier-Parks, 1986; R. G. Wilkinson, 1996).

It is in this spiritually vacuous context that the adaptive challenges to pregnancy and early childhood development take place. When women and children need most to be enmeshed in mutually supportive relationships, they are isolated and alienated by racism, sexism, or social class ostracism. They are bereft of life-sustaining love and relationships as much as they are bereft of practical guidance in the conduct of pregnancy. Under such circumstances their capacity to adapt and transform must be severely limited or stopped entirely. They cannot thrive and realize their greatest potential. They cannot survive.

The premature birth and death of infants is not a problem that is peculiar to African American communities. However, the infant mortality rate is proportionally greater for blacks compared with whites and, consequently, for Americans compared with their industrialized competitors. Specifically, in 2001 the overall infant mortality rate in the United States was 6.8 per 1,000 live births. The rate for white infants was 5.7 per 1,000; the rate for African American infants was 14.0 per 1,000, nearly two and one half times greater. Excluding the data for African American infants, the United States would rank 20th (tied with Ireland) behind industrialized nations such as Austria, Belgium, the Czech Republic, Denmark, France, Germany, and others. Inclusive of the data from African American communities the United States ranks 25th and falls behind Cuba and Taiwan, for example. Alone, the infant mortality rate for African Americans ranks 54th behind such nations as Bahrain, Kuwait, and South Korea (Population Reference Bureau, 2003).

Within the 60 largest cities of the United States, infant mortality rates are greater in those cities with a proportionally larger number of African American births and a proportionally smaller number of Hispanic American births (Haynatzka et al., 2002).

Jan Gates-Williams, an African American woman and medical anthropologist, has examined a broad array of studies of infant mortality. She and her colleagues (1992) found that all of those studies fell into one of three categories: epidemiological studies of demographic risks, studies that advocate prenatal care, and ethnographic studies purporting to show how cultural folklore may interfere with compliance with contemporary, "scientific" medical advice.

None of the studies, Gates-Williams et al. (1992) noted, "bring into focus the experiences and voices of women or how families cope and survive in a society hostile to African Americans and women and indifferent to motherhood and children." If we were to hear their voices — if we were to engage women in the dialogue about an issue that effects them most directly — the message would be unequivocal. For example, Byllye Avery, founder of the National Black Women's Health Network, once asked and answered a question for a journalist: "Why do you think our babies are dying? It's because their mommies are dying. They're in dead relationships" (personal communication, May 13, 2004).

Several anomalous findings are better understood in the light of the foregoing hypothesis. For example, infants born to African American women who are married and educated still die at one and one half to two times the rate of infants born to white women of the same social class. This finding — known as the "paradox of the well-off black woman" — pertains despite receipt of "adequate" prenatal care (Rowley, 1994; Schoendorf, Hogue, Kleinman, & Rowley, 1992).

Neonatologists, Richard David and James Collins (1991), have authored a paper titled "Bad Outcomes in Black Babies: Race or Racism?" In that paper David and Collins dare to ask their readers to look beyond the fallacious concepts of the biology of race and toward the experience of racism as a determinant of poor pregnancy outcomes.

To better understand this tragic dilemma I would suggest that the isolation and alienation experienced as a consequence of racism, sexism, or social class ostracism is a form of psycho-emotional trauma. I draw support for this claim from the separate but related work of Judith Herman, James and Melissa Griffith, and Kai Erikson.

Herman (1992) explored a pattern that connects the experience of women who are battered or raped or both, soldiers in bloody combat, children who are abused physically and sexually, and political prisoners. To her list I would add the community of women who are prisoners of consciousness — the women to whom I have already alluded as oppressed merely because of their gender and whose plight their race or social class standing compounds.

One of the responses to this trauma is what Herman described as "physioneurosis" — hyper-arousal of the autonomic nervous system. In their book *The Body Speaks*, Griffith and Griffith (1994) noted, "Mind-body problems are often consequences of the abuse of power either in personal relationships, such as spouse abuse or childhood sexual abuse, or in societal relation-ships, such as political oppression or racism." (p. 6.) They went on to argue that in the face of unspeakable dilemmas, the body acts out the drama of the conflict. The physioneurosis described by Herman is the body's acting out of the unspeakable dilemma called oppression. This, I believe, is a better explanation for the high incidence of premature births and other complications of pregnancy for disenfranchised women.

Is there other evidence that trauma can be experienced communally? Kai Erikson (1994) has done work that, I believe, makes this perspective plausible. I quote him extensively because he so poignantly and poetically addresses the issue at hand. Erikson wrote (pp. 228–233),

> Trauma is generally taken to mean a blow to the tissues of the body — or, more frequently now, to the structures of the mind — that results in injury or some other disturbance. Something alien breaks in on you, possesses you, takes you over, becomes a dominating feature of your interior landscape, and in the process threatens to drain you and leave you empty ... *collective trauma* ... [is] a blow to the basic tissues of social life that damages the bonds attaching people together and impairs the prevailing sense of communality. The collective trauma works its way slowly and even insidiously into the awareness of those who suffer from it, so it does not have the quality of suddenness normally associated with "trauma." But it is a form of shock all the same, a gradual realization that the community no longer exists as an effective source of support and that an important part of the self has disappeared.... "I" continue to exist, though damaged and maybe even permanently changed. "You" continue to exist, though distant and hard to relate to. But "we" no longer exist as a connected pair or as linked cells in a larger communal body.

I have mentioned the shift in perspective that David and Collins ask us to consider when reflecting on "bad outcomes in black babies." One reason their work is not more widely known or adopted may be that it confronts us with a different set of policy questions — the answers to which may compel us to share if not shift the burden of responsibility for change from the shoul-ders of childbearing women to men.

I turn now to a consideration of the health and well-being of those men as it is reflected in coronary artery disease.

THE BROKEN HEART: A MEDICAL CONSEQUENCE OF LONELINESS

In their comprehensive treatise on population health, Evans, Hodge, and Pless (1994, p. 184) made this assertion:

There is a chain that runs from the behaviour of cells and molecules, to the health of populations, and back again, a chain in which the past and present social environments of individuals, and their perceptions of those environments, constitute a key set of links. No one would pretend that the chain is fully understood, or is likely to be for a considerable time to come. But the research evidence currently available no longer permits anyone to deny its existence.

I will follow their lead in attempting to weave the garment of destiny as it most immediately envelopes white men in America. In doing so I acknowledge my obvious lack of direct experience of white maleness. My understanding of the epidemiology and pathophysiology of coronary artery disease should perhaps be held suspect as well because I have not studied this phenomenon as intensely as I have infant mortality. Nonetheless, I am hopeful that the reader will find this story intriguing if not compelling, and provocative if not credible.

The Behavior of Cells and Molecules

Individual muscle cells of the heart serve to illustrate the way in which whole/parts (holons) work. Each cell is a distinct and recognizable entity and is programmed to contract rhythmically. Yet heart cells will beat slowly and irregularly if isolated from other heart cells in laboratory culture medium. When the cells are allowed to grow together, their beating becomes both regular and synchronized. It is as if heart cells "learn" how to function as heart cells in the company of similar cells. They are dysfunctional in isolation (Jongsma, Tsjernina, & de Bruijne, 1983).

This observation is meant to serve as a metaphor. It symbolizes the argument that I wish to develop regarding the experience of isolation and alienation as a risk factor for premature death from coronary artery disease in men.

Elevated serum cholesterol is perhaps the most oft-cited and best-known risk factor for coronary artery disease and fatal heart attacks. It is important, therefore, to briefly put this matter in perspective.

It is clear that cholesterol contributes to hardening of the arteries. However, cholesterol's contribution to *occlusion* of coronary arteries — a necessary step in the sequence of pathophysiologic events leading to a heart attack — is controversial. Indeed, autopsy studies reveal that individuals may have extensive hardening of the arteries without a history of symptoms of heart failure or heart attack (Evans et al., 1994, p. 191).

It is also important to be mindful of the factors that help to determine the fate of cholesterol in the blood. Specifically, James Lynch reminded us, "Serum cholesterol has been shown to be linked not only to diet but also to emotional stress: people who are more stressed psychologically can have higher levels" (Lynch, 1977, p. 25).

Something other than cholesterol, alone or in combination with other risk factors such as smoking, sedentary lifestyles, or genetic predisposition, contributes to a "choking off" of the heart's blood supply.

A Population Perspective of Coronary Heart Disease

Consider the following story of one white male. I offer it as somewhat analogous to the "paradox of the well-off black woman" mentioned previously. It is the story of W. Thomas Nessa, who died of a heart attack at age 48.

Dr. Nessa was a cardiologist of some repute. He was, in fact, a member of the Boston Celtic's medical team and had helped to convene the "dream team" of cardiologists who initially evaluated and treated the late Reggie Lewis, the once beloved captain of the Boston Celtics. Dr. Nessa was an avid runner who had participated in the Boston marathon on a number of occasions. His colleagues hailed him as "a premier sports cardiologist.... He helped set the standards for cardiac evaluations and care for all NBA athletes."[1]

I must admit to my ignorance of any other information about the man. However, his story quickly brought to mind a question posed by Lynch in a book I have already mentioned, *The Broken Heart* (Lynch, 1997, p. 31): "Why does the United States still rank 24th among industrialized countries in life expectancy for its male citizens?" This despite the availability of and access to arguably the most sophisticated medical technology and care. It is an echo of the question that first began to haunt me in regard to the tragedy of infant mortality. Specifically, it often has been declared shameful that infant mortality rates in the United States rank between 22nd and 24th among industrialized nations. This, too, despite the availability of first-rate medical care, although in this instance concern has been centered on limited access to such care for the women who are at greatest risk. The juxtaposition of these two concerns lends further credence to the growing argument that medical technology and care has made and continues to make nominal contributions to reductions in morbidity and mortality.

How does one begin to account for this paradox? There are a number of population studies that may shed light on this question. The first is a study regarding what has come to be known in public health circles as the "Roseto effect."

Roseto is an Italian American community in Pennsylvania. It came to the attention of public health officials because the men of Roseto had lower rates of death from coronary artery disease than average for American men. A longitudinal study of the relationship of social adjustment to coronary heart disease was begun 30 years ago. The principal investigators of that study noted, "What has been learned seems to confirm an old but often forgotten conviction that mutual respect and cooperation contribute to the health and welfare of a community and its inhabitants, and that self-indulgence and lack of concern for others exert opposite influences."

It is worth expanding on these observations by way of a more extensive quote from *The Power of Clan* (Wolf & Bruhn, 1993, p. vii):

> As important as behaviors such as diet or smoking appear to be from studies of large groups of more-or-less anonymous individuals, they have not been of significant predictive value over a twenty-five year span of time in Roseto. On the other hand, attention directed to broader aspects of behavior of individuals and groups, specifically those that lead to or reflect social disintegration, has suggested a strong influence of individual social values and collective morale on the heart and coronary vessels. The loss of social stability, as reflected in the loosening of family ties and the weakening of community cohesion, appear from the 1985 sociological interviews to have induced a sense of uncertainty about the future among Rosetans, with a variety of accompanying apprehensions and emotional conflicts and perhaps undue variability in vital homeostatic systems. (Wolf & Bruhn, 1993, p. 109)

Lynch (1977, pp. 15–29) argued persuasively that similar dynamics could account for findings in the more widely known Framingham studies. That is, at the outset the community was stable and the death rate from coronary artery disease was lower than average. Over time, Framingham became a less cohesive community. Lynch interpreted the increased rates of divorce, out-of-wedlock births, transience, and deaths from coronary artery disease as symptoms of eroding communal bonds.

Adding to the complexity (and diversity) of these stories, I briefly consider the experience of Mexican American women, Japanese American men, and African American men.

First-generation Mexican American women, who are generally more impoverished economically than African Americans and receive less prenatal care, have infant mortality rates as low or lower than white women. In succeeding generations, with increasing exposure to our American way of life, the infant mortality rate for Mexican Americans begins to climb (James, 1993; Kerr, Verrier, Ying, & Spears, 1995).

A parallel experience has been documented for Japanese men. Despite industrialization and rapid economic growth, the Japanese have had the lowest rates of death from coronary artery disease when compared with people from other industrialized nations. The rates increase for Japanese American men who live in Hawaii, and they are higher still for those men who live in the continental United States. Among the latter group of Japanese men, those who maintain their cultural ties and mores continue to enjoy relatively low rates of death from heart attacks (Evans et al., 1994, pp. 197–200).

Having reflected and speculated on the plight of other identity groups, I turn briefly to a reflection on the group with which I share membership: middle-aged black men. As is the case with infant mortality rates, death from heart disease is not peculiar to blacks or whites. The differential pattern of disease, however, is as interesting as it is instructive. Specifically, hypertensive cardiovascular disease and stroke is more prevalent among African American men, whereas atherosclerotic heart disease is proportionally greater in American white men (Flack, Ferdinand, & Nasser, 2003). In an autopsy study, Onwuanyi et al. (1998) found that hypertensive vascular disease was the cause of death in 42% of blacks compared with 23% of whites. In contrast, atherosclerotic heart disease was the cause of death in 64% of whites versus 38% of blacks. These differences were statistically significant.

Investigators have advanced a number of theories to account for the differential rates of hypertension and its sequalae in African American men including genetic predisposition, excess salt in the diet, and limited access to health care services. Arguably the most intriguing studies (and the studies that resonate with my own experience) are those linking the experiences of racism with cardiovascular disease in African Americans (Clark, Anderson, Clark, & Williams, 1999). In particular, Wyatt et al. (2003) explored three levels of racism — institutionalized, perceived or personally mediated, and internalized — to explain the disproportionate burden of hypertensive disease and mortality in African Americans.

Poets have an ability to capture poignant aspects of life that might otherwise filter through the fine sieve of epidemiological studies. There is, for example, a chorus of African American poets that identify the potential source of despair or anger, or both, attendant to racism and underlying cardiovascular disease and stroke. Georgia Douglas Johnson (1973) wrote of old black men who dream of "glory, love, and power." When their dreams are thwarted, "they have learned to live it down / as though they did not care." Langston Hughes (1973, p. 76) is not persuaded and presses the question, "What happens to a dream deferred?" Hughes answers with a rhetorical question in the closing line of his poem: "Does it explode?" Does the dream deferred explode outward in a homicidal rage (the sixth-leading cause of death among blacks)? Or does it explode inward with sudden cardiovascular death or stroke? Frank Marshall Davis (1973, p. 96) has written a poem about a fictional yet all-too-real character, Robert Whitmore. Whitmore was successful in business, owned a home, and was a leader in a prestigious community organization. Yet he "died of apoplexy / when a stranger from Georgia / mistook him / for a former Macon waiter."

Isolation and alienation is enraging for African American men and constricts the blood vessels. Perhaps the same experience for white American men hardens the blood vessels.

Fashioning a Single Garment of Destiny

In an excerpt from Nikki Giovanni's (1978) poem "Crutches" we glimpse the angst attendant to the American male ethic of rugged individualism, which provides the emotional overtone for the remainder of this essay.

> men are supposed to be strong
> so they have heart attacks
> and develop other women
> who don't know their weaknesses
> and hide their fears
> behind male lovers
> whom they religiously touch
> each saturday morning on the basketball court
> its considered a sign of health doncha know
> that they take such good care of their bodies

In telling the story of women and children I noted that their health was imperiled by the loss of mutually supportive and challenging relationships at a critical juncture in their development. I must, therefore, offer some evidence for similar dynamics occurring in the life of men between 45 and 55 years of age — the time in which the peak incidence of premature death from coronary artery disease occurs. I believe that evidence can be found in the separate works of Daniel Levinson and Philip Slater.

Levinson (1978) was the principal investigator in a pioneering study that culminated in the publication of *The Seasons of a Man's Life*. In this study Levinson was able to show, contrary to popular wisdom, that beyond childhood and young adulthood, man still faced developmental frontiers and challenges.

I am particularly drawn to Levinson's thesis because he begins with the same foundational claim articulated earlier in this presentation. Levinson noted,

> The individual life structure is a patterning of self and world ... self and world are not two separate entities. They are not like billiard balls that, colliding, affect each other's course but not each other's nature. An essential feature of human life is the *interpenetration* of self and world. Each is inside the other.... The structure of society is reflected in the self and the life structure. Every man's life gives evidence of his society's wisdom and integration as well as its conflicts, oppression and destructiveness. (pp. 47–48)

On the basis of extensive and longitudinal biographical interviews with 40 men, Levinson defined four eras in the male lifecycle: childhood and adolescence, early adulthood, middle adulthood, and late adulthood. Each era is separated by a "cross-era" transition period. It is the midlife era and its preceding midlife transition to which I wish to bring your attention, for it is in this time — 40 to 60 years of age — that men are dying prematurely from heart disease. A key developmental task in this time of a man's life is coming to grips with his own mortality. This task is not peculiar to midlife but, like other tasks to be explored in a moment, it is particularly pressing.

In describing the broader, more critical process in midlife transition, Levinson (1978) coined the term "de-illusionment." "The process of losing or reducing illusions [and] involves diverse feelings — disappointment, joy, relief, bitterness, grief, wonder, freedom — and has diverse outcomes" (p. 193).

Indeed, this de-illusionment is a necessary outcome of *individuation* — man's experience of changes in the nature of his relationship to himself and to his world. Moreover, Levinson found that there are four paradoxes to be transcended during midlife individuation. Specifically, one must be open to the experience of (a) being both young and old, (b) being both destructive and creative, (c) being both masculine and feminine, and (d) being both autonomous and interdependent (Levinson, 1978, p. 197).[2]

The latter two paradoxes — integration of the masculine and feminine aspects of the self, and balancing autonomy and interdependence — are especially germane to the argument I am attempting to develop. Philip Slater's (1990) critique of American culture, *The Pursuit of Loneliness*, helps us to appreciate the forces that affect the achievement of the important developmental tasks at midlife defined by Levinson.

Slater wrote of three human desires that are "deeply and uniquely frustrated by American culture." They are the desire for community, attachment, and dependency. These desires are frustrated, in essence, by a credo of rugged (masculine) individualism.[3] An integration of the masculine and feminine aspects of the self is particularly difficult:

> The masculine ideal in our culture ... has traditionally been one of almost complete emotional constipation. Anger might be encouraged in certain settings, but tears or joyous effusions never. Men could choose between a mask of mute stolidity and one of pompous intellectuality ... men even today are stuck with this choice between articulate and inarticulate zombiehood. (Slater, 1990, p. 3)

This difficulty was apparent to Levinson in his study. He observed,

> In its extreme form, this polarization requires a man to be a kind of thinking machine. To be truly masculine, he must devote himself to his occupation in a highly impersonal way. He can allow himself a narrow range of "manly" feelings relating to assertiveness, rivalry and task attainment. But he is not permitted feelings that involve dependency, intimacy, grief, sensuality, and vulnerability. Such feelings are associated with childishness and femininity. (Levinson, 1978, p. 233)

However, as we have seen with the physioneurosis that is the mind-body response to the unspeakable dilemma of trauma, "zombiehood" does not mitigate the ultimate expression of emotion. Slater offered this eloquent and particularly germane observation:

> Whatever the feeling that's tabooed, its suppression causes distress. A certain amount of roundabout relief may be gained vicariously or through discharging other feelings, but some discomfort always remains. Usually it takes physical form in chronic muscular tension. Such tension and its secondary effect cause much illness ... and a lot of the decay we attribute to "old age" is just the erosion caused by each society trying to cram humans into some emotional mold that doesn't quite fit. (Slater, 1990, p. 6)

"Individualistic thinking," Slater argued, "is unflagging in the production of false dichotomies," among which are the very ones we must strive mightily to transcend in midlife.[4]

TRYING ON THE SINGLE GARMENT OF DESTINY

On the surface we are confronted with seemingly disparate causes of premature death in two different groups of individuals: black infants and white men. Is there a common thread to their experiences?

At the very least, both groups are at risk for failing to adapt or transform at a critical, albeit different, stage of the lifecycle. For both groups the failures to adapt and evolve to the next stage of greater integration and complexity is limited. The mothers of black infants are stopped in their development by the experiences of oppression in a race-, gender-, and class-conscious society. A most significant developmental challenge is presented to them early in their lives when they have few illusions about "belonging."

White men, on the other hand, live in a culture that nurtures a sense of belonging — a sense that begins to change in the period of de-illusionment that characterizes the midlife transition. Again I cite Levinson:

> As a man becomes more individuated and more oriented to the Self, a process of "detrib-alization" occurs. He becomes more critical of the tribe — the particular groups, institutions and traditions that have the greatest significance for him, the social matrix to which he is most attached. (Levinson, 1978, p. 242)

As the illusion is shattered, so too may be the heart, especially if the man is not embedded in a mutually supportive and challenging relationship at this critical juncture of his life. This is the crux of the thesis that Lynch attempts to develop in *The Broken Heart*.

I conclude, then, with an African aphorism that reiterates my foundational claim and heralds a warning. It was Desmond Tutu (Tutu, 1989), a South African Anglican Bishop and Nobel laureate who said,

> I would not know how to be a human being at all, except I learned this from other human beings. We are made for a delicate network of relationships, of interdependence. We are meant to complement each other. All kinds of things go horribly wrong when we break that fundamental rule of our being (p. 73).

Death as a sequel to premature birth or coronary artery disease may be among the things that go horribly wrong when we ignore our interdependence.

REFERENCES

Clark, R., Anderson, N. B., Clark, V. R., & Williams, D. R. (1999). Racism as a stressor for African Americans: A biopsychosocial model. *American Psychologist, 54*(10), 805–816.

David, R. J., & Collins, J. W. (1991). Bad outcomes in black babies: Race or racism? *Ethnicity and Disease, 1,* 236–244.

Davis, F. M. (1973). Robert Whitmore. In A. Adoff (Ed.), *The poetry of black America* (p. 96). New York: Harper & Row.

Erikson, K. (1994). *A new species of trouble: Explorations in disaster, trauma, and community.* New York: W. W. Norton.

Evans, R. G., Hodge, M., & Pless, I. B. (1994). If not genetics, then what? Biological pathways and population health. In R. G. Evans, M. L. Barer, & T. R. Marmor (Eds.), *Why are some people healthy and others not?* New York: Aldine de Gruyter.

Flack, J. M., Ferdinand, K. C., & Nasser, S. A. (2003). Epidemiology of hypertension and cardiovascular disease in African Americans. *Clinical Hypertension, 5*(Suppl. 1), 5–11.

Gates-Williams, J., Jackson, M. N., Jenkins-Monroe, V., & Williams, L.R. (1992). The business of preventing African-American infant mortality. *Western Journal of Medicine, 157,* 350–356.

Giovanni, N. (1978). *Cotton candy on a rainy day*. New York: Morrow.

Good, B. J. (1994). *Medicine, rationality, and experience*. Cambridge, UK: Cambridge University Press.

Griffith, J. L., & Griffith, M. E. (1994). *The body speaks: Therapeutic dialogues for mind-body problems*. New York: HarperCollins.

Haynatzka, V., Peck, M., Sappenfield, W., et al. (2002). Racial and ethnic disparities in infant mortality rates—60 largest U.S. cities, 1995–1998. *Mortality and Morbidity Weekly Report, 51*(15), 329–332.

Herman, J. L. (1992). *Trauma and recovery: The aftermath of violence—from domestic abuse to political terror*. New York: Basic Books.

Huges, L. (1973). Dream deferred. In A. Adoff (Ed.), *The poetry of black America* (p. 76). New York: Harper & Row.

James, S. A. (1993). Racial differences in infant mortality and low birthweight. A psychosocial critique. *Annals of Epidemiology, 3*(2), 130–136.

Johnson, G. W. (1973). Old black men. In A. Adoff (Ed.), *The poetry of black America* (pp. 21–22). New York: Harper & Row.

Jongsma, H. J., Tsjernina, L., & de Bruijne, J. (1983). The establishment of regular beating in populations of pacemaker heart cells. A study with tissue-cultured rat heart cells. *Journal of Molecular and Cellular Cardiology, 15*(2), 123–133.

Josselson, R. (1992). *The space between us: Exploring the dimensions of human relationships*. San Francisco: Jossey-Bass.

Kerr, G. R., Verrier, M., Ying, J., & Spears, W. (1995). Proportional differences in births and infant mortality rates among the triethnic population in Texas from 1984 through 1986. *Texas Medicine, 91*(3), 50–57.

King, M. L., Jr. (1968). *Trumpet of conscience*. New York: Harper & Row.

Krieger, N., Rowley, D. L., & Herman, A. (1993). Racism, sexism, and social class: Implications for studies of health, disease, and well-being. *American Journal of Public Health, 9*(Suppl.), 82–122.

Levinson, D. J. (1978). *The seasons of a man's life*. New York: Ballentine Books.

Lynch, J. J. (1977). *The broken heart: The medical consequences of loneliness*. New York: Basic Books.

Meckel, R. A. (1990). *Save the babies: American public health reform and the prevention of infant mortality*. Baltimore: Johns Hopkins University Press.

Onwuanyi, A., Hodges, D., Avancha, A., et al. (1998). Hypertensive vascular disease as a cause of death in blacks versus whites: Autopsy findings in 587 adults. *Hypertension, 31*, 1070–1076.

Pear, R. (1990, August 12). *New York Times*. p. E-5.

Philadelphia Inquirer (1990, August 20). p. A-12.

Pilisuk, M., & Hillier-Parks, S. (1986). *The healing web: Social networks and human survival*. London: University Press of New England.

Population Reference Bureau. (2003). 2003 world population data sheet. Retrieved October 22, 2003, from *http://www.prb.org/pdf/WorldPopulationDS03_Eng.pdf*

Prager, K. (1995, February 1). *Wall Street Journal*, p. A-13.

Rowley, D. (1994). Research issues in the study of very low birthweight and preterm delivery among African-American women. *Journal of the National Medical Association, 86*(10), 761–764.

Schoendorf, K. C., Hogue, C. J., Kleinman, J. C., & Rowley, D. (1992). Mortality among infants of black as compared with white college-educated parents. *New England Journal of Medicine, 26*(23), 1522–1526.

Slater, P. (1990). *The pursuit of loneliness: American culture at the breaking point* (3rd ed.). Boston: Beacon Press.

Sperling, M. A. (1990, August 15). *Pittsburgh Post Gazette*. p. C-3.

Swimme, B., & Berry, T. (1992). *The universe story*. San Francisco: Harper.

Tutu, N. (1989). *The words of Desmond Tutu*. New York: New Market Press.

Wilber, K. (1979). *No boundary: Eastern and Western approaches to personal growth*. Boston: Shambhala.

Wilber, K. (1995). *Sex, ecology, spirituality*. Boston: Shambhala.

Wilkinson, J. (1998). *The Bible and healing: A medical and theological commentary*. Grand Rapids, MI: William B. Eerdmans.

Wilkinson, R. G. (1996). *Unhealthy societies: The afflictions of inequality*. London: Routledge.

Wolf, S., & Bruhn, J. G. (1993). *The power of clan: The influence of human relationships on heart disease*. New Brunswick, NJ: Transaction.

Wyatt, S. B., Williams, D. R., Calvin, R., et al. (2003). Racism and cardiovascular disease in African Americans. *American Journal of Medical Sciences*, 325(6), 315–331.

NOTES

1. *The Boston Globe*. (1995, January 24). Obituaries.
2. For a more detailed look at the nature of the challenge of transcending paradox (and the illusion of opposites) see Wilber (1979).
3. My use of the term *credo* is quite deliberate. The medical anthropologist, Byron J. Good, reminded us, "*Credo*, in the Latin, is literally 'I set my heart'" (Good, 1994, p. 17).
4. Slater made the same foundational claim alluded to already. He stated, "The problem with individualism is not that it is immoral but that it is incorrect. The universe does not consist of a lot of unrelated particles but is an interconnected whole. Pretending that our fortunes are independent of each other may be perfectly ethical, but it's also perfectly stupid" (Slater, 1990, p. 13).

FIVE

Keeping the White Queen in Play

Michael Billig

YOUNGER SON: I don't think he would have married a black girl either.
MOTHER: Oh no.
YOUNGER SON: Or a Chinese girl.
MOTHER: No. [*laughs*]
OLDER SON: Or a Greek. [*Father and Mother laugh*]
MOTHER: Or an I-tie. [*general laughter*]
FATHER: Would you?
YOUNGER SON: So, I mean in that, in that sense, he's dictated to, as to who he can
   fall in love and get married.

It is an English family, sitting in their own home, talking about the British Royal Family. The older son, a 30-year-old photographer, is the only one arguing an antiroyalist position. The conversation is relaxed, with much friendly banter between the older son and the other three members. The talk got round to the question whether Prince Charles, as heir to the throne, would have been free to marry anyone of his choice. They were agreeing that palace authorities would have inspected the background of any prospective wife, checking in particular for her capacity to produce royal offspring. The younger son, much more traditional than his older brother, then raised the issue of race. Prince Charles would not have been free to marry a black girl. In the exchange, which followed, there was the joking and the laughter, outlined above.

Why should laughter accompany the turn toward race? In the exchanges about checking a prospective royal princess, there was little humour. The older son had mentioned that any prospective queen by marriage would have been required to undergo a gynecological examination to see whether she could have children. No jokes were made. The mother had said that, should the tests prove unsatisfactory, Charles would have been required to find another partner. Still no joking. Then the hypothetical black girl is suggested. And the joking begins. Perhaps, the timing was fortuitous. Yet, jokes can often be revealing. They can indicate a breaking of social and discursive codes, as the impermissible is briefly permitted to be uttered in a changed, safely humorous, form (Mulkay, 1988). The codes and taboos are not directly challenged by the jokes, which can protect the codes, which they appear to infract.

Although jokes appear to permit the unsayable to be uttered, some things still remain unsaid. As will be suggested, the family's joking touched upon deep issues of identity and nationhood — issues that are too hedged with social taboos to be spoken directly. Even in the jokes, there is much to be left unsaid, especially in relation to the unsayable assumptions of race and whiteness. In this instance, the unsayable themes indicate how the assumptions of race can deeply permeate conventional talk about British national identity.

The family had been taking part in a research project about the ways in which English families talk about the Royal Family. An interviewer had contacted over 60 families; all but one was white. The resulting discussions were recorded in the families' own homes (for details, see Billig, 1992). Speakers would typically talk at length about the desirability of royalty representing the nation, or setting standards for ordinary people. In the majority of cases the issue of race was not a topic that was raised. But when it was, the discursive turns were revealing, both in terms of what was said and, also, most importantly, what was not said.

In the extract just quoted, the laughter did not start with the mention of a black girl. That was to be considered as a serious possibility. Britain has an estimated population of more than two and a half million nonwhites, of whom more than a half a million could be identified as "African" or "Afro-Caribbean" (Skellington & Morris, 1992). There is evidence of an increase of inter-ethnic couples, so that there are now more people described as "mixed origin" than "West Indian"; almost 40% of those described as "mixed origin" are less than ten years of age (Skellington & Morris, 1992, pp. 39–40). Also, British people, especially whites, consistently overestimate the number of nonwhites in the country (see, for example, the results of the NOP poll, reported in Skellington & Morris, 1992, p. 153). If the idea of white and black falling in love in contemporary Britain is not considered a fanciful prospect, then it is not beyond the bounds of imagination to entertain the possibility that the Royal Family might be faced with the prospect of nonwhite in-laws.

However, the possibility was not seriously discussed in that particular conversation. Jokes turn the conversation away from the topic, after the idea of a black queen is mooted. The mother raises the possibility of Charles falling in love with a Chinese girl. There is laughter. Why is it funny? Certainly, there is a much smaller British Chinese population than black or "Asian" (in Britain, "Asian" generally refers to people from the Indian subcontinent). The idea of a Chinese Queen of England is itself a mixing of codes: a sense of incongruity is invoked by the very idea. The idea is beyond the conventionally possible idea that the heir, in common with increasing numbers of his white subjects, might fall in love with a black Briton. The joke is taken up and pushed further by the older son: "Or a Greek," he says. Slyly, it is back to reality: The Queen's husband was originally Prince Philip of Greece. But the reality is itself a source of jokes: This man, who looks and sounds so aristocratically British, is *really* Greek ("just a Greek").

The mother, far from rebutting the implication (and far from seeing her son's comment as a criticism against the biased customs of royal matrimony) joins in the fun: "Or an I-tie." It's all become a joke. If Greeks are not inappropriate (so long as they appear English), then nor are Italians. But the mother uses the derogatory slang, to reverse the reversal: an "I-tie" is inappropriate, for an "I-tie" would be a most Italian Italian. And the word itself is inappropriate: A breaking of codes is indicated by the socially impolite slang, which can only be uttered in jest. To have used "I-tie" in earnest would be coarse, especially in front of a stranger — the interviewer. It would hardly have conformed to codes of middle-class, English politeness.

The matter is not left as a joke, for these jokes, like most jokes, are not "merely" jokes. The younger son sums up the position, to which the comments, jesting and serious, are leading. "So," he says, using a little word, which conventionally indicates that a point is to be drawn from the preceding remarks (Schiffrin, 1985). So, the prince is dictated to: he cannot choose whom to fall in love with. The point is to sympathise with the prince — not to sympathise with any black, Chinese, or "I-tie" who might be rejected as inappropriate for royal position.

But something is being left unsaid. The jokes allude to, but skirt around, a crucial issue. There is no articulation of the principle, according to which prospective brides might be accepted or rejected. But the principle is understood — and is understood beyond humour. It is, of course, the principle of presumed "whiteness." There can be jokes about Chinese or Italian royal spouses — but not about "blacks." "I-tie" can be uttered, but not the equivalent for blackness. The word "white" is absent in the exchanges. And the jokes move the conversation on from "colour" (black and perhaps "yellow"), so the concluding principle (itself based on an unarticulated principle) can be drawn. The jokes, about the white (or possibly "whitish") foreigners leave the unsayable unsaid, but in place: the future Queen must be white.

According to Pajaczkowska and Young (1994, p. 202), white identity possesses an "absent centre." If identity is discursively constructed (Shotter, 1993; Shotter & Gergen, 1989; Wetherell & Potter, 1992), then this absent centre will be supported by codes of utterance, rather than inner psychic structures. Just as conversations can jointly produce collective memories (Billig & Edwards, 1994; Edwards & Middleton, 1988; Middleton & Edwards, 1990), so, too they can accomplish denials and projections, as speakers combine to move talk away from tabooed topics, jointly protecting what cannot be uttered. In this way, the unsayable will be present, even if marked by its absence.

In the case of British royalty there is a taboo of race and identity. The Royal Family, as many British speakers claim, is to be seen as a symbol of the nation. If nations are, to quote Anderson (1983), "imagined communities," then monarchy occupies a central place in the imagination of contemporary Britain. Often respondents said that Britain would not be Britain without a monarchy; it would be like other countries (for details, see Billig, 1992). As the mother of the family, quoted above, said in another part of the conversation, "It's part of our background, you know as English people." The equation between the nation and the Royal Family is also an equation of identity — it's part of "us," "our" background, "our" selves. If Britain is not Britain without the Royal Family, then "we, the British" would not be British: "We" would not be "us." Imagining "us" as "not-us" was something to be avoided.

In this way the Royal Family is defended as an object of national identification; people would say that they wanted a Royal Family in whom they could see themselves. Royalty should, in many ways, be ordinary — like "you" and "me." But, they should not be too ordinary: They should also be figures of respect. In Nairn's (1988) phrase, royalty should be super-ordinary (see also Edley, 1993). How, as English (or British) people, could "we" recognize "ourselves" in a foreigner? More than this, how could "we" see "ourselves" *as British* in the image of a foreigner — for "we" look to royalty to reflect "our" own sense of national self? The objects of "our" national identification must be objects of national identity. A Greek who looks and talks British is possible. But a Chinese person . . . an "I-tie" . . . a black. . . .

Something, here, cannot be uttered directly because of the conventional dilemmas of race. According to Etienne Balibar, contemporary racism is a "racism without races" (1991, p. 21). Racism itself must be denied, for its cultural undesirability, and more generally that of "prejudice," is firmly established. Denials can be heard as white persons talk about nonwhites. The utterance of complaint has its own etiquette. "I'm not prejudiced but, . . . " a common preface uttered as speakers, especially in European countries, begins their rhetoric of criticism directed against "immigrants" (Billig, 1991; Potter & Wetherell, 1988; van Dijk, 1991, 1992, 1993; Wetherell & Potter, 1992). The phrase itself draws attention to the social undesirability of "prejudice." Speakers claim the credentials of being "unprejudiced." In so doing, they recognize that their words might well be heard as being "prejudiced." In this way, the prefix seeks to disarm criticism in advance. In the United States, it is claimed that whites likewise disavow the open racism of two generations ago (Gaertner & Dovidio, 1986; Kinder, 1986; Kinder & Sears, 1981; McConahay, 1986; McConahay, Hardee, & Batts, 1981). Criticisms of blacks are seldom outwardly made on the ground of race in this new racism. Always some other reason — some deracialized justification — is found (Barker, 1981; Reeves, 1983; van Dijk, 1993).

The phrase "I'm not prejudiced but . . . " also indicates that there is a "prejudice" (the "proper" prejudice) existing beyond speakers' complaints. Speakers are implicitly distancing their own remarks, and their own selves, from the category of "prejudice." Thus, the implied image of some further extreme is justifying their own claims to nonprejudice. In Europe, the *real* prejudices are often presumed to be those of the fascist far-right (Billig, 1991). In the United States, it is the "rednecked" racism of segregation. The image of *real* prejudice, through which white speakers deny their own racism, is an image of racialised racism, with racial epithets and theories of race. There is more. A racism with races is not merely a racism against "them." It is a racism about "us." The fascist groups proclaim a theory of race, openly claiming to defend the racial purity of the white race (Billig, 1991). In this, they go beyond the bounds of politeness and social acceptability of the "normal" discourse of deracialized racism, which denies its own racism. In this denial, whiteness becomes invisible.

When race is talked about by whites in conventional ways, it must be socially managed to prevent the discursive intrusion of "whiteness," while, all the same, permitting the distinction between "whiteness" and "blackness" to be maintained, just out of argumentative reach. In the case of conventional talk about royalty, it is assumed that the nation should be represented by the image of a British, white family. But if the figures of identification are to be white, then this cannot be justified directly. Discursive projections and denials are necessary.

Traces of such denials are visible in the conversations about Royalty. Although more than 60 family discussions were recorded with white families, only on five occasions was the issue of royalty marrying outside their race raised. This, in itself, might be considered as a sign of avoidance. But when the issue was raised, the conversational delicacies became evident. Here was an "ideological dilemma," especially for the majority who were royalists (Billig et al., 1988). The whiteness of royalty was to be protected, but it could not be defended directly. Not only must "we" deny "our" own racism, but so must the racism of royalty be denied. To support a racist royal family — to identify openly with those who practice racial purity — would be to condemn "ourselves," both personally and nationally. Some other code of talking, together with a means of discursive avoidance, must be found.

A denial of choice was sometimes asserted, as if no one was making racial decisions. The older son in the family, already quoted, sums up his family's view: Prince Charles is "dictated to" in his choice of partner. Who is dictating this and why they are doing so are left unsaid. It is as if a hidden hand of necessity is operating in a vacuum. A 68-year-old, retired toolmaker is talking with his daughter and son-in-law. What would have happened if Prince Edward had "wanted to marry somebody from Asia or Africa?" asked the interviewer. "Well, I don't think he would have been allowed to," answered the father. Daughter and son-in-law agreed. Then, the father dismissed the question:

> I don't think the question would ever come up anyway because if they found out that he was involved with a coloured person, then, err, he, think, she would, she would, err, slowly go out of the limelight.

Hesitations and pauses, evident in his remarks, are conventional signs of discursive difficulty. Who was doing the allowing is again unspecified, as the passive tense is used. But one thing could be stated. The father said, "I don't think the Queen would be prejudiced, but I'm sure the old royalty would have been."

In another discussion, the mother, a 68-year-old former cleaner, agreed that royalty would not "be allowed to marry someone coloured." Her son, a 43-year-old school caretaker agreed: "It would all be hushed up ... before it even got to holding hands.... They'd be shipped abroad or somewhere, you know, out of the way." Who would be doing the shipping abroad, or the hushing up, of the nonwhite illicit lover is not specified. Somehow, magically, the black figure would be eliminated, with no questions asked.

Even so there is the problem of racism, conceived not as an injury to nonwhites but as an accusation against whites, including the speakers themselves. The caretaker continued, straight after his remarks about the hushing up and shipping away, to mention the possibility of racism:

I don't think it would happen, not because they're racist, I'm not saying they're racist, you know, 'cause they mix with the [*pause*] um, I can't see it myself, I don't know why.

Not even "blackness" was mentionable here, let alone "whiteness": royals are not racist because they mix with the "urn." No suitable description was at hand. None of the listeners needed to ask for clarification. The speaker's denial of royal racism was, also, a denial of his own racism: he was not supporting a racist figurehead. It wasn't racism; it just wouldn't happen. But why, he couldn't say: "I don't know why."

Neither his mother nor wife pushed him to specify. They were agreeing with him, supporting his point. "I mean it's what's expected of royalty," added his wife. "Yeah, that's it, it's imagery, yeah," added her husband taking up the point: "It wouldn't look right in the public eye." His mother agreed: "Well, it isn't right in the public eye, is it really." A double projection had been achieved. The wish for white royals was projected onto the royals themselves. And, then to escape the possible charge of racism, which the speakers were themselves raising, the royals were claimed to be acting in accordance with public opinion. The speakers did not associate themselves with "the public eye." It was as if this eye were something existing objectively outside of themselves — as an objective necessity beyond criticism. The royal whiteness, which this eye is presumed to need to gaze upon, is left unidentified. It is merely something whose absence would not look right. A discursive collusion enables "us" not to gaze upon (or mention) what is the nature of the right look.

A mother, who works as a cleaner, is talking with her 17-year-old daughter, a factory worker. They had been talking about the way that the young royals have to ask permission to marry. The interviewer asked the mother whether she expected her children to ask her for permission to get married. The mother replied, "As long as the bloke can keep them and look after them, I mean, I don't care if he's black, white, with pink spots or what he is." But what if "they" — royalty — wanted to marry a black person? Now it was a matter for joking — and hesitation:

Oh dear, I doubt it [*pause*], they'd have to scrub the poor devil to get it clean [*laughs*] no I doubt it, I mean, I know sort of [*pause*], well you know, they'll marry different nationalities, but [*pause*] coloured no.

"I don't think the Queen would like it," said her daughter in agreement. "I think she'd put a stop to it." They would "bleach them," joked the mother again.

The components of avoidance are there. "They," not "us," would forbid it; jokes about scrubbing and bleaching draw attention away from the details of forbidding; the mother mocks the irrationality of the prohibition, but the jokes leave it in place. The two women are not criticizing royalty on this issue. The issue is spoken of as a matter of blackness, of colour, but not of whiteness. The term "white" is avoided. Royalty would not marry "coloured," but they would different "nationalities": an opposition between "colour" and nationality is assumed. Listeners are to understand "nationalities" as "white foreigners": Greeks, French, Germans, even Italians or, perhaps, "I-ties." The meaning of race — and particularly of "whiteness" — is conveyed without the word "white."

Significantly, the mother does use "white" in her previous statement, when she is talking of permission rather than prohibition. When she talks about her own daughters, she expresses a tolerance that she does not attribute to royalty. Colour, she said, was irrelevant. Her daughters can marry whom they want: black or white or pink spots. She was speaking in front of her own unmarried daughter, and so her words can be understood as a message of permission. Whiteness is mentioned when it is specified as irrelevant: this message carried no danger of accusation. But when whiteness becomes relevant, as the object of a prohibition, then it must be semantically camouflaged.

In this way "whiteness" is kept in place as an unnamed standard, representing the national self — "colour" is the deviation. The retired toolmaker, his daughter, and son-in-law have already been mentioned. After mentioning that "a coloured person" who might get romantically entangled with a royal would be removed from the limelight, the toolmaker switched the conversation to religion. "They wouldn't be allowed to marry a Roman Catholic," said the old man. After a few exchanges on this theme, the son-in-law said,

> I think the whole issue between different sects, religion, and colours and races is to try and keep things as neutral as possible politically, that's how I personally see it.

The interviewer asked him what he meant. He replied, "Generally as a nation if you introduce something like a Catholic, a Jewish person, a black person, or an Asian, you're immediately putting a bias on the situation." What is neutral is unnamed: it is the normal terrain, the unmarked, national ground against which the biased figures stand out. And the biases, as compared with the pale background, can be identified by name. This identification itself can be claimed as an example of "neutrality," for the speaker, too, is laying claim to a position of neutrality. In this neutrality, race is treated alongside other categories, such as religion, and, thus, the particularities of race are absorbed into an outwardly deracialized general principle. Negative terms are avoided: there is no semantic hint of an "I-tie" here, nothing to attract the accusation of racism, anti-semitism, or whatever. It is a defence of neutrality, which leaves the background in the background, its proclaimed neutrality — "our" neutrality — as the standard, untouched and pure.

In all these defences of the whiteness of the Royal Family (and, thus, the white personification of the nation), the word "white" is avoided. As John Heritage (1988) argued, the conventions of discourse are often revealed in the exceptional case. Thus, the mother revealed the discursive conventions of "whiteness" by including the word in her permissions but not in her prohibitions. There was one discussion, in which the topic of royalty marrying a nonwhite was mentioned and a speaker specifically used the word "white" in this connection. The utterance indicated the assumptions behind the absences on other occasions.

A middle-class mother and father — secretary and salesperson, respectively — were talking with their 16-year-old daughter and her school friend, also 16. They had been discussing the religious restrictions on royal marriages: "They don't allow them to marry into different religions," said the mother, using the impersonal mode, which ascribes power and responsibility to a mysterious "them." The daughter, then, raised the issue of race, the white race:

DAUGHTER: It makes me wonder, right, 'cause, you know, all of the Royal Family are white, it makes me wonder whether they'd allow if they wanted to marry a coloured person; I just thought of that 'cause I don't think they would.
DAUGHTER'S FRIEND: I don't see why not.
DAUGHTER: Yeah, I don't see why not, but I don't think they would.
FATHER: I don't think it would ever happen.
DAUGHTER'S FRIEND: No.

As soon as the daughter introduces the topic and uses the term "white," her friend distances herself from the assumed royal position. She makes it plain that she sees no reason why royals should marry white. And the daughter agrees, distinguishing herself from the position attributed to royalty. The interviewer then asked the question, "How coloured would you have to be?" The daughter replied, "I think you've got to be pure white, I think that's how they'd take it." Again, an expression of distancing accompanies the outward expression of whiteness: that's how they would take it, emphasising that it is not the way she takes the issue. "Pure whiteness" is the sort of phrase to be used in earnest by the open racist: here, the phrase is turned around as critique. If royalty wish to remain "pure white," then they are being exposed: and she, the exposer, distances herself from the exposed racism.

Her mother and father utter no phrases, which either criticise royalty or distance themselves from the presumed royal policy of racial purity. Their words can be heard as evasions. And significantly, the word "white" is absent. The father agrees that royalty would not allow such intermarriage to happen. But he offers no words to criticise the presumed royal stance. Having stated the royal position, he, together with the mother, talk about whether the situation is ever likely to occur. The mother says the possibility hasn't ever cropped up. But it could in the future, says the father, "'cause there's more colours and everything coming into England and now it's a possibility." He did not think that there was "anything stated that they can't do that." The Queen would have the final say, said the mother.

As mother and father talked thus, they only described the Queen's stance, not their own. When their daughter and her friend had made their stance, there had been a parental silence. Words of criticism had not been uttered. Nor had words of "whiteness." Instead, their words were moving the point of conversation to the discussable topic of whether the situation might arise, and who would have the final say. And, finally, there was escape. They settled into discussing whether the royals could marry divorcées. This was a safer topic for the business of giving opinions. The mother now offered her stance: All those years ago, it had been wrong to prevent Princess Margaret from marrying the person of her choice. A divorcée. And, in fact, a white man. But the latter was not said. It was not her point.

In this sort of context, the discursive avoidances of whiteness leave the assumptions of whiteness in place. However, as the statements of the 16-year-old girl and her school friend indicate, the assumptions can be challenged. The issues at stake are not trivial. In Britain, the topic of royalty is centrally bound up with the imagining of the nation. As such, it is a form of banal nationalism and a key theme of national identity (Billig, 1995). As the conversational extracts suggest, this imagining of national identity has its racial aspect. However, the assumption of whiteness is not to be directly expressed, and certainly not directly justified. Hence, there is the projection of the wish for a white Royal Family onto the Queen, onto unspecified "them," or onto "public opinion." It is anywhere but here in "us."

The Royal Family was commonly justified as the personalized representation of national identity (see Billig, 1992). The mother, quoted above, said that it's part of "our" background as "English" people; royalty is part of the national "us." To reflect "our" national selves, this object of identification must offer the possibility that "we" can recognize "our" national selves in their reflection. Too Greek — too "I-tie" — too swarthy: and such recognition is not possible. Blackness, Jewishness, Chineseness absorb the light of British self-reflection — at least for the majority of "us." Here the tones of hegemony are to be heard. The "others" are to recognize themselves in the projected image of the majority, but "we" cannot recognize "our" national selves in "them." There is no equality in this exchange. The exotic peripheries must not be allowed to move toward the centre of Narcissus's nationalist mirror. But, hush. This is "our" background, "our" nation, "our" tolerance. Polite silences are required to keep it thus.

References

Anderson, B. (1983). *Imagined communities*. London: Verso.

Balibar, E. (1991). Is there a "neo-racism"? In E. Balibar & I. Wallerstein (Eds.), *Race, nation, class*. London: Verso.

Barker, M. (1981). *The new racism*. London: Junction Books.

Billig, M. (1991). *Ideology and opinions*. London: Sage Press.

Billig, M. (1992). *Talking of the Royal Family*. London: Routledge.

Billig, M. (1995). *Banal nationalism*. London: Sage.

Billig, M., Condor, S., Edwards, D., Gane, M., Middleton, D., & Radley, A. R. (1988). *Ideological dilemmas: A social psychology of everyday thinking*. London: Sage.

Billig, M., & Edwards, D. (1994). La construction sociale de la memoire. *La Recherche, 25*, 742–745.

Edley, N. (1993). Prince Charles — our flexible friend: Accounting for variations in constructions of identity. *Text, 13*, 397–422.

Edwards, D., & Middleton, D. (1988). Conversational remembering and family relationships: How children learn to remember. *Journal of Social and Personal Relationships, 5*, 3–25.

Gaertner, S. L., & Dovidio, J. F. (1986). The aversive form of racism. In J. F. Dovidio & S. L. Gaertner (Eds.), *Prejudice, discrimination and racism*. Orlando, FL: Academic Press.

Heritage, J. (1988). Explanations as accounts: A conversation analytic perspective. In C. Antaki (Ed.), *Analysing everyday explanation*. London: Sage.

Kinder, D. R. (1986). The continuing American dilemma: White resistance to racial change 40 years after Myrdal. *Journal of Social Issues, 42*, 151–171.

Kinder, D. R., & Sears, D. O. (1981). Prejudice and politics: Symbolic racism versus racial threats to the good life. *Journal of Personality and Social Psychology, 40*, 414–431.

McConahay, J. B. (1986). Modern racism, ambivalence and the Modern Racism Scale. In J. F. Dovidio & S. L. Gaertner (Eds.), *Prejudice, Discrimination and Racism*. Orlando, FL: Academic Press.

McConahay, J. B., Hardee, B. B., & Batts, V. (1981). Has racism declined in America? *Journal of Conflict Resolution, 25*, 563–579.

Middleton, D., & Edwards, D. (1990). *Collective remembering*. London: Sage.

Mulkay, M. (1988). *On humour*. Cambridge: Polity.

Nairn, T. (1988). *The enchanted glass*. London: Radius.

Pajaczkowska, C., & Young, L. (1994). Racism, representation, psychoanalysis. In J. Donald & A. Rattansi (Eds.), *"Race," culture and difference*. London: Sage.

Potter, J., & Wetherell, M. (1988). Accomplishing attitudes: Fact and evaluation in racist discourse. *Text, 8*, 51–68.

Reeves, F. (1983). *British racial discourse*. Cambridge: Cambridge University Press.

Schiffrin, D. (1985). Everyday argument: The organization of diversity in talk. In T. A. van Dijk (Ed.), *Handbook of discourse analysis* (Vol. 3). London: Academic Press.

Shotter, J. (1993). *The cultural politics of everyday life*. Milton Keynes: Open University.

Shotter, J., & Gergen, K. J. (1989). *Texts of identity*. London: Sage.

Skellington, R., & Morris, P. (1992). *"Race" in Britain today*. London: Sage.

van Dijk, T. A. (1991). *Racism and the press*. London: Routledge.

van Dijk, T. A. (1992). Discourse and the denial of racism. *Discourse and Society, 3*, 87–118.

van Dijk, T. A. (1993). *Elite discourse and racism*. Newbury Park, CA: Sage.

Wetherell, M., & Potter, J. (1992). *Mapping the language of racism*. Hemel Hempstead: Harvester/Wheatsheaf.

NOTE

The research reported in this chapter was supported by the Economic and Social Research Council on the project "Socio-psychological analysis of family discourse" (Grant Number R000231228). The author would like to thank, once again, Marie Kennedy for her interviewing skills.

SIX

Making White Right:
Race and the Politics of Educational Reform

Michael W. Apple

In a number of recent books, I have critically analyzed the ways in which neoliberal and neoconservative ideological movements have transformed our common sense. In the process, I have examined a range of proposals for educational "reform" such as marketization, standards, national and statewide curricula, and national and statewide testing. As I have demonstrated, even with the (supposedly) good intentions of the proponents of many of these kinds of proposals, in the long run these policies may actually exacerbate inequalities, especially around class and race. Furthermore, they may paradoxically cause us both to mis-recognize what actually causes difficult social and educational problems and to miss some important democratic alternatives that may offer more hope in the long run (see, e.g., Apple, 2000, 2001; Apple & Beane, 1995, 1999).

It is important to think of this ideological transformation as having been accomplished through the use of a vast socio/pedagogic project, a project that has actively — and in large part successfully — sought to transform our very ideas about democracy. Democracy is no longer a political concept; rather it is wholly an economic concept in which unattached individuals — supposedly making "rational" choices on an unfettered market — will ultimately lead to a better society. As Foner (1998) reminds us, it has taken decades of creative ideological work to change our commonsense ideas about democracy. Not only does it fly in the face of a very long tradition of collective understandings of democracy in the United States and many other nations but it has also led to the destruction of many communities, jobs, health care, and so many other institutions not only in the United States but also throughout the world. I am constantly amazed at the inability of many policy makers to recognize what is happening. By now we should know better. However, hidden assumptions about class and, as we shall see, about the politics of *whiteness* may make it hard for us to face this honestly.

RECOGNIZING RACE

In their exceptional analysis of the way the discourses of race have operated in the United States, Omi and Winant argued that race is not an "add-on" but is truly constitutive of many of our most taken for granted daily experiences.

In the United States, race is present in every institution, every relationship, every individual. This is the case not only for the way society is organized — spatially, culturally, in terms of stratification, and so on — but also for our perceptions and understandings of personal experience. Thus as we watch the videotape of Rodney King being beaten; compare real estate prices in different neighborhoods; size up a potential client, neighbor, or teacher; stand in line at the unemployment office; or carry out a thousand other normal tasks, we are compelled to think racially, to use racial categories and meaning systems in which we have been socialized. Despite exhortations both sincere and hypocritical, it is not possible or even desirable to be "color-blind" (Omi & Winant, 1994, pp. 158–159).

Not only is it not possible to be color-blind, as they go on to say "opposing race requires that we notice race, not ignore it." Only by noticing race can we challenge it, "with its ever-more-absurd reduction of human experience to an essence attributed to all without regard for historical or social context." By placing race squarely in front of us, "we can challenge the state, the institutions of civil society, and ourselves as individuals to combat the legacy of inequality and injustice inherited from the past" and continually re-produced in the present (Omi & Winant, 1994, p. 159).

Although Omi and Winant are analyzing racial dynamics in the United States, I would hope that by now it is equally clear that their claims extend well beyond these geographical borders to include Australia, the United Kingdom, and many other nations. It would not be possible to understand the history, current status, and multiple effects of educational policy without placing race as a core element of one's analysis.

Placing race at the center is less easy than one might expect, for one must do this with due recognition of its complexity. Race is not a stable category. What it means, how it is used, by whom, how it is mobilized in public discourse, and its role in educational and more general social policy — all of this is contingent and historical. Indeed, it would be misleading to talk of race as an "it." "It" is not a thing, a reified object that can be measured as if it were a simple biological entity. Race is a *construction*, a set of fully social *relationships*. This unfortunately does not stop people from talking about race in simplistic ways that ignore the realities of differential power and histories (see, e.g., Herrnstein & Murray, 1994; Kincheloe & Steinberg, 1996). Yet complexity needs to be recognized here as well. Racial dynamics have their own histories and are relatively autonomous. But they also participate in, form, and are formed by other relatively autonomous dynamics involving, say, class, colonial and post-colonial realities, and so on — all of which are implicated in and related to the social construction of race. Furthermore, racial dynamics can operate in subtle and powerful ways even when they are not overtly on the minds of the actors involved.

We can make a distinction between intentional and functional explanations here. Intentional explanations are those self-conscious aims that guide our policies and practices. Functional explanations on the other hand are concerned with the latent effects of policies and practices (see, e.g., Liston, 1988). In my mind, the latter are more powerful than the former.

In essence, this point rightly turns what is called the genetic fallacy in logic on its head, so to speak. Let me be specific here. We are apt to think of the genetic fallacy in particular ways. We tend to castigate authors who assume that the import and meaning of any position is totally determined by its original grounding. Thus, for example, it is clear that E. L. Thorndike — one of the founders of educational psychology — was a confirmed eugenicist and was deeply committed to the project of "race betterment" and had a vision of education that was inherently undemocratic.

Yet, one is on shaky ground if one concluded that every aspect of his work is totally "polluted" by his (repugnant) social beliefs. Thorndike's research program may have been epistemologically and empirically problematic, but a different kind of evidence and a more complex analysis is required to debunk all of it than to simply claim (correctly) that he was often racist, sexist, and elitist (see Gould, 1981, and Harraway, 1989, for how this more complex program might be done). Indeed, it is not difficult to find progressive educators drawing on Thorndike's work for support of what were then seen to be radical positions.

When we are talking about racism and reform in current policies, we need to turn the genetic fallacy around. The overt motivations of the sponsors of Labour's policies in the United Kingdom or of the Clinton and Bush proposals for education such as the establishment of national testing, and increasing "choice," in the United States may not have been about race or may have assumed that such proposals would "level the playing field" for everyone. Their intentions may have been self-consciously "meritorious." (I very much mean this play on words.) Yet, conscious originating motives do not guarantee at all how arguments and policies will be employed, what their multiple and determinate functions and effects will be, whose interests they will ultimately serve, and what identifiable patterns of differential benefits will emerge, given existing and unequal relations of economic, cultural, and social capital and given unequal strategies of converting one form of capital to another in our societies (Apple, 2001; Bourdieu, 1984).

Such differential functions and outcomes are clear in some very recent analyses of race and education in England. For example, in Gillborn and Youdell's report of the results of their investigation of the effects of national benchmarks (standards) and similar "reforms" in schools with significant populations of children of color, they state that the available data suggest that "beneath the superficial gains indicated by a year-on-year improvement against the benchmark criterion ... in some areas there has been a widening of inequality; between students, schools and in some cases, ethnic groups" and that this is especially the case for white and Afro-Caribbean students (Gillborn & Youdell, 1998, p. 7; see also Gillborn & Youdell, 2000).

CREATING EDUCATIONAL TRIAGE

There have been analyses here in the United States that have begun to document similar kinds of effects (Linn, 2000; Oakes, 1992; Oakes, Wells, Jones, & Datnow, 1997; Wells, Lopez, Scott, & Holme, 1999). However, unfortunately, the predominance of relatively unreflective and at times almost self-congratulatory policies around markets, standards, testing, and reductive forms of accountability is exactly that here — predominant. Even given the aforementioned exceptional work that is being done, for example, by Jeannie Oakes, Amy Stuart Wells, and others on the hidden effects of some of these kinds of policies and practices, and even given the fact that there are numerous examples of extremely effective schools in our urban and rural areas that succeed through using much more democratic and critical models of curriculum, teaching, and evaluation (Apple & Beane, 1995, 1999), it still feels as if one has to constantly swim against the tide of conservative modernization.

Given this state of affairs, it is now even more important that we pay attention to material that demonstrates what can happen in situations where the stress on higher standards and higher test scores hits both the realities of schools and the different populations they serve. I shall use David Gillborn and Deborah Yudell's volume *Rationing Education* (Gillborn & Youdell, 2000) as an example of what we can learn by looking beneath the rhetoric of intentions and focusing critically on the actual social functioning of "reforms" of this type. Gillborn and Youdell go into even more detail about the powerful, and often damaging, effects on teachers and students of our seeming fascination with ever-rising standards, mandated curricula, and over-emphasis on testing.

The volume is based on in-depth research on the equivalent of middle and secondary schools in England. It details the overt and hidden effects of policies that are currently being undertaken in the United States as well. These include such things as creating a situation where the tail of a high-stakes test "wags the dog" of the teacher, pressuring schools to constantly show increased achievement scores on such standardized tests no matter what the level of support or the impoverished conditions in schools and local communities, to publicly display such results in a process of what might be realistically called shaming, and to threaten schools that do not show "improvement" on these tests with severe sanctions or loss of control.

Of course, there are poor schools and there are ineffective practices in schools. However, the reduction of education to scores on what are often inadequate measures, often used in technically and educationally inappropriate ways for comparative purposes (Linn, 2000), has some serious consequences. What these consequences are provides the context for the story Gillborn and Youdell tell.

In many ways, *Rationing Education* provides what might be called a micro-economy of school life. It examines the ways in which certain valued commodities are accumulated by schools in a time of intense competition for scarce resources. In this case, the commodities are higher test scores and the resources are both numbers of students and public recognition of being a "good" school. The authors' way of describing this is what they call the "A–C economy."

Like the United States, in England schools exist in what is really a hierarchical ordering, a market, in prestige and reputation. They are valued by the number of students that get passing scores on particular national tests. The national tests are made public as a form of "league tables" in which schools are rank-ordered according to their relative results. Schools with large numbers of students getting grades A–C are more highly valued than those with students whose rates of passing are less — even though everyone tacitly knows that there is a very strong relationship between school results and poverty. (We need again to remember in the United States, for example, that poverty explains *much* more of the variance in school achievement than any school reform.)

This is straightforward and not surprising. However, this situation creates an economy that has certain characteristics. Students with predicted higher test scores are even more valuable. Students with predicted lower test scores are seen as less useful to the school's place in the market. This too is not surprising. The results of such an economy, however, are powerful. There is another key group of students who are focused upon and on whom considerable resources, energy, and attention is devoted — students who are on the border between passing grades and failing grades. These students — often seen as white middle-class "under-achievers" — become objects of great value in the school. After all, if this key group can be pulled across the border into the A–C column, the school's results will be that much more positive.

What could be wrong with an increased focus on students on the border? Here is one of the places where the results are ominous. In such an A–C economy, specific students are seen as moveable. Other students' abilities are seen as increasingly fixed and less worthy of attention. The class and race characteristics of these latter students are striking. Poor and working class students, students of African descent, and other ethnically "different" children are not valued commodities on this kind of market. Even though gender divisions were less pronounced in the schools that were studied, divisions strongly rooted in racializing and class-based structures were not simply mirrored in the schools. They actually were *produced* in these institutions.

Thus, policies that were put in place to raise standards, to increase test scores, to guarantee public accountability, and to make schools more competitive had results that were more than a little damaging to those students who were already the least advantaged in these same schools. Yet, it was not only the students who witnessed these negative effects. The voices of teachers and administrators indicate what happens to them as well. They too begin to harden their sense of which students are "able" and which students are not. Tracking returns in both overt and covert ways. And once again, black students and students in government subsidized lunch programs (the usual measure of poverty in a school population) are the ones most likely to be placed in the lower tracks or given academic and career advice that nearly guarantees that they will not only have limited or no mobility but will confirm their status as students who are "less worthy."

Equally worth noting here is the specific way the A–C economy works to choose those students who are deemed to have worthiness. Often, students whose behavior and test results are quite similar have very different careers in the school. Thus, a black student and a white student may be, say, on the border of the A–C/failing divide, but the black student will not be the beneficiary of the added attention. These situations are all too often characterized by tacitly operating visions of ability, ones that have been hardened by years of discourse on the "problem" of black student achievement and especially by the increased visibility once again of supposedly scientific (and ultimately racist and empirically problematic) "research" on genetic differences in mean intelligence between blacks and whites. Not only would no reputable population geneticist make such a claim but these theories have been discredited multiple times. The fact that they re-enter into our commonsense decision making in schools in times of scarce resources and increased pressure, shows how deeply seated they are in the sets of assumptions educators may unconsciously mobilize in their attempt to be pragmatic in dealing with large numbers of students.

As previous research has clearly indicated, students are not passive in the face of these tendencies. Indeed, as Gillborn and Youdell show, students "interpret, question, and on occasion, resist." However, "the scope for resistance is severely constrained, and pupils are clearly positioned as the subject of numerous organizational and disciplinary discourses in which the young people themselves play little active role" (Gillborn & Youdell, 2000, p. 194). In what is perhaps one of the most powerful messages of the book, the authors summarize the effects of this entire process in the following way. "It is a cruel irony that the processes of selection and monitoring that have been adopted with the aim of heightening attainment are so frequently experienced as disempowering and demotivating by the students" (Gillborn & Youdell, 2000, p. 195). These experiences are turned into feelings of being treated unfairly, of teachers and schools being organized in ways that privilege the already privileged in terms of class and race. If this is the case, some of the most powerful messages "reforms" of this type may send is that not only is the world deeply unfair but schools themselves are prime examples of institutions that simply respond to those who already possess economic and cultural capital. This is decidedly *not* the message that any society that is serious about what might be called "thick" democracy wants to teach. But it may be what our children learn in school systems that are so driven by the assumption that putting place higher standards and higher stakes testing will somehow magically solve deep-seated educational and social problems.

Unfortunately, recent research on the effects of all of this in the United States confirms these worries. Linda McNeil's powerful and detailed investigation of what has actually happened in Texas when state mandated "reforms" involving imposed standards and curricula, reductive and competitive testing, and attacks on teachers' professionalism demonstrates in no uncertain terms that the very children and schools that these policies and practices are supposed to help are actually hurt in the process. And once again, African American and Latino students suffer the most from the hidden effects of such policies (McNeil, 2000).

It should not be surprising at all that Gillborn and Youdell, as well as so many other researchers, find what they call an "educational triage" system at work in the school. Indeed, it would be surprising if they didn't, given what we know about the effects in other institutions of specific racialized patterns of income inequality, of employment and unemployment, of health care and housing, of nutrition, of incarceration, and of school achievement in nations like the United States (see, e.g., Apple, 1996, pp. 68–90). These patterns and effects make a mockery of any claim to a level playing field and one should not be surprised that in times of fiscal and ideological crises multiple forms of triage will be found in multiple institutions.

Yet, Gillborn and Youdell's research should make us extremely skeptical that the constant search for "higher standards" and for ever-increasing achievement scores can do much more than put in place seemingly neutral devices for restratification. As they also demonstrate (though considerably more empirical research would be required to fully substantiate the more general claim), in situations such as these, there is a narrowing of the curriculum. Increasing a school's test scores means focusing both on those subjects and on those students who can contribute to higher school performance. Class, race, and gender interact in complex ways here. White boys' achievement, especially for those on the D–C borderline, is all too often seen as mutable. For black male students, their supposedly "lesser ability" is tacitly assumed. "Valuable" students, then, are not usually black, seemingly by a set of natural accidents (Gillborn & Youdell, 1998, 2000). All of this is not necessarily intended. It is due to a set of over-determined historical relations and to the complex micro-politics over resources and power within the school and between the school and the local and national state, as well of course to the dynamics of power in the larger society.

However, even as I say this, I do not want to suggest that this makes race less powerful. Indeed, my claim is exactly the opposite. It gets a good deal of its power through its very hiddenness. Nowhere is this more true than in the discourse of markets and standards.

Race, Marketization, and the Politics of Whiteness

Although some commentators may be correct that "the competitive schools market in the UK as envisioned by neoliberals was created without reference to implications for ethnic minorities" (Tomlinson, 1998), this may be true only at the level of conscious intentions. Although race talk may be overtly absent in the discourse of markets, it remains an absent presence that I believe is fully implicated in the goals and concerns surrounding support for the marketization of education. The sense of economic and educational decline, the belief that private is good and public is bad, and so on is coupled with an often unarticulated sense of loss, a feeling that things are out of control, an anomic feeling that is connected to a sense of loss of one's "rightful place" in the world (an "empire" either now in decline or under threat), and a fear of the culture and body of "the other." The "private" is the sphere of smooth running and efficient organizations, of autonomy and individual choice. The "public" is out of control, messy, heterogenous. "We" must protect "our" individual choice from those who are the controllers or the "polluters" (whose cultures and very bodies are either exoticized or dangerous). Thus, I believe that there are very close connections between support for neoliberal visions of markets and free individuals and the concerns of neoconservatives with their clear worries about standards, "excellence," and decline (Apple, 2001).

In this regard, I believe that it is the case that under current conditions national curricula all too often actually represent a step backward in antiracist education (although we should never romanticize the situation before; not all that much antiracist education was actually going on I fear). Isn't it odd that just as gains were being made in de-centering dominant narratives, dominance returns in the form of national curricula (and national testing) which specify — often in distressing detail — what "we" are all like? Of course, in many nations the attempts at building national curricula and/or national standards were and are forced to compromise, to go beyond the mere mentioning of the culture and histories of "the other." (Certainly, this was and is the case in the United States.) And it is in such compromises that we see hegemonic discourse at its most creative best (Apple, 1996, 2000).

Take as one example the new national history standards in the United States and the attempt in textbooks to respond to the standards' creation of a multi-cultural narrative that binds "us" all together, to create that elusive "we." Such a discourse, while having a number of progressive sounding elements, demonstrates how hegemonic narratives creatively erase historic memory and the specificities of difference and oppression. All too many textbooks in our schools construct the history of the United States as the story of "immigrants" (Cornbleth & Waugh, 1995). "We" are a nation of immigrants. We are *all* immigrants, from the original Native American people who supposedly trekked across the Bering Strait to more recent people from Europe, Asia, Africa, and Latin America. Well, sure we are. But such a story totally misconstrues the different conditions that existed. Some "immigrants" came in *chains*, were enslaved, and faced centuries of repression and state-mandated apartheid. Others were subjected to death and forced enclosure as official policies. And there is a world of difference here between the creation of (an artificial) "we" and the destruction of historical experience and memory (Apple, 1996).

This destruction and how it is accomplished is again related to how race functions as an absent (at least for some people) presence in our societies. This can be made clearer by directing our attention to the invisibility of whiteness. Indeed, I want to suggest that those who are deeply committed to antiracist curricula and teaching need to place much more of their focus on white identity.

It may be unfortunate, but it is still true that many whites believe that there is a social cost not to being a person of color but to being *white*. Whites are the "new losers" in a playing field that they believe has been leveled now that the United States is a supposedly basically egalitarian, color-blind society. Because "times are tough for everybody," policies to assist "under-represented groups" — such as affirmative action — are unfairly supporting "nonwhites." Thus, whites can now claim the status of victims (Gallagher, 1995, p. 194). These feelings are of considerable importance in the politics of education in the United States, but also in many other nations. The recent attention given to Pauline Hanson's One Nation party in Australia, for example, is a case in point. As it is being shaped by the conservative restoration, whiteness as an explicit cultural product is taking on a life of its own. In the arguments of the conservative discourses now so powerfully circulating, the barriers to social equality and equal opportunity have been removed. Whites, hence, have no privilege. Much of this is untrue, of course. Although undercut by other dynamics of power, there is still considerable advantage to "being white" in this society. However, it is not the truth or falsity of these claims that are at issue here. Rather it is the production of retrogressive white identities.

The implications of all this are profound politically and culturally. For, given the Right's rather cynical use of racial anxieties, given the economic fears and realities many citizens experience, and given the historic power of race on the U.S. psyche and on the formation of identities in so many other nations, many members of these societies may develop forms of solidarity based on their "whiteness." To say the least, this is not inconsequential in terms of struggles over meaning, identity, and the characteristics and control of our major institutions.

How do we interrupt these ideological formations? How do we develop antiracist pedagogic practices that recognize white identities and yet do not lead to retrogressive formations? These are complex ideological and pedagogical questions. Yet these issues cannot be dealt with unless we focus directly on the differential power relations that have created and been created by the educational terrain on which we operate. And this requires an insistent focus on the role of the state, on state policies, on the shift to the right by Labour, and on the reconstruction of common sense in which the Right has successfully engaged.

If we were to be true to the historical record, whiteness is certainly not something we have just discovered. The politics of whiteness has been enormously, and often terrifyingly, effective in the formation of coalitions that unite people across cultural differences, across class and gender relations, and against their best interests (Dyer, 1997, p. 19). It would not be possible to write the history of "our" economic, political, legal, health, educational, indeed all of our institutions, without centering the politics of whiteness either consciously or unconsciously as a core dynamic. Of course, I am saying little that is new here. As critical race theorists and postcolonial writers have documented, racial forms and identities have been and are constitutive building blocks of the structures of our daily lives, imagined and real communities, and cultural processes and products (see, e.g., Fine, Weis, Powell, & Mun, 1997; McCarthy, 1998; McCarthy & Crichlow, 1994; Omi & Winant, 1994; Tate, 1997).

Let us look at this situation a bit more closely. Race as a category is usually applied to "nonwhite" peoples. White people are usually not seen and named. They are centered as the human norm. "Others" are raced; "we" are just people (Dyer, 1997, p. 1). Richard Dyer speaks to this in his telling book, *White*.

> There is no more powerful position than that of being "just" human. The claim to power is the claim to speak for the commonality of humanity. Raced people can't do that — they can only speak for their race. But, nonraced people can, for they do not represent the interests of a race. The point of seeing the racing of whites is to dislodge them/us from the position of power, with all of the inequities, oppression, privileges, and sufferings in its train, dislodging them/us by undercutting the authority with which they/we speak and act in and on the world (Dyer, 1997, p. 2).

"Our" very language speaks to the invisibility of power relations in our ordinary talk about whiteness. "We" speak of a sheet of white paper as "blank." A room painted all white is seen as perhaps "needing a bit of color." Other examples could be multiplied. But the idea of whiteness as neutrality, as a there that is not there, is ideally suited for designating that social group that is to be taken as the "human ordinary" (Dyer, 1997, p. 47). The same is true in many nations. In this sense, for example, the whiteness of "us" enables the white majority in Australia to represent

Aboriginal land claims under the Australian Native Title Act as based on "exotic" cultural values and experience. It is a small step then to represent such claims as indicative of "special treatment" for Aboriginal people that is not available to "ordinary Australians."

In the face of this, in the face of something that might best be called an absent presence, a crucial political, cultural, and ultimately pedagogic project then is *making whiteness strange* (Dyer, 1997, p. 4). Thus, part of our task in terms of pedagogy and political awareness and mobilization is to tell ourselves and teach our students that identities are historically conferred. We need to recognize that "subjects are produced through multiple identifications." We should see our project as not reifying identity, but both understanding its production as an ongoing process of differentiation, *and* most important as subject to redefinition, resistance, and change (Scott, 1995, p. 11).

There are dangers in doing this, of course. As I argue in *Cultural Politics and Education* (Apple, 1996) and *Educating the "Right" Way* (Apple, 2001), having whites focus on whiteness can have contradictory effects, ones we need to be well aware of. It can enable one to acknowledge differential power and the raced nature of everyone — and this is all to the good. Yet, it can also serve other purposes than challenging the authority of, say, the white West. It can just as easily run the risk of lapsing into the possessive individualism that is so powerful in this society. That is, such a process can serve the chilling function of simply saying "But enough about you, let me tell you about me." Unless we are very careful and reflexive, it can still wind up privileging the white, middle-class woman's or man's need for self-display. This is a seemingly endless need among many of these people. Scholars within the critical educational community will not always be immune to these tensions. Thus, we must be on our guard to ensure that a focus on whiteness doesn't become one more excuse to recenter dominant voices and to ignore the voices and testimony of those groups of people whose dreams, hopes, lives, and their very bodies are shattered by current relations of exploitation and domination.

Furthermore, focusing on whiteness can simply generate white guilt, hostility, or feelings of powerlessness. It can actually prevent the creation of those "decentered unities" that speak across differences and that can lead to broad coalitions that challenge dominant cultural, political, and economic relations. Thus, doing this requires an immense sensitivity, a clear sense of multiple power dynamics in any situation, and a nuanced and (at times risky) pedagogy.

Issues of whiteness may seem overly theoretical to some readers or one more "trendy" topic that has found its way to the surface of the critical educational agenda. This would be a grave mistake. What counts as "official knowledge" consistently bears the imprint of tensions, struggles, and compromises in which race plays a substantial role (Apple, 1999, 2000, 2001). Furthermore, as Steven Selden has so clearly shown in his recent history of the close connections between eugenics and educational policy and practice, almost every current dominant practice in education — standards, testing, systematized models of curriculum planning, gifted education, and so much more — has its roots in such concerns as "race betterment," fear of the other, and so on (Selden, 1999). And these concerns were themselves grounded in the gaze of whiteness as the unacknowledged norm. Thus, issues of whiteness lie at the very core of educational policy and practice. We ignore them at our risk.

Of course, this is partly an issue of the politics of "identity" and there has been increasing attention paid over the past decade to questions of identity in education and cultural studies. However, one of the major failures of research on identity is its failure to adequately address the hegemonic politics of the Right. As I have been at pains to show elsewhere, the conservative restoration has been more than a little successful in creating active subject positions that incorporate varied groups under the umbrella of a new hegemonic alliance. It has been able to engage in a politics inside and outside of education in which a fear of the racialized other is connected to fears of nation, culture, control, and decline — and to intensely personal fears about the future of one's children in an economy in crisis. All of these are sutured together in tense but creative and complex ways (Apple 1996, 2000, 2001; Carlson & Apple, 1998). In this way, considerably more socially democratic trajectories of reform are in essence closed off (see, e.g., Apple & Beane, 1995, 1999) and groups of people are pulled into what are implicitly racializing rightist projects by the very success of the Right in institutionalizing its logics and assumptions.

Given this, those of us who are committed to antiracist educational policies and practices and who are engaged in bearing witness to the actual functioning of existing and newly proposed educational "reforms" would be wise to direct our attention not only to the racial effects of markets and standards but just as much to the creative ways neoliberal and neoconservative (and in the United States, authoritarian populist religious fundamentalist) movements work to convince so many people (including many of the leaders of the Labour Party in the United Kingdom and Australia and in the Democratic Party in the United States) that these policies are merely neutral technologies. They're not.

CONCLUSION

In this article, I have argued that we must differentiate between intentions and functions in educational policy and practice. We need to get beneath the rhetorical surface of claims about reforms and examine the *patterns* of differential benefits and losses in the seemingly beneficial educational reforms being proposed in many nations to make education "more effective," "more efficient," and "more accountable." I have used some of the most powerful research now available to deconstruct these claims. I have argued as well that in order to understand the patterns of inequalities that these reforms produce we need to place class and especially "race" at the very center of our critical appraisals of these reforms.

There is a national myth in a number of nations that its citizens live in a "racial democracy." Such a claim may act to cover the ways whiteness works in the daily lives in all too many of its dominant economic, political, and cultural institutions. Certainly, in my own country, such a claim would have to be critically examined with a good deal of scepticism. Given the histories of racial subjugation, inequalities, and current struggles, I would hope that this is true wherever such a claim is made in the Americas, especially in the area of educational reform.

REFERENCES

Apple, M. W. (1996). *Cultural politics and education*. New York: Teachers College Press; Buckingham: Open University Press.

Apple, M. W. (1999). *Power, meaning, and identity*. New York: Peter Lang.

Apple, M. W. (2000). *Official knowledge* (2nd ed.). New York: Routledge.

Apple, M. W. (2001). *Educating the "right" way: Markets, standards, God, and inequality*. New York: Routledge.

Apple, M. W., & Beane, J. A. (Eds.). (1995). *Democratic schools*. Alexandria, VA: Association for Supervision and Curriculum Development.

Apple, M. W., & Beane, J. A. (Eds.). (1999). *Democratic schools: Lessons from the chalk face*. Buckingham: Open University Press.

Bourdieu, P. (1984). *Distinction*. Cambridge: Harvard University Press.

Carlson, D., & Apple, M. W. (Eds.). (1998). *Power/knowledge/pedagogy*. Boulder, CO: Westview Press.

Cornbleth, C., & Waugh, D. (1995). *The great speckled bird*. New York: St. Martin's Press.

Dyer, R. (1997). *White*. New York: Routledge.

Fine, M., Weis, L., Powell, L., & Mun, W. (Eds.). (1997). *Off white: Readings on race, power and society*. New York: Routledge.

Foner, E. (1998). *The story of American freedom*. New York: Norton.

Gallagher, C. (1995). White reconstruction in the university. *Socialist Review, 94*, 165–187.

Gillborn, D., & Youdell, D. (1998). *Raising standards and deepening inequality: League tables and selection in multi-ethnic secondary schools*. Paper presented at the symposium on Racism and Reform in the United Kingdom, American Educational Research Association, San Diego.

Gillborn, D., & Youdell, D. (2000). *Rationing education*. Philadelphia: Open University Press.

Gould, S. J. (1981). *The mismeasure of man*. New York: W. W. Norton.

Harraway, D. (1989). *Primate visions*. New York: Routledge.

Herrnstein, R., & Murray, C. (1994). *The bell curve*. New York: Free Press.

Kincheloe, J., Steinberg, S., & Greeson, A., (Eds.). (1996). *Measured lies*. New York: St. Martin's Press.

Linn, R. (2000). Assessment and accountability. *Educational Researcher, 29*, 4–16.

Liston, D. (1988). *Capitalist schools*. New York: Routledge.

McCarthy, C. (1998). *The uses of culture*. New York: Routledge.

McCarthy, C., & Crichlow, W. (1994). *Race, identity and representation in education*. New York: Routledge.

McNeil, L. (2000). *Contradictions of school reform*. New York: Routledge.

Oakes, J. (1992). Can tracking research inform practice? *Educational Researcher, 21*, 12–21.

Oakes, J., Wells, A. S., Jones, M., & Datnow, A. (1997). Detracking: The social construction of ability, cultural politics, and resistance to reform. *Teachers College Record, 98*, 482–510.

Omi, M., & Winant, H. (1994). *Racial formation in the United States*. New York: Routledge.

Scott, J. (1995). Multiculturalism and the politics of identity. In J. Rajchman (Ed.), *The identity in question*. New York: Routledge.

Selden, S. (1999). *Inheriting shame: The story of race and eugenics in America*. New York: Teachers College Press.

Tate, W. (1997). Critical race theory and education. In M. W. Apple (Ed.), *Review of research in education* (Vol. 22). Washington: American Educational Research Association.

Tomlinson, S. (1998). *New inequalities? Educational markets and ethnic minorities*. Paper presented at the symposium on Racism and Reform in the United Kingdom, American Educational Research Association, San Diego.

Wells, A. S., Lopez, A., Scott, J., & Holme, J. (1999). Charter schools as postmodern paradox: Rethinking social stratification in an age of deregulated school choice. *Harvard Educational Review, 69*, 172–204.

NOTES

An earlier draft of this essay was presented at the symposium on Racism and Reform in the United Kingdom: The Market, Selection, and Inequality, American Educational Research Association, San Diego, April 1998. The arguments in it are expanded considerably in Michael W. Apple, *Educating the "Right" Way: Markets, Standards, God, and Inequality* (New York: Routledge, 2001).

Correspondence may be sent to Professor Michael W. Apple, University of Wisconsin, Department of Curriculum and Instruction, 225 North Mills Street, Madison, WI 53706 or by e-mail at apple@education.wisc.edu.

Living

SEVEN

Whites Are from Mars, O. J. Is from Planet Hollywood: Blacks Don't Support O. J. and Whites Just Don't Get It

James M. Jones

We, the jury in the above entitled action, find the defendant, Orenthal James Simpson, not guilty of the crime of murder . . .

In response to this simple declarative pronouncement of O. J.'s lack of guilt,[1] Black America cheered, raised their fists in victory. White America gasped in horror and pain. Although Black America felt victory, I doubt that White America felt defeat. I suspect they felt more like betrayed. *Those* Blacks on the jury had perverted *our* justice system for group aggrandizement. There was little question, in the mind of White America, that O. J. was guilty (polls showed about 65% of them felt so). In a display of racial arrogance (read racism) they lambasted the jury for deliberating too little, for identifying with the defendant on the basis of race, and for letting that identification gain emotional leverage on their reason, and in the final analysis, for not seeing the evidence the way *they* did!

There were two elements to Black reactions: (1) Legal Retribution for past Injustice, and (2) Existential Reality of the Racism Evidence. For Whites, too, there were two reactions: (1) O. J. was dispositionally and physically capable of the crimes, ergo he was guilty; and (2) Blacks *had to ignore* the evidence to reach that verdict. For Blacks, institutional and cultural context provided reasonable doubt based on the idea that racism provided a plausible alternative explanation for both the evidence and O. J.'s culpability in the crime. For Whites, dispositional characteristics of jealousy, violent temperament, egocentrism, provided the strongest suspicion that DNA evidence confirmed beyond reasonable doubt—O. J. did it!

Although Black America may have claimed victory, they did not embrace O. J. as a hero. In fact, the depth of Black reaction to the verdict is given precisely because O. J. was no hero to Black America. O. J. was a Planet Hollywood celebrity who had abandoned his Black wife, hung out at the Riviera country club with his rich White friends, and forgotten how to find the inner city. Why then did Black America cheer?

The LAPD beat Rodney King on video and walked. For many Blacks, the O. J. trial was about the LAPD, and although they walked when the venue was shifted to Simi Valley, they were *convicted* when it was brought back to downtown LA. Blacks cheered the conviction of the LAPD; Whites lamented the acquittal of O. J. Blacks cheered racism revealed. Whites jeered justice denied. Different worlds, different experiences, different emotions.

In the few pages that follow, I will advance the idea that (1) racial differences in reactions to the verdict stem from cultural differences in social perception, (2) racial differences in experience provide a different database from which to extrapolate the interpretive meaning of evidence, and (3) White ethnocentrism and subtle racism lie behind reaction to the verdict.

FROM DISPOSITIONS TO ACTS: ATTRIBUTIONAL BIASES IN PERCEIVING THE BEHAVIOR OF OTHERS

E. E. Jones and Davis (1965) outlined the process by which people infer causes for the behavior of others under the title, "From Acts to Dispositions." The general idea is that we infer the causes of behavior by working backward to figure out the correspondence between the behavior and a plausible set of underlying dispositions that could have caused it. We are satisfied most when the causes for behavior are located internal to the actor, imply dispositional stability, and correspond best to the act itself.

So important is it to us that we Americans find a dispositional explanation for behavior, that we err in the direction of seeing more disposition than is there. This tendency has been labeled the Fundamental Attribution Error (FAE) (cf. Ross, 1977). This "error" occurs because we see others' actions as dispositional, failing to perceive the possibility that circumstances in their environment may importantly affect their behavior. Behavior, in this view, is a mirror on the soul, a reflection of personal traits and qualities that define one's character and worth. Weiner (1993) suggested that when negative outcomes occur and a dispositional attribution is made, the actor is held accountable and consequently blamed for his *sin*.

Western cultures can be described as "independent"—hardening of boundaries between self and other; focus on internal attributes, preferences, traits, and abilities. In an independent culture, our judgments of others focus on internal or dispositional proprieties of the self and these are seen as defining of character and causal for behavior. It is this hardening of boundaries between self and other that gives rise to the FAE. By contrast, other cultures are less prone to this FAE tendency to the extent that they could be described as "interdependent"—blurring of boundaries between self and other; focus on the interdependent relationships among people where duty, obligation, and responsibility are paramount (Markus & Kitayama, 1991). In an interdependent culture, judgments of others are contextualized by interdependent relationships and expectancies, and these define the self in relation to others and offer contextualized causes for individual behavior.[2]

The point to be made here is that in a cultural-independent context, the biases all operate so as to focus attention on the individual culpability for behavior, and when negative outcomes can be linked to this internal cause evaluative judgments quickly follow. O. J. was guilty for Whites, in part, because over time, the horrendous outcome became attached to dispositional properties of O. J.—the 911 tapes established his violent temper, his self-absorbed egocentrism, his jealousy, and his public self-consciousness (cf. Scheier & Carver, 1980). This tendency to make a dispositional attribution made it all the easier to accept the blood evidence. It was the biological counterpart to the dispositional character evidence. This point only comes together if we assume, as I clearly do, that Whites as a group adopt the cultural-independence beliefs with all the cognitive and evaluative implications outlined above.

But, this is not a one-way street. Blacks, too, made a dispositional attribution—Fuhrman was a racist. His racism was shown just as clearly by his taped interviews with Laura Hart McKinny as O. J.'s violence was shown by the 911 tapes. But whereas O. J.'s dispositional culpability went directly to his murderous acts, Fuhrman's went directly to the context, the community of the LAPD. The evidence of a racist police department is revealed by a racist cop. O. J.'s dispositional character explained his individual act. Fuhrman's dispositional character explained the entire context of racism in the LAPD.

RACIAL DIFFERENCES IN EXPERIENCE: AFFECT CONTROL AND INJUSTICE—
WHITES 2,178, BLACKS 1!

In the previous section I argued that Blacks and Whites activated somewhat different perceptual and cognitive processes as they assessed the evidence and made the critical judgments of guilt. I now make the claim that because of fundamentally different experiences, Blacks and Whites developed different emotional sensitivities that influenced their interpretations of justice in the verdict.

One of the pivotal differences between Blacks and Whites was that Fuhrman's racism, which all could see and abhor, ultimately meant less to Whites than to Blacks. It had the capacity to explain more for Blacks than for Whites. Henry Louis Gates (1995) suggested,

> People arrive at an understanding of themselves and the world through narratives — narratives purveyed by schoolteachers, newscasters, "authorities," and all the other authors of our common sense. Counter narratives are, in turn, the means by which groups contest the dominant reality and the fretwork of assumptions that supports it ... much of black history is simply counter narrative ... fealty to counter narratives is an index to alienation, not to skin color. (p. 57)

Counternarratives tell the story of our dominant cultural reality—freedom, liberty, equality from the other side. That race had nothing to do with the O. J. trial is a narrative told from the dominant viewpoint. In the counternarrative, race had everything to do with it. More important than the perspective, which is important, is the fact that these narratives and counternarratives define reality! They define not only our collective cultural realities but also our individual, personal realities as well. Counternarratives are not simply a reification of skin color as a dividing line; they reflect alienation from the White cultural narrative that marginalizes Blacks as a group, while ambivalently and ambiguously accepting individual Blacks. Black emotions attach to the narratives and specific events that exemplify them.

In the first instance, O. J. was famous, *not* Black. In the final analysis, O. J. was Every Black Man who, in the counternarrative, had been victimized by injustice. The emotional attachment we saw was to the counternarrative. Whites' emotional attachment was to the narrative in which race was not an issue. When the verdict came down, Whites saw what in their mind was an irrelevant feature define reality. Blacks saw an atypical situation where a perspective from their counterreality was given voice. This verdict now is added to the counternarrative that now reads Whites 2,178, Blacks 1.

To put this thinking into a conceptual framework, we offer Affect Control Theory (ACT) (Scher & Heise, 1993) as a plausible basis for differential emotions (see also Izard, 1991; Smith, 1994). ACT proposes that a given situation may arouse justice-related emotions, which once triggered can affect the subsequent judgment of justice. By this reasoning, Whites' perception that the verdict was unjust, and Blacks' judgment that it was just, can be derived from the justice-related emotion that accompanied the trial.

The fundamental ACT proposition is that when people involved in transaction feel anger or guilt, and the emotions are not ameliorated, they may decide that the transaction is unfair or unjust.

Many people were angered by O. J.'s abusive treatment of Nicole. That anger, in their context of the trial for murder, aroused justice concerns. The verdict, then, was judged unfair because of the prior emotion-laden anger held toward O. J.

The same emotion-laden anger may have occurred for those upset by Fuhrman's racism. For them, though, the verdict vindicated their anger and reduced any feelings of justice incongruence (i.e., injustice).

Smith (1993) argued that the experiences of members of our group can evoke emotional feelings in us such that we feel as though we have had their experience. This group-identification basis of emotion may further explain the differential reaction of Whites and Blacks. Blacks have experienced Whites directly or vicariously over hundreds of years — the murder, torture, and abuse of their people at the hands of Whites. The disfigured face of Emmett Till in *Jet* magazine in 1955 is one vivid example.[3] The face of Rodney King rekindled that image, and the failure to convict Till's attackers and to convict the LAPD officers who beat King resulted in emotional anger at justice-related scenarios. Adding fuel to the fire is the image that it is Black men who are violent and who are dangerous. Charles Hughes killed his wife in Boston in 1993, and by simply calling 911 and reporting a Black male attacker, he had the community up in arms searching for a Black man. Susan Smith, a copycat accuser, did the same thing in 1994 when she drowned her two sons in South Carolina. The fact that these stories were plausible and believable attests to the idea that in the counternarrative account, Injustice and Justice trade places. The cultural narrative that pronounces Black men guilty until proven innocent is rewritten innocent until proven guilty. And to this jury, the burden of proof was not met. It is possibly true that the burden of proof is heavier when the evidence is viewed through counternarrative scenario lenses, and the defendant is a Black man.

Whites, by contrast, may have cognitive understanding of these scenarios, but certainly not emotionally laden experiences of a personal nature. Did O. J.'s crime become emotional because his victims were White? Would the anger-mediated judgments have been as severe if his alleged victim had been his Black first wife? Such counterfactual thinking is a bit mushy here, but it does seem intuitively less likely that the media frenzy and the emotional fascination of the American people would have been so great if it were a within-group situation.

Justice indifference is an important concept in ACT. It refers to the extent that a given interaction or situation arouses justice concerns. The high-profile nature of the case certainly made it low (near zero) in justice indifference. Whites were angry at O. J.; Blacks at Fuhrman. Had the verdict been reversed, it would have been Blacks who saw injustice and whose emotions would have been strong.

This ACT analysis suggests that Whites, already angered by O. J.'s behavior toward Nicole, found the verdict escalated the justice-incongruence in their minds. This escalation, mediated by emotional anger, found release and explanation in the perception of unfairness. ACT theory argues that emotion mediates judgments of unfairness and is not simply reactions to what are perceived to be unfair outcomes. Thus it was their anger at his abusiveness and their prior belief in his guilt that triggered the reaction.

For Whites, then, a not guilty verdict was unjust but a guilty verdict would have been just. For Blacks the reverse was true. What we saw in the initial reactions, shown widely on network TV all over the country, was the emotional concomitant of affect control processes.

A second aspect of this case and one of the important principles of ACT is transient impression of actors. The Behavior-Object relationship suggests that behaviors are evaluated more negatively when they are out of character — powerful behaviors are evaluated more negatively when they are directed at weak objects, and behaviors are judged worse when performed by a bad than a good actor.

Put these things together and you have the context for strong, negative emotion associated with O. J. These strong negative emotions then mediate perceptions of unfairness in the verdict and intensify the emotional feelings already present.

One provocative implication of ACT is "that a sequence of negative events might push the transient impressions of participants [O. J.] down sufficiently that even a procedure decided by a 'benevolent judge' would evoke injustice-related emotions." This analysis suggests that perceptions of judicial bias may be triggered by the sequence of emotion-mediated judgments, not by a cognitively objective appraisal of the decision and the rationale's provided by jurors for it.

WHITE ETHNOCENTRISM AND SUBTLE RACISM — EVEN MY ERRORS ARE CORRECT!

The first two analyses above suggest that Whites differed from Blacks in the ways in which evidence was processed, and this difference revolved, in part, around different experiences Blacks and Whites have had in America. These analyses sought to explain, in part, differential perceptions of guilt and innocence as well as differences in the degree of justice perceived in the jury verdict. We now look at White's reactions to the verdict and to the Black's reactions to it. I suggest here that the strong, negative judgments of Blacks and the Black influence on the jury verdict may be associated with White ethnocentrism and subtle racism.

As Gates (1995) put it, "For many Whites a sincere belief in Simpson's innocence looks less like a culture of protest than like a culture of *psychosis*" (p. 56, emphasis added). That is, you got to be crazy to think he is innocent. In fact, one person noted that as a result of this verdict, she would no longer be able or willing to vote for General Colin Powell, because "I don't want to give *them* any more power."

Ethnocentrism refers simply to the preference for aspects of one's own ethnicity or culture. There is a strong tendency for most groups in the world to maintain such ethnocentric attitudes and beliefs. Deviations from this pattern are usually associated with subjugation to hegemonic groups (e.g., Sidanius, 1993). In these instances, it is argued that reduced levels of ethnocentrism can be traced to acceptance of "legitimizing myths," which are stories (narratives) that endorse the structure and extol the virtue of the social hierarchy, embrace its inevitability, and even assert its inherent morality. *The Bell Curve* (Herrnstein & Murray, 1994) can be viewed as such a myth in this light.

The preferences for one's own group's ways of being have been shown to produce a preference for members of one's own group (Brewer, 1979) known as in-group bias. Social psychologists have become quite expert at demonstrating the subtle ways in which such ethnocentrism or in-group bias operates. For example, Dovidio, Evans, and Tyler (1986) showed subjects a slide with the words *white, black,* or *house,* followed by a slide that contained adjective traits associated with positive or negative stereotypes of Blacks or Whites. Subjects had to determine whether the adjective words "could ever be true" of the group shown in the first slide; White subjects responded fastest when they judged whether a positive attribute associated with Whites was true of Whites.

More recently, Fazio, Jackson, Dunton, and Williams (1995) demonstrated a subtle unobtrusive measure of racial attitude. They defined attitude as an affective reaction to a stimulus object. Therefore, a positive attitude toward Blacks could be reflected in a positive affective reaction to a photograph of a Black person. Conversely, a negative reaction would suggest a negative attitude.

Fazio et al. primed subjects with both White and Black photographs just prior to their making judgments about whether specific adjectives were predominately positive or predominately negative. If the picture evoked a positive attitude, they reasoned, this judgment should be facilitated when it was a positive word, and inhibited when it was a negative word. Thus, the speed with which these adjective judgments were made indicated the racial attitude of the subject.

Fazio et al. found that for White subjects, responses were facilitated most when a positive adjective judgment followed a White photo, and next most when a negative adjective judgment followed a Black photo. This is precisely the pattern of in-group bias. Moreover, the more this pattern was true of a given subject, the more likely he or she was to rate a Black experimenter negatively. So this unobtrusive measure of racial attitude actually was manifested in differential race-relevant behavior.[4]

How does this relate to the jury verdict? Specifically, I suggest that the attributional processes, the salience and legitimacy of personal experience, or the emotion-mediated sense of fairness, which could reasonably be shown to differ between racial groups, was largely dismissed by Whites in their reaction to Blacks' reactions to the verdict. From an ethnocentric perspective, the perceptions of Blacks had no merit because the basis on which their view could be correct had little legitimacy within a White ethnocentric context. If a narrative has no meaning within a sociocultural context, it is likely to be ignored or rejected or at best to be tolerated. Within this ethnocentric cultural matrix of reasoning and analysis, legitimate belief in innocence is simply not possible.

But the verdict did *not* confer innocence on O. J.; it merely acknowledged an absence of guilt. But as a White female colleague said, "He was guilty of something" (namely domestic violence). But as a Black female juror noted emphatically, this was not a domestic violence case. So what is the legitimate perspective on the case? What determines the basis of guilt, innocence, and doubt when there are such divergent perspectives operating? How important are violent temperament and racism and how should they be judged? And finally, what about the brutally murdered victims? Someone certainly did it, and we have not legally determined who it is.

The next element of this analysis is the hated *R* word, *racism*. First, we must recognize that racism is a belief in the superiority of one's own group. Nikki Giovanni captured this spirit in her poem, "I am so great even my errors are correct!" I have argued that racism as name-calling is not a very profitable enterprise (J. M. Jones, 1972, 1988). There are, to be sure, individuals who can by any account be considered a racist. Abraham Lincoln comes immediately to mind, as the following quote suggests:

> I am not, nor ever have been, in favor of bringing about in any way the social and political equality of the white and black races; I am not, nor ever have been, in favor of making voters or jurors of Negroes, nor qualifying them to hold office ....
>
> I will say in addition to this that there is a physical difference between the white and black races which I believe will ever forbid the two races living together on terms of social and political equality. And in as much as they cannot so live, while they do remain together there must be the position of superior and inferior, and I as much as any other man am in favor of having the superior position assigned to the white race. (Abraham Lincoln, 1894, pp. 369–370, 457–458)

But what is most important is that racism operates across multiple levels from individual psyches to institutional practices to cultural values and meanings. It is within the fabric of this interlocking network of perceptions, beliefs and values, laws and institutional practices, and cultural expressions that racism lurks.

Racism operates at three levels; *individual* (beliefs in the superiority of one's own racial group), *institutional* (institutional practices that produce systematic advantages for one racial group over another, whether intended or not), and *cultural* (a race-based normative standard of value, merit, and meaning that places one's own group at the apex of a value hierarchy and judges other racial groups deficient in comparison) (J. M. Jones, 1972). The levels are interlocking in that individual beliefs are partially derived from the outcomes of institutional racism, and the power to define racial difference as deficiency, and racial similarity as the exception that proves the rule (J. M. Jones, 1988).

One group's figure is another group's ground. As we saw with the ethnocentrism analysis, own-group standards are figure when concerned with something positive. Other groups become figure when a negative judgment is at hand. Racism is in the end about figure and ground. As one student at my university noted, "The defense brought race into the trial because they needed an issue to divert jurors away from the evidence in the trial." For this White student, the "evidence" was figure and the possibility of racism was ground. Linking blood to O. J. is evidence, but linking racism to the policemen who found and preserved the blood is a diversionary tactic. In the counternarrative that tells the story of injustice and oppression in Black America, racism is the figure and virtually all else is ground.

CONCLUSION

The dramatically different reactions of Black and White Americans to the verdict in the O. J. Simpson murder trial clearly focused our attention on the great racial divide in America. Did it deepen and widen it? I think not. But I think it did most definitely expose the depth and breadth of it. I have tried in the preceding pages to suggest ways in which we may understand this divide using the reactions to the jury verdict as text, and social psychological theory and research as hermeneutic analysis.

As the data from the Fazio et al. (1995) study suggests, Blacks and Whites have different foci of attention. Whites are most strongly biased toward their own experiences, values, beliefs, and the products of their culture. Blacks, who have so often been victimized by those very beliefs and cultural outcroppings, mistrust them and ultimately dislike them. The stories are different, the symbols that attach to them are different, and the experiences from which they are derived are different. The racial divide is deep, wide, and real.

Is this to say there is no hope? Alas, can't we all get along? It seems to me that the starting point is to recognize the profound differences in experiences and the perceptual, emotional consequences to which they give rise. In the jury verdict reaction, there is a profound sense that Whites as a group declared their perspective superior and denigrated the Black viewpoint and the jury itself as an extension of a Black perspective. Such a failure to escape cultural biases reflects the patterns of racism that cause the divide in the first place. Moreover, it suggests that, left unchecked and unexamined, differences will grow rather than recede, and lack of communication will exacerbate the already profound differences in experience and expectation between Black and White Americans.

But I believe that there is a strong positive sentiment in most Americans, Black and White, to make this society a kinder and gentler one. To tone down the race rhetoric, I believe, we must be willing to recognize variations in experience and perspective, and to examine our viewpoints and the *possibility* that other viewpoints not only exist but have merit.

REFERENCES

Brewer, M. B. (1979). In group bias in the minimal intergroup situation: Cognitive-motivational analysis. *Psychological Bulletin, 86,* 307–332.

Dovidio, J. F., Evans, N., & Tyler, R. B. (1986). Racial stereotypes: The contents of their cognitive representations. *Journal of Experimental Social Psychology, 22,* 22–37.

Fazio, R. H., Jackson, J. R., Dunton, B. C., & Williams, C. J. (1995). Variability in automatic activation as an unobtrusive measure of racial attitudes bona fide pipeline? *Journal of Personality and Social Psychology, 69,* 1013–1027.

Gates, H. L. (1995, October 23). Thirteen ways of looking at a Black man. *The New Yorker, LXXI,* 56–65.

Giovanni, N. (2003). *The collected poetry of Nikki Giovanni, 1968–1998.* New York: William Morrow, c2003.

Herrnstein, R. E., & Murray, C. A. (1994). *The bell curve.* New York: Free Press.

Izard, C. E. (1991). *The psychology of emotions.* New York: Plenum.

Jones, E. E., & Davis, K. E. (1965). A theory of correspondent inferences: From acts to dispositions. In L. Berkowirz (Ed.), *Advances in experimental social psychology* (Vol. 2). New York: Academic Press.

Jones, J. M. (1972). *Prejudice and racism.* Reading, MA: Addison-Wesley.

Jones, J. M. (1988). Racism in Black and White: A bicultural model of reaction and evolution. In P. A. Katz & D. A. Taylor (Eds.), *Eliminating racism: Profiles in controversy* (pp. 117–135). New York: Plenum.

Lincoln, A. (1984). *Abraham Lincoln, Complete works.* J. G. Nicolay and J. Hay (Eds.) New York: The Century Company.

Markus, H., & Kitayama, S. (1991). Culture and the self: Implications for cognition, emotion and motivation. *Psychological Review, 98,* 224–253.

Ross, L. (1977). The intuitive psychologist and his shortcomings: Dispositions in the attribution process. In L. Berkowitz (Ed.), *Advances in experimental social psychology* (Vol. 10, pp. 174–221). New York: Academic Press.

Scheier, M. F., & Carver, C. S. (1980). Private and public self-attention, resistance to change and dissonance reduction. *Journal of Personality and Social Psychology, 39,* 390–405.

Scher, S. J., & Heise, D. R. (1994). Affect and the perception of injustice. In E. Lawler, B. Makovsky, & J. O'Brien (Eds.), *Advances in group processes* (Vol. 10). New York: JAI Press.

Sidanius, J. (1993). The psychology of group conflict and the dynamics of oppression: A social dominance perspective. In S. Iyengar & W. J. McGuire (Eds.), *Explorations in political psychology* (pp. 183–219). Durham, NC: Duke University Press.

Smith, E. R. (1993). Social identity and social emotions: Toward new conceptualizations of prejudice. In D. M. Mackie & D. L. Hamilton (Eds.), *Affect, cognition and stereotyping: interactive processes in group perceptions* (pp. 297–315). San Diego, CA: Academic Press.

Weiner, B. (1993). On sin and sickness: A theory of perceived responsibility and social motivation. *American Psychologist, 48,* 957–965.

NOTES

1. I do not take a stand here on the issue of the *actual* guilt or innocence of O. J. Simpson. Rather, my purpose is to explore the basis of dramatically different reactions of Black and White Americans to the verdict.

2. It is curious though, that although the conventional analysis suggests that FAE is more prevalent in Western cultures such as the United States, Whites seem to lose this bias when it comes to themselves and race. That is, they often fail to see the contextual basis for their own situation relative to Blacks. Blacks are less well off because of their dispositional inadequacy as FAE would have it. But, Whites are relatively better off because of their superior character, contrary to FAE's claim that context is more salient in self-attributions. When it comes to race, the environmental context is undervalued in its explanatory power by Whites for the differential standing of *both* Blacks and Whites.

3. In 1955, Emmett Till was a 15-year-old black teenager from Chicago who was visiting his uncle in Money, Mississippi. Allegedly, he whistled at or spoke familiarly to a white woman in a store and that evening, the woman's husband and his half-brother abducted Emmett from his uncle's house. His mutilated, castrated body was found several days later in a stream. The two men were tried and acquitted by an all-white jury after deliberating forty-five minutes.

4. The opposite was true for Black subjects. Their responses were facilitated most when a negative judgment was made following a White photo, and next by a positive response to a Black photo. So, Whites are most affected by positive *in-group* feelings, and Blacks by negative *out-group* feelings. This may be the flip sides of races — Whites feel superior and Blacks hate them for it.

EIGHT

Growing Up Girl: Psychosocial Explorations of Gender and Class

Valerie Walkerdine, Helen Lucey, and June Melody

SOCIAL CLASS REVISITED

Gender, Class, and Labour in New Britain

Manufacturing was supplanted by financial services, which, along with the communications and service sectors, became the mainstay of the British economy. Traditional male working-class jobs dried up and, as the film shows so graphically, many working-class men struggled to find new types of work while coping with the rise of women's employment and economic power, though of course many women were still employed in low-paid, part-time work.

A BBC serial called *The Missing Postman* illustrates well the gendered reactions to the huge and terrifying changes that were taking place. The postman in the title has been made redundant, but he refuses to give up his work and cycles around the country personally delivering his last sack of letters. In the process he becomes a cause celebre and a fugitive. On his travels he meets many men who have also lost their jobs and are now working in the service sector. It is they who most count him as a hero, the man who refuses to give up. The devastating losses suffered by these men have left them with no sense of how to cope or where to move on to. As they struggle to comprehend the savageness of the changes that confront them, many are also overwhelmed by the accomplishment with which their wives cope with these changes and positively face the prospect of self-transformation. Meanwhile the postman's wife "comes to life" after her husband's disappearance. She demolishes the interior of her home and redesigns it with such panache that the media crews sent to interview the postman after his return concentrate instead on her dramatic interiors. She is remade as an interior decorator with a lucrative living at the very moment he is broken by defeat. His only way out is to leave again, this time on an adventure to Italy to deliver one more letter.

Just as for the missing postman's wife, self-invention by women in the new labour market presents opportunities that are not open to men. Like the missing postman, many men can see only loss ahead of them and cannot face what feels like a loss of manhood and feminisation, or what Cohen and Ainley (2000, p. 83) called the loss of "musculatures of the labouring body." The possibilities offered by feminisation are not viewed as positive, but of course for many women, whatever their class location, the opening up of areas of the labour market formerly denied them is exciting and offers many possibilities, even though it also brings the double burden of work and family.

In this essay we shall explore how young women and their families set out to remake themselves inside the practices of self-invention and self-regulation available to them in contemporary Britain. In particular, we want to establish how this moment of transition and transformation is one of loss and uncertainty as well as of hope and excitement. The young women from professional families have to cope with not only the loss of security that the new economy brings, and therefore uncertainty about the reproduction of the middle class, but also their remaking as a new female professional at a time of a labour market shift that puts high-flying men elsewhere and devalues the status of the professions.

Young women from erstwhile working-class families have to face the realm of work throughout their adult lives, unlike any other generation before them. They face a "girl power" that tells them they can be what they want in a labour market that cruelly sets limits on any ambition, together with an education system that classifies them as fit for certain kinds of work depending on their academic capabilities. In the context of Rose's (1991) psychological subject who is capable of bearing the serious burdens of liberty, this will often be understood as a psychological failure, which produces its own wishes, anxieties, and defences. In addition to this, their families face the prospect of a stakeholder democracy with the fantasy that they too might join the middle class, the property- and share-owning class that Thatcherism made possible through the sale of council houses and the privatisation of public utilities such as electricity, gas, rail, and telecommunications. Thus the biggest self-invention of all lies in the possibility of the working class remaking itself as middle class, a possibility that has been ambiguously signaled from at least the 1950s (Gorz, 1983). How, then, is that self-invention approached in our study?

The Reinvention of the Working Class

For some theorists and political pundits, the challenge of articulating the massive societal changes of the past 20 years in terms of class appears too great and it is simpler to give up on the idea that class as a concept has any useful place in the work of sociology and politics (Holton & Turner, 1989; Pahl, 1989). But can there really be a turning away from the living of oppression and exploitation, as if it were only ever an intellectual concept, existing in the minds of academics and the left as elegant and linear theories of history? We shall examine the argument that "class doesn't matter any more" in the light of the dramatic changes in the economic and social structures of post-industrial countries and what the subjects of our study had to say about class.

There is no denying that class is etched deeply into our culture and our psyches. There are of course other aspects to stratification across the developed world, with age, geographical, cultural, and religious differences all acting as the basis of discrimination. However social class, alongside gender and race, remains one of the most powerful factors in the shaping of our lives and dealing our "life chances": how we are born, what illnesses we have and our chances of overcoming them, where we live, and, of course, the work we do, which has been the backbone of stratification schemes since the 1950s (Eder, 1993; Halsey, Heath, & Ridge, 1980; Marshall, Newby, Rose, & Vogler, 1988).

Laying the Groundwork

Within sociological debates, the theoretical ground on how changes in the postwar economy have affected class relations has, until very recently, been carved up between two dominant perspectives: neo-Marxist and neo-Weberian. However the rise of postmodernism posed a serious challenge to "grand narratives" such as Marxism, which were viewed as unable to theorise the diversity and plurality of social experience (Crook, Pakulski, & Waters, 1992; Mercer, 1990). Neo-Weberian models that already contained the notion of "fragmentation" have fared rather better in the deconstructive onslaught of postmodern and poststructuralist enquiry, although some have taken the idea of fragmentation further, arguing that classes have been subject not merely to change but also to disintegration (Beck, 1992). "The educated person," he claims, "becomes the producer of his or her own labor situation, and, in this way, of his or her social biography" (Beck, 1992, p. 93).

For Beck, "There is a *hidden contradiction between the mobility demands of the labor market and social bonds*. This means loosening local and constructing non-local networks. By becoming independent from traditional ties, people's lives take on an independent quality which, for the first time, makes possible the experience of personal destiny" (Beck, 1992, p. 94). He wants to "unite individuals and groups as self-conscious subjects in their own personal, social and political affairs" (p. 101). He asks whether in fact this will lead to social emancipation or political apathy. For Beck then, self-invention is a way to move beyond a stultifying traditionalism, and in this respect it shares much with bourgeois individualism.

In this essay we argue that this particular narrative of the present political conjuncture fails to engage with the complexity of self-invention and the difficult position of women, and it reads class only as an economic category while we understand it as deeply implicated in the production of subjectivity, as written on the body and mind. How, though, is class to be ignored and self-invention produced if the erstwhile working classes in Beck's account cannot actually remake themselves as middle class through occupational mobility? This structural contradiction lies at the heart of some of the problems that, as we shall see, faced many of the young women in this study.

Feminist sociologists, for instance those drawing on the work of Pierre Bourdieu, have challenged traditional mobility studies that used quantitative indices as their empirical base, and have highlighted the ways in which the formation of gendered subjectivities cannot be made sense of without an understanding of the complexities of class positioning and articulation (Butler & Savage, 1995; Devine & Savage, 2000; Hey, 1997; Reay, 1998a; Savage, Barlow, Dickens, & Fielding, 1992; Skeggs, 1996).

What Bradley (1996, p. 143) called the "new sociology of ethnicities" is heavily influenced by postmodern and poststructuralist accounts and focuses on identities, cultural practices, and racist discourses, and has been able to incorporate class as one of the social processes through which racial and ethnic difference is produced and reproduced (Donald & Rattansi, 1992; Gilroy, 1987, 1993; Tizard & Phoenix, 1993). The notion of "hybridity," developed by Homi Bhabha (1990), adds another dimension to the theories of fragmentation and helps us to explore the dynamic formation of contemporary ethnic identities in a post-colonial world.

Indeed Bradley draws up some strategies for the future study of inequalities, which recognise and attempt to go beyond the present disputes about class (Bradley, 1996, pp. 203–204). The first strategy is to accept Lyotard's idea that local narrative should replace grand narratives, and to reject general theories of inequality, looking instead at the study of particular manifestations of inequality in specific contexts, tracing their history and the discourses implicated. Her second strategy is to accept the first but to recognise that the local manifestations of inequality "exist within the framework of powerful and controlling unitary tendencies, notably that of the globalisation of capital." Third, the literature suggests that previous modernist theories were flawed because of their "failure to appreciate the way that different dynamics of inequality intersect." Societies, stressed Bradley, are both fragmented and polarised (p. 210).

It is the deep intransigence of class inequality that demands we adopt a position more akin to her second strategy, while attempting to acknowledge her third strategy. As we shall see, inequality is lived locally by the families in this research, but the globalisation of capital places particular demands on the constitution of subjects that cross those local boundaries.

Throughout the traditional sociological discussions of social class there has been an assumption that the links between structure, consciousness, and action must be the basis upon which both empirical and theoretical work should proceed (Goldthorpe & Marshall, 1992). Such debates have assumed that what is interesting about working-class people is the production of a change in consciousness that will somehow activate their potential as a protorevolutionary group. In fact little attention has been paid, even within the newer approaches discussed above, to the social and psychic practices through which ordinary people live, survive, and cope. To engage with this issue we shall address the practices through which the families in our study were formed, together with an understanding of the emotional and unconscious aspects of their location.

LOCATING ERICA AND SHARON: TWO WORKING-CLASS GIRLS

We shall now explore the lives of two families touched by the transformations of the 1980s. Erica Green was a white working-class girl who first took part in the study when she was 6 years old. Ten years later we found that the family had moved from their council house in London to northeast England, where they had family connections. Mrs. Green gave Helen Lucey instructions on how to find the house: "YOU can't miss us, the sign is on the gate." The sign certainly was on the gate, a gate that opened onto a wide gravel drive that swung across a vast lawn and garden. At the end of the drive, on one side there was a paddock and a stable with a horse in it, and on the other an imposing and attractive detached house that had been renovated and extended. In the drive were two large new, cars with personalised number plates. This was not the modest upward mobility the team had imagined.

Over the next few days, as Helen spent time interviewing the family and recording Erica at work, all the members of the family were keen to show Helen around and, with immense pride, tell her about the fruits of their success: the small business that was doing so well, Erica's horse, the cars (including the one that awaited Erica when she passed her driving test), the beautiful views from their expensively furnished house, the landscaped garden, the new kitchen. They had "made it" and wanted this to be known and recorded.

So what was the Greens' story, and what does it have to do with the changing story of class in Britain? In 1984, when Erica was 6 years old, Mr. Green was a skilled craftsman working for a small firm, and Mrs. Green worked part-time as a dinner lady. They were managing financially, but were by no means wealthy. Then came the breaks. As council tenants the Greens had bought their Georgian terraced house under the Right to Buy Act of 1979. At that time the gentrification of specific locales in the borough (typically areas containing unmodernised properties at far lower prices than in more established or more extensively gentrified middle-class areas) was in full swing (Butler & Savage, 1995; May, 1996). During the early 1980s Mr. and Mrs. Green painstakingly set about a complete interior restoration of the house. Working on a small budget, they did most of the work themselves, with Mrs. Green researching period decor and design with the help of books from the library. Mrs. Green's mother also had a house in the area (though much more modest) but had moved back to northern England a few years earlier. They had been dreaming of moving out of London for some time, but just as the Greens' house was finished, two things happened: Mr. Green hit a health crisis and house prices hit an unthinkable high. In 1986 they decided it was time to sell both houses and join Mrs. Green's mother in the north. With the sizeable profit from the sale of the houses they were able to buy a franchise of the business where Mr. Green was floor manager and go it alone.

Sharon Cole was another white, working-class girl who took part in the study when she was 6 years old. Her father worked for the local council as a security guard and was a member of the Labour Party; her mother worked as a lavatory attendant and was a shop steward in her union. They lived on a large council estate (about half a mile from the Greens), which was gaining a reputation for crime: Mrs. Cole had been mugged once and their flat had been burgled six times. Like the Greens they were worried about their children's future in a poor inner-city borough. As Mr. Cole put it,

> In that year, yeah. I think we were a bit worried about how the children were going to be brought up because Sharon herself was only six, seven at the time, the boy Richard was only ten and we decided then that if they kept living in that environment of so much violence, and it was easier to steal than to work, which happens — you can't blame the kids, it's actually true, it's the government that causes it, you know what I mean. And what we decided then, was that it would be better to move.

As with the Green family, this decision to move coincided with a crisis with Mr. Cole's health and he was medically retired from his job. Unlike the Greens, the Coles had no property on which to capitalise: They had not been tempted to buy their flat on a run-down council estate.

However, with their savings and Mr. Cole's early retirement payment they too managed to escape London and bought an ex-council house in a suburban Thames estuary town. Mrs. Cole ran a small catering business. Mr. Cole showed Helen the extension he was building onto the kitchen, explaining how he was going to do this and that job and what it would look like when it was finished. Both parents stressed how "safe" and "quiet" the area was, how the schools were so much better. They too felt that they had made real improvements in their lives and those of their children. The move out of London and into their own house was a move up and one of which they, like the Greens, were proud.

In 1995 Roy Hattersley, then a senior member of the opposition Labour Party, argued that it was futile to mourn the end of full-blooded socialism and claim that the Labour Party was abandoning working-class values as the working class had already abandoned them themselves (Hattersley, 1995). Hattersley nostalgically referred to the "solidarity" and "community" amongst miners and shipbuilders in order bitterly to counterpose this nostalgic view to "the age of the almost universal middle class — individualistic, self-confident, suburban in attitude and aspiration if not in income and lifestyle." What did his comments have to do with the Coles, the Greens, or the other working-class families in our study, nearly all of whom had achieved some measure of social and/or economic mobility in the past 20 years? Did this necessarily mean the end of the class story for them and their children? Both the Coles' and the Greens' stories, as well as the stories of many other working-class families in our study, spoke directly to the sentiments expressed in Hattersley's article. But his swiping at working-class people through a sentimental contrasting of past and present left the working-class families in this study nowhere to go; they were reproachfully marooned on "individualistic," "aspiring," and "suburban" islands. In that sense their reinvention of themselves as "suburban" signaled precisely that "free individual" that

Rose (1991) and Henriques, Holloway, Urwin, Venn, and Walkerdine (1998) speak of. What these authors say is inevitable; Marxist sociologists take as a signal of "the end of the working class" (Gorz, 1983).

When asked which social class he thought he belonged to, Mr. Green asked, "Where do you draw the line?" To this we could add another question: What do you draw the line with? There are a variety of conceptions that contribute to the enormous lack of clarity that characterises contemporary debates on stratification. However social classes have been generally conceived of as objective entities that can be empirically investigated. To this end the occupational structure has enduringly been seen as providing a framework within which the "class structure" can be mapped (Rose & O'Reilly, 1997). A common feature of all approaches that aim to measure the class structure via the structure of employment is that many of the measures they use, for example the Registrar General's classification scheme, are descriptive schemes devised for social policy purposes rather than as a contribution to debates on theoretical class analysis. Crompton (1993) asserted that one major source of the many confusions that have arisen (and continue to arise) in the various strands of class analysis is the divergence between those who have focused on empirical investigation of the class structure and those who have conflated consciousness and structure into facets of the same phenomenon.

There is a very real sense of course, in which "occupation" is hopelessly inadequate in capturing the nuances of class relations in either a Marxist or a Weberian sense because it can only refer to social relations at work, the technical division of labour. Connell (1977) argued that some of the survey research on class "emasculates" (an interesting choice of word to say the least) the concept of class itself: It makes a claim to empirical understanding, but produces only a "bloodless" knowledge (p. 33), which reduces the lived experience of class to an abstraction for the purpose of statistical treatment. In response to this unhappy situation, sociologists in the 1970s and 1980s (Goldthorpe, 1983; Wright, 1985) began to develop schemes that, in contrast to gradational status or commonsense schemes, claimed to reflect the structure of actual class relations. These "relational" schemes were constructed on the assumption that underlying class processes and relations are reproduced within the employment structure.

It is particularly important to note here that it is in the debates on postmodernity that the importance of consumption has been signaled, of a move away from a stress on production and its links with classes and social communities as categories of modernity. The increasing focus on consumption has become one of the factors contributing to debates on the end of class. The argument has emerged that employment itself is becoming less significant and that people's identities are being increasingly expressed and manifested through consumption (Offe, 1985), and that it is consumption rather than production that is becoming more relevant for the analysis of stratification systems. The importance of class and locality have broken down and young people in particular have looked to consumer goods as means of self-fulfillment and identity (Seabrook, 1978). In recent years, commercial organisations began to focus heavily on ways of locating and targeting existing and potential customers, and it became necessary to devise classification systems that could accurately measure the relationship between structural factors such as location, job, income, and, increasingly important, lifestyle, of which aspects of consumption were taken to be indications. These kinds of scheme, originally devised for the commercial market, were taken up by political parties in an attempt to group and then predict the voting behaviour of sectors of the population (Worcester, 1991).

The new interest in performativity (e.g., see Butler, 1997) has meant that identities are often described as shifting and mobile, not fixed or class related, and as being produced within an arena of consumption. Hence younger people are often understood as being subject to more mobile categories of identity than their parents' generation, in spite of the constraints of class, gender, or race. However, as we shall see, such work ignores the issue of the regulation of identities or subjectivities, which severely limits the apparent freedom to become "who everyone wants to be," which is such a feature of late capitalism. Diane Reay (1998b) went further when she argued that there is an intrinsic deceit in such postmodern accounts which, though concerned to map the changes in media, style, and consumerism in general, show a stubborn unwillingness empirically to address the issue of who can and cannot afford to consume. The ability to enter into and maintain consumption practices is, after all, closely linked to and to a large extent dependent on an individual's class location in the first place.

How then can we understand the girls' and their parents' self-location in the 1990s? The Greens had indeed achieved a material transformation, but did this constitute a transformation of class and therefore of class consciousness? The Coles, like the majority of the working-class parents in this study (67%), had become home owners. Few of the parents worked in what could be described as traditional manual jobs, they had holidays abroad, and a number of them had two cars. Crucially, they hoped for more. Does this mean they had become middle class? And what does "middle class" mean nowadays?

The water is muddy enough, but it gets muddier when we talk about the subjective aspects of class. For naturally enough, people's perceptions of class vary according to age, gender, nationality, ethnicity, and so on. Age is especially significant as each generation constructs and disentangles the different social practices into which it was born in a new way, though this does not mean that socialisation processes are irrelevant. However, neither can we assume that social consciousness is simply reproduced in an unaltered way. The world into which young women enter adulthood is vastly different from the one in which their parents lived as 21-year-olds, so how can they possibly experience and therefore understand class in exactly the same way as their parents?

Emotional Landscapes of Class

We asked all of the young women in our study and their parents what social class they thought they belonged to. The young women were also asked if they thought they would remain in the social class they were in now. Most of the girls, working and middle class, defined themselves accurately in relation to the class scheme that had originally been used to stratify the sample. Jacky said,

> I'm not too sure what working class is and that, but it's like working class is like, in the mines, or like working in an office or something, so . . . I suppose they're working class and middle class because they've got good values and that sort of thing.

Having Something of Your Own: House Ownership and Working-Class Subjectivity

It was common for the working-class parents and their daughters to make direct connections between home ownership and perceived class location. Geographical location fuses powerfully with type of housing tenure to produce a "geography of exclusion" (Massey, 1995), in and through which understandings of space and place provide a sorting mechanism, sifting out the type of people we are and the type we are not. Sharon Cole identified herself as middle class because "this isn't a council house, this is our own house and that's it really."

For Satinder, a British Asian 16-year-old whose family moved from the inner city to the suburbs of London, locality and size of house (rather than tenure) were just as important in the family's project of social mobility.

> SATINDER: I think when we were in Hackney we were working class.... I don't know where the line lies.
> JM: Well what changed for you to start seeing yourself as middle class?
> SATINDER: I suppose having a bigger house. Yeah, I suppose it was probably that.

What is invisible in her account of class mobility is how, not only in Britain but also across Europe, the United States, and Australia, the processes of residential differentiation and, crucially, the imagery of "racial segregation" have played key roles in the social reproduction of race categories and the organisation of objective and subjective space (Back, Cohen, & Keith, 1998; Smith, 1989, 1993).

Sharon Cole pointed to the step upward that the family had taken by moving out of the inner city:

> I'd say we're middle class now we've moved here. And other things like, I don't know, it's a lot cleaner round here and quieter at night. My aunty still lives there and to be honest, I don't really want to go to her place to visit like, I don't want to go back there.

A former council house in a quieter neighbourhood outside London was enough to make them feel different, but was it enough to make others see them as middle class? The painful process of self-transformation may appear to have been easily accomplished in the home-owning, share-owning democracy, but it is just as difficult as it ever was. In some ways more so, because now anything is supposed to be possible. In the new "third way" there appear to be no split and fragmented subjects, caught in the interstices of self-regulation and invention.

Class Codings of Taste and Style

Although neo-Marxist and neo-Weberian theorists continue to engage with the categories and quantifiers of social class, Pierre Bourdieu (1984) contributed to a shift of focus on contemporary theorising of class to include a complex analysis of the interrelationship between class and culture. Within this model the distribution of different kinds of "capital" (economic, cultural, social, and symbolic) locates (and have more potential to move) the owner through social space. The markers of the possession of these different kinds of capital are both abstract and material, encompassing taste, education, lifestyle, accent, and cuisine (see Skeggs, 1997).

The middle-class sample did not mention home ownership and far fewer spoke about money as a defining factor in class location. Instead they prioritised education as central to the determination of class position, and this in turn was likely to surface in comments that brought up and utilised the notion of "privilege" and "opportunity." Importantly, this was also true of the working-class girls who were heading for or were already at university. As Hannah, a white middle-class 16-year-old, said,

I suppose I think of it as being a kind of ethos.... It's about something much bigger than the profession of your parents yeah. And it's also about taste and about dress and about interests. You can spot it a mile off even though it's not to do with money.

Because Bourdieu views the knowledge of taste and style as a possession, as a kind of capital, his analysis can pick up the articulacy of Hannah's remark but it misses something much more subtle and much more painful. If Hannah could "spot it a mile off," it would be ridiculous to assume that the targets of her pejorative evaluations would not also be able to spot it in themselves and others, even if they could not theorise it in the way that Hannah's upbringing had taught her to do for many years. But in this analysis class is in everything about people, from the location of their home, to their dress, their body, their accent. These are not simply matters of capital that one does or does not possess. They are ways in which a kind of subject is produced, regulated, lived. Otherness is in the myriad large and small signs through which people recognise themselves and categorise both themselves and those from whom they seek difference, distance.

Indeed that recognition and the fragile move from pejorative to acceptable classification and judgement is exactly what Sharon Cole described when she called herself middle class because she had moved away from a dangerous council estate. It is what Erica Green talked about when she described the highs and lows of her move to the north of England. Underneath the bright veneer of the success story of upward mobility conveyed by the house and the lifestyle, lurked the possibility that some signs of middle-class status (the house, the horse and so forth) were contradicted by others (dress, style, accent, behaviour, intelligence, for example). Such a move, then, may have produced envy in others but it may not have produced Erica's ambition "to be respected in Hampwick." This extraordinary ambition for a 17-year-old speaks volumes about the way in which she clearly recognised the signs of class location.

Indeed this reading is supported by Erica's feelings about class and her identification as middle class. Erica said that she could be a "bit of a snob" at times and mentioned disliking and "looking down on" some people because they lived in council houses. What an extraordinary statement! Erica had come absolutely to identify with the Other. She was the one who only a few years before had lived in a council house. It was because she knew only too well what that meant that she could now take the position of the middle-class subject and the Other her previous self. This statement revealed the huge amount of shame she felt about that previous self. It also tells us something of how this shame must be defended against. In becoming upwardly mobile she had to attempt to erase every possible mark of what she used to be. She had to become more snobbish than those who had been born middle class, who could afford to say that class didn't matter to them. Her very pain and shame helped to tie her to the very thing she longed to get away from. And more than this, she believed at some level that she did not deserve what she now had, that she was still the stupid little working-class girl:

I've lost a lot of friends since I started to work. Because all they're saying is, you know, I'm getting like a leg up in the business. And, er, they're getting nowhere you know.

Indeed we found that the working-class girls' and their parents' talk on social class generally and their own class location in particular was infused with a desire to distance themselves from the painful position of being "one of them." "They" were the "scruffs," the rough working class, the "underclass," the poor, the homeless, or the hopeless.

The painful recognition of Otherness as marked on the body was displayed by many of the young working-class women, a feeling that they were less, lacking, a lack that had to be carefully hidden in some circles and revealed in others, a complex hide-and-seek game that amply demonstrated both that the working-class subjects knew exactly how they were positioned and that they knew fragmentation for what it was. That is, a complex game in which it appeared possible to be one thing in one circumstance, another in another, a masquerade or passing.

The sometimes baffling complexity (to outsiders and insiders alike) of the British class system is and has always been intricately coded around "taste" and "style," with strong distinctions being made by the middle classes between "old" and "new" money. Amanda, a middle-class 21-year-old who attended a highly exclusive and established boarding school, summed it up when she said,

> I suppose especially now after the '80s and stuff there are a lot of people who've made it big in business and stuff in a way that there might not have been before.... I mean I went to school with a few people like that who like, whose parents have made it really big and they were definitely more into having like a white piano or something than, you know what I mean, 'cos and having quite a showy sort of house and things.

The Green family had undoubtedly made an economic transformation from working class, but the mooning gnomes in their garden, their personalised number plates, and their choice of furniture might well have been seen as "vulgar" by the middle-class families in this study.

Erica desperately wished to see herself as "above" her working-class contemporaries and she had every chance, through her parents' business, to become economically well-off. But the path she was on at the time of the interviews certainly meant that she would not follow the kind of route deemed essential to educate and groom middle-class girls on their path to "well-rounded," seemingly confident, well-travelled maturity. Neither she nor her parents were part of the "chattering classes" or "dinner-party society," and their working-class origins betrayed them at many turns. No easy or painless self-invention there. The economic mobility the Greens had achieved and many other working-class families hoped for was so much more fragile than the educational mobility of both the parents and the girls from working-class families, though both of these routes to upward mobility were fraught with the most painful emotional defences.

Being "In the Middle"

> Working-class people who identify themselves with the bourgeoisie have traditionally been a problem for the left, particularly those for whom Marxist thought was their starting point. Marx conceptualised the bourgeoisie as somehow lying "between" the working and ruling classes in terms of class consciousness, and therefore untrustworthy and vacillating in their allegiances. (Ainley, 1993)

The comments of the working-class girls and their families in this study were shot through with a desire for a respectability that lies in the contradictory and often elusive space of "the middle." Importantly, this safe middle ground not only relies on the actual, discursive, or symbolic existence of the pathological poor but also relies on its equally feared opposite, the rich. So "they" can just as powerfully be "posh," "stuck-up," rich, envied for their privilege. Importantly, this envy is psychically defended against and experienced as contempt (as we discussed in relation to our own envy of the middle-class families in *Democracy in the Kitchen* [Walkerdine & Lucey, 1989]). Whoever "they" are, their otherness is what must be avoided — whether the otherness of poverty or privilege:

> Middle class, I'd say — well, working class to my mind is someone that goes round talking like that. Middle class, they've got a bit more respect for everything, and upper class are just idiots, because they've got no brains and they've got brilliant jobs. (Jenny, 21, white working class)
>
> I don't think I'd be upper class. 'Cos they've got loads of money and that, and um, some of them are right snobs and all that, so I wouldn't like to be like that. I'd like to have their money but not to be like some of their attitudes and that. (Jacky, 21, white working class)
>
> I'd put myself in the middle class I think. I think there is an upper class now and between the upper class and the lower class there's a big gap isn't there? But I'd put myself in the middle class.... Don't get me wrong, I'm a working person and I work for the family and everybody else, you know, so they've got different things indoors, but I work for them. I think — I'm no snob, don't get me wrong, but I suppose I'm middle class yes, but I mix with everybody, so I suppose I'm somewhere in the middle. I get on with life and enjoy life to the best you can. I'm no snob, but I suppose as you say, middle class. (Anna's father, white working class)

We would argue strongly that it is far too simplistic to see those working-class subjects who identified themselves as middle class as somehow under a hopelessly false illusion. However, neither do their self-classifications speak of "collectivism" and community. It is not the language of Marxism, traditional socialism, the trade union movement, or the old style Labour Party. If we consider the practices of regulation, which depend so heavily on the use of normalisation and pathologisation, together with Conservative and other political injunctions against extremism, it is not surprising that being in the middle — not rich, not poor, not Other or extreme — feels like a safe place to be compared with the terrors of other possible positions.

Refusing Class(ification)

An equal number of working-class and middle-class girls and parents at first resisted the question about their class location and expressed frustration at the divisiveness of the concept of class. They felt that it was wrong to categorise people, to "put them into boxes," and felt that individuals should be taken on their own merit rather than judged as being in one class or another. In these comments there was a strong desire to wish class away, but at the same time, there was an uncomfortable awareness of social inequality and difference:

> I don't really put myself into a class.... I think it's all stupid, this class business. I mean it's all um ... material things, isn't it? It's all your ... it's whether you've got money really. Whether you've got a big car, a nice car, a big house and luxury this, luxury that. I mean, what is that? I mean, it's just stupid ... you shouldn't look on somebody as a class, I mean you should look at them for what they are, not class. (Zoe, 16, white working class)
>
> I don't know. I don't really think nothing about class really. I think having class is ... like what class you're in is a bit stupid really. I mean a person's a person. I don't really pay much attention to like working class, upper class, lower class. (Patsy, 21, white working class)

Yeah, it's the kind of thing that you really wish that people weren't aware of, but it is still there. (Amanda, 21, white middle class)

I feel I don't properly belong to any class, I also think there shouldn't be such things anyway. I think the idea of a classless society is what we should be aiming at. (Amanda's father, white middle class)

What came up powerfully in this study was the desperate desire of all the working-class subjects to make their lives "okay," We argue that this desire was central to their identification of themselves as middle class. They were not mistaken in imagining that the middle classes had "enough" materially, or at least more than they had. No wonder they wished, on some but not all levels, to take themselves out of a class that, in Britain, has always had to struggle economically. All the working-class parents and many of the working-class girls spoke of a fantasised future in which they would have "enough" materially and emotionally. The kind of success the Green and Cole families felt they had achieved was precisely articulated around this concept of "enough." What also came up in relation to the working-class girls was that although many saw themselves as working class at the moment, that was not where they wanted to be forever. Much was invested in a hopeful future in which dreams of mobility and release from paid employment featured powerfully:

I'm working class at the moment. [But] not forever. . . . You know, but I'm working class at the moment. No I want to be rich [laughs]. No um — no I don't want to be working class forever. Holding down a nine to five job. That's not what I want to do. That's why — you know, I'm not going to do that forever. (Sarena, 21, black working class)

Indeed, who in the fiction of choice as a life project of self-actualisation (Rose, 1991) would actually want to hold down a nine to five job forever? This is not the picture of "making it" that is held out as a possible dream.

For the working-class parents, many of these desires were focused on their children; a "respectable" and therefore "safe" location for them to grow up in and the provision of a financially secure future for them. The 1980s boom (coming as it did out of a deep recession) promised huge financial profits. Five of the working-class parents in this study did indeed try the entrepreneurial road during that decade, but only one of them achieved the kind of success that the Thatcherite dream promised. Mr. and Mrs. Green, with foresight, good timing, and a heavy helping of luck, managed to ride the 1980s house price boom, escaping from London with a huge profit to set up their own successful business. For the others, financial loss and the slow running down of their small business was the norm.

Nearly all of the working-class parents spoke about the worry they had about their daughters' working futures. Underlying these comments for some (especially fathers) was a sense of impotence at not being able to protect them from unemployment, poor wages, or dead-end jobs. Therefore the Greens' ability to provide a means of training and a future as a partner in a successful business to a daughter who was poorly equipped for academic or employment success was, we suggest, the kind of thing that most working-class parents could only dream of. There was a curious gender-twist in this narrative in that Erica had set out on an occupational path that represents so much of what had been "lost" in terms of traditional working-class masculinity: as an apprentice in a skilled-manual "craft."

But how did it feel to have achieved this dream? Once the dream had come true, did it have to be guarded fiercely? Erica's parents, like most from working-class backgrounds, desperately wished to protect their child from what they had had to do. They wanted her life to be much easier than theirs, with less work and more reward. But the dependence they produced in Erica was closely connected to their own need for protection. We heard from other working-class parents, especially fathers, that everything they had done had been for the children. For example Christine's parents put what little money they had into their children, leaving nothing for themselves — they did not own a car, smoke, drink, or go out for pleasure by themselves. Instead, one of their weekly routines when Christine was 6-years-old was to buy an educational book and go on an "educational visit" (Walkerdine, 1997). They saw themselves as going out into the world and battling (like Mr. Cole) for their sons and daughters. Does their view of their daughters as vulnerable and in need of protection tell us something important about the kinds of unconscious defence they had used to guard against the terrible vulnerability they had felt in their own lives?

The desire of the poor parents for their children to have lives that were better than theirs was very strong, so strong that in many cases the parents psychically denied and wounded themselves in order to offer something better to their children. What was the effect of this on social and psychic relations within the family? For example did Christine simultaneously feel that she had to withstand the jibes of her schoolmates about being middle class while feeling a terrible guilt about letting her parents down because they had given up so very much for her? What was the effect of this on the way she understood her present and her future?

Conclusion

We argue that in the 1980s people did not want to reject the welfare state, rather they simply wanted a share of the good life that the welfare state had promised but failed to deliver. They wanted decent houses that actually felt like homes. They wanted their spirits buoyed. "Social democracy in its shabbiness and torpor failed to replace pride in ownership with pride in community" (Krieger, 1986, p. 86). Mr. Cole described himself mockingly as a "violent midget" and a "fighter" (Walkerdine, 1997). He had strong political and moral beliefs that he strove to act upon, as a member of the Labour Party and as an individual. His identification as someone who fought for his rights at times brought him into direct conflict with the institutions he had contact with (Walkerdine, 1991, 1997).

Some feel that the "zeitgeist" of the 1980s was the ideology of enterprise, as created by the Conservatives, with enterprise presented as the solution to modernisation and the intractable crisis of capitalism. Services that, postwar, had been owned and provided by the state were sold off to private companies, along with bus companies, the railways, and the power and water utilities. Other public services were retained by the state as semi-independent agencies to be run at a profit (as with health and social services). The consumers of those services are now "customers," redefined as "citizens" with individual "rights" enshrined in the contractual relations of "charters."

Market discourses that assert universal freedom of choice are used in defence of discourses of classlessness and serve to obscure the ways in which social advantage is maintained through the free market (Reay, 1998b, p. 261). Far from displacing the logic of class, as some would argue (Pakulski & Waters, 1996), the markets themselves shape and are shaped by social relations of class. The citizens of governmental charters do not participate collectively as informed citizens in a democratic process that decides which goods and services should be provided. Ainley (1993) argued that they merely choose as "passive consumers" between the different commodities the market offers them. If you cannot afford any of the market options then you must fall back on what the run-down, overstretched welfare system can offer.

Class cannot be understood simply through any of the available sociological modes of explanation. The production of subjects from all classes and the way in which they live their subjectification centrally involves a constant invitation to consume, to invent, to choose, and yet even in the midst of their choice and their consumption class is performed, written all over their every choice. From house to dress, from accent to appearance, Eliza Dolittle is as present in the early 21st century as she was in the 19th. And more than this, the living out of these marks of difference is filled with desire, longing, anxiety, pain, defence. Class is at once profoundly social and profoundly emotional, and lived in its specificity in particular cultural and geographical locations.

Reprinted by permission of Palgrave Macmillan. This essay first appeared in *Growing Up Girl: Psychosocial Explorations of Gender and Class* (2001) by Valerie Walkerdine, Helen Lucey, and June Melody.

References

Ainley, P. (1993). *Class and skill: Changing divisions of knowledge and labour.* London: Cassell.
Back, L., Cohen, P., & Keith, M. (1998). "First takes," finding the way home [Working paper]. London: CNER, University of East London.
Beck, U. (1992). *Risk society: Towards a new modernity.* London: Sage.
Bhabha, H. (1990). The third space. In J. Rutherford (Ed.), *Identity* (pp. 253–266). London: Lawrence and Wishart.
Bourdieu, P. (1984). *Distinction: A social critique of the judgement of taste.* London: Routledge and Kegan Paul.
Bradley, H. (1996). *Fractured identities: Changing patterns of inequality.* Cambridge: Polity Press.
Butler, T., & Savage, M. (Eds.). (1995). Gentrification and the urban middle classes. In T. Butler & M. Savage (Eds.), *Social change and the middle classes.* London: UCL Press.
Cohen, P., & Ainley, P. (2000). In the country of the blind?: Youth studies and cultural studies in Britain. *Journal of Youth Studies, 3*(1), 79–95.
Connell, R. (1977). *Ruling class, ruling culture: Studies of conflict, power and hegemony in Australian life.* Cambridge: Cambridge University Press.
Crompton, R. (1993). *Class and stratification: An introduction to current debates.* Cambridge: Polity Press.
Crook, S., Pakulski, J., & Waters, M. (1992). *Postmodernization.* London: Sage.
Devine, F., & Savage, M. (2000). Conclusion: Renewing class analysis. In R. Crompton, F. Devine, M. Savage, & J. Scott (Eds.), *Renewing class analysis.* Cambridge: Blackwells.
Donald, J., & Rattansi, A. (Eds.). (1992). *"Race," culture and difference.* London: Sage.
Eder, K. (1993). *The new politics of class: Social movements and cultural dynamics in advanced societies.* London: Sage.
Gilroy, P. (1987). *"There ain't no Black in the Union Jack": The cultural politics of race and nation.* London: Hutchinson.
Gilroy, P. (1993). *The black Atlantic.* London: Verso.

Goldthorpe, J. H. (1983). Women and class analysis: In defence of the conventional view. *Sociology, 17*(4), 465–488.

Goldthorpe, J. H., & Marshall, G. (1992). The promising future of class analysis: A response to recent critiques. *Sociology, 26*(3), 381–400.

Gorz, A. (1983). *Farewell to the working class.* London: Pluto.

Halsey, A. H., Heath, A. F., & Ridge, J. M. (1980). *Origins and destinations: Family, class and education in modern Britain.* Oxford: Clarendon Press.

Hattersley, R. (1995, April 27). Tone of the times. *Guardian*, p. 8.

Henriques, J., Holloway, W., Urwin, C., Venn, C., & Walkerdine, V. (1998). *Changing the subject: Psychology, social regulation and subjectivity* (2nd ed.). London: Routledge.

Hey, V. (1997). *The company she keeps: An ethnography of girls' friendships.* Buckingham: Open University Press.

Holton, R. J., & Turner, B. S. (1989). *Max Weber on economy and society.* London: Routledge.

Krieger, J. (1986). *Reagan, Thatcher, and the politics of decline.* Cambridge: Polity Press.

Marshall, G., Newby, H., Rose, D., & Vogler, C. (1988). *Social class of the modern Britain.* London: Hutchinson.

Massey, D. (1995). *Spatial divisions of labour: Social relations and the geography of production.* London: Macmillan.

May, J. (1996). Globalization and the politics of place: Place and identity in an inner London neighbourhood. *Transactions of the Institute of British Geographers, 21*, 194–215.

Mercer, K. (1990). Welcome to the jungle: Identity and diversity in postmodern politics. In J. Rutherford (Ed.), *Identity.* London: Lawrence and Wishart.

Offe, C. (1985). Work—A central sociological category? In C. Offe (Ed.), *Disorganized capitalism.* Cambridge: Polity Press.

Pahl, R. E. (1989). Is the emperor naked? Some comments on the adequacy of sociological theory in urban and regional research. *International Journal of Urban and Regional Research, 13*, 709–720.

Pakulski, J., & Waters, M. (1996). The reshaping and dissolution of social class in advanced society. *Theory and Society, 25*, 667–691.

Reay, D. (1998a). *Class work: Mother's involvement in their children's primary schooling.* London: Taylor & Francis.

Reay, D. (1998b). Rethinking social class: Qualitative perspectives on class and gender. *Sociology, 32*(2), 259–275.

Rose, N. (1991). *Governing the soul: The shaping of the private self.* London: Routledge.

Rose, D., & O'Reilly, K. (1997). *Constructing classes: Towards and new social classification for the UK.* Swindon: Office for National Statistics and Economic and Social Research Council.

Savage, M., Barlow, J., Dickens, P., & Fielding, T. (1992). *Property bureaucracy and culture, middle-class formation in contemporary Britain.* London: Routledge.

Seabrook, J. (1978). *What went wrong? Working people and the ideal of the labour movement.* London: Gollancz.

Skeggs, B. (1996). *Becoming respectable: An ethnography of white working-class ideology.* London: Routledge.

Skeggs, B. (1997). Classifying practices: Representations, capitals and recognitions. In P. Mahoney & C. Zmroczek (Eds.), *Class matters.* London: Taylor & Francis.

Smith, S. J. (1989). *The politics of race and residence.* Cambridge: Polity Press.

Smith, S. J. (1993). Residential segregation and the politics of racialization. In M. Cross & M. Keith (Eds.), *Racism, the city and the state.* London: Routledge.

Tizard, B., & Phoenix, A. (1993). *Black, white and mixed race*. London: Routledge.

Walkerdine, V. (1991). *Schoolgirl fictions*. London: Verso.

Walkerdine, V. (1997). *Daddy's girl: Young girls and popular culture*. London: Macmillan; Cambridge, MA: Harvard University Press.

Walkerdine, V. & Lucey, H. (1989). *Democracy in the kitchen*. New York: Random House.

Wilkinson, H., & Howard, M. (with Gregory, S., Hayes, H., & Young, R.). (1997). *Tomorrow's women*. London: Demos.

Worcester, R. M. (1991). *British public opinion: A guide to the history and techniques of political opinion polling*. Oxford: Basil Blackwell.

Wright, E.O. (1985). *Classes*. London: Verso.

NINE

Adolescent Masculinity, Homophobia, and Violence: Random School Shootings 1982–2001

Michael S. Kimmel and Matthew Mahler

> Generally speaking, violence always arises out of impotence.
> It is the hope of those who have no power.
> —Hannah Arendt

> Every year now like Christmas
> Some boy gets the milk fed suburban blues
> Reaches for the available arsenal
> And saunters off to make the news.
> —Ani Difranco

Violence is one of the most urgent issues facing our nation's schools. All over the country, Americans are asking why some young people open fire, apparently randomly, killing or wounding other students and their teachers. Are these teenagers emotionally disturbed? Are they held in the thrall of media-generated violence — in video games, the Internet, rock or rap music? Are their parents to blame?

Indeed, school violence is an issue that weighs heavily upon our nation's consciousness. Students report being increasingly afraid to go to school; among young people ages 12 to 24 years, 3 in 10 say violence has increased in their schools in the past year, and nearly two fifths have worried that a classmate was potentially violent (Penn, Schoen, & Berland, 1999). More than half of all teens know somebody who has brought a weapon to school (although more than three fifths of them did nothing about it), according to one study ("Half of Teens," 2001). And nearly two thirds (63%) of parents believe a school shooting is somewhat or very likely to occur in their communities (Carlson & Simmons, 2001). The shock, concern, and wrenching anguish shared by both children and parents who fear that our nation's schools may not be safe demands serious policy discussions. And such discussions demand serious inquiry into the causes of school violence.[1]

We begin our inquiry with an analysis of the extant commentary and literature on school violence. We argue that, unfortunately, there are significant lacunae in all of these accounts — the most significant of which is the fact that they all ignore the one factor that cuts across all cases of random school shootings — masculinity. Thus we argue that any approach to understanding school shootings must take gender seriously — specifically the constellation of adolescent masculinity, homophobia, and violence.

We go on to argue that in addition to taking gender seriously, a reasoned approach to understanding school shootings must focus not on the *form* of the shootings — not on questions of family history, psychological pathologies, or broad-based cultural explanations (violence in the media, proliferation of guns) — but on the *content* of the shootings — the stories and narratives that accompany the violence, the relationships and interactions among students, and local school and gender cultures. Using such an approach to interpret the various events that led up to each of the shootings, we find that a striking similarity emerges between the various cases. All or most of the shooters had tales of being harassed — specifically gay baited — for inadequate gender performance; their tales are the tales of boys who did not measure up to the norms of hegemonic masculinity. Thus in our view, these boys are not psychopathological deviants but rather over-conformists to a particular normative construction of masculinity, a construction that defines violence as a legitimate response to a perceived humiliation.

MISSING THE MARK

The concern over school shootings has prompted intense national debate, in recent years, over who or what is to blame. One need not look hard to find any number of "experts" who are willing to weigh in on the issue. Yet despite the legion of political and scientific commentaries on school shootings, these voices have all singularly and spectacularly missed the point.

At the vanguard of the debates have been politicians. Some have argued that Goth music, Marilyn Manson, and violent video games are the causes of school shootings. Then-president Clinton argued that it might be the Internet; Newt Gingrich credited the '60s; and Tom DeLay blamed day care, the teaching of evolution, and "working mothers who take birth control pills" ("The News of the Week," 1999). Political pundits and media commentators have also offered a host of possible explanations, of which one of the more popular answers has been violence in the media. "Parents don't realize that taking four-year-olds to *True Lies* — a fun movie for adults but excessively violent — is poison to their brain," noted Michael Gurian (Lacayo, 1998). Alvin Poussaint, a psychiatrist at the Harvard Medical School, wrote,

> In America, violence is considered fun to kids. They play video games where they chop people's heads off and blood gushes and it's fun, it's entertainment. It's like a game. And I think this is the psychology of these kids — this "Let's go out there and kill like on television." (Klein & Chancer, 2000, p. 132)

And Sissela Bok, in her erudite warning on violence, *Mayhem*, suggested that the Internet and violent video games, which "bring into homes depictions of graphic violence . . . never available to children and young people in the past," undermine kids' resilience and self-control (Bok, 1999).

For others, the staggering statistics linking youth violence and the availability of guns point to a possible cause. Firearms are the second-leading cause of death to children between ages 10 and 14 and the eighth-leading cause of death to those aged 1 to 4 (Centers for Disease Control and Prevention, 2001). In 1994, 80% of juvenile murders used a firearm; in 1984 only 50% did (Kelleher, 1998). Barry Krisberg, president of the National Council on Crime and Delinquency, argued that both the media and guns are at fault. He said, "The violence in the media and the easy availability of guns are what is driving the slaughter of innocents" (Lacayo, 1998). Or perhaps, if we are to believe NRA president Charlton Heston, the problem is not that there are too many guns but that there are not enough guns. He argued that had there been armed guards in the schools, the shooting would have ended instantly (Lacayo, 1998). These accounts, however, that blame a media purportedly overly saturated by violence and a society infatuated with guns are undercut by two important facts, which are often conveniently forgotten amongst the fracas. The first is that although the amount of violent media content has ostensibly been increasing, both youth violence, in general, and school violence, in particular, have actually been decreasing since 1980. And second, juvenile violence involving guns has been in decline since 1994 (largely as a result of the decline of the crack epidemic).[2] As Michael Carneal, the boy who shot his classmates in Paducah, Kentucky, said, "I don't know why it happened, but I know it wasn't a movie" (Blank, 1998).

Finally, some have proposed psychological variables, including a history of childhood abuse, absent fathers, dominant mothers, violence in childhood, unstable family environment, or the mothers' fear of their children, as possible explanations (see, for example, Elliott, Hamburg, & Williams, 1998; Garbarino, 1998). Although these explanations are all theoretically possible, empirically, it appears as though none of them hold up. Almost all the shooters came from intact and relatively stable families, with no history of child abuse. If they had psychological problems at all, they were relatively minor, and the boys flew under the radar of any school official or family member who might have noticed something seriously wrong. In a term paper, Eric Harris, of Columbine infamy, quoted Shakespeare's *The Tempest*, "Good wombs hath borne bad sons."

This search for causal variables is also misguided because it ignores a crucial component of all the shootings. These childhood variables would apply equally to boys and to girls.[3] Thus, they offer little purchase with which to answer the question of why it is that only boys open fire on their classmates.

Government-supported investigations—such as the FBI report (O'Toole, 2000), the surgeon general's report on youth violence (*Youth Violence: A Report of the Surgeon General*, 2001), the Bureau of Justice Statistics' report *Indicators of School Crime and Safety 2000* (U.S. Department of Justice, Bureau of Statistics, 2000) as well as the latest new study of bullying (Nansel et al., 2001) all concentrate on identifying potential psychological or cultural antecedents of school violence—for example, media influence, drugs and alcohol behavior, Internet usage, father absence, parental neglect. That is to say, they focus on "form"—who the perpetrators were—not the "content." None examine local cultures, local school cultures, or on gender as an antecedent or risk factor.

Most important for our argument is the fact that these studies have all missed gender. They use such broad terminology as "teen violence," "youth violence," "gang violence," "suburban violence," "violence in the schools," as though girls are equal participants in this violence with boys. Conspicuously absent is any mention of just who these youth or teens are who have committed the violence. They pay little or no attention to the obvious fact that *all the school shootings were committed by boys*—masculinity is the single greatest risk factor in school violence. This uniformity cuts across all other differences among the shooters: some came from intact families, others from single-parent homes; some boys had acted violently in the past, others were quiet and unsuspecting; some boys also expressed rage at their parents (two killed their parents the same morning), and others seemed to live in happy families. And yet if the killers in the schools in Littleton, Pearl, Paducah, Springfield, and Jonesboro had all been girls, gender would undoubtedly be the only story (Kimmel, 2001; see also Klein & Chancer, 2000). Someone might even blame feminism for causing girls to become violent in vain imitation of boys.

But the analytic blindness of these studies runs deeper than gender. We can identify two different waves of school violence since 1980. In the first, from 1982 to 1991, the majority of all the school shootings were nonrandom (that is, the victims were specifically targeted by the perpetrators). Most were in urban, inner-city schools, and involved students of color. Virtually all involved handguns and were sparked by disputes over girlfriends or drugs, and all were committed by boys.

These cases have not entirely disappeared, but they have declined dramatically. Since 1992, only one of the random school shootings occurred in an inner-city school (it was committed by a black student)—whereas the remaining 22 were committed by white students in suburban schools. Virtually all involved rifles, not handguns—a symbolic shift from urban to rural weaponry. However, once again, all shootings were committed by boys.

As the race and class of the perpetrators have shifted, so too has the public perception of school violence. No longer do we hear claims about the "inherent" violence of the inner city, or, what is even more pernicious, the "inherently" violent tendencies of certain racial or ethnic groups. As the shooters have become white and suburban middle-class boys, the public has shifted the blame away from group characteristics to individual psychological problems, assuming that these boys were deviants who broke away from an otherwise genteel suburban culture—that their aberrant behavior was explainable by some psychopathological factor. Although it is no doubt true that many of the boys who committed these terrible acts did have serious psychological problems; such a framing masks the significant role that race and class, in addition to gender, play in school violence.

WHO SHOOTS AND WHY?

Still, most students—white or nonwhite, male or female—are not violent, schools are predominantly safe, and school shootings are aberrations. As a public, we seem concerned with school shootings because its story is not "when children kill" but specifically when suburban white boys kill. To illustrate the distribution of shootings across the country, we have mapped all cases of random school shootings since 1982 (see Figure 9.1). There were five cases documented between 1982 and 1991; there were 23 cases since 1992.

Figure 9.1 reveals that school shootings do not occur uniformly or evenly in the United States, which makes one skeptical of uniform cultural explanations such as violent video games, music, Internet, television, and movies. School shootings are decidedly *not* a national trend. Of 28 school shootings between 1982 and 2001, all but 1 were in rural or suburban schools (one in Chicago). All but 2 (Chicago and Virginia Beach) were committed by a white boy or boys. The Los Angeles school district has had no school shootings since 1984; in 1999, San Francisco, which has several programs to identify potentially violent students, had only two kids bring guns to school.

School shootings can be divided even further—along the lines of a deep and familiar division in American society (see Figure 9.2).

Contrary to Alan Wolfe's assertion that we are "one nation, after all," it appears that we are actually two nations, "red states" (states that voted for George W. Bush in the 2000 presidential election) and "blue states" (states that voted for Al Gore in the 2000 election). Twenty of the 28 school shootings took place in red states (marked with light gray in Figure 9.2). Of those in the blue states (marked with dark gray in Figure 9.2), 1 was in suburban Oregon, 1 was in rural (eastern) Washington, 2 were in Southern California; 1 was in rural and another in suburban Pennsylvania, and 1 was in rural New Mexico. Of those 8 from blue states, half of the counties in those blue states (Santee, CA; Red Hill, PA; Moses Lake, WA; and Deming, NM) voted Republican in the last election.

What this suggests is that school violence is unevenly distributed, and that in order to understand its causes, we must look locally, at "gun culture" (percentage of homes owning firearms, gun registrations, NRA memberships), local gender culture, and local school cultures—attitudes about gender nonconformity, tolerance of bullying, teacher attitudes.

With this as our guiding theoretical framework, we undertook an analysis of secondary media reports on random school shootings from 1982 to 2001. Using the shooters' names as our search

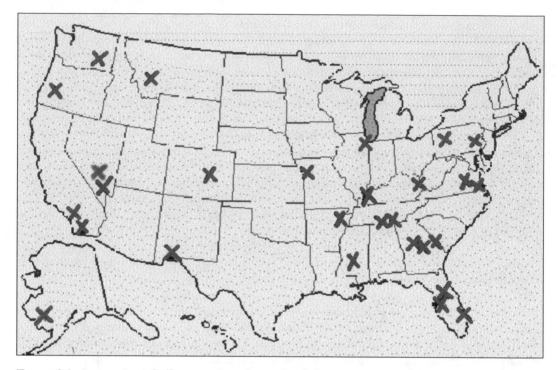

Figure 9.1. A mapping of all cases of random school shootings since 1982.

terms, we gathered articles from six major media sources — the three major weekly news magazines, *Time, Newsweek,* and *U.S. News and World Report* (in order from greatest circulation to least), and three major daily newspapers, *USA Today,* the *New York Times,* and the *Los Angeles Times.*[4] In conducting our analysis, we found a striking pattern from the stories about the boys who committed the violence: Nearly all had stories of being constantly bullied, beat up, and, most significant for this analysis, "gay baited." Nearly all had stories of being mercilessly and constantly teased, picked on, and threatened. And, most strikingly, it was *not* because they were gay (at least there is no evidence to suggest that any of them were gay), but because they were *different* from the other boys — shy, bookish, honor students, artistic, musical, theatrical, nonathletic, "geekish," or weird. Theirs are stories of "cultural marginalization" based on criteria for adequate gender performance — specifically the enactment of codes of masculinity.

Research has indicated that homophobia is one of the organizing principles of heterosexual masculinity, a constitutive element in its construction (see, for example, Epstein, 1995, 1998; Herek, 1998, 2000; Herek & Capitano, 1999). And as an organizing principle of masculinity, homophobia — the terror that others will see one as gay, as a failed man — underlies a significant amount of men's behavior, including their relationships with other men, women, and violence. One could say that homophobia is the hate that makes men straight.

There is much at stake for boys, and as a result, they engage in a variety of evasive strategies to make sure that no one gets the wrong idea about them (and their manhood). These range from the seemingly comic (though telling), such as two young boys occupying three movie seats by placing their coats on the seat between them, to the truly tragic, such as engaging in homo-

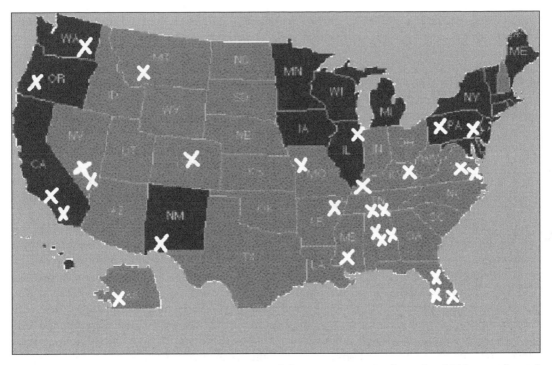

Figure 9.2. The "red states" are states that voted for George W. Bush in the 2000 presidential election and the "blue states" are states that voted for Al Gore in the election. The Xs indicate places where school shootings took place between 1982 and 2001.

phobic violence, bullying, menacing other boys, masochistic or sadistic games and rituals, excessive risk taking (drunk or aggressive driving), and even sexual predation and assault. The impact of homophobia is felt not only by gay and lesbian students but also by heterosexuals who are targeted by their peers for constant harassment, bullying, and gay baiting. In many cases, gay baiting is "misdirected" at heterosexual youth who may be somewhat gender nonconforming. This fact is clearly evidenced in many of the accounts we have gathered of the shootings.

For example, young Andy Williams, recently sentenced to 50 years to life in prison for shooting and killing two classmates in Santee, California, and wounding several others, was described as "shy" and was "constantly picked on" by others in school. Like many of the others, bullies stole his clothes, his money, and his food; beat him up regularly; and locked him in his locker, among other daily taunts and humiliations (Green & Lieberman, 2001). One boy's father baited him and called him a "queer" because he was overweight. Classmates described Gary Scott Pennington, who killed his teacher and a custodian in Grayson, Kentucky, in 1993, as a "nerd" and a "loner" who was constantly teased for being smart and wearing glasses (Buckley, 1993). Barry Loukaitis, who killed his algebra teacher and two other students in Moses Lake, Washington, in 1996, was an honor student who especially loved math; he was also constantly teased and bullied and described as a "shy nerd" ("Did Taunts Lead to Killing?" 1996). And Evan Ramsay, who killed one student and the high school principal in Bethel, Alaska, in 1997, was also an honor student who was teased for wearing glasses and having acne (Fainaru, 1998).

Luke Woodham was a bookish and overweight 16-year-old in Pearl, Mississippi. An honor student, he was part of a little group that studied Latin and read Nietzsche. Students teased him constantly for being overweight and a nerd, and they taunted him as being "gay" or "fag." Even his mother called him fat, stupid, and lazy. Other boys bullied him routinely, and, according to one fellow student, he "never fought back when other boys called him names" (Holland, 1997). On October 1, 1997, Woodham stabbed his mother to death in her bed before he left for school. He then drove her car to school, carrying a rifle under his coat. He opened fire in the school's common area, killing two students and wounding seven others. After being subdued, he told the assistant principal "the world has wronged me" (Lacayo, 1998). Later, in a psychatric interview, he said, "I am not insane. I am angry.... I am not spoiled or lazy; for murder is not weak and slow-witted; murder is gutsy and daring. I killed because people like me are mistreated every day. I am malicious because I am miserable" (Chua-Eoan, 1997).

At Columbine High School, the site of the nation's most infamous school shooting, this connection was not lost on Evan Todd, a 255-pound defensive lineman on the Columbine football team, an exemplar of the jock culture that Dylan Klebold and Eric Harris found to be such an interminable torment. "Columbine is a clean, good place, except for those rejects," Todd said. "Sure we teased them. But what do you expect with kids who come to school with weird hairdos and horns on their hats? It's not just jocks; the whole school's disgusted with them. They're a bunch of homos.... If you want to get rid of someone, usually you tease 'em. So the whole school would call them homos" (Gibbs & Roche, 1999). Ben Oakley, a soccer player, agreed. "Nobody liked them," he said, "the majority of them were gay. So everyone would make fun of them" (Cullen, 1999). Athletes taunted them: "Nice dress," they would say. They would throw rocks and bottles at them from moving cars. The school newspaper had recently published a rumor that Harris and Klebold were lovers.

Both were reasonably well-adjusted kids. Harris's father was a retired army officer and his mother was a caterer — decent well-intentioned people. Klebold's father was a geophysicist who had recently moved into the mortgage services business and his mother worked in job placement for the disabled. Harris had been rejected by several colleges; Klebold was due to enroll at Arizona in the fall. But the jock culture was relentless. "Every time someone slammed them against a locker and threw a bottle at them, I think they'd go back to Eric or Dylan's house and plot a little more — at first as a goof, but more and more seriously over time," said one friend (Pooley, 1999).

The rest is all too familiar. Harris and Klebold brought a variety of weapons to their high school and proceeded to walk through the school, shooting whomever they could find. Students were terrified and tried to hide. Many students who could not hide begged for their lives. The entire school was held under siege until the police secured the building. In all, 23 students and faculty were injured, and 15 died, including one teacher and the perpetrators.

In the videotape made the night before the shootings, Harris said, "People constantly make fun of my face, my hair, my shirts." Klebold added, "I'm going to kill you all. You've been giving us shit for years." What Klebold said he had been receiving for years apparently included constant gay baiting; being called "queer," "faggot," "homo"; being pushed into lockers, grabbed in hallways, mimicked, and ridiculed with homophobic slurs. For some boys, high school is a constant homophobic gauntlet, and they may respond by becoming withdrawn and sullen, using drugs or alcohol, becoming depressed or suicidal, or acting out in a blaze of overcompensating violent "glory" (see Egan, 1998).

The prevalence of this homophobic bullying, teasing, and violence is staggering. According to the Gay, Lesbian, Straight Education Network, 97% of students in public high school in Massachusetts reported regularly hearing homophobic remarks from their peers in 1993; 53% reported hearing anti-gay remarks by school staff (Youth Risk Behavior Surveys, Massachusetts and Vermont; cited in Bronski, 1999). The recent report, *Hatred in the Hallways*, paints a bleak picture of anti-gay harassment, but it pays significant attention to the ways in which gender performance — acting masculine — is perceived as a code for heterosexuality (Human Rights Watch, 2001).

And if we are to believe recent research, the effects of such hectoring should not be underestimated. In a national survey of teenagers' attitudes, students suggested that peer harassment was the most significant cause of school shootings (Gaughan, Cerio, & Myers, 2001). Nearly 9 of 10 teenagers said that they believed that the school shootings were motivated by a desire "to get back at those who have hurt them" (87%) and that "other kids picking on them, making fun of them, or bullying them" (86%) were the immediate causes.

Before we continue, let us be completely clear: Our hypotheses are decidedly *not* that gay and lesbian youth are more likely to open fire on their fellow students. In fact, from all available evidence, *none* of the school shooters were gay. But that is our organizing hypothesis: Homophobia — being constantly threatened and bullied *as if you are gay*, as well as the homophobic desire to make sure that others know that you are a "real man" — plays a pivotal and understudied role in these school shootings. But more than just taking gender performance and its connections to homosexuality seriously, we argue that we must also carefully investigate the dynamics of gender within these local cultures — especially local school cultures and the typically hegemonic position of jock culture and its influence on normative assumptions of masculinity — in order to begin to understand what pushes some boys toward such horrific events, what sorts of pressures keep most boys cowed in silence, and what resources enable some boys to resist.

WHY BOYS AND NOT GIRLS?

Despite the remarkable similarities between the sexes on most statistical measures, the single most obdurate and intractable gender difference remains violence — both the willingness to see it as a legitimate way to resolve conflict and its actual use. Four times more teenage boys than teenage girls think fighting is appropriate when someone cuts into the front of a line. Half of all teenage boys get into a physical fight each year (Kimmel, 2000). Psychological inventories that measure attitudes and ideologies of masculinity invariably score propensity to violence and legitimacy of violence as "masculine." Undoubtedly, violence is normative for most boys (see also Lefkowitz, 1997).

This association of violence and virility starts early for boys, and it takes on particular resonance at around age 7 or 8, according to developmental research conducted by Judy Chu (2000). Unlike girls, boys do not lose their voice, they "gain" a voice, but it is an inauthentic voice of constant posturing, of false bravado, of foolish risk-taking and gratuitous violence — what some have called the "boy code," the "mask of masculinity." The once-warm, empathic, communicative boy becomes, very early, a stoic, uncommunicative, armor-plated male. They "ruffle in a manly pose," as William Butler Yeats once put it, "for all their timid heart."

Historically, no other industrial society than the United States has developed such a violent "boy culture," as historian E. Anthony Rotundo (1993) called it in his book *American Manhood*. It is here where young boys, as early as the 1940s, actually carried a little chip of wood on their shoulders daring others to knock it off so that they might have a fight. It is astonishing to think that "carrying a chip on your shoulder" is literally true — a test of manhood for adolescent boys. And it is here in the United States where experts actually *prescribed* fighting for young boys' healthy masculine development. The celebrated psychologist G. Stanley Hall, who invented the term "adolescence," believed that a nonfighting boy was a "nonentity," and that it was "better even an occasional nose dented by a fist ... than stagnation, general cynicism and censoriousness, bodily and psychic cowardice" (cited in Stearns, 1994). His disciple J. Adams Puffer (1912) was even bold enough to suggest, in his successful parental advice book *The Boy and His Gang*, that it is not unreasonable for a boy to fight up to six times a week. Calling someone a "faggot" means questioning his manhood. And in this culture, when someone questions your manhood, we do not just get mad, we get even.

WHY WHITE BOYS?

There may be a single "boy code," but there are also a variety of ways in which different boys and men relate to it, embrace it, and enact it — in short, there are a variety of young masculinities. The deft interplay between generalized normative constructions and local iterations are vital to explore — and something that is rarely done by the myriad books that have counseled parents to attend to the needs of their boys. Making gender visible ought not to make other elements of identity — age, sexuality, race, ethnicity, class — invisible. It is for this reason that we have come to use the term "masculinities" to denote these differences. What it means to be a 71-year-old black, gay man in Cleveland is probably radically different from what it means to a 19-year-old white, heterosexual farm boy in Iowa.

At the same time, we must also remember that all masculinities are not created equal. All American men also contend with a singular hegemonic vision of masculinity, a particular definition that is held up as the model against which we all measure ourselves. We thus come to know what it means to be a man in our culture by setting our definitions in opposition to a set of subordinated "others" — racial minorities, sexual minorities, and, above all, women. As the sociologist Erving Goffman once wrote,

> In an important sense there is only one complete unblushing male in America: a young, married, white, urban, northern, heterosexual, Protestant, father, of college education, fully employed, of good complexion, weight, and height, and a recent record in sports.... Any male who fails to qualify in any one of these ways is likely to view himself — during moments at least — as unworthy, incomplete, and inferior. (1963, p. 128)

It is crucial to listen to those last few words. When we feel that we do not measure up we are likely to feel unworthy, incomplete, and inferior. It is here, from this place of unworthiness, incompleteness, and inferiority, that boys begin their efforts to prove themselves as men. And it is here where violence has its connections to masculinity. As James Gilligan said in his book *Violence*, violence has its origins in "the fear of shame and ridicule, and the overbearing need to prevent others from laughing at oneself by making them weep instead" (1996, p. 77). *Shame*, inadequacy, vulnerability — all threaten the self; *violence*, meanwhile, is restorative, compensatory.

By pluralizing the term masculinity, we also make it possible to see places where gender *appears* to be the salient variable, but may, in fact, be what sociologist Cynthia Fuchs Epstein called a "deceptive distinction" — something that looks like gender difference but is in fact a difference based on some other criterion. Thus, for example, we read of how male cadets at the Virginia Military Institute or the Citadel would be distressed and uncomfortable by women's presence on campus. Of course, in reality, there were plenty of women on campus — they cleaned the rooms, made and served the food, taught the classes, were readily available as counselors and medical personnel. What bothered the men was not gender, but class — that is, women's institutional equality. (Similar analyses can be made about male doctors or corporate executives who are not at all uncomfortable with female nurses or secretaries, or male athletes who are not at all uncomfortable about female cheerleaders but seem threatened by female athletes.)

Most important for our current discussion though is the fact that failure to see race while looking at gender will cause us to miss the real story. We know that African American boys face a multitude of challenges in schools, from racial stereotypes, formal and informal tracking systems, low expectations, and underachievement. But the one thing they do not do is plan and execute random and arbitrary mass shootings. And this is particularly interesting because the dynamics of the classroom and academic achievement have different valences for African American girls and African American boys. In their fascinating ethnographies of two inner-city public high schools, Signithia Fordham (1996) and Ann Ferguson (2000) discussed these differences. When African American girls do well in school, their friends accuse them of "acting white." But when African American boys do well in school, their friends accuse them of "acting like girls."

We might posit that cultural marginalization works itself out differently for subordinates and superordinates. Even if they are silenced or lose their voice, subordinates — women, gays and lesbians, students of color — can tap into a collective narrative repertoire of resistance. They can collectivize their anguish, so that the personally painful may be subsumed into readily available political rhetorics. White boys who are bullied are supposed to be real men, supposed to be able to embody independence, invulnerability, manly stoicism. In fact, the very search for such collective rhetorics can be seen as an indication of weakness. Thus we might hypothesize that the cultural marginalization of the boys who did commit school shootings extended to feelings that they had no other recourse: They felt they had no other friends to validate their fragile and threatened identities; they felt that school authorities and parents would be unresponsive to their plight; and they had no access to other methods of self-affirmation.

CONCLUSION

In a brilliant passage in *Asylums*, Erving Goffman touched on the interplay between structure and agency, between repression and resistance:

> Without something to belong to, we have no stable self, and yet total commitment and attachment to any social unit implies a kind of selflessness. Our sense of being a person can come from being drawn into a wider social unit; our sense of selfhood can arise through the little ways in which we resist the pull. Our status is backed by the solid buildings of the world, while our sense of personal identity often resides in the cracks. (1961, p. 320)

It is our task, as researchers concerned with race, ethnicity, gender, and education, to understand how those structural forces shape and mold young men's identities, and to explore the seams of resistance, where they might carve out for themselves a masculinity that is authentic, grounded, and confident.

REFERENCES

Adams, J., & Malone, J. (1999, March 18). Outsider's destructive behavior spiraled into violence. *Louisville Courier Journal.*

Anderson, M., Kaufman, J., Simon, T., Barrios, L., Paulozzi, L., Ryan, R., Hammond, R., Modzleski, W., Feucht, T., Potter, L., & School-Associated Violent Deaths Group. (2001). School-associated violent deaths in the United States, 1994–1999. *Journal of the American Medical Association, 286,* 2695–2702.

Blank, J. (1998, December). The kid no one noticed. *U.S. News and World Report,* p. 27.

Bok, S. (1999). *Mayhem: Violence as public entertainment.* Cambridge, MA: Perseus.

Bronski, M. (1999, July). Littleton, movies and gay kids. *Z Magazine.*

Buckley, J. (1993, November 8). The tragedy in room 108. *U.S. News and World Report, 115*(18), p. 41.

Carlson, D., & Simmons, W. (2001, March 6). *Majority of parents think a school shooting could occur in their community.* Gallup Poll Release. Retrieved from *http://www.gallup.com/poll/releases/pr010306.asp*

Centers for Disease Control and Prevention. (2001). Web-based injury statistics query and reporting system (WISQARS). National Center for Injury Prevention and Control, Centers for Disease Control and Prevention. Retrieved from *www.cdc.gov/ncipc/wisqars*

Chu, J. (2000). *Learning what boys know: An observational and interview study with six four-year-old boys.* Unpublished doctoral dissertation, Graduate School of Education, Harvard University, Cambridge, MA.

Chua-Eoan, H. (1997, October 20). Mississippi: In a dramatic turn, an alleged one-man rampage may have become a seven-pointed conspiracy. *Time, 150*(16), p. 54.

Cloud, J. (2001, March 19). The legacy of Columbine. *Time, 157,* p. 32.

Cullen, D. (1999). The rumor that won't go away. *Salon.* Retrieved from *www.salon.com/news/feature/1999/04/24/rumors/index.html*

Did taunts lead to killing? (1996, February 4). *Minneapolis Star Tribune.*

Egan, T. (1998, June 15). Patterns emerging in attacks at schools. *The New York Times.*

Elliott, D. S., Hamburg, B. A., & Williams, K. R. (1998). *Violence in American schools.* New York: Cambridge University Press.

Epstein, D. (1995). Keeping them in their place: Hetero/sexist harassment, gender and the enforcement of heterosexuality. In J. Holland & L. Adkins (Eds.), *Sex, sensibility and the gendered body.* London: Macmillan.

Epstein, D. (1998). Real boys don't work: Underachievement, masculinity and the harassment of sissies. In D. Epstein (Ed.), *Failing boys? Issues in gender and achievement.* London: Open University Press.

Fainaru, S. (1998, December 4). Alaska teen's path to murder. *The Dallas Morning News,* p. 48A.

Ferguson, A. (2000). *Bad boys: Public schools in the making of black masculinity.* Ann Arbor: University of Michigan Press.

Fordham, S. (1996). *Blacked out: Dilemmas of race, identity, and success at capital high.* Chicago: University of Chicago Press.

Garbarino, J. (1998). *Lost boys.* New York: Free Press.

Gaughan, E., Cerio, J., & Myers, R. (2001). *Lethal violence in schools: A national survey, final report.* Alfred, NY: Alfred University.

Gibbs, N., & Roche, T. (1999, December 20). The Columbine tapes: In five secret videos they recorded before the massacre, the killers reveal their hatreds — and their lust for fame. *Time, 154*(25), p. 40.

Gilligan, J. (1996). *Violence.* New York: Vintage.

Glassner, B. (1999a, August 13). School violence: The fears, the facts. *The New York Times.*

Glassner, B. (1999b). *The culture of fear.* New York: Basic Books.

Goffman, E. (1961). *Asylums.* New York: Vintage.

Goffman, E. (1963). *Stigma: Notes on the management of spoiled identity.* Englewood Cliffs, NJ: Prentice Hall.

Green, K., & Lieberman, B. (2001, March 10). Bullying, ridicule of Williams were routine, friends say. *San Diego Union-Tribune,* p. A-1.

Half of teens have heard of a gun threat at school. (2001, November 27). *USA Today,* p. 6D.

Herek, G. (Ed.). (1998). *Stigma and sexual orientation: Understanding prejudice against lesbians, gay men and bisexuals.* Newbury Park, CA: Sage.

Herek, G. (2000). The psychology of sexual prejudice. *Current Perspectives in Psychological Science, 9*(1), 19–22.

Herek, G., & Capitano, J. (1999). Sex differences in how heterosexuals think about lesbians and gay men: Evidence from survey context effects. *Journal of Sex Research, 36*(4), 348–360.

Heslam, J., & Richardson, F. (2001, November 26). Suspect labeled outcast, estranged from family. *The Boston Herald,* p. 6.

Holland, G. (1997, October 3). "I am not insane, I am angry": Suspect in Pearl handed classmate a chilling note. *Biloxi Sun Herald.*

Human Rights Watch. (2001). *Hatred in the hallways: Violence and discrimination against lesbian, gay, bisexual, and transgender students in the U.S.* New York: Author.

Kelleher, M. (1998). *When good kids kill.* New York: Dell.

Kim, R. (2001, March 5). Eminem — Bad rap? *The Nation,* p. 4.

Kimmel, M. (1994). Masculinity as homophobia: Fear, shame and silence in the construction of gender identity. In H. Brod & M. Kaufman (Eds.), *Theorizing masculinities* (pp. 119–141). Newbury Park, CA: Sage.

Kimmel, M. (1996). *Manhood in America: A cultural history.* New York: Free Press.

Kimmel, M. (2000). *The gendered society.* New York: Oxford University Press.

Kimmel, M. (2001, March 9). Snips and snails . . . and violent urges. *Newsday, Minneapolis Star-Tribune, San Francisco Examiner,* p. A41.

Klein, J., & Chancer, L. S. (2000). Masculinity matters: The omission of gender from high-profile school violence cases. In S. U. Spina (Ed.), *Smoke and mirrors: The hidden content of violence in schools and society.* Lanham, MD: Rowman and Littlefield.

Lacayo, R. (1998, April 6). Toward the root of the evil. *Time,* pp. 38–39.

Lefkowitz, B. (1997). *Our guys: The Glenn Ridge rape and the secret life of the perfect suburb.* Berkeley: University of California Press.

Ma, X. (2001). Bullying and being bullied: To what extent are bullies also victims. *American Educational Research Journal, 38,* 351–370.

Nansel, T., Overpeck, M., Pilla, R., Rune, J., Simmons-Morton, B., & Scheidt, P. (2001). Bullying behaviors among U.S. youth: Prevalence and association with psychosocial adjustment. *Journal of the American Medical Association, 285*(16), 2094–2100.

The news of the week in review. (1999, November 15). *The Nation*, p. 5.

Noguera, P. (2001, Summer). The trouble with black boys. *Harvard Journal of African American Public Policy, 7*, 23–46.

Olweus, D. (1978). *Aggression in the schools*. Washington, DC: Hemisphere.

Olweus, D. (1991). Victimization among school children. In R. Baenninger (Ed.), *Targets of violence and aggression* (pp. 45–102). Amsterdam: Elsevier.

O'Toole, M. (2000). *The school shooter: A threat assessment perspective*. Quantico, VA: National Center for the Analysis of Violent Crime, FBI Academy.

Penn, Schoen, & Berland. (1999, April 22). Fear of classmates. *USA Today*, p. A1.

Pooley, E. (1999, May 10). Portrait of a deadly bond. *Time*, pp. 26–27.

Puffer, J. A. (1912). *The boy and his gang*. Boston: Houghton.

Rotundo, E. A. (1993). *American manhood*. New York: Basic Books.

Salmon, G., James, A., & Smith, D. M. (1998, October). Bullying in schools: Self-reported anxiety, depression and self-esteem in secondary school children. *British Medical Journal, 317*, 924–925.

Smith, P., & Brain, P. (2000). Bullying in schools: Lessons from two decades of research. *Aggressive Behavior, 26*(1), 1–10.

Stearns, P. (1994). *American cool*. New York: New York University Press.

U.S. Department of Justice, Bureau of Justice Statistics. (2000). *Indicators of school crime and safety, 2000*. Washington, DC: Office of Justice Programs.

Youth violence: A report of the surgeon general. (2001). Washington, DC: Department of Health and Human Services.

Notes

1. This despite the fact that school shootings — where a young student opens fire on school grounds, apparently randomly, and shoots teachers and students — are the only type of school violence that has increased since 1980 (Glassner, 1999a, 1999b; see also Anderson et al., 2001). More than 99% of public high schools have never had a homicide. In the 1992–1993 school year there were 54 violent deaths on high school campuses; in 2000 there were 16 (Cloud, 2001). Less than 1% of all school-associated violent deaths are the result of homicide (Anderson et al., 2001).

2. This is not to entirely dismiss the potential links between school shootings and the availability of guns. While many boys are frustrated, harassed, and saturated with media violence, not all of them have equal access to guns.

3. This same critique could also be directed at the aforementioned arguments blaming the media and/or the prevalence of guns.

4. These papers were selected because they comprise three of the top four daily newspapers in circulation. The *Wall Street Journal*, which has the highest circulation of any daily newspaper in the United States was not included in our analysis because its substantive focus is on business-related issues. To extend our analysis to local media outlets, we also selectively sampled from smaller regional papers. We recognize that using secondary media reports as indicators of "what really happened" leading up to and during these shootings is

a questionable tactic. To further tease out the causes of these shootings, one would have to conduct firsthand interviews with those directly involved in the shootings — the shooters themselves, classmates, teachers, administrators, parents, and so forth. However, we feel that an analysis of media reports is nevertheless a valuable approach in this instance, because one of our major points is that although virtually all of these accounts contained some evidence indicating the connections between masculinity, homophobia, and violence, they all somehow overlooked this fact.

TEN

Excavating a "Moment in History": Privilege and Loss inside White Working-Class Masculinity

Lois Weis, Amira Proweller, and Craig Centrie

In the past 20 years, we have come a long way toward unraveling the identity production processes among various groups within American society. Feminist work, in particular, has helped us understand the ways in which girls and women fashion their own identities in relation to what Dorothy Smith called textually mediated discourses. Drawing from Foucault, Smith (1988, p. 39) argued,

> Social forms of consciousness, "femininity" included, can be examined as actual practices, actual activities, taking place in real time, in real places, using definite material means and under definite material conditions. Among other matters, this means that we do not neglect the "textual" dimensions of social consciousness. By texts, I mean the more or less permanent and above all replaceable forms of meaning, of writing, painting, television, film, etc. The production, distribution and uses of texts are a pervasive and highly significant dimension of contemporary social organization. "Femininity," I'm going to argue, is a distinctively textual phenomenon. But texts must not be isolated from the practices in which they are embedded and which they organize.

Smith's observations are helpful as we work toward understanding the production of femininity, and work by Linda Valli (1986), Nancy Lesko (1988), Claire Wallace (1987), Valerie Walkerdine, Helen Lucey, and June Melody (2001), as well as others, enhances our knowledge of the production of women's identities. Here we shift our gaze to the production of masculinity, and particularly the production of white masculinity. Although feminists have undertaken work on the production of femininity and theorized it as such, scholars who have focused on the production of boys' and men's identities have not, until fairly recently, theorized their work specifically along gender lines. Well-known work by Paul Willis, for example, although wholly centered on the production of male culture, does not theorize it as such. Rather he employs a class-based paradigm through which he understands the lads' culture as working class and develops an analysis through a distinctly class-centered lens. He fails, however, to employ theoretical work on gender to begin to decode these processes as specifically gender-based practices, although, as Arnot argued, Willis's study set the stage for subsequent work embedded within a sociology of masculinity (Arnot, 2004). When Willis does focus on gender, he employs classic Marxist notions of gender (and race) that speak to the divide-and-rule tactics associated with the capitalist class.

Work on masculinities has become increasingly popular into the 21st century (Jackson, 2002), and, as Connell (2000, p. 24) noted, there has been a "great flowing of empirical research on masculinities." Here we join these recent scholars in that we place the production of masculinity and, in particular, the production of white masculinity, at the center of our analyses, naming our focus as the culture of working-class men in the northeast United States. Along these lines, we highlight the production of white masculinity in this particular class fraction as it takes shape at the intersectionalities of social class, race, and gender. Theoretically this represents a departure from previous work on men and even recent work on the production of masculinity in that we rely heavily on Kimberle Crenshaw's important discussion of intersectionality as being key in the production of identity across variegated sites of meaning making. In short, then, we focus here specifically on the production of white masculinity, but white masculinity inside working-class life at a time of tremendous upheaval in the world economy.

On Being White

Theorists and researchers including Dorothy Smith (1988), Leslie Roman (1983), Stanley Aronowitz (1982), Joel Kovel , Judith Rollins (1985), bell hooks (1985), Toni Morrison (1992), and others have argued for the study of privileged standpoints, for "studying up." Relatively few, however, with the obvious exception of those in this volume, have taken up this challenge. White standpoints, privileged standpoints, are generally taken as an unstated norm, rather than offering a site for theoretical excavation. Certainly the work of Peggy Sanday (1990) in her analysis of fraternity men at an elite university stands out as an exception. Dorothy Smith's (1988) analysis of corporate workplaces excavates privileged standpoint, as does Judith Rollins's (1985) study of domestic workers and their white employers. Roslyn Arlin Michelson, Stephen Smith, and Melvin Oliver (1993) similarly focused on privilege when they studied the ways in which universities, in spite of affirmative action policies, work to exclude the voices of people of color, and Melvin Oliver and Thomas Shapiro (1997) pointed out vividly the racially structured bases of inequality, specifically the privileging of "whiteness," in housing policies and outcomes.

In this discussion, we take up this challenge as we begin to unravel white male identity inside working-class culture in a time of global economic restructuring. Gone are the jobs in heavy industry that sustained white men's fathers and grandfathers and that allowed them to earn the "family wage" that bought them the privilege of dominating their wives and children in the home. Most of the truly "masculine" jobs, those that demand hard physical labor, are gone, replaced by jobs in the service sector, jobs that not only pay less but do not offer the "hard" real confrontation with physicality that was embedded in jobs of former years, jobs that encouraged the production of a certain type of masculinity (Connell, 1995). We wonder, then, not only how white males in the 1980s and 1990s, in the midst of feminism, affirmative action, and gay and lesbian rights, managed to sustain a sense of self, individually and collectively, but also how they sustained a belief in a system that had, at least for working-class and middle-class white males, begun to crumble, eroding their once certain advantage over white women and women and men of color (Newman, 1993).[1] As scholars begin to recognize that "white is a color" (Roman, 1993; Wong, 1994), we write in order to make visible the borders, strategies, and fragilities of white, working-class male culture in insecure times, at, in Dorothy Smith's words, "a moment in history."[2]

Our focus here renders the study of privilege more complex than standpoint theorists generally recognize. Although white working-class men are privileged because of their color, they are relatively less privileged than their economically advantaged white male counterparts. Too, they are currently losing the edge they had in the economy over men of color. White working-class men represent a position of privilege; at the same time they represent the loss of such privilege. It is this simultaneous moment of privilege and loss that we excavate when we turn our attention to the production of white masculinity. It is their whiteness and maleness that privileges them. But it is also in this space of historical privilege that they begin to confront the realities of loss.

Through an analysis of data collected with poor and working-class white, Latino, and African American men and women, ages 23 to 35, as to their concrete experiences in family, job, community, religion, political activism, and schooling (Fine & Weis, 1998), we unearth the territory mapped by white men inside in-depth interviews. We normally conducted the interviews in two segments, each approximately 1 to 1 and one-half hours in length, and we conducted them with low-income people in Jersey City, New Jersey and Buffalo, New York. We drew respondents from meaningful urban communities, to use William Julius Wilson's (1980) term, such as schools, Headstart, literacy centers, churches, and social agencies directly involved with local ethnic and racial communities.

We argue that white working-class men feel themselves to be under siege—in their jobs, in their neighborhoods, in their homes, and in their schools. Whether true or not in material terms, they feel themselves to be decentered, to no longer hold the position of privilege that they sense is rightfully theirs. This is, of course, stated in much more coded language, and no individual alleges that whites deserve more in the society simply by virtue of their skin color. That, unfortunately, may be one of the real outcomes of the civil rights struggle—that whites have to justify privilege in ways other than simply skin color. The expectation of privilege because of whiteness and maleness must be coded differently so that the demand for privilege does not rest on skin color alone, or skin color as related to intelligence. (We do, however, see a resurgence of this latter argument as well; see Herrnstein [1994], *The Bell Curve*.) Rather, these men are involved in the production of elaborate justifications of privilege, justifications that serve, in their minds, to recenter what they argue is the decentered white male. Much of their identity production swirls around the creation and maintenance of the dark "other" against which their own whiteness and goodness is necessarily understood. The social construction of this goodness, then, provides moral justification for privileged standpoints. We do not mean to argue that this type of discursive work has not been done historically. Clearly that is not the case, as Toni Morrison and David Roediger make clear. However, what is important in the late 20th and early 21st century is that these productions coexist with a dismantled apartheid legal system. Discursive productions swirling around race therefore undermine ostensible equality under the law. These discursive productions are, as Dorothy Smith reminded us, textually mediated. They do not arise out of the thin air of class culture, "on the ground," so to speak, but are dialectically linked to the media, popular culture, and other forms of consumerist culture that directly articulate with economic arrangements as they structure daily experience (see McCarthy et al., 2004 [this volume]).

ON WHITENESS

Work by Ruth Frankenberg (1993) is extremely provocative. She argued, "To speak of the social construction of whiteness" reveals locations, discourses, and material relations to which the term "whiteness" applies. She further asserted, "Whiteness refers to a set of locations that are historically, socially, politically, and culturally produced and moreover are intrinsically linked to unfolding relations of domination. Naming 'whiteness' displaces it from the unmarked, unnamed status that is itself an effect of its dominance. Among the effects on white people both of race privilege and of the dominance of whiteness are their seeming normativity, their structured invisibility" (p. 6). As Frankenberg asserted, to analyze whiteness is to focus squarely on a site of constructed dominance.

In the United States, the hierarchies of race, gender, and class are embodied in the contemporary "struggle" of white maleness. As we show, these men work to sustain both an identity within dominance and the very hierarchies that ensure their ongoing domination. Among the varied demographic categories that spill out of this race and gender hierarchy, white males are the only ones who have a vested interest in maintaining both their position and their web of power. The irony here, of course, is that white working-class males are not the biggest beneficiaries of privilege itself. In sustaining the hierarchy, they are reproducing the very conditions that render them relatively expendable in the current economy. The assertion of dominance in one arena (race) implies the lack of such dominance in another (social class). To accomplish the myth of race privilege, white males have had to sustain the notion of egalitarianism or at least the potential for equality. White male power necessitates a commitment on the part of white working-class males to engage the struggle for cultural dominance. Yet the location of struggle is far removed from the actual center of power and privilege residing inside the elite community. Lower income and working-class white males form a necessary buffer that, if eliminated or realigned along class rather than race lines, would destabilize elite domination.

Scholars of colonial discourse have highlighted the ways in which discourse about non-Western "others" are produced simultaneously with the production of discourse about the Western white "self," and this work becomes relevant to our analyses of race and gender domination. Scholarship on West European expansion documents the cultural disruptions that took place alongside economic appropriation, as well as the importance of the production of knowledge about groups of people that rendered colonization successful. As Frankenberg (1993, p. 16) stated, "The notion of 'epistemic violence' captures the idea that associated with West European colonial expansion is the production of modes of knowing that enabled and rationalized colonial domination from the standpoint of the West, and produced ways of conceiving other societies and cultures whose legacies endure into the present." She argued,

> Colonial discourse (like racist discourse) is in many ways heterogeneous rather than univocal, not surprising given the extent and geographical dispersion of European colonizing projects. However, if a common thread runs through the whole range of instances of colonial discourse, it is the construction of alterity along social and/or cultural lines — the construction of others conceived as fundamentally different from, and inferior to, white, European metropolitan selves.... It must also be noted — and this is a point perhaps more difficult to grasp upon first encounter with it — that it is precisely by means of the construction of a range of others that the self or dominant center constitutes itself. White/European self-constitution is, in other words, fundamentally tied to the process of discursive production of others, rather than preexisting that process. (p. 63)

It is precisely this point that gives rise to the voices inside Afrocentric scholarship, particularly the work of Asante (1990; Asante & Mattson, 1991), who asserted that the colonial European has no identity other than that which has been constructed vis-à-vis "others." Mohanty (1988) and Roediger (1992) talked carefully about the production of white racial identity in the United States and the ways in which this identity is intimately tied to the production of black identity. What is important here is that the legacy of colonialism, more specifically the legacy of colonial discourse, rendered the category "white" a simultaneously *empty* but *normative* space — in other words, "white" could only be defined in relation to the constructed other. It is by these very processes of othering that "white" becomes the norm against which all other communities (of color) are judged (usually to be deviant). Colonialism and neocolonialism have sanctioned the normativity and structured invisibility of the West, partially through the production of knowledge but mainly by positioning an "other" as knowledge consumer. This has served to bolster the inscrutability of whiteness through naming and labeling the "other." Internal colonialization in the United States has achieved this same dynamic through the marginalization of people of color and the resulting normativity of whiteness. It is, therefore, possible to name cultures precisely because they are excluded from the normative, thus enabling the dominant "white" to engage in a process of establishing what Trin Min-ha (1989) called "boundedness." Thus much of white identity formation, stemming from colonial times to the present, involves drawing boundaries, engaging in boundedness, and configuring rings around the substantively empty category "white," while at the same time discursively constructing "others." The dominant white self can, therefore, only be understood in relation to the constructed other. Without it, the white self pales into nonexistence.[3]

Central, then, to the colonial discourse and the construction of whiteness in the United States is the idea of the "other" being wholly and hierarchically different from the white self. Discursively inventing the colonial other, for example, whites were parasitically producing an apparently stable Western, white self out of a previously nonexistent self. Gayatri Chakravorty Spivak (1985) argued, "Europe ... consolidated itself as sovereign subject by defining its colonies as 'others,' even as it constituted them for purposes of administration and the expansion of markets" (as cited in Frankenberg, 1993, p. 17). Thus the Western (i.e., white) self and the colonial "other" are products of this discursive construction.

One continuing effect of colonial discourse is the production of an unnamed, unmarked, white, Western self against which all others can be named and judged. It is the unnamed, unmarked, white self that must be deconstructed, named, and marked. We take up this challenge in this essay, as we argue that white male identity is indeed parasitically coproduced as white men continue to name and mark others, thereby naming and marking themselves. At a moment of economic crisis when white working-class males are being squeezed, the construction of others proliferates.[4]

Centered inside these constructions is the white male self—the male "under siege" in the economy, the community, and the family. We now turn to each of these sectors at their complex intersections as we explore the assault on historical privilege as white working-class men forge lives that increasingly appear to hang in the balance.

UNDER SIEGE IN THE ECONOMY

Although it is indeed the case that massive restructuring has taken place in the American economy and white working-class male jobs have been substantially reduced or pay less than they did before (Reich, 1991, 2002), the changes in the economy are due almost entirely to the concrete decisions made by elites in order to compete more profitably in the global market economy. It is the case that there has been some preferential hiring of people of color and that this accounts for some loss of jobs for white males, but the loss of jobs associated with affirmative action policies pales in comparison with job loss associated with massive restructuring and widespread deindustrialization (Perry 1987; Bluestone, & Harrison; Harrison & Bluestone, 1982).

It is most interesting, therefore, that not one of the white men we interviewed held elites accountable for the relocation of industry, closing of industries, and so forth. Rather the finger was always pointed at affirmative action policies that allegedly accorded preferential treatment to minorities, positioned differently as undeserving. This is why, according to white males, they are not working, or not working in jobs for which they feel entitled.

Because of the economy, many working-class white males have had, at times, to seek and obtain welfare benefits. What they do discursively with welfare is very important here. Welfare becomes a site wherein people of color are defined as lazy and undeserving, while at the same time, white men define themselves as hardworking and going on welfare only when absolutely necessary. This set of discursive constructions serves to draw their own boundaries at what constitutes acceptable conditions for "not working," welfare receipts, and government-sponsored programs, thus establishing a state of "boundedness." Having created an "other" who holds a set of unpleasant personal characteristics, white men can, then, at the same time, deny their own participation in the welfare state, their own experiences with unemployment, their own moments on the dole. Race affords them the opportunity to project and deny, defining themselves as the men who know how to take care of the family and not "live off the government." The subordination of women in these families is absolutely essential to the propping up of white working-class men vis-à-vis men of color. This set of discursively drawn distinctions, however, keeps white men from looking carefully at the real source of their difficulties — elites. It encourages them to trade on their whiteness, offers them a way of being white, and therefore dominant, at the expense of seriously analyzing the system and what it has, in fact, done to working-class white men. The white male critique is grounded fundamentally in the notion that people of color do not want to work.

LW: Are there tensions?

LARRY: Probably not so much between them [blacks and Hispanics], but like for us, they think, I mean, it gets me angry sometimes. I don't say I'm better than anybody else. But I work for the things that I have, and they [blacks and Hispanics] figure just because you're ahead, or you know more and you do more, [that it's] because you're white. And that's not really it. We're all equal, and I feel that what I've done, I've worked for myself to get to where I'm at.... If they would just really try instead of just kind of hanging out on the street corners. That's something that really aggravates me, to see while I'm rushing to get to work, and everybody is just kind of milling around doing nothing.

At the heart of the white male critique is the notion that people of color, blacks, in particular, simply do not wish to work, that they are lazy. We can hear the victory of psychology over economics in this explanation. Personal, moral attributions of blame thrive despite rampant evidence of private-sector and public-sector abandonment. This is juxtaposed to notions of self that assert that although white men may be out of a job, they always want to work. From this flows an overt racial critique of affirmative action programs, as well as a somewhat more racially coded critique of welfare abusers and cheats. We — actually they — take up the issue of affirmative action first.

PETE: For the most part, it hasn't been bad. It's just that right now with these minority quotas, I think more or less, the white male has become the new minority. And that's not to point a finger at the blacks, Hispanics, or the women. It's just that with all these quotas, instead of hiring the best for the job, you have to hire according to your quota system, which is still wrong.

LW: Do you have any sense of social movements? Like the Civil Rights Movement?
PETE: Civil rights, as far as I'm concerned, is being way out of proportion.
LW: Talk to me more about that.
PETE: Well, granted, the Afro-Americans were slaves over 200 years ago. They were given their freedom. We as a country, I guess you could say, has tried to, well, I can't say all of us, but most of us, have tried to, like, make things a little more equal. Try to smooth over some of the rough spots. You have some of these other, you have some of these militants who are now claiming that after all these years, we still owe them. I think the owing time is over for everybody. Because if we go into that, then the Poles are still owed [he is Polish]. The Germans are still owed. Jesus — the Jews are definitely still owed. I mean, you're, you're getting cremated, everybody wants to owe somebody. I think it's time to wipe that slate clean.

The critique of affirmative action (often referred to as "quotas") is that it is not "fair"; that it privileges blacks, Hispanics, and at times white women above the white male; and that this contradicts notions of equal opportunity and a flat playing field. It is noteworthy that nowhere in these narratives is there any recognition of the fact that white men as a group have been historically privileged, irrespective of individual merit.

When men give credence to affirmative action, they take highly essentialist forms. John, for example, felt that affirmative action programs "have their place," that they "shouldn't be completely out of the question." For example, he said, "Women can speak with women or children a lot better than men can" and "In the areas of crime, you have to have blacks and Hispanics working in community programs, so you have to have certain jobs and responsibilities where they can deal with people, like say, with people of their own race or background." In other words, women should be privileged for *certain* jobs dealing with women and children, and blacks and Hispanics should be privileged in jobs dealing with crime. That is where, he suggested, affirmative action is useful. In general, though, white men concur with Tom, who stated, "As soon as they [blacks] don't get a job, they yell discrimination. . . . But the ones who are really lazy, don't want it [to become educated and work one's way up], they start yelling discrimination so they can just get the job and they're not even qualified for it. And they might take it away from, whether it's a, you know, a woman or a [white] guy."

The assertions about affirmative action offer white men a way of "othering" African Americans, in particular. "We" whites, even though we might be unemployed, want to work. "They," blacks, just want a free ride — they just want to get the job without having to really work for it. This encourages the discursive coconstruction of blacks as lazy, as wanting a handout, unlike hardworking whites. This theme was further elaborated in discussions of welfare abusers and cheats.

AP: Have you ever applied for welfare?
RON: No.
AP: Or, have you ever had to?
RON: Never had to. I, probably very early in our marriage, when the first company I worked for, and they closed up. And we, we went through a period where we probably could have, had we applied, I think we would have been eligible. I mean, our income was really low enough that we probably should have.
AP: But you didn't. How come?
RON: I guess both of us pretty much feel the same way. You know, we look at welfare as being something less than admirable.
AP: And that's what it would have amounted to for you? Sort of less than admirable?

RON: Yeah, I think, had we been any lower, as far as income and gotten to the point where we absolutely couldn't even afford to eat. I mean, I'm not opposed to doing what I have to do.... But, to me, it should be a strictly a last resort. I think the welfare system is very much abused.

AP: Can you talk to me a little about that?

RON: Well, ... I think for the most part, I think most people get out of life what they put into it. You know, because some people have more obstacles than others, there's no doubt about it. But I think a lot of people just expect things to come to them, and when it doesn't, you know, they've got the government to fall back on.... You know, I think it [falling back on the government] is more common for black people.... I mean social services, in general, I think, is certainly necessary, and Sheila [wife] and I have taken advantage of them. We've got food stamps several times.... But, you know, as soon as I was able to get off it, I did. And not for any noble reasons, but just, you know, I think I'd rather be able to support myself than have things handed to me.

CC: What do you think of welfare?

TOM: I think it's good for people who deserve it. And I think there's a lot of people that don't deserve it. The system stinks. If you're on welfare, I think if you're willing to work, I think the ... you know, I think the state should, I mean look out here, there's a lot of things that need to be cleaned up. Let 'em clean the streets; let 'em do something. Just don't let 'em sit at home and just collect their check. There's some that can't [work]. There's some who deserve it and they have to ... for the most part, yeah. I mean, if you deserved it, fine. But if you don't, don't play the system.

Katherine Newman's (1993, p. 89) insights are particularly helpful here.

American culture is allergic to the idea that impersonal forces control individual destiny. Rather we prefer to think of our lives as products of our own efforts. Through hard work, innate ability and competition, the good prosper and the weak drop by the wayside. Accordingly, the end results in peoples' lives — their occupations, material possessions, and the recognition accorded by friends and associates — are proof of the underlying stuff of which they are made. Of course, when the fairy tale comes true, the flip side of merito-cratic individualism emerges with full force. Those who prosper — the morally superior — deserve every bit of their material comfort.

White men, then, script poor blacks as deserving of their plight and unwilling to work, whereas they [white men] "sincerely" strive for the American Dream. They, that is, white men, are coconstructed as highly deserving, willing to work, and eager to participate in the American economy.

Although there are some exceptions to this, the primary function of discussions about welfare abusers is to draw the boundaries of acceptable welfare receipt *at themselves* — the hardworking white man who is trying to support his family. Pete, for example, stated, "There's definitely some people who abuse the system, I can see that. But then there are people who, when you need it, you know, it's like they have something to fall back on. And they're [the caseworkers] basically shoving everybody into one category. They're [all welfare recipients] all users. But these [the caseworkers] are the same people that if the county closes them off, they won't have a job, and they're going to be there next too." Because most of the caseworkers are white, Pete is discursively aligning himself with the hardworking people who have just fallen on hard times, unlike the abusers, largely black, who exploit the system. His criticism of the caseworkers is that they treat all welfare recipients as cheats, as African Americans, thus denying differential positionality vis-à-vis welfare.

The discussions of affirmative action and welfare abuse enable white men to draw distinctions between themselves and a largely black "other," whom they discursively construct as lazy, unwilling to do what is necessary to get a job, and more than happy to take advantage of government handouts, including affirmative action programs, which they script as a handout, as going to those undeserving. In discursively constructing a black "other," white men simultaneously construct themselves as hardworking and going on welfare and accepting government help only when absolutely necessary.

This splitting of "self" and "other" is reminiscent of Weis's (1990) working-class white high school boys. Boys in Freeway High constructed the black "other" as highly sexualized and drug prone. This construction at one and the same time served to authorize white boys as clean, respectful of women, and definitely heterosexual. Beyond high school, into young adulthood, these discursive constructions layer on top of one another, so that black men, in particular, are now discursively constructed as lazy, unwilling to work, and so forth. This weaves through the high school constructions revolving around drugs and sexuality, ultimately leaving young white men highly resentful not only of blacks in general, whom they see as drug prone, oversexualized, and lazy, but also of affirmative action programs, in particular, which they feel privileges inferior human beings. This, then, is social critique to white men. Interestingly enough, it leaves totally unexamined and even unrecognized the role of whites who self-consciously closed industries or enabled legislation that moved capital across state and international borders, thus interrupting and ultimately displacing far more white male jobs than affirmative action ever could (or has) (Bluestone & Harrison, 1982; Perry, 1987).

Under Siege in the Neighborhood

A felt assault invades the perceptions of many white men in talk about their neighborhoods as they begin to express a sense of no longer belonging or that their neighborhood is "deteriorating" — further evidence that it is no longer a space that belongs to them in both physical and psychological terms. Most often this encroaching instability is attributed to an influx of blacks or Hispanics who they clearly position as the other. Larry said,

> I really feel — I'm not going to say out of place. I do. I've grown up in the neighborhood [the Italian west side], but I don't really feel as though I belong here anymore. I don't know, not strictly because I'm a white male, and there's not many of us. I mean, there's not really that many in my neighborhood that I can say, "Well, I have a neighbor, the guy who lives next door to me or the somebody across the street." There is, I'm kind of like the minority. I'm, I don't really, there's not a lot of people I associate with. There's some people I'll say hello to, or, you know, you talk with your neighbors to associate.

A focus group discussion with three men in a west-side church uncovered similar sentiments:

CC: What was it like when you guys were little?
RON: I think it was different — ten times different.
CRAIG: What did happen? What did you see happen?
RON: I just seen more kids on the streets, more of them starting to dress up like the rappers on TV, white kids, black kids, Hispanic, it didn't matter. I just seen, you know, more hanging out.
PETE: The west side has always been like a low-income type of area, and it's always been a tough neighborhood. But what I think is, more or less, it's getting more violent. We both

went to Belton [high school], so we know what it's like to grow up in kind of like a tough atmosphere, but nothing like it is now. There's a lot of drug dealing, a lot of guns.

RON: The thing is, they're getting younger.

PETE: Thirteen, 14-year-old kids are carrying guns. It's really not that out in the open, but you hear about it. You hear about the shootings.... There was a rape at School 16 [elementary school], maybe about a month ago. I heard it on the news.

RON: I did see a drug bust. As a matter of fact, right on my street. The cop more or less blocked me in my driveway, because they just pull up, and they park unmarked cars, and they just rushed into a couple of houses down.

Ron, in an individual interview, elaborated as follows:

RON: Just look at the school. It's just ... you know ... and you hear the loud music all over the place now. I mean, it's not as bad as I might be making it sound ... but ... my car got broken into, stuff like that ... that never happened back then.

Q: It didn't?

RON: Uh uh. I'd say up to 4 or 5 years ago, it didn't happen.

Q: Interesting. What proportion of the people are still Italian?

RON: There's a lot of older ones still there. Um, oh, my God, I'd say 30 to 40%.

Q: Still? Well that's quite high then.

RON: See, you have the lower west side and the upper west side, say ... you know what I'm talking about ... that's predominantly Puerto Rican. The upper west side still has got a lot of Italians through there.

Q: But you said a lot of the Puerto Ricans and blacks are moving into the upper west side?

RON: Oh yeah, they're coming. I mean, which is ... which is fine. I have no problem with that. A lot of Italians are moving to the north side, so that's starting to be Italian Heaven over there. But there's been a definite change, no doubt about it.

Ron is interesting because he is a border crosser in the sense that his girlfriend (whom he later became engaged to) is Puerto Rican. However this presents no conceptual difficulty for him because she is among those Puerto Rican families that have been there for a while and who also object to the new Puerto Ricans and blacks moving in. He noted, "Yeh, she'll talk to me. Coming from her mouth herself, she would say the same thing I did. It's really sad I can't walk through my old neighborhood, you know, it's really sick. It's ignorant, you know. They, her family, feels the same way. Her mother, because her mother doesn't have a car, so she has to walk a lot of places, and she knows what's going on."

Dave, who during the course of our interview let us know that he was Native American, said the following:

DAVE: It was a real friendly neighborhood. I lived on Janick and Northwood Avenue, and at the time, it was a predominantly Italian neighborhood. It was very close knit. I mean, you could leave your doors open and bikes unchained, and all that kind of stuff, and now it's not like that anymore.

Q: How is it different?

DAVE: Well, now it's a Hispanic and black neighborhood, and you practically have to ... you know ... chain things up, nail them down, put bolts on them, and it's something that shouldn't be ... we should all be able to live together and respect each other's personal artifacts, whatever they are.

Many of the white men interviewed hope to exit the areas they define as "under siege" as soon as they can. In Larry's case, he bought some land in a suburb where his two brothers live, because he cannot imagine raising children where he currently resides. Several others plan to move to the suburbs, or to North Buffalo, when they are married, and especially when they have children. This will not necessarily be easy to accomplish, because many are living in properties owned by their parents, properties bought with monies that white privilege was able to amass in the parental generation, when white men were easily able to secure full-time work in industry. Those who foresee staying in the city are working to establish block clubs, neighborhood watches, and small-scale organizations designed to patrol the borders of their communities. Tom, for example, is very active in the block club in his community.

Q: What is the purpose of the block club?
TOM: To watch the neighborhood. You know, if you see trouble happening, to call 911. Or, if one of the neighbors is having a problem, you know, it's better to come out in groups, you know, don't cause any violence.... And you know, if we see somebody else, like the lady across the street is an older elderly lady. And we watch for her. You know, we see somebody strange up that driveway or at her house, you know, we'll confront them. We'll ask them [who they are]. And I think that shows too. I think people see that.

Although he narrated this as very supportive, and indeed it is in many ways, the borders they are patrolling are those basically encasing the white community against encroaching "others." It is whiteness that people are attempting to protect in these neighborhoods. This does not deny the fact that some blacks live in white neighborhoods as well but rather points out that in these white neighborhoods bordered by the "other," it is the other against whom white communities are attempting to protect themselves. This is also not to ignore the fact that several families of color live in these white neighborhoods but rather to note that these families are considered settled—as "just like us" in the case of the "Spanish" family who lived in the Italian neighborhood. It is the racial "other"—the "other" constructed as lazy, violent, dangerous, not working, hanging around—that is at issue here. And it is this group to whom block clubs are formed in response. Tom said, "If I move, it's going to be because I want to move, not because the kids are going to force me out. You know, I'm not afraid of the kids. I'm not afraid of, you know, people moving in. You know, I'm not afraid of the colored [sic] coming in. They don't bother me. If I'm going to move, it will be because [I want to]." In the meantime, he is organizing with other white men and white women to patrol the borders of his neighborhood, a relatively "safe space," from the onslaught of the "other."

Some, like Bill, recognized that the block clubs can engage in seemingly racist practices:

Q: Do you belong to any groups of any kind?
BILL: No, none.
Q: Any groups that, like anything that tries to change the community? Like, do you belong to a block club?
BILL: Um, the block club I won't join.... I totally hate their views. I mean, they're like, "Get them out, kick their ass," just ...
Q: Who is saying "Get them out, kick their ass?"
BILL: Oh, people who live a few doors from me. And they're very prejudiced.
Q: So, they're whites?
BILL: Yeah.
Q: Whites want to kick out the blacks.
BILL: Exactly. It doesn't matter to them if they're good or bad. You know if they're renters or

owners. They just want them out. And talking to them, I mean their views on good white people is ridiculous, because there's a few streets over, um, off William, and he, well, the guy who, whose main view, he loves that area because it's mostly white.

Q: Is that a place called Kaisertown?

BILL: No. It's off of William by the Dolsky Center. About half way to the Dolsky Center. And, I mean, it's equivalency, it's the equivalency of black people, black kids running around in their underwear, where, here's white kids running around in their underwear. It's like, he thinks it's a much better area. Why, because you can buy your crack there? Which, he does.

White men then take up a protectionist stance in an effort to secure their "turf" from assault in a time of increasing racial diversification and, with that, the fracturing of white working-class neighborhoods. Block clubs emerge as freely organized and co-opted spaces for group meeting and exchange designed to bolster the community, but they also exist as site for the deployment of tactical strategies meant to arm the neighborhood against the other. A "good" community initiative in the interests of engagement across difference thus doubles as a legitimate form of border patrolling. Initiatives on the part of white working-class men need, then, to be seen as counterstrategies for reclaiming lost power and privilege in their communities which they perceive as being under immediate threat of dislocation.

UNDER SIEGE IN THE HOME: CONTESTING GENDER ROLES

White working-class men express strong sentiment about the family and, specifically, about male roles and responsibilities within the family. The family is idealized and even valorized, at least in theory, if not altogether in practice. Men, who have lost real material space inside shop-floor culture, turn to the family and attempt to assert or reassert dominance in that realm. Although this may have always been the case, as Lillian Rubin (1976) and others have argued about the working-class family, the move to sustain dominance in the white working-class home is particularly key at this moment in time when there are genuine material losses in other spheres of working-class life. Men no longer have a clear-cut material sphere in which they can assert lived power. Working-class men are forced, in a sense, into a symbolic realm, the realm of family, which is not their material space, in order to assert a form of symbolic dominance. Turning to the family as the symbolic domain of male power, they insist or reinsist on reclaiming gender privilege. Much of the patrolling of the borders of community must be seen in these terms as well. The borders of community as patrolled by white men are drawn in the name of the family — men are protecting their wives and children (all of whom are constructed as absolutely less than men) from what they construct as an encroaching assault. Thus they envelop the family sphere within their own symbolic dominance, a dominance that they substitute, although not wholly consciously or completely, for their former authority in the material realm.

We conducted the next set of conversations in a focus group in an Italian church located in one of the borderlands of Buffalo. The family is absolutely essential to the construction of manhood in these narratives and, indeed, to the propping up of the discourse of masculinity inside working-class culture:

CC: What do you think the role of the family is right now?

PETE: I think there is definitely a fall in the American family right now.

RON: That's the major contributor to any of the problems, I think.

PETE: What I see it is, is it used to be a man could work, make a paycheck, and the woman could stay home and be a housewife, but now you need either two incomes or a man cannot support the family, he cannot get a job to support the family, so he bolts, he leaves, and goes on his own, and that's what I see.... He takes the easy way out. All the other pressures of the world ...

CC: What other pressures?

PETE: The age itself. Men are tempted away from their wives; wives are tempted away from their husbands because of sex.

CC: Is that new, though?

RON: No. It's not new, but it's more frequent now because of everything — it's just thrown at you no matter what. You could watch TV and you could just turn it — I mean even regular cable — and you could see some gross stuff, even for kids, you know. It's the temptation of bad. It's the temptation of money and it's just, you know, it's the temptation of well, I've got to please myself first.

CC: What do you think is going to happen to the family in the future? Is it going to get better or worse?

RON: I hate to say it, I don't think it's going to get better.

Pete and Ron attribute what they see as the fall in the American family to a variety of factors. In fact, we hear them searching for explanations as they scan popular culture (cable TV), commodified sex, and the lack of jobs. However, it is clear in these narratives that the linchpin of the family is the man as breadwinner and protector of wife and children. The economy and popular culture have made that difficult because two people now need to earn a wage, and sex tempts both men and women away from family commitments. Thus there is a moral component to the breakdown of the American family as well. But the male as provider must, they argue, be restored if the family is to regain its strength. There is a clear valorization of traditional gender-based roles, without which the family is undermined.

CC: Do you think that the roles of men and women are now changing to some extent because of the changes in the family and the changes in society?

PETE: Definitely. There is more of a leadership role for women.

RON: There is nothing wrong — I mean I agree with women being able to be independent and stuff like that, but the women's lib, when that started, it really threw things into a little bit of chaos too because, like you said, the family. For one thing, it took the mother out of the family.

PETE: Right. The role of the woman has definitely changed because the woman has to work now.

RON: Now there are babysitters or the baby is at day care all day long.

PETE: I think for one thing, the roles have changed because again, of the single parent households. There is a lot of that, and the mother has to be the father and the mother at the same time.

RON: Yeah that's true.

PETE: And it's very hard for a mother to discipline a teenage boy.

RON: You need two parents.

CC: Given everything that you just said right now, what is the meaning of maleness?

PETE: First of all, I think the meaning of maleness is more than, you know, helping to produce a child. I still think that the meaning of maleness is to go out, earn a living, support a family. I still feel that should be the meaning of maleness. I don't know if it is, I really don't think it is.

RON: Just like pretty much what he said. Just to keep — a real man will keep what he believes in and not stray from it to please everybody. He'll get a wife. He'll love her unconditionally and she, in return, will respect him and want to do things for him, and vice versa, and just to follow the example of maybe the church or of Christ. That's pretty much it. Just an unselfish provider willing to sacrifice for his family, or sacrifice for whoever, and not take everyone else's values, to please the other person.

PETE: I think they should be responsible. The male should be more responsible for the family.

RON: Right, exactly. That's what he is in society. Like it was back in the days — like the *Leave It to Beaver* times, when the man went out, and the woman stayed home.

PETE: I think that's when there were really no problems in America. I don't know, I wasn't there, but from what I see, it seemed like everything was better.

Men reclaim their waning dominance in the material sector by centering the family in their collective memory of the past as youth coming of age, from which point they move toward its valorization as the main resource for financial, but, even more to the point, emotional, support. These same men continue to draw on their memories and present experiences as they pin their hopes for the future on family as well, protecting their own marriages and their own families while attempting to build lives in neighborhoods and communities in proximity to family and kin.

Conversation that captures the importance of the intact family sets the stage for discussion of the central role played by men in the household as they argue their significance to the home space despite the fact that they understand themselves as only symbolically dominant therein. In other words, these men are left to reclaim the waning privileges of male dominance through a traditional vocabulary of gender roles and relationships:

Q: What's the most important thing in terms of life?
PETE: Family.
Q: Why?
PETE: Because that's your flesh and blood. That's who you grew up with. That's who loves you the most. That's your most trusted, prize possession, your family. That is the most important thing in my life.
Q: Anything else?
PETE: Belief in God and sticking together as a family, and that's basically it.

The centrality of family to the provision of emotional support inside working-class culture is best captured in Pete's admission of family as "your most trusted, prize possession." Attaching material value to the family unit allows white working-class men to position the family as the fulcrum point on which masculine domination hinges. This line of argument is sustained inside Tom's attention to the family as provider of emotional support whose example makes the future possible.

Q: Could you have predicted that your family would have been so important to you? Do you come from a family where your family is . . . ?
TOM: Yes, Yes. Even though my sisters — like I said, the one sister — I mean, we . . . I'm still close. I mean, if she calls me to do something, I'll still do it for her. My parents were close . . .
Q: So you're not surprised to see this in yourself?
TOM: No. My father's brothers and sisters, my mother, on her side, the cousins and that, we're just close. . . . I mean, it just goes from brother and sister, from wife and kids to brother and the whole family.

Establishing the foundational aspects of the family unit, these white working-class men are able to build an argument that validates male authority, albeit symbolic, inside the home. Normalization of working-class cultural forms mandates a vocabulary that subscribes to the traditional sexual division of labor inside the home. Out of these terms, white working-class men position themselves as bordered by white women whom they see as not being in their correct place. Men are trying hard to reassert male dominance in the home, attempting to make certain that they maintain dominance in this symbolic realm. In other words, although the space materially belongs, in large measure, to women, and the men wish it to stay that way, they want to make it absolutely clear that they are dominant symbolically. They are the head of the household even though they do not materially inhabit or take care of the household in ways they expect of their women. Although this has always gone on, the depth to which this is being asserted, we would argue, is due to the erosion of dominance in their own material space, shop floors, and so forth in the wage labor sector.

References

Arnot, M. (2004). Male working class identities and social justice: A reconsideration of Paul Willis' "Learning to Labour" in light of contemporary research. In N. Dolby & G. Dimitriadis (Eds.), *Learning to labour in new times*. Routledge: New York, 17–40.

Aronowitz, S. (1992). *The politics of identity*. New York: Routledge.

Asante, M. K. (1990). *Kemet Afrocentricity and knowledge*. Trenton, NJ: Africa World Press.

Asante, M. K., & Mattson, M. T. (1991). *Historical and cultural atlas of Africans*. New York: Maxwell Macmillan International.

Bluestone, B., & Harrison, B. (1982). *The deindustrialization of America: Plant closing, community abandonment, and the dismantling of basic industry*. New York: Basic Books.

Cesaire, A. (1947). *Cahier d'un retour au pays natal*. New York: Brentano's.

Cesaire, A. (1962). *Discourse sur colonialisme*. Paris: Presence Africaine.

Cesaire, A. (1969). *Return to my native land*. Baltimore: Penguin Books.

Connell, R. W. (1995). *Masculinities*. Cambridge: Polity Press.

Connell, R. W. (2000). Arms and the man: Using the new research on masculinity to understand violence and promote peace in the contemporary world. In I. Breines, R. Connell, & I. Eide (Eds.), *Male roles, masculinities and violence: A culture of peace perspective*. UNESCO: Paris.

Fanon, F. (1963). *The wretched of the earth*. New York: Grove Press.

Fanon, F. (1967a). *Black skin, white masks*. New York: Grove Weidenfeld.

Fanon, F. (1967b). *Pour la revolution*. New York: Africaine Monthly Review Press.

Fine, M. (1993). Sexuality, schooling, and adolescent females: The missing discourse of desire. In L. Weis & M. Fine (Eds.), *Beyond silenced voices: Class, race, and gender in United States schools*. Albany: State University of New York Press.

Fine, M., & Weis, L. (1998). *The unknown city*. Boston: Beacon Press.

Foucault, M. (1980). *The history of sexuality* (Vol. 1). New York: Vintage Press.

Frankenberg, R. (1993). *White women, race matters: The social construction of whiteness*. Minneapolis: University of Minnesota Press.

Harrison, B., & Bluestone, B. (1988). *The great U-turn: Corporate restructuring and polarizing of America*. New York: Basic Books.

Herrnstein, R. J. (1994). *The bell curve: Intelligence and class structure in American life*. New York: Free Press.

hooks, b. (1989). *Talking back, thinking feminist, thinking black*. Boston: South End Press.

Jackson, C. (2002). "Laddishness" as a self-worth protection strategy. *Gender and Education*, 14(1), 37–51.

Lesko, N. (1988). *Symbolizing society: Stories, rites and structure in a Catholic high school*. New York: Falmer.

McCarthy, C., Rodriquez, A., Meecham, S., David, S., Wilson-Brown, C., Godina, H., Supryia, K. E., & Buendia, E. (2004). Race, suburban resentment, and the representation of the inner city in contemporary film and television. In M. Fine, L. Weis, L. P. Pruitt, & A. Burns (Eds.), *Off white: Readings on power, privilege, and resistance* (2nd ed.). New York: Routledge.

Memmi, A. (1965). *The colonizer and the colonized*. Boston: Beacon Press.

Michelson, R. A., Smith, S. S., & Oliver, M. L. (1993). Breaking through the barriers: African American job candidates and the academic hiring process. In L. Weis & M. Fine (Eds.), *Beyond silenced voices*. Albany: State University of New York Press.

Mohanty, C. T. (1988). Under Western eyes: Feminist scholarship and colonial discourses. *Feminist Review*, 30, 61–88.

Morrison, T. (1992). *Playing in the dark: Whiteness and the literary imagination*. Cambridge, MA: Harvard University Press.

Newman, K. S. (1993). *Declining fortunes: The withering of American Dream*. New York: Basic Books.

Oliver, M., & Shapiro, T. (1997). *Black wealth, white wealth: A new perspective on racial inequality*. New York: Routledge.

Perry, D. (1987). The politics of dependency in deindustrializing America: The case of Buffalo, New York. In M. Smith & J. Feagin (Eds.), *The capitalist city: Global restructuring and community politics*. Oxford (Oxfordshire) and New York: Basil Blackwell.

Price-Mars, J. (1928). *Ainsi parla l'oncle*. Port Au Prince: Imprinerie du Comparegne.

Reich, R. (1991). *The work of nations*. London: Simon and Schuster.

Reich, R. (2002). *The future of success*. New York: Alfred Knopf.

Roediger, D. R. (1991). *The wages of whiteness: Race and the making of the American working class*. New York: Verso.

Rollins, J. (1985). *Between women: Domestics and their employers*. Philadelphia: Temple University Press.

Roman, L. G. (1993). White is a color! White defensiveness, postmodernism, and anti-racist pedagogy. In C. McCarthy & W. Crichlow (Eds.), *Race, identity, and representation in education*. New York: Routledge.

Rubin, L. (1976). *Worlds of pain*. New York: Basic Books.

Sanday, P. (1990). *Fraternity gang rape: Sex, brotherhood, and privilege on campus*. New York: New York University Press.

Senghor, L. (1961). *Nation et voi Africaine du Socialisme*. Paris: Presence Africaine.

Smith, D. E. (1988). Femininity as discourse. In L. G. Roman & L. K. Christian-Smith (Eds.), *Becoming feminine: The politics of popular culture*. Philadelphia: Falmer Press.

Spivak, G. C. (1990). Can the subaltern speak? In S. Harasym (Ed.), *The post-colonial critic: Issues, strategies, dialogues* (pp. 271–313). New York: Routledge.

Trinh, M. (1989). *Woman, native, other*. Bloomington: University of Indiana Press.

Valli, L. (1986). *Becoming clerical workers*. Boston: Routledge and Kegan Paul.

Walkerdine, V., Lacey, H., & Melody, J. (2001). *Growing up girl*. New York: New York University Press.

Wallace, C. (1987). *For richer, for poorer: Growing up in and out of work*. London, New York: Tavistock.

Weis, L. (1990). *Working class without work: High school students in a de-industrializing economy.* New York: Routledge.

Willis, P. (1977). *Learning to labour: How working class kids get working class jobs.* Farnborough, England: Saxon House.

Wilson, W. J. (1980). *The declining significance of race: Blacks and changing American institutions.* Chicago: University of Chicago Press.

Wong, M. (1994). Di(s)-secting and di(s)-closing whiteness: "Two tales from psychology." *Feminism and Psychology, 4,* 133–153.

NOTE

This study is supported through generous funds from the Spencer Foundation.

1. A similar erosion of privilege existed for white males in the southern United States after the Civil War. This era found white men "retaliating" for their felt loss of privilege through the organization of hate groups like the Ku Klux Klan.

2. The now classic works of Frantz Fanon, *Black Skin, White Masks* (1967a) and *The Wretched of the Earth* (1963) and Albert Memmi's (1965) *The Colonizer and the Colonized* have undertaken the delicate task of providing a psychological analysis of the colonial identity complex of both the colonizer and the colonized. These authors have laid the foundation for African American and white scholars to examine the complex nature of racial identity as it intersects with class and gender in the current discourse on the loss of privilege inside the culture of white working-class males.

3. The European construction of the colonized identity has given voice to scholars of color who earlier in the 20th century began to question its validity. Authors of Negritude, among them Aime Cesaire (1947, 1962), Leopold Senghor (1961), and Jean Price-Mars (1928), have asked the question—Are we French or are we black?—in protest of the French Metropolitan practice of linguistic and cultural imperialism. This movement has given rise to an impressive body of work that deconstructs the identity construction of Caribbean as well as North and West Africans under French colonial or neocolonial domination, legislating French colonialist identification as the "superior white."

4. One might speculate as to the extent to which these proliferations are linked to social change. One might speculate, for example, that the intensification of such co-productions is strongly linked historically to economic crisis and/or colonial expansion. One could empirically examine this claim.

ELEVEN

Affirmative Action: Diversity, Merit, and the Benefit of White People

Faye J. Crosby and Stacy Blake-Beard

Affirmative action means different things to different people. For too many Americans over too many years the words have connoted a clash of interests between majority and minority ethnic groups or between men and women. Certainly, Whites have been less active in their support of affirmative action than people of color have, and men have been less active than women (Sincharoen & Crosby, 2001). Among African Americans and Latinos, furthermore, the stronger a person's ethnic identity, the stronger the support for affirmative action. This association has been interpreted as being consistent with "realistic group conflict" theory (Schmermund, Sellers, Mueller, & Crosby, 2001). Until recently, most people seem to have assumed that White men stand to gain little from affirmative action.

We are two women — one White, one Black — who believe that Whites (including men) and men (including Whites) have as much to gain from affirmative action as do people of color (including women) and women (including those of color). Our point in this essay is to explain why. In the process, we aim to explain what affirmative action is and how it operates in education and employment and to explicate the recent Supreme Court decisions in *Gratz v. Bollinger* and *Grutter v. Bollinger* (2003).

Our essay has three sections. In the first section we outline the basics of affirmative action in employment and education. In the second section we discuss at length the reasoning of the Supreme Court in the two recent court cases, in which, for the first time, those who set policy have given serious attention to the argument that affirmative action programs benefit Whites. In the Michigan cases, the benefits have been framed in terms of diversity. Such a framing makes it easy to imagine that diversity is achieved by sacrificing, or at least by bending, considerations of merit. In the final section of our essay, we argue that one of the major benefits of affirmative action for majority individuals is that it creates and sustains a real meritocracy to a far greater extent than does so-called equal opportunity. Throughout our essay we rely on data collected in systematic social scientific studies, but we conclude by acknowledging how our interpretations of the accumulated data may be influenced by the realities of our personal lives as citizens in the United States.

What Is Affirmative Action?

General

Although infrequently articulated, a general definition of affirmative action is not usually contested. Affirmative action occurs whenever an organization goes out of its way to ensure the equal treatment of people of all ethnicities and of either sex (Crosby, 2004). Although sharing the goals of equal opportunity, affirmative action differs from simple equal opportunity policies in several ways (Crosby, 1994). First, affirmative action entails the expenditure of effort and resources; equal opportunity is more passive. Second, affirmative action is planful and forward looking, requiring organizations to monitor their existing actions and outcomes and to anticipate future problems, whereas equal opportunity is reactive, requiring corrective actions only after a problem has been alleged or discovered. Finally affirmative action requires that organizations be cognizant of the ethnic and gender characteristics of people, whereas equal opportunity does not. Indeed, equal opportunity seeks to encourage a "color blind" and "gender blind" approach (Brown et al., 2003).

In Business

In business, the classic form of affirmative action derives from Executive Order 11246, signed in 1965 by Lyndon Johnson. EO 11246 applies only to firms that are federal contractors, and only to firms larger than a certain size (with more than 50 employees) that have a contract with the federal government in excess of a certain amount ($50,000). EO 11246 requires federal contractors to be affirmative action employers. To be an affirmative action employer, the firm must have an affirmative action plan that allows it to monitor its workforce. Following prescribed methods, the firm must match incumbency against availability of workers in the targeted classes, including women (as contrasted with men) and African Americans, Hispanic Americans, Native Americans, and Asian Americans (as contrasted with Whites). Availability is usually calculated using government statistics broken down by job classification. When incumbency is too low, relative to availability, remedial or corrective action must be taken. If the action does not produce a result, no penalty is imposed — so long as the firm can demonstrate that it is making a good faith effort.

In Education

Affirmative action in education operates in a general sense in much the same way that it operates in employment. When a school notices that the percentages of ethnic minority students (or, in the past, women) who matriculate or who graduate are smaller than one would expect, the school may take steps to correct the situation. Race-sensitive admissions plans constitute one type of affirmative action in higher education. Outreach programs and specialized scholarships and financial aide are other ways in which many universities and colleges seek to correct the unbalanced numbers.

The University of California (UC) presents a good example of affirmative action in higher education. Currently, the UC has eight undergraduate campuses, serving more than 150,000 undergraduate students. The UC is part of a three-tier system of public higher education; the other two parts of which are the California State College system and the community college system. By law and by practice, the university is supposed to admit the top 12.5% of eligible students graduating from the high schools in California. The state colleges are less selective, and the community colleges are not at all selective but are open to any high school graduate. The UC enjoys many more resources than the state colleges or the community colleges, and a degree from any one of the UC campuses is thought to be more prestigious than a degree from any one of the state colleges.

For a number of years, a formula was used to determine whether a student should be counted as being in the top 12.5% of graduating high school students. The formula took into account standardized test scores and grades, weighted by whether the course was an advanced placement course. In addition, to be eligible for admission to the UC, a high school student was required to have taken a curriculum of courses in the humanities, social sciences, and natural sciences. A statewide board reviewed the course offerings at each high school and granted or withheld approval for specific courses to be accredited for the purposes of determining eligibility.

Careful self-monitoring at the UC in the late 1980s and early 1990s revealed some disturbing patterns. Far more ethnic minority students were in the top 12.5% of high school graduates than were matriculating at the UC. One major problem had to do with the eligibility requirements. Some of the high schools were so poor that they failed to offer the complete spectrum of accredited courses needed for eligibility. The poor schools tended to serve ethnic minority communities. Further investigation also revealed that, on average, White students were advantaged relative to ethnic minority students in another way as well. White students disproportionately attend schools with a relatively great number of advanced placement courses. Because grades achieved in an advanced placement course were awarded more points than the same grades in a comparable nonadvanced placement course, the more advanced placement courses a student could take, the better would be the students' chances of ranking at the top of all grading seniors in the state.

Once the problems were detected, corrective measures were instituted. Rather than using only one path, determined by one formula, the UC instituted a system allowing various paths to admission. Now students who do extremely well on the standardized tests can gain admission, even if they have not taken all the eligibility requirements. Similarly, students with a GPA in the top 4% of their high school gain automatic admission.

Nationwide, race-sensitive admissions plans may affect as many as 6.5 million Americans. Approximately 13 million Americans attend a 4-year institution. About half of the 4-year colleges and universities in the United States are selective in the sense of not admitting 100% of the applicants.

Of course, where affirmative action has been most hotly debated has been in the truly competitive institutions. In their landmark study, *The Shape of the River*, William Bowen, former president of Princeton University, and Derek Bok, former president of Harvard, determined that race-sensitive admissions programs at 28 elite institutions on the East Coast resulted in a decrease in a White applicant's chances of being admitted — causing it to drop from 26.5% chance of admission to 25% chance (Bowen & Bok, 1998; Vars & Bowen, 1998).

THE DIVERSITY ARGUMENT: *GRATZ V. BOLLINGER* AND *GRUTTER V. BOLLINGER*

Background

In October 1997, two White students, Jennifer Gratz and Patrick Hamacher, filed a lawsuit against the University of Michigan because they had been denied admission to the undergraduate college (see Table 11.1). Applicants of color with lower test scores and grades than theirs had been admitted to the school, and so Gratz and Hamacher claimed "reverse discrimination."

Table 11.1 Dates and Events Related the University of Michigan Cases

October 1997	Jennifer Gratz and Patrick Hamacher filed a lawsuit against the University of Michigan, challenging undergraduate admissions in federal district court (Patrick Duggan, judge).
December 1997	Barbara Grutter filed a lawsuit against the law school in federal district court (Bernard Friedman, judge).
February and March 1998	Judges Duggan and Friedman both denied motions to intervene.
August 1999	Sixth Circuit Court of Appeals reversed both district courts' order and allowed intervention. The cases were delayed months to allow for discovery.
November 2000	Oral arguments were heard for summary judgment in the *Gratz* case.
December 2000	Judge Duggan ruled that the admissions policy in place from 1995 to 1998 failed to pass constitutional muster but that the current plan did meet the criteria specified in *Bakke*.
December 2000	Oral arguments were heard for summary judgment in the *Grutter* case. Judge Friedman decided to hold a limited trial.
January and February 2001	*Grutter* trail was held.
March 2001	Judge Friedman ruled against the law school at the University of Michigan.
May 2001	Supreme Court declined to review University of Washington case, in which race-conscious admissions were upheld.
June 2001	Supreme Court declined to review the *Hopwood* case, which struck down the race-conscious policy of University of Texas Law School.
October 2001	Sixth Circuit Court of Appeals granted motion to hear the Michigan cases en banc.
November 2001	University of Georgia announced that it would not seek review of the Eleventh Circuit's decision against its admissions policy.
May 2002	Sixth Circuit overturned Friedman's ruling in *Grutter* and found that the law school's plan was, after all, constitutional.
August 2002	Grutter asked for review by Supreme Court.
December 2002	Supreme Court granted *certiorari* for *Gratz* (on constitutional grounds only) and for *Grutter*.
April 2003	Supreme Court heard oral arguments.
June 2003	Supreme Court rendered decisions.

Gratz and Hamacher charged that the university had denied their constitutional rights to equal treatment, without regard to any sort of group membership. Two months later another White citizen, Barbara Grutter, filed a similar complaint against the University of Michigan because she had been denied admission to its law school. Like Gratz and Hamacher, Grutter asserted that the university had trammeled the rights guaranteed by the equal protection clause of the 14th amendment to the Constitution.

After considerable legal wrangling, both cases made their way to Federal District Courts for the Eastern Division of Michigan. The *Gratz* (undergraduate) case was assigned to Judge Patrick Duggan; the *Grutter* (law school) case went to Judge Bernard Friedman. In December 2000, Judge Duggan rendered his decision. He held that the undergraduate admissions plan of the university was constitutional, although the plan that had been in place from 1995 to 1998 (hence affecting Jennifer Gratz and Patrick Hamacher) was not. The *Grutter* case, decided in March 2001, had the opposite outcome, with Judge Friedman finding that the law school had violated the equal protection clause.

Observers noted that the different decisions seemed to mirror the political orientations of the two different judges. It was also true that the law school's admission plan was not the same as that of the College of Literature, Science, and the Arts. The law school admits about 350 students each year from an applicant pool numbering about 3,500. Meanwhile, between 9,000 and 10,000 students are admitted to the undergraduate school each year. Law school students came from all over the United States. The undergraduates at the University of Michigan came predominantly from the state. With its smaller numbers, the law school conducted reviews of applicants that were individualized and to a certain degree, subjective. The College of Literature, Science, and the Arts, in contrast, used a point system. Applicants were granted points for various achievements along different dimensions. Up to 110 points could be gained on the basis of academic factors; 10 points went to students who had attended academically strong schools and another 8 points were awarded for attending difficult courses. Between 1 and 4 points were granted to legacies, depending on which relatives had attended the school. At issue were the 20 points that were given to any applicant who was poor, who had gone to a minority high school, or who was from an underrepresented minority group.

In March 2002, the Sixth Circuit Court of Appeals, seated in Ohio, agreed to hear the two cases in tandem and en banc. Two months later the Sixth Circuit Court of Appeals overturned the district court ruling in the case of *Grutter v. Bollinger*, declaring that the admissions plan of the law school was, after all, constitutional. The majority was narrow, 5 to 4, and the minority dissent was unusually vicious. Three months passed. The Sixth Circuit still had not rendered a decision in the *Gratz* case when Barbara Grutter petitioned the Supreme Court of the United States for a review of her case.

Court watchers and people interested in issues of affirmative action or of college admissions speculated about whether the Supreme Court would agree to hear the cases. In any given year the Supreme Court accepts for review only a small fraction (between 100 and 150) of the 5,000 to 6,000 cases presented to it. The Court had declined to review two other similar cases. In the spring of 2001, the Court declined to review a case in the Ninth Circuit Court of Appeals that had upheld the race-conscious admissions policies of the University of Washington. The Court declined to review a case in the Fifth Circuit Court of Appeals that had struck down as unconstitutional the race-conscious admissions plan of the University of Texas Law School. That the Court would grant *certiorari* was not at all a foregone conclusion.

Early in December 2002, the Supreme Court announced that it would hear both the *Grutter* and the *Gratz* cases. At this time the Sixth Circuit still had not rendered a decision in *Gratz*. April 1, 2003, was set as the date for oral arguments.

Briefs on Behalf of the University of Michigan

Of course, the university prepared a brief for each case, but the briefs shared some commonalties. In addition, more than 60 amicus briefs were submitted to the Supreme Court from groups who thought the university had not erred in developing and using race-sensitive admissions policies. Two of the amicus briefs proved especially important: one from a group of retired generals and one from a group of Fortune 500 companies.

At the core of the university's argument was a set of propositions. Although not baldly stated, the core propositions numbered three. First, the university maintained that race-sensitive admissions policies were necessary for the achievement of racial-ethnic diversity among the student body. Second, the university maintained that the achievement of a diverse student body constituted a compelling state interest, the constitutionality of which had been established in the famous *Bakke* decision of 1978 (*Regents of the University of California v. Bakke,* 1978). Embedded within the second proposition was the assertion, based on several studies, that both White students and students of color benefit from diversity. Finally, the university maintained that other means for achieving diversity had or would prove inadequate, thus implying that its own race-conscious programs were what lawyers call "narrowly tailored." The arguments rested on a scaffolding of studies conducted by social scientists at the University of Michigan and elsewhere.

On several fronts the university's strategy was a calculated gamble. The legal argument that the state of Michigan, through its agents, had a compelling state interest to achieve a diverse student body had its roots in the 1978 *Bakke* decision written by Justice Lewis Powell. But some maintained that the Powell opinion was not determinative because only a minority of the 1978 Court had signed on to his pronouncement about the state having a compelling interest in diversity. Indeed, in the *Hopwood* (1994) decision concerning the University of Texas Law School, the Fifth Circuit Court of Appeals explicitly refuted the idea that all sections of the Bakke opinion penned by Powell had the force of law. To make matters more grave, William Rehnquist had been among the justices to dissent from Powell's opinion, and now Rehnquist had become the chief justice. It was entirely possible that the Court would reject Michigan's first premise.

It also was possible that the Court would ignore or not accept the assertions about the benefits of diversity. The assertions rested most directly on studies authored by Professor Patricia Gurin, who had been chair of the psychology department at the University of Michigan from 1991 to 1998. Gurin's work had come under intense attack from the right. Particularly vicious was the critique of Gurin's work authored by conservative scholars Stanley Rothman, Seymour Martin Lipset, and Neil Nevitte. Although the critique was published in an obscure journal called the *International Journal of Public Opinion Research,* Rothman and Lipset managed to gain national attention for their opinion that Gurin's work was too subjective (Selingo, 2003).

One of Gurin's studies involved an experiment in which there was an "intervention" during students' first year at the University of Michigan, the consequence of which were tested during the students' senior year. As freshmen, 87 students took part in a special intercultural class. The class met weekly and involved small discussion sections with a diverse mix of students. As seniors, the same students were contacted by the researchers and asked a series of questions. Answers of the students were contrasted with information from another group of students, matched on demographic characteristics, who had not participated in the program. The contrast showed that the students in the diverse discussion groups differed from the other "control" students. Specifically, they had a more sophisticated view of the role of constructive criticism, were better able to take the perspective of the other person, and were less disconcerted by disagreements than students who had not taken part in the special classes (Gurin, Nagda, & Lopez, 2004).

Some of Gurin's work involved large data sets. In one study, she and her colleagues gathered data from more than 1,100 White students at the University of Michigan. The more contact White students had with students of other backgrounds, the more they developed "active" and "engaged" thinking, the kind of thinking that keeps democracy vital. In another study involving more than 10,000 White students from 183 institutions of higher learning around the nation, Gurin and associates were also able to demonstrate that the benefits of diversity were not limited to the Michigan context. Contact with others from diverse backgrounds helped White students develop intellectually (Gurin, Dey, Hurtado, & Gurin, 2002).

Patricia Gurin was not the only researcher to argue, on the basis of quantitative data, that the predominantly White American society benefits from the inclusion of ethnic minority students in erstwhile White student bodies. One of the important findings of Bowen and Bok's (1998) study of 28 elite colleges and universities was that the ethnic minority alumnae in the study tended to have an extremely high level of community involvement. Such involvement was prized in part for its contribution to the quelling of dissent, especially violent dissent, in the United States.

The Court Decisions

On June 23, 2003, the Supreme Court handed down its decisions in the two Michigan cases. The Court found that the race-sensitive admission plan of the undergraduate college did not pass constitutional muster. The problem was the point system. By automatically awarding points to applicants of color, the university was making an impermissible distinction between citizens on the basis of ethnicity or race, according to the Court. Yet, even in the *Gratz* decision, written by Chief Justice Rehnquist, the majority declared that Michigan did indeed have a compelling interest in ensuring racial or ethnic diversity among the student body at the university. The Court declared that it "rejected petitioners' [i.e., Gratz's and Hamacher's] argument that diversity cannot constitute a compelling state interest."

The state's compelling interest in fostering diversity of the student body was also central to the majority opinion, written by Justice Sandra Day O'Connor, in the case pertaining to the law school, *Grutter v. Bollinger*. O'Connor noted that social scientific research showed the importance of having a critical mass of minority students. Only when the student body contained a critical mass of minority students, said O'Connor, could minority students express their varying opinions and still escape stereotyping. When sufficient numbers of ethnic minority students attend a school, according to the Court, White students would come to see a diversity of opinion among minority students and would no longer think that there was such a thing as an African American position on an issue. Contact with a variety of ethnic minority individuals, in other words, would help White students function better in a multicultural world.

Another reason to characterize diversity as a compelling state interest, according to the majority opinion in *Grutter*, involved the keeping of the peace. A much-quoted phrase stated, "In order to cultivate a set of leaders with legitimacy in the eyes of the citizenry, it is necessary that the path to leadership be visibly open to talented and qualified individuals of every race and ethnicity" (*Grutter v. Bollinger*, 2003).

The importance of Gurin's research and of the research of Bowen and Bok for the Court's reasoning could also be inferred by close scrutiny of the dissenting opinions in the law school case. Especially scathing was the dissent of Justice Antonin Scalia. Scalia insisted that the teaching of good citizenship (including well-developed reasoning capacities) was not the job of a university and was better left to the Boy Scouts. Obviously, the idea that diversity in higher education benefits White people by teaching White students to think more deeply about the role of divergence in democracy was not a favored idea with Justice Scalia. That Justice Scalia thought it necessary to ridicule the idea might be an indication of the great importance of the concept and of the social science data in convincing the majority of the Supreme Court justices about the need for affirmative action plans in higher education.

THE MERIT ARGUMENT

Although the recent emphasis on diversity's beneficial effects may have proved the savior of affirmative action in the Supreme Court, such an emphasis may also ensure the continued public battles over the value of affirmative action. It is, alas, all too easy for the opponents of affirmative action to believe that diversity has been bought at the price of fairness. Fairness, say the critics, requires that organizations focus on merit — regardless of the skin color that accompanies merit (Downing et al., 2002).

The critics' point of view raises the question: What is merit? Merit is defined by the dictionary as "the quality of deserving well; excellence or worth; or a thing that entitles one to reward or gratitude." The definition of merit is clearly subjective. What are the qualities that privilege one group over another? Why do we hear outcries when the criteria are race and gender but no such similar uproar when legacy status? By what process do we determine that someone is "entitled to reward and gratitude"?

Not only are the critics of affirmative action naive about the meanings of merit; they also are thoughtless about the assessment of merit. The assertion that equal opportunity is fair is based on two assumptions. The first assumption is that we have precise instruments to measure merit. The second assumption is that we have a clean environment, free from toxins or pollutants, in which the instruments of merit will yield accurate readings of merit.

From our perspective, both of these assumptions are incorrect. All measures of merit include some degree of subjectivity. Even if we could agree generally on what constitutes merit, our measures contain bias, as do our testing environments.

Unpacking the First Assumption: The Measure of Merit

Many Americans assume that we are able to define merit through objective, value-free measures. Such an assumption seems to us to be naive. Tests of talent do not spring ready-made from the heavens. The tests are created by human beings, and almost always by the human beings who are in positions of power. As long as the results of the tests conform with the stereotypes of the test makers, even those test makers who are sincerely trying to be fair may overlook the bias they are building into the tests.

The use of standardized tests in education raises a number of issues, including which tests are selected as gate-keeping tools, how tests are initially validated, and how scores are combined on different tests. One specific challenge arising from using standardized tests is selective system bias. This problem is signaled by a difference when "the standardized racial (ethnic, or gender) gap in job (or school) performance is smaller than the standardized gap in test performance" (Jencks, 1998, p. 477). Selective system bias occurs when, for instance, African Americans perform much worse than Whites on an entrance exam for school. Another example of selective system bias would be that women perform much worse than men on the gate-keeping tests of physical strength but only a little worse than men on the physically demanding job.

Selective system bias is a persistent problem in higher education. Recent research at the UC, for example, has found that the SAT I scores do not predict freshman year grades there (once socioeconomic status is controlled) (Fernald, 2002; Greiser & Studley, 2001). How much weight should this standardized test be given as a means to determine who gains access to selective institutions of higher education if, in fact, it predicts only a small percentage of the variance in college performance?

Bias can creep into the system when admissions officers decide how to combine different measures of talent. Linda Wightman (1998) highlighted a subtle biasing mechanism used in law school admissions. Most law schools base admission on two criteria: LSAT scores and undergraduate GPA. These two factors are traditionally weighted 60% for the LSAT scores and 40% for GPA. This weighting does not appear, on its surface, to be biased against one group more so than another. But closer examination reveals that women are slightly disadvantaged with that weighting. Women tend to do worse than men on the LSAT and they also tend to have higher undergraduate GPAs than men. By overweighting the LSAT scores relative to grades, women are being unintentionally and persistently disadvantaged in their bid to gain admission to law schools. Examination of any one woman's LSAT and GPA would not allow us to see this pattern of differential treatment. It is only with the examination of aggregate data, as called for by affirmative action, that we can uncover subtle and detrimental patterns of differential treatment.

Bias is also a problem for tests that purport to measure talent in the employment situation. Crosby (1996) presented a dramatic example of gender bias in employment testing. Some years ago, the military decided that it needed to be responsive to the cries of feminists about opening to women jobs that had hitherto been closed. As part of the effort to diminish sexism, the military attempted to see if women could function as fighter pilots. Women and men were both tested to see how quickly they could regain consciousness after a loss of gravity. Each candidate donned a "gravitational suit" which had little apparatuses in it to help push the blood back to the head from all parts of the body when sensors detected a change in body posture. Each candidate was spun around in a simulation machine, which resulted in a loss of consciousness, and the officials timed in milliseconds how rapidly the person regained consciousness. The problem was that the suits had been made for men's bodies and ill fit the women's bodies, because women are longer legged than men of comparable heights. What appeared totally objective as a test was in fact quite biased.

Unpacking the Second Assumption: Interpersonal Dynamics and Differential Treatment

Imagine that you are forming a package delivery company and need to hire workers who can move fast with packages in their hands. We tell you that John covered a mile in 10 minutes carrying a package that weighs 5 pounds and that Mark covered a mile in 7 minutes carrying a 5-pound package. It would seem fair and prudent to hire speedy Mark rather than sluggish John. But what if you learn that John was walking up a steep hill carrying a lumpy package with no string around it, whereas Mark was walking on a smooth path with a slight downhill incline carrying a compact and very portable package? The additional information could certainly change your decision.

When we are using present performance to diagnose future performance, we need to take situational factors into account. What can we infer about the future performance of Person X or Person Y without knowing the conditions of their present performance? Yet, prejudiced or not, Westerners rarely factor situational variables into their thinking (Ross, 1977).

Equal opportunity rests on the assumption that individuals are being evaluated under similar conditions. The assumption of similarity in conditions is no less naïve than the assumption of unbiased test measures. The conditions of life for people of color and for Whites in the United States are not similar, and inferences about the talents of individuals from the two groups should not assume that they are.

One reason that people of color have an uphill battle in the United States is that many White people are prejudiced. Numerous controlled studies have demonstrated the deep and persistent nature of prejudice and stereotyping, even among liberal White students who would like to think of themselves as unprejudiced. Frazer and Wiersma (2001), for example, placed White under-graduates in a setting where they thought they were evaluating job applications. When asked later to recall the interview responses of White and Black applicants, the students were likely to recall the responses of the Black applicant as significantly less intelligent than those of the White applicant, even though the responses for Black and White applicants were identical.

These prejudices and stereotypes may be operating outside of conscious awareness. In many cases, White Americans do not express the more overt forms of racial bigotry, but subtle permu-tations have been uncovered. Dovidio and Gaertner (2000) documented a kind of covert prejudice among White Americans: aversive racism. Aversive racists use plausible excuses provided by circumstances to derogate or exclude out-group members. In one pair of studies, replicated over a 10-year period, White college students did not discriminate in favor of White job applicants when the applicants were clearly outstanding or clearly inadequate, but they gave more positive ratings to White job applicants than to minority applicants when the qualifica-tions of the applicants were middling.

Racial prejudices, overt or covert, can and do result in discriminatory behavior. The discrim-inatory behavior is most clearly documented by what are called "tester studies." In a tester study, actors are trained to behave in a standardized way as go to make purchases, rent an apartment, or apply for a job. The researchers then see if the standardized behavior produces standard results for Whites and for people of color.

Typical is a study done by the Fair Employment Council of Greater Washington, which found that White job applicants were treated significantly better than Black applicants in almost 25% of job searches (Crosby, 2004, chap. 6; Crosby & Herzberger, 1996).

Discrimination also can occur in the absence of current prejudice, just simply because there was prejudice in the past and currently no one has gone out of his or her way to dismantle or adjust the discriminatory system. Think back to the example of the antigravitational suit. In the past, prejudiced army personnel were quite certain that women had no place in a fighter plane. When more open-minded people tried to challenge the sexist assumption by seeing if, in fact, women could regain consciousness as rapidly as men, the unprejudiced people did not imme-diate think to change the length of the legs in the suits. Only by devoting a great deal of thought to the subtleties of the situation did anyone in the army discover the flaw in the test. Before the flaw was discovered, unprejudiced people were perpetuating a discriminatory system.

Blindspots

Discrimination calls for remediation. Prejudiced feelings and discriminatory behavior need to be corrected. About this everyone agrees. But why is affirmative action the appropriate remedy? After all, the race-neutral system of equal opportunity allows for people to bring lawsuits to correct the problems of discrimination.

Affirmative action surpasses equal opportunity as a way to correct discrimination. Under equal opportunity, there must be overt discrimination in order to spark action. But the research presented here, and much other research (e.g., Crosby, 2004), suggests that many stereotypes and prejudices operate under the radar screen, not rising to a level that is readily detected without examination of aggregate data. To root out and address challenges and differential treatment arising from deeply held, resistant stereotypes and prejudices, we must use affirmative action as our policy of choice for redressing inequitable treatment.

Even those who stand to benefit from affirmative action may not be able to act as advocates on their own behalf for a couple of reasons. People who complain about problems almost always encounter further problems just by virtue of complaining (Crosby, 1993). Recognition of the punishment of complainers is a power disincentive to people who might otherwise be willing to take action to improve their situation, especially if the potential plaintiffs find themselves in a relatively powerless position (Crosby & Ropp, 2002).

Not only do people who have been harmed make conscious decisions "not to rock the boat" but they also oftentimes impose blinders on themselves so that they fail to see the discrimination that affects them until the situation becomes intolerable. A large number of studies have by now substantiated a phenomenon called "the denial of personal discrimination" (Crosby, 1984) or the minimization of personal disadvantage. Study after study shows that people in disadvantaged groups imagine that they personally are subject to less disadvantage than are others in the group (Crosby, Iyer, Clayton, & Downing, 2003).

Meanwhile, other observers are often unable to detect instances of injustices unless the injustice is blatant or unless they have access to aggregated data in which the pattern of discrimination is apparent (Crosby, Clayton, Hemker, & Alksnis, 1986; Rutte, Diekmann, Polzer, Crosby, & Messick, 1994). Although privilege tends to blind people, there are many instances in which Whites have clearly and incisively seen the realities of power and tried to change the existing power dynamics. Many Whites have stepped forward, sometimes at considerable risk to their safety, to act as allies of affirmative action and as advocates for justice. Consider the freedom riders of the early civil rights movement (Halberstam, 1998). The rides started on May 4, 1961. At times, the freedom riders faced little resistance. As a White rider went into the Black men's room and a Black rider went into the White men's room in Fredericksburg, Virginia, for example, there was no incident of violence or unrest. Other times (especially as they moved deeper into the South), the anger and violence against the freedom riders, both White and Black, was stunning. In Rock Hill, North Carolina, for instance, John Lewis, a young Black man, and Albert Bigelow, an older White man, were beaten the minute they stepped off the bus. Yet, White as well as Black freedom riders continued their journey in the face of government indifference, public enmity, and covert cooperation between the Ku Klux Klan and the police.

More recently, the White writer and filmmaker Michael Moore has become a staunch supporter of affirmative action. Using humor and sarcasm as weapons, Moore points out that affirmative action has existed in the United States for many years in the sense of privileges extended to members of the elite classes. For decades, the use of legacy preferences at selective colleges and universities went unquestioned (Wingert, 2003). The extremes of affirmative action for the wealthy are skewered in Michael Moore's open letter to George Bush. Moore wrote,

Money and name alone have opened every door for you . . .

You learned at an early age that, in America, all someone like you has to do is show up. You found yourself admitted to an exclusive New England boarding school simply because your name was Bush. You did not have to EARN your place there. It was bought for you.

When they let you into Yale, you learned you could bypass more deserving students.... You got in because your name was Bush.

You got into Harvard Business School the same way. After screwing off during your four years at Yale, you took the seat that rightfully belonged to someone else.

You then pretended to serve a full stint in the Texas Air National Guard. But one day, according to the Boston Globe, you just skipped out and failed to report back to your unit — for a year and a half! You didn't have to fulfill your military obligation, because your name was Bush.

Following a number of "lost years" that don't appear in your official biography, you were given job after job by your daddy and other family members. No matter how many of your business ventures failed, there was always another one waiting to be handed to you.

Finally, you got to be partner in a major league baseball team — another gift — even though you put up only one one-hundredth of the money for the team. And then you conned the taxpayers of Arlington, Texas into giving you another perk — a brand-new multi-million-dollar stadium that you didn't have to pay for.

So it's no wonder that you think you deserved to be named President. (Moore, 2001, pp. 44–45)

As the contrast between Michael Moore and George Bush shows, not every White male in North America imagines that the benefits showered on White people and on men derive solely from their outstanding merits.

Affirmative action in employment promotes the collection of systematic statistics and requires that its affirmative action office scrutinize the aggregated information for patterns of discrimination. With affirmative action, but not with equal opportunity, small problems can be detected — and corrected — before explosive encounters occur. Organizations and the individuals within them benefit from evolutionary, nonrevolutionary, change.

FINAL CONFESSIONS

In an earlier edition of the present book, one of us had an essay titled "Confessions of an Affirmative Action Mama" (Crosby, 1997). The time has come for more confessions. Although we hope you have experienced our narrative as one that is rooted in consensual reality and not simply as the rantings of two extremists, we must acknowledge at the end, as we did at the outset, that all knowledge is situated. We have seen the world of social scientific studies through the lens of our own individual experiences.

What are the relevant experiences of Faye Crosby, the first author? Obviously, they are too numerous to be mentioned here. But we would be remiss if we did not mention a couple of circumstances in Crosby's life that favorably predispose her toward affirmative action. As a woman (albeit a White woman) in a man's world, Crosby encountered a lot of subtle and not very subtle sexism. She remembers sitting in the office of Professor Allen Wagner, the chair of the psychology department at Yale University, and being told that the senior professors would be "embarrassed" to put her name forward for consideration for a promotion because her "early promise" had not been fulfilled. When Crosby asked, "What is the problem?" she was told, "We have no problem with the quantity of your publications or with the quality. It is the nature of the publications that is a problem for us." Nature? Could it be that they did not take seriously her studies because they were very feminist in nature?

Soon after, Crosby accepted a job at Smith College. Smith's job was available to her because the college had instituted an initiative to hire senior women professors after a self-monitoring study revealed that an unacceptably low proportion of full professors at Smith (a women's college!) were women. After being slapped in the face by sexism, Crosby was helped by affirmative action.

Of course, long before she was the direct beneficiary of a formal institutional initiative, Crosby had befitted from other, unlabelled forms of affirmative action. She had grown up as a White upper-middle-class girl in the post-World War II United States. As a girl, Crosby had called all her parents' friends by their last names but had been told to address the cleaning woman by her first name. Because of her White skin, doors were open to Crosby that would otherwise have remained closed. And because the doors were open early in life, Crosby enjoyed the ultimate privilege of allowing herself to imagine that all of her successes came simply by virtue of her own sweet self. So deep and so expansive was the privilege that it had simply become part of the landscape and the very air around her.

Stacy Blake-Beard's avenue to affirmative action support differed in clear ways from Crosby's. Blake-Beard has seen the invisible hand of affirmative action help at every juncture of her career, in both the corporate and academic arena. Very early in her career, Blake-Beard participated in a program designed to attract people of color to fast-track brand management in a well-known manufacturing company. On her first day with this company, she attended a national conference of more than 300 employees in her division. She realized that she saw few if any people who looked like her. This company also realized the dearth of people of color in their ranks. It was for this reason that they had taken the initiative to attempt to attract a more diverse pool of potential employees.

Blake-Beard's career in higher education was similarly touched by affirmative action. Blake-Beard did her graduate work at University of Michigan. She credits her acceptance to Michigan, in part, to the psychology department's conscientious efforts to recruit and retain doctoral students of color. The Black Student Psychological Association, a graduate student support and advocacy group, was heavily involved in recruiting and attracting students of color from around the country to apply to Michigan. Blake-Beard applied to many schools but of all of the places, Michigan, by and far, had the most students of color and faculty of color. The psychology department was also ranked first in the country at that time. So there was no loss of quality as a result of the open and inclusive environment that was created at Michigan.

Blake-Beard's time at the University of Michigan was not a walk in the park. As she taught undergraduate psychology courses, there were times when students would tell her that they'd never had a Black person in a position of authority in their lives. Some were appreciative of the opportunity to learn from a leader who looked different from the White men to whose presence at the front of the class they had become accustomed. Others were not so welcoming—challenging and pushing Blake-Beard in ways that they would never have done with a White male faculty member. At times, there were tensions with White students who resented the presence of a substantive number of graduate students of color. Yet, Blake-Beard would not trade her time at Michigan for anything. The University of Michigan was a place of incredible learning and intellectual growth. Because of the nurturing presence of a supportive community of color, both within Michigan and in the Ann Arbor community, Blake-Beard thrived in her graduate career.

Growing up, Blake-Beard was given two messages. One message was "You can do anything that you want to as long as you work hard." The second message was "Don't ever forget that you can work as hard as you want to and sometimes you still will not get what you deserve. You will have to work five times harder to be seen as competent and sometimes that is still not enough." These seemingly incompatible messages are the reason that we still need to have affirmative action.

Neither one of us espouse activism simply for ourselves. We both share the conviction that affirmative action helps create a better world not just for ourselves and our friends but for future generations. It would be a grave mistake to think that only the ethnic minority children will benefit from affirmation. So will the White children, both as children in today's world and as adults in tomorrow's.

Crosby's children are already adults. Although they are not the direct beneficiaries of affirmative action, they certainly are its indirect beneficiaries. Crosby's two sons need to come in contact with people from all backgrounds. Diversity benefits them. But the rewards of affirmative action go beyond diversity. The White men to whom Crosby gave birth also need to know that they function in worlds that are more truly meritocratic, rather than meritocratic in appearance only; more fair, rather than less fair. They need to see that their own accomplishments are due to something beyond the privileges that they enjoy in society. And they need a true chance, not just the illusion of a chance, to study, work, and live with others who, like Matt and Tim Crosby, are genuinely talented and capable, no matter what the wave of the hair, the shape of the nose, or the color of the skin.

REFERENCES

Bowen, W. G., & Bok, D. C. (1998). *The shape of the river: Long-term consequences of considering race in college and university admissions.* Princeton, NJ: Princeton University Press.

Brown, M. K., Carnoy, M., Currie, E., Duster, T., Oppenheimer, D. B., Schultz, M. M., & Wellman, D. (2003). *Whitewashing race: The myth of a color-blind society.* Berkeley: University of California Press.

Crosby, F. J. (1984). The denial of personal discrimination. *American Behavioral Scientist, 27,* 371–386.

Crosby, F. (1993). Why complain? *Journal of Social Issues, 49*(1), 169–184.

Crosby, F. J. (1994). Understanding affirmative action. *Basic and Applied Social Psychology, 15,* 13–41.

Crosby, F. (1996). A rose by any other name. In K. Arioli (Ed.), *Quoten und Gleichstellung von Frau und Mann* (pp. 151–167). Basel, Switzerland: Helberg & Lichtenhan.

Crosby, F. J. (1997). Confessions of an affirmative action mama. In M. Fine, L. Weis, L. C. Powell & L. M. Wong (Eds.), *Off white: Readings in race, power, and society* (pp. 179–186). New York: Routledge.

Crosby, F. J. (2004). *Affirmative action is dead; Long live affirmative action.* New Haven, CT: Yale University Press.

Crosby, F., Clayton, S., Hemker, K., & Alksnis, O. (1986). Cognitive biases in the perception of discrimination: The importance of format. *Sex Roles, 14,* 637–646.

Crosby, F. J., & Herzberger, S. D. (1996). For affirmative action. In R. F. Tomasson, F. J. Crosby, & S. D. Herzberger (Eds.), *Affirmative action: The pros and cons of policy and practice* (pp. 5–109). Washington, DC: American University Press.

Crosby, F. J., Iyer, A., Clayton, S., & Downing, R. (2003). Affirmative action: Psychological data and the policy debates. *American Psychologist, 58,* 93–115.

Crosby, F. J., & Ropp, S. (2002). Awakening to discrimination. In M. Ross & D. T. Miller (Eds.), *The justice motive in everyday life* (pp. 382–396). New York: Cambridge University Press.

Dovidio, J. F., & Gaertner, S. L. (2000). Aversive racism and selection decisions: 1989 and 1999. *Psychological Science, 11*, 315–319.

Downing, R., Lubensky, M. E., Sincharoen, S., Gurin, P., Crosby, F. J., Quierolo, S., & Franco, J. (2002). Affirmative action in higher education. *The Diversity Factor, 10*(2), 15–20.

Fernald, J. (2002). *Preliminary findings in the relationship between SAT scores, high school GPA, socioeconomic status, and UCSC freshman GPA.* Retrieved November 15, 2002, from *http://senate.ucsc.edu/cafa/SATGP.htm*

Frazer, R. A., & Wiersma, U. J. (2001). Prejudice versus discrimination in the employment interview: We may hire equally, but our memories harbour prejudice. *Human Relations, 54*, 173–191.

Greiser, S., & Studley, R. (2001). *UC and the SAT: Predictive validity and differential impact of the SAT I and SAT II at the University of California.* Retrieved November 16, 2002, from *http://ucop.edu/sas/research/researchandplanning/pdf/sat_study.pdf*

Grutter v. Bollinger et al. (2003). *Daily Journal Daily Appellate Report* 6800.

Gurin, P., Dey, E. L., Hurtado, S., & Gurin, G. (2002). Diversity and higher education: Theory and impact on educational outcomes. *Harvard Educational Review, 72*, 330–366.

Gurin, P., Nagda, R. A., & Lopez, G. E. (2004). The benefits of diversity in education for democratic citizenship. *Journal of Social Issues, 60*, 17–34.

Halberstam, D. (1998). *The Children.* New York: Ballantine Publishing Group.

Hopwood v. Texas. (1994). 21 F. 3d 603.

Jencks, C. (1998). Racial bias in testing. In C. Jencks & M. Phillips (Eds.), *The Black-White test score gap* (pp. 457–479). Washington, DC: Brookings Institution.

Moore, M. (2001). Dear George: An open letter to "President" George W. Bush. In *Stupid White Men* (pp. 29–46). New York: HarperCollins.

Regents of the University of California v. Bakke. (1978). 438 US912.

Ross, L. (1977). The intuitive psychologist and his shortcomings: Distortions in the attribution process. In L. Berkowitz (Ed.), *Advances in experimental social psychology* (Vol. 10, pp. 174–221). New York: Academic Press.

Rutte, C. G., Diekmann, K. A., Polzer, J. T., Crosby, F. J., & Messick, D. M. (1994). Organizing information and the detection of gender discrimination. *Psychological Science, 5*, 226–231.

Schmermund, A., Sellers, R., Mueller, B., & Crosby, F. (2001). Attitudes toward affirmative action as a function of racial identity among African American college students. *Political Psychology, 22*, 759–774.

Selingo, J. (2003, March 28). New study questions educational benefits of diversity. *Chronicle of Higher Education, 49*(29), 23.

Sincharoen, S., & Crosby, F. J. (2001). Affirmative action. In J. Worell (Ed.), *Encyclopedia of gender* (pp. 69–79). San Diego, CA: Academic Press.

Vars, F. E., & Bowen, W. G. (1998). Scholastic Aptitude Test scores, race, and academic performance in selective colleges and universities. In C. Jencks & M. Phillips (Eds.), *The Black-White test score gap* (pp. 457–479). Washington, DC: Brookings Institution.

Wightman, L. (1998). An examination of sex differences in LSAT scores from the perspective of social consequences. *Applied Measurement in Education, 11*, 255–277.

Wingert, P. (2003, October 27). Legislating legacies. *Newsweek*, p. 10.

Representing

TWELVE

Race, Suburban Resentment, and the Representation of the Inner City in Contemporary Film and Television

Cameron McCarthy, Alida Rodriquez, Shuaib Meecham,
Stephen David, Carrie Wilson-Brown, Heriberto Godina,
K. E. Supryia, and Ed Buendia

Much contemporary mainstream and radical theorizing on race and popular culture places television, film, and advertising outside the circuits of social meanings, as though these practices were preexisting, self-constituting technologies that then exert effects on an undifferentiated mass public (Parenti, 1992; Postman, 1986). This essay counters that tendency. We see television and film as fulfilling a certain bardic function, singing back to society lullabies about what a large hegemonic part of it "already knows." Like Richard Campbell (1987), we reject the vertical model of communication that insists on encoding/decoding. We are more inclined to theorize the operation of communicative power in horizontal or rhizomatic terms. Television and film, then, address and position viewers at the "center" of a cultural map in which suburban, middle-class values "triumph" over practices that drift away from mainstream social norms. In this arrangement, the suburb, in the language of Christopher Lasch (1991), becomes "The True and Only Heaven": the great incubator and harbinger of neo-evolutionary development, progress, and modernity in an erstwhile unstable and unreliable world.

Suburban dweller here refers to all those agents traveling in the covered wagons of post-1960s white flight from America's increasingly black, increasingly immigrant urban centers. White flight created settlements and catchment areas that fanned out farther and farther away from the city's inner radius, thereby establishing the racial character of the suburban-urban divide (Williams, 1994). As tax-based revenues, resources, and services followed America's fleeing middle classes out of the city, a great gulf opened up between the suburban dweller and America's inner-city resident. Into this void contemporary television, film, and popular culture entered creating the most poignantly sordid fantasies of inner-city degeneracy and moral decrepitude. These representations of urban life would serve as markers of the distance the suburban dweller had traveled away from perdition. Televisual and filmic fantasies would also underscore the extent to which the inner-city dweller was irredeemably lost in the dystopic urban core. Within the broad vocabulary of representational techniques at its disposal, the preference for the medium shot in television tells the suburban viewer, "We are one with you," as the body of the television subject seems to correspond one-for-one with the viewer.

As Raymond Williams (1974) argued in *Television: Technology and Cultural Form*, television, film, advertising, textbooks, and so forth are powerful forces situated in cultural circuits themselves — not outside as some pure technological or elemental force or some fourth estate, as the professional ideology of mainstream journalism tends to suggest. These are circuits that consist of a proliferation of capacities, interests, needs, desires, priorities, and commitments — fields of affiliation and fields of association.

One such circuit is the discourse of resentment, or the practice of defining one's identity through the negation of the other. This essay will call attention to this discourse in contemporary race relations and point to the critical coordinating role of news magazines, television, the Hollywood film industry, and the common sense of black filmmakers themselves in the repro- duction and maintenance of the discourse of resentment — particularly its supporting themes of crime, violence, and suburban security.

Drawing on the theories of identity formation in the writings of C. L. R. James (1978, 1993) and Friedrich Nietzsche (1967), we argue that the filmic and electronic media play a critical role in the production and channeling of suburban anxieties and retributive morality onto its central target: the depressed inner city. These developments deeply inform race relations in late-20th- century society. These race relations are conducted in the field of simulation as before a putative public court of appeal (Baudrillard, 1983).

Standing on the Pyres of Resentment

> I feel deadly faint, bowed and humped, as though I were Adam, staggering beneath the piled centuries since Paradise. (Ahab in Herman Melville's *Moby Dick* [1851, p. 535])

These words uttered in a moment of crisis in the 19th-century canonical text of Herman Melville's *Moby Dick* (1851) might well have been uttered by Michael Douglas as D-fens in the contemporary popular cultural text of *Falling Down* (1993), or by Douglas as Tom Sanders in the antifeminist, proto-resentment film, *Disclosure* (1995). Douglas is the great 20th-century suburban middle-class male victim, flattened and spread out against the surface of a narcotic screen "like a patient etherized upon a table" (Eliot, 1964, p. 11).

In two extraordinary texts, *Mariners, Renegades, and Castaways: The Story of Herman Melville and the World We Live In* (1978) and *American Civilization* (1993), C. L. R. James made the provocative observation that American popular cultural texts — popular film, popular music, soap operas, comic strips, and detective novels — offered sharper intellectual lines of insight into the contradictions and tensions of modern life in postindustrial society than the entire corpus of academic work in the social sciences. For James, comic strips such as *Dick Tracy* (first published in 1931) and popular films such as Charlie Chaplin's *Modern Times* (1936) and John Huston's *The Maltese Falcon* (1941, based on the novel by Dashiell Hammett) were direct aesthetic descendants of Melville's *Moby Dick*. These popular texts removed the veil that covered 20th- century social relations "too terrible to relate," except in the realm of fantasy and imagination (Morrison, 1990, p. 302).

For James, these popular texts foregrounded the rise of a new historical subject on the national and world stage: the resentment-type personality. This subject was a projection of the overrationalization and sedimented overdeterminations of the modern industrial age ("the fearful mechanical power of an industrial civilization which is now advancing by incredible leaps and bounds and at the same time mechanization and destruction of the human person- ality" [James, 1978, p. 8]). James's new subject articulated an authoritarian populism: the mutant, acerbic, and emotionally charged common sense of the professional middle class (Douglas with a satchel of hand grenades in *Falling Down*, Harry and Louise of the anti-health care reform ads). This authoritarian personality was, in James's view, willing to wreck all in the hell-bent prosecution of his own moral agenda and personal ambition. According to James, what was unusual and egregious about the resentment personality type in *Moby Dick* and the 19th-century world of Melville had become pseudonormative by the time of *The Maltese Falcon* in the 1940s—a period marked by the rise of what James (1993) called "nonchalant cynicism" (p. 125).

Thus in *The Maltese Falcon* (1941), detective Sam Spade (Humphrey Bogart) puts the woman he loves in jail for the murder of his corrupt partner, Miles Archer. Their love is overridden by the ideology of professionalism and the socionormative priority of making wrongdoers pay. As the paranoid Spade says plaintively to his lover, "I don't even like the idea of thinking there might be one chance in a hundred that you'd played me for a sucker" (Spade, quoted in James, 1993, p. 125). In Sam Spade's world, lovers do not have any special privileges beyond the domestic sphere. Spade is playing by his own ethics and chucking human relations and feelings as encumbering eruptions of irrationality. This is a tart dish of public common sense. As the eternal proxy for middle-American values, Spade holds the line against the threat of invasion by the morally corrupt other, the socially different, and the culturally deviant and deprived.

Contemporary popular discussion of crime and violence also follows this logic of closed narrative where the greatest fear is that the enemy will be let into our neighborhoods. And the greatest stress on public policy may be how to keep the unwanted off the taxpayer-dependent welfare rolls and out of our town, safely in prisons, and so forth. Sam Spade's worries have had a meltdown in our time at late century. And they have become a potent paranoid resentment brew that spills over from the fantasyland of television and film into the social world in which we live.

What James's astute comments point us toward is the fact that the filmic and televisual discourse of crime and violence is not simply about crime or violence. Art is not here simply imitating life in some unthinking process of mimesis. Art is productive and generative. Televisual and filmic discourses about crime and violence, as Gerbner (1970) and others argued, are fundamentally urban fables about the operation of power and the production of meaning and values in society. They are about moral re-evaluation, about our collective tensions, crises, and fears. They are about how we as a society deal with the social troubles that afflict us: sexism, racism, and the like. In this sense, popular culture—the world of film noir and the grade B movie, of the tabloids, and of the mainstream press—constitutes a relentless pulp mill of social fictions of transmuted and transposed power. At late century, Sam Spade has been replaced by the towering popular and preternatural intelligence of Sweeney Erectus, our guide into the moral inferno. James wrote almost prophetically about resentment mutations and the time lag in the modern world in the late 1940s (Bhabha, 1994). The aim of this essay is to describe the operation of resentment a half century later in our time—a time in which racial antagonism has been the host of a particular resentment stoked in the media and circulating in popular culture.

DANGER IN THE SAFETY ZONE

> The crisis of the middle class is of commanding gravity.... The crisis is hardening the attitude of the middle class toward the dependent poor, and to the extent that the poor are urban and black and Latino and the middle class suburban, and white, race relations are under a new exogenous strain. (Beatty, 1994, p. 70)

Within the past year or so, *Time* magazine published two articles that together document the contemporary rise of suburban middle-class resentment. In these articles, crime and violence are fetishized, transmuted in the language of the coming invasion of the abstract racial other. According to the first article, "Danger in the Safety Zone," murder and mayhem are everywhere outside the suburban home: in the McDonald's restaurant, in the shopping mall, in the health club, in the courtroom (Smolowe, 1993, p. 29). The article also quoted and displayed statistics indicating that crime in the major cities had been declining somewhat while residents of the suburbs — the place where the middle classes thought they were safest — were now increasingly engulfed in random violence.

The second article is titled "Patriot Games." It is about the mushrooming of heavily armed white militias in training, preparing for the war of wars against the federal government and nameless invading immigrants and foreign political forces that the Clinton administration has somehow, unwittingly, encouraged to think that America is weak and lacking in resolve to police its borders. About these armed militias we are told:

> In dozens of states, loosely organized paramilitary groups composed primarily of white men are signing up new members, stockpiling weapons and preparing for the worst. The groups, all privately run, tend to classify themselves as "citizen militias." . . . On a home video promoting patriot ideas, a man who gives his name only as Mark from Michigan says the fears that America will be subsumed into "one big, fuzzy, warm planet where nobody has any borders." Samuel Sherwood, head of the United States Militia Association in Blackfoot, Idaho, tells followers, absurdly, that the Clinton administration is planning to import 100,000 Chinese policemen to take guns away from Americans. (Farley, *Time*, December 19, 1994, pp. 48–49)

What does all of this mean? These articles announce a new mood in political and social life in the United States: a mood articulated in suburban fear of encirclement by difference, and increasingly formulated in a language and politics of what James and Nietzsche call "resentment." The dangerous inner city and the world "outside" are brought into the suburban home through television and film releasing new energies of desire mixed with fear. As we approach the end of the century, conflicts in education and popular culture are increasingly taking the form of grand pan-ethnic battles over language, songs, and the occupation and terrorialization of urban and suburban space. The conflicts intensify as the dual mode of the rich-versus-poor city splinters into fragmentary communities signified by images of the roaming homeless on network television. For our late-20th-century Sweeney Erectus, standing on the pyres of resentment in the culturally beleaguered suburbs, the signs and wonders are everywhere in the television evening news. Sweeney's cultural decline is registered in radically changing technologies and new sensibilities, in spatial and territorial destabilization and recoordination, in the fear of falling, and in new, evermore incorrigible patterns of segregation and resegregation (Grossberg, 1992). Before his jaundiced eyes, immigrant labor and immigrant petty bourgeoisie now course through suburban and urban streets — the black and Latino underclasses after the Los Angeles riots, announces one irrepressibly gleeful news anchor, are restless. The fortunes of the white middle classes are, in many cases, declining. And the homeless are everywhere.

This new world order of mobile marginal communities is deeply registered in popular culture and in social institutions such as schools. The terrain to be mapped here is what Hal Foster (1983) in *The Anti-Aesthetic* calls postmodernism's "other side" — the new centers of the simulation of difference that loop back and forth through the news media to the classroom, from the film culture and popular music to the organization and deployment of affect in urban and suburban communities — Sweeney's homeground.

THE POLITICS OF AFFECT

> The America of the diverging middle class is rapidly developing a new populist anti-politics. (Beatty, 1994, p. 70)

You will recall that Fredric Jameson (1984), in his now famous essay "Postmodernism, or, the Cultural Logic of Late Capitalism," maintained that a whole new emotional ground tone separated life in contemporary postindustrial society from previous epochs. He described this ground tone as "the waning of affect," the loss of feeling. Although we agree with Jameson that emotions, like music, art, film, literature, and architecture, are historically determined and culturally bound, we disagree with his diagnosis that contemporary life is overwhelmingly marked by a certain exhaustion or waning of affect. We maintain that a very different logic is at work in contemporary life, particularly in the area of race relations. Postmodernism's other side of race relations — of the manipulation of difference — is marked by a powerful concentration of affect, or the strategic use of emotion and moral re-evaluation.

Like James, Nietzsche regarded the deployment of retributive morality as central to the organization and mobilization of power in modern industrial society. He also called this use of retributive morality resentment. In his *Genealogy of Morals* (1967), Nietzsche defined resentment as the specific practice of defining one's identity through the negation of the other. Some commentators on Nietzsche associate resentment only with "slave morality." We are here taken genealogically back to "literal slaves" in Greek society, who being the most downtrodden had only one sure implement of defense: the acerbic use of emotion and moral manipulation. But we want to argue along with Robert Solomon (1990) that contemporary cultural politics are "virtually defined by bourgeois resentment" (p. 278). As Solomon maintains, "Resentment elaborates an ideology of combative complacency — a 'leveling' effect that declares society to be 'classless' even while maintaining powerful class structures and differences" (p. 278). The middle class declares there are no classes except itself, no ideology except its ideology, no party, no politics, except the politics of the center, the politics of the middle, with a vengeance.

A critical feature of discourses of resentment is their dependence on processes of simulation (Baudrillard, 1983). For instance, the suburban middle-class subject knows its inner-city other through an imposed system of infinitely repeatable substitutions and proxies: census tracts, crime statistics, tabloid newspapers, and television programs. Last, the inner-city other is known through the very ground of the displaced aggressions projected from suburban moral panic itself: It is held to embody what the center cannot acknowledge as its own (Beatty, 1994; Reed, 1992). Indeed, a central project of professional middle-class suburban agents of resentment is their aggressive attempt to hold down the moral center, to occupy the center of public discourse, to stack the public court of appeal. The needs of the suburbs therefore become "the national interests." By contrast, the needs of the inner city are dismissed as a wasteful "social agenda." Resentment is therefore an emotion "distinguished, first of all, by its concern and involvement with *power*" (Solomon, 1990, p. 278). And it is a power with its own material and discursive logic. In this sense it is to be distinguished from self-pity. If resentment has any desire at all, it is the "total annihilation ... of its target" (p. 279). Sweeney offered his own homemade version of the final solution: Take the homeless and the welfare moms off general assistance. Above all, build more prisons!

A new moral universe now rides the underbelly of the beast — late capital's global permutations, displacements, relocations, and reaccumulations. The effect has meant a material displacement of minority and other dispossessed groups from the landscape of contemporary political and cultural life. That is to say, that increasingly the underclass or working-class subject is contemporaneously being placed on the outside of the arena of the public sphere as the middle-class subject-object of history moves in to occupy and to appropriate the identity of the oppressed, the radical space of difference. The center becomes the margin. It is as if Primus Rex had decided to wear Touchstone's fool's cap; Caliban exiled from the cave as Prospero digs in. Resentment operates through the processes of simulation that usurp contemporary experiences of the real, where the real is proven by its negation or its inverse. Resentment has infected the very structure of social values.

This battle over signs is being fought in cultural institutions across the length and breadth of this society. We are indeed in a culture war. We know this, of course, because avatars of the right like Patrick Buchanan (1992) and William Bennett (1994) constantly remind us of their books of values. As Buchanan put it bluntly, sometime ago, "The GOP vote search should bypass the ghetto" (quoted in Omi & Winant, 1986, p. 124). From the cultural spiel of the 1992 and 1994 election campaigns — from family values to Murphy Brown, to the new Corporate multicultural advertising — from rap music to the struggle over urban and suburban space — from the Rodney King beating, to Charles Stuart, to Susan Smith, to O. J. Simpson — a turf battle over symbolic and material territory is under way. The politics of resentment is on the way as the suburbs continue to draw resources and moral empathy away from the urban centers.

Of course, a fundamental issue posed by the theories of resentment of James and Nietzsche is the challenge of defining identity in ways other than through the strategy of negation of the other. This, we wish to suggest, is the fundamental challenge of multiculturalism, the challenge of "living in a world of difference" (Mercer, 1992). Education is a critical site over which struggles over the organization and concentration of emotional and political investment and moral affiliation are taking place. The battle over signs that is resentment involves the articulation and rearticulation of symbols in the popular culture and in the media. These signs and symbols are used in the making of identity and the definition of social and political projects. Within this framework the traditional polls of left versus right, liberal versus conservative, democrat versus republican, and so forth are increasingly being displaced by a more dynamic and destabilizing model of mutation of affiliation and association. A further dimension of this dynamic is that the central issues that made these binary oppositions of race and class conflict intelligible and coherent in the past have now collapsed or have been receded. The central issues of social and economic inequality that defined the line of social conflict between left and right during the civil rights period are now, in the post–civil rights era, inhabited by the new adversarial discourses of resentment. Oppositional discourses of identity, history and popular memory, nation, family, the deficit, and crime have displaced issues concerning equality and social justice. New Right publisher William Rusher articulates this displacement by pointing to a new model of material and ideological distinctions coming into being since the 1980s:

> A new economic division pits the producers — businessmen, manufacturers, hard-hats, blue-collar workers, and farmers [middle America] — against a new and powerful class of non-producers comprised of the liberal verbalist elite (the dominant media, the major foundations and research institutions, the educational establishment, the federal and state bureaucracies) and a semipermanent welfare constituency, all coexisting happily in a state of mutually sustaining symbiosis. (Rusher, quoted in Omi & Winant, 1986, p. 124)

Let us examine some manifestations of one of the principal articulations of resentment: the discourse of crime, violence, and suburban security. In the next section of this essay, we will discuss examples from television evening news, film, and popular magazine and newspaper features that show the variability, ambiguity, and contradiction in this discourse of conflict. We will see that signifiers of the inner city as the harbinger of violence, danger, and chaos loop into the mass media and the suburbs and Hollywood and back again in the constructions of black male directors of the reality of the "hood."

"REFLECTING REALITY" AND FEEDING RESENTMENT

> Too often, Black artists focus on death and destruction arguing that it is what's out there so we got to show it! Please!! What needs to be shown is the diversity and complexity of African-American life. (*Syracuse Constitution*, 1993, p. 5)

The logic of resentment discourse does not proceed along a straight line in a communication system of encoding/decoding. It does not work one-way from text to audience. Its reach is more diffuse, more rhizomatic, deeply intertextual. Resentment processes work from white to black and black to white, from white to Asian and Asian to white, and so on, looping in and out and back again as second nature across the bodies of the inhabitants of the inner city — the black world available to the black director who delivers the black audience to Hollywood. The inner city is thereby reduced to an endless chain of recyclable signifiers that both allure and repel the suburban classes.

But there is also the shared ground of discourses of the authentic inner city in which the languages of resentment and the reality of "the" hood commingle in films of black realism of black directors such as John Singleton and the Hughes brothers. This is a point that Joe Wood (1993) makes somewhat obliquely in his discussion of the film *Boyz 'N the Hood* (1992) which is set, incidentally, in South Central, Los Angeles. In a recent article published in *Esquire* magazine titled "John Singleton and the Impossible Greenback Bind of the Assimilated Black Artist," Wood noted the following:

> *Boyz's* simplified quality is okay with much of America. It is certain that many whites, including Sony executives and those white critics who lauded the film deliriously, imagine black life in narrow ways. They don't want to wrestle with the true witness; it might be scarier than "hell." Sony Pictures' initial reaction to *Boyz* is instructive: John confides that the studio wanted him to cut out the scene in which the cops harass the protagonist and his father. "Why do we have to be so hard on the police?" they asked. An answer came when Rodney King was beaten; the scene stayed in — it was suddenly "real." (Wood, 1993, p. 64)

Here we see the elements of repeatability, the simulation of the familiar, and the prioritization of public common sense that evening television helps to both activate and stabilize. Hollywood drew intertextually on the reality code of television. Television commodified and beautified the images of violence captured on a street-wise camera. Singleton's claim to authenticity, ironically, relied not on endogenous inner-city perceptions but, exogenously, on the overdetermined mirror of dominant televisual news. *Boyz 'N the Hood* could safely skim off the images of the inner city corroborated in television common sense. For these Hollywood executives, police brutality became real when the Rodney King beating became evening news. As Wood (1993) argued,

> What Sony desired in *Boyz* was a film more akin to pornography ... a safely voyeuristic film that delivered nothing that they did not already believe.... But how strenuously will they resist his showing how Beverly Hills residents profit from South Central gangbanging, how big a role TV plays in the South Central culture. (p. 65)

Of course, what even Joe Wood's critical article ignores about a film like *Boyz 'N the Hood* is its own errant nostalgia for a world in which blacks are centered and stand together against the forces of oppression; a world in which black men hold and practice a fully elaborated and undisputed paternity with respect to their children; a world that radically erases the fact that the location of the new realist black drama, Los Angeles, South Central, the memories of Watts, and so forth, are now supplanted by an immigrant and migrant presence in which, in many instances, black people are outnumbered by Latinos and Asian Americans (Davis, 1992; Fregoso, 1993; Lieberman, 1992).

Like the Hollywood film industry, the mainstream news media's address to black and brown America directs its gaze toward the suburban white middle class. It is the gaze of resentment in which aspect is separated from matter and substance undermined by the raid of the harsh surfaces and neon lights of inner-city life. In the sensation-dripping evening news programs of the networks — CBS, NBC, and ABC, and CNN — as they pant to keep up with the inflamed journalism of the tabloids — black and Latino youth appear metonymically in the discourse of problems: "kids of violence," "kids of welfare moms," "car jackers," the "kids without fathers," "kids of illegal aliens," "kids who don't speak 'American.'" The skins of black and brown youth are hunted down like so many furs in the grand old days of the fur trade. The inner city is sold as a commodity and as a fetish — a signifier of danger and the unknown that at the same time narrows the complexity of urban working-class life. You watch network evening news and you can predict when black and brown bodies will enter and when they will exit. The overwhelming metaphor of crime and violence saturates the dominant gaze on the inner city. News coverage of the cocaine trade between the United States and Columbia routinely suggests that only poor and black inner-city residents use cocaine, not rich suburban whites who are actually the largest consumers of the illegal drug.

The mass media's story of inner-city black and Latino people pays short shrift to the stunning decline of opportunity and social services in the urban centers within the past 15 years: poor public schools, chronic unemployment, isolation, the hacking to death of the public transportation system, the radical financial disinvestment in the cities, and the flight of jobs and resources to the suburbs. All of these developments can ultimately be linked to government deprioritization of the poor as middle-class issues of law and order, more jail space, and capital punishment usurp the Clinton administration's gaze on the inner city. Instead, the inner city exists as a problem in itself and a problem to the world. The reality of the inner city is therefore not an endogenous discourse. It is an exogenous one. It is a discourse of resentment refracted back onto the inner city itself.

It is deeply ironic, then, that the images of the inner city presented by the current new wave of black cinema corroborate rather than critique mainstream mass media. Insisting on a kind of documentary accuracy and privileged access to the inner city, these directors construct a "reality code of being there" after the manner of the gangster rappers. But black film directors have no a priori purchase on the inner city. These vendors of chic realism recycle a reality code already in the mass media. This reality code operates as a system of repeatability, the elimination of traces, the elaboration of a hierarchy of discourses — the fabrication and consolidation of specular common sense.

Menace II Society (1993), created by Allen and Albert Hughes, is the capstone on a genre that mythologies and beautifies the violent elements of urban life while jettisoning complexities of gender, ethnicity, sexuality, age, and economy. Instead of being didactic, like *Boyz 'N the Hood*, the film is nihilistic. The reality of the hood is built on a trestle of obviousnesses. Its central character, Caine Lawson (Tyrin Turner), is doomed to the life of drug running, car stealing, and meaningless violence that claims young men like himself (and before him, his father) from the time they can walk and talk. It is a world in which a trip to the neighborhood grocery can end in death and destruction, and gangbangers demand and enforce respect at the point of a gun. This point is made at the very beginning of the movie when Caine and his trigger-happy buddy, 0-Dog (Larenz Tate), feel disrespected by a Korean store owner. The young men had come to the grocery to get a beer but are provoked into a standoff when the store owner hovers too close to them. The young men feel insulted because the Korean grocer makes it too obvious that he views them with suspicion. In the blink of an eye, 0-Dog settles the score with a bout of unforgettable violence. When Caine and 0-Dog leave, the store owner and his wife are dead. And one act of violence simply precipitates another: By the end of the film, Caine too dies in a hail of bullets — a payback by the gang of a young man that Caine had beaten up mercilessly earlier in the film.

This film sizzles with a special kind of surface realism. There is a lot of blood and gore in the 'hood in *Menace II Society*. Shot sequences are dominated by long takes of beatings or shootings almost always shot in extreme close-ups. Caine's life is supposed to be a character sketch of the inevitability of early death for inner-city male youth reared in a culture of violence. We have already seen it on television evening news before it hits the big screen. Black filmmakers therefore become pseudo-normative bards to a mass audience, who, like the Greek chorus, already knows the refrain. These are not problem-solving films. They are films of confirmation. The reality code the code of the 'hood, the code of blackness, of Africanness, of hardness, has a normative social basis. It combines and recombines with suburban middle-class discourses such as the deficit and balancing the federal budget; taxes; overbearing, overreaching, squandering government programs; welfare and quota queens; and the need for more prisons. It is a code drenched in public common sense. The gangster film has become paradigmatic for black filmic production out of Hollywood. And it is fascinating to see current films like Singleton's *Higher Learning* (1995) glibly redraw the spatial lines of demarcation of the inner city and the suburbs onto other sites such as a university town: *Higher Learning* is *Boyz 'N the Hood* on campus.

It is to be remembered that early in his career, before *Jungle Fever* (1991), Spike Lee was berated by mainstream white critics for not presenting the inner city realistically enough — for not showing the drug use and violence. Lee obliged with a vengeance in *Jungle Fever* in the harrowing scenes of the drug addict Vivian (Halle Berry) shooting it up at the "Taj Mahal" crack pint and the Good Doctor Reverend Purify (Ossie Davis) pumping a bullet into his son (Samuel Jackson) at point-blank range (Kroll, 1991).

By the time we get around to white-produced films like *Grand Canyon* (1991) or *Falling Down* (1993), the discourse of crime, violence, and suburban security has come full circle to justify suburban revenge and resentment. In *Falling Down*, directed by Joel Schumaker, we now have a white suburban male victim who enters the 'hood to settle moral scores. Michael Douglas as the angst-ridden protagonist, D-fens, is completely agnostic to the differences within and among indigenous and immigrant inner-city groups. They all should be exterminated as far he is concerned — along, of course, with his ex-wife who won't let him see his infant daughter. D-fens is the prosecuting agent of resentment. His reality code embraces Latinos, who are supposedly all gangbangers, and Asian store owners, who are portrayed as compulsively unscrupulous. In a bizarre parody of gang culture, he becomes a one-man gang — a menace to society. In a calculated cinematic twist, the world of D-fens is characterized by a wider range of difference than the world of the films of black realism. However, ironically, blacks are for the most part mysteriously absent from this Los Angeles (Douglas, apparently, feels more confident beating up on other racial groups). On this matter of the representation of the "real" inner city the question is, as Aretha Franklin puts it, "Who's zooming who?"

What is fascinating about a film like *Falling Down* is that it too is centered around a kind of hyper-normative, anomic individual, who is "out there." He is the purveyor of what Jacques

Lacan calls "paranoiac alienation" (Lacan, 1977, p. 5). Singlehandedly armed with more socio-normative firepower than any gangbanger could ever muster, D-fens is ready to explode as everyday provocations make him seethe to the boiling point. We learn for instance that he is a disgruntled laid-off white-collar employee — a former technician who worked for many years at a military plant. Displaced as a result of the changing economy in the new world order — displaced by the proliferation of different peoples who are now flooding Los Angeles in pursuit of the increasingly elusive American dream — D-fens is part of the growing anxiety class that blames government, immigrants, and welfare moms for its problems. He is the kind of individual we are encouraged to believe a displaced middle-class person might become. As Joel Schumaker, the director, explained,

> It's the kind of story you see on the six o'clock news, about the nice guy who has worked at the post office for twenty years and then one day guns down his co-workers and kills his family. It's terrifying because there's the sense that someone in the human tribe went over the wall. It could happen to us. (Morgan, 1993)

D-fens is a kind of Rambo nerd, a Perot disciple gone berserk. *Newsweek* magazine, that preternatural barometer of suburban intelligence, tells us that D-fens is the agent of suburban resentment. D-fens's actions while not always defensible are "understandable":

> *Falling Down*, whether it's really a message movie or just a cop film with trendy trimmings, pushes white men's buttons. The annoyances and menaces that drive D-fens bonkers — whining panhandlers, immigrant shopkeepers who don't trouble themselves to speak good English, gun-toting gangbangers — are a cross section of white-guy grievances. From the get-go the film pits Douglas — the picture of obsolescent rectitude with his white shirt, tie, specs and astronaut haircut — against a rainbow coalition of Angelenos. It's a cartoon vision of the beleaguered white male in multicultural America. This is a weird moment to be a white man. (Gates, 1993, p. 48)

D-fens's reactions are based on his own misfortunes and anger over the anticipated disempowerment of the white middle class. Despite his similarities with the neo-Nazi, homophobic army surplus store owner in the movie, they are not the same type of social subject. Unlike the neo-Nazi, D-fens reacts to the injustices he perceives have been perpetrated against him. Like his alter ego Tom Sanders in *Disclosure* (1995), he is the post–civil rights scourge of affirmative action and reverse discrimination.

With *Falling Down*, Hollywood places the final punctuation marks on a discursive system that is refracted from the mainstream electronic media and the press onto the everyday life of the urban centers. Unlike D-fens in *Falling Down*, the central protagonist in *Menace II Society*, Caine, has nothing to live for, no redeeming values to vindicate. He is preexistentialist — a man cut adrift in and by nature. What *Menace II Society* and many other black new wave films share with *Falling Down* are a general subordination of the interests and desires of women and a pervasive sense that life in the urban centers is self-made hell. Resentment has now traveled the whole way along a fully reversible signifying chain as black filmmakers make their long march along the royal road to a dubious Aristotelian mimesis in the declaration of a final truth. The reality of being black and inner city in America is sutured up in the popular culture. The inner city has no interior. It is a holy shrine to dead black and brown bodies — hyperreal carcasses on arbitrary display.

CONCLUSION

There is a country-and-western song popular, we are told, among the rural suburban dwellers of the Southwest. Its refrain is an urgent plea to God to keep the penitent middle American on the straight and narrow. "Drop kick me Jesus through the goal posts of life," the song goes. Here, the importunate penitent draws down lines of social location in an edict of moral specificity and separateness from the contagion of all that dwells outside the security of the home and the neighborhood. The fictive goalposts morally keep the unwanted out. The trope of resentment exists in the empty space of the center, between the homoerotic legs of the goalposts, so to speak.

In many respects, then, the resentment discourse of crime, violence, and suburban security that now saturates American popular cultural forms, such as the country-and-western song quoted above, indicates the inflated presence of suburban priorities and anxieties in the popular imagination and in political life. It also indicates a corresponding circumscription of the control that blacks and Latinos (particularly black and Latino youth) and other people of color have over the production of images about themselves in society — even in an era of the resurgence of the black Hollywood film and the embryonic Latino cinema. The discourse of crime, violence, and suburban security also points to deeper realities of abandonment, neglect, and social contempt for the dwellers in America's urban centers registered in social policies that continue to see the inner city as the inflammable territory of "the enemy within" and the police as the mercenary force of the suburban middle classes. Those who articulate the anxieties repressed in and by their own privileged access to society's cornucopia of rewards — dwellers of the suburban city and the parvenu masters of the fictive hyperrealisms of the 'hood — bear some responsibility to the urban city that their practices of cultural production and overconsumption both create and displace. In these matters, to use the language of the Guyanese poet Martin Carter, "All of us are involved, all of us are consumed" (1979, p. 44).

REFERENCES

Baudrillard, J. (1983). *Simulations*. New York: Semiotext(e).
Beatty, J. (1994, May). Who speaks for the middle class. *The Atlantic Monthly*, 65–78.
Bennett, W. (1994). *The book of virtues*. New York: Simon and Schuster.
Bhabha, H. (1994). *The location of culture*. New York: Routledge.
Buchanan, P. (1992). We stand with President Bush. In C-Span Transcripts (Eds.), *1992 Republican national convention* (pp. 6–9). Lincolnshire, IL: Tape Writer.
Campbell, R. (1987). Securing the middle ground: Reporter formulas in 60 Minutes. *Critical Studies in Mass Communication*, 4(4), 325–350.
Carter, M. (1979). You are involved. In *Poems of resistance* (p. 44). George Town, Guyana: Guyana Printers Limited.
Davis, M. (1992, June 1). Urban America sees its future: In L. A. burning all illusions. *Nation*, 254(21), 743–746.
Dunn, T. (1993). The new enclosures: Racism in the normalized community. In R. Gooding-Williams (Ed.), *Reading Rodney King* (pp. 178–195). New York: Routledge.
Eliot, T. S. (1964). The love song of J. Alfred Prufrock. In T. S. Eliot, *Selected poems* (pp. 11–16). New York. Harcourt Brace Jovanovich.
Farley, C. J. (1994, December 19). Patriot games. *Time*, 48–49.
Fedarko, K. (1993, August 23). Holidays in hell. *Time*, 50–51.

Foster, H. (1983). *The anti-aesthetic*. Seattle, WA: Bay Press.

Fregoso, R. L. (1993). *The bronze screen. Chicana and Chicano film culture*. Minneapolis: University of Minnesota Press.

Gates, D. (1993, March 29). White-male paranoia. *Newsweek*, pp. 48–53.

Gerbner, G. (1970). Cultural indicators: The case of violence in television drama. *Annals of the American Association of Political and Social Science, 338*, 69–81.

Grossberg, L. (1992). *We got to get out of this place*. New York: Routledge.

James, C. L. R. (1978). *Manners, renegades, and castaways: The story of Herman Melville and the world we live in*. Detroit, MI: Bewicked.

James, C. L. R. (1993). *American civilization*. Oxford: Blackwell.

Jameson, F. (1984, July-August). Postmodernism, or, the cultural logic of late capitalism. *New Left Review*, no. 146, pp. 59–82.

Kroll, J. (1991, June 10). Spiking a fever. *Newsweek*, pp. 44–47.

Lacan, J. (1977). The mirror stage as formative of the function of the I. In A. Sheridan (Trans.), *Ecrits* (pp. 1–7). New York: Norton.

Lasch, C. (1991). *The true and only heaven: Progress and its critics*. New York: Norton.

Lieberman, P. (1992, June 18). 52% of riot arrests were Latino, study says. *L.A. Times*, p. B3.

Melville, H. (1851). *Moby Dick: Or the white whale*. New York: Harper.

Mercer, K. (1992). "1968": Periodizing postmodern politics and identity. In L. Grossberg, C. Nelson, & P. Treichler (Eds.), *Cultural studies* (pp. 424–449). New York: Routledge.

Morgan, S. (1993, March). Coastal disturbances. *Mirabella*, 46.

Morrison, T. (1990). The site of memory. In R. Fergusson, M. Gever, T. T. Mmh-ha, & C. West (Eds.), *Out there: Marginalization and contemporary cultures*. New York: The Museum of Contemporary Art.

Nietzsche, F. (1967). *On the genealogy of morals* (Trans. W. Kaufman). New York. Vintage.

Omi, M., & Winant, H. (1986). *Racial formation in the United States*. New York. Routledge.

Parenti, M. (1992). *Make believe media: The politics of entertainment*. New York: St. Martin's Press.

Postman, N. (1986). *Amusing ourselves to death*. New York: Penguin.

Reed, A. (1992). The urban underclass as myth and symbol: The poverty of the discourse about the discourse on poverty. *Radical America, 24*(1), 21–40.

Smolowe, J. (1993, August 23). Danger in the safety zone. *Time*, 29–32.

Solomon, R. (1990). Nietzsche, postmodernism, and resentment: A genealogical hypothesis. In C. Koelb (Ed.), *Nietzsche as postmodernist: Essays pro and con* (pp. 267–294). New York: SUNY.

The Syracuse Constitution. (1993, August 2). A menace to society, p. 5.

Williams, D. (1994). Society, spatiality, and inner city disinvestment in a large U.S. city. *International Journal of Urban and Regional Research, 17*, 578–594.

Williams, R. (1974). *Television, technology and cultural form*. New York: Schocken Books.

Wood, J. (1993, August). John Singleton and the impossible greenback of the assimilated black artist. *Esquire*, 59–108.

THIRTEEN

The Revolution of Little Girls

Pat Macpherson

Ann-Margret has more than a boyfriend by the end of *Bye, Bye, Birdie* (1963). She has a body that sings and dances with her own erotic energy. From the girdled, coiffed, and pinned-to-a-steady model of wifedom-in-training that was the highest attainment of 1950s femininity, Ann-Margret throws herself off the white family pedestal and into the streets. She runs with a crowd of rocking and rolling teenyboppers and shrieks and faints in sexual ecstasy at a rebel hero sex object. She dramatizes the shift in heterosexuality itself in the early 1960s, from a (sexual) male protecting his (asexual) female loving object, to a permissive reciprocal current of desire and initiative between two interested parties.

In 1962 Helen Gurley Brown announced in *Sex and the Single Girl* that career girls were as entitled to sex as were Hugh Hefner's playboys (Ehrenreich, Hess, & Jacobs, 1986). In 1963 Betty Friedan announced in *The Feminine Mystique* that women were human underneath their aprons, and therefore entitled to work outside family (Bowlby, 1987). In 1948 and 1954, Albert Kinsey reported that heterosexual experiences were more similar than different for males and females, and that lots of sex was "natural" for all (Irvine, 1990). Progressives like these three were proposing a basic human nature underneath socially imposed gender roles. This radically challenged the 1950s consensus that gender was the most basic natural essence — mother's milk flowing from the ladies, sexual fluids spurting from the gents. Nobody was yet challenging the invisible assumptions that human nature was white, middle class, and male.

Meanwhile teenage girls, taught to be the virgin bait and to put the brakes on their premarital sexual experiences, were beginning to find the ways and means to define and act on their own (rather than their boyfriends') sexuality. The sexual revolution began, I am arguing, when young women effected this change in themselves from innocent little girls to sexually motivated people. I take my title from Blanche McCrary Boyd's (1992) novel *The Revolution of Little Girls*, which explores the cross-class and cross-race roots of revolt in one young white girl whose family lost one protector and was abused by another.

Five films of the early 1960s show the sexually significant differences emerging in the nature and roles of single white females. Natalie Wood starred in *Splendor in the Grass* (1961), *Love With the Proper Stranger* (1964), and *Sex and the Single Girl* (1965). Audrey Hepburn starred in *Breakfast at Tiffany's* (1961), and Ann-Margret starred in *Bye, Bye, Birdie* (1963). All are the girl's story of how she found and claimed a sexuality that then disrupts the traditional family and its rituals of reproduction. This revolution of little girls challenged two central postwar norms: the male dominance of heterosexuality, and the invisible white racial dominance embodied in the safe family norm protected by the suggestive white picket fence.

These contemporary films reveal how sexual norms work through the body itself. Body language speaks the desire or desirability, action or reception meant by that gendered body. Retrospective accounts, on the other hand, reveal the racial base of the stakes of this revolution. Young white women were the family jewels of middle-class gentility and racial purity (Breines, 1992). When a few disgraced themselves they disappeared. But when enough of them dirty danced their sexuality in public and then insisted on a seat at the family dinner table — as Baby does in *Dirty Dancing* (1987) — a change *in* the family has occurred. The story of these films and later accounts, then, is the story of how little girls changed the white family's most basic signifier — white female purity as whiteness itself — and had "the time of their lives" doing it, as *Dirty Dancing* sings it. By refusing to take on sexual guilt, they redefined female innocence to include an active sexuality that was off white.

Splendor in the Grass was written by the gay playwright William Inge and starred Warren Beatty in his first film. Natalie Wood plays Deanie, Bud's girlfriend, and their teen heat was the extra scandalous subject of the film when their affair during the filming was publicized. In turn, when parents forbade teens to see the film, illicit viewings reinforced rebellion and the importance of film and sex to identity.

Teen sex is mostly the girl's problem, and Deanie and her mother fight over its nature and limits. The daughter won't accept her mother's version of unwilling wifehood for the sake of motherhood:

> "Boys don't respect a girl they can go all the way with. Boys want a nice girl for a wife. Wilmadean, you and Bud haven't gone too far already, have you?"
>
> "No Mom ... Mom, is it so terrible to have these feelings about boys?"
>
> "No *nice* girl does."
>
> "Doesn't she?"
>
> "No nice girl."
>
> "But Mom, didn't you ever? I mean — feel that way about Dad?"
>
> "Your father never laid a hand on me until we were married.... I just gave in because a wife has to. A woman doesn't enjoy those things the way a man does. She just lets her husband — come near her — in order to have children."

The pair replay this scene after the daughter's sexual frustration mounts and she has abandoned all good girl behavior of eating, studying, fixing her hair. Again her mother asks, "Did he spoil you?" "Yes! No Mom, I'm just as fresh and virgin as the day I was born — naked." Because Deanie is in the bathtub, her bodily purity and its social truth about herself seems poignantly apparent. "I'm a good little girl — I've always done everything Daddy and Mommy told me — and I hate you!"

Rebellion erupts in her as she flings her flailing body out from the tub and down the hallway. But censors wouldn't allow the full shot of her running nude, director Elia Kazan writes in his memoir (Kazan, 1988). White girls' bodies, especially in all-too-naked resistance, were not for public consumption in 1961. But the real rebellious point has already been made. The Victorian past, embodied in the sex-denying mother, is bad. The daughter's bold bodily rebellion is good — which means, crucially for femininity, still innocent, pure, white.

Bud's sister in the film is a bad rich girl who gets drunk at parties and does it indiscriminately.

Deanie is a poor middle-class girl who only wants to do it with her boyfriend — especially after he's done it with the local not-white-enough-to-count Juanita. Deanie's nervous breakdown is expressed as bad-girl party behavior like the sister's, only for Deanie it's unnatural, a sign of her desperation rather than her badness.

The film argues for Deanie, in the form of a waterfall, that it's natural and healthy for her to seek and find sexual release. The 1950s social proprieties of femininity look as Victorian as the furniture darkening and crowding her family house. Her mother's denial of female sexuality, and fathers' enforcement of the double standard, drive the kids crazy. The mental hospital where Deanie spends the next 2 years is, luckily for her, a modern institution where a hip father figure guides her therapeutic self-reconstruction. She emerges in a stunning white hat and chic dress — autonomous, adult, beautiful. Upward mobility is her reward. She bids a fond farewell to the past and its punishing castrations, in the person of a rurally ground-down Bud, toiling the farm for the pregnant ex-waitress Italian wife he met in New Haven. Deanie hatches herself and emerges a poised white woman with an even brighter white future that includes paid-in-full sexual entitlement.

Audrey Hepburn's first outfit in *Breakfast at Tiffany's* resembles Natalie Wood's final outfit in *Splendor*, a broad-brimmed white hat and a slim dark sheath dress. Holly Golightly wears effortlessly the sexual self-possession that it takes most girls a long adolescence to compose. Actually Holly first appears without a dress: She's just answered her door in a tuxedo shirt when George Peppard rings in the middle of the afternoon. Talk about a kooky bohemian life in New York! "How do I look?" she asks when she's quickly and casually transformed herself into the sophisticated working girl. But (as Helen Gurley Brown warned) she's hardly been waiting for him — she's off to work, he's just a new tenant in the apartment building. Their similarities make them friends rather than lovers, each struggling to survive with integrity when patronage is how they support their bohemian lifestyles. (He's a rich woman's gigolo to support his writing, she's paid by a gangster to visit him in jail.) He's enchanted with her insouciance; he's captivated because she's a free spirit. She's trying to marry rich, but he knows she's really innocent of such cynicism or material appetite.

As with Natalie Wood and all the heroines, a pure — yet still sexual — innocence is essential to her character's sexually dubious position. She avoids the 1950s caricatures of single women, either frigidly afraid of sex or guiltily slutty in getting it. She is innocent of Helen Gurley Brown's *Cosmo* girl's ambition and appetites. Audrey Hepburn plays an androgynous pubescent virgin sprite with no virginity at stake, a new social possibility: a sexually active woman who's Teflon-coated inside and out so neither guilty regret nor sexual reputation stick to her. Her (guilty) secret is revealed by the arrival of Fred:

> "She was Lulumae Bonner. I'm her husband.... Them's her chirren: four. When I married Lulumae she was goin' on 14. Never could understand why that woman run off."
> "I love you — but I'm not Lulumae anymore," she tells him.

As a figure of Holly's hickest of pasts, he and his plot development are improbable at best. But its shock value measures the social change from a backward rural past entrapping and impoverishing women, to a liberating present where fragile birds like Holly can find freedom in the city's pleasures and opportunities.

Holly's complex innocence might have to work overtime with this adult material, but the effort never shows in Audrey Hepburn. She seems impervious to charges that could be brought by a 1950s morality: adultery and abandonment of family, semi-sexual racketeering, and gold digging. Her appetite itself is innocent and androgynous, seeking only experience, arty bites of life, like not naming your cat and wanting breakfast at Tiffany's. When they take off their Woolworth's masks after a day adventuring through the city being spontaneous, their kiss is fresh with the sincere wonder of it all, not groping for possession or broiling with lusty longings unleashed. They are like children who have not learned that sex is a gender business deal. They pioneer the promise of the sexual revolution that humans enjoy better sex when they take off their social masks and gender roles.

Credit the complex gay sensibility of Truman Capote, who like William Inge, made the hero as beautiful and desirable a sexual object as the heroine, and the heroine even more hungry for experience outside conventional arrangements, and determined to pursue it, whatever the social costs, than the hero. The beautiful man plays more of the woman's traditional role: lovely to look at, interested in sex once romance has secured the partner's affections, and blooming like a flower into a having-and-holding nurturant center for future family procreation. And the woman plays more of the man's — and none of the mother's — role. Most radically, she's innocent of maternal instinct and emotional possessiveness, the sine qua non of 1950s femininity. So she turns down marriage when it's offered:

> "Holly I love you. You belong to me."
> "I'll never let anyone put me in a cage. . . . I don't know *who* I am."
> "You're chicken. . . . People do fall in love. People do belong to each other. That's the only way they find happiness . . ."

Finally in the rain, amongst the woman's tears and retrieval of her lost cat, they kiss, and — the camera pans back and the credits roll. Cohabitation is more likely than marriage.

In both films the moral justification for "free sex" is "nature," the "human nature" of sexual appetite and fulfillment. Left behind are old-fashioned gender roles and prohibitions and hypocrisies and separate spheres for women and men. Sex is nature, love awakens sex in woman and man, and — if no archaic relatives stand in the way — fulfillment follows.

Love With a Proper Stranger has Natalie Wood again fighting her parents for a better life than their domestic death. Only this time she's the Italian (Angie) and is already pregnant from a one-night stand with a stranger, Steve McQueen. Angie starts off off-off white, in other words. She asks him to help pay for an abortion, and he gets money from his parents, then rescues her from imminent butchery on the floor of an empty room. *Love With a Proper Stranger* was filmed in black and white for a gritty urban "ethnic" (off-white) realism: lots of crowded streets and buildings and cold winds of alienation, especially before the abortion.

Angie's revolt is to remain resolutely single. She refuses two marriage offers. Dominic her suitor says of McQueen, "When he told me my whole stomach turned over on me. He came to me like a man and he's willing to marry yah."

"Why?" Angie asks. "Do you want to get married?"

"I said I would," McQueen answers. But, "Who wants to get married? . . . I'm willing to take my medicine."

"And I'm the medicine?" Angie challenges him — his attitude, the "old" deal of unwilling husband, anxious entrapping wife. "It may come as a shock to you but underneath this hair and skin is a human girl." Essentially human, not female, the key innovation of permissive heterosexuality: the promise of sex without gender. "I don't want to be a warden all my life. As long as you feel that being married is being in jail then you're not happy."

The rest of the film follows McQueen's awkward fighting courtship of the independent (and still pregnant) Angie. She moves out of her Italian-speaking mother's apartment where boiling spaghetti and a steaming clothes iron fog the air. She serves McQueen a modern dinner in her working girl's modest apartment, wearing a scoop neck black dress. "Man you look wild. You look like a woman," he raves. "This is kind of a test run for me," she confesses shyly. "If you didn't try so hard to play against it you'd be a really nice person," he says as they kiss. As in the other films, *he* seems to offer the having and holding, complementing her "business girl" talents.

Earlier he had asked her, "Why did you go with me — up in the mountains?" (Their sex, like everyone's it seems, is in "nature.") She answers that it was "just a stupid experiment." He concurs in their mutual disappointment: "Boy, how they build things up in all the books and movies." Their attempt at the illusions of romance and glamour and independence landed them in more trouble than their marginal lives can support. For him, "bells and banjos playing" is "how they brainwash you" into marriage. The husband becomes "the prisoner of Zenda." For her, "the dead" are the people who live alone, without love to support them. How does real love grow from gritty working-class lives? Together they resist the separate spheres of gender in their parents' lives, the men playing bocci, the women silently waiting. Together they move into a partnership based on mutual needs, for "human" interdependence both emotionally and economically, and for more distance from the bondage of the past — their parents' ethnicity a symbol of both their dead-end working class, and their premodern entrapped gender types. By moving them up and out, middle-class marriage promises to turn off white to white.

In *Sex and the Single Girl* Natalie Wood plays Helen Gurley Brown and Tony Curtis plays Bob, a magazine writer intent on exposing her as a virgin marriage counselor. He'll do anything to get his (1950s) story: the lead career girl who advocates sex for single women is actually a frigid old maid terrified of sex and men. He disguises himself as an impotent married man and seeks treatment from her.

Her story is more modern (with a 1960s heroine): "Single women should stop being ashamed of sex and of being single." From that challenge, problems (like Bob) pursue her. Joseph Heller's screenplay (with David Schwartz) identifies the catch-22 for single working women: If she's sexually experienced, her suited career girl autonomy is splattered all over with her "sex." If she's a virgin, as rumored, she's not only suspect psychologically and socially as old-maid frigid, but her authority as a marriage counselor is completely shot. As his editor suggests, "Make your grab for her, let her tell you she's not that kind of a girl — and we'll sue to make her prove that she *is* that kind of a girl. . . . I'm going for a Pulitzer Prize." The gender stakes are explicit. If women "stop behaving like mice and start behaving like men," as Helen advocates, "Who's going to take care of all of us married men?" Bob wants to know.

Helen's dilemma in the film is resolved by marriage to Bob, in the tradition of 1950s sex comedies such as *Pillow Talk*. She is relieved to discover she wants sex (because his cons succeed in turning her on), and he is relieved to discover he wants marriage (because her energetic and sincere struggles as a professional and a woman can be "solved" by his intervention). The fighting couple get tangled in the conflicts of a married couple with a similar issue: Does the wife's working make or break the marriage? Although the comedy makes hay from its gender misunderstandings, disguises, and different interests, it moves the characters toward happy marriage as mutual recognition. In this "modern" tale, they recognize the human nature or sameness of desire and need and ability in each other, rather than the difference of gender.

The comedy explores the sexual politics that occur when single career women interrupt the old gendered arrangements of the working world. Helen Gurley Brown claims the privileges of men, and an identity that dumps the deficits of old-fashioned femininity:

"I wouldn't give up my career for marriage."

"I have work I care about much more [than marriage]."

"When I marry it won't be for love or romance or sex — I can get those things outside of marriage — just like you."

"I'm not going to give up one iota of freedom or dignity for a man."

"I won't be dominated by any man."

Bob gradually acquires the sensitivities and values formerly associated only with femininity: "For me it's only the beginning," he tells his boss when he's fired for refusing to run his original story on Helen Gurley Brown. "You may have the money and power and sex. But I've got love."

From the predator using the double standard to track down and expose his prey as "that kind of girl" (female object degraded by sexuality), he comes to the permissive conclusion that "Dr. Helen Brown is a decent human being. It would be indecent to malign her." He respects the doctor's (ungendered) professionalism and (ungendered) humanity.

When he gets Helen drunk on champagne and they are happily necking, he confesses his love for her, his dirty little secret as a bachelor supposedly only interested in scoring. As in the other films, the cynical bachelor finds his arms outstretched, chasing after the free spirited working woman.

Bob dons Helen's frilly robe while she dries his wet clothes after a comic contrived splash in the river. As they drink and neck on her sofa in her robes, they joke that he looks like Jack Lemmon in *Some Like It Hot* (1959). But close as he got to the woman in impersonation and intimate contact, Jack Lemmon never got to neck with Marilyn Monroe. Sex in the 1950s was sex segregated. In the Victorian mode, the playboy drooled over the naughty sex object. The difference between Monroe's "real woman" and Jack Lemmon's fake woman highlight the very different nature of women from men. Monroe's particular female "innocence" was that she played a desirable woman with no desires of her own. Her 1950s gender identity is archaic by 1963. The revolution of such little girls has already occurred.

The couple's modern moves on the sofa of the sexual single girl include her emerging erotic capacity (and disinterest in possession) and his emerging emotional capacity (and disinterest in scoring). Predator and sex object gender — Clothes off, same-sex robes on, what comes out is hetero heat, a reciprocating current of sexual and emotional initiatives and hesitations. They are more alike than different.

A Summer Place (1959) reveals what goes missing by the early 1960s: the good father. In *A Summer Place* the father remains central as moral arbiter and protector and point of view. Fathers are disappointing in *Splendor* and *Proper Stranger*, missing in *Tiffany's* and *Single Girl*. In *Bye, Bye, Birdie*, Paul Lynde is a fair fool who is schooled by his clever daughter in what's modern and fun.

A Summer Place was written by Sloan Wilson (whose *Man in the Gray Flannel Suit* was also made into a movie). The film's point of view makes for fascinating social history: the first divorced father coping with his angry teen kids. Two enlightened adults divorce archaic spouses (a drunk and a prude) and marry each other (as they should have when they had their affair as teens) and sponsor the affair of their teen children. Molly (Sandra Dee) gets pregnant, Johnny (Troy Donohue) marries her, and they take over running the summer place where their parents consummated their teenage lust. What's at stake here? Whiteness is actually made whiter by the two blond children reproducing.

The battle over sex is waged between Molly and her "frigid" mother, who makes her wear "an armor-plated bra and girdle" because "she says I bounce when I walk. Do I?" she asks her father.

"In a pleasant and unobjectionable way," Mr. Natural assures her. Her mother's advice on premarital sex is meant to sound cold blooded and prehistoric, but it merely exposes the economics of the maidenhead and the marriage deal:

> "Don't you ever underestimate the value of a good reputation. . . . You could do worse [than Troy Donohue]. Play your cards right. You can't let him think your kisses come cheap. You're a good girl. You have to play a man like a fish. You have to make him want you and never betray that you want him — that's what's cheap — wanting a man. Love should be more than just animal attraction. Promise me you won't let him kiss you till I say it's time."

As in *Splendor*, the mother "denies" female desire before marriage, and there's no sign in her feeling it inside marriage either — perhaps from the strain of so much premarital inhibition and manipulation, a real psychic problem of real couples in the 1950s (Breines, 1992).

Molly tells her father what she thinks of her mother's point of view. She does not tell her mother. "She's anti-sex. She says it's all a boy wants out of a girl and when they marry it's something she has to endure. I don't want to think like that. She makes me ashamed of even having a body." Her mother is the "dismissed" archaic model of denied (or vindictively killed) female desire. She's excluded from the current of father-daughter conversation. The father represents the modern view that sex is part of love: "To love and be loved — that's our sole reason for existence." What Molly and Johnny are left to figure out on their own is whether sex can be safe outside marriage. The film's answer seems to be, as in *Proper Stranger's* pregnancy, that it's not, unless "love" can ensure that marriage will follow.

What's interesting about *A Summer Place* is its lecturing advocacy of women's entitlement to sex — provided the father approves and the boyfriend protects. With all the film's 1960s style permissive tolerance for rolling joyously amongst the waves, and living the modern (second marriage) way in a Frank Lloyd Wright house on the beach, Molly is still dated 1955. She parades and puckers and withholds like a doll, the clean and saintly boyfriend still wins possession through declaring love, and the father still hands over his daughter to the boyfriend: the prerevolutionary hetero contract of male protectorship in exchange for the woman's freely given body. Molly's stepmother accurately described the deal (to Molly's father) at the very moment of exchange (in the boathouse on the dock), "I'm perfectly willing to come when you want me." Molly says the same to Johnny before they do it in the beach shack: "If you need me then I need you — only twice as much." Desire: his. Security: hers.

Revealingly, race — in the form of racism — raises its ugly head right at the moment of their tender gender contract, right when they're about to break her virgin vessel. The extra-blond Molly reminds the fair Johnny that *King Kong* is the movie they're supposedly seeing, so she'll summarize the plot so they won't get caught. "Now about *King Kong*," she says as they kiss. "There's this giant ape ... but they kill him." Scene dissolves in kisses, while we ponder *King Kong's* implicit question: Doesn't every beast in the jungle want the whitest and squishiest of blonds, and doesn't her all-innocent heart bleed for the victims of her own desirability? The crudest myth of white supremacy waves its giant arms in *King Kong* — showing what's at stake in the maidenhead even in the most liberally furnished of summer places.

What's radical about *Bye, Bye, Birdie* is the new source and the disrupting effects of desire in teen heterosexual culture. Conrad Birdie represents not just Elvis but the impact of several emerging "off-white" cultures on the protect-the-pedestal formation of the all-American family. As Barbara Ehrenreich, Elizabeth Hess, and Gloria Jacobs explained about Beatlemania in *ReMaking Love* (1986), Wini Breines explained about cross-class and cross-race relationships in

Young, White and Miserable (1992), and Susan J. Douglas explained about cross-over music in *Where the Girls Are* (1994), white middle-class girls were exploring the possibilities in a newly desegregated teen culture for re-making their sexuality.

Some used a 'hood boyfriend, as in Alice McDermott's retrospective novel (1987) and then the film *That Night* (1994); John Sayles's film *Baby, It's You* (1983), from a story by Amy Grant; the film *Dirty Dancing* (1987); and Ann Imbrie's memoir *Spoken in Darkness* (1993). Some had a black friend or lover, as in Lyn Lauber's novel *White Girls* (1990), Hettie Jones's memoir *How I Became Hettie Jones* (1990), and Alice Walker's novel *Meridian* (1977). Some had abusive father figures: Sylvia Fraser's *My Father's House* (1988) and Dorothy Allison's *Bastard Out of Carolina* (1992). Most had depressed mothers: Janet Vandenburgh's *Failure to Zigzag* (1989) and Marilyn Robinson's *Housekeeping* (1982).

What such retrospective accounts explore is exactly what was so successfully denied in the common culture (like Hollywood movies) of the time that it was (almost) invisible. Supposedly, white girls needed white men's protection from King Kong — all those off-white muscle-packed predators drunk and delirious from the desirability of white femininity.

White girls who seek pleasure from off-white men take from the family the purity that is the justification for all protection of "innocent" privilege. They destroy denial, the illusion of (racial) innocence that covers racial discrimination and inequality. Crossing and recrossing the tracks, white girls unpinned their bodies from the boyfriend/father protector. In pursuing off-white men, in enjoying the mass female hysteria of lusting after writhing male performers, little girls renounced innocence and purity and gentility — but not necessarily goodness or membership in the family. And after their own desire and sexual experience, the passivity and purity of "desirability" are revealed as the second-hand experiences that they are. This radically rewrites the grammar of the hetero sentence: who's desiring subject and who's desirable object in sex.

Bye, Bye, Birdie celebrates the "mass jailbreak" of white girls using rock 'n' roll. In the "before" (rock 'n' roll) scene, Ann-Margret's coy freshly pinned miss (Kim) is "happy to be a woman" in the best tradition of prerevolutionary consciousness. Kim's best friend does perky till it's bubbling out her swinging blond ponytail. "How do you absolutely feel in your deepest secret soul?" she asks Kim about being pinned. "Like I've been reborn. Like all my life until this very moment I was nothing — and now I'm alive. Now I know what it means to be a woman!"

What's revolutionary about *Bye, Bye, Birdie* is that it's ironic, even *campy* about teen rituals and desires, about parents' limited control, and about safe-family norms and defenses — all the components of heterosexuality and whiteness. So all the singing celebrations are quite caricatured and gaily enjoyed — the phones buzzing with Kim and Hugo's playing-at-marriage "steady" contract, Kim's song of self-loveliness at now being a woman, which includes her wifely plan "to pick out a boy and train him . . . and then when you are through, you've made him the man you want him to be." As for her desires, "It gives you such a glow just to know you're wearing lipstick and heels," and "how marvelous to wait for a date in simply beautiful clothes." Even while she's singing about 1950s femininity, she strips off her orange chiffon and slides into 1960s casual — a bulky sweater and capris and fluffy slippers. She loosens her coiffed do and piles her masses of red hair aside for a baseball cap on sideways.

She goes downstairs and greets her parents the modern way by their names and tries to bum a cigarette. "Times are changing," she informs them of Bob Dylan's news. But unlike the beat and folk countercultures, her teen rebellion is offered and taken in the greatest of good humors by her "modern" parents, played by Jennifer Leigh and Paul Lynde. This sets the comic tone for all further family conflict. As one song goes, it's "Kids Today," but it's entirely benign, ritualistic, and even — once you get the archaic relatives out of the way — fun. A deep, bitter, thorough, and long-lasting cultural conflict is here made into dancing confrontations and singing resolutions rich and resonant in the details of white middle-class family politics. Enormous good fun, with backup singers and dancers multiplying the significance of the nuclear family's spats, fields and gyms and bars full of teens dancing through their dilemmas using full body language.

Conrad Birdie has been drafted and Kim has been selected to receive Birdie's "Last Kiss" and song on the *Ed Sullivan Show*. Kim's white purity is ensured by her location, Sweet Apple, Ohio, her all-American family portrait, and her blondest of blond boyfriends Hugo. Hugo is already his father. He's all letterman sweater and crooning about love as if it were only about loyalty. Even when he later joins the dance "I've Got a Lot of Livin' to Do" it's hard to spot even a twitch of sexual impulse. Hugo embodies the security premise of the safe family: trade sex for security. Purity is maintained by exclusive possession.

Birdie and his crowd ride motorcycles right into the crowd of milling — and willing — girls. He dismounts between two raised electric guitars and hardly waits for the official welcome before blasting into his song. "You've gotta be sincere — you've gotta feel it here," he gestures with a pointed pelvic thrust, and the girls start vibrating into ecstatic frenzies. His gold lamé body suit and boots, song and delivery, are more Las Vegas than Memphis (certainly a sign of where Elvis and Ann-Margret were actually headed the following year, *Viva Las Vegas!* [1964], and an affair during the filming).

Birdie refers to Elvis as Elvis referred to black music and culture with his brilloed pompadour and pelvic swivel-and-thrust dancing and sexually coded lyrics and erotic 4/4 rhythms. At the same time, Birdie caricatures the white cleanup act exploiting the black sexuality that was the heart of the whole white youth rebellion against white sexual purity. And he caricatures the way whites saw black music as real and honest, "sincere." "Yah gotta feel it here, honestly sincere.... In everything I do, my sincerity shows through.... When I sing about a girl, I really feel that." And he caricatures sincerity by looking bored with the scene even as he lays waste to the town-folk in a final swooning mass. The mayor's wife in particular keeps fainting with spread legs. Even the next day her knees seem to have been permanently disreputably separated.

The boredom was showing in Elvis by 1963, and the Beatles's fresh sincerity was imported the following year, with the same white-boy coverage of black beat/black heat. For girls who couldn't afford to cross the tracks, the culture of rock 'n' roll had transgressive opportunities that could be explored without leaving home.

Symbolically this is what happens to Kim. Her dance numbers become increasingly sexual-ized and far-flinging and publicly broadcast. She manages her nervous boyfriend by singing that he's her "one special boy," between bouts of Birdie fever and fainting fits from Birdie's kisses. Her mother helps convert her father to the fun of Birdie fandom by arranging for him to join his daughter on the ultimate family hour, the *Ed Sullivan Show*, after Birdie's rock 'n' roll number. As for Elvis and the Beatles, this show helped these boys "enter" the white family home.

Bye, Bye, Birdie is about the transformation of Kim by consuming the rock 'n' roll body language of Birdie. At the beginning when she sings "Bye, Bye, Birdie" she is the coyest of little girls. Each regret is about her lack when he's gone, the ultimate female dependency. "I'm gonna miss ya so." She promises to write every night, and guesses "I'll always care." At the end of the film, Birdie has left town and she is reunited with Hugo, back in the premarital virgin loyalty mode, her head on his shoulder. But when she sings "Bye, Bye, Birdie" by herself directly to the camera, wind machine blowing her orange chiffon, her body is now fully alive and offered as evidence of the difference Birdie made. Her good-bye is grateful for "Your swivel and your sway, your superduper Class." Her loyalty isn't about regret or waiting: "No more sighing each time you move those lips, No more dying (shimmying) each time you twitch those hips." Instead it's now

"Time for me to—FLY!" As she sings "fly-ay-ayayeee" she shakes her breasts like a pro. Continuously walking forward in an exhilarated self-arousal, Ann-Margret throws her woman's body behind the revolution of little girls.

In the best and worst tradition of white middle-class feminism, these heroines' revolutionary act is to claim the (sexual) privileges of white middle-class men. By 1960, they can start from a position of relative economic and social equality—in the family as teens, or in the workforce as adults. The Pill came on the market in 1960, and though it's never mentioned in these films, it made possible women's equal access to permissive sex.

For those women living off camera, outside the white picket fences of the affluent suburbs, the battles over their bodies and futures were very differently waged. Their stories and studies are just beginning to be written. Hollywood film, that most expensive of cultural products, did not often focus its camera on off-white girls.

West Side Story (1962) is the story of Puerto Rican and Anglo boys in gangs and the interethnic conflicts that keep them in their dog-eat-dog "culture of poverty and juvenile delinquency," as Barbara Ehrenreich (1989) described the early 1960s liberal view of those who can't get organized to pass into the ever-open doors of the vast middle class. Although the musical mocks this view of juvenile delinquency, and explores dilemmas of immigration and family conflict over sex and prospects, the solution remains the suburbs. This is Tony and Maria's "place for us," where "peace and quiet and open air waits for us." Their primary loyalty to ethnic roots cuts off their escape route. The girls' sexuality remains tied to their boyfriends, their marriage chances, and their future economic prospects. Their revolt or escape from such circumstances is yet to come.

References

Allison, D. (1992). *Bastard out of Carolina*. New York: Penguin.

Bowlby, R. (1987, Autumn). The Problem with No Name: Rereading Friedan's "The Feminine Mystique." *Feminist Review*, no. 27.

Boyd, B. (1992). *The revolution of little girls*. New York: Random House.

Breines, W. (1992). *Young, white and miserable: Growing up female in the fifties*. Boston: Beacon Press.

Douglas, S. (1994). *Where the girls are: Growing up female in the mass media*. New York: Time Books, Random House.

Ehrenreich, B. (1989). *Fear of falling: The inner life of the middle class*. New York: HarperPerennial.

Ehrenreich, B., Hess, E., & Jacobs, G. (1986). *Re-making love: The feminization of sex*. New York: Anchor Press.

Fraser, S. (1988). *My father's house*. New York: Ticknor and Fields.

Imbrie, A. (1993). *Spoken in darkness: Small-town murder and a friendship beyond death*. New York: Hyperion.

Irvine, J. (1990). *Disorders of desire: Sex and gender in modern American sexology*. Philadelphia: Temple University Press.

Jones, H. (1990). *How I became Hettie Jones*. New York: E. P. Dutton.

Kazan, E. (1988). *A life*. New York: Alfred A. Knopf.

Lauber, L. (1990). *White girls*. New York: Norton.

McDermott, A. (1987). *That night*. New York: Harper and Row.

Newman, K. (1993). *Declining fortunes: The withering of the American dream.* New York: Basic Books.

Robinson, M. (1982). *Housekeeping.* New York: Bantam Books.

Snead, J. (1994). Spectatorship and capture in *King Kong:* The guilty look. In *White screens, black images: Hollywood from the dark side.* New York and London: Routledge.

Spigel, L. (1992). *Make room for TV: Television and the family ideal in postwar America.* Chicago and London: University of Chicago Press.

Vandenburgh, J. (1989). *Failure to zigzag.* New York: Avon Books.

Walker, A. (1977). *Meridian.* New York: Pocket Books.

FOURTEEN

Representations of Race and Social Responsibility: News Stories about Neglect and Failure to Protect

Sarah Carney

Each year, hundreds of women — and a handful of men — are prosecuted for "failing to protect" their children (Swift, 1995). "Failure-to-protect" has become a broad charge that covers a multitude of offenses, from negligence, neglect, child abuse to murder. At this particular moment in the United States, cases that fall under the umbrella of failure to protect are growing exponentially, and they range in type from parents who abandon their children to mothers who use drugs or abuse alcohol while pregnant; they include mothers who "allow" boyfriends, partners, or husbands to abuse their children, mothers whose children drown in bathtubs, and even, most recently, mothers whose children commit suicide. This broader conception of neglect, and the resulting increased criminalization of mothers, coincides, unsurprisingly, with a current social and political moment that favors the withdrawal of public support. The effect of the shrinking public sphere — what Eisenstein (1997) called the "politics of privatization" (p. 142) — is that, as the state relinquishes its social responsibility, it places the burden for care back on the families themselves and, within families, specifically, on the shoulders of women. Fine and Carney (2001) wrote, "We suggest that it is during these periods of conservatism ... that women are particularly burdened and doubly threatened" (p. 405). The inherent, gendered nature of "the new neglect" makes it clear that it is women who are responsible for caring for and managing the family, because men are only rarely charged with failure to protect, failure to act, or failure to resist. When families erupt in violence, and when children get hurt — most often by fathers, stepfathers, partners, and so forth — women will often be the target of blame (Fine & Carney, 2001). The vividness of accounts of female neglect works to overshadow an absence of comparable accounts about male culpability; fathers and male partners will not be held similarly responsible when mothers murder their children.

Although it is true that "contemporary women across racial and ethnic groups are considered accountable to care for 'public' and 'private' life" (Fine & Carney, 2001), it is also true that some women are more accountable than others. Poor mothers and mothers of color are scrutinized more carefully by the state than white middle-class women, whose standard of mothering is seen as ideal. Among those who, by reason of race or social or economic circumstance, lack the resources or privileges that accompany whiteness or social class (e.g., privacy or the ability to pay others to do caring work; see Fine & Weis, 2000) it becomes far too easy to find examples of "bad mothering" (Blackman, 1990, 1994; Chamallas, 1992; Fraser, 1993). Blackman (1994) stated, "Those without the resources to ensure that their rights are protected are the most likely to be held individually responsible when they act ... destructively or self destructively" (p. 148). Recent feminist research makes a clear and convincing argument that the response of the criminal justice system to cases of neglect and failure to protect is thus deeply influenced by "racist, classist, and sexist assumptions, with women, particularly poor women of color, being blamed and held responsible most often" (Fine & Carney, 2001, p. 402). Those charged with neglect who currently fill criminal and family courtroom dockets across the country are, most likely, women; and, nested within gender, they are, more often than not, poor and of color.

I began my analysis of news stories about women charged with neglect, abuse, and failure to protect their children guided by several very well-established lines of research in addition to the feminist work already mentioned. There is, currently, a great deal of psychological and sociological research that demonstrates the overrepresentation of people of color within the criminal justice system (Humphries et al., 1995; Hutchinson, 1990; Jaynes & Williams, 1989; Nagel & Weitzman, 1972; Sokoloff & Price, 1995). Defendants of color are arrested (Mann, 1995; Pokorny, 1965), found guilty (Sutherland & Cressey, 1978), and imprisoned (Hawkins, 1986; Whitaker, 1990) more frequently than whites. In addition, recent critical race work has highlighted the cultural discourses and social representations of (and surrounding) race that become visible in media stories about criminals and crime (Chancer, 1998). Defendants of color are portrayed in the media in ways that perpetuate racial stereotypes and prejudices (Bhabha, 1989; hooks, 1992; Squire, 1997). Findings regarding the existence and prevalence of racial bias both in the courts and in the news are almost taken for granted. These now well-documented findings, and the statistics that accompany them, have become so accepted in mainstream U.S. culture that they have become a part of a national discourse on crime; the idea that whites and people of color are treated differently — both within the criminal justice system and by local and national news outlets — can no longer be considered a revolutionary statement.

With this substantial literature as a foundation, I expected my own work — an examination of the ways in which women charged with neglect are represented in mainstream media narratives — to become, essentially, a study of news stories about black and Latina mothers. I planned a fairly straightforward piece of research, focusing on different ways women of color and white women — their crimes, as well as their homes, families, children, and histories — were described in the news. Anticipating a fierce media condemnation of mothers of color, I predicted a more gentle treatment of white women who were similarly charged. I believed that stories about white women might be written from a more contextualized perspective, with social circumstances such as mental illness or domestic violence included in her story and potentially moderating her guilt. Any such context and mitigating circumstances would be, I thought, stripped from narratives about defendants of color, leaving readers with the impression of a woman isolated and incomprehensible — a subhuman "monster." As so often is the case in qualitative research, the data both confirmed and complicated these beginning suppositions. The most fundamental assumption of this research, that media representations of women defendants would vary in style and content and that these variations would be profoundly influenced by race, did hold true. However the way in which media narratives about crime are constructed, and the ways in which blackness or whiteness — and maleness and femaleness — operates within them, defies any further theoretical aspirations about simplicity or elegance. Attempts to understand cultural notions about criminal mothers became much more complicated than simply comparing terms like "monster" (i.e., black or Latina) with "postpartum depression" (i.e., white). Context was not something that was simply included or excluded in news accounts of crime — there or not there — and news stories were far from being dispassionate, impartial accounts of a crime.

In fact, there was no evidence that any woman, regardless of her race, received sympathetic treatment in the media — all were fiercely condemned. Furthermore, the voice and perspective of the various newspapers was not even remotely neutral; news coverage of cases of neglect or failure to protect tended to be much more thorough in its descriptions of — and thus more favorable toward — the prosecution's account than they were regarding defense narratives. The addition of context in news stories about women defendants was, indeed, integrally related to race, with much more background information included in stories about neglectful white women than in articles about women of color; however, although it was true that this presence of background information could, hypothetically, lead to alternate understandings about women and crime, the inclusion of context did not function straightforwardly to exonerate white women. In fact, the inclusion (in the case of white women) and exclusion (in the case of black women) of context in news stories about cases of neglect actually seemed to net the same narrative result: to effectively promote the legal and moral isolation (and, therefore, imprisonment) of individually "responsible" mothers.

Understanding the ways in which race, poverty, and gender interact and intersect in news stories to set up and maintain a national consciousness about maternal neglect makes two lines of theorizing necessary. First, a more thoughtful theorizing of context is needed; in other words, what part of a defendant's background or current circumstances are seen by reporters as relevant to the story on crime? What information finds its way into news on crime, and what does not? For whom are these pieces of context inserted? Second, analysis is needed regarding the ways in which these various kinds of context then function within stories to shape the public debate on crime and to sustain a national consciousness about mothers, race, and responsibility. The first requirement is a fairly straightforward task of coding and classifying the background information reporters choose to include; the second is more complex because it involves studying the effect of the presence of context and circumstance in stories about white women, as well as analyzing the effect of its absence in stories about women of color.

With these two lines of theorizing in mind, I began my examination of mainstream newspaper stories about cases of failure to protect. I analyzed 15 cases that led to media-produced crime narratives — 14 of those cases described women defendants (5 white, 3 African American, 2 Latina, 1 Caribbean, and 3 race unknown) and 1 involved a white man. All of the cases occurred between 1989 and 2001, with the majority having taken place in the late 1990s; most described murder charges directed toward women whose husbands, partners, or boyfriends actually perpetrated the abuse. The amount of newspaper coverage for each story varied tremendously, from one paragraph in a "Briefly Noted" section to the 456 articles that followed the arrest of Pauline Zile, who was implicated in the beating death of her 7-year-old daughter. I coded these 15 cases and paid close attention to the ways context might be used differently according to the race or gender of the defendant.

OPENING CRIME STORIES ABOUT NEGLECT: THE MANY FACES OF CONTEXT

Beginning the Story of a White Mother

October 1994. "A Saturday outing turned into a nightmare for a Riviera Beach, Florida, woman whose 7-year-old daughter was abducted from a restroom at the Fort Lauderdale Swap Shop" (Fretz & Walker, 1994). Florida headlines broadcast the frightening news: Christina Holt, daughter of Pauline Zile (age 24), and stepdaughter of John Walter Zile (age 32), had disappeared from the flea market while on a shopping excursion with her mother. The community began a massive search: local television broadcast pictures of Christina and workers from the Adam Walsh Center for Missing Children printed and distributed fliers with Christina's picture and description, while a tearful Pauline, clutching what she said was a doll belonging to her daughter, was interviewed, pleading for the safe return of her daughter.

A few days into the search, the appalling truth was revealed and John Zile was arrested, charged with murdering his stepdaughter. After intensive questioning, Pauline Zile, who had been given immunity for her statement, admitted her husband had beaten the child to death. The kidnapping tale, she stated, had been the hoax they had concocted to hide the crime. Detectives suggested that Pauline had seen, but not participated in, the fatal beating.

Beginning the Story of a White Father

October 2000. Thirty-seven-year-old Paul Wayment of Summit County, Utah, left his 2-year-old son, Gage, asleep in the truck while he went to scout out a potential hunting site. While he was gone, Gage woke up, managed to free himself from his car seat, and wandered off into the woods, perhaps looking for his father. The child disappeared. What began as a local story of a missing boy quickly exploded on to the national news desk as search and rescue teams organized, combing the forest for any sign of the boy, fearful that the cold, wet weather — with temperatures that dipped below freezing at times — would lessen the likelihood that Gage would be found alive. A nation held its collective breath as professional rescue teams, helicopters, and local volunteers hunted frantically in what all agreed was a race against time. As fire chief Tom Moore put it, "Hope fades every minute, every hour" ("Police, Rescuers," 2000).

Five days after Gage's disappearance, the worst was realized. Reports published indicated that volunteer searcher James Wilkes had located Gage's body in the woods. He was found, newspaper articles claimed, buried underneath a 4-inch layer of snow. The tragic details — for example, the feet of his pajamas were apparently worn through — were described repeatedly. The medical examiner ruled the cause of death unofficially as due to hypothermia, pending further toxicology results and other findings (Vigh & Curreri, 2000).

The Story of a Black Mother

January 1996. Local news anchors for WGN News at noon, Dave Eckert and Roseanne Tellez, reported that Chicago mother Sharon Burton and her then unnamed boyfriend had been charged with the murder of Sharon's 3-year-old daughter. The couple had, according to reports, drowned the child because she would not potty train.

Headlines mark the new story: "Six Children Killed in House Fire; Mother Charged With Manslaughter" ("Six Children Killed," 2001); "Parents Charged in Death of Girl, 4, Bronx Pair Face Murder Counts" ("Parent's Charged With Death," 1994); "Police Find Body of 2-Year-Old Girl in Home" ("Police Find Body," 1999); "Mom of Boy Who Died of Head Injury Arrested" (Barton, 2000); "Stepfather, Mother Held in Boy's Death" (Landry & Bellandi, 1989). News coverage of incidences of child neglect, abuse, or failure to protect begins with horrific events and sketchy information. They are written, most typically, with a heavy reliance on details provided by police and police spokespeople (Hancock, 2000), and their early task is to frame the events and facts as an easily understood — and recognizable — crime story for their readers. From this "police blotter" type of beginning, most stories of failure to protect fade from media and public consciousness; however, some cases of neglect or failure to protect generate a great deal of community interest, and they will build in momentum, accompanied by a corresponding swell of media-based discussion. In other words, in the case of some select crime stories, particular types of context may enter the news narrative, and therefore the realm of public discussion. Christina Holt's murder, like the dramatic search for 2-year-old Gage Wayment, marked the beginning of a lasting public fascination with their neglecting parents; news coverage about Sharon Burton, however, like so many stories of women of color, ended abruptly after her arrest.

The Story of a White Woman Continues

November 1994. Reports indicated that Pauline had had a fairly troubled upbringing. Just 16 years old when Christina was born, she struggled to raise a child she had not wanted with a husband she was not in love with. Pauline struggled with drug and alcohol abuse, but she had no criminal history. John Zile, however, had had multiple run-ins with the law — for burglary, drug and alcohol abuse, and probation violations. They had met in the mid-1980s in Florida, where Pauline had moved to live near her mother and to try to start her life over. They were married in 1990, settled into Singer Island, Florida, and had two sons.

When a news story grows past initial arrest reports, context is added to flesh out a story of neglect. Background information may be added to crime narratives in two ways: first, through individually specific and vivid descriptions of the defendant and her family, and, second, with the inclusion of legal, psychological, and cultural analyses and interpretation. Reporters insert context, first, by painting a picture of the event for their readers, writing a rich and detailed account of the days leading up to and including the crime. Reporters describe the defendant herself — what she looks like; where she is from; the neighborhood in which she lives; her marital, employment, and criminal history; her educational level; her history of drug or alcohol abuse, or both; and the condition of the family home — as well as the child victim and other involved family members. In their breaking — and growing — stories about failure to protect, reporters also typically include grim information about injuries inflicted, graphic autopsy reports, and emotionally wrenching accounts of funerals and grief-stricken families. The use of vivid description often extends to documenting the response of the local community to the crime, many of whom will provide colorful — and quotable — reactions, and who, therefore, become the focus of a great deal of media attention. Finally, reporters will struggle to aptly describe the trial scene itself and to describe the dramatic exchange between accuser and accused, as well as the depth and variety of emotions floating inside the courtroom.

The goal of vivid description is to construct a clear, unambiguous account of the criminal event — to establish the facts of a case of neglect. Vivid description rarely stands on its own, however, and many reporters will take on an additional task: placing the specific event of abuse into some sort of wider cultural, psychological, or legal perspective. This task may be accomplished by quoting local police, attorneys, judges, and other experts (psychologists, educators, etc.), who explain, analyze, and interpret the event for their readers. For example, in some cases the woman defendant's documented history with mental illness (see Andrea Yates) or domestic violence (see Hedda Nussbaum) enters the story as context and partial explanation. In others, local departments of children and families may be implicated in, perhaps even partially responsible for, the tragedy. Inserting the voices of experts and including their analyses in news narratives about local crime work to frame the story by placing it alongside familiar themes. Criminologists and psychologists educate reporters — and thus readers — about the nature and behavior of the typical sociopath or about battered woman syndrome, doctors explain post-partum psychosis, local attorneys explain the difference between abuse as an act of commission versus abuse as an act of omission, judges outline the standards for legal insanity, sociologists speculate on the response of the local community, and detectives defend common police assumptions about the link between narrative consistency and truthfulness.

The wide variety of contextual information that could potentially be included in narratives of failure to protect might suggest a widening cultural perspective on crime and even reflect a public willingness to entertain alternative versions of blame and responsibility. Unfortunately, with very few exceptions, reporters use these statistics, sources, and types of context, as well as "the power of story choice" (Hancock, 2000, p. 79) to influence a conservative public conversation on crime and to further shape a limited national perception regarding neglectful mothers. With the focus on her depression, her messy home, her erratic employment history, and so forth, child neglect, more than ever, continues to be framed by the mainstream media as individually based (deviance or illness) and personally caused (Swift, 1995) by a woman.

Some research, however, criticizes this individualist perspective on child neglect, stating that, in effect, these types of narratives hide the ways in which powerful social realities contribute to its occurrence (Fine & Carney, 2001; Fine & Weis, 2000; L. Gordon, 1988; Swift, 1995). Scrutinizing only individual mothers — as either deviant or ill — ignores (or erases) other particular kinds of historical context, in particular, long histories of oppression and racism as well as the day-to-day struggles of living in conditions of poverty. A. Gordon (1997) might call these histories "ghosts," and she described the invisible impact of power relations as a "seething presence" (p. 8). Addressing the same kinds of erasures, Fine (2002) wrote on "the presence of an absence."

Hancock (2000) named some particular ghosts, reminding us that there are some kinds of contextual questions that are rarely (but more often, never) asked or included in crime narratives, including questions about available child care, for instance, or the role of quality schooling. News stories on crime do not address issues such as the lack of decent housing, the difficulty of obtaining adequate health care (including treatment for drug and alcohol abuse), or the ineffectiveness of standard parenting programs. Framed by the kinds of contextual information reporters choose to include — which function to effectively prohibit any perspective that addresses the larger social context in which crimes occur — published news stories often reproduce stereotypical versions of neglect that objectify, individualize, and dehumanize defendants, creating cardboard criminals (Hancock, 2000). In fact, the types of context reporters choose to include in their stories allow them to continue to cover crime in a manner that leads to easy clichés and to draw simple conclusions; the public will cry for a focused crackdown on abusive parents, while occurrences of neglect get treated as though they happen in a bubble — disconnected from any social, economic, or family history or circumstance. When women are charged with failure to protect their children, the inclusion of context works more frequently to shut down her story than to open up a socially critical public debate.

ISOLATE AND BLAME OR MODERATE AND FORGIVE: THE FUNCTION OF CONTEXT IN NARRATIVES OF NEGLECT

The Story of a White Woman Continues

October and November 1994. Florida neighbors, citizens, and coworkers were angry, mostly at Pauline, and, it seemed, even more particularly, at her involvement in the kidnapping hoax. Swap Shop vendor Lorraine Bukowski stated, "She had us fooled. I thought I was a better judge of character. She was shaking and crying. Your first instinct is to look for the child. I would like to know how she is going to live with that little girl looking at her before going into convulsions and then dying" (Ellicott, Pickel, Morrissey, & Gienger, 1994). Fellow resident Susan Ritz said, "I think she should rot in hell right along with him. I can't understand why, if they didn't want her, they didn't give her to somebody. I would have taken her" (Ellicott et al., 1994). Local citizen Lisa Nurkowski added, "I feel the same. The mother should rot in hell the same as the stepfather" (Wiggins, 1994).

Almost immediately a narrative shift occurred. Although John Zile was arrested as the murderer and Pauline as a bystander — culpable in her failure to act — in local news stories about the crime, Pauline came to be described as the murderer. For example, one local reporter wrote, "What had been a tale of cruelty wreaked by the unknown turned into the unimaginable — cruelty apparently inflicted by the most familiar, the protector, the mother" (Kastor, 1994).

The Story of a White Man Continues

October and November 2000. Many who wrote letters to the editor of the local paper, the *Deseret News*, argued that what had happened to the Wayments could have happened to any family. One reader wrote, "Because the unthinkable happened, we are quick to judge Paul Wayment. But parents need to stop and ask themselves if their excuse for leaving their child alone is going to sound any more reasonable when broadcast on the evening news. The lesson to be learned is that it could happen to you" ("Don't Leave Children Alone," 2000). Another had this to say: "He's going to beat himself up for a long, long time. But my personal opinion is if what he did is child abuse, then each one of us is guilty. I think each of us puts our kids in dangerous situations from time to time. We don't think about it, and seldom does it turn tragic, but we do it" (Benson, 2000).

The Story of a Black Woman

November 2001. Shiara Worsham was arrested and charged with child endangering when she failed to intervene in her husband, Joshua Brissett's, abuse of their 5-month-old son. Brissett apparently had been trying to reshape his son's skull with his hands so that it would look more like his own. Worsham, police reported, waited 3 days to take him to the hospital after he began vomiting because of a fractured skull (Tobin, 2001).

Although the forms of context in standard media stories about child abuse and neglect may be fairly straightforward, their functions, once added, are not. Gender and race influence reporter's choices about what types of context to include or exclude. Even more important, they influence the messages and implications contextual information will carry, once it becomes a part of the story. For example, although erratic employment history was written in local news as evidence of Paul Wayment's honorable and humble lifestyle (allowing him to stay home with Gage daily), Pauline Zile's various temporary and low-paying jobs were described in the local media in a manner recalling Loch's (1906) notions of poverty as "a weakness of will and a poverty of the spirit" (cited in C. Jones, 1979, p. 74)—her poverty became evidence of her guilt. Narrative context, then, seemed to mitigate against full condemnation or blame in the case of Paul Wayment. His grief, as well as that of his family and the rest of the community, was highlighted daily, and the majority of news stories focused on drawing clear connections between his "mistake" and the ways in which any loving parent might be similarly neglectful. For Pauline Zile, however, the inclusion of context worked to an opposite effect, shoring up cultural notions of an individually responsible, evil, aberrant mother, isolated in her culpability. Meanwhile, when women of color, such as Sharon Burton or Shiara Worsham, abuse or neglect their children, details about the crime and their subsequent arrests mark the end of their stories rather than the beginning. With few details and little information other than police speculation, a brief description of the crime will be constructed, and it is there that, for most, the story will end.

Context works differently within each of these stories depending on the gender of the defendant—its presence exonerates Paul Wayment but condemns Pauline Zile. Furthermore, the dearth of articles that grow beyond single sentence arrest reports about women of color who are charged with neglect suggests that the use of context also reflects differences in how racial groups are represented. If Pauline Zile is an incomprehensible monster, whose behavior, according to literally hundreds of news stories, flies in the face of cultural beliefs about natural, maternal instincts, what does it mean that mothers of color—Sharon Burton and Sherain Bryant, for example—are in need of no explication in the media? In the remainder of this essay I examine three specific contextual functions that are visible and hard at work across media narratives about failure to protect. First, I discuss the ways in which context is used in the news to frame current cultural understandings of, and explanations for, crime. Next, I demonstrate how context may be used to justify the banishment of a defendant and, alternatively, how context may be added that invites some defendants back into the community. Finally, I address the ways in which notions like intention versus mistake or accident are represented through the use of context. Each of these three functions operates differently depending on race and gender, and each tends to reinforce stereotypical notions about who commits crimes in general. All of them make the "ghostly" presence (A. Gordon, 1997) of unequal power relations momentarily visible.

EXPLANATIONS OF CRIME AND FRAMES OF DEVIANCE

Child neglect has been described in the psychological literature, primarily as a characteristic of the individual, endemic to the personality of the mother; as such it has been typically viewed as a clinical, treatable, or at least punishable, problem (Myers, 1998; Polansky, Borgman, & De Saix, 1972). Although some psychological understandings about why mothers abuse have shifted historically, beliefs about the individualized nature of their crime have not. This individualized focus is mirrored in news representations of crime; when women abuse their children they are represented as solely responsible, and, when the men in their lives are the abusers, women are often described as equally responsible. Thus, media representations continue to describe child abuse or neglect as the unfortunate result of the deviant behavior (evil choices) or psychopathology (mental illness) of aberrant, violent, and unnatural individuals. In news articles, context functions, then, to support cultural beliefs about the naturalness of the mothering instinct, all the while taking individual-centered explanations for crime for granted.

Although the individualized nature of crime in general is assumed and remains unquestioned, it is also true that events like failure to protect or neglect are explained differently according to the race and gender of the defendant under consideration. Pauline Zile (a white woman), Paul Wayment (a white man), and Sharon Burton (a black woman) were all charged with various types of manslaughter or murder and were each considered by the media through (at least initially) an individualized lens. However, it is quickly apparent that, in each of these cases, a reporter's choices about which contextual pieces to include and which to leave out actually ended up framing responsibility — and explanations for crime — in different ways.

From the beginning, stories about Pauline Zile included context that explained her actions as those of a depraved and evil mother. Through a compilation of news stories, a picture of Pauline emerged; her lack of education, her frequent moves (from ramshackle apartment to ramshackle apartment), her early marriage (and then divorce), her various unskilled jobs, her drug use, her relationship with John Zile (then a known criminal) — all of these pieces of background information tap into deeply entrenched cultural beliefs about what a typical abuser looks like. They are — and therefore she is — recognizable to [white] readers. When viewed alongside pretrial articles revealing Pauline's concern with prison roommates and requests for a mirror (Stapleton, 1995) and trial reports that contrasted her choice of a white, "girlish" bow in her hair with her flat, emotionless, and stoic presence during the proceedings, the overall impression constructed is that of an ignorant, selfish, self-absorbed woman, one who, it is not difficult to believe, allowed her own needs and desires to supercede those of her daughter. Although John Zile, it is true, inflicted the beating that eventually killed Christina Holt, the media-created image of Pauline Zile is that of a clearly evil — and unnatural — woman, and she can, therefore, be viewed as (at least) equally responsible.

In contrast with Pauline Zile, for Sharon Burton — and for other women of color who are similarly charged — such explicit narrative work seems to be unnecessary. Burton's media-told story, for example, ends upon arrest. When women of color abuse their children, the story is not "how could she do that" but becomes one of arrest statistics and conviction rates. Context and background are not added to the story, perhaps because they are assumed — and familiar. Readers already know what Burton's home looks like, and they simultaneously presume her probable drug use, her lack of education, and her lack of steady employment. So entrenched are cultural notions linking abuse with race and poverty that readers conclude that, although it may be true that Burton's boyfriend actually inflicted the beating that led to the child's death, her own participation seems likely, and therefore unremarkable. Pauline's whiteness brings her closer to idealized versions of motherhood, making the interpretations of, and explanations for, her behavior necessary. Her presence slaughters a collective fantasy; it represents the death of the "good mother." The vast amount of description written indicates that reporters are well aware that her actions are somewhat surprising, and that readers will want to know how and why Pauline has "gone bad." No such fantasy exists for black women, and therefore little work is needed to explain Sharon Burton. Regardless of whether context is added (Pauline) or deemed unnecessary (Sharon), both ultimately join the masses of women charged with neglect who are depicted in a way that supports current cultural notions of criminal mothers as evil and depraved. When Paul Wayment left his 2-year-old alone sleeping in the car, however, and his son subsequently left the car, wandered into the woods, and eventually died of hypothermia, the context added to media stories about him functioned very differently from the way it had in the cases of Pauline Zile and Sharon Burton.

From the beginning Paul was described as a terrific father; even his lack of a steady job became evidence of good parenting — he could spend all day with his son. As neighbors, friends, and his ex-wife attested to his devotion to Gage, reporters described Paul's frantic search for his son, his grief, and his tearful contrition in their stories about the event. Very few articles questioned his judgment, let alone condemned him, and none implied that he was evil or unnatural or that his actions were incomprehensible. Many, in fact, argued that what had happened to Paul could have happened to any otherwise responsible parent. The problem, summarized one reporter, is that communities are isolated. If only, she added, others — friends, neighbors, or family — had offered to help the single father raising his child alone (Cortez, 2001). She continued,

> Seemingly every parent I know has experienced a momentary crush of panic when their child has slipped away from them at the store or walked over to a neighbor's house without their knowledge. These things happen even to the most attentive parents.... I don't think anything is gained by scolding a grieving father. It's not our responsibility to cast judgment on Paul Wayment. I believe the best we can do in these situations is assess our own circle of friends and family and offer our help so they do not become overwhelmed and take chances they ordinarily wouldn't. We should pause and consider the occasions that our actions or inaction — regardless of intent — have put our children in harm's way. ("Don't Leave Children Alone," 2000)

Thus, in the story of Paul Wayment, context did not function to underline the individual, and inherently evil, nature of his crime of neglect; rather, context mitigated against such a conclusion and hinted at more community-centered notions regarding social responsibility. Unlike Sharon Burton, his actions did require explanation; however, unlike Pauline Zile, Paul's maleness opened up the possibility that a different, more forgiving, less individually focused type of narrative could be written.

A COMMUNITY REACTS: ISOLATION OR INCLUSION?

The Story of a White Mother Continues

November and December 1994. Reaction to the news of Christina Holt's death and Pauline's arrest were uniformly horrified. Poolesville, Maryland, family and friends were, predictably, shocked and saddened. Meanwhile, in Florida, mourners turned the sandy grave site into a makeshift monument, and reports described the mountains of flowers, stuffed animals, Virgin Mary statues, and balloons that had been left there. There were cards, notes, a stick of Wrigley's spearmint gum, and a bottle of peach Snapple. One visitor, it was reported, left a sign next to the site that read, "RIP Christina. John Zile should pay for his crime with his pathetic life" (Ellicott et al., 1994). Another note read, "Dear one, May God hold and rest you in his arms. I pray for you now to find peace and love from us who deeply care for you. My guardian angel, please protect the daughter I love most deeply" (Ellicott et al., 1994). Local citizens interviewed had perhaps always been particularly harsh in their condemnation of Pauline; however, their voices grew even louder at the time of her arrest: "If there is any justice [she] will suffer greater pain, not only for betraying her child, but for betraying motherhood, the rest of the country, and particularly all the frightened little children who will be lost or kidnapped from now on" (Recchi, 1994).

The Story of a White Father Continues

October 2000. Neighbors, friends, and fellow church members testified to Paul Wayment's deep commitment to Gage and described their devotion to one another. One neighbor, for example, stated, "I've been in their home and I've seen them playing together. Paul is really good with his son. This sounds like a terrible accident" (Curreri, 2000b). Paul's brother told reporters that Paul was devastated by the disappearance: "He's terribly remorseful he left him in the car seat for even five minutes" (Reavy, 2000). His sister Valerie Burke said, "I know this is a terrible thing.... He was a totally devoted father to this child. He would never purposely put his child in danger. It was a horrible mistake. Nobody loved Gage more than he did" (Reavy, 2000). Later, she added, "I know what my brother did was not the best. But that little boy was absolutely his whole life. He's not the irresponsible, terrible person that a lot of people are concluding" (Newell, 2000a). Even Paul's ex-wife, Gage's mother, vouched for him, saying she is sure he would not do anything to hurt his child (Curreri, 2000a).

Many local citizens wrote letters to the editor supporting Paul and expressing their sense of solidarity with him. These letter writers identified themselves as potentially fallible parents themselves, and many talked about the inevitability of mistakes along the way. "Parents are human," one reader wrote, "and parenthood is a learning process where, invariably, mistakes are made" ("Parents Make Mistakes," 2001). He continued, "Even the wisest and most diligent parents cannot prevent all such tragedies. A child's quick dart into the street, a curious climb into a trunk, a trusted sitter distracted by the other children. I pray that life, with its myriad dangers, may also bring a bit of luck to keep my children safe when I, in my humanness, may fail." Another wrote,

> As parents, let's reflect on every negligent thing we've done, and continue to do, as we raise our children. Our homes, cars, yards, and lives are hazardous. Dangerous things are on, out and open. We leave kids in a running car as we dash to a neighbor's door, we vacation on a houseboat at Lake Powell with toddlers, we buy pocket knives, BB guns and trampolines. Our old cribs fail current safety standards. We don't fingerprint our baby-sitters. We let the kids build tree houses. I must have 30 tiny things on my floor that a crawling baby could choke on. ("Parenthood Is Risky," 2001)

The Story of a Black Mother

November 2001. Christie Rene Greenwood, age 24, was arrested and charged with manslaughter when her six children, left home alone, died in a house fire. News sources indicated that Christie had been playing cards with friends, and that she had left her children sleeping in the "shotgun shack" that evening. According to firefighters, the fire broke out in a makeshift wood-burning heater constructed out of a 55-gallon drum.

When Pauline Zile was arrested, news reports about legal explanations and criminal justi fications sat alongside descriptions of neighborhood shock, local outrage, and man-in-the-street expressions of grief. Articles describing local reactions suggested the existence of a community-wide sentiment, asserting that Christina had been a child of the community itself and that, therefore, the public shared in a powerful sense of grief and anger over the terrible event. Because news of a child's murder is always emotionally charged, perhaps particularly so for the members of the community in which such an appalling event occurred — the crime having occurred "too close to home" — articles about community grief and local reactions such as these perform a specific contextual function: They reconstruct the clear line between a criminal mother and the rest of the local citizenry. They reconstitute the dichotomies of bad and good, irresponsible and responsible. With surprise and outrage, locals remind each other that theirs is not a community of violence, and they disassociate themselves from the evil acts of the child's mother. The community takes in the child, saving the innocent after her death. Stories about community grief tighten the connections between local citizenry — if only temporarily — because they draw the public together, united in its condemnation of a criminal mother and in its cries for her expulsion.

When white women like Pauline Zile fail to protect their children, community shock — and local anger — is a big part of the news. Because articles about community grief appear more often in stories about white defendants than in those involving defendants of color, it is likely that the isolating function performed by these types of stories is connected with a particular type of public vehemence, one reserved for white women who defy social expectations and middle-class norms. When the mother-defendant is black or Latina, the lack of coverage suggests that her story does not appear to inspire the same level of local anxiety, shock, or anger, and less work is required to isolate her from the community at large.

Christie Greenwood's moment in the media spotlight, unlike Pauline Zile's, is brief and ends upon arrest. There were no published reports about neighborhood shock or surprise, and articles including descriptions of Greenwood made by friends, family, and coworkers did not appear. According to news coverage the tragic death of Greenwood's six children did not seem to have inspired local citizens to create or visit a makeshift grave site or shrine, and reporters did not fill articles with the statements of an angry community demanding swift punishment. Perhaps, if viewed in isolation, Greenwood's story seems unremarkable — it is just one more tragic case of neglect. However, when we place it alongside the story of Pauline Zile, for whom community reactions (and rejections) became fully developed narratives, the absence of such contextual descriptions about Christie Greenwood becomes glaring. The story of Pauline Zile is simultaneously the story of a community; alternatively, Greenwood and her family are represented as community-less and ungrounded. By stripping local context from stories about defendants of color, articles describing women like Christie Greenwood end up reflecting stereotypical notions about who commits crimes such as neglect and failure to protect. And Greenwood's children died unnoticed because, in the end, they were not children of the white, middle-class (and news-reading), local population. When women of color neglect their children it is not news, it's confirmation.

The volume and ferocity of the anger that accompanies stories about white women, and the ways in which women across races are removed — narratively and literally — from their communities, stands in marked contrast to the ways in which stories about local reactions functioned throughout the case and trial (and, it must be noted, the eventual suicide) of Paul Wayment. Although articles describing local grief certainly served to unify the community in its expressions of sorrow and loss, tightening the connections between community members did not mean an obligatory banishment of Paul. In fact, it meant the opposite: the local population rallied behind Paul Wayment. The *Deseret News* (the local, Salt Lake City paper) published multiple letters to the editor, and reporters wrote column after column, in which Paul's neglect was represented as the sort of mistake any reasonable parent might make. And when, despite the public opinion to the contrary, Paul Wayment was officially charged with, and eventually found guilty of, negligent homicide, even the prosecutor handling the case told reporters he would not ask for jail time saying, "I think it would be personally difficult for me to argue for jail time. He lost his son, and under the circumstances, I'm sure he has suffered" (Blake, 2001). Many argued that Paul was driven to suicide because he had been criticized unfairly, and that the guilty verdict and the 30-day jail sentence was overkill. This is what happens, articles like these argued, when courtrooms take the place of community support. One reporter wrote, "With the compassion of a freight train running over a penny on a railroad track, the state of Utah chose to compound the tragedy by flattening Paul even more.... While helplessly on the ground writhing in pain at his loss and at his unintentional role in it, Utah kicked him repeatedly with criminal charges, prosecution and blame" (*Deseret News*, 2001). Similarly, in one letter to the editor, the author argued, "They hounded Paul because they had to prove once again that what they scribble on paper — the law — is always more important than mercy or the well-being of their fellow man" (*Deseret News*, August 1, 2001). Thus, for Paul Wayment, articles describing contexts of community grief and local reactions did not function to isolate him in his guilt; rather, they worked to effectively reaffirm a sense of connection, between Paul and the community and between his regrettable neglectful actions and the misguided but noncriminal risks taken by any parent. Gender and whiteness play a significant role in Paul's redemption. Paul, as a single parent to a 2-year-old boy, challenges the social notion that men cannot care for their children alone; his actions do not fly in the face of fundamental cultural beliefs about paternal instincts, and they do not threaten the status quo. A father without a wife is already a saint. Thus, his neglect is represented as an almost endearing, fumbling mistake, and he is showered with accolades for having even tried to take on such a nontraditional responsibility. In the end, the community mourns, not just for the lost of 2-year-old Gage, but for Paul as well.

REPRESENTATIONS OF ACCIDENTS AND INTENTION

The Story of a White Woman Continues

Attorneys for the prosecution and defense summed up their positions succinctly: Although Scott Cupp, lead prosecutor stated, "She knew punishment was about to happen. She'd been there and she'd seen it before. She's the child's mother. She should have had her out of there a long time ago" (Ellicott, 1995), defense attorney Guy Rubin asked, "Where is the proof that Pauline was aware of what was going on until a minute or two after Christina's last sounds? There's not a scintilla of evidence that she could have prevented it" (Ellicott, 1995). As the jury began their deliberations, Cupp stated again, "It's very clear under the Florida law. The defendant owed not only a moral and ethical obligation, but a legal duty to protect her biological child" (Testa, 1995).

The Story of a White Man Continues

After the medical examiner's report was issued, Detective Berry told reporters that Paul Wayment had agreed to take a lie detector test, although it appeared to be a mere formality. The medical examiner's report "appears to end suspicions that the boy was killed by his father," said Berry ("Boy, 2, Froze," 2000). Lieutenant Joe Offret added, "We're leaning toward believing this was just a really tragic accident" (Vigh & Curreri, 2000).

Erik Luna, a professor of criminal law and criminal procedure at the University of Utah, said, "This is a tragic case of incredibly poor judgment on the part of the father, but it's unlikely to be a crime" (Newell, 2000b). Luna explained that legally, the question is first, whether this was an intentional crime, and second, whether Paul's conduct was reasonable. He continued, "Although it shows incredibly poor judgment to leave a child in a car in those conditions, it doesn't look on its face as though his conduct dropped below a level of care that we require of parents" (Newell, 2000b). Luna concluded, "Utah is a very family-oriented state and very community-oriented in its values. I suspect that the people are going to see this as an unmitigated tragedy and feel a great deal of sympathy for the parents rather than a need to punish them" (Newell, 2000b).

In cultural debates on crime, questions about intention always figure prominently. Did the defendant knowingly intend to commit a crime, or, alternatively, was this simply a tragic accident? In fact, although legal definitions may make intent theoretically irrelevant, whether the defendant meant to cause harm may be the most important factor taken into consideration when determining guilt or innocence. Morally, ethically, philosophically — and emotionally — intent always matters. Proving intention means social condemnation will be guaranteed, and it can mean the difference between life in prison (Pauline Zile) or 30 days in the county jail (Paul Wayment). The accidental or inadvertent criminal is more likely to be forgiven, or even found innocent.

The charge of failure to protect, in and of itself, brings questions of intention to the moral and legal forefront right from the beginning. Both the jury and the larger culture face this question: Was this mother negligent because she willfully failed to act reasonably, and, if so, can we then, as a society, hold her criminally responsible? For example, in Pauline Zile's case, did she intend to stand by and allow John Zile to beat Christina Holt so severely that she eventually died? Did Sharon Burton knowingly allow her boyfriend to drown her 2-year-old daughter? Was Shiara Worsham aware that her husband was abusing their newborn son and yet chose to do nothing? Did Christie Greenwood understand the risks inherent in leaving her six children home alone? Did Paul Wayment intend for his son to get out of his car seat and wander into the woods?

News stories about cases of failure to protect focus, almost exclusively at times, on questions about criminal intent, and they are therefore good places from which to extract a national discourse — and to view the social debate — about crime and its relationship with cultural notions about individual choice. The complicated task of determining intention, however, becomes visible right away. Although it is possible to prove that someone failed to act, it is much more difficult to prove that they meant to — or chose to — fail to act. Intention has an opaque quality to it; it is, after all, an internal state that can only be inferred and is never seen. As such, it is a difficult undertaking to operationalize intention or to provide concrete evidence for any internal, psychological process of "choice making" a defendant may have gone through. The difficulties encountered in making intentions concrete and provable means, in turn, that there is a great degree of flexibility and choice involved in how failing parents get represented — both in the courts and in the news. For some, the goal of proving intent means proving that the defendant acted with purposeful and determined action — this is intent as it is traditionally understood and commonly defined. For others the question is not necessarily whether the defendant meant for the child to die but whether she acted irresponsibly, choosing to ignore the clear risks that would have stopped, or at least altered, the behavior of more reasonable people. This latter definition represents a shift away from the more fixed and straightforward question about purposeful action, toward the more slippery slope of "should have knowns" or "could have dones." It is a definitional and conceptual swing that has had enormous repercussions, however, since it has made it legally possible to prosecute women who are either unable to, or for some reason fail to, protect their children from the abuse of others. It meant, for instance, that Shiara Worsham could be sentenced to 3 years in prison for child endangerment and, even more dramatically, that Pauline Zile could be convicted of first-degree murder and sentenced to life in prison without the possibility of parole. Meanwhile, by keeping the focus on whether Paul Wayment had meant for his 2-year-old son to leave the car and wander away — "of course not," agreed both prosecution and defense — Utah prosecutors paved the way for Gage's death to be framed as an accidental tragedy rather than intentional murder.

Media representations of a crime as the result of purposive action, as neglect, or as a regrettable accident have tremendous power to either exonerate or condemn. These various representations of failure to protect have huge implications for how the defendant will be perceived, and judged, by the public, perhaps even by the jury. However, choices about how to frame the death of a child — as a murder or as a horrific accident — are not neutral; they are deeply political, and they turn out to be closely intertwined with race, class, and gender.

When women are charged with failure to protect, the broader, hazier definition of intent as neglect or irresponsibility is almost always invoked. The use of this more open-ended conception of intent in cases of women defendants makes sense given current cultural conceptions that define female responsibility broadly (Fine & Carney, 2001) and blame women, almost exclusively, when violence erupts in the home. Women, regardless of race, are presumed responsible for controlling the behaviors of the men in their lives. Fathers, however, are not similarly charged if it is mothers who abuse their children; men are not supposed to run the household or manage its occupants.

If, as was the case with Pauline Zile, the defendant is a white woman, further evidence about her intention to commit a crime will mostly likely become a part of the story, often through the use of complicated legal explanations and rationalizations. The presence of such detailed justification anticipates — and reaffirms — common social understandings about normal and expected maternal behavior; it demonstrates the ways in which she violated those norms, and it outlines, in the simplest terms possible, the ways in which Pauline's behavior was intentional, and therefore criminal. See, for example, the following.

One week after accepting immunity for telling police about the kidnapping hoax and her husband's fatal beating of her daughter, Pauline Zile was in fact arrested and charged with first-degree murder and aggravated child abuse. State Attorney Barry Krischer explained the charges, referring to a Florida Supreme Court ruling from 1992, and reasoning that she had been present during the beating and failed to promptly notify authorities. He stated that failure to act — acts of omission in child abuse case — was "tantamount to an act of commission" (Beyers, 1994). "In other words," he stated, "by not doing something you've done something. And whenever aggravated child abuse leads to death, it is felony murder" (Beyers, 1994). Krischer later added that his office would seek the death penalty for both John and Pauline.

If the presence of contextual narratives documenting legal definitions of intent works to establish a woman's guilt, the absence of such narratives about black and Latina mothers suggests that questions of intention — and guilt — are unnecessary if the women involved are of color. Sharon Burton, like Pauline Zile, was charged with failing to protect her child from her husband.

Unlike Pauline, however, whether she intended for her husband to kill her daughter goes undiscussed in the brief, one-paragraph news story covering the crime. There are no questions asked in the media about what she may have (or may not have) done to prevent the drowning and no descriptions of her grief over the death of her child are given. Burton's — and Christie Greenwood's and Shiara Worhsham's — intent to harm is implied.

Strict adherence to the more conventional definition of intent as desire, however, made it possible to reframe Paul Wayment as a victim himself. Media discussion centered on Gage's death as a horrifying accident, rather than on what Paul should have, or should not have, done. From the beginning of the reporting on the case, Paul's grief and remorse was featured prominently. For example, reporters noted his tireless search for his son and described his sense of personal guilt and clearly tormented state of mind by quoting parts of his conversation with police: "I should never have left the truck. I should never have done that; that is the stupidest thing I've ever done in my life, and I should be skinned and shot for that" (Curreri & Vigh, 2000). Neighbors, family, and friends testified to Paul's grief and profound remorse. For example, his sister Valerie Burke told reporters, "We just feel like it was a very unfortunate accident. But we understand that there are consequences even to accidents. . . . Paul lost the only thing that meant the world to him. Charges now are a really small thing. They can't hurt him any more than he's already been hurt." And Paul's attorney reportedly said, "I don't know a client who's been more emotionally distraught over a crime as this one. He was vomiting and sobbing at the scene. I have seldom seen greater remorse than in this client" (Blake, 2001). At sentencing, Paul read a statement that said, "In one brief and monumental moment while Gage slept in the truck, I made the biggest mistake of my life. . . . If I could change places with my son, I would give up my life in a second" (Wolfson, 2001).

Grief and remorse are at the heart of the media story about Paul Wayment, and they work to support the narrative theme of tragic accident rather than intentional crime. News stories about Paul Wayment, unlike those about Pauline Zile, Sharon Burton, or Christie Greenwood, represent Gage's death as a mistake, a lapse in judgment, a slip, an unfortunate twist of fate, rather than murder. Evil and twisted, Pauline Zile was represented as having actively participated in abusing Christina Holt when she failed to stop her husband from beating her; Paul, however (so said reporters, columnists, and letters to the editor), was guilty of making a bad choice. There, but for the grace of God, go I, wrote many, who concluded rhetorically, Who among us has not made similar mistakes?

Grief, remorse, and, therefore, intention, all operate differently (and more or less explicitly) in media stories about child neglect. For white mothers, intention is narratively and specifically proven, whereas for mothers of color it need only be assumed. For white men like Paul Wayment, intention is blurred with desire, and this combination perhaps opens the door for a serious conversation about legal conceptions of responsibility versus social understandings about accident or tragedy. Although Pauline Zile's and Sharon Burton's stories take existing conceptions of crime and punishment for granted, Paul's story, as it is written in the news, questions fundamental cultural assumptions about the place of courts as the final determiners of guilt, responsibility, and innocence.

On Ghosts

In her book *Ghostly Matters* (1997) Avery Gordon wrote about the enormity and the importance of finding the shapes that are described by absence or "the paradox of tracking through time and across

all those forces that which makes its mark by being there and not being there at the same time....
This is a particular kind of social alchemy that eludes us as often as it makes us look for it" (p. 6).
Patricia Williams (1991) called it a search for her great-great-grandmother's shape and the hand of
the slave owner who kept her. Michelle Fine (2002) called it the search for the presence of an
absence. For these authors, and for many others, the task is to uncover invisible steel — the solid,
heavy object that is power. A study of social reality, they suggest, is partial at best without an understanding about the forces, hidden but powerful, that give it structure.

Gordon (1997) suggested that ghosts become less transparent through the study of social
reality and its modes of production. In this essay I describe one such effort to make the invisible
visible and look to the mainstream media as one site where reality is structured and shaped.
Looking for what is produced — therefore what is included and what is excluded — in dominantly
crafted news media links the epistemological with the social (Flax, 1992; Lubiano, 1991), and,
in this project, the connections between language, narrative, and discourse and the more
concrete applications of the law make privilege and existing wells of power temporarily observ-
able — perhaps even alterable. By making visible the ways gender, class, and race influence the
ways representations get made — and guilt or innocence get assigned — I seek in this project,
admittedly ambitiously, to uncover the ghosts that shape a persistent and growing oppression of
women, particularly women of color. Perhaps even more ambitiously, I aim not only to document the presence of haunting but also to uncover the process by which social reality gets
"ghosted" — the ways in which discrimination is normalized and privilege is maintained. Avery
Gordon wrote, "Ghostly matters are a part of social life" (p. 23); I agree with her: It does matter
what we see or think we see. If we are truly committed to social justice, we must, at some point,
wrestle with ghosts.

REFERENCES

Barton, A. (2000, September 6). Mom of boy who died of head injury arrested. *Palm Beach Post.*
Benson, L. (2000, November 5). 2 endings — one happy, one tragic. *Deseret News.*
Beyers, D. (1994, November 5). Mother faces Fla. murder charge; Her delay of telling of
daughter's fatal beating prompts case. *Washington Post.*
Bhabha, H. (1989). Signs taken for wonders. In H. Gates (Ed.), *Race, writing and difference.*
Evanston, IL: Northwestern University Press.
Blackman, J. (1990). Emerging images of severely battered women and the criminal justice
system. *Behavioral Sciences and the Law, 8,* 121–130.
Blackman, J. (1994). At the frontier: In pursuit of justice for women. In B. Sales & G. Vandenbos
(Eds.), *Psychology in litigation and legislation. The master lecturer.* Washington, DC:
American Psychological Association.
Blake, C. (2001, June 5). Wayment pleads no contest to negligent homicide in son's death.
Associated Press State and Local Wire.
Boy, 2, froze to death in the woods. (2000, November 2). Associated Press.
Chamallas, M. (1992). Feminist constructions of objectivity: Multiple perspectives in sexual
and racial harassment litigation. *Texas Journal of Women and the Law, 1,* 95–142.
Chancer, L. (1998). Gender, class and race in three high-profile crimes: The cases of New
Bedford, Central Park, and Bensonhurst. In S. Miller (Ed.), *Crime control and women:
Feminist implications of criminal justice policy.* Thousand Oaks, CA: Sage Publications.

Cortez, M. (2001, January 13). Offer help to busy parent — it may save a life. *Deseret News*.

Curreri, F. (2000a, October 29). No sign of toddler missing in woods; boy, 2, vanished in the wild on Thursday. *Salt Lake Tribune*.

Curreri, F. (2000b, October 28). Toddler vanishes after dad leaves him alone while hunting; Boy left in pickup while dad is hunting. *Salt Lake Tribune*.

Curreri, F., & Vigh, M. (2000, December 14). Father charged with misdemeanor in tot's hypothermia death. *Salt Lake Tribune*.

Don't leave children alone. (2000, November 3). *Deseret News* [Opinion column].

Eisenstein, Z. (1997). Women's publics and the search for new democracies. *Feminist Review, 57*, 140–167.

Ellicott, V. (1995, April 8). Judge drops child abuse count. *The Palm Beach Post*.

Ellicott, V., Pickel, M., Morrissey, S., & Gienger, V. (1994, October 30). Flowers, teddy bears decorate grave. *Palm Beach Post*.

Fine, M. (2002). 2001 Carolyn Sherif award address: The presence of an absence. *Psychology of Women Quarterly, 26*, 9–24.

Fine, M., & Carney, S. (2001). Women, gender, and the law: Toward a feminist rethinking of responsibility. In R. Unger (Ed.), *Handbook of the psychology of women and gender*. New York: John Wiley.

Fine, M., & Weis, L. (2000). Working without a net but with a spotlight: Mothering in poverty. In G. Noblit (Ed.), *Post-critical ethnography*. Cranhill, NJ: Hampton Press.

Flax, J. (1992). The end of innocence. In J. Butler & J. Scott (Eds.), *Feminists theorize the political*. New York: Routledge.

Fraser, N. (1993). Clintonism, welfare, and the antisocial wage: The emergence of a neoliberal political imaginary. *Rethinking Marxism, 6*, 9–23.

Gelles, R. (1973). Child abuse as psychopathology: A sociological critique and reformation. *American Journal of Orthopsychiatry, 43*, 611–621.

Gordon, A. (1997). *Ghostly matters: Haunting and the sociological imagination*. Minneapolis: University of Minnesota Press.

Gordon, L. (1988). *Heroes in their own lives*. New York: Penguin.

Hancock, L. (2000). Framing children in the news: The face and color of youth crime in America. In V. Polakow (Ed.), *The public assault on America's children, poverty, violence and juvenile justice*. New York: Teachers College Press.

Hawkins, D. (1986). Black and white homicide differentials: Alternatives to an inadequate theory. In D. F. Hawkins (Ed.), *Homicide among black Americans*. New York: New York University Press.

hooks, b. (1992). *Black looks: Race and representation*. Boston: South End Press.

Humphries, D., Dawson, J., Cronin, V., Keating, P., Wisniewski, C., & Eichfeld, J. (1995). Mothers and children, drugs and crack: Reactions to maternal drug dependency. In B. Price & N. Sokoloff (Eds.), *The criminal justice system and women: Offenders, victims, and workers* (2nd ed.). New York: McGraw-Hill.

Hutchinson, E. O. (1990). *The mugging of black America*. Chicago: African American Images.

Jaynes, G., & Williams, R., Jr. (1989). *A common destiny: Blacks and American society*. Washington, DC: National Academy Press.

Jones, C. (1979). Social work education, 1900–1977. In N. Parry et al. (Eds.), *Social work, welfare, and the state*. London: Edward Arnold.

Kastor, E. (1994, November 5). The worst fears, the worse reality; for parents, murder case strikes at heart of darkness. *Washington Post.*

Landry, S., & Bellandi, D. (1989, July 30). Stepfather, mother held in boy's death. *St. Petersburg Times.*

Lubiano, W. (1991). Shuckin' off the African-American native other: What's "po-mo" got to do with it? *Cultural Critique, 18,* 149–186.

Mann, C. (1995). Women of color and the criminal justice system. In B. Price & N. Sokoloff (Eds.), *The criminal justice system and women: Offenders, victims, and workers* (2nd ed.). New York: McGraw-Hill.

Myers, J. (1998). *Legal issues in child abuse and neglect.* Thousand Oaks, CA: Sage Publications.

Nagel, S., & Weitzman, L. (1972). Double standard of American justice. *Transaction: Social Science and Modern Society, 18,* 18–25.

Newell, L. (2000a, October 30). Authorities re-interview father of missing boy a day after search halted. Associated Press State and Local Wire.

Newell, L. (2000b, November 2). Criminal justice expert: Father unlikely to be charged in son's death. Associated Press State and Local Wire.

Parenthood is risky. (2001, August 10). *Deseret News* [Opinion column].

Parents charged in death of girl, 4, Bronx pair face murder counts. (1994, March 30). Associated Press.

Parents make mistakes. (2001, August 3). *Deseret News* [Opinion column].

Pokorny, A. (1965). A comparison of homicide in two cities. *Journal of Criminal Law, Criminology, and Police Science, 56,* 479–487.

Polansky, N., Borgman, R., & De Saix, C. (1972). *Roots of futility.* London: Jossey-Bass.

Police find body of 2-year-old girl in home. (1999, November 22). Associated Press.

Police, rescuers searching for missing toddler. (2000, October 27). Associated Press.

Reavy, P. (2000, October 29). Father and son — real buddies. *Deseret News.*

Recchi, R. (1994, November 11). True crime: Hysteria slows search for any lasting solutions. The greatest pain. *Atlanta Journal and Constitution.*

Six children killed in house fire; mother charged with manslaughter. (2001, November 10). Associated Press.

Sokoloff, N., & Price, B. (1995). *The criminal justice system and women.* New York: McGraw Hill.

Squire, C. (1997). Who's white? Television talk shows and representations of whitness. In M. Fine, L. Weis, L. Powell, & M. Wong (Eds.), *Off white: Readings on race, power, and society.* New York: Routledge.

Stapleton, C. (1995, February 15). A "coffee klatch" of accused moms. *Palm Beach Post.*

Sutherland, E., & Cressey, D. (1978). *Criminology.* Philadelphia: J. B. Lippincott.

Swift, K. J. (1995). *Manufacturing "bad mothers": A critical perspective on child neglect.* Toronto, Canada: University of Toronto Press.

Testa, K. (1995). Both sides rest in Zile case. *The Ledger,* April 8.

Tobin, M. (2001, November 2). Dad faces charge for trying to shape son's head. *The Plain Dealer.*

Utah at fault for suicide. (2001, August 1). *Deseret News* [Opinion column].

Vigh, M., & Curreri, F. (2000, November 2). Boy likely died of hypothermia; police theorize toddler walked 2 miles from truck before laying down; toddler's body found under 4 inches of snow. *Salt Lake Tribune.*

Was Wayment a criminal? (2001, August 1). *Deseret News* [Opinion column].

Whitaker, C. (1990). *Black victims*. Washington, DC: U.S. Department of Justice.

Wiggins, R. (1994, November 1). Is there any excuse? *Palm Beach Post*.

Williams, P. (1991). *The alchemy of race and rights*. Cambridge, MA: Harvard University Press.

Wolfson, H. (2001, July 17). Wayment found dead after failing to show up at jail. Associated Press State and Local Wire.

FIFTEEN

Finding a Place to Pee and Other Struggles of Ethnography: Reflections on Race and Method

Mitchell Duneier

Hakim Hasan is a book vendor and street intellectual at the busy intersection of Eighth Street, Greenwich Avenue, and the Avenue of the Americas — aka Sixth Avenue. He is a sturdy and stocky five-foot-seven African American, 42 years old. In the winter, he wears Timberland boots, jeans, a hooded sweatshirt, a down vest, and a Banana Republic baseball cap.

Hakim is one of many street book vendors throughout Greenwich Village and New York City generally. Most of these vendors specialize in one or more of the following: expensive art and photography books, dictionaries, *New York Times* best-sellers, "black books," new quality mass-market and trade paperbacks of all varieties, used and out-of-print books, comic books, pornography, and discarded magazines.

On Sixth Avenue alone, among the vendors of new books, a passerby may encounter Muhammad and his family, who sell "black books" and an incense known as "the Sweet Smell of Success" at the corner of Sixth Avenue and Eighth Street. Down the block, an elderly white man sells best-sellers and high-quality hardcovers on the weekends. At Sixth and Greenwich (across the street), one encounters Howard, a comics vendor, also white, and Alice, a Filipina woman (Hakim's sometime business partner), who sells used paperbacks and current best sellers.

It goes without saying, perhaps, that one good way to find out more about people is to get to know them first hand, but this is more easily said than done. When I began, I knew that if I was to find out what was taking place on the sidewalk, I would have to bridge many gaps between me and the people I hoped to understand. This involved thinking carefully about who they are and who I am. I was uneasy.

One of the most notorious gaps in American society is the difference between people related to race and the discourse revolving around this volatile issue. Though there were also differences between our social classes (I was raised in a middle-class suburb, whereas most of them grew up in lower- and working-class urban neighborhoods), religions (I am Jewish and most of them are Muslim or Christian), levels of education (I hold a Ph.D. in sociology and attended 2 years of law school, whereas some of them did not graduate from high school), and occupations (I am a college professor of sociology and they are street vendors), none of these differences seemed to be as significant as that of race. Actually, the interaction between race and class differences very likely made me uneasy, though I was unaware of that at the time.

When I stood at Hakim's table, I felt that, as a white male, I stood out. In my mind, I had no place at his table, because he was selling so-called black books. I thought that his product formed the boundary of a sort of exclusionary black zone where African Americans were welcome but whites were not.

It is interesting that I felt this way. African Americans buy products every day from stores owned by whites, often having to travel to other neighborhoods to acquire the goods they need. They must shop among whites, and often speak of enduring slights and insults from the proprietors of these businesses. I myself rarely have to go to neighborhoods not dominated by whites in search of goods or services. None of the book vendors ever insulted, offended, or threatened me. None of them told me I was not welcome at his table. None of them ever made antiwhite or anti-Semitic remarks. Yet I felt unwelcome in ways I had not felt during previous studies that had brought me into contact with African Americans. This was because many of the conversations I heard were about so-called black books and because the people participating in them seemed to be defining themselves as a people. (Actually, there were also white customers at Hakim's table, though I didn't know it at the time.) I felt out of place. Also, I wanted the trust that would be necessary to write about the life of the street, and race differences seem a great obstacle to such trust.

One day, before I knew Hakim and after I had concluded that these tables were not an appropriate place for me to hang out, I walked by his book table on my way to an appointment. I was surprised to see for sale a copy of *Slim's Table*, my own first book.

"Where did you get this from?" I asked, wondering if it had been stolen.

"I have my sources," Hakim responded. "Do you have some interest in this book?"

"Well, I wrote it," I responded.

"Really? Do you live around here?"

"Yes. I live around the corner, on Mercer Street."

"Why don't you give me your address and telephone number for my Rolodex."

His Rolodex? I wondered. This unhoused man has a Rolodex? Why I assumed that Hakin was unhoused is difficult to know for certain. In part, it was due to the context in which he was working: Many of the African American men selling things on the block lived right there on the sidewalk. There was no way for me to distinguish easily between those vendors who were unhoused and those who were not, and I had never taken the time to think much about it. I gave him my telephone number and walked off to my appointment.

A few weeks later, I ran into an African American man, Carl Thomas, who had been in my first-year class at the New York University School of Law. (Carl went on to be the lawyer who would bring the beating of Abner Luima to the attention of the press and was the first attorney to represent him before Johnny Cochran took over the case.) Purely by coincidence, he told me that he was on his way to see a book vendor from whom he had been getting some of his reading material during the past year. It was Hakim.

I told my classmate about my interest in getting to know Hakim and explained my reservations. He told me that he didn't think it would be as hard as I thought. Hakim had apparently gone through spells of sleeping at my classmate's home with his wife and children.

A few days later my classmate brought him to meet me in the law-school lounge. When I told Hakim that I wanted to get to know him and the people at his vending table, he was circumspect, saying only that he would think about it. A few days later, he dropped off a brief but eloquent note at my apartment, explaining that he didn't think it was a good idea. "My suspicion is couched in the collective memory of a people who have been academically slandered for generations," he wrote. "African Americans are at a point where we have to be suspicious of people who want to tell stories about us."

During the next couple of months, Hakim and I saw each other about once a week or so on our own. On a few occasions we met and talked at the Cozy Soup & Burger on Broadway. It seemed that we had decided to get to know each other better.

Early one morning a few months later, I approached his table as he was setting up and I asked, "What are you doing working on Sixth Avenue in the first place?"

"I think there are a number of black folks in these corporate environments that have to make this decision," he replied. "Some are not as extreme as I am. Some take it out on themselves in other ways."

It had not occurred to me that Hakim had come to work on the street from a corporate environment. Learning this about him has been significant, as I have worked to understand his life on the street. In the universities where I teach, I meet many African American students who believe that it will be very difficult for them to maintain their integrity while working in corporate life. Many of them have come to this conclusion by hearing of the experiences of relatives and friends who have already had problems; others have themselves sensed racial intolerance on campus. Yet, in choosing to work on the street, Hakim had clearly made what would be a radical, if not entirely incomprehensible, decision by the standards of my African American students. Once we had discussed some of these issues in depth over the subsequent weeks, Hakim volunteered that he felt comfortable letting me observe his table with the purpose of writing about it, and I began to do so.

In fact, Hakim probably did not feel comfortable. In an afterward to *Sidewalk*, he later wrote,

Mitchell Duneier recalls that he was thoroughly surprised when, during our first conversation at my book vending table, I told him that I had a Rolodex. His surprise was a matter of social context. But what if I had not mentioned the word Rolodex to Mitch? Because the word Rolodex is associated with people who work in offices, and because I was perceived as a "street person," my use of it stood out. It caused a shift in Mitch's perception of me. I am now inclined to suggest that this book would never have been written if it had not been for this conversation, which challenged his assumptions about me and my social status.

In the first chapter Mitch recalls his difficulty in convincing me to become a subject — at the time the sole subject — of the book. Indeed, I found myself hearing the decree of my mother, whenever she had to leave my siblings and me at home alone: Do not open the door for anyone while I'm gone.

If I defied the maternal decree and opened this door, on what basis would I weigh Mitch's intentions? How could I prevent him from appropriating me as mere data, from not giving me a voice in how the material in his book would be selected and depicted? How does a subject take part in an ethnographic study in which he has very little faith and survive as something more than a subject and less than an author?

Because I believe my disastrous experience in the corporate world was the effect of racism (a claim many whites these days liken to that of the proverbial boy who cried "Wolf!"), I asked myself, "Can I expect Mitch, as a white sociologist, to understand why that experience led me to work as a book vendor on Sixth Avenue in the first place?" The idea of race as a lived experience could not be avoided; at the same time, if I made the mistake of denying Mitch his humanity on the basis of race, without giving him a fair chance, there would have been no way for me to know whether he could write about my life accurately.

I did not know how Mitch would construct an account of my life on these blocks. Would he conduct his research as a descendent of a sociological tradition which historically has found it all but impossible to write and theorize about blacks, especially poor blacks, as complex human beings? I worried this way, oddly enough, even after reading Mitch's first book, *Slim's Table*, despite its insights into the lives of working-class black men, because my life, not the lives depicted in that book, was at stake....

I am still trying to understand how Mitch and the people whose lives he documented developed relationships on several New York City Streets where race and class conflicts derail most efforts to transcend such barriers. Does this mean that people sometimes find ways — the will, actually — to work through their phobias and prejudices on these streets? Is it a matter of being willing to listen to one another with respect? Does it hinge on the sheer willpower of a subject, in this case myself, who was determined not be reduced to theoretical formulations or mere "data"? Given the vast inequalities, racial misunderstandings, and violence found on the street at every turn, I believe there was some measure of good luck involved here — the kind of luck scholars and "subjects" of different races, classes, and genders will need when they encounter one another in the field.

I could not imagine a more eloquent statement on these topics than Hakim's. When we use the word "luck," we often are referring to mere good fortune, but we are also referring to factors that have not yet been identified. While acknowledging that there is a tremendous amount of luck involved in any fieldwork project actually coming to fruition, it is essential to characterize the concrete things we actually *can* do in order to increase the chances that good fortune will be on our side. In reflecting on my field experiences researching race and racism as a white male, I have developed a few rules for myself as I go about doing my work.

First, don't begin with the assumption that special rapport or trust is always a precondition for doing successful fieldwork. And don't be so presumptuous as to believe that you have trust or even special rapport with the people you are trying to write about, even when it seems you do.

On June 8, 1996, I appeared on Sixth Avenue at about 6:00 A.M. Ron, whom I recognized from the time I had spent on the block (but whom I had never met), was already there. I had heard enough about his violent episodes to think that I had better wait until Marvin arrived before I approached.

Marvin appeared half an hour later. He greeted me and introduced me to Ron, who, it turned out, had been expecting me. As the two men began unpacking magazines from crates that a "mover" named Rock had transported from Marvin's storage locker, Marvin told me to watch how the magazines are displayed, with the foreign fashion titles placed at the top of the table where they will catch the eyes of passersby.

As I joined in the work, I removed a tape recorder from my bag. Ron looked down at the machine and scowled. He hardly spoke that day. I put the tape recorder back in my bag, never having turned it on.

I was wearing the same clothes I had been wearing in the classroom a few days earlier: a blue button-down shirt, beige pants, and black shoes. Even if I had dressed differently, I would have stood out. My speech and diction alone would have made me seem different. Had I tried to downplay these differences, though, Ron would have seen through such a move immediately.

So right away on the block I was being a person not unlike the person I am with my friends in casual settings, my family at home, and my colleagues at work. Of course, in each of these settings, I adapt somewhat, accentuating some traits and downplaying others. In small ways I am not aware of, I doubtless did the same as I began my work.

Using myself as a participant observer, I was there to notice by taking part, trying to observe and retain information that others in the setting often thought unimportant or took for granted. I had research questions vaguely in mind, and I was already making mental comparisons between what I was seeing and what the sociology literature had to say. I was there simply to observe and record, and I was asking the people working the sidewalk to let me be there.

One of the most difficult situations I faced as I tried to make an entry into these blocks was avoiding the conflicts that already existed. Hakim, with whom I had become closely associated, got along well with everyone on Sixth Avenue except Muhammad. But if I was to get to know all the men on the block, it was essential that I not be viewed as especially associated with Hakim.

The act of "getting in," then, sometimes led me to be less than sincere about my connection to Hakim. Fieldwork can be a morally ambiguous enterprise. I say this even though I have never lied to any of the persons I write about. The question for me is how to show respect for the people I write about, given the impossibility of complete sincerity at every moment (in research as in life).

The gulf between the other vendors and me was much greater than it was with Hakim. How could I expect these men to trust me? The vendors were wondering the same thing. One conversation captured on my tape recorder illustrates this. I had been interviewing one of them, who had been holding my tape recorder, when I got called away. While listening to the tapes a few months later, I came across the conversation that ensued after I left. (The participants, who forgot the tape was running, have asked me to conceal their identities in this instance.)

"What you think he's doing to benefit you?" X asked.

"A regular black person who's got something on the ball should do this, I would think," said Y.

"He's not doing anything to benefit us, Y."

"I'm not saying it's to benefit us," said Y. "It's for focus."

"No. It's more for them, the white people."

"You think so?" said Y.

"Yeah. My conversations with him just now, I already figured it out. It's mostly for them. They want to know why there's so much homeless people into selling books. . . . I told him because Giuliani came in and he said nobody could panhandle no more. Then the recycling law came in. People voted on it."

"Case in point," said Y. "You see, I knew he had to talk to you. I can't tell him a lot of things 'cause I'm not a talker."

"I told him in California there's people doing the same thing that we're doing. They do it on a much more higher level. They are white people. You understand?"

"Yeah."

"They have yard sales."

"Yeah."

"They put the shit right out there in their yard. He knows. Some of them make a million dollars a year. But what they put in their yard, these are people that put sculptures. They put expensive vases. These are peoples that drives in their cars. All week long, all they do is shop."

"Looking for stuff," said Y. "Like we go hunting, they go shopping."

"Right. Very expensive stuff. They bring it and they put it in their yard and sell it. And they do it every weekend. Every Saturday. Every Sunday. So they making thousands. He's not questioning them: How come they can do it? He's questioning us! He want to know how did the homeless people get to do it. That's his whole main concern. Not really trying to help us. He's trying to figure out how did the homeless people get a lock on something that he consider lucrative."

"Good point," said Y.

"You gotta remember, he's a Jew, you know. They used to taking over. They used to taking over no matter where they go. When they went to Israel. When they went to Germany. Why do you think in World War II they got punished so much? Because they owned whole of Germany. So when the regular white people took over, came to power, they said, 'We tired of these Jews running everything.'"

"But throughout time the Jewish people have always been business people. But they love to take over."

Y laughed.

"Of course," X said, laughing hysterically. "That's what he's doing his research on now. He's trying to figure out how did these guys got it. How come we didn't get it?"

Y laughed.

X continued laughing hysterically, unable to finish his next sentence.

"I don't think so," said Y.

"But he's not interested in trying to help us out."

"I'm not saying that, X. I'm saying he's trying to focus on the point."

"I told him that, too," said X. "Everyone he talk to, they're gonna talk to him on the level like he's gonna help them against the police or something like that. They're gonna look to him to advocate their rights."

"No. I don't think that, either. I think it's more or less to state the truth about what's going on. So people can understand that people like you and I are not criminals. We're not horrible people. Just like what you said, what happens if we couldn't do this? What would you do if you couldn't sell books right now?"

Hearing those stereotypes invoked against me made me realize that—conventional wisdom to the contrary—participant observers need not be fully trusted in order to have their presence at least accepted. I learned how to do fieldwork from Howard S. Becker, and one of the things he taught me—I call it the Becker principle—is that most social processes have a structure that comes close to ensuring that a certain set of situations will arise over time. These situations practically require people to do or say certain things because there are other things going on that require them to do that, things that are more influential than the social condition of a fieldworker being present. For example, most of the things in a vendor's day—from setting up his magazines to going on hunts for magazines to urinating—are structured. This is why investigators like me sometimes can learn about a social world despite not having had the rapport we thought we had, and despite the fact that we occupy social positions quite distinct from the persons we write about.

It was hard for me to know what to make of that discussion between X and Y. Maybe they were "just" having fun, but I don't think so. Though I was not astonished by what I heard, I had no idea that X harbored those suspicions toward me as I had gone about my work on the blocks throughout the summer. In this sense, fieldwork is very much like life itself. We may *feel fully* trusted and accepted by colleagues and "friends," but full acceptance is difficult to measure by objective standards and a rarity in any case. If we cannot expect such acceptance in our everyday lives, it is probably unrealistic to make it the standard for successful fieldwork.

At the same time, participant *observers like* me who do cross-race fieldwork must, I think, be aware that there are many things members of the different races will not say in one another's presence. For blacks in the United States, it has been necessary to "wear the mask," to quote the black poet Paul Laurence Dunbar, who wrote,

> We wear the mask that grins and lies,
> It hides our cheeks and shades our eyes,
> This debt we pay to human guile;
> With torn and bleeding hearts we smile,
> And mouth with myriad subtleties.
>
> (Braxton, 1993)

Dunbar's words are no less relevant today, for, as a survival mechanism, many blacks still feel that they cannot afford to speak honestly to whites. Surely, it would have been a methodological error for me to believe that apparent rapport is real trust, or that the poor blacks I was writing about would feel comfortable taking off the mask in my presence.

I believe that some of the vendors may have let me work out on Sixth Avenue with them because they eventually saw what I was doing nearly the way I did; others merely wanted to have me around as a source of small change and loans (something I discuss later); and a few others may have decided to put up with me so that there would be a book about them and the blocks. But it would be naive for me to say that I knew what they were thinking, or that they trusted or accepted me fully, whatever that might mean.

Second, begin research with a humble commitment to being surprised by the things you learn in the field, and a constant awareness that your social position likely makes you blind to the very phenomena that might be useful to explain.

Once while listening to tapes I had made on the street, I came across a dialogue between two unhoused men — Mudrick telling Keith that the assistant manager kicked him out of McDonald's for not being a "customer" when he tried to use the bathroom. A comparison I did not plan to make was suddenly evident: Mudrick is an unhoused vendor. He works on the street. I am a professor. I work in an office building. The unhoused vendor, a 57-year-old black man, has just relied on the goodwill of a teenage black boy with the title "assistant manager" to let him use the bathroom. I, by contrast, had been using the bathrooms of local restaurants whenever I pleased.

We are told by the methods literature to ask questions that will enable us to dialogue with theory, that are important in the real world, or that make some contribution to the literature. What we are not told is how to overcome blinders that may derive from differences between us and the people we write about. These blinders influence the conception of questions, and the determination that certain topics should be noticed in the first place.

I had often seen men urinating against the sides of buildings or in cups during my years working with the vendors, but this had never registered as important enough to jot on a note pad or think about twice. It was so much part of my taken-for-granted reality that it did not bear note. I had probably assumed that the men who were peeing against the side of the Washington Square Court condominium were just lazy, and no different, by the way, from all my upper-middle-class male friends who do the same thing when they are in the middle of the golf course and are too lazy to go back to the clubhouse to take a piss. This is the kind of male behavior I have taken for granted throughout my life. And the things we take for granted often do not end up in our field jottings.

On the tape I had just listened to, I was confronted with a single conversation that posed a challenge to my taken-for-granted assumptions. Mudrick had been *excluded from* the McDonald's bathroom. As an unhoused man he was not peeing against the condominium out of the same kind of laziness I had observed in my upper-middle-class white friends on the golf course. But why, if I had been working out on the street every day and night with these men, had I not *understood* this to be a problem? How was it that while working with the housed and unhoused vendors I had not noticed this basic aspect of their lives, let alone conceived of it as a research issue?

As an upper-middle-class white male, I had skin and class privileges that the men I was working with did not have. As I thought back to the previous summer on these blocks, I thought of the hundreds of times I had crossed the street and darted to the back of Pizzeria Uno without once wondering if anyone would deny me entrance. Though we were occupying the same physical space and engaging in common activities out on the street, my experience of urinating (and, I would later learn, of defecating), had been radically different from that of the men I worked with. This is part of the reason I did not perceive it as a research topic. The fact that I *did* finally consider it, that I did ultimately recognize a research issue, came from a constellation of lucky circumstances, one of which being that while listening to the tape in my office far away I happened to have been in need of using the bathroom, which made me particularly sensitive to the issue of peeing when I heard that 5-second snippet of tape that might have otherwise run by unnoticed.

Now here is a question. What if I had not belonged to a more privileged social position than my subjects? What if, instead, I was poor and black and similarly excluded? I would surely have understood this to be an aspect of daily life, but would I have understood it to be a topic? I don't know the answer, but one possibility is that being excluded from public bathrooms is so taken for granted on the street that it is rarely discussed. I never heard discussions about it during the previous summer, and the discussion I *did* hear on the tape was hardly a discussion, more like a reference to an incident that did not deserve elaboration. I do not believe that someone from the same social position as the vendors would necessarily have seen exclusion from bathrooms as a research topic, any more than my colleagues at the university would see the circumstances of bathroom use on the eighth floor of the social science building as an interesting research issue.

I suspect that a black male professional researcher might have had less difficulty than these men gaining access to local public bathrooms, but I cannot be certain. Researching race usually entails researching class and it is often difficult for researchers to know if they are being treated differently from the people they write about because of skin, class, gender privileges, or by some interaction between them. Despite the social differences between us, it is possible that I would have arrived at an understanding of this situation if the men had talked about it. They did not. I remain uncertain as to how to interpret their silence. Did they simply find this to be an unremarkable aspect of their struggles as unhoused men, since this form of exclusion was so routine? Or did they want to protect me (and themselves) from further humiliation and embarrassment by not discussing my own racial and class privileges as a white upper-class academic? I have routinely noted that people who experience race and class discrimination tend to be quite sensitive toward the feelings of those who do not share their experiences. In fact, in my experience neither blacks nor whites in the United States talk honestly about race in the other's presence.

Though I constantly obsess about the ways that my upper-middle-class whiteness influences what I see, I must emphasize my uncertainty about what I do not see and what I do not know I missed.

Third, try to overcome the disadvantages that derive from your social position by consulting with your research subjects, as well as with scholars and intellectuals who once shared the social position of the people you are writing about.

After completing the draft of the original *Sidewalk* manuscript, I gave it to Hakim and asked him for his comments. He read it and brought to my attention a major limitation. As he saw it, my study focused too closely on him and not enough on the vendors who occupied other spaces on Sixth Avenue. As I listened to what he had to say, I realized that we needed to have a sustained conversation about the material in the manuscript. I proposed that we teach a course together at the University of California–Santa Barbara, where I was that year. Hakim was clearly well read, and I had admired his pedagogical relationships with young men like Jerome. Surely my students in Santa Barbara could benefit from working closely with him. I told my idea to Bill Bielby, the chair of my department, who arranged for Hakim to receive a lecturer's salary for the 10-week course.

Hakim and I taught a seminar for undergraduates called "The Life of the Street and the Life of the Mind in Black America." In it, we discussed a number of books that Hakim had sold at his table and spoke in detail from the draft manuscript, showing the students how "black books" entered into the lives and discussions of people who came to Hakim's table. As a teacher, Hakim was organized, insightful, and patient with students on subjects of race, class, and gender, although the discussions were sometimes quite heated.

My research focus was evolving in the seminar as I continually listened to Hakim and came to get a sense of what might be gained if the book included a more comprehensive view of the street.

Sometimes it was the suggestions of African American scholars that led me back to the field with new ideas and questions I had not thought to ask. In trying to understand why black women don't get entangled to the same extent as white women by street harassment in encounters with poor black men, for example, I was helped by the suggestion of a black Wisconsin sociologist, Franklin D. Wilson. He thinks that because the black women share a racial history with the men on the street, they do not feel responsible or guilty for the men's plight and so are less willing to excuse the men's behavior toward them. Surely a white scholar could have had that insight, but none of those who read my chapter did. I suspect it comes out of Wilson's particular life experience, from situations and people he has known.

Another thing that has helped me has been my collaboration with the African American photographer Ovie Carter, whose professional and life experiences enable him to give me good advice. Ovie is 52 years old, was born in Mississippi, and grew up in Chicago and St. Louis, before serving in the Air Force. He joined the *Chicago Tribune* at the age of 23. He has worked in Africa as a photojournalist but has spent most of his career covering poor neighborhoods in Chicago. Shortly before our work began on *Sidewalk*, his brother moved in with him from the streets as he made his way off crack. Consequently, Ovie has a deep appreciation for the anguish and problems associated with addiction. Ovie read and commented on all the chapters in *Sidewalk* as I wrote them, and the long hours we have spent together helped me to understand aspects of life on Sixth Avenue that I would otherwise have been blind to.

All these circumstances have worked for me at times, but there is no simple way to overcome ingrained racial bias, inexperience, or others' suspicions. Perhaps the best starting point is to be aware that a different social position can have a serious effect on one's work, and one can do better work by taking them very seriously.

REFERENCES

Braxton, J. (1993). *The Collected Poetry of Paul Laurence Dunbar*. Charlottesville, VA: University Press of Virginia.

SIXTEEN

White Experimenters, White Blood, and Other White Conditions: Locating the Psychologist's Race

Jill G. Morawski

The contours of America's long-standing obsession with race have been mirrored in psychologists' studies of race. Scientific psychology has not simply reflected dominant cultural understandings of race but has reconfigured race through the discipline's evolving theoretical commitments. In an era of research fascinated by individual differences, for instance, race conveniently stood as a "natural" category for comparing differences, whereas in a research climate attuned to social problems, race comprised a crisis to be rectified. In the spirit of laboratory practices, psychologists literally experimented with race, alternately designating it a conceptual category, a variable, a genetic entity, a methodological problem, or a cognitive process.

Among these changing foci of scrutiny was the occasional consideration of the scientist's race. There exist writings, spanning nearly 75 years, which examine the race of scientists, be they acting as examiners, testers, interviewers, observers, or experimenters. Having encountered several instances where psychologists observed their own racial identities, I suspected that much could be learned from these cases but it soon became apparent that they were anomalies. Aside from approximately 100 studies devoted to the subject, few research reports published during the period even mention the investigator's race. Save a minuscule subset, then, experimental psychology reports including over 90% of the research on race indicate no race of experimenter (Graham, 1992; McLoyd, 1991).

Logic and facts reined and reigned in on my initial project. Indeed, during the period there were but a few gestures of researchers' serious self-reflection on their race. Moreover, the predominant tendency in these studies was to deflect self-appraisal away from examining whiteness. Over time, the experimenter's race was routinely treated as a discrete variable or a factor of secondary interest. Routinization of this issue had become a tactical means to shift and manage scientific visions and identities, not to interrogate them. Toni Morrison described the dismissal of race matters in American literature "as a kind of trembling hypochondria always curing itself with unnecessary surgery" (1992, p. 13). Most of the interrogations of the experimenter's race look like such unnecessary surgery, removing once and for all some ambiguous race from nearly abstracted and careless experiments.

The foremost finding of my historical analysis, then, is that the matter of the experimenters' race has been deferred to a politics of epistemology. The epistemic commitment to an abstracted, formless observer preponderated. Questions about the observer's identity have been overshadowed by this prevailing commitment. A second finding of the historical analysis is related to this quiet dismissal of the race of experimenter issue. In the process of taking up and ultimately rejecting consideration of the experimenter's race, these studies transferred scientific attention to the race of the subjects. The subjects' racial status, skin color, degree of "white blood," racial psychology, or attitudes eventually gained primary consideration. In the end, the vast majority of race of experimenter studies have been about the other, not the self of the investigator. Gazing outward and not inward, these studies have sustained a focus on the raced subject — the broad subject of race and/or the particular racialized subjects who participate in experimentation.

Until very recently, race research comprised a psychology of the "other" wherein nonwhite races were the targets of investigation. That research presumed, but did not interrogate, a normative psychology of whiteness. Instead, it demonstrated a keen regard for the nature of otherness, all the while largely neglecting the meanings and implications of whiteness. Studies on the race of experimenter, while sporadic in occurrence, nevertheless correspond to this dominant approach to race in North American psychology. Given this correspondence, the essay proceeds from a survey of conventional conceptions of race to an examination of how and when the experimenter's race was acknowledged. Awareness of experimenter's race was not a random event, but tended to arise at junctures when the political implications of psychological research became particularly pronounced. For many psychologists, the objective observation of experimenter's race represented efforts to ensure that truly scientific data — objective and value-free facts — were brought to these political concerns. For a few psychologists, analyzing the experimenter's race was expressly intended as a means to examine the politics of science. Regardless of psychologists' specific motivations, the general outcome of these studies was the erasure of politics, either by ignoring, minimizing, or forgetting the experimental problem.

"Race" in American Psychology

To claim that race has been one preoccupation of psychology in America over the past century comprises a fair statement, one readily supported by historical evidence. To claim that race is difficult to locate, even that it has been invisible, in experimental work in that time span also would stand as credible even as it seems to contradict the first claim. Race in psychology, if viewed from a historical vantage point, has a now-you-see-it-now-you-don't quality. The simultaneity of prominence and invisibility is neither illusion nor happenstance but is the product of the variegated intellectual traditions and political inclinations which have influenced American experimental psychology. German psychophysics, developed in the mid-19th century, aimed to discover universal laws of mental life. These laws would govern all minds regardless of people's cultural or individual particularities. By contrast, a concomitant engagement with individual difference research ensued from Darwinism thinking and its presupposition of evolutionary determinism, chance variation, and selection of particular mental attributes. From its inception Darwinism was applied to race, deeming it a natural variation readily accessible to assessment and comparison. American psychology was not shaped only by these two traditions: It also matured with an indigenous aspiration to be a useful science, to be practicable in the everyday world. Race has been one of those practical problems for psychology, emerging most frequently in response to policy issues of immigration, education, social welfare, and integration.

The confluence of these intellectual traditions has had two notable effects on the treatment of race in psychology. One peculiar effect has been the aforementioned feature of race as at once visible and invisible within psychology. The introspection movement of the early 20th century, for instance, paid little attention to race matters in its search for universal qualities of the mind, whereas the concurrent work on intelligence testing quickly identified race as a possible determinant of group differences in mental ability. In the present, research on cognition and memory rarely features considerations of race, whereas studies of school achievement and addiction research routinely assess race differences. A second effect of psychology's plural traditions has been the mobility, even mutability, of the concept. At various times and in various investigative venues race has been taken to be a natural, kind, genetic entity, personal attribute, attitude, or an interpersonal perception. Some of these variations in the meaning of race in research transpired sequentially (i.e., the change from early-20th-century interests in race differences to studies of prejudice by the early 1940s), but they also have coexisted within a single time frame. Thus, current studies of the genetic bases of race coincide with investigations of the social bases of race and racism. The resultant conceptual confusions are substantial and are described in recent recommendations for clarifying the notion of race and distinguishing it from concepts of genetics, ethnicity, and culture (Betancourt & Lopez, 1993; Helms, 1992; Yee, Fairchild, Weizmann, & Wyatt 1993; Zuckerman, 1990).

The alterations and multiplicity of race concepts complicate the construction of any simple historical narrative of the psychology of race, yet some overarching patterns in research can be discerned. Evident over the past 75 years are three trends: a shift in emphasis from bodily and material phenomena to mental (cognitive) phenomena, a primary focus on African Americans as racial others, and an unremitting preoccupation with methodology (Gaines & Reed, 1995; Henriques, 1984; Samelson, 1978).

Intellectual commitments, then, guided psychological investigations of race. However, these commitments along with the general interest in race were configured through sociopolitical concerns. Interest in race waxed and waned with changes in the cultural climate. The fact that African Americans have been the predominant racial group studied (J. M. Jones, 1991), the minority that is most often the subject of political debate, intimates the motivations underguiding research. The personal and political attitudes of individual scientists further attest to linkages between race research and sociopolitics (Pastore, 1949; Samelson, 1978; Tucker, 1994). The fact that these sociopolitical matters were at odds with a chief edict of psychology's scientific epistemology — that rational scientists put aside politics and identity matters, including their race — may be the source of an intriguing duality of vision. That is, many research programs harbor a dual model of persons: at least when the experimenter is white, the race of *experimenter* is held to be unrelated to his or her cognitions, whereas the race of the *subject* is held to possibly affect his or her cognitions.

LOCATING THE PROBLEM: EPISTEMOLOGY OR METHODOLOGY?

Empiricism holds that the social status of the observers, given adequate training, is irrelevant to scientific practice. Epistemological traditions like empiricism, however, are historical and social products: Just as objectivity has had different meanings at different historical moments, so have conceptions of the objective scientist or scientific observer. Our modern understanding of objectivity, fashioned in the 19th century, is based on aspirations for censuring the personal (subjective) and eliminating the observer's presence as well as on the ideals of precision, sustained scrutiny, and sensory acuity. Objectivity thus defined guided the mundane tasks of scientific work, but it also constituted "a profoundly moralized vision, of self-command triumphing over the temptations and frailties of flesh and spirit" (Daston & Galison, 1992, p. 83).

Psychologists' considerations of experimenters' race need to be viewed in terms of the then-current conceptions of scientific observers — scientists' construals of scientists. However, although the observer's status and capabilities constitute epistemological concerns, in scientific practice they often have been translated into methodological problems. The race of the experimenter was treated as one such problem. Before considering its treatment as a methodological concern the general beliefs about the experimenter's status as objective observer warrant review.

By the end of the 19th century, science was conceived not just as a means to acquire a certain kind of knowledge or as a profession but also as a moral enterprise (Hollinger, 1989). Karl Pearson, in his popular 1892 philosophy of science text, captured this conception in claiming, "Modern science, as training the mind to an exact and impartial analysis of the fact is an education specially fitted to promote sound citizenship" (1892/1937, p. 9). Pearson claimed that although the "savage" deifies trees and water to account for natural events, the "civilized man" expresses "his emotional experience in works of art and his physical and mental experience in the formulae or so-called laws of science" (p. 36). Pearson's description aims to depict a universal attitude, but in actuality it casts the scientist as a distinct personality, one associated with a specific social class. In most depictions of the era, the scientist was educated, broad-minded, serious, and manly. The writings of the first generation of experimental psychologists mirror this image of the scientist. Edward Titchener described the necessity of "long-training" to overcome the "ignorance" that he observed in the untrained mind (1910, p. 350). E. W. Scripture encouraged the "education of men, instead of bookworms and mummies" (1894, p. 570). To G. S. Hall, research training "emancipates the mind from error and superstition" and, above all, "gets the mind into independent action, so that men can become authorities and not echoes" (1910, p. 350). George Trumbell Ladd wrote, "It is not arrogant to claim that the trained psychologist *understands* not only the child, the idiot, the madman, and the hypnotic subject, but also the artist, the scientist, the statesman, and the thinker, as psychological beings, far better than any of these classes understand each other, or even themselves" (1894, p. 21). Robert Woodworth observed in 1910 that "members of the inferior races" were suitable, indeed, "admirable subjects for the psychologist," providing that the psychologist understood that he should not try to secure "elaborate" responses from them (introspections being one such elaborate response). Instead, "If tests are put in such form as to appeal to the interests of the primitive man, he can be relied on for sustained attention" (Woodworth, 1910, p. 179). The desirable scientific observer shared cultural ideals of manliness and middle-class professionalism (Rotundo, 1993), along with certain qualities of the late-Victorian gentleman.

The experimenter's status, one privileged by gender and race as well as education, was just one of the myriad problems in race research that initiated methodological discussions. Whether it be the establishment of group norms, statistical methods to account for variance, control of dialect effects, representative sampling, or test-forming, race research generated methodological disputes. Some areas of race research have become virtually ongoing contestations over methodological issues. For instance, the now nearly century-long investigation of race differences in intelligence looks like an ongoing pattern of confrontations over a series of methodological problems, from attaining representative sampling to constructing culture-free tests. Likewise, the classic studies of doll preference, conducted by the Clarks and used in the *Brown vs. Board of Education* decision, initiated many alterations in procedure, evoking numerous questions about methodology (for example, Banks, 1976). Among the sciences and social sciences alike, the discipline of psychology has a long-standing reputation for its intense concern with methods, even a "method fetish" (Toulmin & Leary, 1985), but the fixation on methodological matters in race research exceeds even this reputation.

Two specific methodological concerns relating to the race of the experimental actors emerged during this century and have perplexed the design, as well as the interpretation, of experiments. The first problem entails the subjects (now usually called participants) in research. In particular, the problem concerns the fact that subjects' racial status has been recorded and examined in relatively few studies beyond those expressly investigating race. Even when this status has been reported, it has been done in an inconsistent manner. The simplest solution to this problem has been to include subjects of more than one race (white) and to report these data routinely. Assessments of the presences of African American participants in psychology journal articles over the past three decades concur that the percentage is somewhere between 3.6 and 5% (Graham, 1992; J. M. Jones, 1983; McLoyd & Randolph, 1986). Related to this representation problem is the larger concern about whether inclusion is done in order to conduct race-comparative or race-homogenous studies. Graham's (1992) analysis of selected APA journal articles that were published between 1970 and 1989 found approximately three times as many articles devoted to race comparisons as to race homogeneous investigations. In these considerations of the race of subjects, what might be held as simple matters of inclusiveness or even simply representative sampling can be seen upon closer inspection to be guided by metatheoretical commitments. Such methodological issues are tied, on the one hand, to beliefs about whether race is related to psychological experiences and processes, and on the other hand, to questions about whether race itself or the differences among races warrant attention.

A second methodological concern that has figured in the race research enterprise is the race of the investigator. On first appearance this problem might resemble that of the race of subject: It might well be conceived as a problem requiring greater attention to representativeness, inclusiveness, and comparisons of investigators. But, both the historical and epistemological conditions of the researcher problem do not parallel those of subjects. Neither do the solutions. The history of race in America has been such that although there has been no shortage of subjects of differing races, researchers have been overwhelmingly, at times exclusively, white (Guthrie, 1976; Wispe et al., 1969). The practical consequences of this labor problem, however, mostly have gone unappreciated, perhaps because they have been overshadowed by a troublesome epistemological dilemma. In the empiricist tradition to which modern psychology has cleaved itself (a tradition that is kept alive in the sciences), the social status of the observer is held to be irrelevant: With appropriate training in the scientific method, any person can observe the world, and observe it in the same way. Objectivity requires removal of the subjective or personal and can be practiced by any appropriately trained observers, regardless of their particular social status. Suggesting that different sorts of persons, that is, persons of different genders, ages, nationalities, or races, observe differently violates the epistemological premises of empiricism (Harding, 1986) and the attendant goals of objectivity. Acknowledging the observer's racial status also increases the pressure to address other identity differentials, thus potentially producing an unending list of qualifiers, such as ethnicity, age, economic status, attractiveness, gender, and so forth. Such admissions thus complicate the research process just as they necessarily implicate a subjectivity of the researcher that has been long denied in psychology.

These two lingering methodological issues, the race of subjects and the race of investigators, then, have not methodology at their roots but history, metatheory, and epistemology. Nevertheless, these problems routinely have been rendered as mere (albeit often debated) technical difficulties. Conceptualized as methodological matters, these problems obscure the more substantial "methodological horrors" (Woolgar, 1988) of the scientific practice they represent. Woolgar's term, methodological horrors, refers to the realization that we, as observers, have no final assurance that our representations of objects in the world accurately reflect those objects in the world. One such real horror is reflexivity — that back-and-forth process whereby our representation depends on preexisting knowledge of what that representation refers to and vice versa. In the human sciences reflexivity is even more complex because the objects of inquiry are humans or human activities; representations thus refer back to the observer as well as to others who are being observed. Reflexivity, in the end, is a self-referential activity (Morawski, 1994). Yet, scientific practices are structured to hide methodological horrors such as reflexivity. Strategies for doing so include construing the horrors as a mere technical difficulties or presenting the problem as a problem for others, for instance as a problem of the subjects but not for the researcher (Woolgar, 1988). As a consequence of the latter strategy, the psychologist and the ordinary person are taken to be different, again perpetuating a dual model of persons. One introductory textbook candidly depicted this duality in racial terms by drawing an analogy between Robinson Crusoe's relationship with his man Friday and the psychologist's relationship with his "other-one" (Meyer, 1921).

Psychological studies of the race of experimenter constitute an example of research strategies created to mask the problems associated with reflexivity. Researchers' self-awareness of their own racial membership, or their self-construals of race more generally, could open the way for intentional (and productive) reflexive analysis, but the studies on experimenter's race reveal, at most, minimal self-awareness. These studies have deflected self-appraisal by making a transference: The problem of the experimenter's race is and has been conceptualized as a problem of the participants. Transferred to the participants, that problem is then construed either as a technicality (experimental artifact) to be controlled if not eliminated and/or an enduring psychological attribute of the participants. Of course, given changes in psychological theorizing about race and in psychology's investigative procedures, interpretations of the race of experimenter problem have varied across the century. Despite these variations, the deflection of self-appraisal has persisted, and the problem of the experimenter's race has been perceived as technical and/or as residing with the subjects.

These omissions, obscurations, and transferences of the researcher's race have notable implications for theory as well as for empirical findings. Most obvious of these consequences is the subterranean existence of our understandings of whiteness and an accompanying fixation on racial "others" and their "differences." Whiteness is buried. Likewise sacrificed are the generative possibilities for reflexive practices on the part of researchers. We have, for instance, not developed ways through which I, as an interrogator of the racial identities of earlier psychologists, can begin to assess the meaning of my own whiteness for these interrogations (or vice versa).

Experimental Dramas: Earlier Studies

Twentieth-century psychology proceeded with an epistemic commitment that served to deflect attention from the social identities of observers. Yet it also thrived on an attitude of empirical curiosity in which the game permitted, even encouraged, the manipulation and control of variables to ascertain previously unknown outcomes. As a discipline replete with theoretical debate, empirical studies were the chief means to resolve such conflicts as well as to explore hunches (later formalized as hypotheses). The possibility that the race of the investigator influenced research results was one such hunch. To date, my research assistant Jessica Smock and I have located 86 empirical studies that address this hunch. The exact number of such studies is difficult to ascertain as it is undoubtedly the case that there is other research in which the race of experimenter was an auxiliary interest; such studies would go undetected because we used subject indices, titles, and citations to locate our cases. Our analysis of the 86 studies indicates a long history of awareness and evasion.

The first report on race of experimenter did not appear until 1916. Although the account was published in a major journal, the author chose anonymity. However, timeliness and authorship become moot points in light of the comprehensiveness and prescience of this brief report that carried the understated title "Some Suggestions Relative to Study of the Mental Attitude of the Negro." The article opens with a quote from Nietzsche on the erroneous tendency of persons to treat the unknown as "strange" and as warranting study. According to Nietzsche, the reality of the matter of strangeness is actually the reverse because "The known is the accustomed, and the accustomed the most difficult of all to understand, that is to say, to perceive as a problem, to perceive as strange, distant, outside of us" (quoted in Anonymous, 1916, p. 201). With Nietzsche's reflexive reversal of the relations of self and other, known and unknown, the author undertook a sweeping appraisal of race psychology that moves from an inquiry into the definition of race to a psychological analysis of experimenters — white and Negro experimenters alike. The typical question of "who is the Negro" is usually answered by some likely social-scientific responses, ranging from "anyone who is not a Caucasian" to the estimation of relative degrees of white and Negro blood. On the problem of explaining race differences in intelligence, the author noted the impossibility of any adequate experimental controls to test the nature-nurture alternatives. Such a definitive experiment would require control of all environmental conditions, and, if for no other reason, it would be impossible because "where are we to find a negro and a white child who have had even approximately the same environment, one a member of the ruling race, the other kept in subjection?" (p. 201).

The crucial dilemma posed in the article entails yet another problem: the scientist. To the author, "the most serious objection to the present methods of investigation is based on the fact that white people conduct the investigation; especially is there danger if the investigator is a stranger" (Anonymous, 1916, pp. 201–202). The mere presence of the white investigator, even a "friendly" one, is shown to elicit certain attitudes from Negro subjects. These attitudes include the Negro's determination "not to let a white person know anything about him" (p. 202), as well as the way that the Negro subject is "proficient in interpreting the moods of the overlord and in devising ways and means to placate him" (p. 202). The investigator too brings other relational dynamics to the research setting. The general tendency of people, including scientists, to want to confirm their suspected beliefs is augmented in this case by an "unconscious mental bias" toward a belief that Negroes are of inferior intelligence. The author concluded that it is impossible for members of the "white race" to conduct fair studies.

This short essay foreshadows the variety of explanations that would be given to the race of experimenter issue over the remainder of the century. The author named what some other investigators would later describe: the potential psychological reactions of the Negro subject (although not the white subject) and the limitations of both black and white investigators. With impressive prescience, the author also attempted to move beyond these problems of racialized roles to imagine a solution in the form of a collaborative objectivity wherein scientists of different racial memberships "each could supply what the other lacked." Albeit through the notion of "each," the author broached an account of whiteness.

Within the decade following this essay, several relevant articles were published. Each article engaged one of two types of treatments of the experimenter's race. The first type of treatment can be referred to as "rhetorical disregard," for it entailed recognition and then dismissal of concerns about the experimenter. Sometimes rhetorical dismissal entailed a direct claim that the matter of the experimenter's race is a concrete methodological problem. In one of the earliest studies

222 Jill G. Morawski

to discuss how subjects of different races may react differently to test situations, that is, to acknowledge the "white" context of testing, authors Pressey and Teter (1919) noted, "The tests were given by white examiners, to colored children in a school showing no adaptation to the particular needs of this race, and in communities where there is sufficient race consciousness for the colored people to be a distinct class by themselves" (p. 278). Through the application of logic, however, the problem was dismissed because "certain of the differences found seem to be too marked to be explainable as the result of such factors alone" (p. 278). Seemingly satisfied with noting implications of the scientist's race, none of these experimenters put their observations of observers to an empirical test.

A second type of treatment of the race of experimenter problem entailed empirical, rather than simply rhetorical, work. In 1927 Horace Bond reported a study of Negro children's intelligence that was conducted by a Negro investigator. The results diverged significantly from most race comparison studies of intelligence: Not only did Negro children display a wide distribution of I.Q. scores but a fair number tested in the "exceptional" range. Bond's data were challenging, but his framing of the study and its results were even more so. His study ensued not simply from a methodological worry but from a unique appraisal of the entire program of race psychology research. That program was portrayed as a rule-bound "game":

> First one must have a *white* examiner; a group of *Negro* children; a test standardized for white children tested by *white* examiners; and just a few pre-conceived notions regarding the nature of "intelligence," the degree with which Negro children are endowed, if at all, with this faculty and the *fact* that the social status of Negro children need not be considered as an extra allowance for scores different from whites. (Bond, 1927, p. 257)

The game includes special logic rules, especially the axiom that high-scoring white children come from high social status families because the family was highly intelligent (and, therefore, intelligence is inherited). Another rule is one that states that examiners must carefully establish "rapport" with white subjects "but for some reason, perhaps the docility of the Negro subjects, or the innate superiority of the race to which the examiner belongs, this caution is not to be regarded in Negro children" (p. 257). Bond sarcastically confessed that he broke a rule in surmising that "as white investigators are able to gain fullest rapport with white children, the same thing might be true of Negro testers with Negro children" (p. 258). In the end, Bond's insider-outsider status as a trained psychologist and a Negro enabled him to construct a radically different and multiple framing of the experimental situation.

Exercises of critique such as Bond's and the aforementioned 1916 critique may have been only that — exercises. They appeared in a period of expansion and professional legitimation during which psychologists were struggling to certify their scientific status and to find markets for their products (Camfield, 1970; O'Donnell, 1985; Sokal, 1987). White psychologists' understandings of themselves as scientists were infused with ideals of middle-class professionalism, including implicit assumptions about race. In this atmosphere of professional progress, the 1916 anonymous review might well have gone unheeded. Readers who held the dominant image of the magnanimous, objective scientist would logically reject the appeal to reflect on their conceptions of "others." After all, given objective training that would allow one to see the world clearly and at a distance, such reflection would be unnecessary. Bond's critique and nonconforming data most likely received quite different responses. For one thing, it appeared not in a mainstream psychology journal but in *The Crisis*, a Negro intellectual journal created and edited by W. E. B. Du Bois (Guthrie, 1976). The actual responses of white investigators are unknown, for it appears that only black researchers replied to it in print. What would it mean to a white psychologist, familiar with the plentiful findings about the inferiority of Negro intelligence to hear about discordant data — and to hear it from a Negro psychologist? Just as Bond's study reported anomalous results about Negro intelligence, so did his racial identity make him conspicuous in a crowd of psychologists whose scientific identity covered their race.

METHODOLOGICAL AND SOCIAL SOPHISTICATION: THE 1930S AND 1940S

During the first four decades of this century, psychology rapidly accrued intricate methodological norms and eventually moved toward exploring social-psychological, as well as psychological dimensions, of thought and action. Among the methodological advances made by the late 1930s was procedural attention to the psycho-social dynamics of the experimental situation. The use of confederates, Rosenzweig's identification of "experimental artifacts," and various forms of experimenter bias were among the discovered dynamics (Suls & Rosnow, 1988). The first experiment (using systematic manipulation of variables) to test the notion that the race of investigator influenced the experimental outcome appeared in 1936. Inspired by the anonymous 1916 article and by Bond's analysis, Herman Canady (1936) conducted a study in which a race comparison of children's intelligence was coupled with a race comparison of the experimenter's influence on the testing results. By this time, making the problem of the experimenter's race a variable was a logical procedural step mandated by empirical research. Adhering to these mandates, Canady reasoned that the influence "can be determined only by recourse to facts, and until the present time the problem has been discussed wholly as a matter of opinion" (pp. 210–211). The opinions previously voiced in the literature had been about the (white) experimenter's influence on Negro children, but Canady included white subjects in his sample because he logically inferred that if white examiners could not establish adequate rapport with Negro subjects, then it also might be true that a Negro examiner could not gain the full cooperation of white children. One Negro and 20 white examiners were used, and each child was tested by a Negro and a white examiner (the sequence was varied). The subjects were unaware that the experiment was about "rapport" (p. 211). The study was qualified with the caveat that the subjects were from (relatively) integrated Evanston, Illinois, and not the South with its "race friction" (p. 218) and its separation between the two races "as though they lived on different continents" (p. 211). The results, too, were qualified. With a Negro examiner the Negro children's I.Q. increased an average of six points and white children's I.Q. decreased by approximately the same amount of points; the change was reported as "haphazard rather than progressive upward and downward" (p. 219). The results were not quite unequivocal: Canady found that there were effects, but they did not neatly confirm unexplained hypothesis of "rapport."

Rapport became perceived as a problem of race research: Although the word was rarely defined, it soon became an unproblematic concept, a buzzword, in the psychological literature. The term was used without elaboration in several early discussions of I.Q. testing situations, was described at some length in Klineberg's 1935 *Race Differences*, and thereafter acquired the status of a known phenomenon. It generally was taken for granted that rapport was a problem when the subject was not white, a belief following from a tacit assumption that experimenters were white. The rare instances when writers imagined otherwise, that the experimenter was not white, had a sensational impact. For example, in his social psychology text Britt fortified the concept by asking the assumed (white) reader, "Would it make any difference in your performance if an intelligence test were administered to you, a white person, by a very dark Negro?" (Britt, 1941, p. 433).

The rising concerns with rapport indicate several changes in investigative practices that took place by the late 1930s. In keeping with the general transition from the study of race differences to race prejudice (Samelson, 1978), the race of experimenter issue too became a social-psychological phenomenon. Likewise, consistent with the growing efforts to cover concrete problems that threatened the validity of human experimentation (primarily by making them technical problems), the experimenter's race came to be considered a methodological matter. Two significant reconfigurations accompanied this transition to the social and technical domains. First, emphasis on the experimenters themselves was transferred from the experimenter as an individual to the social interaction; only a few psychologists continued to note the problem of the possible assumptions of racial superiority on the part of white scientists (i.e., Gilliland & Clark, 1939, p. 184). Second, as rapport came to be a code word for the complex racial dynamics of the experimental situation, it was transfigured into a variable, a technical detail that was related as much or more to the subjects as to the experimenters. Both reconfigurations transposed the experimenter's attributes or actions onto those of the subjects.

These reconfigurations occurred amid an atmosphere of reformism: Many psychologists shared the optimistic cultural belief that social injustices to minority groups and the underprivileged should and can be removed. There was considerable faith that such amelioration could be effected largely through education of minorities and the majority alike. It was at this moment of its identification as a specific experimental concern that the race of experimenter was reduced to a variable of minor methodological concern. Transfigured into a social-psychological phenomenon, the concern then was transferred to the minds of the subjects, who, after all, were the targets of eventual remediation in order to improve race relations in America.

THE SOCIAL AS COMPLEX: POST–WORLD WAR II

The interest in race prejudice, along with studies of the experimenter's race, continued on a steady course until the early 1960s. The research produced during this period yielded further refinements both in the social psychology of race perceptions and in the technicalities of experimental procedures (methods). Above all, what had been tacitly conveyed through the term "rapport" was fashioned into intricate accounts of the dynamics of racial interaction. In so refining models of racial interaction, whatever problems had been associated with the race of experimenters were largely transferred to the subjects. Placing the weight not only of the experimenter's race but of the subjects' race as well in the subjects' heads yielded a new and remarkably coherent victim psychology. Although it would be another decade before the structure and implications of victim psychology were identified (Ryan, 1971), much of the postwar research converged to conceptualize minorities in general, and black subjects in particular, as the cause of their own problems. In victim psychology the victim's stigma or problem is seen as environmentally determined, but "the stigma, the defect, the fatal difference — though derived in the past from environmental forces — is still located *within* the victim, inside his skin" (p. 7).

As rapport and related racial interactions were addressed, the social situation was more precisely located in the subjects. Even while rapport was systematically examined, the homogeneity of researchers (in their class, age, sex, and race) was seen as advantageous; to one methodologist, the exception was the problem of "the reluctance of Negroes to express their opinions freely to whites" (Hyman, 1954, p. 159). Anxieties accompanying the very subject of race were rapidly becoming a problem residing with the subjects. Thus, the reported "fears" that the study of racial attitudes cause anxiety or socially desirable responses (MacKenzie, 1948;

Reynolds, 1949) were submitted to empirical scrutiny. Between 1945 and 1965 at least 16 studies explored the race of experimenter effect, most of them producing significant results. And the effect was no longer a problem for intelligence research alone but also was found in numerous subject areas, including TAT, frustration-aggression, GSR, and verbal tasks; it became a concern of polling researchers, interviewers, and psychotherapists as well as of experimenters and test examiners (Bernstein, 1965; Heine, 1950; Katz, Robinson, Epps, & Waly, 1964; Rankin & Campbell, 1955; Riess, Schwartz, & Cottingham, 1950; Treat, 1954; F. Williams & Cantril, 1945; J. A. Williams, 1964; Winslow & Brainerd, 1950). During this period the problem also earned a place in review articles (Dreger & Miller, 1960; Katz, 1964; Masling, 1960; Shuey, 1958).

The studies include both majority and minority psychologies to explain the persistence of prejudice and discrimination, often suggesting that members of both races had to change in order to reduce race conflict. However, the growing fascination with the minority personality tipped the balance of attention, which had already been slanted by the methodological focus on subjects and not experimenters. Herman aptly described the overarching theme of the postwar period: "If white attitudes were in need of change, black personalities were the proof that change was both mandatory and long overdue" (1995, p. 183). Posited in an era when psychoanalysis occasionally was comingled with social psychology, the depiction of the Negro subject as ego-defended and anxious was an amenable one. Most of the empirical studies concurred in surmising that not only did Negro subjects have less rapport with white experimenters than with Negro experimenters but Negro subjects also tended to be fearful, defensive, withholding, and ingratiating with such mixed-race experimenters (F. Williams & Cantril, 1945). Textbooks of the period elaborated on this interpretation, weaving it into the new theories of prejudice. By "growing up in the shadow of race," as two textbook authors described the origins of prejudice, Negro youth develop defense mechanisms to protect themselves from the discrimination they must endure (Sargent & Williamson, 1958, p. 654). In presenting this new minority psychology, Sargent and Williamson simply designated the race of experimenter as a *variable*, a "complicating" one (p. 656). By confining a victim psychology with methodological language focused on experimental situations and subjects, whiteness and white experimenters faded from the analysis.

From 1945 to the 1960s, researchers from a variety of specialties seemed to concur on the problem of race in psychology studies, yet this emerging consensus that the problem resided with the subjects (and to some extent with black researchers) was not shared universally. A few investigators differed in their assessments, pointing to the possible effects of personality that could trigger experimenter bias or to the conditions of social reality. In a study of the Negro Version of the TAT, Schwartz, Reiss, and Cottingham (1951) considered both of these factors. On the basis of their study using Negro and white subjects, Negro and white test administrators, and Negro and white TAT cards, they emphatically concluded, "We do not believe that skin color replaces the more important factors of social reality in determining, facilitating, or impeding the reactions of Negroes and whites to Negro and white cards and to Negro and white examiners" (p. 400). In an era in which investigators were intrigued by cognitive or intrapsychic processes and victim psychology, the idea of a social and material reality was not to flourish.

CIVIL RIGHTS IN THE LAB: THE 1960S AND BEYOND

The question of the race of experimenter continued and, by the mid-1960s, became one of a host of race issues receiving attention from psychologists. The civil rights movement, underway in the 1950s, soon influenced psychological research in multiple ways: Most important, it offered an opportunity for psychologists to utilize their expertise in policy making. Research on black psychology and race conflicts scrutinized the family, masculinity, and urban life to uncover what eventually became known through the 1965 Moynihan report as a "tangle of pathology." Psychological experts were persuasive in their demonstrations of the psychological bases of social problems, convincing policy makers, citizens, and activists alike that the psychological realm needed adjustment.

Sensitivity to race matters, and to their psychological dynamics in particular, also was manifested in the escalated concern with the race of experimenter. Between 1966 and 1975, 46 studies on the subject were published; in the following decade, 1976 to 1985, 26 studies appeared. Despite this increased regard, the matter of the experimenter's race was neither resolved nor illuminated. Approximately 20% of the studies report no significant effects of the race of investigator. Several of these studies submit that purported race effects are really due to some other characteristics of the examiner; notably social class, personality, or personal bias (J. E. Williams, Best, & Boswell, 1975; Womack & Wagner, 1967). Others suggest that characteristics of subjects (other than race), or a combination of such characteristics of subjects and those of experimenters, are more influential in the experimental setting (Samuel, 1977; Sattler & Theye, 1967). Something is amiss in the experiment, these studies deduced, but it is not race.

During the 25-year period of 1965 to 1990, a significant majority of the studies reported a race of experimenter effect. These studies yield no simple assessment of the race of experimenter effect because they vary substantially in methodology: They differ in races examined, subject and experimenter variables, and dependent measures. What is probably more important is that, although the studies rely on diverse explanation of race effects, they nevertheless tend to converge in emphasizing the subjects' psychological processes or reactions to the experimenter (and not the experimenter's actions or reactions). Against and above a methodological cacophony, then, one apparent message is clear: The subjects and not the experimenters are the source of interest. If the race of experimenter is an effect, it is not being examined in the experimenter but in the subject.

During this period psychological depictions of the nonwhite (still typically African American) subject were modified. Earlier portrayals of the resistant — withholding yet ingratiating — Negro subject were altered to accommodate political and cultural awareness of black identity. The black subject was coming to be recognized as having a unique heritage and as living in a duplicitous world. Negro students and patients were no longer only seen as deprived and excluded but also as oppressed (Smith, 1967). Hence, the black subject of psychological analysis was ascribed with an apparent degree of agency and a positive identity. Pettigrew, who in 1964 had written extensively about the Negro "role," including his or her role in research, with its defenses of withholding, stupidity, and slowness, reconsidered this role in light of subsequent events. In 1970 he said that "the Negro's own protests and assertion of civil rights, his increasing educational and economic opportunities, the findings of social science, and the emergence of proud new African nations all have salved the old wounds" (Pettigrew, 1970, p. 151). The emergence of a visible black intelligentsia, a group deeply concerned about race, fostered historical and cultural exploration of black identity (Goodman, 1976; Guthrie, 1976; R. L. Jones, 1972).

With these changes in the model black subject, the experimenter's race faded even more. Empirical studies emphasized the cognitive and affective processes of subjects, deflecting analysis from the experimenter. The technical detailing of experimental artifacts, indeed, the very relegation of race to the category "artifact," further diminished the experimenter's self-awareness, and deflected attention away from the investigator in general. Rendering race an experimental "condition" made it all seem ephemeral or at least mobile, hence movable and removable. Continued focus on the minority psyche, even through a proactive identity politics, served to detract critical regard away from the investigator. So successful were these transferences of gaze that only occasionally did more conservative researchers need to argue that the race of experimenter did not matter (Jensen, 1980, pp. 596–603).

CONCLUSION

The experimental method, adopted from neighboring sciences, provided psychology with a protocol for work as well as for professional legitimation. Psychologists took that method to be a genuinely liberating practice. The experiment permitted the researcher to control the messiness of human life in order to locate its underlying causal mechanisms. It also provided a place where researchers could perfect *acts of self-control*, where they could conduct observations cleansed of personality, biases, and expectations. As such, the human psychology experiment constituted a new form of social relations in which authority and abilities were differentially named and distributed. Many of the risks of experimentation that such social relations consequently imposed upon subjects have been identified and addressed in an elaborate code of ethics. Regarding the investigators, these experimental social relations and their consequences have received less attention.

There are now plentiful studies, however, demonstrating that what psychologists have taken to be an interesting experimental phenomena, and how they perceived those phenomena, have been shaped by their culture. The experimenter's race has been one such experimental phenomenon that has changed dramatically in response to the political and social climate. In the early years of the century, the need for psychologists to establish a market for their skills encouraged them to investigate salient social concerns such as the race aspects of schooling, reform, and immigration. During the interwar years, changes in the population of psychologists (namely, the increase in emigres from Europe), along with the liberalized politics of the depression, fostered new interests in improving human relations. After World War II, psychologists were able to expand their place in policy making, persuasively demonstrating that race, along with other social matters, was a psychological problem. Throughout these involvements, psychologists' conceptions of race were transfigured through changing sentiments and politics.

The presence (or absence) of African American psychologists also has been influential in the history of seeing (or not seeing) the experimenter's race. Although psychologists of diverse races addressed the matter of the effect of the experimenter's race, African American psychologists (despite their near invisibility in the profession) were the first to produce a comprehensive critical analysis (Bond, 1927) and a systematic experiment designed to assess the effect (Canady, 1936). More recent theoretical work has led some social scientists, particularly feminist and minority investigators, to a new quandary related to the experimenter's race. These researchers self-critically acknowledge the identity of the experimenter. Thus, reluctant to abandon the scientific epistemology that denies the observer as a particular, historically situated person, they are equally resistant to dismissing their own personal and political attributes.

The race of the investigator, in the end, simultaneously reveals and conceals the race (whiteness) of psychologists. The epistemic project to create a position of nowhere from which to observe human life at once illustrates the vibrant dualism of secularism and anxiety, democracy and class privilege, progressive reformism, and ethnocentricity. Yet, investigations of the race of the experimenter also have concealed much. Study of these studies is revealing: It shows how we as investigators become educated to step out of our skin (or other features of our bodies), how we conceptualize the skin of others, and how we confine our self-reflections — ignoring our positions as cultural actors and segregating our "lived" experiences from our "experimental" ones. These acts of concealment may be as telling about whiteness as our invention of the objective observer.

REFERENCES

Anonymous. (1916). Some suggestions relative to a study of the mental attitude of the Negro. *Pedagogical Seminary, 23,* 199–203.

Banks, W. C. (1976). White preference in blacks: A paradigm in search of a phenomenon. *Psychological Bulletin, 83*(6), 1179–1186.

Bernstein, A. S. (1965). Race and examiner as significant influences on basal skin impedance. *Journal of Personality and Social Psychology, 1*(4), 346–349.

Betancourt, H., & Lopez, S. R. (1993). The study of culture, ethnicity, and race in American psychology. *American Psychologist, 48*(6), 629–637.

Bond, H. M. (1927). Some exceptional Negro children. *The Crisis,* 257–259.

Britt, S. H. (1941). *Social psychology of modern life.* New York: Rinehart and Company.

Camfield, I. M. (1970). *Psychologists at war: The history of American psychology and the First World War.* Unpublished Ph.D. dissertation, University of Texas at Austin.

Canady, H. G. (1936). The effect of "rapport" on the I.Q.: A new approach to the problem of racial psychology. *Journal of Negro Education, 5,* 209–219.

Daston, L., & Galison, P. (1992). The image of objectivity. *Representations, 40,* 81–128.

Dreger, R. M., & Miller, K. S. (1960). Comparative psychological studies of Negroes and whites in the United States. *Psychological Bulletin, 57*(5), 361–402.

Gaines, S. O., & Reed, E. S. (1995). Prejudice: From Allport to Du Bois. *American Psychologist, 50*(2), 96–103.

Gilliland, A. R., & Clark, E. L. (1939). *Psychology of individual differences.* New York: Prentice Hall.

Goodman, J. (1976). Race, reason, and research. In L. M. King, V. J. Dixon, & W. W. Nobles (Eds.), *African philosophy: Assumptions and paradigms for research on black persons.* Los Angeles: Fanon Center Publication.

Graham, S. (1992). "Most of the subjects were white and middle class": Trends in published research on African Americans in selected APA journals, 1970–1989. *American Psychologist, 47*(5), 629–639.

Guthrie, R. V. (1976). *Even the rat was white: A historical view of psychology.* New York: Harper and Row.

Hall, G. S. (1894). The new psychology as a basis of education. *Forum, 17,* 713.

Harding, S. (1986). *The science question in feminism.* Ithaca, NY: Cornell University Press.

Heine, R. W. (1950). The Negro patient in psychotherapy. *Journal of Clinical Psychology, 6,* 373–376.

Helms, J. E. (1992). Why is there no study of cultural equivalence in standardized cognitive ability testing? *American Psychologist, 47*(9), 1083–1101.

Henriques, J. C. (1984). Social psychology and the politics of racism. In C. Henriques, C. Hollway, C. Urwin, C. Venn, & C. Walkerdine (Eds.), *Changing the subject: Psychology, social regulation, and subjectivity.* London: Methuen.

Herman, E. (1995). *The romance of American psychology: Political culture in the age of experts.* Berkeley: University of California Press.

Hollinger, D. A. (1989). Inquiry and uplift: Late nineteenth-century American academics and the moral efficacy of scientific practice. In T. L. Haskell (Eds.), *The authority of experts: Studies in history and theory* (pp. 142–156). Bloomington: Indiana University Press.

Hyman, H. H. (1954). *Interviewing in social research.* Chicago: University of Chicago Press.

Jensen, A. R. (1980). *Bias in mental testing.* New York: Free Press.

Jones, J. M. (1983). The concept of race in social psychology. In L. Wheeler & P. Shaver (Eds.), *Review of personality and social psychology* (pp. 117–150). Beverly Hills, CA: Sage.

Jones, J. M. (1991). Psychological models of race: What have they been and what should they be? In J. D. Goodchilds (Ed.), *Psychological perspectives on human diversity in America* (pp. 5–46). Washington, DC: American Psychological Association.

Jones, R. L. (Ed.). (1972). *Black psychology*. New York: Harper and Row.

Katz, I. (1964). Review of evidence relating to effects of desegregation on the intellectual performance of Negros. *American Psychologist, 19*, 381–399.

Katz, I., Robinson, J. M., Epps, E. G., & Waly, P. (1964). The influence of race of the experimenter and instructions upon the expression of hostility by Negro boys. *Journal of Social Issues, 20*(2), 54–59.

Klineberg, O. (1935). *Race differences*. New York: Harpers and Brothers.

Ladd, G. T. (1894). *Primer of psychology*. New York: Scribner.

Mackenzie, B. K. (1948). The importance of contact in determining attitudes toward Negroes. *Journal of Abnormal and Social Psychology, 43*, 417–441.

Masling, J. (1960). The influence of situational and interpersonal variables in projective testing. *Psychological Bulletin, 57*, 65–85.

McLoyd, V. C. (1991). What is the study of African American children the study of? In R. L. Jones (Eds.), *Black psychology* (pp. 419–429). Berkeley, CA: Cobb and Henry.

McLoyd, V. C., & Randolph, S. M. (1986). Secular trends in the study of African-American children: A review of child development, 1936–1980. In A. B. Smuts & J. W. Hagen (Eds.), *History and research in child development: Monographs for the society of research in child development*. Chicago: University of Chicago Press.

Meyer, M. F. (1921). *Psychology of the other-one, an introductory text-book of psychology*. Columbia, MO: Missouri Book Company.

Morawski, J. G. (1994). *Practicing feminisms, reconstructing psychology: Notes on a liminal science*. New Haven, CT: Yale University Press.

Morrison, T. (1992). *Playing in the dark: Whiteness and the literary imagination*. New York: Vintage Books.

O'Donnell, J. (1985). *The origin of behaviorism: American psychology, 1870–1920*. New York: New York University Press.

Pastore, N. (1949). *The nature-nurture controversy*. New York: King's Crown Press.

Pearson, K. (1937). *The grammar of science*. New York: Meridian Books. (Original work published 1892)

Pettigrew, T. F. (1964). *A profile of the Negro American*. Princeton, NJ: D. Van Nostrand Company.

Pettigrew, T. F. (1970). The role and its burden. In R. V. Guthrie (Ed.), *Being black: Psychological-sociological dilemmas* (pp. 146–155). San Francisco: Canfeld Press.

Pressey, S. L., & Teter, G. F. (1919). A comparison of colored and white children by means of a group scale of intelligence. *Journal of Applied Psychology, 3*, 277–282.

Rankin, R. E., & Campbell, D. T. (1955). Galvanic skin response to Negro and white experimenters. *Journal of Abnormal and Social Psychology, 51*, 30–33.

Reynolds, R. T. (1949). Racial attitudes revealed by a projective technique. *Journal of Consulting Psychology, 13*(1), 396–399.

Riess, B. F., Schwartz, E. K., & Cottingham, A. (1950). An experimental critique of assumptions underlying the Negro version of the TAT. *Journal of Abnormal and Social Psychology, 45*, 700–709.

Rotundo, E. A. (1993). *American manhood: Transformations in masculinity from the revolution to the Modern Era*. New York: Basic Books.

Ryan, W. (1971). *Blaming the victim*. New York: Vintage Books.

Samuel, W. (1977). Observed IQ as a function of test atmosphere, tester expectation, and race of tester: A replication for female subjects. *Journal of Educational Psychology, 69*(5), 593–604.

Samelson, F. (1978). From "race psychology" to "studies in prejudice": Some observations on the thematic reversal in social psychology. *Journal of the History of the Behavioral Sciences, 14*(3), 265–278.

Sargent, S. S., & Williamson, R. C. (1966). *Social psychology: An introduction to the study of human relations* (2nd ed.). New York: Ronald Press Company.

Sattler, J. M., & Theye, F. (1967). Procedural, situational, and interpersonal variables in individual intelligence testing. *Psychological Bulletin, 68*(5), 347–360.

Schwartz, E. K., & Riess, B. F. (1951). Further critical evaluation of the Negro version of the TAT. *Journal of Projective Techniques, 15*, 394–400.

Scripture, E. W. (1894). Methods of laboratory mind-study. *Forum, 17*, 558–570.

Shuey, A. M. (1958). *The testing of Negro intelligence*. London: Holborn Publishing Company.

Smith, D. H. (1967). The white counselor in the Negro slum school. *School Counselor*, 268–272.

Sokal, M. M. (Ed.). (1987). *Psychological testing and American society, 1890–1930*. New Brunswick, NJ: Rutgers University Press.

Suls, J. M., & Rosnow, R. L. (1988). Concerns about artifacts in psychological experiments. In J. G. Morawski (Ed.), *The rise of experimentation in American psychology* (pp. 163–187). New Haven, CT: Yale University Press.

Titchener, F. B. (1910). *A textbook of psychology*. New York: Macmillan.

Toulmin, S., & Leary, D. E. (1985). The cult of empiricism in psychology and beyond. In S. Koch & D. F. Leary (Eds.), *A century of psychology as science* (pp. 594–617). New York: McGraw-Hill.

Trent, R. D. (1954). The color of the investigator as a variable in experimental research with Negro subjects. *Journal of Social Psychology, 40*, 281–287.

Tucker, W. H. (1994). *The science and politics of racial research*. Urbana: University of Illinois Press.

Williams, F., & Cantril, H. (1945). The use of interviewer rapport as a method of detecting differences between "public" and "private" opinion. *Journal of Social Psychology, 22*, 171–175.

Williams, J. A. (1964). Interviewer-respondent interaction: A study of bias in the information interview. *Sociometry, 27*, 335–352.

Williams, J. E., Best, D. L., & Boswell, D. A. (1975). The measurement of children's racial attitudes in the early school years. *Child Development, 46*, 494–500.

Winslow, C. N., & Brainerd, J. F. (1950). A comparison of the reactions of whites and Negroes to frustration as measured by the Rosenzweig Picture-Frustration Test. *American Psychologist, 5*(7), 297.

Wispe, L., Ash, P., Awkward, J., Hicks, L. H., Hoffman, M., & Porter, I. (1969). The Negro psychologist in America. *American Psychologist, 24*, 142–149.

Womack, W. M., & Wagner, N. N. (1967). Negro interviewers and white patients: The question of confidentiality and trust. *Archives of General Psychiatry, 16*, 685–692.

Woodworth, R. S. (1910). Racial differences in mental traits. *Science, 31*(788), 171–186.

Woolgar, S. (1988). *Science: The very idea*. New York: Tavistock.

Yee, A. H., Fairchild, H. H., Weizmann, E., & Wyatt, G. F. (1993). Addressing psychology's problems with race. *American Psychologist, 48*(11), 1132–1140.

Zuckerman, M. (1990). Some dubious premises in research and theory on race differences: Scientific, social, and ethical issues. *American Psychologist, 45*(12), 1297–1303.

NOTE

Jessica Smock assisted in coding and analysis of the race of experimenter studies. Scott Plous and Karl Scheibe gave insightful comments on a draft of the essay. Michelle Fine and Mun Wong's encouragement made the project happen. To all these people I give thanks.

Educating

SEVENTEEN

The Achievement (K)not: Whiteness and "Black Underachievement"

Linda Powell Pruitt

INTRODUCTION

The extensive literature on Black academic underachievement has a very specific focus. The research looks either at the stresses and conditions of individual Black students in a racist society (see for example Fordham, 1988, 1993; Howard, 1985; Steele, 1992) or at the ways in which schools could be more effective for these students (Comer, 1988; Edmonds, 1979, 1986). On rare occasions, the exploration of this phenomenon turns itself on its head to examine Black excellence (Hilliard, 1995). Occasionally, researchers will also investigate the organizational dynamics of schools that combine to "create" academic achievement (notably Fine, 1990; Guinier, Fine, Balin, Bartow, & Stachel, 1993; Lightfoot, 1990; Mack, 1995).

Although efforts to understand and reverse the failure experience of minority students have been intense and sustained, the phenomenon of "Black underachievement" is stubborn, pervasive, and extraordinarily complex. We know a great deal about what is effective for Black students, their schools, and families, yet it remains extremely difficult to mobilize the resources and will required to make a systemic difference in their lives.

What may be missing from this literature and from various interventions is a better understanding of the role that whiteness plays in the knot of minority student failure. This essay explores the hypothesis that "Black underachievement" is not a simple knot tied within and among the Black community but is actually composed of many strands of differently weighted rope, some of them black and some white. The white strands are woven into the black in a convoluted way that can passively prevent the knot from loosening. Thinking of the entire knot as a whole — using group-as-a-whole theory (Smith & Berg, 1987; Wells, 1985) — may provide an additional lens in the consideration of this phenomenon; if we can begin to identify a dynamic relationship between Whiteness and the phenomenon that is then labeled "Black underachievement" we might find additional levers for change in Black children's lives.

The centerpiece of this essay is a partial description of a class experience about Whiteness from the perspective of the instructor; it is incomplete and intended to be heuristic and evocative. Any complete exploration would include the reflections of the students and the three teaching assistants and the group relations conference staff on a wide range of topics.[1] I frame the case with two experiences, from almost 30 years ago, and from the present, which I carried into the classroom.

THE HISTORIC KNOT

In 1968 I was a high school senior planning to attend college. By virtue of SAT scores I was both a State Scholar (one of the top students in the state) and a National Achievement Semifinalist (a student of African American descent). I received recruitment letters from colleges around the country. One of the most prestigious universities in my state sent me two letters. The first was addressed to the State Scholar and assured me that I was among the best and the brightest; they were delighted to consider offering me admission, and it would be their honor to train me for the leadership that I would (inevitably) provide for my community and my country. This letter tails squarely into what I will call the *discourse of potential*. The second letter was addressed to the National Achievement scholar; it focused on what a wonderful university it was, how fortunate I would be to have the chance to attend, and how many remedial and supportive programs were in place to help me when I (inevitably) ran into difficulty at this world-class university. This letter was a perfect example of the *discourse of deficit*.

Many White people laugh nervously when I tell this story, and rush to mistakenly compare it with the cases of young White people offered admission to prestigious colleges if they are thought to be Black yet denied admission if they are White. Upon examination, these cases are not comparable at all. That selection decision raises a question about the equitable distribution of scarce resources. The *existence* of two letters raises questions about institutional racism and its expression.

There are at least three ways of understanding this episode. First, it was simply a computer error and was without further meaning. This explanation often accompanies the laughter I get following this story. Just a glitch of little import. It isn't meaningful to these listeners that this university didn't recognize that one could be *both* African American and a top student in the state. Perhaps the organization unconsciously wanted me to see both letters (or didn't care enough to prevent it), so that I might understand my place and be assured that I was not leadership material.

Another hypothesis is that the incident is a coded discourse on competence. Perhaps the university could not simply send the first letter because it was deeply conflicted about educating a talented African American woman at the close of the 1960s. It was simply too painful for a "world-class university" to admit that it might be incapable of preparing me for leadership.

The psychological mechanisms of splitting and projection may play important roles in this incident. Obviously every student has both potential and developmental needs. It is the task of education to recognize both in every student. Rather than admit that the social and political changes of the 1960s were making the task of education increasingly complex and that there was concern in the university about its ability to effectively educate all people, the worry about incompetence is projected into students of color through the discourse of deficit. Although this diminishes the potential of these students and privileges their deficits, it preserves the university's sense of value. The students become the only ones with possible incompetence. Likewise, White students are supported, empowered, and affirmed through the discourse of potential (as though they had no deficits) and it just feels like "they earned it." Black students, their families, and their communities are burdened with the "rumor of inferiority" (Howard, 1986) in a subtle and stifling way. White students remain unfettered by the complexities of race and their Whiteness, believing that meritocracy must be real because it has always rewarded *their* hard work. Black students are keenly aware of unfairness, expected to keep silent and continue to perform if they seek the benefits that the White world offers.

Under normal circumstances, White students get the "white" letter and never know that the second letter exists, whereas Black students are absolutely clear that theirs is a race-coded letter. Black and White students meet at the same college in the same classes but with fundamentally different messages about their right and ability to be there. In this way, Black students carry a burden of awareness and clarity about race on behalf of all.[2]

The Knot—Live and in Living Whiteness

I offered a new course[3] at a graduate school of education to explore leadership and authority in urban schools. There was a special emphasis on the challenge of change in these institutions and on the issues of race, poverty, and power. The design of the course was drawn from the tradition of laboratory learning that provides insight and practice for leadership (see Heifetz, 1994; Schall, 1995). Unlike many courses that are highly structured with regard to classroom dynamics, this class was not organized to be "safe" in the popular sense or to help students (or faculty) feel comfortable. The course was designed with much of the ambiguity and dynamic of "real life." In previous courses, I had discovered that students and I would enact in real time the content-related material; process often *was* content when race and power were under study. The task in this class was to attend closely to what actually happens in the here and now and make meaning from it.

The course was also an example of my change-oriented professional development efforts in urban public schools (Powell, 1996; Powell & Barry, 1995; Powell, Barry, & Davis, 1996). Professional development with adults involved in systemic change efforts must be designed with four key attributes. With *experiential* learning, experiences and values must be engaged by paying increasing attention to the "here and now." With *parallel process*, dynamics in class can give us valuable clues to the experiences of those working in urban schools. With *holding environment*, individuals and groups need psychological support to experience and work through the predictable conflicts that arise during this kind of learning, and with the *strategic use of theory*, the utility of research can be greatly enhanced by placing it squarely within the context of immediate experience and application.

The 17 Black, White, and biracial students enrolled in the course created a microcosm of the academic community; all areas of the school were represented, as well as one other graduate school in the area. Most students were connected to schools during the course, although only one of them was a full-time teacher in an urban school. The teaching staff included two doctoral students and a recent alumna, all of whom had taken similar classes and worked with me previously. The lead teaching fellow (African American male) took primary responsibility for the administrative and logistic issues of the course. The two other teaching staff (White French male and Japanese American female) supported the task of interpreting our experience over time during the semester.

A central learning experience in this course was a 2-day group relations conference (Banet & Hayden, 1977; Powell, 1996; Rice, 1965; Rioch, 1975). This experiential conference focused student attention on the exercise of leadership and followership and the difficulties encountered in the exercise of authority. Group relations conferences give an actual experience of splitting, projection, introjection. This is qualitatively and quantitatively different from reading about these mechanisms and can be extremely disorienting. This intense and unusual experience was later evaluated by most of the students in the class as an incredibly powerful — if unexpected — learning experience.[4]

The conference served as an intervention in the class' ability to express and explore conflict.

Prior to the conference, the predictable conversation about race used students of color to express strong feelings about race while White students responded to them. Although this response was often honest, tortured, and searching, it still veiled Whiteness in the potential discourse while the Black students spoke from the pain of the deficit discourse. The racial identity of the White students (Carter & Helms, 1990) often seemed less developed as Whiteness was solely defined as a reaction to color. It was always individual (no racial group identity) and ahistoric (in this moment in time). The relative inability of White students to talk about their own racial identity was covered by their discovery of and interest in the issues raised by students of color.

During the group relations conference, some students were surprised to discover that they held ideas and values about race (and gender, age, and authority) that remained outside of their immediate awareness but were potent nonetheless. Students of all racial backgrounds discovered that they had feelings about their own race as well as about the race of others. This process of discovery seemed both enlivening and confusing.

Because of, or despite, the innovative teaching methods, I chose to base the course grade on two academic papers with explicit criteria for grading. I also required weekly memos. These communications were not required to take any particular form nor were they graded. Students were free to choose their style and content. Most took the memos as an opportunity to communicate a wide range of ideas, experiences, and reactions to the class. The memos informed me that every student wrote and thought clearly; no one seemed hesitant to say what they thought. I felt certain that, regardless of the material, they would all be able to demonstrate their learning and do well in the class.

This was not true. After grading the midterm papers on their conference experiences, I noticed that there was a wider range of grades than I had ever given, from A's to a C–. The lower graded papers were similar in that they were not carefully prepared; sentences were left unfinished, complex thoughts were not explained. Most had not been spell checked. Very important ideas were presented in their most strongly felt and least digested form. I was compelled by the raw power of their ideas and by a respect for their experience, but I was working much too hard to understand these papers.

Many students reported great difficulty writing this paper. Perhaps there had been an unconscious expectation that anything taught by a Black woman would be easy. I certainly didn't appreciate the impact of the return of repressed material that normally stays unconscious on the traditional task of writing an academic paper. What I didn't realize was that this assignment might have exacerbated the traditional split between thinking and feeling. Students admitted later that they struggled with doing "good" academic writing, writing that is by definition bloodless, heady, and disconnected.[5] Conflict, passion, and values were cut in the ruthless search for some imagined search for objectivity. This writing assignment may have increased the traditional split of feeling and thinking, leaving Black students holding the feelings that had been devalued by the task (and thereby having their thinking impaired) and White students more free to do the thinking in the heady academic assignment.

While reviewing the papers, the lead teaching fellow literally swore out loud and asked if I had noticed the grading pattern. The African American students had gotten the lowest grades. The Japanese American woman on the teaching staff noticed what neither of us as African Americans could bear to see: The biracial and lightest skinned Black people had earned the highest grades within that group. A "pigmentocracy" had emerged among the students who were not White.

Stunned, I reread all the papers, looking carefully at the distribution of grades. Knowing from the memos that all my students wrote well, my immediate hypothesis was that this pattern revealed something flawed and shameful about me as a teacher and as an African American. I reread the papers, looking for unreliability or a pattern of bias. I compared the papers with previous memos, which were not formally evaluated. When I felt confident that the grade distribution was not "natural," I was left with an ethical dilemma.

I had offered this class with the explicit understanding that our experience was a source of learning about urban schools (parallel process). I had provided a theoretical perspective that group behavior could be understood as organic, with individual members taking on roles on behalf of the whole (group-as-a-whole theory). I had provided a capacity for interpretation of complex experience (holding environment). With this in place, we had reproduced the most relentless feature of urban schools yet the data was entirely "in" the teaching staff. Could we bring this up for discussion? *Should* we bring it up? Because grades might be considered private property, did we have the right to "out" students' grades without their permission, even in a group-oriented course? What would be the productive outcome of such a discussion?

Colleagues I consulted admitted that this racial grading pattern occurred in their classes as well, and that they had no strategy for dealing with it. They suggested various actions, all of which had to do with my relationships to the *Black* students. "Doing something" with and for them was the consistent theme: Why not meet with them individually and give constructive feedback with the opportunity to redo the paper? Or why not get them together as a subgroup so as not to "shame" them publicly, airing *our* dirty laundry?

This didn't feel right. How could I teach a theory about the group as a whole, without at least considering the involvement of *all* students in the creation of this outcome? What would happen if we included the White students in the analysis? I realized how few White students had been directly angry at me. Difficult experiences with the larger institution and with me as its representative had been publicly expressed by the students of color. The intense conversations about race had been led by students of color. Perhaps they had also been organized to protect and shield the fragility and incompetence of Whiteness while fronting the confusion, passion, and hurt of Black students.

I consulted several students of color, seeking their reaction to the possibility of class discussion. None of them seemed especially surprised by the grade distribution and several were curious about the possibility of a class conversation. Heartened by the reaction of these students (whom we still mistakenly thought had the most at risk), the teaching staff decided to present the grade distribution as opening data for a conversation in class. We were far from certain that it was the right thing to do; it was too important not to discuss.

This conversation was not based on the scientific method of moving toward a single right answer. Instead, we employed the interpretive stance (Shapiro & Carr, 1991) to build an understanding of what had happened, "moving from uncertainty to uncertainty." As a group, the class worked together to generate "mutually exclusive and alternative explanations" (Wells, 1985) of the grading distribution; we also tried to understand what our experience might mean in urban schools and in the larger societal context. In retrospect, I believe our ability to have this conversation, to work through ambiguity, discomfort, and rage, was a powerful demonstration of what had been learned in the class.[6]

The simplest explanations looked at the individual: the individual Black students' backgrounds talents, skills, and motivations somehow interacted to create their low grades. Or the hardworking, well-organized White students worked hard for their deservedly high grades. Or, my own self-hatred emerged in the grading; as a sellout of Black people, I was functioning in a gatekeeper role to ensure that none of my Black students would succeed, thereby solidifying my position as "one of the few."

More complex hypotheses centered around subgroup behavior. Perhaps the Black students as a group were testing me: Would I really hold them to the published grading standards? Would I risk affirming their competence by refusing to accept less than excellent work? I wondered if the

Black students had withheld their best work to prevent me from feeling successful as a teacher. Their "underachievement" might be a way to act out rage — projecting their own feelings of incompetence and confusion so that I might know precisely what life in this organization feels like for them (Kahn, 1993).

The White students as a subgroup seemed less encumbered by conflicts about authority and were better able to use me in my role as professor. White students who were overwhelmed and unable to finish the paper asked for an extension. Several of them took an extra 24 hours and turned in A papers, receiving an A–. Black students also reported lack of time as a major difficulty in completing the paper; however, none of them considered asking for an extension, which as one Black woman said, (1) would put *me* in an awkward situation and (2) would feel like "asking for welfare."

These ideas were quite useful, but felt partial. One of the most explosive and painful moments in a generally intense discussion came as a White woman expressed her sense that she had "worked hard and deserved" her grade; she resented the implication that she was in any way involved with or responsible for the Black students' work. This same woman also spontaneously reported that she had been furious at me for several weeks. I had forgotten an appointment to meet with her; when she arrived at my office, I was involved in something else and asked if we could reschedule. Although she reacted casually, she had actually gone to great inconvenience and expense to keep the appointment. She repressed this anger at me. Once she got fully in touch with it, she later reported developing a very unusual writer's block.

When this student was "unaware" of her anger at me, where had it "gone"? One hypothesis is that it is borne by those with a greater and more complex experience about race. These strong feelings are projected into students of color, who then hold and express them on behalf of all, leaving White students free for "raceless" work.

A single experience of unfairness or disrespect with a person of another race (and with greater authority) had an impact on this student; lacking the inoculation of a lifetime of the racial discourse of deficit, the experience with me was painful and her response to it may have affected her performance. If bearing the full complexity of race, including rage and the experience of disrespect and inequity, affects students' ability to perform, then it is not surprising that Black students "underachieve."

After further reflection on this moment, I developed a more complex hypothesis influenced by McCollum's (1990) theory of group development. Placing task, leadership, and environment in a dynamic interaction might yield the following: A Black leader/"colored" teaching staff in a White organization is likely to increase the already tremendous anxiety that is generated by the study of the "evaded curriculum" (American Association of University Women, 1992) of race, power, authority. Any evaluation task that splits affect and cognition may differentially enable student performance, when students of color are holding more of this anxiety about race.

There is a covert and unacknowledged conversation about stigma occurring in the absence of a candid public conversation about Whiteness. This may allow White people to use Black people as receptacles for their concerns about deficit, while holding on to their grip on the discourse of potential.[7]

THE KNOT TIGHTENS

Last fall I found myself in an all-White community in the Heartland evaluating a program in the local high school. This school had won state awards for excellence in academics and sports and had a drop-out rate of less than 10%. No children were lost; even those few who failed to graduate could be traced: They were working at local stores and gas stations. The school was almost completely White, with fewer than 5% minority students and faculty of color.

This school also had every "at-risk" program known to humankind, including some extraordinary role shifts for a public school: food programs, clothes closets, and an ongoing support group for students in abusive relationships. When I asked school personnel how these unusual programs had come about, they said simply that the kids needed them to be successful in school. In a late-night phone call to an East Coast colleague, I was perplexed: Why did they do all of this at-risk stuff when the drop-out rate was so low? My friend pointed out that I had the equation reversed — there were so few dropouts because the supports were there for students to succeed.

The students in this school did not get labeled — were not required to enter the discourse of deficit — in order to receive this support. They did not have to present themselves for the projections of "needy" or "at risk"; they remained simply (White) students, formed and supported within the discourse of potential. Teachers acknowledged their inability to continue business as usual, admitted their professional limitations; but where did their anxieties and concerns about change and competence go?

Why did this picture differ so strikingly from the urban scenes with which I was more familiar? How had this organization freed itself from the tremendous conflicts that urban teachers have when confronting similar dilemmas? How could these teachers simply see the students as valuable and respond to their needs? One clue came during a public meeting when a speaker mentioned the "really troubled" Black families who lived in the state capital; they had difficult problems. But here, the argument went, everything was basically fine; their community was not like that. The unnamed, unknown Black people 150 miles away were convenient vessels for anxiety about change or meeting students' needs. This projection freed this community to do more of whatever was necessary — no matter how innovative or expanded the role public schools — or the success of their children. This was projection on a societal level. Urban schools get filled with these projections of deficit and take up the role of the "violent, hopeless" schools (as if this was all they are), freeing other organizations to be more responsive and creative (as if they have no similar problems). No wonder, then, that urban schools have tremendous difficulty making needed changes; they have become the symbolic containers for all of our difficulties. We need them to fail, for if not, all schools would be required to examine their own difficult experiences about race (including Whiteness), change, and achievement.

LOOSENING UP

Although extremely difficult, the class conversation about grades was worth the risk because something very important shifted. Their final papers were uniformly fabulous: creative, passionate, beautifully written. On a hopeful note, perhaps we reproduced this situation in order to understand and possibly change it; this would parallel the phenomenon in psychotherapy that clients often repeat a difficult or maladaptive experience in order to understand and perhaps master it.

Although I was nervous about evaluation, the final grades were all high primarily because the papers *as a group* were stronger. Several interracial pairs emerged to work together on projects, using the lenses from the class to explore real-world questions.

James Baldwin said not every problem faced can be solved, but no problem can be solved until it is faced. Our experience in this course suggests that we need to open a far deeper conversation about academic achievement, which acknowledges how Whiteness uses Blackness as a receptacle for fragility and conflict. The evasion of an authentic conversation about Whiteness in specific and race in general may have a disproportionate impact on the performance of Black students. This evasion may lower our ability to tackle complex problems of equity and change.

This case highlights many serious dilemmas about teaching for social change. What is the place of controversial classroom work? I had taken every possible precaution regarding holding environment, theory, relationships, provision of a teaching staff–student ratio of 1:6, and so forth. If I couldn't responsibly open up this conversation, then it simply can't be had — and it must be had often if we are to improve the academic achievement of Black students. Some believe that doing work involving the unconscious in an academic environment is irresponsible. On the other hand, to continue to teach as though everything important lies in our awareness is also irresponsible. Finally, "casualty" is not simply a word used to identify someone psychologically hurt in group work; if children are suffering and dying at alarming rates in this country, maybe the benefits we would accrue toward change would be worth the risk of psychological discomfort in our classrooms. Kids are already taking the risks. Maybe educators could take more.

The ongoing conversation in this culture about race is sometimes notable in its silences or its perversions, but it is always in progress by virtue of each of our physical embodiment and identity development. Regardless of what we intend to teach or learn we each import our part of this conversation into our classrooms. That conversation must be directly engaged, as in the class we I may miss the remarkable possibilities of stronger work, of deeper collaboration, of actually making change.

A new visual metaphor of Black underachievement would be a knot with many strands in both black and white. There are tiny intermediate twists that have been in place for many years and are hard and tight. Some of the twists are brand new and have been tied over the old. The black strands and the white operate like a hoist, holding each other in place. Pulling at the black strands alone will not untie the knot, and may actually tighten it. The white strands must loosen as well. This loosening will inevitably involve pain and learning for Whites as they explore their privilege, incompetence, and profound interrelatedness with people of color; they will need to explore their own discourse of deficit. Blacks will also need to explore our dangerous ability to lead, creating and owning our discourse of potential. We must also face those areas of fear of and collusion with the larger social system that we both love and hate. Teachers have the privilege and responsibility of creating new conversations in our classrooms that go beyond a description of risk and capacity, to actually demonstrate and develop them.

REFERENCES

American Association of University Women. (1992). *How schools shortchange girls*. Washington, DC: Author.

Banet, A., & Hayden, C. (1977). The Tavistock primer. In J. E. Jones & J. W. Pfeiffer (Eds.), *The 1977 annual handbook for group facilitators*. CA: University Associates.

Carter, R. T., & Helms, J. E. (1990). White racial identity attitudes and cultural values. In J. E. Helms (Ed.), *Black and White racial identity: Theory, research and practice*. Westport, CT: Greenwood Press.

Comer, J. (1988). School power: A model for improving Black student achievement. In W. O. Smith & E. W. Chunn (Eds.), *Black education: A quest for equity and excellence*. New York: Transaction Publishers.

Edmonds, R. (1979, October). Effective schools for the urban poor. *Educational Leadership, 37*, 15–24.

Edmonds, R. (1986). Characteristics of effective schools. In U. Neisser (Ed.), *The school achievement of minority children: New perspectives* (pp. 93–104). Hillsdale, NJ: Lawrence Erlbaum.

Fine, M. (1990). *Framing dropouts: Notes on the politics of an urban high school.* Albany: State University of New York Press.

Fordham, S. (1988). Racelessness as a factor in Black students school success: Pragmatic strategy or pyrrhic victory. *Harvard Educational Review, 58*(1), 54–84.

Fordham, S. (1993). Those loud Black girls: (Black) women, silence, and gender "passing" in the academy. *Anthropology and Education Quarterly, 24*(1), 3–32.

Guinier, L., Fine, M., Balin, J., Bartow, A., & Stachel, D. L. (1994). Becoming gentlemen. Women's experiences at one Ivy League law school. *University of Pennsylvania Law Review, 143*(1), 1–110.

Heifetz, R. A. (1994). *Leadership without easy answers.* Cambridge, MA: Belknap Press of Harvard University.

Hilliard, A., & Delpit, L. (1995). *Panel presentation, "Black excellence in education."* Paper presented at the annual convention, American Educational Research Association.

Howard, J. (1985). *Rumors of inferiority.* Atlantic Monthly Press.

Kahn, W. (1993). Facilitating and undermining organizational change: A case study. *Journal of Applied Behavioral Science, 29*(1), 32–55.

Mack, C. (1995). *Leadership and improving student performance in a multi-ethnic, cultural, and linguistic public school district: There's going to be bedlam if we get 'em.* Unpublished manuscript.

McCollum, M. (1990). Reevaluating group development: A critique of the familiar models. In J. Gillette & M. McCollom (Eds.), *Groups in context: A new perspective on group dynamics.* Reading, MA: Addison-Wesley.

Powell, L. C. (1994). Interpreting social defenses: Family groups in an urban setting. In M. Fine (Ed.), *Chartering urban school reform: Reflections on public high schools in the midst of change.* New York: Teacher's College Press.

Powell, L. C. (1996). Authority, leadership and organizational change. In A *group relations conference in the Tavistock tradition.* Cambridge, MA: Harvard University Graduate School of Education.

Powell, L., & Barry, M. (1995). *Professional development for change: A working paper.* Philadelphia: Resources for Change.

Powell, L. C., Barry, M., & Davis, G. (in press). Facing reality in urban public schools: Using racial Linda C. Powell identity theory in family group. *Racial identity theory: Applications for individual, group and organizational interventions.* Hillsdale, NJ: Lawrence Erlbaum.

Rice, A. K. (1965). *Learning for leadership: Interpersonal and intergroup relations.* London: Tavistock Publications.

Rioch, M. (1975). All we like sheep. In A. D. Coleman & W. H. Bexton (Eds.), *Group relations reader I.* Washington, DC: A. K. Rice Institute.

Schall, E. (1995). Learning to love the swamp: Reshaping education for public service. *Journal of Policy Analysis and Management, 14*(2), 202–220.

Shapiro, E. R., & Carr, A. W. (1991). *Lost in familiar places.* New Haven, CT: Yale University Press.

Smith, K., & Berg, D. (1987). *Paradoxes of group life: Understanding conflict, paralysis, and movement in group dynamics.* San Francisco: Jossey-Bass.

Steele, C. (1992). Race and the schooling of Black Americans. *Atlantic, 269*(4), 68–73.

Wells, L. (1985). A group-as-a-whole perspective and its theoretical roots. In A. D. Coleman & M. H. Geller (Eds.), *Group relations reader 2*. Washington, DC: A. K. Rice Institute.

Wells, L. (1989). *On the praxis of group-talking: Consultants as nautical navigators*. Unpublished manuscript, Howard University, Washington, DC.

Notes

Many thanks to my students who encouraged me to write about the class experience; to the teaching staff who contributed: Leon Braswell, Francois Guillieux, and Betsy Hasegawa; and to the colleagues who commented on drafts at various stages: Anne Scheibner, Kito Peters, Debra Noumair, William Kahn, Gwendolyn Davis, Margaret Barry, Lola West, Donelda Cook, Scott Barg, and Laure Cassidy.

1. I repressed this entire experience until Michelle Fine and Emily Style drew it out in conversation 20 years later. An understanding of power and a sense of support are important for the recovery of these memories. Without community or interpretation, we repress these experiences because there is no environment that is prepared to hear it.

2. Other key issues that emerged were poverty and spirituality. I have invited students and teaching staff to collaborate on an extended examination of the course and its impact on their change agent efforts in urban schools.

3. The development of this course was made possible by a faculty fund that supports teaching and curriculum innovation.

4. Colleagues from the Kennedy School of Government, Harvard University, and from the New York and Boston Centers of the AKRI volunteered their time to make this conference possible. More information on group relations conferences is available from the A. K. Rice Institute, P. O. Box 1776, Jupiter, FL, 33468–1776.

5. Students found Kahn's (1993) article tremendously helpful as a demonstration of the powerful use of personal experience in scholarly writing.

6. Beyond the earliest moments of this class, I cannot create a linear reconstruction of what followed. The discussion was tightrope walking without a net; I entered an altered state unlike teaching in any previously experienced sense and more like group relations consulting (Wells, 1989). I certainly assume that others present might recall the 90 minutes very differently.

7. The two people in class who defined their racial identity outside the Black-White dichotomy played important roles. The discussion seemed greatly helped by a woman who did not describe herself as either Black or White using her bicultural identity as a position to take leadership in this discussion. She uttered the unspeakable and contributed to a holding environment that enabled difficult positions to be expressed and faced. Another biracial woman felt victimized by what she identified as an exclusive Black-White conversation feeling silenced because her experience was not directly named. Group-as-a-whole theory suggests that Blacks and Whites may be working on behalf of an increasingly complex culture to sort out a fundamental question about achievement and merit. Although they are not the "only" groups to have these concerns, Blacks and Whites may have been unconsciously nominated to hold this split on behalf of the larger culture. In that case, those groups *both* need help to work as well as a reminder to our status as representatives, not sole stakeholders.

EIGHTEEN

Witnessing Whiteness/Gathering Intelligence

Michelle Fine

November 2003. As I sat at my second-grade son's soccer game, trying to focus on the game and thinking about revising this essay, a young father of a teammate asked, "Was your [high school] son at the party on Valley Road last night?" I answered that he wasn't, and Joe continued, "Because I heard there were no parents there, and lots of drinking. A friend from the police department called me about 10:30 and said, 'Joe, is your daughter at a party on Valley? Just want you to know we'll be rolling some cars over there in about 10 minutes and you may want to get her out.' So I picked her up. But I hear some kids were taken downtown." Amazed by the story, and the telling, I couldn't help thinking, do people in the South (Blacker) end of town get these calls?

The everyday privilege of witnessing Whiteness . . .

It is to the question of "witnessing Whiteness" that I chose to turn in this essay. Itchy for better theorizing about racial formations, with debt acknowledged to Howard Winant (2004 [this volume]), Patricia Hill Collins (1990), and bell hooks (1984), I avert my gaze, for a moment, from the inequities produced through "colors," where my work has lingered for so long. I turn, instead to the "merit" that accumulates within the hue of "Whiteness," pausing to theorize the ideological and material production, and the reification, embodiment, and denial of inequitable racial formations in U.S. schools. I worry that by keeping our eyes on those who gather disadvantage, we have failed to notice the micropractices by which White youth, varied by class and gender, stuff their academic and social pickup trucks with goodies not otherwise available to people of color.

Although Toni Morrison (1992), Ruth Frankenburg (1993), Christine Sleeter (1993), Michael Novick (1995), and many others have argued that Whiteness and "other colors" must be recognized in their shadowy interdependence, if not in their parasitic webbing, I find myself trying to understand the micromoves by which Whiteness accrues privilege and status within schools; how Whiteness grows surrounded by protective pillows of resources and second chances; how Whiteness — of the middle-class and elite variety, in particular — provokes assumptions of and then insurance for being seen as "smart."

In this essay I focus on two sites, both within schools, in which I have had the opportunity to witness not only the ways in which "youth of color" accumulate "deficits" but also the ways in which White adolescents and young adults gather "intelligence" or "merit" (see Burns, 2004 [this volume], for a theoretically sophisticated analysis of privileged ambivalence).

Historically, in both psychology and education, Whiteness was unmarked and unstudied. More recently, some scholars have elevated "Whiteness" to the status of "independent variable," tested as a predictor of academic outcomes. In this essay I want to reverse this formulation conceptually by tracing the everyday practices by which educational institutions produce "Whiteness" as merit through power and relations, the practices by which youth embody, even as they resist, these racial-ized identities, and then the ways in which institutions deny the systematic production of "Whiteness" as merit or advantage. In this essay I surveil the institutional, ideological, and material triplet of production, embodiment, and denial in the everyday practices of schooling.

Let me be clear about the assumptions that drive this work. As so many authors in this volume argue, Whiteness, like all "colors," is being manufactured, in part, through educational arrange-ments; specifically, within and across institutions designed "as if" hierarchy, stratification, and scarcity were inevitable, natural, and essential. Schools do not merely inherit or manage racial and ethnic identities; they create and enforce racial meanings. Schools, as contested spaces, structure the conditions for the embodiment, performance, and/or interruption of sustained and inequitable racial formations (Weis & Fine, 2003). In such institutions, whether or not the build-ings are in fact "integrated," Whiteness is coproduced with other colors, usually alongside Black, Asian American, and Latino identities, in symbiotic relation. Where Whiteness grows as a seem-ingly "natural" signifier for quality, merit, and advantage, the Asian American identity runs a close second — always never quite achieving Whiteness — dressed in "model minority" wear; the African American and Latino identities, as signifiers, disintegrate to embody deficit or "lack."

Although individual youth routinely trespass these heavily guarded and institutionally subsi-dized borders, the ideological categories persist, hold, seduce, and smother. The trespassers may be glorified or vilified, but they are viewed as if *they* hold the conflict. In schools, "Whiteness" and "color" are therefore not merely created in parallel but are fundamentally relational in (in)equity. They need to be studied as a system. They must, in statistical terms, be considered "nested" rather than coherent or distinct entities.

As you will see in the material I present, the institutional design of Whiteness, like the produc-tion of all colors, at once creates an organizational discourse about and an institutional denial of race(ism), launching waves of personal embodiments of race and ethnicity, affecting percep-tions of self and others, enabling racial "identities" as well as collective experiences of "tensions" and coalitions to be displayed. Once this process is sufficiently institutionalized and embodied, with ample ambivalence, all that remains plainly visible are the miraculous ways in which quality seems to rise to the glistening white top.

To understand this production, I import Pierre Bourdieu's (1991) writings, in which he invokes the word institution:

> The act of institution is an act of magic. [p. 119] ... An act of communication, but of a particular kind: it signifies to someone what his identity is, but in a way that both expresses it to him and imposes it on him by expressing it in front of everyone and thus informing him in an authoritative manner of what he is and what he must be. [p. 121] This is also one of the functions of the act of institution: to discourage permanently any attempt to cross the line, to transgress, desert, or quit. [p. 336]

This essay is a plea to re-search institutions webbed inside structural and historic relations of power: to notice, to remove the White glaucoma that has ruined scholarly vision, as we lift up the dynamics of schooling that make Whites and other racial groups seem so separable and yet so relentlessly ranked.

SCENE ONE: PRODUCTION OF "WHITENESS" THROUGH POWER AND RELATIONS

White Lies in Alabama

The scene is Wedowee, Alabama, the site where the principal Hulond Humphries was charged in 1994 with racial harassment. My involvement emerges because I am among those representing the U.S. Justice Department; I met with students at Randolph County High School (RCHS). Callie is a young White woman. She's a junior at RCHS: "My mother asked for someone, you know the principal, to watch me and find out if I'm dating a Black boy. So Mr. Humphries called me in and he told me if I kept on dating John I wouldn't be able to get any White boys. No one else would go out with me. We could have a child who's not very smart. And if I go to a family reunion, I may be the only White woman there and no one's going to even talk to me. Then I'd be an outcast." Trina, an African American 11th grader, jumped in: "He called us all into the auditorium after their talk and asked how many of us are going to the prom with someone of the other race. Lots of us raised our hands. Then he asked Rovanda [a biracial student at the school], 'Rovanda, who you taking to the prom?' And Rovanda said, 'I'm taking Chris,' her White boyfriend. And he just looked up in the bleachers, and he said, 'I won't have it. No interracial dating in my school.' And Rovanda said, 'Who *would* you like me to take to the prom?' He said, 'You were a mistake, and we don't want other mistakes like you.'" Tasha joined in, "He said he was canceling the prom." King said, "When he called Rovanda a mistake, it was like he took an axe and cut through the heart of a tree. The heart of our school."

Moving from prom to academics, I pressed on with questions about tracking at this high school. This high school has an "advanced" and a "standard" track. Knowing something about the (unfortunately predictable) racial splitting by track, I asked the students in the group—White and African American—What track are you in? The White kids raised their hand when I said "advanced"; then the African American kids raised their hands when I said "standard." I later learned how profoundly the aggregate numbers, over time, bore out that simple hand-raising exercise.

In my never-satisfied search for the sadistic educator who places kids in tracks and opportunity structures by race, I am never fulfilled. At this school, like many schools, students have what is considered a race-neutral "choice" about which track they opt into. And they "chose" by race. White racism here — and elsewhere — is so thoroughly institutionalized and embodied that young people, when given an opportunity, "choose" their "place," and seemingly with little protest. I asked, "Why did you choose the standard track? The standard track doesn't allow you to attend a four-year college like University of Alabama. You don't take enough math or science to make it into a four-year college." African American students offered a litany of painful, if predictable, responses. "Because I was scared." "Because we thought it [advanced] was too hard." "Because my friends were in the standard track." When Tigray mumbled, "Because maybe they are smarter than we are," Callie, the young White woman who opened the scene, responded, "That's the scam they pull on you. There are plenty of dumb White kids in my classes, but they would never go to the standard track." I pressed Callie, "What would happen if you told your guidance counselor you wanted to be in a standard track?" She laughed, "She'd say, 'Callie, what are you talking about? You're not going into the standard track, you're going to college.'" Indeed in this "integrated" school the advanced track is almost all White; no varsity cheerleader has ever been Black; an African American boy who ran for president of the student council talks of harassment from the principal; almost all the faculty were White. Every strata of school life — academics, social relations, postsecondary opportunities, and sexuality — was layered by race: visually apparent and vigilantly enforced (see Fine et al., forthcoming; Fine, Burns, Payne, & Torre, 2004; Oakes, 1988; Rosenbaum, 1976).

Wanting to understand the principal's motive for his public performance of racializing, I met with Hulond Humphries. We met in the basement of the school district building. Clear that I represented the team for the Justice Department, I probed with pen in hand, "Why did you say what you said about the prom? You must have known it would cause the kind of hysteria that it did." To which he said, "It's not that I have anything against interracial dating.... It's just that those Black boys really want our White girls." He continued, "Now with that feminism, Black girls are wanting our White boys."

Clear lines. Blacks as sexual predators. Whites as prey. Bourdieu's verb *institution* spreads to sexuality. The night before I went to the school, I had the privilege of visiting the African Zion Church just outside of town. I sat, stood, sang for hours, ecstatic and anxious to be part of chanting, singing, praying, preaching, and testifying about what it was like to be a student, a parent, a community member, a Black, within reach of those schools. Then the most elder Reverend booms, "Every 10 years or so God tests the racial waters of the United States. We are privileged that this year he chose Wedowee for His test. And what is our job? To love those people to death."

That was the racial tapestry of schooling in Wedowee, Alabama; the fabric in which young Whites and African American children's lives were intimately interwoven. What is striking is how much the students, White and Black, knew their place and rarely dared to protest aloud. White students' place was just "north" of Black students'. Black students' place was just below White students'. In this small working-class town, southern affect and congeniality allowed little anger to seep explicitly into cross-racial interactions. The Black church was the "safe space," the emotional safety valve, the place to put and contain anger, the "sanity check" on Sunday evening that would allow all to return to the perverse, hostile, if sometimes congenial stratification that many explained constitutes community life Monday through Friday.

Discursively and materially Whiteness is here produced and maintained through the withholding of opportunity from, and the derogation of, that which is Black. The prom was simply a metaphor for all the attempts to separate and sanitize White from Black, to ensure privilege. But being White, in and of itself, in troubled economic times, guaranteed little in Alabama, at least for these poor and working-class families. Unemployment and poverty rates run high across racial groups. Therefore — and this is my major point — this racial formation was filled with parasitic interdependence such that Whites needed Blacks in order to become privileged. African American students were getting less than White students. However, as true, nobody was getting a very rigorous academic education. No one was taking math courses more difficult than advanced algebra, and still none of the African American students had been enrolled even at this level. One might cynically argue that the White students were "lucky" to have the Black students so they could imagine themselves enjoying any "privilege." The purifying of Whiteness — in class tracks, dating, cheerleading, and college opportunities — was the job of the institution.

Two theoretical insights warrant attention. One is that these poor and working-class racial identities and concomitant "racial tensions," perhaps even "desires," were invented and sustained through the privilege and power of withholding. Whiteness was produced through the exclusion and denial of opportunity of people to color. In other words, giving Blacks access to White opportunities would stain, indeed blacken, that which is white. Access is a threat to Whiteness when Whiteness requires the exportation (and subversion) of color.

Furthermore, this case points up evidence of how institutional leadership and seemingly race-neutral policies and practices work to ensure White privilege. The leader of this institution, Hulond Humphries, articulated publicly what he fundamentally believed about race, capacity, sexuality, and who deserves to be educated. In a racially hostile environment, it's very hard for biracial and African Americans to participate with full heart and mind. As devastating, in such environments, White students develop a profoundly false sense of superiority premised almost entirely on denigration which requires opposition to sustain the racial hierarchy. Opposition and denigration became a fix, a steroid to White identity. This public school, in its leadership, policies, and daily practices, did little to interrupt — and much to distribute — this steroid. All in the name of creating and maintaining merit and "quality."

As the work of Sam Gaertner et al. (1995) reveals, we may be witnessing today a reassertion of pro-White policies and practices rather than (or in addition to) actively hostile discrimination targeted at people of color. If this is the case, that Whiteness is "catching" privilege, then where we look for evidence of discrimination and prejudice will have to move to the cumulative benefits of being White, rather than the (exclusive) tracking of blatant racism against, in this case, Blacks. Documenting racism against, as if separable from racism for, may be a diversionary strategy by which our eyes have been averted from the real prize.

SCENE TWO: THE STAKES

In the year 2003, a national fetish billows out of testing mandates and Bush's legislation No Child Left Behind. In New York State, public high school students (but not private high school students) confront a high-stakes testing requirement for high school graduation. Students who have completed 12 years in public school nevertheless must pass a series of five content specific Regents examinations in order to earn a diploma. Or they don't graduate. Predictably, and denied vociferously by the state, drop-out and push-out rates have begun to spike, particularly in urban communities, poor communities, Black and Latino communities, immigrant communities (Haney, 2003). Large urban high schools report between 1,500 and 2,000 ninth graders but 66 to 150 seniors (Fine et al., forthcoming).

In spring 2003, a full two-thirds of the students in New York failed the Math A exam of the State Regents. After much public outcry, the exam was declared invalid and the scores annulled. A young African American student from Bushwick, Brooklyn, during an interview, asked me, "How come when the rich White kids fail the tests, the tests get thrown out. But when we fail the tests, we get thrown out?"

Although these examinations aren't wholly responsible for the fundamental miseducation of poor youth of color, or even for the racialized drop-out patterns, these exams systematically and dramatically exacerbate, and reveal, the race and class inequities that constitute public education in the state (Fine et al., 2003). Asked to testify at state hearings in Albany, I used this opportunity to argue that the high-stakes testing regime creates a statewide educational environment, a "science," and thereby a false popular consensus, that manufactures White and wealth as smart, and deserving of advantage. In my testimony, I sought to reveal the perverse knotting of three theoretical moves that ensure the sustainability and silencing of varied forms of White privilege in education: the *redlining* of opportunities, the *privatization* of (White/elite) student supports and the Teflon-like *lamination* that protects middle-class White youth from the stick of adverse outcomes. Below I extract from my testimony. This was my attempt to unveil the policy and practice workings of White privilege in the name of "merit," to reveal how the testing industry has colonized public education and at whose expense.

Good afternoon. My name is Michelle Fine, and I am a professor of social psychology at the Graduate Center, CUNY. For the past 20 years I have been involved in research on urban schools and more recently prisons. In the early 1990s, I wrote a book entitled, *Framing Dropouts* on the devastating problem of lost bodies; a problem that, it seems, refuses to go away.

Earlier this week I was startled to read Commissioner Mills' testimony before this body, when he stated that, "In 1996, fewer than 40 percent earned Regents diplomas. In 2002, the figure was 55 percent. (And that was 8 exams at 65 or better!)." In this statement, Commissioner Mills failed to tell you that in that same time period, graduation rates plummeted in New York. Today New York ranks 45th among states in graduation rates with rates of less than 40% for Black and Latino students. It was shocking to hear the commissioner speak about survivors' test scores without paying attention to the disposable bodies — mostly youth of color — who are metaphorically being tossed out the windows of public schools, as the state marches toward a full regime of high-stakes testing.

The implementation of the full Regents requirements for graduation has facilitated an explosion in the urban drop-out rates, as documented by Professor Walter Haney (2003). This explosion has been particularly dramatic and devastating within African American and Latino communities. Not only are drop-out rates elevating but we are witnessing a rise in the numbers of "disappeared" eighth graders who never reach high school. The loss of unaccounted for bodies combines, today, with charges that schools are cleansing the records so that long-term absentees are now being cleared, after extended absences, from the books. Franklin Lane and Martin Luther King High Schools are being sued for removal/discharge of underage students considered "off track" for graduation.

Under severe pressures to keep test scores high, these underfunded, high-surveillance high schools appear to be discharging students in order to boost standardized scores and graduation rates. Cumulative evidence from GED educators confirms that the average age of the GED student is dropping, with many well below the legal age of 16, young people "discharged" from their neighborhood high schools, looking for an alternative way to earn a diploma (American Council on Education, 2001; Greene & Winters, 2002). The loss of bodies, in drop-out rates and in the "disappeared," is, of course, not random. These young people are disproportionately youth of color, attending underresourced schools, in low-income neighborhoods. In New York State — on the national cutting edge of regressive social policy — we have developed a system of high-stakes examinations, Regents, which, in practice, mocks the notion of accountability. These are standards based on exclusion, not inclusion; accountability with a wink — as long as we don't notice the missing bodies.

So I ask today, who gets to achieve "smart" in contexts of severely unequal educational opportunities, and with what costs for those who aren't allowed to compete?

Below I unpack the structures and practices of production, embodiment and denial of White privilege within public schools — in an effort to track that ways in which testing crudely legitimates and exacerbates these already overdetermined structural inequities. We begin with academic redlining.

Redlining access to rigor: Drop-out rates notwithstanding, Black and Latino children in New York are not only exiting at elevated and alarming rates. As devastating, those who stay are being redlined out of academic rigor; that is, they are disproportionately denied the public resources necessary to achieve at high levels.

As of 2001, the Board of Regents and the State Education Department reported that the average per pupil expenditures through NYS in 1998–1999 was $10,317, but in Great Neck it was $17,620, in Scarsdale $13,923, and in New York City $9,623. Poor and working-class children of color are most likely to be educated in underfunded schools by underqualified educators. Lankford, Wyckoff, Boyd, and Loeb (2003) find that less-qualified teachers, such as those failing the general knowledge certification exam, are more likely to teach in schools with higher numbers of non-White, poor, or low-performing students. Across schools we see that Black and Latino students have the very least access to qualified educators and rigorous curriculum. White students enjoy disproportionate access to qualified and certified educators.

The material contours of redlining are most apparent across schools, with this gap ensured through finance inequity. But even *within* presumably desegregated schools, we have found that access to rigor and quality education to be starkly racialized. Evidence collected in the Opportunity Gap Project — a broad-based survey of 9,174 youth attending racially integrated suburban high schools in 13 suburban and urban districts in the New York and New Jersey metropolitan area (Fine et al., 2003) — demonstrates that within the same integrated schools, White and Asian children are far more likely to be enrolled in AP and honors classes than African American and Latino students. Nationally, the U.S. Department of Education has found that "Black students were much less likely than White or Asian Pacific Island to complete a rigorous curriculum." In the New York metropolitan area we found that 58% of Asian Americans, 56% of White Americans, 33% of African Americans, and 27% of Latinos were enrolled in high level (AP and honors) courses. Some have argued that these discrepancies are due to class differences and not race or ethnicity. So we probed further. We selected out those students with college-educated parents, and found that the patterns of racialized inequity persisted: 69% of Asian Americans, 65% of White Americans, 42% of African Americans, and 43% of Latinos with college-educated parents enrolled in high level classes (Fine et al., 2003).

Ten years after Wedowee, 50 years after *Brown vs. Board of Education*, within school segregation indices suggest that racially integrated schools, once a national dream, may ironically, worsen racial inequities by undermining the academic trajectories of so many middle-class Black children. These schools may propel cycles of downward mobility for African American and Latino youth, in a society already set up against them.[1]

Privatization: Were redlining not enough, as public schools advantage White and elite Asian American youth, in stunning (not surprising but frightening harmony), the private resources of these families are quietly and meticulously brought to bear to ensure that these same youths succeed, or perform success, often at others' expense (see Burns, 2004 [this volume]). Strategies of privatization, by which middle-class and elite families use networks, money, pressure, influence, external supports, tutoring services, and therapy, circulate in a curious doubling; that is, as public institutions differentially advantage White and middle-class families (for fear they will exit), these same families dedicate private resources to create the magic of "merit," and then further privatize this mobilization of resources as a family secret. As anticipated, privileged children show up at school as if they are simply capable, smart, and worthy of advanced placement.

When we asked students to identify private supports, for example, tutors and test prep, that their families provide, the very stark racialized differences evidenced in what White, Asian, Black, and Latino American students get from the public sector were not only mirrored but extended by the private supports that families provide. Asian and White students report significantly greater access to private tutors and SAT prep (38%) than African American and Latino students (26%). Those most in need are least likely to receive the supports.

Redlining secures inequitable and always-advantaged White access; privatization guarantees a network and staff designed (in a whisper) for success, and then lamination, the third strategic move of privilege, ensures that when trouble brews (for no system is fail-safe), White and elite youths are *relatively* immune.

If it takes a public and private village to get a middle-class White child into a good college, with all of his or her staff of tutors, special sessions, and help, then why are we surprised when we bump into evidence of a "gap"?

Lamination: I turn my attention to the life-long racialized *stakes* that endure, in the aggregate, from these inequities. Today having no high school diploma bears dramatic, adverse economic, social, and potentially criminal justice consequence — for anyone, and especially for African American and Latino young adults. On every indicator of economic and social difficulty, high school dropouts, compared to high school graduates, are substantially more likely to live in poverty, to be unemployed, to be among the working poor and the growing mass of "discouraged" workers, and to serve time in local, state, or federal jail or prison. But African American and Latino dropouts fare far worse than Whites.

The 2000 Census reveals 28.1% of Whites and 31.6% of Latinos, compared with a full 45.6% of Blacks (age 25 to 34) without high school diplomas live in poverty [see Table 18.1].

**Table 18.1 Percentage Living in Poverty
by Race or Ethnicity and Educational Attainment**

	Percentage Living in Poverty		
	Whites	Blacks	Latinos
No degree	28.1	45.6	31.6
High school diploma	10.0	20.0	15.5
Some college	6.2	9.7	8.4

So too, as we examine who constitutes the working poor, we find that 12% of Whites without high school diplomas, 21% of Blacks without diplomas, 4% of White high school graduates, and 11% of Black graduates are among the working poor. In other words, Black high school graduates are as likely to be among the working poor as are White high school dropouts.

Assessing the stakes of inequitable education by turning to criminal justice data, we see the same pattern: high school dropouts, compared to high school and college graduates, are substantially overrepresented within the criminal justice system. And dropouts of color (African American and Latino) are disproportionately overrepresented.

The U.S. Department of Justice, Bureau of Justice Statistics (Harlow, 2003) reports that the "numbers of prison inmates without a high school education increased from 1991 to 1997" and that "Three quarters of State prisoners have not earned a high school diploma" (pp. 2, 3).

But again we see just how much race and ethnicity complicate an already dire situation. While just over a quarter of White prisoners have no high school diploma or GED, a full 44% of Black prisoners and 53% of Latinos have neither diploma nor GED. Without a diploma, there are almost no options for survival for Black and Latino young adults. The absence of a diploma signifies, disproportionately, a biography of miseducation, a state that has declared war on poor communities of color. Lack of education overpredicts that Black and Latino youth and young adults will end up in the criminal justice system.

Once a young person is arrested within the juvenile justice system, race and ethnicity again kick in to overdetermine the trajectory in terms of likelihood of arrest, being detained, and being sent to adult facilities. Poe-Yamagata and Jones (2000) examined rates of detention for White, African American, and "Other" youth arrested for the same crime. Their analyses reveal that race and ethnicity significantly influence detention rates even for youth charged with the same crime:

"Detention was used more often for African American youth (27%) and youth of other races (19%) than for White youth (15%). This was true among each of the four major offense categories as well. Thus, for youth charged with comparable offenses — whether person, property, drug, or public order offenses — minority youth, especially African American youth, were locked up in detention more often than White youth. Consequently, cases involving African American youth were more than twice as likely to be detained for a drug offense than were cases involving White youth or youth of other races (38%, 14%, and 16%, respectively)." (p. 7)

The New York State Regents project places poor youth, urban youth, and youth of color at a terrible risk. It is, indeed, a failed experiment accomplishing none of its original goals and producing a cascade of irreparable damage, severely scarring those communities that most need a strong public sector. At the moment, the Regents have come to symbolize the distortions produced by a state that has refused to listen to educators, parents, and students; a state that is paving the roads to poverty and crime for Black and Latino youth in under-resourced schools, and even those in relatively affluent suburbs. We cannot in good conscience proceed on this path any longer. We are cresting toward an explicit educational assault on Black and Latino communities — in drag as accountability.

With local variation, redlining, privatization, and lamination are practices that routinely accompany the production, embodiment, and denial of privilege by race, ethnicity, class, or gender (see Fine & Burns, 2003). Given these three conditions, high-stakes standardized tests mandated in a system of severe inequity, legitimate ideologies of racial or cultural superiority and inferiority, mask unequal educational conditions, and ensure unchallenged, racialized, and classed consequences in the economy and within the criminal justice system.

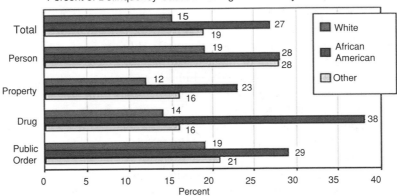

Percent of Delinquency Cases Involving Detention by Race, 1997

Source: *Easy Access to Juvenile Court Statistic; (1988-1997)* [data presentation and analysis percentage]. Office of Juvenile Justice and Delinquency Prevention (1999).

In middle-class and elite schools, these large structures and micropractices collude to produce "White" as merit. These structures, policies, and practices, over time, bear significant material, social, and psychological consequence for all. Youth of privilege come to feel entitled to success, expect supports, and anticipate and appreciate the help that they expect, accurately, will materialize. They construct selves in relatively warm relation to structures of power and networks of support and view mistakes as an opportunity for revision; they know that rules bend and that success is relatively guaranteed (see Burns, 2004 [this volume]). Even when they resist school or break a law, these young people encounter a relatively thicker padding to catch their fall.

In contrast, most youth who have been redlined out of academic opportunity view success as unlikely — perhaps desirable, but out of reach. They view structures and adults in positions of public authority with substantial suspicion (Fine et al., 2003). They rarely seek help from adults in school and view mistakes as occasion for shame. The drip feed of privilege and exclusion bear dramatic, corrosive effects on the soul, the wallet, and the capacity to dream (Fine et al., forthcoming).

But note an exception: Studies in New York City, Chicago, California, and Philadelphia document an important "exception" to these trends: those poor and working-class urban youth who attend small schools dedicated to rigorous curriculum for all, student inquiry, and performance assessments are significantly more likely to persist in high school (not drop out), graduate, go on to college, trust adults, and seek help than are their peers in large underfunded urban high schools and their peers in racially integrated suburban high schools. Working out of an ethic of educational rigor and civic engagement for the neediest youth in the nation, rigorous small schools help their students resist the racist drip feed of the larger culture and challenge the undertow of race and class inequities in public education (see Fine et al., forthcoming).

CONCLUSIONS

These scenes of racial bifurcation in schools raise important questions about the theories, methods, and ethics by which we study and challenge what Winant (this volume) calls racial formations — the relation of Whiteness and other racial and ethnic groups. If we persist in our analyses "as if" races and ethnicities were distinct, separable, and independent rather than institutionally produced, coupled, and ranked, then we will continue to "discover" that most White students "have it" (whatever it is) and most students of color don't. Many have well documented inequities in academic outcomes and the disparate treatment of students by race (Banks & Banks, 2002; Delpit, 1993; Schofield, 1989), class (Fine, 1991; Weis, 1990), and gender (Biklin & Pollard, 1993). We have advocated interventions "for" those historically oppressed to gain access to culturally hostile institutions. But the material I presented in this essay cautions us to problematize such "access" to historically inhospitable institutions.

As is often the case, when the institutional life of schools is essentially constituted through stratification and exclusion, strategies for access, without transformation, are dangerously flawed. If institutions, such as schools, designed to be public and democratic are, in fact, organized to be porous to the replicative winds of racial and class stratification; if, in such institutions, being White (or male or elite) buys protection, and if this protection necessitates the erosion of opportunities for persons of color through policies and practices that appear race-neutral, then those who have been historically excluded may be invited in but most will "fail" to perform "to standard." Some will drop out. A few will go nuts. A handful will survive as "the good ones" with questions of structural and psychological loyalty littering their souls. The institutional mantra of deficit and merit will triumph, bolstered by the hand wringing of "we tried."

Today the cultural gaze of surveillance around academic achievement falls on students of color. Whether we consider the school in Wedowee or the students of color in suburban integrated schools where people whisper the "Even the middle class Black students don't seem to achieve at the same levels of Whites" questions of (in)adequacy, as Foucault (1978)foretold, fall squarely on those who are marked: Colored. In this essay I have argued that social scientists too have colluded in this myopia, legitimizing the fetish, turning away from opportunities to surveil "White," refusing, therefore, to notice the institutional choreography that renders Whiteness meritocratic and other colors deficient.

With this essay I invite colleagues to consider not only the unfair disadvantages that accrue institutionally to darker hues but also the institutionalized pillows and profit that surround and grow embodied by "White." Social scientists need to interrupt the cultural gaze, not make a science of it.

REFERENCES

American Council on Education. (2001, August). *Who took the GED? Statistical report.* Washington, DC: General Educational Development Testing Service.

Aronowitz, S., & Difazio, W. (1995). *The jobless future.* Minneapolis: University of Minnesota Press.

Banks, J. A., & Banks, C. M. (2002). *Multicultural education: Issues and perspectives.* New York: Wiley.

Biklin, S. K., & Pollard, D. (1993). *Gender and education.* Chicago: National Society for the Study of Education.

Bluestone, B., & Harrison, B. (1982). *The deindustrialization of America.* New York: Basic Books.

Bourdieu, P. (1991). *Language and symbolic power.* Cambridge, MA: Howard.

Burns, A. (2004). The racing of capability and culpability in desegregated schools: Discourses on merit and responsiblilty. In M. Fine, L. Weis, L. P. Pruitt, & A. Burns (Eds.), *Off White: Readings on power, privilege, and resistance* (2nd ed.). New York: Routledge.

Collins, P. H. (1990). *Black feminist thought: Knowledge, consciousness, and the politics of empowerment* (pp. 221–238). Boston: Unwin Hyman.

Delpit, L. (1993). The silenced dialogue. In L. Weis & M. Fine (Eds.), *Beyond silenced voices.* Albany: SUNY Press.

Fine, M. (1991). *Framing dropouts.* Albany: SUNY Press.

Fine, M., Bloom, J., Burns, A., Chajet, J., Guishard, M., Perkins, T., & Torre, M. (forthcoming). Dear Zora: *Brown v. Board of Education* fifty years later. *Teachers College Record.*

Fine, M., & Burns, A. (2003). Class notes. *Journal of Social Issues, 59,* 4, 841–860.

Fine, M., Burns, A., Payne, Y., & Torre, M. (forthcoming). Civics lessons: The color and class of betrayal. *Teachers College Record.*

Fine, M., Freudenberg, N., Payne, Y., Perkins, T., Smith, K., & Walzer, K. (2003, Spring). "Anything can happen with the police around": Urban youth evaluate surveillance in public spaces [Special issue]. *Journal of Social Issues, 59,* 1.

Foucault, M. (1977). *Discipline and punish.* New York: Vintage.

Frankenberg, R. (1993). *White women, race matters.* Minneapolis: University of Minnesota Press.

Gaertner, S. L., Davidio, J. F., Banker, B. S., Rust, M. C., Nier, J. A., Mottola, G. R., & Ward, C. M. (1995). Does White racism necessarily mean anti-Blackness? Aversive racism and pro-Whiteness. In M. Fine et al. (Eds.), *Off White: Readings on race, power and society.* New York: Routledge.

Greene, J., & Winters, M. (2002). *Public school graduation rates in the US*. New York: Manhattan Institute for Policy Research.

Haney, W. (2003, September 23). *Attrition of students from New York schools.* Invited testimony at Public Hearing "Regents learning standards and high school graduation requirements," New York.

Harlow, C. (2003). Educational corrections population. US Department of Justice Programs, NCJ 195670. January 17, 2003.

hooks, b. (1984). *Feminist theory from margin to center.* Boston: South End Press.

Lankford, H., Wykcoff, J., Bond, D., & Loeb, S. (2003). *Understanding teacher labor markets: Implications for equity.* Albany, NY: University at Albany's Education Finance Research Consortium.

Morrison, T. (1992). *Playing in the dark.* New York: Harvard.

Novick, M. (1995). *White lies, White power.* Monroe, ME: Common Courage Press.

Oakes, J. (1988, January). Tracking: Can schools take a different route? *National Education Association*, 41–47.

Poe-ya Magata, E., & Jones, M. (2000). *And justice for some.* Washington, DC: Building Blocks for Youth.

Rosenbaum, J. (1976). *Making inequality.* New York: John Wiley.

Schofield, J. W. (1989). *Black and White in school.* New York: Teachers College Press.

Sleeter, C. E. (1993). How White teachers construct race. In C. McCarthy & W. Crichlow (Eds.), *Race, identity and representation in education.* New York: Routledge.

Weis, L. (1990). *Working class without work.* New York: Routledge.

Weis, L., & Fine, M. (2003). *Silenced voices and extraordinary conversations: Re-imaging public education.* New York: Teachers College Press.

Winant, H. (2004). Behind blue eyes: Whiteness and contemporary U.S. racial politics. In M. Fine, L. Weis, L. P. Pruitt, & A. Burns (Eds.), *Off White: Readings on power, privilege, and resistance* (2nd ed.). New York: Routledge.

NOTE

1. A systematic analysis was undertaken with the full senior classes of two suburban high schools to determine racialized access to advanced placement and honors math classes and to calculate the relationship of rigorous curriculum to passage of the Regents examinations. Seventy-three percent of Asian American seniors, 41% of European Americans, 12% of Latinos, and 11% of African American seniors were enrolled in AP math courses. Enrollment in AP courses was highly correlated with scores on the New York States Regents exams in math ($r = .609$, $p = .000$), English ($r = .390$, $p = .000$), and science ($r = .586$, $p = .000$). Although we make no claims that AP teaching is exemplary or even to be considered a model, it is nevertheless shocking to recognize how systematically Black and Latino students are fenced out of "rigor" by virtue of finance inequities (across schools) and tracking (within schools); that is, Asian American and European American students are significantly overrepresented, whereas African American and Latino students are systematically underrepresented in those courses which are considered the academic gold standard in the state — the very gold standard highly correlated with the Regents exam.

NINETEEN

Color Blindness in Teacher Education: An Optical Delusion

Pearl M. Rosenberg

Through the fog of a color-blind ideology one perceives the outline of a picture of a post–civil rights era where race is no longer viewed as a major obstacle to social, political, and economic participation. According to Eduardo Bonilla-Silva (2003), a new racial ideology has emerged in our country that, in contrast to Jim Crow racism (or the ideology of the color line), avoids direct discourse about race — but safeguards racial privilege. According to this view, racism is no longer a structural problem of society but now has been reduced to the attitudes and behaviors of particular individuals, thereby masking an insidious form of racism. Moreover, as Bonilla-Silva asserted, color blindness "is as effective as slavery and Jim Crow in maintaining the racial status quo" (p. 272). Those who favor a color-blind society fail to see that race, especially skin color, has consequences for a person's status and well-being. That blindness to skin color and race remains a "privilege" available exclusively to White people highlights the reality that color blindness only serves to perpetuate and institutionalize the very divisions between people that it seeks to overcome.[1]

Color blindness, then, is a very disturbing yet revealing metaphor for the dominant ideology of race in America. Laying aside the metaphor for a moment, people who are really color blind have an optical defect that limits their ability to see. Clinically color-blind people have to make guesses in order to fill in the gaps of information missing from their visual field. Their vision is imperfect, their experience incomplete. Thus, to be color blind is to suffer a loss. It makes no sense, therefore, to embrace color blindness as an ideal for the teacher in the classroom. And, yet, that is exactly where many of our preservice teachers begin.

Awareness of the problem of color blindness as an urgent matter in the training of teachers is not new. A number of educational researchers, among them Vivian Paley (1979), Lisa Delpit (1988), Gloria Ladson-Billings (1994), and Marilyn Cochran-Smith (1995), have passionately called for classroom teachers to become more culturally responsive to their racially and ethnically diverse students.[2] In her work on successful teachers of African American children, Gloria Ladson-Billings (1994) recognized the impulse in some White teachers who explain their color blindness in relation to their African American students as their way of being fair. But, as she explained, "The notion of equity as sameness only makes sense when all students *are* exactly the same" (p. 33).

Here I continue this conversation about the need for preservice teachers to be armed to confront persistent racial inequalities that belie the dominant color-blind ideology of our time.

This discussion reflects my ongoing efforts to represent the ways in which my preservice teachers traverse beyond their stuck points in constructing questions about race, culture, and teaching.

Preservice teachers committed to the goal of repositioning themselves as culturally aware teachers tend to progress through three discernable stages. Rosalinda Quintanar-Sarellana (1997) outlined the three stages of cultural awareness for teachers. The "culturally unaware" stage characterizes teachers who are unaware of the differences that may exist between the culture of their students and the school, and who may reject the language and culture of their students either "overtly or covertly" (p. 44). In addition, these teachers may blame students for their own failures and see students and their families as needing to change in order to be successful in school. These teachers do not see that it may be their responsibility to locate culturally relevant educational experiences for their students. Teachers who are in a "transition" stage begin to gain insight into the culture and language of their students, often through their own professional attempts at growth and development. At the other end of the spectrum are the "culturally aware" teachers who are characterized as those who are not only aware of the differences between the cultural capital of the students and the school but also try to incorporate the students' own language and culture into the learning process.[3]

What follows are snapshots in the life of preservice teachers both in the teacher training classroom and in the field. First we can see how a color-blind ideology may impact early stages of teacher training. These portraits of classroom life in a predominantly White teacher education program illustrate the dangers of this ideology in the socialization of teachers. Finally, the comparative success of Adria and Joslyn (the two preservice teachers working as tutors in an urban alternative school setting), as well as Devon Allen (visiting artist and teacher in the same setting), illustrates the incomplete attempts at social change that serve as, nevertheless, openings. Their promising relationships with a group of high school students different from them in terms of race, class, and culture embody the notion of teacher as culturally aware and responsive to all students.

TEACHER EDUCATION IN THE "PRESENCE OF AN ABSENCE"

> It could be important for those individuals with color vision deficiency to know about their abnormality, especially if considering an occupation that depends on color. . . . In particular, the person who is severely color deficient can potentially be dangerous in some jobs. (Clayman, 1989, p. 292)

In my teaching practice and research, I have been concerned about how White students primarily learn about race and racism in environments where minority representation is very low. For most of my career as a teacher educator, I have found myself teaching in academic spaces that embody the notion of the "presence of an absence" (Rosenberg, 1998). For people of color may be virtually absent from the immediate scene, but the presence of issues of race and racism are never far from any American scene.

Much of my work in the past 10 years has been an attempt to shed light on the dominant Whiteness of the preservice teaching force and how their narratives and privileges often reinforce the significance of race whether diverse others are present or not (Rosenberg, 1997, 1998). In that work, I have told stories of students from predominantly White teacher education programs who have struggled to give voice to their experience of coming to terms with educational biographies that were, for the most part, colored by privilege.

The socialization process of these preservice teachers around issues of race and racism would often get played out in their hallway confessions of their own racist families or in parking lot disclosures of their worries about not knowing enough about the students and their families that would one day soon be in their care. Unfortunately, what should have been the central texts of these classes (in this case, educational psychology with a field site component) soon became discussions that went "underground" (Rosenberg, 1997). I came to realize that "underground discourses" are discourses, nevertheless. And, as discourses, they could be shared and repaired. Eventually, I would discover some solutions for working with that population of preservice teachers. But, I have also learned that this work often takes form in a dance of two steps forward, three steps back — four steps forward, five steps back. Nevertheless, part of our responsibility as teachers and teacher educators is to stay in the dance, finding ways to become critical of our own educations so that one day we can be creators of caring classrooms for those who may not be like us in terms of race, class, or culture.

In my educational psychology class (the site for this discussion as well), we spend considerable time looking at various ways in which the ideology of equal opportunity and access obscures the actual unequal distribution of resources and outcomes for a variety of individuals based on social categories pertaining to gender, race, class, and culture. Students are asked to read, write, and think about (in this case) racism as a system of advantage based on race. In short, they are asked to begin to understand the Other not as a category of person but as a process of domination. This is the landscape against which we proceed to look at classical topics in the field of educational psychology (e.g., cognitive, social, and moral development; thinking and learning; achievement and motivation; assessment; ability grouping; student resistance to authority, to name a few).

As I try to bring issues of race and racism to consciousness in my students, I view race as a set of social relations that are socially and historically constructed and subject to political tensions and contradictions. Thus, race is not taken as a stable category (Omi & Winant, 1986).

Race comes up in this program in one of three ways: (1) Students may be required to consider issues of race in readings, class discussion, workshops, or field site assignments; (2) students may choose race as a topic for required papers or lesson plans; and (3) students may not choose purposely to think about race, but in the process of studying or discussing other issues, or by working in the field, race reveals itself or is revealed by another as a relevant issue.

WHITEWASHING RACE IN TEACHER EDUCATION

> Most people with defective color vision have no reason to suspect there is anything abnormal about the way they see, because they have no ready access to how other people see the world.... Most cases come to light only when a person is noticed making mistakes with color discrimination. (Clayman, 1989, p. 292)

For many White students, thinking about race becomes a highly charged emotional experience resulting in resistance, misunderstanding, rage, and/or feelings of inefficacy (Tatum, 1994). Although emotional responses to the issue of race should be viewed as a potential source of energy for learning about a multicultural society, too often, in my students, I have seen these feelings be reduced to empathy for and identification with groups not present. These feelings may be in response to the helplessness that they often feel when learning about race, racism, and teaching or the genuine desire to know or understand the other. Nevertheless, the tolerance of many White students for learning about those different from themselves in race, culture, and ethnicity appears to be dependent on the extent to which they can reconstruct those others in the image of themselves.

The following scenario characterizes the preservice teachers I have worked with in predominantly White teacher education programs (Rosenberg, 1998). It is a primary example of how preservice teachers may whitewash the issue of race.

In my educational psychology class (that term, a primarily White class except for one Chinese American male named David), a group of students were showing a clip from the film *Boyz 'N the Hood* as part of their class presentation on stress and adolescence. The student group announced that their choice of this film was based on their collective opinion that this film portrayed adolescent life in an honest way. There was no mention of the fact that the story took place in a Black community in general or that it dealt with gang violence in particular.

Boyz 'N the Hood involves a young male protagonist named Tre (pronounced "Trey"), a sensitive, promising teenager, who is portrayed in relation to his father, friends, and community as one engaged in a towering struggle of how to grow into a Black man with integrity in racist America. The segment that the student group shared with the class on this day shows Tre driving home one night and he is pulled over by a policeman and harassed for apparently no other reason than his race. The policeman is Black as well. After the policeman lets the young man go, the young man returns to his girlfriend's house in great emotional pain; the harassment has catalyzed the daily pain and torment that he lives with and tries so hard to rise above. He writhes and screams in the doorway inside of his girlfriend's house; heavy metal bars form a cross on the door that frames the background of the scene of the young man who ultimately collapses into his girlfriend's arms, sobbing inconsolably.

The class watches this episode respectfully and listens to the presentation that follows. Students in the audience appear eager to talk after the group finishes presenting their formal comments, which included trying to link the ages of the young men in the film to the theories of social development we have been reading about in class. There has been no mention of the course theories about ways of coping, including various forms of resistance and accommodation to oppressive circumstances; nor has there been any recognition of the cultural context for these adolescents in the film, even though we spent time in class reading and discussing all of these ideas in preparation for these presentations. As I am deciding how long to allow this conversation to continue, the students in the audience begin to talk about how adolescents feel powerless in their daily lives in general, and, in particular, how teenage boys are often harassed undeservingly by police officers. Students are relaying simultaneous stories about their experiences of being at suburban parties that have been raided or being stopped by police while driving.

Just as I take a breath to interrupt the student conversation, David (the Chinese American student) directs the class' attention to the fact that these characters in the film are Black. He expresses his concern about the class not viewing Tre's struggle in that context. Students who have been silent in class begin to speak, as if for the first time. One student exclaims fervently that no one should be treated the way Tre was treated. Another student, Jennifer, describes her sadness about racism in our country, after seeing this character portrayed on film. She expresses great empathy for his pain. Another student adds that she feels bad too. A number of students interrupt this small group's emotional expression of empathy for those who suffer because of race to insist that most people in America are not racist. One of them insists that the best way to deal with racists is to "just ignore them so as not to encourage them."

The response of the class to watching scenes from *Boyz 'N the Hood* raises a number of issues. The extent to which these students are unaware of cultural differences may not be evident to the naked eye. But all the labor it takes to NOT see it and to NOT mention it is impressive.

The ability of the class to identify with the main character of Tre in relation to his father and friends is a testament to the level of art achieved in the film as depicting universal themes of adolescence, for sure. But the pedagogical question remains — How do we build on this emotional recognition of sameness toward an intellectual understanding or critique of differences in the presence of color blindness?

Not seeing Tre in his particular struggle as a young Black man facing enormous odds in his community and his world may allow White students to indulge in the pleasure of identification with Tre, but at the expense of challenging the dominant limits on all of our sight. To appropriate Tre's struggle as their own, preservice teachers need to believe that Tre has had the same opportunities that they have had. Of course, all this serves to do is reinforce the racial inequalities between them. The fact that David, the one person of color in the class, is the one who acknowledges publicly the class' color blindness is noteworthy. Not only does David help us put the film in a necessary context for understanding adolescent stress but, by his example, he teaches us a much needed lesson in cultural difference. And, finally, a small group of students can explain away racism as the behavior of a diminishing number of misguided individuals because they are buttressed by the dominant ideology of individualism, which is organized around a belief in equal opportunity.

Joyce King (1991) explained this "uncritical habit of mind" as a form of racism called "dysconsciousness." In her article, "Dysconscious Racism: Ideology, Identity, and Miseducation of Teachers," King defined "dysconscious racism" as the "limited and distorted understandings ... students have about inequity and cultural diversity" (p. 134). Even in their attempt to be well-intentioned, individuals who are "dysconscious" engage in an "uncritical habit of mind (including perceptions, attitudes, assumptions, and beliefs) that justifies inequity and exploitation by accepting the existing order of things as given" (p. 134). In the case of future teachers, "dysconsciousness" is tied to self-identity and an emergent professional identity that includes "emotionally aberrant responses to cultural diversity" (p. 135).

COLOR BLIND, OR COLOR CONSCIOUS?

> "Color dysnomia" is an inability to name colors despite an ability to distinguish them. It may be caused by "expressive dysphasia," an impairment of speech where the individual cannot articulate words. (*Mosby's Medical & Nursing Dictionary*, 1986, p. 371)

America is an overtly race-conscious society, and yet many White folks subscribe to the color-blind ideal when it comes to race and express their wish to live in a society where race is not an issue.[4] This contradiction of claiming not to see race while being conscious of it, as well as constituted by it, is seen frequently in the early days with preservice teachers leaving the teacher-training classroom and crossing borders into the public school classroom. These classrooms are sometimes less than a mile away from the college but are light-years away in terms of cultural differences.

I am talking here about how difficult it is for some White preservice teachers to simply acknowledge another's race. For example, one of my preservice teachers admitted ashamedly one day in her written field site analysis that she felt self-conscious in her urban field site school in relation to the librarian who was African American. This librarian was helping her plan for a series of library lessons with her cooperating teacher's second-grade class. Lauren claimed that she was unable to even use race as a descriptor in reference to the helpful librarian with whom she had a fun working relationship. After a week of getting valuable help in the school library from the same librarian, she returned one last day hoping to firm up her plans with the same librarian for the next day's student workshops. She admitted that she had never gotten the name of the helpful librarian, even though they had laughed together and connected on a personal level. When she got there, another group of librarians was on duty. She described (in writing) how she "bent over backward" trying not to name the previously helpful librarian as a "Black woman" because of her own discomfort. She wrote, "I thought I was being helpful by asking, 'You know that nice lady who's short?' 'You know that lady who wears red a lot?' until I saw the weary, incredulous looks on the three librarians' faces. Practically in unison they wailed, 'Do you mean Shirley, the short Black woman who sits at the main desk??!'"[5]

This vignette raises some concern about how and when White preservice teachers can learn these lessons of fairly benign social discourse with members of other races and ethnicities, let alone larger lessons of power and privilege. For example, White preservice teachers are often hesitant to ask obvious questions from their field experiences (e.g., "Why are all the after-school detention kids students of color?") that are key to helping children in their lives both in and out of school.

White preservice teachers may have had the luxury of putting off these lessons. However, a preservice teacher waiting to develop a critical consciousness about their tendencies toward color blindness will undoubtedly stand in direct contrast to their potential students of color. Because children of color have been raised in the United States where they are bombarded with messages proclaiming fairness and equality for all, parents are more likely to prepare children at young ages for discrimination (Peters, 1985).

Janie Victoria Ward (2000) spoke to this issue in her article, "Raising Resisters: The Role of Truth Telling in the Psychological Development of African American Girls." She referred to the "home-space" as the socializing setting for Black children to learn early about how to deal with racism and prejudice. According to Ward, children are raised to "construct an identity that includes Blackness as positive and valued" (p. 52). This process of creating the self is dependent upon the individual being able to summon what bell hooks (1992) called an "oppositional gaze." Ward explained that this "oppositional gaze" makes it possible for the child of color to "observe the world critically, and to oppose ideas and ways of being that are disempowering to the self" (p. 52).

This potential mismatch between the goals and expectations of the preservice teacher in relation to his or her students and colleagues has profound implications for building community.

In their article, "Colorblindness as a Barrier to Inclusion: Assimilation and Nonimmigrant Minorities," Markus, Steele, and Steele (2000) articulated their concern for the viability of the color-blind model in the formation of community in America with people of diverse backgrounds that is relevant to educators. They highlighted the contradiction that we all sit at the nexus of as American citizens. For even though America is often thought of as a "haven" for diverse others, we are at the same time engaged in an ongoing but silenced struggle with difference. Although we need to have clear vision in our relations with others, as well as ourselves, we too often opt for color blindness as a supposed solution toward equitable outcomes.

The authors suggested that societal settings like work or school, so central to any groups' movement into mainstream American life, are experienced differently by minorities because of the experience of what they called the "one-way nature of assimilation" (p. 239). Here, members of minority groups must assimilate to the goals, standards, or culture of the mainstream, whereas the mainstream is not "required" to take an interest in the corresponding goals, standards, or culture of the minority group. Furthermore, members of nonimmigrant minorities often experience this "one-way assimilation" as an "identity threat" (p. 239). As members of the dominant group in our society, we may take for granted what nonimmigrant minority groups go through in order to achieve inclusion in the workplace or the school. Yet, believing that *not seeing* difference will reduce inequalities and ensure assimilation may constitute what the authors called a "cultural injunction" (p. 235). To counteract "identity threat," the authors proposed an alternative model of inclusion called an "identity safety model," where differences of a group's identity are first acknowledged and then serve as the basis for respect (p. 235). In this type of community then, we need to notice differences and create environments that use this acknowledgment as a point of departure toward inclusion and interdependence, both essential to maintaining a stable society.

Toward "Culturally Relevant Teaching"

> No treatment, whether drugs, vitamins, or exercises, has any demonstrable effect in improving deficiency in color vision. (Clayman, 1989, p. 292)

The notion of an "identity safety model" as a remedy to counteract "one-way assimilation" (as defined by Markus, Steele, & Steele, 2000) is translated by pedagogical theorists as "culturally relevant pedagogy."[6] This model is described by a wide variety of scholars, including Gloria Ladson-Billings (1994) and Geneva Gay (2000), among others.

Ladson-Billings's (1995) scholarly work in the area of exemplary teachers of African American children yields three broad categories of belief that characterize the culturally relevant teacher. These areas include the following: (1) the *conceptions of self and others*, (2) the manner in which *social relations* are structured, and (3) the *conceptions of knowledge* (p. 478).

Culturally relevant teachers who have high self-esteem and a high regard for others embody the *conceptions of self and others*. These teachers believe that all students are capable and can achieve. These individuals see teaching as "pulling knowledge out," like the Freirean (1973) notion of "mining" that is in contrast to "depositing" information. At the heart of the culturally relevant classroom is the acknowledgment of how cultural identity and heritage has an effect on students' attitudes, beliefs, and approaches to learning. Teachers use this cultural knowledge to help students to understand and value their own culture, as well as that of others.

The teacher structures *social relations* in the culturally relevant classroom in order to connect with students individually and collectively. The goal is to create a community of learners, where individuals may teach each other, feel responsible for each other. According to the *conceptions of knowledge*, knowledge is shared and constructed by all participants. Culturally relevant teachers inspire their students to be passionate about knowledge and help students to obtain the skills and dispositions in order to become critical thinkers in their complex world. What needs to be emphasized here is that in order for educators to achieve the "culturally relevant classroom," they need to create "cultural continuity" by "accepting the validity of these students' cultural socialization and prior experiences" (Gay, 2000, p. 25).

The narrative vignettes presented below describe some examples of how preservice teachers in weekly visits to an alternative school setting attempt to accomplish some of the goals of the culturally relevant classroom. Preservice teachers/tutors Adria and Joslyn are seen in relation to a group of high school students who are labeled "at risk" in a precollege outreach program. These high school students have shown promise both cognitively and socially, even though their educational biographies have gotten played out at the margins of opportunity and hope.

The vignettes presented here take place midway through the year, during the 3 weeks of instruction on the play *The Crucible*. This unit is taught by the preservice teachers/tutors Adria and Joslyn, as well as by Devon Allen, a visiting professor, actor, and director from the college's theatre department. The Community Admissions Program (CAP) students know me as a visiting faculty member who serves as the supervisor of Adria and Joslyn, as well as teacher of special workshops on writing, and as the one who is documenting the program.[7]

An early excerpt from my field notes describes their on-site English teacher, Mr. Pittman,[8] whose class we take over as visiting tutors and supervisor every Wednesday. This descriptive snippet serves as counterpoint for the "culturally relevant teaching" snapshots of Adria, Joslyn, and Devon Allen, to be seen shortly.

Their teacher, Mr. Pittman, is a White man in his early 30s, high on the "Authoritarian Personality" scale, who is a bully with a necktie. A baby-faced blond with a buzz cut, pumped-up muscles, and a square jaw, he personifies the notion of "chomping at the bit." He walks around the perimeter of the classroom like an urban gladiator, wrapping his long key cord tightly around his forearm so the flesh of his arm is bulging through the rope, raw with anticipation of a fight, or just to prove he can withstand the pain.

For Mr. Pittman, it appears easier to punish students than to listen to them. Moreover, he tends to leave the room just as his students begin to open up, or perform their new understandings, or respond with enthusiasm to the tutors or visiting professors from the college. Students that we find to be full of life, with a deep curiosity for learning, are reduced to what Mr. Pittman refers to as "bad kids" in his presence.

The teacher has created a culture of fear and shame for his class of predominantly African American students by exhibiting a deep distrust of these young people, often reprimanding them in public. I could swear one day he purposely waited for me to arrive so he could perform his anger at one of the students in front of me. He seemed proud of himself. A few times while the tutors were teaching, students were called out of the room. Some returned crying; all returned dejected. The visiting college tutors and professors registered their concern about Mr. Pittman's treatment of his students with the director of the program and her assistant. We were told that the administration was not happy with Mr. Pittman either, but that he would have to stay until they could find a replacement.

Henry Giroux (2001), in his article "Zero Tolerance: Creating a Generation of Suspects," provided an important frame for thinking about students who have been identified as "at risk." He suggested, "Rather than being 'at-risk' in a society marked by deep racial, economic and social inequities, youth have become 'the risk'" (p. 30). He explained,

> Young people are quickly realizing that schools have more in common with military boot camps and prisons than they do with other institutions in American society.... As schools become militarized and fenced off from the communities that surround them, they lose their ability to become anything other than spaces of containment and control. (p. 32)

During class breaks, the college tutors and the visiting professors would encourage the students to articulate their frustration with the school. The students seem to take it in stride, just glad for a reprieve from Mr. Pittman. We would take turns engaging the students in conversation about their experience in this alternative setting, their plans for the future, and their critique of Mr. Pittman.

JOSLYN (college tutor): Why are you all here?
STUDENTS (a few in unison): Attitude problems.
JOSLYN: Is it helping?
JEN (avoiding the question): We love our tutors.
COLLECTIVE EXCLAMATION: Yeah, yeah, we love all you. We love Wednesdays!
KATRINA: But not Mr. Pittman. He doesn't like us. He thinks we're losers.
ANDRE: He doesn't respect us; thinks we're stupid.

Herbert Kohl (2002) would call Mr. Pittman's teaching performance "playing at being the teacher" (p. 150). According to Kohl, Mr. Pittman has imagined the way that teachers should talk to students. Here we see him in relation to what he perceives to be students with "attitude problems"—students who are not very bright, have no future, and need to be contained. Kohl could be talking about Mr. Pittman in his description of a teacher during an observation: "Looking above the heads of his students, not making eye contact, and pushing on with the lesson whether students were listening or not.... [This] was a function of his insecurity though, unfortunately, he saw it as the student's inability to pay attention" (p. 150).

The college tutors, Adria and Joslyn, had been employed to review with the students whatever they were learning in writing and literature from their other classroom teachers. Shortly after beginning the academic year, however, they soon began to create weekly lessons of their own for the CAP students. This was because they thought it would be good experience for themselves to prepare for their upcoming professional semester in the field and because the students were so hungry to learn. They did not mind the extra work because they knew how much the students appreciated it and because they had grown to love working with them.

A substantial amount of time was being spent on reading, writing, and role-playing in response to Arthur Miller's play *The Crucible*. This was all in anticipation of the theatrical production of the play on the college campus, to which the students were invited to attend.

On this day, the students were to have read the entire text of *The Crucible*. Adria and Joslyn begin the class by showing the class the opening 10 minutes of the recent film version of *The Crucible* (starring Winona Ryder and Daniel Day Lewis), as a way of starting a conversation about the play. The following is in response to the opening scene, which focuses on a character named Tituba who is at the center of a group of girls dancing around a fire,

EISHA: Why is she the only Black girl?
ADRIA (college tutor): She's a slave from Barbadoes in a small New England town.
EISHA: What year is it?

Many of these interactions that hold great promise for further exploration are interrupted by other questions or by overflowing enthusiasm for talking about anything and everything in the film (e.g., the costumes, why these actors were chosen for the roles, Winona Ryder's arrest for shoplifting, etc.).

When the word *wrath* comes up in the text, Adria asks them if they know that word. She begins to explain it after they shake their heads "no." As Adria begins to help them understand what the word means, Elenika interrupts,

ELENIKA: How do you know that word?

She appears eager to know how Adria knows a "big" word.

ADRIA: In eighth grade I had to read the *Grapes of Wrath* and I didn't know what *wrath* meant so I looked it up in the dictionary. (Then in a teasing voice she adds) The dictionary is my friend!

The students listen respectfully. They are hungry to know things. I later learn that Adria often was taken aback by their serious questions and their thirst for knowledge. Even though she never doubts that they were smart, Adria admits that she was so busy trying to manage the collective, that, at times, she found herself unsure how to answer individuals.

Adria brings the group back on track after much laughter and silliness about the idea of her having a relationship with a dictionary.

ADRIA: Come on you can do it. Let's figure this out. So what's Abigail's problem.
KATRINA: She's so mentally ill it's not even funny.
VALERIE: She's a ho.
ADRIA: What's going on here?
KATRINA: A lot of crap.

Adria and Joslyn spoke often about the challenge of trying to lead a discussion with the CAP students in the large group. They believed that their students were smart; they just had other ways of performing their smartness that were not part of the school script that was familiar to Adria and Joslyn. The culturally different discourse structures exhibited by the CAP students were in direct contrast to the more conventional classroom discourse to which they were accustomed.

Geneva Gay (2000) explained, "African Americans 'gain the floor' or get participatory entry into conversations through personal assertiveness, the strength of the impulse to be involved, and the persuasive power of the point they wish to make, rather than waiting for an 'authority' to grant permission. They tend to invest their participation with personality, power, actions, and emotions" (p. 91). The CAP students trusted their tutors and appeared to believe that, at least when Adria and Joslyn were there, the classroom space belonged to them. Perhaps this sense of care and belonging contributed even more to their exuberance.

Ladson-Billings (1994) reminded us "the notion of 'culture relevance' moves beyond language to include other aspects of student culture and teaching" (p. 16). This is evident in view of the next picture of classroom life with the CAP students.

As part of the unit on *The Crucible*, Devon Allen (actress, director, and professor from the college's theatre department) has been invited to spend 2 class days with the group to illuminate their work with some workshop activities around the play.

Devon enters the room wearing a big black coat, a long flowing scarf, and sunglasses. She is a woman with pale white skin that is contrasted strongly to her long raven hair and big dark eyes. She has a commanding presence and proceeds to introduce herself as she apologizes for being 10 minutes late. Still in her sunglasses, Devon begins, "You know what it's like when you are rushing and you have an appointment and you don't want to be late. . . . Well, I got held up by a 'bigwig.' You know what a 'big wig' is?" No answer. The students seem incredulous in the presence of a person who enters a room this way, who talks to them this way.

She continues: "You know, when someone has authority over you and you can't leave." Collectively, they sort of nod in agreement, but appear mesmerized by this character. Devon removes her sunglasses, and introduces herself as an actress and a director. She announces that she is here to work with them today on *The Crucible*, because she knows they have been reading it.

One student calls out: "Are you gonna make us act?" This question has obviously been on their minds because they all look up. And, for what seems like the first time ever, they are speechless.

DEVON: Well you act all the time, don't you? You're acting right now. Do you always act like this wherever you are? Do you think I do?

No answer. They seem nervous.

Devon asks everyone to go around the room and say their names as she proceeds to take off her coat. With each name, she responds, "Thank you," or "I like your hair," or "What's that written on your shirt?" or "That's a beautiful name (Elenika, Jylissa, Eisha, Katrina, Cassandra)," or "Do you know what your name means?" One student named Cassandra says that she knows that her name means "Greek princess who could foresee the future."

DEVON: That's right. She could foresee the future. Of course, they killed her ...

The class bursts into laughter, although, a few are sitting with their arms folded across their chests, trying to keep their squinty-eyed glances and tightly pressed lips from breaking into smiles. Cassandra looks around at her classmates with her face lifted up in the air. She seems to be proud to be named after a Greek goddess, no matter what her fate.

Although it is heartwarming to see the students so animated and free (compared with their "Mr. Pittman" faces), the group's enthusiasm has reached a chaotic level. Devon responds quickly with a litany of firm encouragement, directing her words to specific individuals and pockets of pandemonium around the room. The following phrases were recorded within a 10-minute period:

"Control yourself. You can do it."
"I'll wait for you, so you'll wait for me."
"Come back. Come back. Elevate yourself."
"Be sweet. Be nice."
"Come up here. I want to look at those nails more."
"I know you're just excited and that's why you can't sit still."
"You're all smart."

After a student says, "I can't see," Devon responds with, "Great that you asked for what you want."

Devon trusts that the students will be aligned with her, rather than compliant or oppositional. If she makes them nervous initially, it might be because they have known so few people in authority who can talk *with* them and not *at* them. Ultimately, she reveals to them that they are worth knowing.

Devon begins her workshop on *The Crucible* with a question:

DEVON: What's *The Crucible* about?
EISHA: We all have a witch in us.
DEVON: You all have a lot in common with this place. We're going to build a situation here. What's a "rumor"?

After they acknowledge they all know what a rumor is, Devon presents a challenge to them:

DEVON: What would happen if someone started a rumor about a person in your high school?

The group decides to use the topic of "hair lice" as the reason for a rumor in their high school. Devon asks for the group to choose two main characters to role play "Rumor girl" and "Lice girl," while the remaining students will role-play the rest of the high school.

DEVON: Okay you two fabulous creatures. Move over here. Now this one has fab hair. She has the nicest hair in the school. And how would you feel if your hair wasn't as nice, and here's this girl with fab hair. If someone told you she had lice, why would you believe her?

CLASS MEMBERS: M-m-m-m-h-m!

DEVON: We naturally pick on people who are natural outsiders. And aren't we all sensitive?

JYLISSA: I'm so sensitive you don't know.

DEVON: What about you guys? Is it true, fellas, you can't show people you're sensitive or they'll go after you? You have to hide your sensitivity from your peers.

Some of the boys nod slowly until they realize that some of their classmates have turned around to look at them. I scan their faces one by one. From where I am sitting, I can see some of the boys — Andre, Anthony, James, Hector, all of them quieted by Devon's question. The girls are also quiet. They are all looking at each other with a gentleness, a sweetness, a recognition.

Devon's attention to both the male and female students in the class regarding their sensitivity is remarkable. Even though the males seem self-conscious initially about being "outed" in terms of their sensitivity, Devon has legitimated their feelings. Her sensitive "attunement" to their language, their culture, themselves, allows them to learn.

Herbert Kohl (2002) focused on the teacher-student relationship at the level of language in the classroom. In a recent essay, "Topsy-Turvies: Teacher Talk and Student Talk," Kohl reminded us that students are sensitive to the language of their teachers — the words, the tone, its trust-worthiness — whereas teachers are more likely unaware of how they are being heard and understood. Not surprisingly, a classroom can come undone when "vigilant" students detect what they perceive to be the insincerity of their teachers. Because of the focus that most teachers place on how the students are talking, or responding to teacher talk or other "official" texts in the classroom, teachers engage students in a distinctly one-way relationship. "Teaching requires listening, not merely to your students but to yourself being listened to," said Kohl (p. 159). He urged teachers to consider how they are presenting themselves to their students and then make a 180-degree shift in order to construct how their students may hear them. He called this a "topsy-turvy," which he explained is "an attempt to pay attention to how you are heard at the same time you are talking" (p. 153).

FINAL REFLECTIONS

Many White Americans, preservice teachers among them, believe that race is less relevant today than it ever was in determining the status and well-being of people of color. Contrary to what many would like to believe, America is still organized around structures that perpetuate racial inequality. If anything, these structures may be just as pervasive than ever before, yet harder to identify, especially if our eyes are closed. To not see skin color or race is not to see racism either. For to be color blind is to be blind to White culture, and, thus, blind to one's own White privilege. Yet, that being said, America is an overtly race-conscious society.

Claiming not to see race and skin color while being conscious of it, as well as constituted by it, is a trait that characterizes too many White preservice teachers at the beginning of their teacher socialization process. These individuals are often well-intentioned and caring persons who are, nevertheless, at a loss for how to enter into a teaching environment with those individuals not like them in terms of race or culture. As painful or difficult as this knowledge of self and society may be, it is vital to learn if we, as educators, hope to interrupt how we may be complicit (whether intentionally or not) in maintaining the cycles of oppression for students of color.

Had Adria, Joslyn, or Devon been color blind to their students, they would have missed the full complexity of not just who their students are but who they are in relation to them. As culturally aware teachers, they know that to be blind to race and skin color is neither respectful, nor sensitive, nor fair. It is life-denying. To acknowledge it is to challenge the dominant limits on all of our sight.

Maxine Greene (1995, p. 113) inspires us to "teach for openings." She recalled Martin Buber speaking about teaching and the importance of what he called "keeping the pain awake." She illuminated his notion when she said, "I suggest that the pain he had in mind must be lived through by teacher as well as student, even as the life stories of both must be kept alive. This, it seems to me, is when real encounters occur."

REFERENCES

Au, K., & Jordan, C. (1981). Teaching reading to Hawaiian children: Finding a culturally appropriate solution. In H. Trueba, G. Guthrie, & K. Au (Eds.), *Culture and the bilingual classroom: Studies in classroom ethnography* (pp. 139–152). Rowley, MA: Newbury House.

Banks, J. A., & Banks, C. A. M. (Eds.). (1995). *Handbook of research on multicultural education* (pp. 570–581). New York: Macmillan.

Bonilla-Silva, E. (1996). Rethinking racism: Toward a structural interpretation. *American Sociological Review, 62*, 465–480.

Bonilla-Silva, E. (2001). *White supremacy & racism in the post-civil rights era*. Boulder, CO: Lynne Rienner Publishers.

Bonilla-Silva, E. (2003). "New racism," color-blind racism, and the future of whiteness in America. In A. W. Doane & E. Bonilla-Silva (Eds.), *White out: The continuing significance of race* (pp. 271–284). New York: Routledge.

Boykin, A. W. (1994). Afrocentric expression and its implications for schooling. In E. R. Hollins, J. E. King, & W. C. Hayman (Eds.), *Teaching diverse populations: Formulating a knowledge base* (pp. 243–256). Albany, NY: State University Press.

Brown, M. K., Carnoy, M., Currie, E., Duster, T., Oppenheimer, D. B., Shultz, M. M., & Wellman, D. (2003). *Whitewashing race: The myth of a color-blind society*. Berkeley: University of California Press.

Clayman, C. B. (1989). *The American medical association encyclopedia of medicine*. New York: Random House.

Cochran-Smith, M. (1995). Color blindness and basket-making are not the answers: Confronting the dilemmas of race, culture, language and diversity in teacher education. *American Education Research Journal, 32*, 493–533.

Cochran-Smith, M. (2000). Blind vision: Unlearning racism in teacher education. *Harvard Educational Review, 70*(2), 157–190.

Delgado-Gaitan, C., & Trueba, H. (1991). *Crossing cultural borders: Education for immigrant families in America*. New York: Falmer.

Delpit, L. (1988). The silenced dialogue: Power and pedagogy in educating other people's children. *Harvard Educational Review, 58*, 280–298.

Delpit, L. (1995). *Other people's children: Cultural conflict in the classroom*. New York: The New Press.

Doane, A. W. (2003). Rethinking whiteness studies. In A. W. Doane & E. Bonilla-Silva (Eds.), *White out: The continuing significance of race*. New York: Routledge.

Doane, A. W., & Bonilla-Silva, E. (Eds.). (2003). *White out: The continuing significance of racism*. New York: Routledge.

Ebert, K. L. (2004). Demystifying color-blind ideology: Denying race, ignoring racial inequalities. In C. Herring, V. M. Keith, & H. D. Horton (Eds.), *Skin deep: How race and complexion matter in the "color-blind" era* (pp. 174–196). Chicago: University of Illinois Press.

Fine, M. (1997). Witnessing whiteness. In M. Fine, L. Weis, L. Powell, & M. Wong (Eds.), *Off White: Readings on race, power, & society* (pp. 57–65). New York: Routledge.

Foster, M. (1998). *Black teachers on teaching*. New York: The New Press.

Freire, P. (1973). *Education for critical consciousness*. New York: Seabury Press.

Gay, G. (2000). *Culturally responsive teaching: Theory, research, & practice*. New York: Teachers College Press.

Giroux, H. A. (2001, March/April). Zero tolerance: Creating a generation of suspects. *Tikkun*, *16*(2).

Greene, M. (1995). Teaching for openings. In *Releasing the imagination: Essays on education, arts, and social change* (pp. 109–121). San Francisco: Jossey-Bass.

Heath, S. B. (1983). *Ways with words: Language, life and work in communities and classrooms*. Cambridge, England: Cambridge University Press.

hooks, b. (1992). *Black looks: Race and representation*. Boston: South End Press.

Irvine, J. J. (2002). *In search of wholeness: African American teachers and their culturally specific classroom practices*. New York: Palgrave Macmillan.

Irvine, J. J. (2003). *Educating teachers for diversity: Seeing with a cultural eye*. New York: Teachers College Press.

King, J. E. (1991). Dysconscious racism: Ideology, identity, and miseducation of teachers. *Journal of Negro Education*, *60*(2), 133–146.

Kohl, H. (2002). Topsy-turvies: Teacher talk and student talk. In L. Delpit & J. K. Dowdy (Eds.), *The skin that we speak: Thoughts on language and culture in the classroom* (pp. 145–161). New York: The New Press.

Ladson-Billings, G. (1994). *The dreamkeepers: Successful teachers of African American children*. San Francisco: Jossey-Bass.

Ladson-Billings, G. (1995). Toward a theory of culturally relevant pedagogy. *American Educational Research Journal*, *35*, 465–491.

Markus, H. R., Steele, C. M., & Steele, D. M. (2000). Color blindness as a barrier to inclusion: Assimilation and nonimmigrant minorities. *Daedalus*, *129*(4), 233–259.

Mosby's Medical & Nursing Dictionary. (1986). St. Louis, MO: C. V. Mosby.

Nieto, S. (1999). Critical multicultural education and students' perspectives. In S. May (Ed.), *Critical multiculturalism: Rethinking multicultural and antiracist education* (pp. 191–215). Philadelphia: Falmer.

Omi, M., & Winant, H. (1986). *Racial formation in the United States*. New York: Routledge.

Paley, V. G. (1979). *White teacher*. Cambridge, MA: Harvard University Press.

Peters, M. F. (1985). Racial socialization in young Black children. In H. P. McAdoo & J. McAdoo (Eds.), *Black children* (pp. 159–173). Beverly Hills, CA: Sage.

Philips, S. U. (1985). Participant structures and communicative competence: Warm Springs children in community and classroom. In C. B. Cazden, V. P. John, & D. Hymes (Eds.), *Functions of language in the classroom* (pp. 370–394). Prospect Heights, IL: Waveland.

Powell, L. (1997). The achievement knot. In M. Fine, L. Weis, L. Powell, & M. Wong (Eds.), *Off White: Readings on race, power, & society* (pp. 3–12). New York: Routledge.

Quintanar-Sarellana, R. (1997). Culturally relevant teacher preparation and teachers' perceptions of the language and culture of linguistic minority students. In J. E. King, E. R. Hollins, & W. C. Hayman (Eds.), *Preparing teachers for cultural diversity* (pp. 40–52). New York: Teachers College Press.

Rosenberg, P. M. (1997). Underground discourses: Exploring whiteness in teacher education. In M. Fine, L. Weis, L. C. Powell, & L. M. Wong (Eds.), *Off White: Readings on race, power & society* (pp. 79–89). New York: Routledge.

Rosenberg, P. M. (1998). The presence of an absence: Issues of race in teacher education at a predominantly White college campus. In M. Dilworth & M. Bandele (Eds.), *Being responsive to cultural differences: How teachers learn* (pp. 3–20). Thousand Oaks, CA: Corwin Press.

Sleeter, C. E. (1993). How White teachers construct race. In C. McCarthy & W. Crichlow (Eds.), *Race, identity and representation in education.* New York: Routledge.

Smitherman, G. (2002). Toward a national public policy on language. In L. Delpit & J. K. Dowdy (Eds.), *The skin that we speak: Thoughts on language and culture in the classroom* (pp. 163–178). New York: The New Press.

Tatum, B. D. (1994). Teaching White students about racism: The search for White allies and the restoration of hope. *Teachers College Record, 95,* 462–476.

Ward, J. V. (2000). Raising resisters: The role of truth telling in the psychological development of African American girls. In L. Weis & M. Fine (Eds.), *Construction sites: Excavating race, class, and gender among urban youth* (pp. 50–64). New York: Teachers College Press.

NOTES

1. See Bonilla-Silva (1996, 2001, 2003); Brown et al. (2003); Doane (2003); Doane and Bonilla-Silva (2003); Ebert (2004) for further discussions of contemporary critiques of color-blind ideology and the continuing significance of race.
2. Some of the work on "culturally responsive teaching" focuses on the relationship between teachers and students within the same cultural community (Foster, 1998; Irvine, 2002, 2003). Other studies describe how teachers find more "culturally appropriate" methods of working with students of a different culture (Au & Jordan, 1981; Banks & Banks, 1995; Boykin, 1994; Delgado-Gaitan & Trueba, 1991; Delpit, 1995; Heath, 1983; Nieto, 1999; Philips, 1985). Although others investigated those who have lived and worked within environments characterized by dominant Whiteness (Cochran-Smith, 2000; Fine, 1997; Rosenberg, 1997, 1998; Sleeter, 1993), these researchers ask questions about how as White educators we may be complicit (intentionally or not) in maintaining the cycles of oppression for students of color.
3. See Smitherman (2002) for further discussion of a National Public Policy on Language.
4. According to Bonilla-Silva (2001), White people "seem to be rather 'color-conscious' in terms of their choice of significant other," friends, housing, and other life choices; but, when confronted with their contradictory behavior, Whites argue that it is social class and not race that determine their choices (p. 141).
5. Linda Powell (1997) pointed out that it is likely that students of color are "stuck" *until* race is brought up, whereas White students are "stuck" *once* race is brought up.
6. According to Geneva Gay (2000), even though "culturally relevant pedagogy" may be called by many different names, including "*sensitive, centered, congruent, reflective, medi-*

ated, contextualized, synchronized, and *responsive,* the ideas about why it is important to make classroom instruction more consistent with the cultural orientations of ethnically diverse students, and how this can be done, are virtually identical" (p. 29). In this discussion, I refer to Gloria Ladson-Billings's theory of "culturally relevant teaching" throughout as being *aware, sensitive,* and *responsive.* I use these words less as an indication of a specific theorist who may be attached to a particular version of the idea and more to indicate the variety of ways to affirm the culture of students.

7. This work has been part of a larger research effort on the part of the college and the Allentown school community to understand the role of the Community Admissions Program (CAP) in helping students who are identified as "at risk" to graduate from high school and apply for college. In the spirit of ethnographic analyses, the documentation of this program has included participants, including high school students, preservice teachers/tutors, and visiting college professors, in the research process as well. I have been interested in how the college tutors negotiate their expectations and intentions with a population of students who are unlike them in terms of privilege and experience, as well as how the urban high school students respond to the contradictions they face in trying to carve out their own biographies as precollege students. The relationship of the college tutor with the high school student is central to this experience. For the college student tutors are the first and most intimate reflection back to these young people about whether they can be successful in an environment that may hold great promise for them but for which they do not yet know or embody the rules for participation. Needless to say, the small liberal arts college and large urban public high school in this story share the same literal neighborhood, yet are worlds apart in terms of educational biographies of the young people who inhabit them.

8. All participants (tutors, college professors, and students) in the alternative school setting are referred to by their real names except for the teacher, "Mr. Pittman." The CAP students begged to be referred to by their actual names when they learned that stories of their class would be published in a book.

TWENTY

Resisting Diversity:
An Alaskan Case of Institutional Struggle

Perry Gilmore, David M. Smith, and Apacuar Larry Kairaiuak

INTRODUCTION

In the following discussion an incident provoked by alleged comments regarding the preferential grading of Alaskan Native students at the University of Alaska Fairbanks (UAF) is described and analyzed as a case study in the cultural-racial politics of education. As such it provides a vivid, even chilling, example of the techniques a white institution will marshal to resist cultural diversity and maintain its whiteness by completely missing, misunderstanding, and ultimately ignoring the responses, concerns, and actions of an aggrieved minority population in imposing its own institutional perceptions and interpretations of events. A deeply problematic and painful aspect of this resistance is that it is primarily accomplished through actions that the institution actually believes support minority success but in fact negate it. It is therefore necessary to illustrate and describe examples of the complexities and subtle machinations of white institutional privilege in order to begin to combat its devastating effects.

The authors, an Alaskan Native graduate student and two white professors, present this case in order to raise the level of the discourse from one about individuals, specific programs, and groups to one that focuses on a critical self-examination of institutional practices that consciously and unconsciously undermine diversity and nurture white privilege. (For a fuller discussion of this case and its historical and epistemological context see Gilmore and Smith [2002], Gilmore [1987], and D. M. Smith [2002].) This then is not a discussion about individuals, villains, or heroes but about institutional postures, policies, and practices that on the surface may seem to be about race-neutral issues but, in fact, carry significant and damaging racial-political consequences.

Each of the authors knew well the "grading controversy" on campus in 1991. It had been our own poignant and powerful example of institutional silencing and resistance. We had each, along with many others in the university community, felt passion, rage, and confusion during the months of turmoil surrounding the fractured public discourse. Each of us had entered that discourse both on campus and in the media. Each of us could vividly recall our own sense of exclusion, as the institution "from whom we expected better" (Fine, 1993) seemed to surround elite interests. We offer the following description and discussion of this controversial incident to interrupt an oppressive silence and to create a public place for repair. It is imperative that we take individual and institutional responsibility for critically examining the practices of our own institutions and for initiating and maintaining an open dialogue that will ultimately nurture the possibilities for growth and change within our institutions. This dialogue is a difficult one to initiate. For example, after a limited circulation of an earlier draft of this essay, we had two very different sets of reactions. Members of the Alaska Native community (and the editors of this volume) felt we were extremely generous and diplomatic with regard to the institution and its actions, whereas administration and faculty tended to see our position regarding the institution as particularly harsh. We have tried to find a platform from which to speak that neither diminishes our critique nor inhibits our potential for repair.

In the first section of the essay, we present a description of the incident primarily through the public discourse that surrounded it through its depiction in the dominant culture narrative created and portrayed by the local media and institutional texts. Gates (1995), in a *New Yorker Magazine* essay that examines the national racial discourse surrounding the O. J. Simpson case and Million Man March, pointed out, "People arrive at an understanding of themselves and the world through narratives — narratives purveyed by schoolteachers, newscasters, 'authorities,' and other authors of our common sense" (p. 57). In this essay, the local Alaska media headlines, through which we document the incident, capture a sense of the dominant culture reality in this particular community.

In the final sections of the essay we argue that the incident itself functioned to maintain hegemonic practices at the university and to obscure the demonstrated successes of the Alaska Native student population there. We argue that the university, by almost exclusively focusing their responses to the incident on issues of academic freedom, standards, and grading practices, abdicated their responsibility to resist racial slurs and stereotypes and to provide a safe learning environment for the growing minority population. Although issues of academic freedom, standards, and grading practices are worthy concerns, they are not the focus of this essay. What is of concern to the authors is the fact that despite an official university investigation finding (reported early in the chronology of the incident) that there was *no* evidence to suggest any differences in grading practices for Native and non-Native students, the public discourse continued to almost exclusively concentrate on standards and grades. This dominant culture "grand narrative" managed to effectively squelch any analysis of the damaging racial politics at the core of the incident.

THE INCIDENT

The event that set off the incident occurred on September 5, 1991. In a report to the Board of Regents four months later, the chancellor described it in the following way:

> At a meeting off-campus, [a professor] was invited to present views on methods of teacher certification. During a lively discussion that followed the presentation [the professor] apparently stated that UAF was under equity pressure to pass (graduate) Native students. No tapes of the meeting exist and accounts differ, but her remarks were interpreted as an attack on the integrity of grades and degrees awarded to Native students at UAF. [The professor] was not speaking as a representative of UAF at the meeting. (January 8, 1992)

The comments made at that "lively discussion" and the reactions to them became the focus of a heated and intense discourse that was spotlighted and stirred by the local media and lasted for an entire academic year. Though rumors of the event were circulating, it was a month before the first article that made reference to the event was actually published. This was a letter to the editor in the student newspaper, which was run with the headline, "Concerned With Speaker" (*Sun Star*, October 4, 1991). The professor and a colleague replied in the following issue. Their letters to the editor were headlined, "Inaccurate Rumor Rectified" and "Let's All Work Together," respectively (October 11).

Although the tone of these early student newspaper captions appears mild and almost under-stated, the drama was building across the campus and the community in private discussions, meetings, phone calls, letters, memos, and undocumented dialogues. In a letter to the chancellor, the executive director of the local Native Association wrote, "It is incredulous that statements like this can be made by one of the University's professors, and no reaction by anyone so far" (October 4, 1991). No official or public response from the administration was forth-coming.

Weeks later, on the first of November, the story broke in an Anchorage paper, a city 400 miles away from Fairbanks. The headline was big, bold, and almost unforgettable: "Professor Alleges UAF Graduating Unqualified Native Students" (*Anchorage Times*, November 1, 1991). The article characterized the turmoil, reporting, "A professor's comments about grading standards for Native students at the University of Alaska Fairbanks has sharply split the community, pitting academic freedom against what some say is the devaluation of a degree in education." The director of the Native Association mentioned above was quoted as being "concerned about the effect the statement has on Native students at the university. It has caused them great anxiety and concern — they don't want to have any doubt passed on their education, which the state-ment did."

The torrent of statewide headlines and media attention that followed for the next 7 months must have surprised even the media. The following headlines appeared in the local Fairbanks and Anchorage newspapers and in the UAF student paper between November and December 1991 and captured some of the focus of the controversy: "Professor's Remarks Raise Ruckus: Educators, Students Hit Comments about Native Performance at UA"; "UAF Students Want Investigation"; "Charge of Favoritism Riles Natives at UAF"; "Students Demand Probe of Lenient Grading Claim"; "UAF Grading Policies Face Close Examination"; "Debate Centers on Preparation"; "Native Teacher Shortage Worries Educators"; "Natives Express Anger, Hurt at Forum"; "Controversy Reaches Fever Pitch"; "Regents Seek Report on UAF Grading"; "Racial Animosity"; and "Savage Attack."

The headlines continued through December and final exams with articles, letters to the editor, and guest editorials each taking some position for or against the professor, the faculty, the education department, the Native students, the administration, and so forth. Accusations of racism, stereotyping, and cultural insensitivity, and defenses of academic freedom, university standards, and program quality were dominant themes. Residents in the immediate community as well as those across the state followed the daily headlines. In remote Native rural communi-ties, residents are reported to have waited over fax machines for friends and relatives to send the most recent news reports. Even at a distance the incident carried an "electric" quality.

In January, after the holidays and at the start of a new semester, a report from the chancellor stirred the intensity of the headlines again. Debate continued and accusations were made anew: "Grading Dispute Continues: UAF Chancellor Report Finds No Overall Pattern"; "Professor Slams Study: Says UAF Failed in Analysis of Grading Natives"; "Professor Bolsters Favoritism Charge: Inquiry Does Little to Quell Controversy"; "UAF Grading Charges Fly."

The incident persisted and continued to create controversy and stir emotion and argument, and appeared not only to be irrepressible but also unresolvable. Most everyone felt wounded in some way. Law suits, threat of litigation, and legal action surrounded every interaction, further silencing a substantive or meaningful discourse.

In April a headline read, "Natives Voice Complaints on [the professor]." The newly appointed Native advisory committee, in meetings with the chancellor, were reported to have said that "the controversy over Native student academic abilities has not been resolved and they want to see action." Comments about the professor's "racial remark" were quoted. In response to much of the focus on academic freedom one committee member raised issues of academic responsibility, saying, "Academic freedom does not permit infringing on the rights of others. We have academic freedom of speech but we can also be judged by what we say." After almost a full academic year, despite committee reports, university plans, and investigations, nothing seemed resolved; no one was satisfied.

In May 1992, in response to the Native advisory committee's concerns, the chancellor issued a statement in which she acknowledged, "Many Native students do not believe that the matter has been brought to satisfactory closure." With regard to grading practices she stated,

> We believe without any doubt that, as a standard practice, UAF students, specifically including Native students, earn the grades and credentials they receive. We believe that there is no reason to question the efforts of faculty in general to grade all students fairly. The controversy was unfortunate, and on behalf of the University of Alaska, I apologize to the Native students for any discomfort they may have felt.

These words and the public apology, however, came too late. The semester was over. Many students were gone. In the *Fairbanks Daily News-Miner* on June 28, 1992 (9 months after the alleged remarks about preferential grades were made, and when most students were not on campus), a large ad was placed by the Alaska Native Education Student Association in order to have the chancellor's announcement made public. No articles, letters, or editorials accompanied or were forthcoming in response to the ad. Though the announcement carried large letters declaring "FAIR GRADING OF NATIVE STUDENTS AFFRIMED," the damage had already been done. One might only speculate about what might have been if such a statement had been forthcoming from university officials early in the controversy.

To the Alaska Native students the year's headlines had read like a catechism of hegemony, a litany of shame, a pedagogy for the oppressed (Friere, 1973). Questioning minority credentials and standards is unfortunately not a new or unfamiliar response to minority achievement. Nor are these discussions new to academia. (Unfortunately these are the common responses to interrupting any "gatekeeping" practices where race, class, and gender lines are crossed.) Remarks such as these must have been uttered many other times. But the intensity and persistence of this controversy and its continuous media frenzy with its unending stream of headlines seemed to surprise (and eventually exhaust) everyone.

OVERCOMING CLASHES OF EPISTEMOLOGY, EXPECTATION, AND STYLE

The seriousness of the controversy as measured by the pain and disruption it caused to Native students and their community of supporters demonstrated the separateness of the conflicting worlds they inhabit as subordinate participants in a white institution. This conflict resulted in clashes on several fronts.

In any conflict situation, the parties act according to their perceptions of the meaning of issues raised. Their reactions to the other's actions are colored by a complex set of expectations each has developed of the other. The mutual set of expectations that has evolved between Alaska Native students and the institution is far from simple, involving issues of academic expectations, silencing, and standards for assessment.

To the professor who had made the remark, and to most of the university community, the intense reaction seemed to come as a complete surprise. Comments about the abilities or inabilities of students and opinions about grading policy are the stock-in-trade of academic discourse. Many faculty members had often expressed similar concerns without serious consequence.

For most Alaska Native students the academic experience is loaded with import of a different sort. A pervasive expectation of failure confronts Native students and to a large extent governs how they are viewed and treated by the institution. But in many cases the institutional view is internalized by the students themselves. Many of the students on campus during the controversy represented the first generation of those who attended high school in their own villages[1] and the first generation of Alaska Natives to attend university. These students had much to prove, to themselves and to their families, by their academic success. In their eyes and those of their families that they were earning good grades and graduating means that they have reached a major watermark in striving for success.

This is more the case because for many of them the approbation of professors, in the awarding of successful grades, bespeaks a deep cultural affinity they have experienced with elders or respected relatives in the village. In these contexts when a younger person is told to accept a responsibility by an older relative or elder, he or she accepts the assignment with pride, knowing that he or she would not be asked until they had proved themselves capable. Being told that they didn't deserve their successes, not only by the professor in question but, through its reactions, by the institution itself, created not only palpable pain but a serious betrayal.

The institution treated the matter as purely academic, part of an ongoing debate about grading. It appeared taken back by the strong reaction of the Native community. One professor commented on the "hysteria" in the Native community. The institution didn't seem to know how to read the cues of, respond to, or acknowledge the Native community response. At least part of this reaction can be attributed to a serious and deep-seated clash of expectations. The institution expected that the university community would see the issue as academic and not personal, that it would welcome the proposed, impassionate, and rational attempts to sort out the "facts" as a positive contribution to resolving an ongoing debate.

Native students who had labored under a pervasive expectation of failure and who had, against all odds, registered impressive academic successes, expected the institution to celebrate these successes with them and to censure the faculty who betrayed them. At the very least they expected the institution to hear their pain, understand the shame they risked bringing upon their families and communities, and take the steps to address these concerns.

However, the institution's response to the conflict surfaced another underlying conflict, a clash of conceptions of the nature of the university. On of the tenets of the positivism that characterizes Western institutions is the need to separate facts from values or feelings and to make decisions based on facts alone. Universities celebrate their abilities to make academic distinctions, to look at issues "objectively" and dispassionately. The very bedrock of scientific inquiry is the ability to separate the investigator from the object of study — the need for objectification taken as unproblematic — and to eschew any emotional involvement.

This epistemology seriously clashes with that of Alaskan aboriginal society.[2] It is at the root of a number of other issues facing Alaska today, including the continuing debate of Native subsistence rights, which are seen as economic matters by the dominant majority, not matters of ideology and personal identity as they are perceived by Alaska Natives.

To the administration, and to much of the rest of the university community, the standards controversy was simply a matter of getting the facts and then finding a technistic resolution of the matter. For example, the chancellor repeatedly stated that this was an academic issue and would be addressed through academic channels. This impassionate, rationalistic, and technistic approach, in a Habermasian (1962) sense, clashed with Native students' views of reality as shaped both by their early experiences in traditional villages and by learning to succeed in an oppressive, often condescending and hostile educational environment. In the following examples several dimensions of these views are illustrated.

First, to these students grades, diplomas, and academic successes are not simply objective and depersonalized facts but valued personal accomplishments owned and celebrated not only by them but by their extended families and communities as well, and are important to demonstrating self-worth. Many of the students came from traditional communities that allow for a pedagogy that provides room for error but goes to great pains to arrange for success. Noncompetitive and cooperative learning opportunities characterize the traditional pedagogy of a subsistence lifestyle that holds learners in high esteem and maintains high expectations for them (see Gilmore & Smith, 2002). Although the institution views the students as individuals, the students, in contrast, view themselves as part of a connected web of family and community. As one Native student explained, "The Native family infrastructure is fairly extensive ... aunts, uncles, and grandparents play a vital role ... when you finish school they value it very highly. Because it's seen as part of the family, an accomplishment of the family. It's not just the individual."

Second, contrary to the institutional assumption, the grading incident could not be seen as isolated and aberrant but was connected to other events as a whole to define the nature of their university experience. Their experiences of racism, the stigma of being treated as potential failures, and their marginalization at the university form a connected web. Often Native people would recount several other seemingly (to many non-Natives) unrelated events of violence along with the grading controversy as a related cluster. There had been a drive-by shooting of a Native man in the town and the accused had been acquitted. A yet unsolved murder of a young Alaskan Native woman student in the university dormitory had shocked, saddened, and traumatized the population on campus. These events along with the departure of several Native professors, a restructuring of the Rural College, and the grading controversy were all talked about in the Native community as part of the same problem.

The grading controversy could not be "taken care of" simply by ferreting out the facts, remediating the immediate breech, and proceeding with business as usual. To address it meant addressing the entire pattern of behaviors that constituted their experiencing of university existence. Virtually no one in the administration and few of the faculty or white students ever grasped, or acknowledged, the legitimacy of this reality.

Third, the roles some of the students were thrust into, as spokespersons and leaders, were for them inappropriate given their age and kinship statuses. Students went to the administration and to faculty asking for explanations as to what was happening and for assurance that the issue was being addressed. They got little satisfaction. One student was told by his professor that he had deserved the grades he received but that he was different from other Native students. Many of the professors to whom they looked for direction appeared weak and helpless in the turmoil. The faculty were unable to vindicate themselves or the students. As a result the students found themselves having to serve as their own spokespersons. They organized meetings, wrote letters to the media and the university committees, drafted position papers, and, most difficult of all, were called upon to explain what was happening to their families.

Although these were stressful and time-consuming roles, causing several students to drop classes and even drop out of programs, the net results were not all negative. Several students found a voice to surface what for them had been subjugated knowledge (Foucault, 1980). Some were able to challenge what had been a long-standing matter of conflict for them; that is, the way "white people" fragment reality and look at pieces of the whole. These examples illustrate Lather's (1991) contention that situations of this sort can result in the "historic 'others' mov[ing] to the foreground, challenging and shaping what we know as knowledge." Many of the students assumed leading roles in newly organized student organizations and on advisory committees.

Finally, the confrontational style of the institution and the involved faculty was at first shockingly inappropriate and intimidating. In large part, the student response to the accusation was first to consult with faculty to see if it were true. On hearing it was not, they asked the administration to deal with the professor who made the accusation. As the institution failed to respond and the concern escalated both within the university and the larger community, the students began to participate in meetings and discussions with the media, in student organizations, and with student support service programs, faculty, and administration. The main topic at these meetings was the expression of their hurt, bewilderment, and feelings of betrayal. The response to their initially expressed grievances, even though the administration repeatedly claimed that there was no evidence to support the accusation, was neither apology nor retraction. Rather statements of policy were forthcoming from the institution and real or implied threats of legal action from the professor having made the accusation.

CONCLUSION: COUNTERING INSTITUTIONAL HEGEMONY WITH CULTURAL RESILIENCE AND COLLECTIVE RESPONSIBILITY

The data and discussion we have presented in this essay suggest that the unusual length and intensity of the incident described in this essay can best be understood as an institution's resistance to the increasing successes of a visibly growing minority population on campus. The incident itself functioned to maintain hegemonic practices at the university and to obscure the demonstrated and increasing accomplishments of the Alaska Native population. The university, by almost exclusively focusing its responses to the incident on issues of academic freedom, standards, and grading practices, abdicated its responsibility to resist racial slurs and stereotypes (especially as depicted in news headlines), and to provide a safe learning environment for the growing minority population.

Consistent with theories of resistance and reproduction in education (e.g., see Bourdieu & Passeron, 1977; Friere, 1985; Giroux, 1983), when it could no longer be predicted that Native students would "flunk out" or "get homesick" in their first year at the university, and when graduation statistics included growing percentages of Native students, the discourse shifted to questions of grading and unearned degrees.

Claude Steele (see Waters, 1995) proposed the notion of "stereotype vulnerability." He argued that minority student performance is negatively affected when they have to "contend with this whisper of inferiority" (p. 45). In the case of the Native students on the Fairbanks campus this was not a whisper to contend with but a loud chorus that lasted through midterms and finals of two semesters. What then might be the effects of stereotype vulnerability be when the cues are bold, public, and clearly humiliating as they were throughout the incident described?

By not interrupting the damaging public discourse, the university failed to protect the educational lives and reputations of its Native student population. Many speculated about the damaging impact of the dominant public narrative on the students' potential for professional employment. Given these circumstances, the students demonstrated an unusual and inspiring amount of resilience throughout and after the incident. They displayed a remarkable ability to resist the public discourse.³ The students seemed to draw their strength and direction primarily from their traditional values, families, and communities.

Many Alaskan families want their children to be educated but are cautious about the potential vulnerability of their children in a white man's world, often far from home at the university. A poignant and illustrative example of this was shared in one of the open forums organized at the university during the grading controversy. A young Yup'ik woman came to the podium wearing a full-length traditional fur parka. She stood proudly and explained that when she was leaving her village to come to the university to continue her education, her grandfather spoke to her. He said that she was Yup'ik and that she was beautiful. Because of that, he told her, the white people might try to harm her. (One might argue that this grandfather predicted the incident.) He continued, saying that the parka her grandmother made for her would protect her from harm. At the podium, she turned to model the full beauty of the parka she was wearing and told the audience that she always wears her parka and thinks of her grandparents and their protection.

Though the university had not created a free or safe space, the students were able to maintain their traditional ties and seize a context for themselves. They learned the value of situated freedom, which is not granted but seized and created in the context of many obstacles. For the most part students appeared to be able to transform anger, hurt, and confusion into professionalism and academic effort. That they could so strongly resist the stigma and vulnerability in such a hostile and assaulting environment is a remarkable story of resistance and resilience.

We have much to learn from these events and from the surrounding stories that were never told. If the incident and out reflections on it don't transform us, teach us, warn us, then we have not learned anything. Peggy McIntosh (1988) in a discussion of white privilege asserted, "To redesign social systems we need to first acknowledge their colossal unseen dimensions. The silences and denials are the key tool here."

CODA (BY PERRY GILMORE)

It has been more than a decade since the events described in this essay have occurred. The slightly abridged version above, of a previously the published essay (Gilmore, Smith, & Kairaiuak, 1997), demonstrates early evidence of the assault on affirmative action in the university and gentrification of the academy so prevalent in university communities today. The situation at UAF today is much improved. There is a new chancellor who has demonstrated great sensitivity and support for Native students and faculty. Many programmatic and structural advances have been made that have improved the circumstances for Alaska Native students and faculty. But one thing remains the same at UAF and elsewhere in the academy — the need to be continuously vigilant in locating, identifying, and resisting institutional policies and practices that may on the surface look neutral but are actually organized around hierarchical race politics. These hegemonic practices are invisibly built into the "grand narratives" of the dominant culture and are woven into the fabric of our daily lives in ways that often make it difficult and challenging to uncover, track, and resist. Although white academic institutions continue to resist diversity, marginalized and excluded groups continue to defy those Foucauldian dividing practices and boundaries. Universities cannot afford to be, nor should they be allowed to be, the academic "gated communities" of our society — designating themselves on the highest and most restrictive levels of "perfection" in a misguided modern day revisiting of the pernicious ordering of the Great Chain of Being (see Lovejoy, 1972, for a detailed discussion of the history of the idea). We have a responsibility to be prepared to resist injustice repeatedly and to recognize the realignments of institutional resistance that may even come in the guise of reform and transformation.

My late husband David Smith and I have subsequently examined the discourse surrounding this grading incident in much richer detail through a sociolinguistic analysis of the counternarratives of resistance and resilience in the voices of UAF Alaska native students (see Gilmore & Smith, 2002). That analysis provided (1) a deeper critical understanding of the political struggle that was being waged in the educational arena (see D. M. Smith, 1998), and (2) the identification of the epistemological, linguistic, and cultural resources from which the students drew the strength and tenacity to resist injustice and to interrupt entrenched hierarchical arrangements in the academy.

But it is not enough to document these counternarratives. David Smith (2002) urged that our challenge as researchers is "not only to surface the narratives of oppression, resistance and resilience, but for the edification of the academic community it must develop approaches that put these narratives to use in addressing the oppressive equation ... they must become the basis for a radical new pedagogy, one that is based on and privileges these narratives and local knowledge" (p. 81).

In the spirit of that new pedagogy and partially as a result of this incident, all three of the authors of this essay changed their conceptual understandings, ways of knowing, and ways of working in educational contexts. Larry Apacuar Kairaiuak, now based in San Francisco, has been a leading educator and activist working with indigenous populations across the United States. David Smith and I continued our mentoring experiences and collaboration with indigenous students working to develop "culturally safe" (L. Smith, 1999) localized research approaches that attempted to facilitate the attainment of academic credentials and scholarly recognition without sacrifice of real cultural identity. In addition to our continued work with indigenous students in Alaska we spent a sabbatical in 1998 at the Centre for Aboriginal Studies at Curtin University in Perth, Western, Australia. There we were privileged to be mentors to 20 indigenous Aboriginal students in a unique postgraduate program focused on indigenous research and development. Elsewhere (Gilmore, 2002; Gilmore & Smith, 2004; D. M. Smith, 2002) we provide detailed examples of the strategic discursive work our indigenous students in Alaska and Australia are accomplishing in academic settings in order to maintain autonomy and integrity within Western academic institutions and knowledge systems which represent well-established systems "grounded in histories of colonialism, and the subjugation of indigenous knowledges" (Abdullah & Stringer, 2001). Indigenous scholars have had to continuously resist ascribed stigmatized status for themselves, their communities, and for the linguistic and cultural knowledge they bring. They also must seize opportunities for academic power, privileging their own marginal positions, and legitimizing their own subaltern knowledge. Finally, they must continuously negotiate with dominant culture institutions to reconfigure and scrutinize the range of complex and specific strategies of structure and power they must struggle with in everyday local settings (e.g., see Dobkins, 1999, p. 181).

The incident described in this essay is only one in an unending series of events of exclusion that play out in "white" institutions across the globe. But despite these obstacles over the past decade there has been a steadily growing indigenous presence in the academic community. Newly formed indigenous conferences, research networks, publications, and associations reflect the strong cultural identity and solidarity among indigenous international populations. In the face of global challenges, indigenous peoples are transforming the nature of what we count as knowledge and research. The results have been and promise to continue to be enriching not only for the entire academic community but also for the global community of which we are all a part.

REFERENCES

Abdullah, J., & Stringer, E. (2001, April 15). *Decolonizing university discourses: Indigenous knowledge and indigenous experience as core components of a graduate program.* Paper presented at the American Education Research Association, Seattle.

Bourdieu, P., & Passeron, J. (1977). *Reproduction in education, society and culture.* Beverly Hills, CA: Sage.

Dobkins, R. (1999). Strong language, strong actions: Native American women writing against the federal authority. In M. Bucholtz, A. C. Liang, & L. A. Sutton (Eds.), *Reinventing identities: The gendered self in discourse.* Oxford: Oxford University Press.

Fine, M. (1993, August). *Gender, race, class and culture: The politics of exclusion in schooling.* Lecture. University of Alaska Fairbanks.

Foucault, M. (1980). *Power/knowledge: Selected interviews and other writings, 1972–77.* New York: Pantheon.

Friere, P. (1973). *Pedagogy of the oppressed.* New York: Seabury Press.

Friere, P. (1985). *The politics of education.* South Hadley, MA: Bergin and Garvey.

Gates, H. L. (1995, November). Thirteen ways of looking at a black man. *New Yorker Magazine.*

Gilmore, P. (1987). *Academic literacy in cultural context: Issues for higher education in Alaska.* Paper presented at the American Anthropology Association Meetings, Chicago.

Gilmore, P. (2002). Methodological challenges of critical ethnography: Insights from collaborations on an indigenous counter narrative. In H. Trueba & Y. Zou (Eds.), *Ethnography and schools: Qualitative approaches to the study of education.* Lanham, MD: Rowman & Littlefield.

Gilmore, P., & Smith, D. M. (2002). Identity, resistance and resilience: Counter narratives and subaltern voices in Alaskan higher education in 1991. In D. C. S. Li (Ed.), *Discourses in search of members: In honor of Ron Scollon.* Lanham, MD: University Press of America.

Gilmore, P., & Smith, D. M. (2004). Seizing academic power: Indigenous subaltern voices, metaliteracy, and counter narratives in higher education. In T. L. McCarty (Ed.), *Language, literacy and power in schooling.* Mahwah, NJ: Lawrence Erlbaum.

Gilmore, P., Smith, D. M., & Kairaiuak, A. L. (1997). Resisting diversity: An Alaskan case of institutional struggle. In M. Fine, L. Weis, L. Powell, & L. M. Wong (Eds.), *Off white: Readings on race, power, and society.* New York: Routledge.

Giroux, H. (1983). *Theory and resistance in education.* South Hadley, MA: Bergin and Garvey.

Habermas, J. (1962). *Strukterwandel der Offenlichkeit.* Neuwied: Luchterhand.

Kwageley, O. (1995). *Yup'ik world view: A pathway to ecology and spirit.* Prospect Heights, IL: Waveland Press.

Lather, P. (1991). *Getting smart: Feminist research and pedagogy within the postmodern.* New York: Routledge.

Lovejoy, A. O. (1972). *The great chain of being: A study of the history of an idea.* Cambridge, MA: Harvard University Press.

McIntosh, P. (1988). *White privilege and male privilege: A personal account of coming to see correspondences through work in women's studies* [Working paper No. 189]. Wellesley, MA: Wellesley College Center for Research on Women.

Smith, D. M. (1998). Aspects of the cultural politics of Alaskan education. In H. Trueba & Y. Zou (Eds.), *Ethnic identity and power: Cultural contexts of political action in school and society.* Albany: State University of New York Press.

Smith, D. M. (2002). The challenge of urban ethnography. In H. Trueba & Y. Zou (Eds.), *Ethnography and schools: Qualitative approaches to the study of education.* Lanham, MD: Rowman & Littlefield.

Smith, L. T. (1999). *Decolonizing methodologies research and indigenous peoples.* London: ZED Books.

Waters, E. (1995, September 17). Claude Steele has scores to settle. *New York Times Magazine.*

NOTES

1. The Molly Hootch ruling in 1975 was responsible for mandating that K-12 education was provided in small villages in Alaska where previously children had to leave their homes and communities to attend boarding schools at great distances and for long periods of time in order to get an education.
2. A provocative treatment of this issue is found in Kwageley (1995).
3. Although it is difficult to capture accurately, it appears that neither the grades nor the drop-out rates of the Alaska Native students were significantly affected by the incident. One can only speculate how much better grades might have been in the absence of such negative stereotyping and attention.

TWENTY-ONE

"We Didn't See Color": The Salience of Color Blindness in Desegregated Schools

Anita Tijerina Revilla, Amy Stuart Wells, and Jennifer Jellison Holme

During this 50th anniversary year of the Supreme Court's landmark decision *Brown v. Board of Education*[1] we continue to consider the lessons learned from school desegregation policy. In trying to answer these questions, most researchers have focused on student outcomes as a result of desegregation, especially the test scores of students in racially segregated versus desegregated schools (see Crain, 1976; Levin, 1975; Orfield, 1978). Another, smaller body of research has examined so-called intergroup relations within racially mixed schools — namely, how students of different racial or ethnic backgrounds "got along" and how their school experiences shaped their racial attitudes (see Schofield, 1991, for a review). And finally, there is an even smaller body of work on the long-term effects of desegregation on African American graduates in terms of their aspirations, their college-going rates, and where they live and work as adults (see Wells & Crain, 1994, for a review). Yet very little research has looked directly at how students in desegregated schools learned about race per se and how these lessons on race influenced their understandings of race as adults.

In other words, we know very little about how race and issues of racial privilege were discussed (or not) in school settings where students were dealing with race on a daily basis by virtue of attending schools to which they were assigned often based on their race. In an effort to answer these and other qualitative questions about students' experiences within desegregated schools, our team of researchers from Teachers College, Columbia University, and the University of California Los Angeles (UCLA) set out to study what school desegregation meant to the people who lived through it during the late 1970s in six racially mixed high schools[2] across the country. We conducted a total of 550 interviews with people in these six communities who were involved in desegregation efforts, including policy makers, educators who taught in these six high schools at that time, and 245 students who graduated from these schools in the spring of 1980.

We learned that the educators, administrators, and graduates we studied had rarely talked about issues of race back in the late 1970s. Instead, virtually all of the educators, and to a slightly lesser extent, the students, adopted a color-blind motto — an argument that "we are all the same" and that "race does not matter." Two main reasons were given for their vested interest in being "color blind." First of all, such a perspective was seen as a way to avoid racial conflict and blatant racism — a way to try and "keep the peace," especially in those schools where racial tension had existed just years before. Second, many of the educators and graduates we interviewed argued that this color-blind perspective helped them to reach out over racial boundaries to share common human experiences across the color line — to see people as people.

Yet as appealing as these arguments may be, we saw the many ways that this color-blind motto served to leave many important issues about race unexamined. In fact, many of the adult graduates we interviewed noted that there were many times during their high school years when they would have appreciated the educators' being more open to talking about race and helping students deal with underlying racial tensions and misunderstandings. And often, it seems that *not* talking about race allowed the educators and students — particularly the white educators and students — to act as though race did not matter in the context of schools in which students were being brought together, often for the first time, from racially segregated neighborhoods and a very racially divided and unequal society. We argue, based on our data and social theory related to race and white privilege in the U.S. context, that when race goes unexamined in this way, whiteness becomes the de facto "norm" and those who are not white or do not "act white" are seen as not normal — substandard on several levels. In such a situation, the goal of racial equality and the dream of a truly color-blind society are illusive.

In the following sections of this essay, we first provide a short description of our study and a theoretical framework, grounded in critical race theory and theories of racial privilege. Then we present the findings that emerged from our data related to the theme of color blindness. These findings explain not only what color blindness looked like in the six schools but also how it shaped and was shaped by the experiences of the educators and students within these schools. And finally, we argue, based on additional findings from our larger study and our theoretical framework, that the color-blind ideology perpetuated in these schools contributed largely to the uncertainty and contradictions about race that many of these graduates, especially the white graduates, express today.

This helps to explain how the whites we interviewed in particular can simultaneously argue, in the course of one interview, that "people are people" and thus "everyone is the same" while at the same time trying to explain that a larger percentage of African Americans and Latinos or Latinas in our society are poor because of their problematic culture or the fact they do not place enough emphasis on education and getting ahead, or both. In this way, our study provides a window into the soul of the American society's ongoing dilemma in terms of race. On one hand, white Americans want to think about race only on the individual level — how individuals treat each other — but on the other hand, they lack any broader, societal level explanations for ongoing racial inequality. Thus, they try to explain away this inequality by blaming the victims of it for not acting white, while simultaneously swearing we are all the same in this, our color-blind society.

THE "UNDERSTANDING RACE AND EDUCATION STUDY"

The six cities or towns where we conducted our case studies were Austin, Texas; Shaker Heights, Ohio; Topeka, Kansas; Englewood, New Jersey; Pasadena, California; and Charlotte, North Carolina. The six high schools that we studied within those communities were Austin High School, Shaker Heights High School, Topeka High School, Dwight Morrow High School in Englewood, John Muir High School in Pasadena, and West Charlotte High School in Charlotte. We show the racial makeup of these six high schools in Table 21.1. As we demonstrate in this table, these six schools varied widely in terms of their racial makeup, and two of the schools, Muir and Dwight Morrow, were 50% or more African American in the late 1970s.

Table 21.1 Racial Demographics Then and Now: Six High Schools (in percentages)

	Late 1970s	Late 1990s/Early 2000s
Austin High School (Austin, TX)		
African American	15	8
Hispanic	19	37
White	66	54
Asian/Pacific Isle		2
Dwight Morrow High School (Englewood, NJ)		
African American	57	65
Hispanic	7	32
White	36	1–2
Asian/Pacific Isle		2–3
John Muir High School (Pasadena, CA)		
African American	50	49
Hispanic	11	40
White	35	9
Asian/Pacific Isle	5	1
Shaker Heights High School (Shaker Heights, OH)		
Minority (mostly African American)	39	
African American		52
Hispanic		1
White	61	43
Asian/Pacific Isle		3
Topeka High School (Topeka, KS)		
African American	20	20
Hispanic	8	15
White	69	61
American Indian		3
Asian/Pacific Isle		1
West Charlotte High School (Charlotte, NC)		
African American	50	75
Hispanic		10
White	50	10
Asian		5

Using a multitiered methodology, we first conducted historical case studies of the districts and schools we studied. These case studies included interviews with school district officials, lawyers, community leaders, activists, and parents who were both for and against school desegregation. We also interviewed principals, counselors, teachers from different departments, and other school personnel to learn about the school culture and the impact of desegregation on the school social environment, curriculum, and discipline. In addition to interviews, we collected documents and archives about the historical context of the school desegregation case in each city or town.

The second tier of data collection involved in-depth interviews with 40 to 50 graduates of the class of 1980 from each of the high schools. These graduates were sampled across racial lines roughly in proportion to the racial makeup of their high schools. In Table 21.2 we provide the racial makeup of the graduates we interviewed. These graduates were also sampled to reflect the diversity of their schools in other ways, including a mixture of graduates — within and across the different racial or ethnic groups — who were from different social class backgrounds as well as a mixture of those from high- and low-level classes. We also attempted to interview graduates who reflected a range of involvement in extracurricular activities when they were in high school — from those who were not involved in such activities at all to those who were athletes to those who were Key Club or Chess Club members. In short, we were trying to look at these schools and the students' experiences within them from as many different standpoints as possible.

And finally, the last tier of data collection entailed lengthy "portrait" interviews with 4 to 6 of the graduates who were originally interviewed.[3] In selecting these second, in-depth portrait interviewees from among the 40-plus graduates interviewed initially at each site we again sampled for diversity in terms of race. But we were also sampling for graduates who embodied the central themes that had emerged at each site during the first two tiers of data collection. This form of thematic sampling allowed us to explore these core issues in more detail through the experiences of a small number of graduates.

Table 21.2 Overview of Graduate Interviews by Race

African American	White	Latino	Asian	Other	Total
81	137	21	1	5	245

In our 5 years of traveling the country and tracking down people who had been affiliated with these six school districts and schools more than 20 years ago, we learned some very important lessons about school desegregation policy. We learned how it was implemented in diverse local contexts, how people made meaning of what it was and what is was supposed to be, and how they reflect back on it more than two decades later. Although we focus this essay on the color-blind theme that emerged from our data, we intertwine and interconnect this theme with several other important themes from our study. Thus, we present our theoretical framework for the color-blind theme followed by the color-blind findings that emerged as educators and graduates looked back on their time in these schools in the late 1970s. Next we provide a brief overview of other findings from our study that relate to this central theme of color blindness.

A FRAMEWORK FOR UNDERSTANDING THE POWER
OF THE COLOR-BLIND IDEOLOGY

Although in theory a color-blind society can be construed as a progressive movement toward racial justice, critical race theorists have argued that in practice it legitimates the erasing of cultures, histories, and injustices in a manner that has very real consequences in our society. They further have asserted that assimilation and racial denial do not eliminate white privilege; they maintain it. In fact, these critical race theorists have argued that a color-blind ideology similar to that espoused by the respondents in our study "can be traced to pre–Civil War debates, the modern concept developed after the passage of the Thirteenth, Fourteenth, and Fifteenth Amendments and matured in 1955 in *Brown v. Board of Education*" (Gotanda, 1991, p. 3). Both Gotanda (1991, p. 3) and Crenshaw (1997) critiqued the U.S. Constitution and much of the legal system founded by that Constitution as the basis of color-blind ideologies that help maintain white privilege in U.S. society.

For instance, Gotanda (1991) found that so-called color-blind constitutionalism purposely does not recognize race, ignores the social realities and implications of race, attempts to eliminate racial tension by disregarding race altogether, and thus permits ongoing racial discrimination in the private sphere (p. 8). Likewise, Crenshaw (1997) indicated, "Law in its almost infinite flexibility can assist in legitimizing hierarchy simply by labeling the realm of social equal, declaring victory, and moving on" (p. 282). She argued that the U.S. Supreme Court's rulings, by virtue of their power, imply to the public that once the ruling "comes down," the problem is solved and inequality has been addressed. Thus, the court's decision in *Brown* sent a message to the public that discrimination was eliminated and therefore race was no longer a factor of oppression in the United States.

Gotanda (1991) concluded, "As a means, color-blind constitutionalism is meant to educate the American public by demonstrating the 'proper' attitude towards race. The end of color-blind constitutionalism is a racially assimilated society in which race is irrelevant" (p. 54).

Of course, today, as 25 years ago, we are far from being a society in which race is irrelevant. All we need to do is look at the unceasing degree of racial segregation in housing as well as increasing segregation in the public schools to know that race still matters a great deal. But, at the national level, laws and policies set the tone for color blindness that we saw at the school level. Indeed, color-blind constitutionalism establishes an attitude of racial assimilation and denial that permeates the country and was adopted by the majority of the people in the desegregated schools we studied.

The work of sociologist Bonilla-Silva (2001) illustrates several aspects of racial ideologies that further a color-blind argument and are pervasive in American society today. He wrote, for instance, about the strong-held belief among the majority of whites in the United States that our society already, in a de facto manner, extends equal opportunities to all and that today, we live in a race-neutral society. Therefore, he argued, they exhibit either little support for, or outright resentment toward, policies such as affirmative action, race-targeted government programs such as school desegregation, or minorities' demands for their fair shares.

In other words, Bonilla-Silva (2001) wrote, because whites have a perception that the United States is founded on equality and a color-blind meritocracy, they resent any governmental programs that promote equal access and opportunity for people of color. Of course, he argued, once whites have abandoned discrimination, racism, or racial injustice as the explanation for racial inequality in this society, they need to come up with alternative, race-neutral explanations for facts such as the higher poverty rates of blacks and Latinos. Such explanations include the argument that "blacks' plight is the result of blacks' cultural deficiencies (e.g., laziness, lack of the proper values, and disorganized family life)" (p. 161).

In this way, Bonilla-Silva (2001) explained, contemporary racial ideologies have taken on a new form in that they are framed in race-neutral language. He stated,

> Taken together, whites' views represent nothing less than a new, formidable racial ideology: new because the topics of color blindness have replaced, for the most part, those associated with Jim Crow racism; formidable because these topics leave little intellectual, moral, and practical room for whites to support the policies that are needed to accomplish significant racial change in this country. (p. 162)

Rather than outright racist language and conflict, the new form of racism is covert and apparently race neutral or color blind, thus, making it evermore difficult to challenge from a racial justice perspective. He indicated that this new form of racism was identified as early as the mid-1970s, noting the "increasingly covert nature of racial discourse and racial practices; the avoidance of racial terminology in racial conflicts by whites; and the elaboration of a racial agenda about political matters (state intervention, individual rights, responsibility, etc.) that eschew any direct racial reference" (p. 94).

Thus, according to Bonilla-Silva (2001), people who claim to be color blind often blame the victims of racism, and although they may recognize a minimal degree of discrimination, they often normalize it as a natural occurrence or they minimize its power and presence. Many of such explanations of racial inequality were prevalent in our data from the racially mixed high schools we studied.

Color-Blind Ideology in Desegregated Schools

As Bonilla-Silva (2001) noted, color-blind ideology was detected as early as the 1970s, and one of the areas of social science research and theory in which it first appeared was in the school desegregation literature. For instance, in the early 1970s, Rist (1974) found that a color-blind ideology in desegregated schools inhibited teachers and students from having meaningful cross-race interaction. In a study of a desegregated middle school in the 1970s, Schofield (1989) found that teachers' ideologies about race, especially their color-blind orientation, helped shape students' perceptions and actions about race.

By emphasizing academic student achievement as their "first, last, and only" goal for this racially diverse school, several teachers in Schofield's study excused themselves from confronting racial tension between African American and white students in their classes and school and in society in general. In fact, the few times that teachers made efforts to foster cross-race interaction in class, students and parents objected, arguing that activities that called for student interaction were not necessary for maximizing educational progress. Teachers often opted to instead focus solely on teaching academics and avoiding altogether the discussion of race. This orientation often resulted in resegregation within classrooms and social spaces in the school.

Schofield (1996) explained that educators at the school believed that the best approach for dealing with race in desegregated schools was to adopt a color-blind perspective. In this way, they thought that they would be eliminating the possibility of discrimination against people of color. Schofield (1996) argued that although there are some positive attributes of this perspective, there were negative effects as well. For instance, she noted that the color-blind perspective can reduce, at least in the short term, the potential for overt racial or ethnic conflict by generally deemphasizing the salience of race and encouraging the even-handed application of rules to all students. Furthermore, she acknowledged that such a perspective may reduce the potential for discomfort or embarrassment in racially or ethnically mixed schools by vigorously asserting that race does not matter.

However, Schofield (1996) wrote that this perspective also had a number of negative effects. Most important, "the decision to try to ignore racial considerations — to act as if no one notices, or should notice, race — means that policies that are disadvantageous to African Americans and other nonwhites are often accepted without much examination or thought" (p. 105). For example, Schofield (1996) wrote that when educators are trying so hard not to see color, problems such as disproportionate suspension rates for African American and other students of color may not be read as a sign of the need to examine discipline policies. In other words, patterns of discrimination may go unnoticed if "school faculty and staff think of students only as individuals rather than facing the difficult issue of whether the school may be treating certain categories of students differently than others" (p. 105).

Thus, Schofield (1989, 1996) argued that a color-blind perspective reduces initial discomfort and tension in daily interactions between students and teachers, but it has detrimental consequences in the long run, especially affecting school policies and curriculum.

More than 20 years later, we heard in our interviews with educators and former students from racially diverse high schools many echoes of Schofield's important research. Our work, however, goes beyond Schofield's, as we investigated the beliefs that were in hindsight of both former students (now graduates) and educators in six different sites. We were able, therefore, to examine the issue of color blindness within a larger historical context and to consider its influence, more than 20 years later, on the lives of graduates of desegregated high schools.

FINDINGS FROM THOSE WHO LIVED THROUGH SCHOOL DESEGREGATION

After a resounding echo of responses from educators and graduates — particularly in Topeka, Charlotte, and Austin, but to a lesser extent in the other three sites as well — cited color blindness as *the* central goal for these six desegregated schools in the late 1970s, we sought to understand why and how this had become such an important theme in these schools. Although this goal of color blindness seemed to be more imperative for the white graduates and educators than for those of color, what was so striking about this finding is that it was not simply a "white thing" but it had a powerful ideology that permeated these schools and silenced any discussions of race.

And thus, color blindness was often seen as the "fair" and "right" thing to do in the context of these schools, especially in the southern schools, where a system of legal, race-based segregation had just ended. In these contexts, it seemed wrong to talk about the very thing that had divided the members of different racial groups for so long. We also learned that the vast majority of the graduates and educators we interviewed said that all the students in their racially mixed high schools "got along" across color lines because, in part, of the fact that they did not see race. They also told us that, in reality, it was easier for the graduates and educators to be color blind than it was to learn how to talk about race and to deal with the discomfort and anxiety that they felt when such sensitive issues were discussed.

And thus, the vast majority of the people we interviewed were convinced that their success in eliminating racism was based on their ability to transcend or even deny race and to be color blind. As a white former student of Austin High School noted when we asked her if her teachers talked about race in class, "Race wasn't a big deal. I mean, it really wasn't something we talked about, it wasn't a big deal."

Despite such quotes — and there are many just like this one in our data — it was also clear from our interviews that the color-blind goal only took these students and educators so far. Thus, although color blindness may have helped in some ways to bridge the racial divide in terms of individual relationships and to keep a lid on potential racial fights or conflicts, we also saw that the color-blind ideology left many things unsaid, many misunderstandings unresolved, and many feelings deeply hurt. Furthermore, as we demonstrate below, the goal of color blindness did nothing to promote greater understanding of the role that race had and was playing in these students' local communities and the society at large. Thus, as the theorists we cited previously noted, color blindness as a goal can often be used to maintain white privilege by allowing educators and students to avoid addressing the many ways in which whiteness becomes the norm and thus goes unchallenged. Meanwhile, that which is not white is seen as not only different but also deficient.

In the following sections we illustrate, first of all, the way in which the educators, in particular, made sense of their color-blind goal and their degree of investment in it. We follow this with a section on the students' (now adult graduates) memories of how color blindness promoted peace and "getting along" but at the same time left them feeling like there were important issues or tensions that were not being discussed. In the final section we provide an overview of some of the other central themes of this study — a glimpse at the many racial issues that were *not* being discussed as a result of the color-blind goal and the many missed opportunities to confront racial discrimination and inequality as a result.

Being Color Blind as the Central Goal in Racially Mixed Schools

The quest for color blindness clearly began with the teachers and administrators in all six high schools that we studied and was then handed down to the students. In fact, it was a very rare exception to find an educator who had taught in one of these six schools in the late 1970s who did not espouse this color-blind ideology.

Furthermore, there were two central themes that emerged from their explanations of *why* being color blind was so important. The first had to do with their prior experiences, particularly in the early 1970s, when in several of the districts and schools we were studying there had been a great deal of racial tension and even so-called rioting and fighting. In these settings, particularly Topeka, Austin, Pasadena, and Charlotte, color blindness was seen as the best way to "keep the peace" and to "keep a lid on things" that might otherwise erupt. By not talking about race and being color blind, the rationale went, educators could prevent such incidents from happening.

The educators' second major rationale for the color-blind perspective was the simple and well-meaning argument that "people are people" no matter what color they are and that we need to treat people as individuals and not as members of a particular racial or ethnic group. This view was then seen as the most helpful way to get people to look beyond race and to emphasize personal connections across racial and ethnic groups.

In this section we also examine the students' (now adult graduates) perspective on color blindness. We find that they, too, highly valued this perspective, even as they sometimes felt they needed more support dealing with day-to-day experiences that related to race.

Been There, Done That—Keeping a Lid on Racial Tension by Not Talking about It

According to many of the educators we interviewed, by the late 1970s, there was no need to talk about race because the period of racial tension and fighting in most of these schools and communities had already passed. Thus, in all of these sites, the late 1970s was a relatively tranquil period compared with prior years. In the towns that had seen a great deal of racial fighting or rioting — most notably Topeka, Austin, Pasadena, and Charlotte — the years of the greatest turmoil had occurred prior to the class of 1980 entering high school.

Furthermore, because all six of these schools had already been racially mixed well before the class of 1980 arrived on the scene, most of the teachers remembered that the bulk of the staff development on race and dealing with racial diversity had occurred earlier, in the early 1970s. In these early days of desegregation, some district and school leaders were trying to ease the transition into desegregation through teacher workshops, small student group activities, added course electives, or one-time events. Some teachers recalled (sometimes vaguely) participating in such workshops. They also remembered some student assemblies, new courses, special student or faculty committees, or other mandates from the district including racial quotas for activities such as cheerleading or student government (these were in place in varying degrees in Topeka, Austin, Pasadena, and Charlotte). But by the late 1970s, except for the racial quotas for activities in four of the six schools we studied, such efforts had declined drastically, and the assumption was that the work for racial desegregation was behind them. As one white teacher who taught English at Austin High School explained, "I think in 1980 everything was all over, anything controversial or any unhappiness, you know, that was all settled, and we were settled in as a school."

Thus, the relative calmness of the late 1970s reinforced the general belief among the educators that there was no need to talk about race because everyone "got along" across racial and ethnic lines. As long as there were no racial riots or physical conflict, teachers were under the impression that the social environments of their schools were positive. In Pasadena, Shaker Heights, and Austin, we heard educators and community members compare their racial situations with those of Boston and of "the South" (meaning the Southeast), indicating that in comparison, their schools were in much better shape in terms of people getting along across racial lines. According to white social studies teacher at Muir High School in Pasadena,

> I think there were probably black kids and white kids who had horrid, horrid things happen to them at Muir. But these were not the norm; these, these were the exceptions. And I know that . . . my middle son is in Florida . . . he said, "Dad, you would not believe race relations in Florida. You would not believe how horrid they are. Black people don't like white people. White people don't like black people." He said, "It's not at all what life was like when I was growing up in Muir — at Muir."

And thus, it came to be in these desegregated high schools that a lack of fighting or any form of violence was a sign that everything was OK. Furthermore, so many of these educators told us they believed that this peace — as superficial as it may have been in some instances — was a direct result of their concerted efforts to not see race and to be color blind.

People as People

Thus, in the absence of any perceived need to be otherwise, educators were, for the most part, very proud of their vision of color blindness, especially as they reflected on the historical presence of racism in their schools, communities, and homes. In fact, they recall being very vested in seeing "people as people."

For instance, a white teacher who worked at West Charlotte High School when the class of

1980 attended said she believed that being color blind meant that people — not just students but also faculty — were capable of loving and caring for one another. She explained that this was the spirit of that school in the 1970s and 1980s:

> We just saw each other as people. I don't think so much.... I guess to be corny about it we were color blind. We saw people as people and ... and the potential they could offer, and loved and cared for each other. Again, it just seemed like color didn't seem to make a difference to anyone.... We just, again, viewed people as people. Not emphasizing, I guess would be the fact.... I mean, we emphasized the fact that we were not emphasizing color of skin.

Emphasizing this lack of attention to skin color was echoed in the omission of racial discourse in the classroom. In fact, the majority of the educators insisted that race was not an issue and that it did not matter to teachers what color their students were. A white teacher from Shaker Heights High School in Ohio said,

> I always thought it was a great integration [in Shaker Heights]. I was always very impressed by it. [When I was] at Ohio State studying education, I wrote a lot of papers on integration and ... and what's going to become of the two races and can we all live in peace and was it too much to ask for? I never had a problem with color. I was raised to see people as who and what they are.

An art teacher from Topeka High said that desegregation resulted in their school becoming a much better place after people learned to trust and stop fearing one another. He noted that many people worked hard to make these changes, so that race would not be an issue at their schools:

> I think that it became a much nicer place to be.... At first I think there was [a] certain amount of lacking of trust, but I think that has changed. The lack of trust or fear that ... I think there [were] some real efforts by people to try to make it so that it is more equal. [Silence] I think for a lot of people there, race isn't a matter. It's more of how is this individual doing? How can we help them with what's going on?

Interestingly enough, in many instances, it was both black and white teachers who spoke of their desire to see their students as students rather than by color. We discovered that the first African American teacher at Austin High School had a strong color-blind stance. When asked to summarize the themes and highlights of desegregation in Austin, Texas, she answered,

> People have said to me, "There are not many people [of color] who could have gone to Austin High and fared the way you fared.... But I was not over there for social priorities, social promotion, or advancement of the races. I was there to teach, and I taught them all the same way, so I just didn't separate.... So you know, I think I made a name for myself for just being different. I would prefer to see no White, no Black, no blue, no purple. I just wanted to be the best human being that I could be.

This teacher, much like all but a handful of the approximately 150 teachers we interviewed, made a concerted effort to *not* consider or be considered by race. Clearly, she wanted to extend her desire for color blindness to her students. What we see when we look at the data from the interviews with these former students who are now adults is that in many ways they did adopt similar color-blind perspectives as their teachers and administrators. Still, they were more likely to question the value of this perspective in light of what they were living through on a daily basis in their schools.

Students' Views: Being Color Blind Was Important, but Was It Always the Best Thing?
Given the attitudes of the educators in these six high schools, it should come as no surprise that these school administrators and teachers played virtually no role in helping students deal with or better understand the racial issues they were faced with in their racially mixed schools. Furthermore, we find that this was not just a high school phenomenon. In fact, these class of 1980 graduates — most of whom had been desegregated since elementary school — said that, except for a few occasions, racial issues or desegregation was never talked about in any of their schools. They said they went to their racially mixed schools without ever really understanding the goals of integration or desegregation.

Overwhelmingly, the graduates said they did not attempt to talk with their teachers about racial issues in their schools. As a white graduate of West Charlotte High School explained when asked if he remembered ever talking about school desegregation in school, "No, I don't remember [laughs]. I don't remember anybody ever mentioning anything, really. We just all knew that we were being bused to try to balance out ... the racial lines or whatever."

Thus, although it appears that race was salient on a daily basis and students knew that for many of them, where they went to school depended on their race and ethnicity, it was not discussed in school.

On one level, most of the graduates seemed fine with this color-blind orientation. They reported that generally students "got along" with one another in these high schools in spite of the fact that there were students, parents, and community members who did not agree with the racial integration of the schools. As students, they seemed to understand — almost intuitively — why so many of the educators wanted to avoid talking about race. And looking back on the experience 20 years later, they saw some value in the efforts on the part of the teachers to "keep a lid on" racial tension and to see people as people. In fact, the people-as-people theme comes through loud and clear in their discussions of race today and how they get along with people of different racial and ethnic backgrounds (see Wells, Holme, Revilla, & Atanda, forthcoming).

Furthermore, it was clear from our interviews that the graduates — like many of the educators — saw race as a delicate issue that was to be avoided in part because students and adults of all racial backgrounds felt vulnerable in talking about something that had divided society for so long. For instance, a white graduate of Dwight Morrow High School in Englewood, which was predominantly African American by the time the class of 1980 arrived, indicated that race was a "terrible topic" that he could not discuss in school. When asked why, he said, "Why was it a terrible topic? 'Cause you didn't want to offend people. You didn't want to say something stupid. You didn't want to get into fights. You know, I think it was a culmination — that's kind of, that's a U.S. thing. In the U.S., it's kind of like a topic you don't talk about very much."

Students, therefore, did not expect race to be discussed by their teachers. Instead they assumed that color blindness was a much more "natural" approach to dealing with race. Another white graduate of Dwight Morrow High School said, "It is a very touchy, a delicate issue. How could a public school, an integrated public school that is predominantly black go try to tell or try to encourage something that might not be natural? I don't know if that is possible. And how much more natural can you be by just letting it happen?"

Thus, many graduates said they believed that ignoring race was the "right" thing to do, and although teachers and administrators never actually instructed them to do so, they did it by example. Yet on another level, underlying their insight into why this was necessary, lay the graduates' own sense that maybe talking more about race would have been helpful. For instance, there were some graduates who remembered their schooling experiences as racially tense or chaotic and who would have liked for the educators at these schools to have played a larger role in helping students work through such issues. Others spoke of greatly valuing the few teachers who did talk about race. A white graduate of West Charlotte High School gave an interesting account of how race was or was not discussed in school. She noted that teachers avoided the subject and tried to maintain the status quo, but that some teachers were better at helping students with disputes — racial or otherwise:

> I think everybody wanted to keep [his or her] jobs and keep things on the status quo. I find, too, looking back that I think a lot of teachers were just there. They had their job. They just wanted to get through it without dealing with any extracurricular problems. Some teachers that really would stand out ... Mr. Jones — he would make an effort ... a special effort to ... he'd be an arbitrator for students having problems, and then he didn't care if you were white, black, or purple. He was just that way. My homeroom teacher ... I loved him to death. He was color blind also. He didn't care. He just ... he was funny. You could talk to him about anything. You know, you had those special teachers, but in general, on the whole, the school itself did not advocate discussing racial issues at all.

She applauded one of her teachers for being different because he made an effort to reconcile race-related problems. However, she said that the teacher was "color blind" and "did not care" what race his students were. Thus, in one instance, the graduate was critical of maintaining the status quo and the lack of discussion of race, but on the other, she recognized that the teachers who were color blind were the ones who would be willing to talk about anything, including race. In this manner, color blindness represents equal treatment rather than racial denial.

Meanwhile, a white 1980 graduate of Muir High School in Pasadena said race was a "nonissue" for her, but she admitted that she was very fearful of being bullied by students of color in school. She said,

> I guess it — for me, [school desegregation] was a nonissue, too, 'cause I didn't know any different. And I assumed people across the nation went to schools with people of ... all different colors. I did kind of wish that ... I didn't have so much fear in school. And there didn't seem to be much ... support, like I said, from the administration or from teachers. You know, if you were, if you were bullied by someone ... you were basically afraid to tell anybody for fear of getting even more bullied.... So what did that experience do for me? I don't really know! Except maybe, I mean, the experience of, of going, going to school where I felt kind of threatened, I don't think, served me much. Going to a school where there was, you know, diversity, I think, helped me a lot.

Clearly this graduate, even as she proclaimed that race is a nonissue, would have benefited from discussions about race and racial tensions in her racially desegregated school. Twenty years later, she and many of her classmates are still trying to make sense of their past experiences. But even many of the graduates who did not experience such racial tensions said that more dialogue or discussion about race would have been helpful to them.

In Austin, an African American graduate who has fond memories of his experience at Austin High School recalled that to the extent the students came together across racial lines, they did it on their own with no support or encouragements from the educators. He recalled, for instance, the changes that occurred over time while he was a student. He said that initially, in the lower grades, students were very separated by race, but eventually they learned to get along with one another. However, he argued that the administrators did nothing to assist the students in this process of making connections across race. He described the social environment of his high school:

> At the beginning there was a little ... it was different, it was separated basically ... at the end I think it was ... a more of a togetherness ... so ... and I can't give the administrators credit on any of it, 'cause I can't think of anything that they did. ... I think the students just took it amongst themselves to ... to make it happen ... you know ... break down some stereotypes about the school and stuff. ... That wasn't created by the administration at all ... that was definitely the students just ... being real, you know, and hey, you friend, we're friends ... we're not looking at color and stuff, and that's the way it went down.

In this way, the students adopted their own form of color blindness — of not looking at color even though they were extremely aware of color and which students were "mixing" and "not mixing." Graduates on all sides of the color line evoke pride and a sense of accomplishment in their cross-racial friendships that suggest that although they wanted to see people as people, they were keenly aware of race and aware of when and how someone crossed this line.

The African American graduate of Austin High School, quoted previously, expressed such optimism about his cross-race friendships, which he said grew out of his participation in athletics, as a member of the football team. Like many of the athletes at our six schools, this graduate found such team involvement to do more to facilitate cross-racial friendships than anything the teachers discussed (or failed to discuss) in class (see Wells et al., forthcoming).

Still, they were living race, even if they were not talking about it. This was evident when graduates discussed issues of ownership. For example, in cases where the schools were predominantly white, many students of color indicated that they felt no ownership of the school and that they were less likely to become involved in extracurricular activities or to feel that they had the ability to change things at their school. In the two schools with larger populations of students of color, some white students reported feeling unsafe or threatened. Hence, issues of ownership and belonging created some racial tensions that were rarely discussed in classrooms or by graduates unless pushed to consider such issues.

In Austin, the African American student mentioned previously felt that he could talk about race with his classmates but noted that the teachers would not condone such discussions. He said,

> I could probably talk to the students, but I don't think the teachers would appreciate that or would allow it ... and it could be ... through their beliefs or it could be that they're scared to let something like that happen in their classroom ... because like [I] say it was back in the '70s, so everyone was still touchy feely ... walking on eggshells ... they didn't wanna stir up anything ... and ... so I can't remember any of the teachers offering us an opportunity to share ... you know ... what is [this student] about? What is her culture about? What is [this other student] about? What is his culture about? What is [this other student] about? And his culture ... you know ... they didn't. ... No ... no ... they said, "Let's just get along" ... and that's why I say the administration gets no credit for that school coming ... so diverse and the cultures being able to get along with each other. It was strictly on the students.

Again, this student reminds us that the administrators and educators of his school were not fulfilling their obligations to the students in this racially mixed environment. In his opinion, they were not helping students interact with one another and they were not helping students understand themselves, their own culture or history. Students had to take responsibility for considering issues of diversity and difference and working through the difficulty of talking about race. As this student argued, teachers were "scared" to let students talk about race in the classroom.

In fact, we interviewed a scared white teacher from Austin High School who told us she was extremely afraid of talking about race in faculty meetings because she did not want to offend her black colleague. "We had a black teacher, and I was chairman then, and I remember in the meetings I would try so hard, it was just silly, but I tried so hard not to say anything that might offend her at faculty meetings." It was this fear of offending that prevented her and many others from engaging in meaningful dialogue about race.

Furthermore, this African American Austin High School teacher — the same one we mentioned previously who made an extra effort to *not* be considered by race — was remembered by so many teachers and students as the black teacher who had problems with the black students. When students went to her asking that she sponsor a black student organization, she refused, not wanting to be accused of favoring the students. She noted, "And although they wanted me to sponsor a black club, I wouldn't. I wouldn't, because I told them, 'You are here because you want to integrate. And I don't want to have something black sitting out — we want to try and integrate.'" African American students resented what they perceived to be neglect from this teacher. Nevertheless, she was very well liked and accepted by her colleagues, and often, when they noted that race did not matter at Austin High, they cited this particular teacher as one who set the example of color blindness.

Thus, we see from this careful analysis that although the goal of color blindness transcended racial boundaries and was embraced by educators and students alike, it was the educators who adopted it in a more religious way, whereas the former students (now adult graduates) of these schools sometimes saw that being color blind only took them so far. Yet, as we see in the last section of this essay, despite a racially diverse group of students' sometimes frustration with the color-blind perspective, such a view ended up serving the white students far better than the students of color.

Color Blindness Relates to Other Findings From Our Study: Ignoring Race in Theory Leads to Perpetuating White Privilege

One of the most interesting aspects of the color-blind theme that emerged so clearly from our data is that it relates closely to many other emerging themes from our study. This is especially the case for those themes that demonstrate the way in which white privilege is reasserted into desegregated spaces.

For instance, we learned that in these six cities and towns, like so many across the nation, that the burden of desegregating schools was placed primarily on the African American and Latino communities. Furthermore, once students arrived at these high schools that were "desegregated" in terms of having racially diverse student bodies, they were often racially "resegregated" inside the schools across high- and low-level classes, with very few students of color in the high-level or high-track classes. And of course, in contexts in which race is not discussed or debated, such resegregation was rarely if ever talked about — it was seen as the "norm" to always have the white students on top.

Furthermore, we learned that for the most part, the curriculum at these schools continued in its "Dead White Man" mode as if nothing had happened to the racial makeup of the students (Wells et al., forthcoming). In general, a white, male-dominated Euro-centric perspective on the world was taught in most academic departments at all six schools. Occasionally, there were isolated course add-ons such as black history or African American literature. But when changes were made to the curriculum, they were usually marginal changes in reaction to racial unrest. And although the schools with larger populations of students of color were able to maintain or improve on some of the early changes made in the curriculum, for the most part, these seemingly color-blind schools only taught the curriculum of one color — white — not to mention one gender and one area of the world. Again, this was the "norm" (see Wells, Revilla, Home, & Atanda, 2003).

Yet we also learned that despite this resegregation and thus reassertion of white privilege in these schools and communities the students often times did make important cross-race connections and friendships, even if these friendships did not always carry over into their social lives outside of the schools. And thus, it is not totally surprising that we learned that 20 years later, most members of the class of 1980 — including Latinos and Latinas, African Americans, whites, and the few Asian Americans we interviewed — reflected on their experiences in racially diverse schools as mostly positive with wonderful opportunities for learning how to participate in a racially diverse society. Most of these graduates noted that in high school "we all got along," and they believe that attending a desegregated school, although some times challenging, was nonetheless "worth it" (see Wells et al., forthcoming). Again, it is more than a little paradoxical that these graduates were attending color-blind schools while they noted how much they valued their cross-racial friendships, even if these friendships only went it "so far" and virtually all of their "outside of school" friends were of the same race.

Furthermore, the vast majority of these graduates find that in adulthood they are living in fairly racially segregated neighborhoods and, in most cases, are sending their own children to far more segregated schools than the ones they attended. Indeed, we found that the majority of graduates we interviewed thought it was more than a little ironic that they had attended desegregated schools in part to prepare them for the "real world" but that their real worlds as adults were far more segregated than their high schools had been (see Wells, Holme, Revilla, & Atanda, 2003).

Yet when asked about how they came to lead more segregated adult lives, these graduates, for the most part, lacked a broader understanding of racial inequality and segregation in the U.S. society that would have helped them understand how things had come to be that way. This was especially true for the white graduates who were too quick to slip into explanations that either blamed the victims — for example, because blacks do not work as hard — or saw racial segregation as the "natural" outcome of individual choices (see Wells et al., forthcoming). As time went on, therefore, the white graduates, lacking any formal education in the racial structure of inequality in the United States, became more and more like the white respondents studied by Bonilla-Silva (2001) — proclaiming "we are all equal" while coming up with all sorts of white supremacy-based explanations for why society is so unequal.

Thus, it is clear why, among the major findings from our study (see Wells et al., forthcoming), the color-blind finding we discussed in this essay is one of the most salient to the experiences of educators and students (now adult graduates) in the six high schools. This finding is critical because not only did the desire and goal to become color-blind pervade their experiences in the late 1970s but, according to our interviews with these graduates and their former teachers, many continue to struggle toward a goal of color blindness as the answer to an unequal society. We found many graduates — whites more than the graduates of color — and their former educators today proudly assert their vision of color blindness as a motto for racial justice.

In fact, many of the graduates and educators thought that school desegregation was the first step toward creating a color-blind society. Many of them credit the experience of attending and teaching in a racially mixed school with their current views of racial equality or, more specifically, "race as a nonissue."

We wonder, therefore, to what extent their present-day struggles to make sense of race are legacies of a high school experience in which race was positively framed as a nonissue and everyone strived to be more and more color blind. Given the findings of Bonilla-Silva (2001), such a color-blind view is embraced by graduates of segregated schools as well. So, we are not arguing that the experiences in racially mixed schools had a negative impact on these adults as they try to make sense of race in the early 21st century. Indeed, the data on the extent to which the graduates valued their cross-racial friendships and exposure in racially mixed schools strongly suggest the opposite (Wells, Holme, et al., 2003).

Rather, we are saying that the color-blind ideology of their high schools represents more of a missed opportunity for the generation of students who lived through school desegregation to reconcile the contradictory lessons they learned (or failed to learn) about race in school — namely, that they know "individuals" of other races whom they admire and were friends with while they grope for explanations for the broader and systemic racial inequality and segregation in the United States. Perhaps the greatest irony of all is that now that many schools in this country are more open to multicultural curriculum and celebrating issues of diversity — even in a superficial way — they are becoming more racially segregated (see Orfield, 2001).

Furthermore, a small number of the graduates we interviewed were trying, 20 years later, to figure out some of this racial confusion on their own. These graduates, amidst their busy adult lives, look back and wonder whether the color-blind perspective has served them well, especially in light of the increasingly diverse national population of the 21st century. According to one white graduate of West Charlotte,

> [We] knew our mission was to make us all color blind. That was the objective in that day, time.... In the late '70s, early '80s the objective was to be color blind and everyone be the same. That has since changed to embracing the differences through diversity, and it was [a] very different time and different objective.

Yet this graduate, like so many we interviewed, felt unprepared for this paradigm shift because the color-blind view had served so many of them (especially the white graduates) so well for so long.

CONCLUSION

Granted, many aspects of color-blind racism are confirmed through our data and white supremacy was maintained throughout many policies, practices, and norms of the schools and cities we studied, but the nuances of the data also revealed color blindness as an early attempt to deal with race, racial tension, and racism in school communities that were often educating the first generation of students to matriculate through desegregated schools.

The vast majority of the people we interviewed earnestly believed that if they denied the existence of race, they were making progress. Given the fact that many of the teachers we interviewed were, for the first time, working in desegregated environments and that they were entrenched in socially evolving color-blind ideologies in the late 1970s, the then-students of these schools could not look to their educators for guidance. Color blindness may have been the best option at that time — the progressive view in an otherwise still blatantly racist society.

Thus, we argue that there was a lost opportunity in these racially mixed schools of the late 1970s and that racial consciousness could have helped in many ways, especially as students and educators were trying to understand conflicted views of race, harboring and resenting negative experiences that many of them never spoke about until the day we asked them about their high school experiences.

So little of this story of school desegregation in the United States is known because, as we noted previously, most school desegregation research has ignored what happened inside of schools. This lack of information and understanding left school desegregation policy open to a strong critique by African Americans, as ignoring sociocultural experiences or views of students of color (see Shujaa, 1996).

Yet we have learned in our research on these six high schools that what was happening in the classrooms, hallways, playing fields, and auditoriums of racially mixed schools during the late 1970s was much more than a de facto process of ignoring the sociocultural experiences and needs of students of color. Rather, it was a proactive effort on the part of many educators in these schools to "move beyond racial differences" — to keep the peace and to foster a sense of "common ground" of human connections across race. As compelling as calls for such connections and common ground might be — especially after years of racial tension and fighting — these proactive efforts to be color blind did not result in a situation in which race did not matter. Twenty years later, it is clear that it mattered and continues to matter a great deal.

REFERENCES

Bonilla-Silva, E. (2001). *White supremacy and racism in the post-Civil Rights era*. Boulder, CO: Rienner Publishers.

Crain, R. L. (1976). Why academic research fails to be useful. *School Review, 84*, 337–351.

Crenshaw, K. W. (1997). Color blindness, history, and the law. In W. Lubiano (Ed.), *The house that race built*. New York: Pantheon Books.

Gotunda, N. (1991). A critique of "Our Constitution is Color-Blind." *Stanford Law Review, 44*, 1.

Lawrence-Lightfoot, S. L., & Davis, J. H. (1997). *The art and science of portraiture*. San Francisco: Jossey-Bass.

Levin, H. M. (1975). Education, life chances, and the courts: The role of social science evidence. *Law and Contemporary Problems, 39*, 217–240.

Orfield, G. (1978, Summer). Research, politics and the antibusing debate. *Law and Contemporary Problems, 42*(3), 141–173.

Orfield, G. (2001, July). *Schools more separate: Consequences of a decade of resegregation* (Report from the Harvard Civil Rights Project). Cambridge, MA: Harvard University.

Rist, R. (1974). Race, policy and schooling. *Society, 12*(1), 59–63.

Schofield, J. W. (1989). *Black and white in school: Trust, tension, or tolerance?* New York: Teachers College Press.

Schofield, J. W. (1991). School desegregation and intergroup relations: A review of the literature. In G. Grant (Ed.), *Review of research in education* (Vol. 17, pp. 335–409). Washington, DC: American Educational Research Association.

Schofield, J. (1996). Promoting positive peer relations in desegregated schools. In M. Shujaa (Ed.), *Beyond desegregation: The politics of quality in African American schooling* (pp. 91–114). Thousand Oaks, CA: Corwin Press.

Shujaa, M. (1996). *Beyond desegregation: The politics of quality in African American schooling.* Thousand Oaks, CA: Sage.

Wells, A. S. & Crain, R. (1994). Perpetuation theory and the long term effects of school desegregation. *Review of Educational Research, 64* (4), 531–555.

Wells, A. S., & Holme, J. J. (2002, August). *No accountability for diversity: Standardized tests and the demise of racially mixed schools.* Paper presented at the Resegregation of Southern Schools? Conference, Chapel Hill, NC.

Wells, A. S., Holme, J. J., Revilla, A. T., & Atanda, A. K. (2003, August 30–September 1). *Looking back on desegregation from segregated lives: A study of adult graduates of racially mixed schools.* Paper presented at the Harvard Civil Rights Project Colorlines Conference, Cambridge, MA.

Wells, A. S., Holme, J. J., Revilla, A., & Atanda, A. K. (forthcoming). *In search of* Brown. Cambridge, MA: Harvard University Press.

Wells, A. S., Revilla, A. T., Holme, J. J., & Atanda, A. K. (2003). *In search of* Brown: *The unfulfilled promise of school desegregation in six racially mixed high schools.* Paper presented at the annual meeting of the American Sociological Association, Atlanta, GA.

NOTES

1. *Brown v. Board of Education,* 347 U.S. 483 (1954).
2. By "racially mixed," we mean between 40% and 75% of any one race, and no more than 25% off the racial balance of the city or town for any one race.
3. See Lawrence-Lightfoot and Davis (1997).

TWENTY-TWO

Narrating the Multicultural Nation: Rosa Parks and the White Mythology of the Civil Rights Movement

Dennis Carlson

Spike Lee's *Bamboozled,* a film that unsettled both black and white audiences when it was released in 2000, is about black actors learning to perform white representations of blackness, to in effect put on a black face for a white audience. In using the minstrel show as a central metaphor or trope in the movie, Lee was making an important point about "blackness" as a production of "whiteness." The minstrel show, performed by whites in "black face" more than a century ago and through the late 1920s in films such as *The Jazz Singer* with Al Jolsen in black face, demonstrated the dominant culture of whiteness recognized all along that blackness was a representation, and one they had produced at that. So, whites could perform blackness, and arguably better than blacks. When whites put on black face, they became their own Other, and an Other who could be expected to stay in character. The minstrel show reinforced and policed rigid racial stereotypes that were oppressive. At the same time, however, it seemed to parody these stereotypes, revealing them as no more than an illusion, a performance, and an exteriorization of part of the white self.

In his film Lee suggests nothing too much has changed since the minstrel show days, except that blacks are now the ones performing in black face. The movie concerns the creation and production of a television show called *The Man-Tan New Millennium Minstrel Show,* a variety show set on a plantation in the antebellum South. One of the most intense moments in the movie is when two black performers undergo the transformation into the black Other, the minstrel, by rubbing burnt cork across their faces. Here, parody plays an important role in denaturalizing "blackness," and (by implication) "whiteness," revealing them to be ritualized performances, representations of self and Other. To view and critically discuss a film like this, one must also study and discuss a whole history of white representations of blackness in Hollywood films. Lee points to just such a project in the concluding segment of the film, which consists of a montage of Hollywood images — from Stepin Fetchit, to animated cartoons depicting blacks in exaggerated forms and actions, to Al Jolson in blackface singing "Mammy" in *The Jazz Singer,* to Bing Crosby and Judy Garland playfully "blackening up" with shoe polish, to the "great" epic of D. W. Griffith's *Birth of a Nation.* Surely this last film is the barely visible but always present Other in Lee's film. In Griffith's film whites in blackface portrayed blacks as fools and rapists.

Whiteness as a hegemonic form of Eurocentrism and racism in the United States has changed, and in some significant ways. White Americans, along with many black Americans, are proud of the progress that has been made in challenging oppressive forms of whiteness that relied on degrading stereotypes. The civil rights movement of the 1950s and 1960s forced many whites, including southern whites, to revise their sense of who they were in relation to blacks. Whites began to see, haltingly to be sure, that the continuation of such negative stereotypes was part of the problem, part of what stood in the way of overcoming a historical legacy of conflict and tension with blacks. They also began to acknowledge the role that positive images and role models can play in countering the stereotypes of the past. Certainly, no one would produce a movie like *The Birth of a Nation* today, and African American producers like Lee are making films like *Bamboozled* that help both white and black audiences "unthink" the taken-for-granted cultural logic of whiteness (Shohat & Stam, 1994). Nevertheless, the fact that *Bamboozled* made many people uncomfortable suggests that perhaps things have not changed as much as they seem on the surface, that whiteness only has taken on a new form, revising its narrative of the national history to make room for racial Others but still telling the story in ways that legitimate continued inequalities.

This brings us to the subject of multicultural education in a post–civil rights era. We might view dominant or mainstream forms of multicultural education as the outgrowth of an accord or a settlement reached in the civil rights era between the dominant culture and various Others — particularly race, gender, and sexual identity Others — in which the dominant culture agreed to change oppressive representational practices and to counter negative stereotypes with positive role models (Carlson, 1995). Public education has been one of the primary sites assigned responsibility for carrying out this accord, although popular culture (including Hollywood) also has agreed to live by the general terms of the accord. One might then ask, How are the public schools and the mass media doing at keeping the accord that holds together whiteness as a hegemonic discourse and practice in American life? If whiteness was "saved" by this civil rights accord rather than overthrown, should we not expect to find that it still is engaged in the production of white history, albeit a multicultural version of white history? Might we find continuities in the representational practices of whiteness across the decades, even in the new multicultural history of the United States?

To address these questions, I focus my comments on Rosa Parks, the "mother" of the civil rights movement, and how her story is being narrated within certain "texts" often used in teaching about multicultural education and the civil rights movement in public schools. Specifically, these texts are in the general field of children and adolescent's literature. I also examine one popular film, the 2002 CBS made-for-TV movie *The Rosa Parks Story*. In both cases a similar representation or "myth" of Rosa Parks emerges, one that tells her story in ways that are not threatening and unsettling and that reinforce some familiar if reworked tropes of whiteness. In both children's literature and the mass media, Rosa Parks is integrated within a "writing of the nation," to use Homi Bhabha's (1990) term. Dominant Eurocentric forms of historicism involve telling individual stories as expressions of the formation of a unified national culture and national cultural identity. The national narrative of whiteness is, in its most generic form, about the molding and shaping of the "American character" in the reflective image of the Enlightenment, and thus of the slow but inevitable triumph of reason over ignorance, of tolerance over intolerance and prejudice, and of equality of opportunity over discrimination. Within this narrative, I argue, the myth of Rosa Parks serves to confirm some predictable tropes of whiteness. There are, however, counternarratives of Rosa Parks — narratives written by African Americans — that challenge in significant ways the hegemonic narration of her life. I will conclude this essay by saying something about these counternarratives, the Montgomery Bus Boycott, and the civil rights movement. My point is that Rosa Parks, as a mythological character, can mean different things within different narratives of nation. But it is clear that progressives will need to interrogate the dominant myth of Rosa Parks and ask why she has been elevated within the multicultural education curriculum to the "mother" of the civil rights movement, right along side of the "father" of that movement, Dr. Martin Luther King. When conservative social critic William Bennett (1993), in the *Book of Virtues*, elevated Rosa Parks to the status of a hero for her quiet courage, then we have to wonder what is going on. We have to wonder whether multicultural education is being integrated within a renarration of the nation that does not seriously challenge whiteness precisely because it is produced by whiteness.

The enunciation of the nation's narrative is, from the beginning, to be understood as a selective process, one that will require both remembering and forgetting, both inclusion and exclusion, both speaking and keeping silent. Why, then, are Rosa Parks and the events that surrounded her refusal to surrender her seat to a white man on a Montgomery, Alabama, city bus on December 1, 1955, remembered rather than forgotten? The obvious answer is that her subsequent arrest sparked a 386-day boycott of buses by Montgomery's black community, and an NAACP suit against the city that eventually led to a Supreme Court ruling desegregating public transportation and repealing the South's Jim Crow laws. Two factors are noteworthy about Rosa Parks's actions as told within a conservative discourse of whiteness: They signal the "end of history," and they separate the public and the private.

The conservative historian Francis Fukuyama (1992) articulated the post-civil rights era philosophy of whiteness in his argument that American society was reaching the "end of history." This is a reference to Hegel's philosophy, and to Hegel's conception of history as a long road leading through the dialectic of progress toward a final "happy ending," when all those who have been oppressed and dominated are freed and the story of history will, in effect, come to an end (Carlson, 2002). Hegel argued that the story of history is about recognition — recognizing the Other as an equal human being deserving full human rights and freedoms. The difference between conservative Hegelianism and radical democratic Hegelianism is that the former associates recognition with equal treatment under the law whereas the latter has something far more encompassing in mind, involving a reconstruction of self and Other that is ongoing and that moves beyond legalistic remedies to the interrogation of inequality and privilege in everyday life and popular culture. Fukuyama and other social conservatives have argued that history has come to an end, at least to the extent that there is no transformative or revolutionary alternative to liberal, democratic, capitalist society. From this perspective, the grand narrative of American history, and the subnarrative of civil rights struggles for equality, begins to come to an end with Rosa Parks's heroic act of resistance. Supposedly with the establishment of a "color-blind" law throughout the United States, nothing more stands in the way of equality of opportunity. So the events of December 1, 1955, are presented as if they were the fulfillment of a dream. The national past is made to coalesce, to crystallize into an immediately readable moment, in which the ideals of the "founding fathers" are affirmed — strict equality before the law and the rule of the law. This helps explain why conservatives like William Bennett can elevate Rosa Parks to the pantheon of national heroes. The national narrative of progress thus reaches a high, final peak, in the striking down of legal inequalities between blacks and whites. Since then, again from this perspective, the nation has entered a phase of decline and fall. Conservative scholars such as Thomas Sowell (1984) have argued that as the leaders of the civil rights movement shifted their focus from equal treatment under the law to a demand for equal results regardless of differences in merit or ability (as affirmative action supposedly mandates), the movement was delegitimated (see Crenshaw, 1995). The rhetoric of whiteness now becomes, as Michael Dyson (2000) says, the language of "equal playing field," "racial justice," "equal opportunity," and "color blindness." He finds irony in the fact that even former supporters of the system of segregation in the South now rally around Rosa Parks and Martin Luther King in defense of a color blindness and in opposition to the "reverse discrimination" of affirmative action (p. 11).

Rosa Parks's story is also articulated with a conservative discourse on whiteness by framing it within a narrative about the public and the private. Is it coincidental that Rosa Parks's act of resistance occurs on a public bus, or does this fact enter into the meaning of the story, explicitly or implicitly? How else do we account for the reduction of the ongoing struggle over civil rights in Montgomery to the events of one afternoon on a public bus? In Bennett's (1993) account of Rosa Parks, the bus is a recurring motif. We learn, for example, that Rosa and her husband woke each morning "to the familiar sound of a City Lines bus pulling up to a stop across the road." The green and white bus stands at the stop for more than a minute as black and white workers climb aboard and prepare for their day's labor. The bus takes them to work each day, Bennett said, and brings them back each evening, so that the way people behave on buses is linked to the way they supposedly relate, or should relate, as workers once they get off the bus. After the boycott begins, Bennett wrote, "empty buses bounced around for everyone to see" (p. 491), visible symbols of the collapse of a common public life.

Legally, but also culturally, the public bus is a powerful signifier of the public and of public space, and it is also perhaps not coincidental that public schools were legally desegregated through court-ordered busing. In fact, the struggle to desegregate public schools was represented and understood very much in the way that the struggle to desegregate public buses was represented and understood — as a struggle over the rights of all citizens to use public facilities and institutions without regard to "race, creed, or national origin." The desegregation of public schools would provide everyone a right to a seat in the public school classroom, just as Parks had won the right to a seat in a public bus. As a symbol of the public, the bus served to advance some important democratic projects in that era, and it continues to signify some important democratic values. When Atlanta baseball player John Rocker commented that he did not take the subway when he played in New York City, he was pointing to the fact that public buses and subways can be very diverse and thus democratic sites. People uncomfortable with diversity avoid subways and public buses. Nevertheless, by locating the drama in a public bus, Parks's story is integrated within a writing of the public that is severely restrictive and individualistic. The public bus is a space in which people acknowledge each others' rights to be there but may choose to ignore each other completely or even harbor hostility toward one another. Ironically, in the intimate environment of the bus, the public often has a very limited, impersonal meaning. Whiteness now must tolerate its Other, but it is required to do nothing more. Furthermore, this expectation of tolerance, this sharing of a common space as equals, is understood to be limited to the explicitly public space of buses, schools, and businesses. In the "private" world, segregation was to continue as a way of life. Whiteness would give ground in the public, so long as the public could be reconstituted in terms of a restrictive rather than expansive discourse of rights.

Now that I have commented on the setting of the story, it is time to turn to Rosa herself, and more specifically to Rosa as she emerges as the central actor in a historical master narrative. This means turning to her life as it has been represented by others and as she herself represented it in her autobiography, written primarily for adolescent readers, *Rosa Parks: My Story* (1992). Although there are a number of different tropes and codes embedded in these different texts, I have organized my comments here around a discussion of two primary binary oppositions that to lesser or greater degrees govern the production of truth about race within the texts: good blacks–bad blacks and good whites–bad whites. My intent is not so much to dismiss the idea that there are "good" people and "bad" people. It may even be useful for members of marginalized groups, including inner-city poor black and Hispanic youth, to construct their identities in opposition to "bad" youth, defined as those who lack self-respect and are in one way or another living up to the self-destructive expectations established for them in the dominant culture. I do, however, want to trouble this good-bad binary and reveal some of the interests it has served, and continues to serve, in legitimating systems of racial domination in the United States.

Bennett's (1993) writing of the Rosa Parks story includes a scene in which, shortly after the Boycott began, Rosa was driven to the courthouse, where she was met by a crowd of supporters. According to Bennett, while Parks was inside "the crowd was getting restless. Some of them were carrying sawed-off shotguns, and the policemen were beginning to look worried" (p. 492). Here we have the image of white fear and *ressentiment*: the impulsive, violent, nihilistic, black mob. It is a particularly ironic trope of whiteness in that blacks have had to fear white mobs more than whites have had to fear black mobs. But it remains a powerful trope in the conservative discourse on race in the United States. Parks is celebrated, along with King, as one of the "good" blacks who help calm angry black crowds, who are able to steer blacks away from their presumed inclination to riot and act violently and to disrespect authority and the law. She represents a voice of reason, according to Bennett, in a community that was about to explode.

Goodness, in this case, is related to normality, to acting normal, to adhering to the normal or expected performance of race. In the language of Michel Foucault (1979), dominant Western discourses of power have been associated with "normalization" and thus with the establishment of a binary that separates the normal from the abnormal. Those who conform to gendered and racialized norms of self-presentation are seen as deserving full rights, and those who "act up" are not. Thus, an article for social studies teachers on how to integrate the study of the Montgomery Bus Boycott into the curriculum notes that Rosa Parks "was not the first person to be prosecuted for violating segregation laws on city buses in Montgomery. She was, however, a woman of unchallenged character who was held in high esteem by all who knew her" (Bredhoff, Schamel, & Potter, 1999, p. 207). In her autobiography, Rosa Parks participates to at least some degree in promoting this image of herself as Rosa the normal. But at times she also expresses a keen awareness of the strategic advantages of acting normal, even if black folks should not have to. She notes that the NAACP leadership in Montgomery had decided that the best plaintiff to challenge the segregated bus laws "would be a woman, because a woman would get more sympathy than a man. And the woman would have to be above reproach, have a good reputation, and have done nothing wrong but refuse to give up her seat" (Parks, 1992, pp. 110–111). Elsewhere she wrote, "I had no police record.... I wasn't pregnant with an illegitimate child." Consequently, whites could not say that there was anything she had done to deserve such treatment, "except to be born black" (p. 125). In her book to black youth, *Quiet Strength* (1994), Parks quoted from the Bible (Titus 2:7–8) to support her argument that to be a role model you must "show integrity, seriousness and soundness of speech that cannot be condemned." The aims of blacks, in her view, should be to make white people ashamed because they have "nothing bad to say about us" (p. 45).

Part of the goodness associated with Rosa Parks, and part of what makes her nonthreatening to many whites, certainly has to do with her performance of gender as well as race. This comes through very powerfully in the made-for-television movie *The Rosa Parks Story*, directed by Julie Dash. Much of that movie focused on her relationship with her husband Parks, as she called him, and so her story is transformed into a modern love story. He is the assertive one and she is the shy one, the one who lets herself be courted. Later, the character Rosa Parks defines herself primarily as a good wife to her husband, someone who never meant to get caught up in so much fuss and disturb their domestic tranquility. Parks is represented as her guiding star, at least initially, until he becomes disillusioned and cynical after the Scottsboro Boys, accused of raping a white woman, were not acquitted. Throughout everything, Rosa is a model of endurance in the face of sometimes overwhelming hardship and suffering. She is Rosa the meek and humble, and behind her public stoical face, the film suggests, Rosa is really a frightened little girl who is trying to hold back her tears — not very successfully. All of this makes Rosa Parks a very "normalized" woman, one who seems to accept her role as a subordinate, both in her relationship to Parks and in her working life. Rosa is a seamstress in a big department store in downtown Montgomery, where she is often shown literally on her knees, mending a skirt on a middle-class white patron or on one of the store's white middle-class mannequins. She is the good subservient worker who never questions her white boss, who is always ready to do overtime or come in on one of her days off if he should ask her to. Rosa's involvement in the NAACP is also in the role of a secretary. She listens quietly at meetings, takes notes, and stays late in the NAACP office typing and organizing papers. The president of the NAACP chapter, on leaving the office one evening, remarks to Rosa that she should go home. "Lord knows," he says, "a woman don't need to be nowhere but home and in the kitchen." But Rosa does not go home, and therein lies one of the central contradictions or tensions in the film, and perhaps in Rosa Parks's real life. She is the good black and the good woman, and as a black woman her subservience is amplified. Yet she does have another side, a double consciousness. She is a resister at her core, and she was raised to be a resister. She was encouraged by parents and grandparents from an early age to stand up for what she believes in, never let anyone tell her she couldn't be anything she wanted to be, and always do what she thinks is right. This, of course, is bound to get her into trouble with white folks and the law. If the film version of her story leans heavily on the side of representing Rosa Parks as basically subservient and meek, it at least acknowledges the contradictory nature of this subservience, given what she did to resist, time and again, the norms of life in Jim Crow South. At issue, however, is the very real possibility that Rosa Parks has been valorized precisely because she is not "uppity," precisely because she can be situated within a long history of representations of subservient (and thus "good") African Americans and women.

Right alongside of such a history of white representations of the "good"-"bad" black person, we may locate a corresponding history of white representations of the "good"-"bad" white person. By identifying racism with "bad" whites, stereotyped as Southern "red necks" and a few Northern bigots, the dominant culture of whiteness disassociates itself from racism and diverts attention away from an analysis of how racism is part of the deep fabric of American culture and is maintained through institutional structures. By emphasizing the role played by "good" white people in support of the civil rights movement of African Americans, whiteness revises history in ways that get it off the hook and that do not implicate it in the perpetuation of racism in the United States. Thus, the dominant myth of Rosa Parks emphasizes the role "good" white people played in the Montgomery Bus Boycott and indeed throughout Rosa's life. Rosa Parks might seem an unlikely candidate to confirm the thesis of the "goodness" of many white people. After all, her own experiences as a youth led her to have a deep-seated distrust of whites that she admits in her autobiography never completely went away, although she did learn to see connections between the struggles of African Americans and other groups, chiefly poor southern whites. This was particularly so after her experiences at the Highlander Academy in Monteagle, Tennessee, in the summer of 1955, where she, King, and other civil rights leaders worked with Myles Horton and other whites, including those involved in the Southern Poverty Law Center. On the whole, however, Rosa Parks never moved much outside the black community, never emphasized alliance building with whites as much as she did black mobilization and solidarity.

In spite of all of this, the "good" white person working hand in hand with blacks is an almost ubiquitous and unquestioned trope in most tellings of Parks's story. In the movie version of her life, the "good" white person is everywhere, and not just in the background of the story. The movie opens with an extended flashback scene from Rosa's childhood, which recurs at times throughout the movie. The setting is the Montgomery Industrial School for Girls, in which Rosa has been enrolled. The school is run by a group of white Quaker women from New York who are on a mission to help educate poor black girls. Significantly, the school is led by Mrs. White, and the school is informally referred to as Mrs. White's school. The first classroom scene shows Rosa as a girl, sitting in a class of other black girls, being taught by a benevolent and always-smiling white woman. One student questions why they should have to work so hard to learn to read and write when they're only going to be doing white folk's laundry when they graduate. Instead of answering the question, the teacher poses it to the class, asking if anyone can give the student a reason why they should bother to study and work so hard. Rosa raises her hand, is recognized, and proceeds to say, "We bother so we can be equal to everyone else. . . . If I put my mind to it, I can do anything I want to in this world. . . . Can't nobody take your dignity from you but you." The teacher tells the class that if they learn nothing else at Mrs. White's school, "may the blessed Lord help you remember what Rosa just taught you." But what is being taught here? One of the primary myths being taught is that black people in the South benefited from, and perhaps even depended on, benevolent white patrons to educate and "elevate" them. Here, that elevation takes the form of an education that is all about discipline and subservience; about learning to cook, set tables, and mend clothes; about learning how to say "yes, ma'am," and "no, ma'am," to speak only when spoken to.

Rosa is made into the model student, the one who sides with her good white teachers against some of her own peers and affirms the official ideals of the school. One of her friends in the school who also is a good student tells Rosa, "My mother thinks that Mrs. White is a saint for putting up with what she does, for keeping the school open." Many white teachers, she says, would not teach colored girls. Mrs. White, as a saint in the church of whiteness, is represented as providing Rosa the kind of character education she would need later in life. It is around this firm foundation of an education by "good" whites that the film builds its story of Rosa as a civil rights leader. Rosa also learns in the film that not all whites are alike. Her friend tells her that some city bus drivers are "mean spirited" and others are not. Later, in 1942, she is seen boarding a bus and taking a seat up front. In this case, the bus driver is depicted as mean spirited, and Rosa does not forget it. So, she chooses his bus to board that fateful day in December 1955, to get her revenge. Perhaps, the film suggests, if she had boarded another bus in 1942 and had a different experience, if the bus driver had been a "good" white instead of a "bad" white, the events that transpired might not have happened. At another important point in the film, a "good" white steps in to save Rosa. After she is arrested and taken to the city jail, her husband calls the jail and demands that she be allowed to speak with someone. The police officer on the other end of the line simply hangs up on him. So Parks calls a white friend of the NAACP, a rich local businessman, and when he calls the police station, Rosa is immediately released.

The notion that white people were inextricably involved in, and even at times leaders of, the civil rights movement is pervasive in the literature on Rosa Parks. Let me point to just one example here. In the late 1980s, the progressive educator Herbert Kohl happened to be visiting an elementary school in Southern California at a time when the children were performing a dramatic rendering of Parks's arrest and the subsequent Montgomery Bus Boycott as part of African American History Month. As he wrote about the presentation, the play ends with mostly white, middle-class children marching around the stage carrying signs that read, "We Shall Overcome" and "Blacks and Whites Together." The narrator says that the bus boycott in Montgomery was resolved by "people coming together to protest peacefully for justice" (Kohl, 1991, p. 36). Kohl talked with the teacher after the performance to point out that the drama misrepresented the civil rights movement as an interracial struggle. The teacher's response, according to Kohl, was to agree that the play "took some liberties with history," but that the play was presented as part of an effort to bring black and white kids together in the school. The teacher feared that if the play were presented as blacks against whites it might lead to racial strife in the classroom. Kohl disagreed, suggesting that by dramatizing the bus boycott as an organized movement by the African American community in Montgomery, "it might lead all of the children to recognize and appreciate the strength oppressed people can show when confronting their oppressors" (p. 37). I do not want to suggest (although perhaps Kohl did) that there is one and only one truth here: either whites played a significant role in the black civil rights movement or they did not. Nor do I want to argue that all white people are basically alike, that all can be painted with a common brush as equally racist. Certainly, if white-identified young people, in both the North and South, are to reclaim some pride in their heritage, it must be tied to a history of real white support for black struggles. As the black feminist scholar Patricia Hill Collins (2000, p. 37) has argued, the empowerment movement of black people in the United States always has had some support from white "race traitors," those who are willing to question their own racial privilege and view their role as confronting social justice. In particular, those whites who have been oppressed or marginalized in some other way and are engaged in similar social justice projects may be able to identity points of connection. This points to the importance of coalition building across lines of difference — race, class, gender, and sexual orientation, for example — in building a more powerful movement in the United States that challenges systems and structures of domination across a number of axes of struggle, identity, and affinity. At the same time, the history of "race traitors" is not the primary history of whiteness in the United States, even in the "enlightened" North. By emphasizing the important role of whites in the civil rights movement of the 1950s and 1960s, we tell a story that whites like to hear, but it also distorts the reality of what happened and has the effect of getting those who consider themselves "good" whites off the hook for the continuation of racism.

The Rosa Parks Story ends with some real footage of Rosa in Washington, D.C., in 1999, receiving the Presidential Medal of Freedom from President Clinton. In introducing Rosa, the president said, "For most of us alive today, in a very real sense the journey began 43 years ago." Rosa Parks is, in these words, transformed into a national hero for everyone, someone has become such part of the canon of heroes inaugurated into the newly revised narration of the nation's past. Her journey is our collective and individual journey. It should perhaps not be surprising, then, that as Rosa Parks has been integrated into this official narrative of national progress and a unified cultural identity, many black Americans, perhaps particularly black youth, have begun to question and trouble the dominant myth of Rosa Parks. In 2002, the same year that *The Rosa Parks Story* won an Emmy for Best TV Movie of the year, the movie *Barbershop* was released — a film targeted primarily to black audiences and made with a black sensibility. In that film, one character, played by Cedric the Entertainer, tells the other black men in the barbershop that Parks was merely tired rather than heroic and that she was given too much credit because of her association with the NAACP. The implicit charge is that the NAACP historically has been timid in its defense of blacks' rights, that it has lost touch with the rage of many sectors of the black community. This indicates that in elements of the black community a critique of the politics of timidity and meekness has developed and that this is tied to a critique of some of the symbols of the civil rights movement. The fact that Rosa Parks was angered by this reference to her in a popular movie also suggests that she now sees herself as a protector of her image as a "positive" role model.

This leads me to another reference to Parks in contemporary popular culture, this time by the Atlanta-based rap group Outkast, one of the most creative and progressive forces in hip-hop culture.

"Rosa Parks" is the name of one of the more popular tracks on Outkast's 1998 album *Aquemini*. The song lyrics contain no further references to Parks, although the recurring refrain includes the words, "Hey, there, hush that stuff; everybody move to the back of the bus." The song also includes profanity, including the word "nigger." The video that accompanies the song includes footage of Outkast boarding a bus and assertively taking the front seats, telling others to move to the back. Parks has since sued Outkast for commercially exploiting her name in a personally degrading manner, and she hired big-name lawyer Johnny Cochran to defend her, in a case that is still pending as of this writing. Dyson, in writing about the incident, made the point that Parks (like King) can no longer be a very useful symbol for black youth if she is turned into a sacred symbol of goodness. "They [Outkast] appeal to her symbolic presence to warn all pretenders to their hip-hop throne that they would have to move to the back of the bus" (Dyson, 2000, p. 308). What Outkast did in their song was attempt to reappropriate Rosa Parks, turning her into a "useful hero, a working icon, a meaningful metaphor" for a new generation of assertive black youth (p. 310). In doing so, Outkast inverted the normal reading of Parks as a meek, quiet, "good" black and transformed her into an assertive and even loud "bad" black. The song is thus also an insipient critique of a whiteness and its representation of good and bad blacks.

This, at least, must be taken as a hopeful sign. At the same time, little of this critique of whiteness has yet entered the discourse of multicultural education and diversity. Rosa Parks is valorized in that discourse precisely because she can be represented as nonthreatening, docile, subservient, and morally upright. The transformation of Rosa Parks into Rosa the Good has accelerated over the past decade, as has her integration into a normalizing discourse. For example, an elementary school unit of study on the Montgomery Bus Boycott recently posted on the Web page of the Alabama Department of Historical Archives includes a lesson on "good manners and courtesy." According to the lesson, students are to be asked questions such as, "Why do you think that good manners would be important during a situation like this [blacks and whites riding a public bus together]? Why are good manners and courtesy important to all people?" This is a type of multiculturalism of whiteness, a multiculturalism that would seek to integrate the civil rights movement within a state and regional narrative of good manners and courtesy, a narrative that suggests that blacks and whites have always gotten along when they did not abandon a heritage of good manners. These manners, according to the lesson plan, apply to "riding a school bus or working together in the classroom." The clear implication is that good manners could have gone a long way to resolving the conflict that led to the Montgomery Bus Boycott. What the lesson plan fails to remember is that good manners did not save Rosa Parks from being arrested, nor did good manners protect her from the threats on her life that forced her and her husband to flee Montgomery and take up residence in Detroit. The bus she rode on that December morning in 1955 has moved as well. It now sits in the Henry Ford Museum in nearby Dearborn, Michigan, where it has been appropriated within a corporate multicultural history. A Ford bus was there at one of the great moments of American history, playing its part.

All of this points to the importance of a democratic multiculturalism that is anchored in the critical, deconstructive reading of popular culture texts. In place of a multiculturalism of "positive" role models and heroes, we need a multiculturalism that questions whose interests are served by the production of positive representations and what projects they advance. In place of a multiculturalism that transforms civil rights leaders into universal moral or ethical heroes, we need a multiculturalism that is interested in the specificity of historical struggles, the specific ways in which the language of social justice, freedom, and rights is given meaning within concrete contexts of usage — both by dominant and by oppositional groups. In place of a multiculturalism that brings only the Other under its gaze, we need a multiculturalism that turns its gaze on the master narratives and tropes of whiteness. In the end, only oppositional knowledge and counternarratives produced by African Americans, along with Latinos, Latinas, and American Indians, can help white people "unthink" the master narratives that have shaped their collective memory, their sense of self in relation to Other. Until the subaltern began to speak, no light was shining on whiteness, and so whiteness did not have to name itself or acknowledge itself and thus interrogate its own privilege. This suggests that in order to develop a critique of whiteness, white folks will need to read a lot more about themselves written from the standpoint of the Other. My own reeducation as a white person began during the civil rights era, when I was a teenager. I was taught first by William Baldwin, who spoke to me across the racial divide in a voice of both rage and love, and later by Eldridge Cleaver and Franz Fanon, who helped me understand a politics of resistance and a discourse of empowerment, and still later by Toni Morrison who spoke to me of endurance and strength in the face of oppression. As a white man, and more particularly a white gay man of working-class background, I have grown to understand the racial Other as an ally and a teacher, and as another human being. I have also learned to respect those, like Rosa Parks, who reach a point where they will no longer participate in being treated like less than human, and who, in resisting what seems unresistable, remind us that hegemonic discourses such as whiteness are forged out of resistance and oppositionality and that they are never stable and secure.

REFERENCES

Bennett, W. (1993). *The book of virtues: A treasury of great moral stories.* New York: Simon & Schuster.

Bhabha, H. (Ed.). (1990). *Nation and Narration.* New York: Routledge.

Bredhoff, S., Schamel, W., & Potter, L. A. (1999). Teaching with documents: The arrest records of Rosa Parks. *Social Education, 63*(4), 207–211.

Carlson, D. (1995). Constructing the margins: Of multicultural education and curriculum settlements. *Curriculum Inquiry, 25*(4), 407–432.

Carlson, D. (2002). *Leaving safe harbors: Toward a new progressivism in American education and public life.* New York: RoutledgeFalmer.

Collins, P. H. (2000). *Black feminist thought. Knowledge, consciousness, and the politics of empowerment.* New York: Routledge.

Crenshaw, K. (1995). Race, reform, and retrenchment: Transformation and legitimation in anti-discrimination law. In K. Crenshaw, N. Gotanda, G. Peller, & K. Thomas (Eds.), *Critical race theory* (pp. 103–126). New York: The New Press.

Dyson, M. (2000). *I may not get there with you: The true Martin Luther King, Jr.* New York: Free Press.

Foucault, M. (1979). *Discipline and punish: The birth of the prison* (Alan Sheridan, Trans.). New York: Vintage.

Fukuyama, F. (1992). *The end of history and the last man.* New York: Free Press.

Kohl, H. (1991). The politics of children's literature: The story of Rosa Parks and the Montgomery Bus Boycott. *Journal of Education, 173*(1), 35–50.

Parks, R. (with Haskins, J.). (1992). *Rosa Parks: My story.* New York: Dial Books.

Parks, R. (1994). *Quiet strength: The faith, hope, and the heart of a woman who changed a nation.* New York: Zondervan Publishing.

Shohat, E., & Stam, R. (1994). *Unthinking Eurocentrism: Multiculturalism and the media.* New York: Routledge.

Sowell, T. (1984). *Civil rights: Rhetoric or reality?* William Morrow.

Contesting

TWENTY-THREE

Through the Looking Glass: Implications of Studying Whiteness for Feminist Methods

Aída Hurtado and Abigail J. Stewart

I'll tell you all my ideas about Looking-glass House. First, there's the room you can see through the glass — that's just the same as our drawing-room, only the things go the other way. I can see all of it when I get upon a chair — all but the bit just behind the fireplace. Oh! I do wish I could see *that* bit!

—Lewis Carroll (1946, p. 199)

Feminist methods were developed to provide an accurate reflection of women — in fact, to bring women, usually absent, into the center of research. Feminist methods also emphasized the need to have women studying women to provide an accurate reflection of women's lives. However, in studying whiteness, feminist methods have to go beyond providing undistorted knowledge about women, to simultaneously look behind the privilege that whiteness provides — to try to see "that bit" which has not been central to the study of race. Like Alice in Wonderland, going through the looking glass will be necessary to see how the study of whiteness is and is not the same as the study of "race."

Whiteness is suddenly interesting — to social scientists and politicians — in the 1990s. Implied, but concealed, in the concept of "race," whiteness has rarely before been interrogated. In *Playing in the Dark*, Toni Morrison (1992) brilliantly exposed how whiteness operates in public and literary discourse; it remains for social scientists to build on her work by exploring how whiteness operates in individual psyches and social relations. As we try to do that, we must consider the possibility that analytic tools and research methods that helped us understand systems and experiences of oppression may not be as appropriate for understanding privilege.

When social scientists began to study "race" they first examined the operation of prejudice and stereotypes — that is, individuals' racist attitudes about blacks or people of color (see, e.g., Allport, 1958). The focus, then, was on attitudes about people of different (nonwhite) "races." This individual-focused approach eventually yielded to examination of how racism operated as an impersonal system of discrimination and institutionalized disadvantage (e.g., Feagin & Feagin, 1978). This important shift to a systemic analysis continued to obscure "whiteness," because social scientists explored the impact of institutional racism on those who "had" race in the sense that their race was marked, noted, taken as "other" in U.S. society (e.g., Pettigrew, 1964; Wilson,

1987; Zweigenhaft & Domhoff, 1991). Whiteness, like maleness, was viewed as background; being of color, like being female, was understood to shape and define one's personality, as one's life. To be white or male was simply to be, in fact to be subject to highly idiosyncratic, individualized shaping processes. As we move now to considering the significance of whiteness (and maleness) for individuals' lives and personalities, we may be tempted to rely on the analytic tools and research methods that have proved so useful both in identifying racist and sexist limitations in social science theory and research, and in studying the experience of women and people of color.

Feminist social scientists made a case for the need for new methods and approaches by showing that the apparently, or supposedly, "neutral" studies of sex differences were riddled with bias and sexism (see, e.g., Sherif, 1979). As antiracist social scientists did for race, feminist social scientists showed that the scientific method alone did not guarantee gender neutrality; they demonstrated how distorted our understanding of "women" was, when men were taken as the human norm. To build an alternate account, feminist scholars developed and honed strategies for uncovering bias and identifying aspects of female experience that were devalued or ignored (Fonow & Cook, 1991). In particular, the value of adopting a female "standpoint" or position, or actually empowering women to articulate their own perspective, was developed as a methodological ideal (see, e.g., Harding, 1991). By bringing women "to voice," missing experiences — of groups of women, even of all women — could be articulated and understood. These methods have yielded enormous value in our understanding of rape, sexual harassment, women's work, and family roles.

They have been equally useful as feminist scholars increasingly recognized that women were not all alike, and that therefore it was important to study the experience of different groups of women directly. Thus, the standpoint or voice of each group — lesbians, poor women, women of color, women with disabilities — must be identified and articulated (Hurtado, 1989; Landrine, Klonoff, & Brown-Collins, 1992; Reid, 1993). The processes of bringing these standpoints and voices into social science is far from complete. Nevertheless, defining them has inevitably made clear how the viewpoints previously seen as neutral are in fact inflected by class (upper), race (white), and gender (male). Therefore, feminist scholars have made efforts to shift their gaze to the privileged side of oppression (see especially Ostrander, 1984; Ostrove & Stewart, 1994; Sturgis, 1988). At the same time, some scholars' efforts to bring the experiences of understudied groups of women into social science research and theory have resulted in sophisticated reflections on the importantly different standpoints of the researcher and the researched (see, e.g., Belle, 1994; Fine, 1989; Lykes, 1989). As feminist social scientists begin to study whiteness (and other markers of privilege), we think they must continue to reflect on the different — and similar — standpoints of the researcher and the researched; even more important, we must think about the implications of sharing and not sharing a *privileged* standpoint for the use of methods that have been used to study people whose lack of privilege was our focus in the past.

Some of our most cherished "feminist research methods," and the implied or explicit standpoint epistemology associated with them, must be rethought as we approach the study of a culturally valued characteristic. Issues of voice, empowerment, and standpoint, as well as objectivity and distance, are particularly relevant here. Thinking about how best to study whiteness should also help us identify features of feminist methodological discussions that apply with equal, or greater, force to the study of whiteness. These will surely include tools for critical analysis, and attention to the perspective and social characteristics of the researcher as an integral part of the method. We will begin by reviewing what we know about how whiteness matters, turning after that to an analysis of methodological issues raised by this research.

CONTRIBUTIONS TO OUR UNDERSTANDING OF WHITENESS: PREVIOUS RESEARCH

No clear paradigm and method has emerged to study whiteness, although the few studies that address whiteness directly give us more than the expressed knowledge the mostly white authors purport. The unintended outcomes of these studies on whiteness are the revelations of the researchers themselves, thus making the results multilayered — that is, they tell us more than the authors intended and more than the respondents knew they were revealing. With this notion in mind, we address what we consider the best contributions these studies have made to how we study and conceptualize whiteness in the United States.

Denaturalizing Whiteness

A recurrent finding in the study of whiteness is the fact that white respondents do not consider their "whiteness" as an identity or a marker of group membership per se. That is, whiteness is a "natural" identity because it has not been problematic and therefore salient to most respondents in these studies. In fact, most white respondents are hard-pressed to define whiteness and the privileges that it brings to those who own it. Interestingly enough, whiteness becomes much more definable when the privilege it accords its owners is lost. For example, Fine and her colleagues (Fine, Weis, & Addelston, 1997) documented white working-class men's frustrations as they see their jobs "being taken over by people of Color. It is in the loss of their way of life, which includes their jobs, that they begin to articulate what it means to be white." Tatum (1992) and Gallagher (1995) described how students in multicultural college classrooms similarly, and painfully, "discover" their whiteness.

Ironically, although race is a central organizing component of U.S. society — whether someone is white, black, Asian, or brown — there has been a norm of explicitly ignoring race as a form of denying its importance in the subordination/domination process (Tatum, 1992). However, Toni Morrison (1992) appropriately pointed out that even in this nonmention, the racialization process continues. For example, Morrison observed, in analyzing the Africanist presence in American literature, that intellectuals are sometimes proud they have not read any African American texts, a feeling tied to the notion that not noticing race is polite and humanistic; that it indicates a certain political consciousness. So not "seeing" is turned on its head to mean "politeness" or generosity when in fact it only reinforces the existing racist power arrangements.

Morrison's (1992) point (made in reference to U.S. literature) is also well documented in Frankenberg's (1993) research on what their race means to white women from all walks of life. Almost all her respondents mention having been socialized not to "see" people of color. However, not "seeing" is an integral part of their identity formation because the privilege of "whiteness" is based on the availability of "surrogate, serviceable Black bodies for her [their] own purposes of power without risk, so the author[s] employs them in behalf of her [their] own desire for a safe participation in loss, in love, in chaos, in justice" (Morrison, 1992, p. 28). People of color are the serviceable others who are the blank slates on which white people can project all those fears, emotions, and attitudes that give whiteness purity because there are others to live out that which would taint whiteness. Roediger (1991) described in detail how this process worked for different groups, at different times in U.S. history in the construction of white working-class men's self-hood. If whiteness is never articulated, then it is people of color, *as a group*, who can be scrutinized and blamed to exalt the perfection of that which is "natural" and left unexamined.

Precisely because of the "naturalness" of white identity and because of the cloaked secrecy of its manifestation, it is difficult to take the time and energy to listen to whiteness. It isn't viewed as problematic, given that it provides privilege (we are much more passionate about injustice; it makes us feel we are doing something worthwhile) and that it is "natural" and therefore difficult to describe. It also seems like useless "work," like pressing the already ironed dress or putting clean dishes in the dishwasher — because it isn't a problem and everybody knows what it is, why indulge in introspective angst that leads nowhere? Privilege has the semblance of naturalness that in itself defends it from scrutiny. Much of the struggle in the 20th century has been to problematize "the natural," and progressive scholarship has accomplished an admirable body of research revealing many forms of oppression. But the challenge of the 21st century will be to continue the work of the enlightenment — when royalty was scrutinized and the privilege of lineage was dismantled to provide avenues for democracy to flourish. Race privilege has substituted for lineage of royalty in our time. It countervails class, at times, just like "royal blood" did in the past. We believe in its goodness as former subjects believed in the direct connection to God through their kings.

The Documentation of the Dynamics of Power

The power that whiteness holds for its owners (Harris, 1993b) has not been explicitly documented — it is a birthright that is socialized from generation to generation in the largely racially segregated living arrangements that exist in the United States (McIntosh, 1992, p. 77). Like the construction of manhood through lifetime socialization in sports (Kimmel, 1993), the process is largely hidden, unless you have been admitted to this exclusive club. The current research on whiteness begins the process necessary for understanding both the power of whiteness and the beginning of its deconstruction. It can draw from research on social class that has already identified some of the mechanisms used to pass on class privilege. This is not to suggest that race and class can or should be collapsed, but rather that the mechanisms used to conceal and perpetuate one kind of institutionalized privilege may have counterparts in the analysis of other kinds of institutionalized privilege. It is important to note, though, that the intersection of privilege and subordination will always complicate things. Thus, the mechanisms associated with race privilege will be affected by its co-occurrence with poverty or wealth, maleness or femaleness, and so forth. Nevertheless, we must begin to identify and define the mechanisms so we will be able to recognize them in the many forms in which they appear.

Distancing

Ostrander (1984), in her study of upper-class women, gives us an intimate portrait of how women in the upper crust of U.S. society make sense of their class privilege. In this particular instance, class privilege is inextricably tied to race privilege because Ostrander's definition of her sample required them to have had wealth in their families for generations as measured by their membership in registered clubs. However, it should be noted that many of her observations are echoed in Wellman's (1993) case studies of white racism in various social classes, as well as Roediger's (1991) analysis of the social construction of white identities in working-class men. The women Ostrander interviewed consistently distance themselves from the origins of their race/class privilege by claiming that it was based on an accident of birth that they had nothing to do with creating. Their class and race membership was not borne out of a conscious intention on their part; therefore, they do not take any responsibility for the costly consequences of their privilege for others. The respondents in Ostrander's (1984) study *distance* themselves from the phenomenon as if it were a natural disaster they had nothing to do with creating and resent having to clean up. Even though these women recognize their privilege, most feel it is the "natural" arrangement of things and they do their personal best to help those less fortunate through their charity work.

Denial

Many researchers have documented the psychological strain in "passing" from a subordinate group to a dominant group, say fair-skinned blacks passing as whites (Harris, 1993b). The same strain has been documented for those individuals who become conscious of racism and perceive the omnipresence of its effects in all areas of social life. That's one of the reasons individuals resist acquiring a "double" consciousness, because becoming conscious of power and domination creates enormous psychological strain and pain (Du Bois, 1961; Harris, 1993b, p. 1711; Tatum, 1992). It is not surprising, then, that many of the white respondents in these studies claim that "whiteness" does not bring unearned privileges — that is, that whatever privileges are accorded to whiteness are earned through merit because whites, as a group, perform better than people of color in all kinds of arenas. In fact, denial of white privilege is only fully documented when it is lost. It is in the process of being dislocated and making sense of that dislocation that white respondents begin to fully acknowledge the privileges they previously denied whiteness brought them (Fine et al., 1994; Gallagher, 1995).

Superiority

The articulation of exactly what whiteness constitutes is difficult for most respondents in these studies. However, what is not as difficult for them to articulate is the superiority they feel in comparison to nonwhite people. For example, McIntosh (1992) tried to articulate precisely what white privilege provides for her, giving us insight into the superiority that most white people come to expect in almost all social contexts. Because white privilege is perceived as the "natural" state of affairs then by definition it embodies an attitude of superiority: "Whites are taught to think of their lives as morally neutral, normative, and average, and also ideal, so that when we work to benefit others, this is seen as work that will allow 'them' to be more like 'us'" (McIntosh, 1992, p. 73). In other words, even though McIntosh does not see herself as oppressing anybody, the list of privileges she was socialized to expect in almost all daily interactions have trained her to feel and act superior to nonwhite people.

Ostrander (1984) similarly found in her sample of upper-class women a feeling of unquestioned superiority that is their birthright. Because they do not feel they had much to do with constructing the structure of inequality, these women feel that their superiority is "natural." Furthermore, these women are very conscious of the pleasures that their material privilege affords, which is intertwined with their feeling of superiority at the same time that they don't see how it is related to whiteness. The legitimacy of their superiority because of their birthright allows them not to question their class position. Many of these respondents proudly announced that "The door opens for position" and that access to every sphere is "just a phone call away" (Ostrander, 1984, p. 29). As Wellman (1993) argued, racism is not only a "system of exclusion and privilege" but also "a set of ultimately acceptable linguistic or ideological constructions that defend one's location in that system" (p. 25).

The pleasure upper-class women feel in their superiority prevents them from challenging the class and race legitimacy on which it is based. In Ostrander's study, these women do not challenge their husbands because they recognize that these men "know how to rule and are masters of the exercise of power" (Ostrander, 1984, p. 151). The women understand that masters rarely recognize their dependency on slaves. Furthermore, if they are not likely to be shaken from their positions of power outside the home, how likely are they, really, to be successfully challenged as heads of their households? Ostrander (1984) astutely pointed out that in the unlikely event that these women successfully challenged their husbands on their gender superiority, they might be putting their own class status in peril. Therefore these women submit to their husbands: "They will do so perhaps in part because the gains of *gender* equality would not be enough to balance the losses of class equality" (Ostrander, 1984, pp. 151–152).

These women are not passive recipients of their class privilege but actively participate in maintaining it. First and foremost is the code of silence to hide imperfection (Ostrander, 1984, p. 30). The code is intricately related to what these women refer to as "social graces" that define their class (race) status (see also Domhoff, 1983; Ryan & Sackrey, 1984). Ostrander observed, "These social graces are not just optional amenities of upper-class life; they are essential to the ways in which the upper-class persons are able to control — with great civility and charm — virtually any social situation in which they find themselves" (Ostrander, 1984, p. 89).

Similarly, Wellman (1993, p. 26) argued that "European Americans have advantages that come from their social location in the racial hierarchy, and . . . they explain, or ignore, their privileged position in socially acceptable terms."

Belongingness

One of the major advantages of privilege is the sense of absolute belonging and importance. Belongingness can be communicated in a variety of ways. Sturgis (1988), in her autobiographical essay, beautifully discussed how the unmarked history she was taught in school provided a direct measure of her importance as a descendant of "founding fathers" and of the importance of those who can make history. The historical lessons she learned about whites' (mostly male) accomplishments gave her a sense of their centrality and belonging to the mainstream of life. Not to belong, because of race or class, or both, is a way to control and diminish those who are outside this well-defined mainstream. Again, when the sense of belonging is taken away, white respondents immediately "see" how belonging is an integral part of their whiteness and they openly complain about being robbed by the invasion of minorities tainting their neighborhood or demanding equal participation in the mainstream (Fine et al., 1994, pp. 8–9). It is clear, then, how dependent this sense of belonging is on processes of exclusion. Gallagher (1995) quoted one white student as saying, "We can't have anything for ourselves anymore that says exclusively White or anything like that. But everyone else can" (p. 177).

Solidarity

Ultimately, white privilege depends on its members' not betraying the unspoken, nonconscious power dynamics socialized in the intimacy of their families. White solidarity may on first sight appear to be an oxymoron. However, many of the respondents and essayists covered in our review reveal a tacit understanding of white solidarity (see especially Gallagher, 1995, and Roediger, 1991). Although whiteness is "natural" and although few can articulate the privileges that whiteness brings, most can detect when whiteness is being questioned and its privilege potentially dismantled. Therefore, solidarity on the basis of whiteness will have to be fully understood and dismantled for the deconstruction of race privilege to continue. In fact, it is precisely when that solidarity dissolves that differences *among* whites (class, sexuality, etc.) emerge — a process viewed as liberating by some and upsetting or frightening by others.

In summary, some of the mechanisms of power employed in the exercise of whiteness, like class privilege, are distancing, denial, superiority, belongingness, and solidarity, all of which are daily practices and psychological processes that simultaneously support and reflect the position — justifying beliefs Wellman (1993) and others find whites hold about race. Thus these mechanisms are geared to the maintenance of structural power for white people as a whole. Whether individual whites use these mechanisms is irrelevant to the outcome of the white group's superiority, and certainly the studies conducted so far suggest that most whites are socialized to employ, whether or not they actually do.

THE USE OF WHITENESS TO MAINTAIN STRUCTURAL PRIVILEGE AND TO PROMOTE RACISM

The objective of the mechanisms of power described in the research on whiteness is to maintain the very real structural privilege of whiteness. An integral part of maintaining structural privilege is racism — the belief that whites are superior to other nonwhite "races." The superiority of whiteness is codified into law as a form of property whose value has not been thoroughly articulated (Harris, 1993b). In fact, law professor Cheryl Harris claims that whiteness has been an exclusive club that has been protected by the courts more than any other kind of property (Harris, 1993b, p. 1736). Whiteness, codified in law, by definition coerced nonwhites into denial of their identity to ensure survival (see also Williams, 1995); therefore, it makes no sense to study race as if the mechanism of construction were the same for all groups (Harris, 1993b, p. 1744).

But how exactly does the construction of whiteness form the basis for the maintenance of structural privilege for its owners? It is especially pressing to find answers when apparently its possessors are so oblivious to its effects and some of its nonpossessors seem to agree it is not whiteness per se that confers privilege as they strive to climb into the (white) mainstream wagon. The answer may lie in the different functions groups serve in the domination/subordination process as outlined by Apfelbaum (1979). In her theory of intergroup relations, the formation of groups in industrialized society is not independent of the process of enforcing power. The dominant group de-emphasizes its function as a group and instead portrays its existence as the "norm" or as "natural" to mystify how its members obtain power by their group membership. Apfelbaum (1979) named this as the "universal rule" where supposedly *anybody* who "acts" according to prescribed standards is meritorious and deserving of societal and economic rewards. The "universal rule," in theory, is open to everybody and, in fact, applies primarily to those who possess whiteness, and secondarily to those who "act" as white as possible. An unspoken double standard gets set up in which, as Harris (1993b) pointed out, democracy and rules are exclusively for whites (or those who act as white as possible), whereas tyranny is justified for blacks. This double standard is dictated not by the democratic state but by the "inherent" difference between blacks and whites. The "inherent difference" is biological race, which is codified into law through the one-drop rule — those individuals with at least one drop of black blood are *legally* considered black. Belief in a biological basis for whiteness ensures that it will take many generations of intermarriage with "pure" whites before individuals can legally possess the privileges of whiteness; meanwhile, they are without its property (Harris, 1993b).

On the other hand, the subordinate group is marked or stigmatized. The value attached to being white and the devaluation of being nonwhite makes group membership in a nonwhite ethnic or racial group problematic for its members. In effect, the nonwhite ethnic or racial group is (de)grouped and cannot serve the usual positive functions that groups serve — providing a basis for positive social identity, group solidarity, a sense of belonging, and empowerment (Apfelbaum, 1979). At the same time, whiteness does serve those functions for its possessors (McIntosh, 1992; Sturgis, 1988). Degrouping as a basis for group subordination is also a very effective means of sabotaging resistance to domination. Although ethnic or racial membership is not supposed to matter in the United States, all privilege and power is distributed according to race, class, and gender (Harris, 1993b, pp. 1741, 1761): "In effect, the courts erected legal 'No trespassing signs' — passing, therefore, is largely a phenomenon from subordinate to dominant group rather than the other way around." This is reminiscent of the movie *La Cage Aux Folles II*, in which a gay man passes as a woman in Italy and, having to do grueling woman's work, he looks up from the floor he is scrubbing and states, "I want to be a man!"

Apfelbaum (1979) argued that a critical stage in overthrowing domination is when the subordinate group, which has been degrouped, begins to use its own norms and standards for positive identity formation and political mobilization. When a previously degrouped group begins to fight back, the dominant group steps up its restrictive controls. Therefore, it is not surprising that when there are increasing numbers of people of color in the United States, as well as increasing awareness of how "race" is socially constructed and therefore not about inherent merit — that is, at the very moment when race is on the verge of taking center stage in the analysis of oppression — all of a sudden, race doesn't matter and we should be color blind (Harris, 1993b, p. 1768). In fact, the deconstruction of white privilege has brought a backlash of countercharges of reverse racism. The increasingly openly expressed response to charges of racism is the assertion that whiteness is a legitimate criterion of resource allocation because merit is color blind and it is coincidence (or inherent superiority) that most meritorious persons happen to be white and male. Nowhere are the unmentioned assumptions of the "inherent" merit of whiteness more clear than in the legal battles on reverse discrimination. For example, in the now famous Bakke case, the defendant only claimed discrimination on one criterion — whiteness. Other selection criteria like applicants being the offspring of wealthy donors went unchallenged, largely because these hierarchies are perceived as legitimate. Whiteness as property is possessed by all members of the defined group and lends itself to race solidarity. Wealth is possessed in varying degrees and doesn't lend itself to being the criterion for solidarity — not universal enough. In fact, whiteness may be the only uniformly unifying characteristic of the dominant group (Harris, 1993b, p. 1773). In Professor Harris's (1993b) words, "Bakke expected that he would never be disfavored when competing with minority candidates, although he might be disfavored with respect to more privileged whites" (p. 1773). That is, competition among whites is fair because they are his equals.

The inherent right for whiteness to serve as valuable property is based on biology; it is therefore property that groups of color cannot possess immediately, and results in *a priori* structural privilege. To treat white identity as no different from any other group identity when, at its core, whiteness is based on racial subordination ratifies existing white privilege by making it the referential baseline (Harris, 1993b, p. 1775). Not only is this done in the courts and throughout the legal system but this is the same thing that has been done in the study of whiteness in the social sciences. When whiteness, because of its "natural" order and its elusive nature, remains unquestioned, we have *racial realism*, leaving no room to question whiteness/privilege (Harris, 1993a).

The Relationship between Privilege and Subordination in Defining a White Identity

Because whiteness is the "natural" state of affairs, or mainstream, nonwhites are the outsiders or the marginals. In the United States, national identity has been constructed as white (Harris, 1993b, p. 1790; Roediger, 1991). To be nonwhite is to be non-American. Congruently, "normal" to white people means "normal" as defined by their worldview (McIntosh, 1992, p. 73). The same is true about being a "good" person. However, this country's national identity, normality, and superiority are not independent of the existence of nonwhites. An integral part of defining free Americans is by contrasting them to those who are non-American and unfree. White identity is largely constructed through social comparison of those less fortunate (mostly nonwhites). White identity supersedes other identifications — poor white people at least have the consolation that they are not black (see Roediger, 1991, for several detailed accounts of this process in U.S. history). A white woman at least has the consolation that her status is above nonwhites — at least she is not a woman of color.

Many of the studies focusing on whiteness explicitly use social comparison between whites and nonwhites to delineate white identity. For example, McIntosh (1992), in her brutally honest essay on whiteness, listed the nonconscious "privileges" that whiteness brings her on an everyday basis. Perhaps, not surprisingly, the list is shaped by *comparisons* to people of color rather than an introspective focus on herself and her group. (McIntosh is not alone in this practice.) As a result, the list is an account of privileges based on what people of color do not have, rather than what whites possess in the absence of the presence of people of color. The element of superiority comes through because people of color in this paradigm have no subjectivity and the dominant assumes that what he or she wants and has is exactly what all people desire. The notion that people of color may have a different "list" of what a good life is, or what a "good person" is, is not acknowledged in a paradigm where whiteness is obviously considered superior (McIntosh, 1992, pp. 73–74). McIntosh is fully aware of this contradiction and her essay is an attempt to deconstruct the privileges of whiteness. Again, her honesty, which may be perceived as betrayal by some whites and offensive to some people of color, allows her to begin to rethink whiteness and by definition the inferiority assigned to nonwhites.

The use of people of color for the exaltation of whiteness, although gendered, still is used by both men and women. Whiteness and maleness are defined in opposition to "color" and "femaleness" — the other has to exist to exalt the centeredness of the subject. If the other refuses to be the other, it creates chaos in the subject because they have to reconstitute themselves (Fine et al., 1994, p. 2). The presence of nonwhites creates a "humanity" scale in which white men are the pinnacle of human development — they are rational, logical, unemotional, industrious, adventurous, in control, creators (Harris, 1993a) — all of these characteristics would be difficult to judge if it were not for the presence of nonwhites. Even the gender relations between whites are more "human" because of the presence of people of color. Morrison (1992) illustrated this when discussing Hemingway's *To Have and Have Not*. In the novel Harry and his wife Marie are making love. Marie asks her husband,

> "Listen, did you ever do it with a nigger wench?"
> "Sure."
> "What's it like?"
> "Like a nurse shark."

Morrison (1992) went on to remark that for Hemingway, the black woman is

> the furthest thing from human, so far away as to be not even mammal but fish. The figure evokes a predatory, devouring eroticism and signals the antithesis to femininity, to nurturing, to nursing, to replenishment. In short, Harry's words mark something so brutal, contrary, and alien in its figuration that it does not belong to its own species and cannot be spoken of in language, in metaphor or metonym, evocative of anything resembling the woman to whom Harry is speaking — his wife Marie. The kindness he has shown Marie is palpable. His projection of black female sexuality has provided her with solace, for which she is properly grateful. She responds to the kindness and giggles, "You're funny" (pp. 84–85).

It is in the owning of people of color, historically through slavery, not through their labor, that white men's manhood was transformed in the new world (Roediger, 1991). As Morrison (1992) pointed out, "Whatever his social status in London, in the New World he is a gentleman. More gentle, more man. The site of his transformation is within rawness: he is backgrounded by savagery" (p. 44). The presence of people of color and the potential threat of their darkness and their concomitant "savagery" opens the gateways for white people to assume their color burden and protect the "civilized world" through the use of brutality that by definition is not uncivilized. This tautology leads to the most brutal acts, like the imprisonment and execution of more poor black people in the United States than in any other country — all done in the name of civilization.

Morrison (1992) argued that the use of people of color, historically, to give whiteness its identity is largely because there was no "royalty" in the United States as there was in Europe from which to draw a counterdistinction:

> Americans did not have profligate, predatory nobility from which to wrest an identity of national virtue while continuing to covet aristocratic license and luxury. The American nation negotiated both its disdain and its envy in the same way Dunbar did: through the self-reflexive contemplation of fabricated, mythological Africanism. For the settlers and for American writers generally, this Africanist other became the means of thinking about body, mind, chaos, kindness, and love; provided the occasion for exercises in the absence of restraint, the presence of restraint, the contemplation of freedom and of aggression; permitted opportunities for the exploration of ethics and morality, for meeting the obligations of the social contract, for bearing the cross of religion and following out the ramifications of power. (p. 47)

Morrison (1992) quoted sociologist Orlando Patterson's observation that "we should not be surprised that the Enlightenment could accommodate slavery; we should be surprised if it had not. The concept of freedom did not emerge in a vacuum. Nothing highlighted freedom — if it did not in fact create it — like slavery" (p. 38). The significance of white identity is still in reference to the presence of dark others — the definitions of social issues are as well. For many whites the passion that propels their lives stems from the need to "help" save, and by default indirectly control, the dark others. In Morrison's (1992) words, "Africanism is the vehicle by which the American self knows itself as not enslaved, but free; not repulsive but desirable; not helpless, but licensed and powerful; not history-less, but historical; not damned, but innocent; not a blind accident of evolution, but a progressive fulfillment of destiny" (p. 52).

In sum, people of color are the experimentation ground where real lives get hurt, trashed out, dumped, and disposed of, while whites psyches remain intact — or do they? It is not their children who have been killed in disproportionate numbers by drugs, guns, or war, but will their children not inherit their consequences? Will the anger whites have been systematically cultivating for so long be unleashed on those they care about most because they represent their immortality — future generations of white children?

METHODOLOGICAL ISSUES

In reviewing both direct accounts of whites' experience of race, and more indirect accounts of other kinds of privilege, we have been struck by the challenge this research poses to our understanding of "feminist methods." Feminist methods have grown out of efforts by researchers to dismantle privilege — both gender and scientific privilege. An integral part of feminist epistemology and methods has been to create an activist scholarship at the root of which is the hope of changing existing power relations. Analytic and procedural techniques flowing from these goals have been used to great advantage in studying subordinate groups; they are, however, much more problematic in the study of "dominants." Recognition of this fact may help feminist social scientists articulate more precisely the conditions under which various research approaches are useful or appropriate.

Research as Empowerment

Many feminist scholars have thought hard about the intertwined ethical and methodological issues involved in conducting research with people who are disadvantaged in terms of gender, class, and/or race (see Bowles & Duelli Klein, 1983; Fonow & Cook, 1991; Nielsen, 1990; Reinharz, 1992; Roberts, 1981). Thus, for example, Oakley (1981), in an important early paper, described the importance of not withholding crucial information and knowledge from research participants who needed it. Generally increased openness with research participants about the purposes and goals of the research has been advocated (Cook & Fonow, 1986). Mies (1983) argued early on for the importance of research participants' role in shaping and defining the research questions. Many worried about how to encourage those who have been "shut up and shut out" to tell what they know (Belenky, Clinchy, Goldberger, & Tarule, 1986; Reid, 1993). As a result, there has been considerable — and critical — development of methods that support and affirm participants' perspective and leave plenty of space for its articulation.

Parallel recommendations have been made about how we write up what we learn. Thus, feminist scholars have recommended that we avoid representing research participants' experience, but instead permit those participants — who often have not been heard directly before — to speak "in their own voice." This concern has been expressed in extensive quotation from participants, provision of richly detailed accounts of the context (or "ethnography"), as well as in inclusion of participants' own reflections on the researchers' claims (see Franz & Stewart, 1994; Stacey, 1990).

How do these suggestions, flowing as they do from a concern about the power imbalance between the researcher and the researched, fare when we turn to research on whiteness? Many of these studies have employed open-ended interview, or ethnographic, techniques of data collection *from people who are white* and therefore already "empowered" at least with respect to their location in the racial hierarchy, and they have included extensive quotations from the research participants. These techniques can leave researchers in the ethically complex situation of eliciting, recording — and not challenging — participants' racist views. On the one hand this approach seems consistent with feminist methodological preoccupations with supporting and encouraging participants' "voices" and with facilitating identification of multiple "standpoints." However, we doubt that recording, and repeating, racist views of whites in a racist society could ever have the same moral or ethical standing as recording and repeating the views of those whose opinions are not institutionalized and reified throughout the culture (and we note that feminist researchers have not been interested in documenting sexist views in rich detail). Moreover, for an antiracist researcher simply to record racist sentiments is certainly not open or honest. Wellman (1993) discussed an interesting case in which a black interviewer repeatedly presses a white respondent to explain her views on race more clearly. The interview sounds uncomfortable but "honest" in a way not quite envisioned in most writing on feminist methods.

Quoting hate-filled sentiments puts scholars in the position of giving those sentiments more "air time" than they already have. This is not to say it is never justified, but here we must ask not for "thick" description or empowerment and giving voice but for "thick" analysis (Wellman, 1993, provided a good model of this ratio of analysis to quotation). The repetition of certain opinions will, in itself, inflict pain on some who read them; that pain must be justified by a gain in understanding provided by explication and critique. An appropriate strategy for reporting may be to provide minimal documentation, when views are all too familiar and oppressive, while holding ourselves and others to a very high standard of analytic depth when work carries such a high risk of causing suffering in those who are already the objects of daily racism.

Who Are the Experts on Whiteness?

Research on whiteness carried out with people of color has very different risks and benefits. We have seen that many whites are not able to articulate any clear meaning of whiteness in their lives. In contrast, we suspect that people of color have a rather well-developed understanding of how "whiteness matters" (just as women tend to have a clearer sense of male privilege than men do). In fact, Dill (1988), Rollins (1985), and Romero (1992), in their studies of domestic workers, often provided perspectives on whiteness. Even more directly, Philomena Essed (1990) set out to study "racism" from the perspective of women of color (in the Netherlands and the United States). She adopted a "feminist method": "I wanted the women to describe and illustrate their experiences at length. With this in mind, I tried to direct the interviews as little as possible" (p. 3). In her study of racism from the perspective of women of color, she certainly identified many important features of whiteness. She identified three main forms of "everyday racism": inferiorization, social or spatial distancing, and social or physical aggression. Each of these tells us something important not only about the experiences of racism of women of color but also about the experience of whiteness of white women and men. In addition, Essed suggested,

> Everyday racism implies that people of color can, potentially, experience racism every day. As a result, people of color learn to systematically observe the behavior of whites. They develop expertise in judging how whites behave toward them. They also gain insight into the white delusion of superiority and the ideology defining people of color as inferior. They have daily opportunities to test new insights, because they have contact with all sorts of whites every day. (p. 258)

In short, people of color are experts about whiteness, which we have learned whites most emphatically are not. We suggest that feminist methods used to study whiteness from the perspective of people of color are likely to produce substantial knowledge, without posing the same kinds of ethical dilemmas they pose when studying the perspective of whites.

Revisiting the Researchers' Perspective

Attention to the perspective of the researched must be matched by attention to the perspective of the researcher. It is critical for scholars exploring the meaning of whiteness to articulate the implications of their own relation to whiteness. Essed (1990) discussed what it meant for her research:

> Doing research among one's own group has the advantage of making it easier to discuss negative views about an "out group," in this case whites. Thus I was in an advantageous position as a black researcher of experiences of racism. (p. 3)

In this case, then, she is able to encourage and support expression of negative views not normally sanctioned by the larger culture. In the reverse case — as a white person, facilitating the expression of negative views of people of color by whites — the researcher is on much less defensible ground, both in terms of the likelihood of uncovering previously invisible features of the social landscape and in terms of the ethics of the situation, given her own social position. Interestingly, Wellman (1993) experimented with having black interviewers interview whites about race; at least some of these interviews were brilliantly successful.

One technique for addressing the limitations of one's own standpoint is actively to seek out literature written from other standpoints. Thus, for example, Caraway's (1991) analysis of "racism and the politics of American feminism" employs a brilliant strategy of combining thoughtful recognition of her own position as a white female feminist and the rich literature written by feminists of color. She argued for a "crossover politics" in which

> feminists try (but never truly succeed) to see and hear from "other" vantage points, perhaps sharing some of their experience and knowledge with someone else, some of whose own experience and knowledge might rub off. (p. 172)

The argument that precedes her case for a "multicultural feminist politics of solidarity" is powerful precisely because she presents — in respectful detail — the viewpoints of feminist theorists of color and reacts to them from her own perspective. Studies of whiteness by white scholars would not be so likely to create a sense of eavesdropping on a particularly ugly conversation if they incorporated at least this academic form of "walking in others' shoes" — reading, taking seriously, citing, quoting — the scholarship by people of color about race.

Reinventing Feminist Methods

It is, then, crucial for researchers to keep the power dimension of standpoints or perspectives in focus. Methods that serve constructive aims when used with subordinates may have very different implications when used with dominants. We do not advocate the use of different methods for different groups because they are "different" in an essentialist way but rather that social location gives access to power. In progressive scholarship where the goal is to dismantle oppression, social location is crucial in determining our research methods. In fact, this is one of the main cornerstones of feminist epistemology — that women's subordination, historically, did not permit the use of Western positivist, male paradigms and methods without inevitably eclipsing women's experiences and therefore distorting their lives. One way to mitigate the impact of one's own social position may be to employ more complicating collaborative research practices. Methods in which whites are provided an opportunity to express views about race *while being held accountable for them* can be created, as Wellman (1993) showed. Focus groups constructed to include individuals with different views could offer one such approach; interview techniques involving two (or more) interviewers from different social locations might be another. In any case data collected can always be analyzed — by focus groups, collaborators, other participants — from multiple perspectives. And written reports can include those multiple perspectives in a single "voice" or in several. When exploring hegemonic experiences like whiteness, the trick is to find ways to retain a critical, counter-hegemonic presence in the research. Recognizing the complexity of that task will help us enrich "feminist methods" to include techniques that more fully acknowledge the complexity of the power relations among and between women and men.

REFERENCES

Allport, G. (1958). *The nature of prejudice*. Garden City, NJ: Doubleday.

Apfelbaum, E. (1979). Relations of domination and movements for liberation: An analysis of power between groups. In W. G. Austin & S. Worchel (Eds.), *The social psychology of intergroup relations* (pp. 188–204). Monterey, CA: New York: Plenum.

Belenky, M. E., Clinchy, B. M., Goldberger, N. R., & Tarule, J. M. (1986). *Women's ways of knowing: The development of self, voice and mind*. New York: Basic.

Belle, D. (1994). Attempting to comprehend the lives of low-income women. In C. Franz & A. J. Stewart (Eds.), *Women creating lives*. Boulder, CO: Westview.

Bowles, G., & Duelli Klein, K. (1983). *Theories of women's studies*. London: Routledge.

Caraway, N. (1991). *Segregated sisterhood: Racism and the politics of American feminism*. Knoxville: University of Tennessee Press.

Carroll, L. C. (1946). *Through the looking glass*. New York: Random House.

Cook, J. A., & Fonow, M. M. (1986). Knowledge and women's interestests: Issues of epistemology and methodology in sociological research. *Sociological Inquiry*, (1), 2–29.

Dill, B. T. (1988). "Making your job good yourself": Domestic service and the construction of personal dignity. In A. Bookman & S. Morgen (Eds.), *Women and the politics of empowerment* (pp. 33–52). Philadelphia: Temple University Press.

Domhoff, G. W. (1983). *Who rules America now?* Englewood Cliffs, NJ: Prentice Hall.

Du Bois, W. E. B. (1961). *The souls of black folk*. Greenwich, CT: Fawcett Publications.

Essed, P. (1990). *Everyday racism: Reports from women of two cultures*. Alameda, CA: Hunter House.

Feagin, J., & Feagin, C. B. (1978). *Discrimination American style: Institutional racism and sexism*. Englewood Cliffs, NJ: Prentice Hall.

Fine, M. (1989). Coping with rape: Critical perspectives on consciousness. In R. K. Unger (Ed.), *Representations: Social constructions of gender* (pp. 167–185). Amityville, NY: Baywood.

Fine, M., Weis, L., & Addelston, J. (1997). White loss. In M. Zeiler & L. Weis (Eds.), *Beyond black and white: New faces and voices in U.S. Schools* (pp. 283–301). Albany: State University of New York Press.

Fonow, M. M., & Cook, J. A. (1991). *Beyond methodology*. Bloomington: Indiana University Press.

Frankenberg, R. (1993). *White women, race matters: The social construction of whiteness*. Minneapolis: University of Minnesota Press.

Franz, C. E., & Stewart, A. J. (1994). *Women creating lives*. Boulder, CO: Westview.

Gallagher, C. A. (1995). White reconstruction in the university. *Socialist Review, 24*(1–2), 165–185.

Harding, S. (1991). *Whose science? Whose knowledge? Thinking from women's lives*. Ithaca, NY: Cornell University Press.

Harris, C. I. (1993a). Bell's blues. *University of Chicago Law Review, 60*, 783–793.

Harris, C. I. (1993b). Whiteness as property. *Harvard Law Review, 106*, 1707–1791.

Hurtado, A. (1989). Relating to privilege: Seduction and rejection in the subordination of white women and women of color. *Signs, 14*, 833–855.

Kimmel, M. S. (1993). Invisible masculinity. *Society, 30*, 28–35.

Landrine, H., Klonoff, E., & Brown-Collins, A. (1992). Cultural diversity and methodology in feminist psychology: Critique, proposal, empirical example. *Psychology of Women Quarterly, 16*, 145–163.

Lykes, M. B. (1989). Dialogue with Guatemalan Indian women: Critical perspectives on constructing collaborative research. In R. K. Unger (Ed.), *Representations: Social constructions of gender* (pp. 167–185). Amityville, NY: Baywood.

Mcintosh, P. (1992). White privilege and male privilege: A personal account of coming to see correspondences through work in women's studies. In M. L. Andersen & P. Hill Collins (Eds.), *Race, class, and gender* (pp. 70–81). Belmont, CA: Wadsworth.

Mies, M. (1983). Towards a methodology for feminist research. In G. Bowles & R. Duelli Klein (Eds.), *Theories of women's studies* (pp. 117–139). London: Routledge.

Morrison, T. (1992). *Playing in the dark*. New York: Vintage.

Nielsen, J. M. (1990). *Feminist research methods*. Boulder, CO: Westview.

Oakley, A. (1981). Interviewing women. In H. Roberts (Ed.), *Doing feminist research* (pp. 30–61). London: Routledge.

Ostrander, S. (1984). *Women of the upper class*. Philadelphia: Temple University Press.

Ostrove, J. M., & Stewart, A. J. (1994). Meanings and uses of marginal identities: Social class at Radcliffe in the 1960s. In C. Franz & A. J. Stewart (Eds.), *Women creating lives* (pp. 273–288). Boulder, CO: Westview.

Pettigrew, T. F. (1964). *Profile of the Negro American*. New York: Van Nostrand.

Reid, P. T. (1993). Poor women in psychological research: Shut up and shut out. *Psychology of Women Quarterly, 17*, 133–150.

Reinharz, S. (1992). *Feminist methods in social research*. New York: Oxford.

Roberts, H. (1981). *Doing feminist research*. London: Routledge.

Roediger, D. R. (1991). *The wages of whiteness*. New York: Verso.

Rollins, J. (1985). *Between women: Domestics and their employers*. Philadelphia: Temple University Press.

Romero, M. (1992). *Maid in the U.S.A.* New York: Routledge.

Ryan, J., & Sackrey, C. (1984). *Strangers in paradise*. Boston: South End Press.

Sherif, C. W. (1979). Bias in psychology. In J. A. Sherman & E. T. Beck (Eds.), *Prism of sex: Essays in the sociology of knowledge* (pp. 93–133). Madison: University of Wisconsin Press.

Stacey, J. (1990). *Brave new families*. New York: Basic.

Sturgis, S. J. (1988). Class act: Beginning a translation from privilege. In C. McEwan & S. O'Sullivan (Eds.), *Out the other side: Contemporary lesbian writing* (pp. 7–13). London: Virago.

Tatum, B. D. (1992). Talking about race, learning about racism: The application of racial identity development theory in the classroom. *Harvard Educational Review, 62*(1), 1–24.

Wellman, D. T. (1993). *Portraits of white racism* (2nd ed.). New York: Cambridge University Press.

Williams, G. H. (1995). *Life on the color line: The true story of a white boy who discovered he was black*. New York: Dutton.

Wilson, W. J. (1987). *The truly disadvantaged: The inner city, the underclass, and public policy*. Chicago: University of Chicago Press.

Zweigenhaft, R. L., & Domhoff, G. H. (1991). *Blacks in the white establishment?* New Haven, CT: Yale University Press.

NOTE

We would like to thank the following individuals for their throughtful comments: Linda Blum, Michelle Fine, Pat Gurin, Gerry Gurin, Rosario Ceballo, Lois Weis, Joan Ostrove, and Mun Wong.

TWENTY-FOUR

Racism and "Whiteness" in Transitions to Peace: Indigenous Peoples, Human Rights, and the Struggle for Justice

Maria De Jesus and M. Brinton Lykes

Yet the problem there [in Chiapas] is not really a religious one. It is derived from [ ] corruption, plunder, the take-over of traditional indigenous lands. It arises out of racism, social injustice and oppression. (Menchú Tum, 1998, p. 217)

As an indigenous person I feel important as a Mexican, because we count with the history of our first parents, the fact that they were indigenous and they also fought, as we fight, to not disappear. As indigenous women we are not going to give up the fight until we are recognized in the Constitution and we are no longer treated as animals. (Comandanta Yolanda, Tzotzil Zapatista delegate, *http://zapatistas.net/comandantes/*)

The latter half of the 20th century has witnessed the emergence of multiple social movements, including armed struggles, wherein communities traditionally marginalized from access to power and resources have organized, often in identity-based groups, to denounce these exclusions and to demand their rights. Many of these actions seeking to redress economic inequalities, structural poverty, and institutionalized racism were met by brutal, sometimes violent, resistance from governments, often supported by international forces, resulting in massive violations of human rights and loss of human life. Despite this, a growing, at least tacit, acceptance of the UN Declaration on Human Rights has created conditions wherein governments are increasingly willing to enter into peace negotiations with insurgents, sign accords, and participate in truth commissions to document the impact of armed conflict and facilitate "transitions to democracy."

Psychologists have been increasingly present in these late-20th-century conflict and postconflict contexts, offering crisis intervention strategies and psychosocial services to survivors and their families. Post-traumatic stress disorder as a primary psychological effect of contemporary warfare for children and adults (see, e.g., Eth & Pynoos, 1985) informs much of this work. However, some mental health professionals have argued that the effects of state-sponsored violence are not only individual phenomena but also collective, social phenomena. Specific critiques of individualizing psychological approaches to trauma include liberation psychologists' theories of psychosocial trauma and the public health-based critique of an individually based tertiary intervention that addresses only a small proportion of those affected while leaving devastated communities and even whole societies unattended (see, e.g., Bracken, Giller, & Summerfield, 1995; Martín-Baró, 1994).

One critical approach to the individualism and acontextualism underlying many psychologists' roles in postwar contexts has been developed by the second author and illustrated by her work accompanying communities in their searches for a just peace in Guatemala and South Africa (see, respectively, Women of ADMI & Lykes, 2000; Lykes, TerreBlanche, & Hamber, 2003). Drawing on human rights discourse, this work ruptures the increasingly normative psychological response to trauma that reduces collective processes to individual suffering and contributes to a developing liberatory community psychology.

In this essay we explore some of the ways in which, despite its liberatory promise, this community-based and human rights discourse and praxis often fails to uncover the submergence of racism and privileging of "whiteness" that characterize much global conflict and, when left unchallenged, persist through transitional and reconciliation processes. The case of the Zapatista uprising in Chiapas, México, and the stalemated peacemaking process is presented as a concrete site for exploration of how one social movement sought to organize at the intersections of racism and class oppression, on the one hand, and local and global political realities, on the other.

We begin with a brief overview of human rights, clarifying how the struggle for indigenous rights transcends classic human rights discourse pushing the boundaries of Euro-American understanding. We situate the Chiapas struggle within this global debate and then we locate ourselves, privileged, North American psychologists, whose work is increasingly situated as aspiring liberatory psychologists in the field of human rights and mental health. We next examine the Zapatista struggle for indigenous, collective rights, and communal lands as one site for understanding contemporary challenges to racism and class oppression. We argue that the Zapatistas sought to develop an alternative to the mass-based movements and armed struggles for economic and racial justice and social transformation that characterize previous struggles both in the United States and in Latin America. To understand the race-class dialectic at the center of their struggle, we briefly review constructions of race and *mestizo* within México. We argue that the contemporary relations between the Mexican government and the indigenous leadership are reflective of a long-standing and entrenched privileging of *mestizaje* or "whiteness" and a refusal to acknowledge institutionalized racism that date back to colonial times. Central to each of the arguments presented here is a tension between our understandings of racism and white privilege developed within the context of our lives and work within North America and the emerging alternatives posited by indigenous groups. We seek to interrogate the contributions of an antiracist discourse for better understanding the Zapatista struggle and for resituating the work of liberatory psychologists who seek to work with those engaged in or affected by social movements such as theirs.

Four Generations of Human Rights

The Zapatista movement's claims as indigenous peoples are rooted not only in their history but in a developing human rights discourse. The Universal Declaration on Human Rights adopted by the United Nations General Assembly on December 10, 1948, is the basis of much human rights activism. It was not, however, until 1996 that two international covenants — the Covenant on Civil and Political Rights and the Covenant on Economic, Social, and Cultural Rights — were approved, thus establishing the Universal Declaration's principles in law. These documents extended what were initially thought of exclusively as *protections from* (e.g., extreme abuse and punishment) to focus on more positive, or second-generation, rights (economic, social, and cultural) and rights *to* development, self-determination, and a sustainable environment, also known as third-generation rights (Berting et al., 1990, cited in Messer, 1995; van der Gaag, 1998). Many countries from Africa, Latin America, or Asia were still under colonial rule during the period in which the initial declaration was drafted. The views of the majority world were not, therefore, well represented in the initial documents (Messer, 1997; for a discussion of evolving conceptions of rights that extend civil and political rights as articulated by the first covenant, see also Kam, 1998; Menchú Tum, 1998; Nagengast, 1997).

Leaders within newly forming nations as well as women and indigenous groups throughout the world have fought to expand the two original human rights covenants to include demands for women's and children's rights and for indigenous rights. This most recent draft declaration (*Draft Declaration on the Rights of Indigenous Peoples*, 1994), whose implementation is still under debate, would establish collective rights; that is, "a right that adheres to certain groups *because* it is not reducible to individuals" (Thompson, 1997, p. 789), if adopted.

These collective rights, also known as fourth-generation rights, challenge Euro-American assumptions about the autonomy and centrality of the individual as a locus of human rights, asserting "the collectivity" as a locus of rights (see "Universal Human Rights," 1997). Indigenous groups and pan-national and global organizing among these groups have contributed to this evolving understanding of human rights. The 2001 UN World Conference against Racism, Racial Discrimination, Xenophobia, and Related Intolerance (see *http://www.un.org/ WCAR/*) engaged this discussion, exploring links among the struggles of Africans at home and in the Diaspora and indigenous peoples worldwide. In their Final Declaration those gathered in Durban, South Africa, affirmed their support of a range of recommendations about indigenous groups (Issues 203–209) and urged the rapid conclusion of a Draft Declaration of the Rights of Indigenous Peoples.

VIOLATIONS OF CIVIL-POLITICAL RIGHTS: INDIVIDUAL AND INSTITUTIONALIZED VIOLENCE

Despite these developments, it is perhaps not surprising that most "UnitedStatesians"[1] typically think of human rights abuses in civil or political terms, that is, as violations of our rights to free speech, as arbitrary arrest, or as cruel, inhuman, or degrading treatment or punishment. Messer (1997) argued convincingly that the U.S. government persistently equates civil liberties and human rights, selectively enforcing the violation of those rights relative to its economic interests, while ignoring or even rejecting social welfare guarantees that are part of its own legal history. Furthermore, these attitudes influence the agenda of the largest and most influential human rights nongovernmental organizations (NGOs), Amnesty International and Human Rights Watch, who define their missions in terms of these first-generation rights. It is of note that despite this focus on the individual, Amnesty International has moved, *de facto*, to expand its conception of individual rights by its inclusion of indigenous rights within its defense of civil and political rights (see, e.g., Amnesty International, 1992).

Moreover, systematic violations of civil-political rights often have antecedents or roots in institutional violence. Examples include the massacres of one's own citizens by the state (e.g., in Guatemala, see CEH, 1999) and the policies and practices of the International Monetary Fund and World Bank wherein countries in the majority world pay more money to service their foreign debt than they can invest in national health or education for their citizens, thereby institutionalizing poverty (*Jubilee 2000*, 1998). Others (see, e.g., Pereira, 1997) have argued that civil-political rights and their violation or abuse are not aberrations from the norm but rather official directives, legally enacted and implemented over centuries to ensure oppression against the majority of the world's people. First-generation rights, rather than protecting all individuals, protect the interests of only some individuals; that is, the elite of the First [*sic*] World, thereby contributing to the marginalization and oppression of all others. We argue here that the indigenous activists' focus on collective and cultural rights not only shifts the discourse of rights but also surfaces the submerged individualism and discourse of "whiteness" underlying civil-political rights. We discuss this more fully in our presentation of the case of Chiapas.

SITUATING OURSELVES: PSYCHOLOGY AND HUMAN RIGHTS PRAXIS

Ignacio Martín-Baró argued for an understanding of liberation of the whole people; that is, one that includes personal liberation as well as a new epistemology wherein the "truth of the popular majority" (Martín-Baró, 1994) is not to be found but to be created, "from below" (see, e.g., Freire, 1970, and Gutiérrez, 1973/1988, for the roots of this perspective). He described a new praxis, wherein psychologists place themselves alongside the dominated or oppressed rather than alongside the dominator or oppressor (Martín-Baró, 1994). "Taking sides" or "the preferential option for the poor" is not, therefore, bias but rather ethical positioning and action.

The work of black psychiatrists (Fanon, 1967) and psychologists (see, e.g., Gordon, 1973; White & Parham, 1990), feminist psychologists (see, e.g., Burman, 1998), community psychologists (Seedat, 1997; Watts & Serrano-Garcia, 2003) as well as critical psychologists (see, e.g., Fox & Prilleltensky, 1997) also challenges psychologists' exclusive attention to individual persons abstracted from a multilayered social, historical, and cultural context that is coconstitutive of the person. Moreover, these works urge both the engagement in dialogue with marginalized and oppressed populations and the interrogation of dominant, mainstream psychological theory and research. These liberatory theories and praxes have informed more recent work among survivors of war and state-sponsored violence (see, e.g., Lykes et al., 2003), work that seeks to engage with local communities in transformative praxis to redress social injustice and create well-being.

We situate our work as teachers, as researchers, and as human rights activists within this liberatory psychological praxis. Our explicitly activist work as psychologists is defined, in part, within the Ignacio Martín-Baró Fund for Mental Health and Human Rights. The fund supports local grassroots organizations whose psychosocial praxis within ongoing and postwar situations includes community organizing and community and economic development. Groups in local communities from the Philippines to Guatemala challenge us to rethink our theories and inform our ongoing praxis and research. Closer to home, we seek to educate U.S.-based psychologists about this work and about the role of the U.S. government in creating and supporting conditions of violence and oppression in these communities (see *www.martinbarofund.org*).

As teachers we are currently collaborating in a field-based project wherein a service-learning course for undergraduates and a graduate seminar in participatory action research are yoked and co-taught with members of Cooperative Economics for Women, a Boston-based community development and organizing NGO that works with immigrant women and children. We participated with other Boston-based organizers in a 2-day workshop organized by the People's Institute to explore the historical roots of institutionalized racism in the United States and to relocate ourselves, relative to differing privileges and experiences of oppression that frame our developing collaborations as researchers and activists. Such engagement demands ongoing and systematic exploration of the privilege-oppression dialectic in which we differently situate ourselves and are differently situated by others.

As white academics whose relative status (Ph.D. student, Ph.D. professor) and ethnic-national diversities (Portuguese Canadian daughter of immigrants, Southern UnitedStatesian mixed ethnicity) differentially shape our privilege, we situate ourselves within the cultural, racial, and linguistic realities of the communities with whom we work. We have learned some of the languages of these communities and developed our understandings of cultural particularities and singularities in dialogue with cultural psychology, anthropology, and key informants who include indigenous healers. We also have drawn heavily on human rights discourse to inform our local collaborations in struggles against oppression and in the co-development of programs that facilitate survival.

For both of us, our primary praxis has been in communities beyond U.S. borders where a major site of struggle, including armed struggle, has been focused on the dramatically unequal distribution of land within countries whose majority population is "indigenous" or "of color" (e.g., in South Africa, Guatemala, and Chiapas, México). We have lived among these communities in contexts of ongoing war and, more recently, as they have been "transitioning" from war to "democracy."

As we argued previously, the case of Chiapas offers one example of a revolutionary struggle that foregrounds the rights of indigenous people and an analysis of the institutionalized racism that contribute to their ongoing marginalization. We briefly explore the construction of "whiteness" in the Mexican context and the ways in which white privilege operates to submerge and sustain institutional and cultural racism. We describe the struggles of the Zapatista movement and government responses, the stalemated peace processes, and possible interpretations for better understanding contemporary fractures in the local struggles of survivors. Within that context we offer suggested provisional guidelines for a liberatory psychological praxis for work with survivors and activists in local communities. Our purpose in this essay is not to dismiss the important work of existing human rights activists or of individual-based psychological practice in the context of liberation movements or in the wake of armed conflict. Rather we seek to bring an antiracist praxis and a consciousness of white privilege into dialogue with a cross-national praxis that draws heavily on human rights and liberation discourses and explore a potential dialogue.

History of *Mestizaje* within Mexico: Social Constructions of Identity

Although racial categories are fluid political and social constructs that change over time and context, and not clear-cut fixed biological traits, there are direct and indirect consequences to how one self-identifies and, more important, how one is identified by others. Language forms a way of thinking and interpreting reality. Moreover, race classification underpins how resources are distributed in society. The South African architects of apartheid, for example, both constructed and drew on racial categories and used them for purposes of white political and economic domination (Dawes, 2001). Those who were Japanese were classified as "honorary whites" and granted more privileges than blacks. Impoverishment of those not classified as whites was achieved by reserving 86% of the land for whites and limiting educational and job opportunities for blacks (Dawes, 2001). Racial groups are accorded differential statuses and this makes it easier to justify the marginalization of lower status racial groups.

In México, as in many other postcolonial societies, the concept of race is entangled with the concept of national identity. Historically, race has been used as the basis for nationhood (De Castro, 2002). Specifically, the political ideology of *mestizaje* was introduced in Latin America to create a common semantic field in which the discourse about "nation" could be grounded. This ideology is rooted in and arose from European nationalist thought and action and, as such, it functions as a political tool used to "melt" the reality of racial and cultural heterogeneity into a unified concept of the nation.

However, similar to the rhetoric of assimilation and the "melting pot" in the United States, the discourse of *mestizaje* maintains a racial hierarchy with whites at the pinnacle. Although it proposes to ground the nation in a racial unity that can be achieved by the fusion of white, Amerindian, and black populations, the "national culture" is defined by the ruling, *mestizo* classes. Furthermore, for the *mestizo* governing elite a superior "tripartite identity" exists wherein Spanish is the nation's language; Catholicism, its religion; and white, its ideal (De Castro, 2002). In fact, many critics (e.g., Kahn, 1995) have claimed that the discourse of the *mestizo* is a facade that permits the oppression of indigenous and blacks by the elite ruling classes under the banner of their inclusion into the national community. This parallels the argument of Pereira (1997), cited previously, wherein an ostensibly positive human rights discourse of civil-political rights privileges a minority elite while legitimating the marginalization of a majority population.

Recently, scholars (see Perry, 1996) have documented the Mexican state's constructions of generic categories of identity such as *indio* and *campesino*—terms that are considered pejorative and connote "backward masses." *Indios* typically speak indigenous languages rather than Spanish, wear local rather than European styles of clothing (women more so than men), and are part of indigenous communities. Indigenous peoples themselves, in contrast, have historically centered their identities on locality, common language, kinship ties, and access to *ejidos*.[2]

Although many Mexicans are, arguably, a mixture of white European (typically Spanish) and Indo-American descent, most do not self-identify as *indio*, thus denying their indigenous heritage (see Foley, 1999, for a similar point in Guatemala). This denial of any Indian blood reflects a rejection of the negative connotations that this particular identity conjures up: backward, inferior, uncivilized masses or *campesinos*. Furthermore, it is grounded in the history of colonialism, the construction of identity described previously, and in a socialization of *blancofilia* (i.e., love for white); that is, the valuing of "Europeanness" or "whiteness."

For well over 500 years, *mestizos* have ruled over the indigenous peoples in a nation that values "whiteness" and "Europeanness" over native culture (see Adams & Bastos, 2003, and Taracena Arriola, 2002, for similar points in Guatemala). Furthermore, a Eurocentric racial hierarchy and a belief in white superiority have provided *mestizo* elites a psychological basis for denying their indigenous heritage and for morally excluding nonwhites (see Opotow, 2001, for a similar point). Historically, indigenous peoples have been denied full citizenship rights based on their presumed racial inferiority and are treated as second-class citizens, at best, and animals, at worst. This racial hierarchy contributed to and was used to justify indirect (structural, e.g., denial of collective rights to land) and direct violence (e.g., ethnocide, see Lykes, 2001; genocide, see CEH, 1999) against the indigenous people of Chiapas for centuries. Furthermore, despite Chiapas's majority indigenous population, *indios* endure ongoing political and economic exclusion.

CHIAPAS: THE STRUGGLE FOR INDIGENOUS RIGHTS AND ECONOMIC EQUALITY

The Zapatista rebellion in Chiapas (the poorest state in México) emerged within a legacy of repeated violent attacks on indigenous ideas and civilizations by missionaries, European colonial powers, and the Mexican government. The uprising was sparked by indigenous resistance to centuries of deep-seated injustice.

Zapatista Uprising and Its Unique History

In 1992, the Mexican Congress, supported by President Salinas de Gortari (PRI),[3] revised Article 27, the agrarian reform section of the Mexican Constitution, thereby allowing the privatization of *ejidos* (Hansen, 2002). This decision legalized the government's refusal to resolve *campesinos'* long-standing land claims (Collier, 2000) wherein indigenous sought to legalize *ejidos*, lands on which their livelihoods, and, as we argued previously, their identities, depend. Thus these indigenous *campesinos* were forcibly displaced and left landless (Ross, 1995).

Although many of these *campesinos*, including Tzeltal, Tzotzil, Chole, Zoque, Tojolabal, Chamula, Lacandon, and other Maya Indians from central Chiapas, speak different dialects and had previously felt little in common with one another, their forced displacement and their leaders' participation in pan-indigenous movements contributed to the development of a broader sense of shared identity (Perry, 1996). By 1994, they formed a pan-indigenous revolutionary movement and *Zapatismo* came to symbolize their struggle for indigenous rights. Zapata, after whom this movement was named, was a leader of the agrarian revolt in México in the early 1900s. He was a *criollo*[4] from Morelos, thus neither Maya nor from Chiapas. The movement's autoidentification or self-naming thus situated it within México's revolutionary history, reflecting a desire to appeal to principles and issues that while grounded in local indigenous concerns transcended them (Perry, 1996).

Twentieth-century *Zapatismo* focused not only on land as a resource for material survival but also on land as central to the survival of the indigenous *campesinos* as a people. This appeal to collective as well as cultural rights reframes long-standing *campesino* land claims within the discourse of second-, third-, and fourth-generation human rights and an identity politics that has informed other late 20th-century pan-indigenous global movements (see, e.g., Warren, 1998, for a discussion in postwar Guatemala). Thus, at the heart of the Zapatista movement in Chiapas was the denunciation of the root causes of indigenous oppression: racism and economic and political exclusion (Ross, 1995).

Given our previous analysis, it is of particular note that the first public phase of the Zapatista armed uprising was initiated on January 1, 1994, when former Mexican President Carlos Salinas de Gortari signed the North America Free Trade Agreement (NAFTA) with the United States and Canada. As national and international leaders gathered in México City, a group of representatives from different localities and dialect groups who called themselves the Zapatista Army of National Liberation (EZLN or *Ejército Zapatista de Liberación Nacional*) gathered in the city of San Cristóbal de las Casas and protested the ongoing unfair treatment of indigenous peoples in Chiapas by an oppressive elite government. The Zapatistas presented a list of specific demands that included work, land, shelter, food, health, education, independence, freedom, democracy, justice, and peace (Chomsky, 1995). The demand for autonomy and cultural rights that permeated the language of these demands reframes revolutionary struggle, thus challenging not only the economic and political rule but also the cultural dominance of elite *mestizos* in México (Ross, 1995). The ensuing year was marked by several cease fires, repeated government repression, massive demonstrations, armed encounters, and multiple failed efforts at dialogue (for details see *www.globalexchange.org*).

On January 15, 1995, in meetings in the Lacandon jungle, representatives of the Zapatistas and of the Mexican government agreed to work for the establishment of a stable cease-fire and a return to negotiations. Less than 1 month later the federal government launched a new wave of repression and violent attacks against the EZLN and their communities of supporters, both inside and outside Chiapas. On March 11, 1995, the Mexican Congress acknowledged the failure of this military operation and passed the *Law for Dialogue, Reconciliation, and a Just Peace in Chiapas*, which was subsequently signed by PRI-party president Ernesto Zedillo (Navarro, 2002).

Later that year, the first phase of talks on indigenous rights and culture was held between the EZLN and the federal government. Four months later (on February 16, 1996), the *San Andrés*

Peace Accords on Indigenous Rights and Culture[5] were signed, incorporating the central basis of the Zapatista demands: autonomy. By signing, the government recognized two key Zapatista demands — the official recognition of the right of indigenous communities to choose their own forms of leadership and administration of justice, and their right to control the natural resources in their territories.

The Zapatistas do not wish to secede from México but rather they call for recognition of their unique, indigenous identity and respect for indigenous, collective rights. They root their demand for autonomy in their right to live according to their own "practices and customs." This right would be accorded all indigenous peoples if the fourth-generation rights currently being debated by the United Nations were confirmed and adopted by participating nations. However, as we argue next, neither President Ernesto Zedillo nor subsequent governments nor the Mexican Congress adhere to the terms of the San Andrés Accords.

AUTONOMY AND THE CONSTRUCTION OF GRASSROOTS POWER

Despite the government's ongoing failure to respect these negotiated accords, indigenous peoples of Chiapas have undertaken the construction of autonomous counties and regions to make their demands concrete. Autonomy has been embodied through several different political arrangements. For example, Zapatistas have formed their own autonomous municipalities, developing economic, political, and cultural organizations with no formal contact or collaboration with the Mexican government. Inhabitants of these Zapatista-governed municipalities elect their own authorities, refusing to participate in government-organized elections. They do not accept aid from the Mexican government, stating that they could not accept assistance from the same government that organizes and supports military and paramilitaries forces that attack them (Stahler-Sholk, 1998). In this case, autonomy reflects an organized resistance against a government that refuses to recognize them as a parallel governing force and a commitment to structural change and social transformation (SIPAZ Report, 2002).

In late 1994, other indigenous groups that do not form part of the EZLN established autonomous municipalities organized through Multi-Ethnic Autonomous Regions (*Regiones Autónomas Pluriétnicas*, RAPs). In contrast to the Zapatista municipalities, they accept government aid and participate in government-run elections (Castro & Hidalgo, 1998). Indigenous, peasant, political, and social organizations within the RAP municipalities push for change from within the system. The RAPs argue that their decision to accept government support was necessary to ensure their survival, but Zapatistas accuse them of having been co-opted by the government. These local differences have created and reflect tensions and conflicts among indigenous groups in Chiapas.

ZAPATISTA AUTONOMOUS REGIONS

By 1998, there were 32 Zapatista autonomous counties functioning primarily in rural areas of Chiapas; that is, in the highlands, the northern and border regions, and the Lacandon jungle (Castro & Hidalgo, 1998). These self-governing entities include villages and towns and elect representatives to an Autonomy County Council. They exist parallel to the constitutionally recognized counties and the RAPs. Justice is administered according to indigenous practices and customs. For example, reparation for harm caused in and to the community is redressed through community service rather than a jail term or a fine. These parallel government structures thus function without legal recognition by the federal government.

The autonomous counties are regularly targeted by the federal government, the police, and the Mexican army from nearby military camps. Violent attacks and repression have resulted in more than 7,000 indigenous peoples being displaced in 1997 alone (Stahler-Sholk, 1998). On December 22, 1997, a group of nonviolent indigenous people, *Las Abejas* (The Bees), living in a refugee community called Acteal in the municipality of Chenalhó were attacked. Forty-five Tzotzil indigenous people, mostly women and children, were brutally massacred by paramilitaries, who cut open the wombs of pregnant mothers with machetes and cut the unborn children into little pieces in front of mothers' eyes. Days later, state police fired on demonstrators who were protesting this massacre in the town of Ocosingo, killing an indigenous woman and wounding two children. The government justified this use of military force against the indigenous peoples to reestablish "the rule of law" (see the following section) (Stahler-Sholk, 1998).

CHIAPAS TODAY: FRACTURED REBELLIONS AND ONGOING RACISM

Many towns within the Zapatista autonomous communities fractured along pro-PRI and pro-EZLN lines (Stahler-Sholk, 1998). The acceptance or not of government funds lead to either expulsion or a decision by those who joined the PRI to abandon resistance (SIPAZ Report, 2002). Some argue that the national government is actively seeking to foment divisions within local indigenous communities by lavishing subsidies on those who will accept them (Stahler-Sholk, 1998). The Mexican government distributed a subsidy of $55 per hectare of corn and coffee and $1,125 per family as compensation payments. Some have argued that these transfers, provided by government-sponsored economic aid programs (e.g., PROCAMPO), were made exclusively to PRI supporters (Stahler-Sholk, 1998). In a communiqué dated October 1, 2000, the members of *Las Abejas* in the municipality of Chenalhó[6] denounced this alleged government tactic:

> [PRI committees of Chenalhó] are forcing people to affiliate with the PRI, ... so that our municipality of Chenalhó will continue being governed by that party in upcoming elections. The persons who make up the committees are deceiving and manipulating the people through the PROGRESA and PROCAMPO programs, and they are delivering benefits, saying that the PRI is the party which helps the people. (see *www.jaguar-sun.com/chiapas/chiapas55*)

MESTIZO POWER, MEXICAN HEGEMONY, AND HUMAN RIGHTS RESPONSES

Negotiations between the EZLN and the current administration of President Vicente Fox are stalemated and a low intensity conflict marked by constant death threats and periodic killings continues, particularly targeting those who refuse to align with the party in power in the state of Chiapas. Indigenous peoples live in ongoing insecurity and fear and more than 20,000 displaced persons in Chiapas lack adequate food supplies (Stahler-Sholk, 1998). In response to the demands put forth by the EZLN, the government referred to the EZLN as a "political force in formation." Clearly, those in power do not have any interest in entering into a genuine dialogue with the EZLN.

In addition to direct violence, the government has delegitimized the pan-indigenous movement by characterizing the struggle of a majority population as either "radical intellectuals" or "refugees from neighboring Guatemala" (Perry, 1996). A closer analysis of some of these and other responses to the Zapatistas, particularly at the local level, evidence a discourse of privilege and oppression. For example, the former governor of Chiapas, Armado Avendaño, responded to the Zapatista political demands for rights by labeling the indigenous of Chiapas as "ungovernable" (Ross, 1995) and indigenous governance and customs as "primitive" (SIPAZ Report, 1998). This "official view" is blatantly discriminatory and rooted in a legacy of colonialism that values "Europeanness" over indigenous culture.

Repeated military attacks carried out in the name of "restoring order" and an official discourse that characterizes autonomous structures as "primitive" reflect an entrenched, institutionalized, and cultural racism. Responsibility for the government's *de facto* and *de jure* racist treatment of indigenous peoples is thereby buried in a language that privileges the elite; that is, the *mestizo* and a civil-political rights discourse that guarantees them protections. As Subcomandante Marcos, the Zapatista leader, stated in a communiqué dated June 10, 1994,

> The government tried to reduce the demands for autonomy to the indigenous communities, and thereby leave intact the centralist power structure that magnifies the power of the federal executive in a dictatorial manner. The demand for the autonomy of the townships was tossed aside. The law promised by the government to recognize the political, economic and cultural autonomy of the Indigenous communities follows the usual line: a law that doesn't resolve the deep-rooted problems, that isn't consensed upon within the Indigenous movement, and that is to be approved undemocratically. (Subcomandante Marcos, 1994)

Violent force and militarization, including massacres and forced displacement, have been used to repress México's indigenous peoples. These brutal strategies and tactics are combined with political strategies that fracture communities. As significantly, the dominant government discourse reduces the EZLN demands to local, isolated concerns, delegitimizing their collective struggle and their demands for cultural rights. This indirect violation of collective rights of indigenous peoples through political processes within a powerful *mestizo*-dominated government complements the direct violence and terror we described previously. Both are entrenched within unacknowledged institutionalized and structural racism and a privileging of "Europeanness" or "whiteness." The human rights discourse defended by the government is deracialized and devoid of any recognition of institutional and cultural racism and white/*mestizo* privilege.

The Zapatista movement's demand for indigenous autonomy breaks with traditional political structures based on civil-political rights. The agrarian grassroots democracy rooted in communal land ownership that they assert further challenges the current political system long dominated by one political party controlled by *mestizo* urban elites. Without an understanding by the *mestizo* ruling elites of the racial dynamics underlying the marginalization of indigenous peoples, genuine change is beyond reach.

Challenges Facing Psychologists Committed to Human Rights Work

In contexts of war and postwar, massive human rights violations are most frequently described in terms of violations of civil-political, individual rights (i.e., first-generation rights). This discourse minimizes or ignores the range of cultural and collective rights we discussed previously. Indigenous peoples of Chiapas organized themselves within the Zapatista movement and demanded recognition and respect for their traditions and customs; that is, for their second-, third-, and fourth-generation rights. They denounced institutionalized racism and the legacy of colonialism and developed communities wherein the traditional systems of land ownership and justice could be practiced. They were met by government repression and direct and indirect violence wherein thousands were displaced and hundreds wounded and murdered.

As we previously suggested, some psychologists, working here and in similar contexts, provide individual and small group work with victims of human rights violations. Others, including the authors of this essay, have sought to accompany survivors in rethreading local community as they struggle for social justice and transformation (see, e.g., Lykes et al., 2003). Yet our analysis of the Zapatista resistance and subsequent repression suggests that community-based mental health work among indigenous populations seeking to redress injustice is additionally challenged. Liberatory praxis must recognize and address the dynamics of racism and the privileging of whiteness that are frequently buried within a first-generation human rights discourse and a struggle for economic justice. Failure to address the all-too-frequent submergence of racial dynamics, such as we have described previously in the case of Chiapas, contributes to maintaining rather than challenging the systemic causes of the exploitation and oppression of indigenous groups.

The Zapatista movement — with autonomy at its center — challenges institutionalized racism and economic oppression and demands structural change. By deracializing human rights discourse and praxis, some psychologists and human rights activists may be promoting, inadvertently, the dominant power structure. Those who position themselves as "ethically neutral" are challenged to develop solidarity relations with indigenous peoples. Within a position of solidarity they can critically analyze their whiteness and racism, actively denouncing racism and *mestizo* power and promoting collective indigenous rights to autonomy. "Ethical positioning" rather than "ethical neutrality" is central to liberation psychology and to a liberatory praxis. In the case of Chiapas, liberatory psychologists would align themselves with indigenous communities and "stand under" (Lykes, 1997) their realities in order to accompany them in their struggle for social change.

A human rights discourse and practice rooted exclusively or primarily in civil-political rights *de facto* submerges racism and *mestizo*/white privilege. It fails to understand the direct (e.g., ethnocide) and indirect (e.g., institutional and cultural racism) violation of four generations of rights and their consequences for indigenous peoples. Below we suggest several provisional guidelines that inform our work and that serve as suggestions for psychologists and human rights practitioners. The guidelines seek to incorporate four generations of human rights within an antiracist and liberatory agenda and direct how we position ourselves and evolve within the dialectic of action-reflection that characterizes a psychological praxis striving for liberation. The guidelines include:

- recognizing and critically examining local, regional, and national racial dynamics, with particular focus on how racism and white privilege create and sustain oppressive structural inequalities;
- situating oneself as "other" and questioning one's own identity politics and privileges within a praxis of solidarity with oppressed communities;
- engaging with a more radical peace-building agenda by accompanying oppressed communities in social change efforts that seek to transform institutionalized racism and cultural and economic exploitation in order to promote a lasting peace with justice;
- collaborating with local oppressed communities in combining creative resources and traditional indigenous practices toward action research that analyzes root causes of social oppression; and

- actively contributing toward the co-development of community-based programs that transform structures of institutional racism and cultural and economic exploitation.

These are orienting principals, not formulas for action. Chiapas offered us a "cautionary tale." Social justice for indigenous peoples requires a dramatic rethinking of the meaning of human rights and human rights violations. As significantly, it requires a deepening understanding of traditional indigenous values and customs. A liberatory psychology or human rights praxis of accompaniment must, therefore, be explicitly antiracist and reflexive. As outsiders we are challenged to situate ourselves within an antiracist praxis, interrogating our whiteness and privilege as well as that of the power structures within which we work.

REFERENCES

Adams, R., & Bastos, S. (2003). *Las relaciones étnicas en Guatemala, 1944–2000* [Ethnic relations in Guatemala, 1944–2000]. Antigua, Guatemala: CIRMA.

Amnesty International. (1992). *Human rights violations against indigenous peoples of the Americas.* London and New York: Author.

Bracken, P. J., Giller, J. E., & Summerfield, D. (1995). Psychological responses to war and atrocity: The limitations of current concepts. *Social Science and Medicine, 40*(8), 1073–1082.

Burman, E. (Ed.). (1998). *Deconstructing feminist psychology.* London: Sage.

Castro, G., & Hidalgo, O. (1998, May 6). The future of "deep" Mexico: Reflections on autonomy. *CIEPAC, 108.* Retrieved from *http://ciepac.org/bulletins/ingles/ing108.htm*

CEH (Commission for Historical Clarification [Comisión para el Esclarecimiento Histórico]). (1999, February). *Report of the CEH.* Guatemala: Author. Available from *http://hrdata.aaas.org/ceh*

Chomsky, N. (1995). Time bombs. In E. Katzenberger (Ed.), *First World, ha ha ha! The Zapatista challenge* (pp. 175–182). San Francisco: City Lights.

Collier, G. A. (2000, March/April). Zapatismo resurgent: Land and autonomy in Chiapas. *NACLA Report on the Americas, 33*(5), 20–25.

Dawes, A. (2001). Psychologies for liberation: Views from elsewhere. In J. D. Christie, R. V. Wagner, & D. D. Winter (Eds.), *Peace, conflict, and violence: Peace psychology for the 21st century* (pp. 295–306). Englewood Cliffs, NJ: Prentice Hall.

De Castro, J. E. (2002). *Mestizo nations: Culture, race, and conformity in Latin American literature.* Tucson: University of Arizona Press.

Draft Declaration on the Rights of Indigenous Peoples. (1994). Available from *http://www.un.org*

Eth, S., & Pynoos, R. S. (1985). *Post-traumatic stress disorder in children.* Washington, DC: American Psychiatric Press.

Fanon, F. (1967). *Black skin, white masks.* New York: Grove Press.

Foley, N. (1999, May 28). A fledgling democracy confronts the legacies of racism. *Chronicle of Higher Education,* p. B7.

Fox, D., & Prilleltensky, I. (Eds.). (1997). *Critical psychology: An introduction.* Thousand Oaks, CA: Sage.

Freire, P. (1970). *Pedagogy of the oppressed.* New York: Seabury Press.

Gordon, T. (1973). Notes on white and Black psychology. *Journal of Social Issues, 29*(1), 87–95.

Gugelberger, G. M. (Ed.). (1996). *The real thing: Testimonial discourse and Latin America.* Durham, NC: Duke University Press.

Gutiérrez, G. (1973/1988). *A theology of liberation: History, politics, and salvation* (Sister C. Inda & J. Eagleson, Trans. and Eds.). Maryknoll, NY: Orbis Books.

Hansen, T. (2002). Zapatistas: A brief historical timeline. In T. Hayden (Ed.), *The Zapatista reader* (pp. 8–15). New York: Thunder's Mouth Press.

Jubilee 2000: A year of the Lord's favor; a reflection on forgiveness and reconciliation. (1998). Washington, DC: United States Catholic Conference.

Kahn, J. S. (1995). *Culture, multiculture, postculture.* London: Sage.

Kam, A. L. N. (1998). Sticks, stones and smokescreens. *New Internationalist, 298,* 34–35.

Lykes, M. B. (1997). Activist participatory research among the Maya of Guatemala: Constructing meanings from situated knowledge. *Journal of Social Issues, 53*(4), 725–746.

Lykes, M. B. (2001). Human rights violations as structural violence. In J. D. Christie, R. V. Wagner, & D. D. Winter (Eds.), *Peace, conflict, and violence: Peace psychology for the 21st century* (pp. 158–167). Englewood Cliffs, NJ: Prentice Hall.

Lykes, M. B., TerreBlanche, M., & Hamber, B. (2003). Narrating survival and change in Guatemala and South Africa: The politics of representation and a liberatory community psychology. *American Journal of Community Psychology, 31*(1/2), 79–90.

Martín-Baró, I. (1994). *Writings for a liberation psychology* (A. Aron & S. Corne, Eds.). Cambridge, MA: Harvard University Press.

Menchú Tum, R. (1998). *Crossing borders* (Ann Wright, Trans. and Ed.). New York: Verso.

Messer, E. (1995). Anthropology and human rights in Latin America. *Journal of Latin American Anthropology, 1*(1), 48–97.

Messer, E. (1997). Pluralist approaches to human rights. *Journal of Anthropological Research, 53,* 293–317.

Nagengast, C. (1997). Women, minorities, and indigenous peoples: Universalism and cultural relativity. *Journal of Anthropological Research, 53,* 349–370.

Navarro, L. H. (2002). Mexico's secret war. In T. Hayden (Ed.), *The Zapatista reader* (pp. 61–68). New York: Thunder's Mouth Press.

Opotow, S. (2001). Social injustice. In J. D. Christie, R. V. Wagner, & D. D. Winter (Eds.), *Peace, conflict, and violence: Peace psychology for the 21st century* (pp. 102–109). Englewood Cliffs, NJ: Prentice Hall.

Pereira, W. (1997). *Inhuman rights: The Western system and global human rights abuse.* New York: Other India Press.

Perry, R. J. (1996). *From time immemorial: Indigenous peoples and state systems.* Austin: University of Texas Press.

Ross, J. (1995). *Rebellion from the roots: Indian uprising in Chiapas.* Monroe, ME: Common Courage Press.

Seedat, M. (1997). The quest for liberatory psychology. *South African Journal of Psychology, 27* (4), 261–270.

SIPAZ Report (Servicio Internacional Para la Paz [International Service for Peace]). (1998, August). *The autonomous counties in Chiapas: The rock in the shoe of the Mexican government, 3*(3). Retrieved from *http://www.sipaz.org*

SIPAZ Report (Servicio Internacional Para la Paz [International Service for Peace]). (2002, December). *Autonomy: Source of conflict or the road to peace? 7*(4). Retrieved from *http://www.sipaz.org*

Stahler-Sholk, R. (1998, March/April). The lessons of Acteal. *NACLA Report on the Americas, 31*(5), 11–14.

Subcomandante Marcos. (1994, June 12). The rejection of the dialogue for peace and reconciliation in Chiapas. *La Jornada.*

Taracena Arriola, A. (2002). *Etnicidad, estado y nación en Guatemala, 1808–1944* [Ethnicity, state and nation in Guatemala, 1808–1944] (Vol. 1). Guatemala: Nawal Wuj.

Thompson, R. H. (1997). Ethnic minorities and the case for collective rights. *American Anthropologist, 99*(4), 786–798.

Universal human rights versus cultural relativity [Special issue]. (1997). *Journal of Anthropological Research, 53*(3), 269–381.

van der Gaag, N. (1998). No hiding place. *The New Internationalist, 298,* 7–11.

Warren, K. B. (1998). *Indigenous movements and their critics: Pan-Maya activism in Guatemala.* Princeton, NJ: Princeton University Press.

Watts, R., & Serrano-Garcia, R. (2003). The community psychology of liberation: Responses to oppression [Special issue]. *American Journal of Community Psychology, 31*(1/2).

White, J. L., & Parham, T. A. (1990). *The psychology of blacks: An Afro-American perspective* (2nd ed.). Englewood Cliffs, NJ: Prentice Hall.

Women of ADMI (Asociacion de la Mujer Maya Ixil [Association of Mayan Ixil Women]), & Lykes, M. B. (2000). *Voces e imágenes: Mujeres Mayas Ixiles de Chajul/Voices and images: Mayan Ixil women of Chajul.* Guatemala: MagnaTerra.

NOTES

1. The term is a translation of the Spanish term *estadounidense* (see Gugelberger, 1996, p. 4, also Note 4, p. 119). It is used here rather than the more common "American" because this latter term includes reference to all citizens of the Americas, that is, of Canada, México, Central and South America, and the United States of America.

2. *Ejidos* are communal landholdings where indigenous communities produced food for their own subsistence, selling a few cash crops whenever possible.

3. PRI is the Spanish acronym for the Mexican political party, Institutional Revolutionary Party (*Partido Revolucionario Institucional*). Established in 1929, it changed names several times and since 1946 all Mexican presidents and most local and regional elected officials have belonged to the PRI, which often has been accused of corruption, electoral fraud, and government inaction. In 2000, Vicente Fox Quesada (PAN — National Action Party [Partido Acción Nacional]) became México's president ending 71 years of rule by the PRI. Local elections have been hotly contested as the PRI seeks to retain power and regain the presidency.

4. *Criollo* refers to a Mexican-born Spaniard.

5. These accords marked a first concrete step toward peace and a dialogue process. What was to follow was a series of discussions that would eventually lead to the construction of further accords addressing other demands to the improve conditions for indigenous communities in Chiapas and further transform political, economic, and social life. These accords included Democracy and Justice, Well-Being and Development, and the Situation of Women.

6. In Chenalhó, as in all Chiapas villages, there was only one political party, the PRI, which typically won close to 100% of votes in local and national elections. After 1994, however, villagers openly supported the EZLN, casting votes for their candidates (see *http//lanic.utexas.edu/la/region/news/arc/lasnet/1997/0340.html*).

TWENTY-FIVE

Racial Wrongs and Restitutions: The Role of Guilt and Other Group-Based Emotions

Aarti Iyer, Colin Wayne Leach, and Anne Pedersen

Racial inequality is everywhere. Throughout the world, people of color tend to be disadvantaged relative to those classified as "white." There is little doubt that the historical indenture, enslavement, and colonization of people of color has contributed to this systemic inequality. It is also clear that contemporary forms of group privilege and discrimination carry racial inequality into the present and future. This seeming intransigence has led many an observer to conclude that racial inequality is an unavoidable product of diverse societies (e.g., Sidanius & Pratto, 1999).

Given the apparent inevitability of racial inequality, one might wonder how anyone is able to muster opposition to it. Yet, a subset of people in every society opposes racial inequality, sometimes at great personal risk. This surprising, and extremely important, fact is our focus. We want to know why people oppose racial inequality. We are especially interested in why members of advantaged groups oppose systems of inequality from which they benefit.

In this paper we examine how members of advantaged groups come to recognize, and react against, the illegitimacy of racial inequality. We give special attention to group-based guilt as one way in which the advantaged respond to racial wrongs. The first section reviews the conceptual and empirical arguments for *what racial guilt is*. Because it is an unpleasant feeling of self-blame that people prefer to assuage, group-based guilt is associated with efforts to make restitution to those harmed. This is *what guilt does* to motivate opposition to racial inequality. In the second section, we examine the relationship between guilt and two forms of racial restitution at issue in contemporary politics: apology and compensation. After characterizing what racial guilt is and what it does, we describe the *limits of guilt* in the third section. We argue that, despite its association with restitution, guilt is neither a frequent response to racial advantage nor a basis of general opposition to racial inequality. Given these limits, we move *beyond guilt* in the last section to consider other emotional reactions to racial inequality. Group-based emotions such as sympathy and moral outrage do not emphasize self-blame, and thus should be important bases of support for general efforts against racial inequality.

GUILT IS . . .

Available theory and research suggest that group-based guilt is characterized by three interrelated properties: a focus of attention on the group self, a sense of group responsibility for an immoral act, and an extremely unpleasant feeling that people prefer to assuage through restitution or avoidance.

. . . Self-Focused

Several approaches to emotion conceptualize guilt as focused more on the self than on other people (see Ortony, Clore, & Collins, 1988; Salovey & Rosenhan, 1989; Weiner, 1982). Personal guilt, for example, is a self-conscious reflection of one's immoral behavior as an individual (Tangney & Fischer, 1995; Weiner, 1982). This self-focus leads people who feel guilt to attend less to those they have wronged and more to how they themselves feel about their transgression. Those who feel personal guilt think about themselves much more than they think about others (Baumeister, Reis, & Delespaul, 1995). Thus, the relatively self-focused nature of guilt makes it seem more a selfish concern for one's own pain than a sympathetic concern for others (Batson, 1998; Steele, 1990).

Feeling guilty about what one's group has done should also focus attention more on the self than on the victimized other (Leach, Snider, & Iyer, 2002). Unlike personal guilt, however, group-based guilt focuses attention on the group self rather than on the individual self (Branscombe, Doosje, & McGarty, 2002). This self-focus is suggested by several studies that have produced group-based guilt by directing the advantaged group's attention to their position relative to disadvantaged or harmed outgroups. For example, Montada and Schneider (1989) assessed the guilt Germans felt when thinking about their economic advantage over migrant workers; Doosje, Branscombe, Spears, and Manstead (1998) assessed the guilt felt by in-group members when they were told that previous in-group members had mistreated an out-group; and Swim and Miller (1999) assessed the guilt European Americans felt in response to the inequality between "whites" and "blacks" in the United States.

Although these studies relied on (group) self-focus to produce (group-based) guilt, none of them directly examined focus of attention. The self-focus of attention presumed in group-based guilt has been more directly examined in recent research by Iyer, Leach, and Crosby (2003), who used both self-focused and other-focused beliefs about inequality to predict general feelings of "white" guilt (see the left half of Figure 1 for a conceptual representation of this model). Iyer et al. (2003, Study 1) measured European American students' belief that their group enjoyed privileges and benefits because they are "white." Taken from Swim and Miller's (1999) research, these questions assessed belief in a self-focused form of racial inequality by emphasizing European Americans' systemic advantages. Iyer et al. also assessed participants' belief in an other-focused form of racial inequality. These other-focused questions measured the belief that African Americans face racial discrimination in several important domains, such as housing and employment (see Swim & Miller, 1999).

Confirming the self-focused nature of guilt, only the self-focused belief in privilege independently predicted feelings of "white" guilt. The other-focused belief that African Americans face discrimination did not independently predict general feelings of "white" guilt. These findings were confirmed in a second study using different methods and measures (Iyer et al., 2003,

Belief in Inequality   Group-based Emotion   Intention/Action

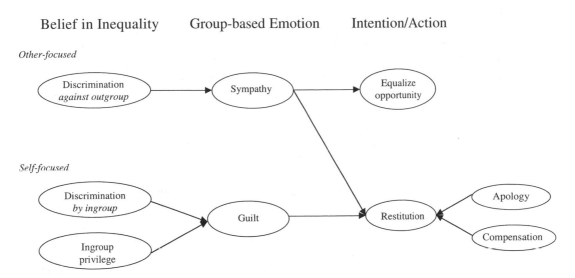

Figure 1. Conceptual model predicting support for restitution and equal opportunity strategies.

Study 2). Rather then presenting European Americans with scales to assess their belief in self-focused privilege and other-focused discrimination, Iyer et al. manipulated focus of attention with a subtle linguistic change in a measure of perceived racial discrimination. To encourage a self-focus, the researchers asked European American participants if they believed that European Americans discriminated on the basis of race. To encourage an other-focus, the authors reworded the items slightly to ask if African Americans faced racial discrimination. This change in the subject of the sentences was expected to lead participants to focus either on their fellow European Americans as perpetrators or on African Americans as targets. As in their first study, Iyer et al. (2003, Study 2) found higher levels of "white" guilt when participants (self-) focused on their group as perpetrators than when they (other-) focused on the targets of the group's discrimination. Thus, Iyer et al.'s research on European American guilt regarding racial inequality shows this form of group-based guilt to be self-focused in nature. As we discuss below, this self-focus has important implications for guilt's other characteristics.

... Based in Group Responsibility for an Immoral Act

Feelings of personal guilt focus people's attention specifically on their personal responsibility for an immoral act (Kugler & Jones, 1992; Roseman, Spindel, & Jose, 1990). Although those who feel guilty wish that they had not acted immorally (Roseman, Wiest, & Swartz, 1994), their sense of guilt is based in taking responsibility for what they have done to harm others (Frijda, Kuipers, & ter Shure, 1989; O'Connor, Berry, Weiss, Bush, & Sampson, 1997; C. A. Smith & Ellsworth, 1985; Weiner, 1982). Similarly, group-based guilt is grounded in the belief that one's group is responsible for an immoral act against another group (Leach et al., 2002).

This sense of responsibility may operate more or less directly in group-based guilt (Leach et al.,

2002). A rather indirect form of group-based guilt can occur when people's group membership *associates* them with those who have committed moral violations (Branscombe et al., 2002). For example, Doosje et al. (1998, Study 2) induced "guilt by association" by giving Dutch students clear evidence that Dutch colonists had treated Indonesians unfairly *in the past*. Although these Dutch participants did not feel directly responsible for the injustices their ancestors had perpetrated, they felt guilty because the perpetrators had been Dutch like them. This type of "guilt by association" seems likely in situations where group members are made to face their ancestors' harmful actions, and it may lead people to take steps to acknowledge their group's past wrongdoing. Such actions include contemporary discussions of replacing Columbus Day with Indigenous people's day in the Americas, the building of a monument to slavery in the Netherlands, and "sorry day" to remember the European invasion of Australia and its negative repercussions.

Group members may also feel responsible for their group's *collective misdeeds in the present*. This kind of shared responsibility for current wrongs should promote a more direct kind of guilt, or "guilt proper." Guilt proper can be based in the belief that one's group benefits illegitimately from institutionalized privilege. For example, some "white" people believe that they as a group enjoy unearned group privileges in racially biased societies. These may vary from the privilege of seeing one's group well represented in the media to the privilege of not fearing the possibility of racial discrimination (Lipsitz, 1998; McIntosh, 1989). Given that this kind of group privilege is accorded all people ascribed to the social category "white," all those who see themselves as belonging to this group can believe that they benefit from illegitimate racial inequality (Hoffman, 1976; Leach et al., 2002). Believing that this kind of group privilege benefits one as a group member has recently been shown to promote group-based guilt. For example, Swim and Miller (1999) showed European American students' level of guilt over racial inequality to be strongly associated with the degree to which they believed European Americans benefited from racial privilege (see also Iyer et al., 2003, Study 1; relatedly, see Branscombe's 1998 study of gender privilege).

Guilt proper can also be based in the belief that one's group is (collectively) responsible for discrimination against another group. As mentioned above, Iyer et al. (2003, Study 2) showed that perceiving one's group as responsible for racial discrimination leads to greater levels of group-based guilt than does simply acknowledging the existence of discrimination. Again, in this study Iyer et al. asked European American students one of two sets of subtly different questions regarding contemporary racial discrimination. In one form of questioning, they asked participants to indicate the degree to which they believed that *"whites" discriminate on the basis of race* in housing, employment, college admissions, and other dimensions. These self-focused questions identified European Americans as those responsible for racial discrimination. In an other-focused version, these questions were rephrased to ask if African Americans faced racial discrimination in these same areas. The other-focused questions emphasized only the existence of discrimination against African Americans. Iyer et al. (2003, Study 2) found that participants assigned to the self-focused questions were more likely to experience guilt than those assigned to the other-focused questions. Thus, European Americans faced with questions that focused attention on the in-group's responsibility for racial discrimination were more likely to report feeling guilty about racial inequality.

... An Unpleasant Feeling That People Prefer to Assuage Through Avoidance or Restitution

People do not enjoy feeling guilty. Personal guilt is associated with a "sinking feeling" (Roseman et al., 1994), mainly because it is uncomfortable to focus on oneself as personally responsible for an immoral act (Baumeister, Stillwell, & Heatherton, 1994). Indeed, personal guilt is experienced as an extreme dysphoria because accepting responsibility for a transgression threatens one's self-image as a good person (Tangney & Fischer, 1995).

This unpleasant self-blame motivates people to rid themselves of the personal guilt they feel (Estrada-Hollenbach & Heatherton, 1998; Frijda, 1986). People often seem to rid themselves of guilt by challenging the reasons they feel guilt in the first place. Thus, guilt may be most easily assuaged by undermining the basis for the guilt feeling itself (Leach et al., 2002). This can be accomplished by perceiving less personal responsibility for an immoral act or by shifting attention away from the self (Batson, 1998; Estrada-Hollenbach & Heatherton, 1998; Schmitt, Branscombe, & Brehm, 2004).

Sometimes, however, guilt is not so easily escaped. In such cases, guilt can be most directly assuaged by providing restitution to those harmed (O'Connor et al., 1997; Salovey, Mayer, & Rosenhan, 1991; Tangney, Miller, Flicker, & Barlow, 1996). Efforts at restitution seek to repair the damage done by one's wrongdoing by restoring morality to the intergroup relation. In this way, attempts at restitution seek a "restorative justice" for both perpetrator and victim. Archbishop Desmond Tutu, a central figure in the South African Truth and Reconciliation Commission's efforts to cope with the great injustices of apartheid, contrasts the notion of restorative justice to the concern for punishment central to retributive justice:

> Retributive justice is largely Western. The African understanding is far more restorative —
> not so much to punish as to redress or restore balance that has been knocked askew. The
> justice we hope for is restorative of the dignity of the people. (Minow, 1998, p. 81)

Given their sense of responsibility for immorality, those feeling guilt are highly motivated to make restitution. Emotion research has shown guilt to be associated with two particular forms of restitution: apology (Roseman et al., 1994) and material compensation (Baumeister et al., 1994; Niedenthal, Tangney, & Gavanski, 1994). By apologizing for wrongdoing, perpetrators show their (restored) respect for morality and justice (Minow, 1998). Perpetrators' attempts to compensate victims for the harm they have caused seek to restore morality in a similar way. By compensating victims, perpetrators acknowledge that something tangible was destroyed by their injustice. Material compensation may seek to restore both the material and the moral loss.

As with guilt in general, group-based guilt should motivate these same forms of restitution. Unlike personal guilt, however, group-based guilt should motivate apology and compensation to the out-group on behalf of the in-group. That is, group-based guilt should be associated with group efforts at restitution, in the form of collective apology or compensation to the aggrieved group (but see McGarty & Bliuc, 2004).

GUILT DOES ...

... Promote Group Apology

Several official group representatives have stated that they feel bad about their group's mistreatment of other groups. For example, on a recent visit to South Korea, Japan's Prime Minister Junichiro Koizumi expressed his "heartfelt remorse and sorrow over the great pain and suffering inflicted on South Koreans by Japan's colonial rule" ("Japanese Premier," 2001, p. B6). Remorse is a term closely related to guilt, in that both express a sense of responsibility for wrongdoing (Wierzbicka, 1992). By stating his remorse, the Japanese prime minister was accepting collective responsibility for his country's misdeeds.

Across the world, those harmed by racial inequality and their allies are asking for formal apologies, because apologies imply responsibility and guilt. At the 2001 UN Conference, for example, a number of African delegates expressed disappointment that the former slave-trading countries did not apologize for their role in slavery (Constable, 2001). Political efforts have been mobilized worldwide in an effort to force societies — and the governments that represent them — to admit guilt and to apologize for collective wrongdoing. In the United States, for instance, there is a growing political and legal effort to pressure the government into offering an official apology for the enslavement of the Africans from whom most African Americans have descended (V. E. Smith, 2001; for a review see Brooks, 1999).

In Australia, there is serious debate over whether the Australian federal government should apologize to Indigenous Australians for the injustices they have endured. In two recent studies, McGarty et al. (2002) examined the emotional basis of Australians' support for a government apology. In one survey of 164 randomly selected non-Indigenous residents of Perth, Western Australia, they used Swim and Miller's (1999) measures of perceived "white" privilege and guilt to predict support for an official government apology. It is important to note, however, that the overall level of support for an apology was low. That is, only 27% of the Perth sample believed the federal government should apologize for the treatment of Indigenous Australians.

Given that feelings of personal guilt are strongly associated with the desire to apologize to those harmed by one's actions (Roseman et al., 1994), McGarty et al. (2002) reasoned that a similar process should operate at the group level. Thus, the (limited) support demonstrated for apology should be associated with guilt. Indeed, McGarty et al. (2002, Study 1) showed "white" guilt to independently predict support for an official government apology to Indigenous people. Importantly, a mediation analysis showed that the belief that "whites" are advantaged relative to Indigenous people predicted support for an apology in part because perceived advantage was associated with greater guilt. Thus, believing in "white" advantage predicted guilt, which in turn predicted support for an official government apology. The structure of this conceptual model is shown in the bottom half of Figure 1.

McGarty et al.'s findings confirm group-based guilt as a self-focused feeling of responsibility that serves as the basis for restitutive apology (see also Zebel, Doosje, & Spears, 2004). The results of this questionnaire study are also corroborated by a recent qualitative study of everyday discourse in Australia. In an analysis of personal opinions e-mailed to a newspaper Web site, Lecouteur and Augoustinos (2001) found that people opposed to saying "sorry" defined an apology as implying responsibility and guilt. Thus, opposition to an apology was explained as opposition to the acceptance of responsibility and, by extension, opposition to feelings of guilt.

... Promote Material Compensation

Providing material compensation for the damage done is another form of collective restitution that can assuage group-based guilt (Baumeister et al., 1994; Niedenthal et al., 1994). By compensating those victimized by one's (group's) immoral actions, the guilty seek to make restitution by providing some material equivalent of the harm done. In the United States, tens of thousands of African Americans have applied for tax credits from the government based in the myth that this is an available form of compensation for the enslavement of their ancestors (Kristof, 2002). More formally, several groups are currently pursuing legal action against the government and private corporations as illegitimate beneficiaries of slavery (V. E. Smith, 2001; for a review see Brooks,

1999). These groups hope to gain legal judgments that will force the responsible parties to compensate the descendants of the slaves upon whose labor the parties made profit. Winning this kind of court-ordered compensation is dependent on a legal demonstration of the perpetrator's responsibility for the harm done. In this way, victims of injustice appeal to perpetrators to accept responsibility and (legal, if not emotional) guilt.

Although current efforts to force reparations for slavery in the United States are meeting with little success, there is supportive precedent for the provision of compensation as restitution. In the 1980s, for example, the Japanese American Citizens League lobbied the U.S. Congress for both an apology and financial reparations for the wrongful internment of Japanese Americans during World War II. In 1988, the Civil Liberties Act awarded each survivor $20,000 and an official letter of apology from President Bush (Minow, 1998; Nagata, 1990). Although the United States took more than 40 years to make reparations to the interned Japanese Americans, soon after World War II the United States and its allies forced Germany and Japan to compensate those countries damaged by invasion and war. War reparations are perhaps the most long-standing precedent for such direct material compensation to victims of injustice (Minow, 1998).

Postapartheid South Africa provides another example of timely efforts at collective compensation. In 1995 the first democratically elected parliament in South Africa created a Committee on Reparation and Rehabilitation as part of the larger Truth and Reconciliation Committee. This committee was empowered to fund direct financial compensation as well as the provision of health and social care to victims of apartheid (Minow, 1998). In addition, South Africa's postapartheid Constitution (1996) and the more recent Employment Equity Act (1998) enable affirmative action to be used to compensate those hurt by past discriminatory laws (Tummala, 1999). The notion that victimized groups can be compensated by favoring them in hiring, promotion, and educational access decisions is codified in South African law. Similarly, India has practiced a system of "reservation" since its independence in 1947 to compensate for past and present discrimination on the basis of caste (Hodges-Aeberhard, 1999).

Social psychological research is consistent with the notion that guilt is associated with efforts at compensation. For example, research by Doosje et al. (1998, Study 2) supports the idea that "guilt by association" motivates efforts at restitution. Doosje et al. (1998) found that Dutch students who felt guilty about their country's colonial exploitation of Indonesia were more likely to support compensation by giving money to a "good cause" in Indonesia.

There also is evidence that the more direct form of group-based guilt motivates support for the adoption of compensatory state policies. Iyer et al. (2003, Studies 1 and 2) examined the predictors of European Americans' support for compensatory affirmative action, a policy that frames preference for African Americans in hiring and college admissions as compensation for racial discrimination. In both studies, Iyer et al. showed that guilt independently predicted support for compensatory affirmative action. Guilt also partially mediated the relationship between belief in "white" privilege and support for compensatory affirmative action (Study 1). This suggests that support for compensation can be based more straightforwardly in the belief that group inequality exists and also that group-based guilt is an important basis of the desire to compensate for injustices.

Guilt Is Not . . .

We have argued that guilt is an extremely unpleasant feeling based in a self-focused sense of responsibility for immorality. This self-focus motivates those who have harmed others to make up for their wrongdoing. As such, people who feel guilty seek to provide restitution. In the case of racial wrongdoing, "white" guilt promotes efforts to compensate and/or apologize to those disadvantaged by racial inequality. We believe that this is what group-based guilt is and what group-based guilt does.

Despite its role in efforts at restitution, however, guilt has serious limitations as a response to group wrongs (Leach et al., 2002). In our view, this is due to two factors. The first is that guilt is, in fact, infrequent. Given the extreme dysphoria caused by this self-focused and self-blaming emotion, guilt is avoided when possible. Thus, by its very nature, guilt is rare (Branscombe et al., 2002; Leach et al., 2002). This infrequency limits guilt as a basis for action against group inequality. Second, even when experienced, guilt's narrow concern for restitution may limit it as a basis for other efforts against inequality and injustice. Thus, the many nonrestitutive efforts against inequality in operation at present may find little support among those feeling group-based guilt.

... Frequent

Members of racially advantaged groups try to avoid the experience of group-based guilt (Branscombe et al., 2002; Leach et al., 2002). Such avoidance may occur even in situations where the group's responsibility for inequality is indisputable. South Africa's handling of racial inequality is one particularly striking case. Although the postapartheid South African Constitution encourages the consideration of membership in disadvantaged groups in employment and education decisions, several judges have still questioned this form of compensation in recent lawsuits (Hodges-Aeberhard, 1999). Even in a society that had such clear and brutal forms of institutionalized discrimination that were only recently repealed, many members of the groups advantaged by these systems fail to experience guilt (Leach, 2002).

The low prevalence of guilt is likely due to the fact that "white" people, as members of the advantaged group, do not tend to believe that people of color are disadvantaged as a group. As discussed above, group-based guilt is based on the notion that one's group has done something wrong. If many group members do not believe that the in-group enjoys systemic advantages, there is little reason to feel guilt.

In a recent study, McGarty et al. (2002, Study 1) found that group-based guilt is infrequent among the non-Indigenous residents of Perth, Western Australia. Indeed, only 14% of the sample expressed explicit agreement with questions assessing guilt regarding inequality between Indigenous and non-Indigenous people. These low levels of guilt appear to be due to the fact that very few non-Indigenous people believe that the Indigenous are, in fact, disadvantaged. Thus, less than half of the respondents (36%) perceived Indigenous Australians to be disadvantaged relative to non-Indigenous Australians. Much more prominent is the belief that Indigenous people have an unfair advantage over other Australians. In fact, nearly half of McGarty et al.'s (2002) "white" respondents (44%) saw themselves as disadvantaged compared with Indigenous people.

It seems that this reversal of perceived disadvantage is based in the belief that there is "reverse racism" against "white" people. An analysis of open-ended questions asked of McGarty et al.'s sample of Western Australians supports this notion (see Waller, Mansell, Koh, Raja, & Pedersen, 2001). For example, one respondent said, "They [Indigenous Australians] are paid to attend school, driving lessons and licenses are paid for, school excursions, etc. Whites don't get these benefits." Another complained, "As we are all considered to be 'Australian' we should all be treated the same and all the extra benefits and privileges for the Aborigines — mostly money ones — should be stopped. At the moment the discrimination is against non-Indigenous people — who have to work for everything they get. It's not handed to them on a platter — as is with the Indigenous people."

The belief that it is non-Indigenous people who are disadvantaged appears to be perpetuated by the notion that the government provides outlandish support to Indigenous Australians. For example, one respondent said, "I understand that the Government spends over $50,000 a year on each of the people who claim they are Indigenous." Another seemed to agree, stating, "Aborigines should pay land tax and rates on the land." Such beliefs appear to be widespread. Indeed, Pedersen, Contos, Griffiths, Bishop, and Walker (2000) recently showed two randomly selected samples of non-Indigenous Australians to have completely unfounded beliefs that Indigenous people are granted illegitimate advantages by the government. For example, 65% of respondents erroneously believed that Indigenous Australians get more social security benefits than do non-Indigenous Australians.

Denying that racial inequality exists is a straightforward way to prevent feelings of group-based guilt. Often, however, members of advantaged groups do recognize racial inequality and turn to other strategies to avoid feeling guilty about it. For example, they may deny responsibility for inequality or avoid responsibility for inequality by distancing themselves from the disadvantaged. Both of these strategies may be based in an attempt to preserve a sense of positive group identity.

Refusing responsibility. Although the advantaged may believe that group inequality exists, they can refuse any responsibility for it and thus avoid experiencing group-based guilt. Iyer et al. (2003, Study 2) examined the extent to which European American students believe in racial discrimination when it was framed explicitly in terms of in-group responsibility or out-group disadvantage. Half the participants completed a measure of the self-focused belief that European Americans discriminate against African Americans, and the other half completed a measure of the other-focused belief that African Americans face racial discrimination. Participants in the self-focused condition were less likely to believe in the existence of racial discrimination than were participants in the other-focused condition. In other words, European Americans were less likely to believe that racial discrimination is a problem when their own group was held responsible for the wrongdoing.

Most official expressions of dysphoria over group wrongs appear to avoid direct acceptance of collective responsibility and, thus, also avoid feelings of guilt. For example, Australian Prime Minister John Howard has recently expressed "regret" about the past treatment of Indigenous Australians. In a similar fashion, the 2001 United Nations Conference Against Racism, Racial Discrimination, Xenophobia, and Related Intolerance expressed "profound regret" for modern slavery (Constable, 2001). The semantics here are important because, unlike "guilt" or "remorse," terms such as "regret" and "sorrow" imply no sense of responsibility for wrongdoing (Ortony et al., 1988; Wierzbicka, 1992). To regret what has happened is simply to wish that it had not happened. To express guilt or remorse on behalf of the group is to accept collective responsibility for a misdeed.

The absence of guilt (and thus felt responsibility) in these official statements suggests that these advantaged groups have made no attempt to apologize for the mistreatment they acknowledge. Formal apologies are based in perceived responsibility and guilt. When guilt is not felt because responsibility for wrongdoing is not acknowledged, there is no desire for restitution through apology or compensation.

Avoidance through distance. The unpleasant state of guilt may also be avoided by physically or psychologically distancing oneself from those harmed by one's immorality (for a review see Batson, 1998). That is, one can simply walk away from, or ignore, the harm one has caused others. This may be accomplished by seeing those harmed as less than human (Baumeister et al., 1994) or by blaming the disadvantaged for their (group's) low status (Branscombe et al., 2002). In this way, the disadvantaged are perceived as outside of one's moral system and therefore not worthy of any attention or assistance (Opotow, 1990). This kind of dehumanization appears to have allowed many European and European American slave holders; for example, to deny basic human rights to large classes of people without guilt (Leach, 2002).

Protecting group identity. People who are highly identified with their group may be especially motivated to avoid feeling group-based guilt. This is due to the fact that the experience of guilt threatens group members' social identity, as it calls attention to the misdeeds or illegitimate advantages of their group. In a study of Dutch students' feelings of group-based guilt, Doosje et al. (1998, Study 2) presented participants with somewhat ambiguous evidence of the Netherlands' past misdeeds in Indonesia. Participants who were highly identified with the in-group experienced less group-based guilt than did those who were less identified with the in-group. Doosje et al. (1998) argued that the high identifiers were more invested in the positive image of the in-group, and thus were more defensive about their group's past actions.

... A Basis of General Opposition to Inequality

There are many reasons that members of advantaged groups will not feel guilt in response to racial inequality. On the rare occasions that they do, however, we have argued that guilt is associated with group efforts at restitution, typically in the form of apology or material compensation. As outlined above, group-based guilt is associated with restitution mainly because the experience focuses attention on the in-group self's responsibility for wrongdoing. Both apology and compensation have the potential to restore justice and morality to the intergroup relation by addressing the group's responsibility for the harm done. Through restitution, those feeling guilt can assuage their extremely unpleasant feelings of self-recrimination. Restitution is only one strategy against group inequality, however. Guilt's narrow focus on restitution may limit its role in other forms of opposition to inequality.

Compensation, for example, is only one type of policy that seeks to combat racial inequality. There are other strategies that may be just as, or more, effective at opposing racial inequality. Most affirmative action programs that seek to reduce racial inequality in the United States are not characterized by compensation. Such programs might focus on monitoring hiring practices to detect discrimination or on increasing the opportunities of disadvantaged groups by recruiting them to apply for positions they would not otherwise know about (Kravitz et al., 1997). Given its narrow focus on restitution through compensation, group-based guilt should not provide a basis of support for these equal opportunity policies that do not explicitly focus on compensation. This has been shown recently in the previously mentioned research by Iyer et al. (2003).

Iyer et al. (2003, Study 2) used feelings of "white" guilt to predict support for two kinds of affirmative action programs. One form of affirmative action was described as compensating for past and present racial discrimination by encouraging preferential treatment for African Americans in employment and education. Another type of policy was presented as an equal opportunity program that sought to encourage African Americans to apply for positions and to provide limited support to qualified applicants. This latter, noncompensatory, form of affirmative action is by far the most commonly used and most-supported program in the United States (Kravitz et al., 1997). Despite its prevalence and popularity, however, support for affirmative action aimed at increasing opportunities was not predicted by "white" guilt over racial inequality. European American guilt was associated only with support for affirmative action that sought to compensate African Americans for racial discrimination and injustice (Iyer et al., 2003, Study 2).

Why should guilt be limited in this way? As we argued above, guilt is associated with restitution because it can restore morality to the intergroup relation. In this way, restitution can reestablish the moral value of both perpetrator and victim. Those feeling guilty, however, appear to be particularly concerned with their sense of themselves as moral and good people. Acts of restitution may be more focused on restoring a sense of self that has been challenged by self-blame. Noncompensatory policies are not concerned with restitution and therefore should not serve to assuage feelings of guilt. Guilt thus should not serve as a basis of support for such policies.

Guilt's particular association with compensation can be taken as a sign of its narrow self-focus. This strong concern for self-redemption through restitution is the main reason that some characterize guilt as a potentially selfish motivation to help others (Batson, 1998; Steele, 1990). Research on helping behavior has shown self-focused negative emotions, such as guilt, to provide only limited motivation to help the disadvantaged (Batson, 1998; Salovey & Rosenhan, 1989). This research suggests that emotions that focus on the plight of the disadvantaged themselves provide bases of more general support for helping behavior. For these same reasons, other-focused emotional reactions to racial inequality may provide a basis of opposition to a wider range of strategies against inequality.

Beyond Guilt

Sympathy

Sympathy is an emotional reaction to recognizing and understanding the thoughts, feelings, and intentions of others (Salovey & Rosenhan, 1989).[1] As a response to another's distress, sympathy is based in identification with another and his or her misfortune. It is a relatively other-focused emotion, as attention is paid to the victim's suffering rather than to one's own position in the inequality (Leach et al., 2002). For these reasons, group-based sympathy offers an important contrast to the more self-focused feeling of group-based guilt.

Iyer et al. (2003, Study 2) compared group-based sympathy with group-based guilt. As a first conceptual step, Iyer et al. examined the other-focused nature of group-based sympathy. Half of their European American participants completed a measure of the self-focused belief that European Americans discriminate on the basis of race. The other half completed a measure assessing their other-focused beliefs that African Americans are discriminated against (without naming specific perpetrators). Participants who were considering their other-focused belief in discrimination were more likely to experience feelings of sympathy than were participants concentrating on their self-focused belief in discrimination. This finding confirms that group-based sympathy is relatively other-focused in orientation.

Directing attention to the victim tends to increase helping behavior (for reviews see Batson, 1998; Salovey & Rosenhan, 1989). This is why sympathy has been suggested as a motivation for sustained prosocial activism (Hoffman, 1991). Thus, when members of socially advantaged groups focus on those disadvantaged by inequality, they should wish to help them (as illustrated in Figure 1). In the case of racial inequality in the United States, affirmative action can be regarded as one way of helping the disadvantaged (Pratkanis & Turner, 1999). As both compensatory and equal opportunity affirmative action policies seek to help the disadvantaged, sympathy should serve as a basis of support for both types of policies. This sets sympathy apart from guilt, which is associated only with compensatory approaches to opposing inequality.

In their comparison of group-based guilt and sympathy, Iyer et al. (2003, Study 2) found support for these ideas. European American sympathy for African Americans was strongly associated with support for equal opportunity affirmative action and was somewhat associated with support for compensatory affirmative action. This is in sharp contrast to guilt, which only predicted support for compensatory affirmative action. Thus, sympathy appears to serve as a broader impetus than guilt of support for racial equality.

Sympathy is, however, a helping emotion (Batson, 1998; Weiner, 1982). It does not excite the same kind of direct action against systems of inequality that is part of other system-focused emotions such as a specific kind of anger called moral outrage (Montada & Schneider, 1989; see also Frijda, 1986; Ortony et al., 1988; Weiner, 1982).

Moral Outrage

As a response to relative advantage, moral outrage is quite similar to guilt. Both group-based emotions are based in recognition of illegitimate inequality, and both are directed at placing blame for this inequality. The key difference between them, however, is focus of attention: moral outrage places blame for the inequality on the system or a third party — it is a more system-focused response (Leach et al., 2002). This means that the experience of moral outrage does not include self-recrimination. Rather, because there is no self-blame involved, people who experience moral outrage have no qualms about demanding a change in the existing status system. Indeed, this justice-oriented emotion is both a statement against illegitimate advantage and a call to action (Leach et al., 2002). Moral outrage thus should be a powerful motivator of efforts toward justice and equality (Goodman, 2001).

Anger at the system or the government for racial inequality is a basis for action for many activists who are members of privileged groups. Tim Wise, a European American antiracism activist said, "My job is to do everything in my power to resist collaborating with what I consider a truly evil system — nothing more, nothing less. It's really about using my white (and male) privilege — as a weapon against the very system that bestows the privileges to begin with" (Brasel, 1999, p. 1). The Anti-Racism Campaign, a Dublin-based group of native Irish people formed "to combat anti-refugee and anti-immigrant hysteria," proclaimed, "The Irish government is determined to pursue a mean-spirited and penny-pinching attitude to asylum seekers and immigrants. The deportation of asylum seekers and the stirring up of racism is part of this. That is why it is important that a strong and vibrant anti-racism movement is built" (Anti-Racism Campaign, 2000, p. 1). Jeff Hitchcock argued that anger and moral outrage are important to galvanizing antiracism actions among all "white" people: "When white people finally free ourselves from the blinders our culture imposes upon us, we feel … anger. In time the anger gets channeled into activism, words and deeds intended to make our country live up to its values of freedom and democracy" (Hitchcock, 1999, p. 1).

Very little empirical work has examined moral outrage as a response to relative advantage. In one of the few studies on group-based moral outrage, Montada and Schneider (1989) found that feelings of moral outrage predict efforts at social change. In their study, German nationals' feelings of moral outrage at social inequality were a strong predictor of a commitment to helping disadvantaged groups. In fact, moral outrage was a stronger predictor than guilt of every prosocial activity in the study, including giving monetary contributions, signing a petition, or participating in demonstrations. The system focus of moral outrage makes it a better predictor than guilt of general support for social change strategies (Montada & Schneider, 1989).

Our recent research in Australia is also suggestive of the way that moral outrage against a system of inequality can motivate political action. Pedersen, Iyer, and Leach (2002) conducted a survey of nearly 200 residents of Perth, Western Australia, who identified themselves as politically active in Aboriginal issues. These respondents saw Indigenous people in Australia as extremely disadvantaged compared with non-Indigenous people. This belief in racial inequality was strongly associated with feelings of anger and outrage. As one 31-year-old woman said in an open-ended response, "I feel sad and angry that politicians and the media demonstrate no strong leadership in the changing of public opinion." For these politically active pro-Indigenous people, their moral outrage was predictive of greater support for a federal apology and greater intentions for political action in support of an apology (e.g., writing letters to the editor, marching in protest, voting). Although guilt over racial inequality was positively associated with this moral outrage, guilt was not itself strongly related to support for an apology or intentions of political action. Thus, there is some preliminary evidence that moral outrage over racial inequality motivates political action against it in a way that self-focused guilt does not. Obviously, this issue is in need of further research.

CONCLUSIONS

Guilt is one (emotional) reaction members of advantaged groups can have when faced with the fact of group inequality. It is important because it is based in a felt responsibility for moral wrongdoing and therefore has potential for motivating efforts to bring about equality. It is, however, a relatively self-focused emotion. Unlike sympathy or moral outrage, which focus attention more on the plight of the disadvantaged and the system that perpetuates inequality, guilt focuses more on the advantaged group and their feelings about being immoral.

As a relatively self-focused sense of responsibility for group immorality, this extremely unpleasant experience motivates people to assuage their guilt. If group-based guilt cannot be escaped easily, it is strongly associated with efforts at restitution. This is what guilt does. Guilt-based restitution can take the form of apology or material compensation. Both of these forms of restitution attempt to restore morality to the previously immoral intergroup relation. Its role in promoting efforts at restitution makes group-based guilt important to intergroup relations. "White" guilt, for example, is central to support for an official federal apology to Indigenous Australians for historical mistreatment (McGarty et al., 2002, Study 1). "White" guilt also appears to be an important basis of support for affirmative action that seeks to compensate African Americans for systems of racial privilege and discrimination in the United States (Iyer et al., 2003). Thus, group-based guilt seems to motivate members of advantaged groups to take responsibility for inequality, and thus work to make restitution.

Despite its important role in efforts at restitution, guilt does not provide a basis for many other efforts against inequality. Indeed, its narrow concern for restitution may limit guilt's role in more general social change strategies. For example, "white" guilt in the United States is not associated with support for affirmative action programs that seek to increase opportunities for those facing racial discrimination. This is a disturbing finding, because such opportunity-oriented policies are some of the least controversial, most widely supported policy efforts designed to combat racial inequality (Kravitz et al., 1997). It seems, however, that guilt's focus on the self prevents it from serving as a basis of support for such policies that are not explicitly focused on compensation.

This suggests that other emotional responses that focus on the plight of the disadvantaged themselves may provide a broader basis of support for efforts against inequality (Leach et al., 2002). We discussed one study by Iyer et al. (2003) that provides support for this notion. They showed that other-focused sympathy was associated with support for both compensatory- and opportunity-oriented affirmative action in the United States. These results support Leach et al.'s (2002) argument that other-focused group emotions are better than self-focused guilt as a general basis of action against group inequality.

It is clear that we have offered an ambivalent rendering of group-based guilt. We believe that guilt is an important basis for the disavowal of group advantage. We also believe that group-based guilt has serious limits. Like all other emotions (group or personal), guilt is a specific way of interpreting group relations (Montada & Schneider, 1989; E. R. Smith, 1993). The phenomenological and conative specificity of guilt are what make it a useful characterization of intergroup relations. When we know a group is guilty, we know that the group members feel bad about the harm that they have done, and that they are likely to intend restitution. This specificity is also, however, a reason not to expect more from guilt than it can provide. What guilt *is* relates to what guilt *does* (Frijda, 1986). This is why guilt is associated with a (narrow) concern for restitution and is not a basis for more general efforts to combat inequality.

The specific experience of guilt is only one way in which group members can experience their group position. Sympathy and moral outrage are other ways that group members can interpret their relation to disadvantaged groups. These feelings have their own phenomenological and conative specificity; that is, emotions are different things and do different things (Leach et al., 2002). This is the main advantage of the intergroup emotion approach to intergroup relations. Specific group-based emotions offer a nuanced and textured rendering of group experience that enables a more detailed analysis of the ways in which groups interpret and act toward one another. By studying the way people use emotion language to characterize the specific ways they experience their group's position relative to that of other groups, we may better understand how psychological experience interacts with social structure and politics to maintain inequality.

REFERENCES

Anti-racism campaign. (2000). *Stand up against racism*. Retrieved from *http://flag.blackened.net/revolt/arc/leaflets/stand_up_oct00.html*

Batson, C. D. (1987). Prosocial emotion: Is it ever truly altruistic? In L. Berkowitz (Ed.), *Advances in experimental social psychology: Vol. 20* (pp. 65–122). New York: Academic Press.

Batson, C. D. (1998). Altruism and prosocial behavior. In D. T. Gilbert, S. T. Fiske, & G. Lindzey (Eds.), *The handbook of social psychology: Vol. 2* (pp. 282–316). Boston: McGraw-Hill.

Baumeister, R. F., Reis, H. T., & Delespaul, P. A. E. G. (1995). Subjective and experiential correlates of guilt in daily life. *Personality and Social Psychology Bulletin, 21*(12), 1256–1268.

Baumeister, R. F., Stillwell, A. M., & Heatherton, T. F. (1994). Guilt: An interpersonal approach. *Psychological Bulletin, 115*, 243–267.

Branscombe, N. R. (1998). Thinking about one's gender group's privileges or disadvantages:

Consequences for well-being in women and men. *British Journal of Social Psychology, 37,* 167–184.

Branscombe, N. R., Doosje, B., & McGarty, C. (2002). Antecedents and consequences of collective guilt. In D. M. Mackie & E. R. Smith (Eds.), *From prejudice to intergroup emotions: Differentiated reactions to social groups* (pp. 49–66). Philadelphia: Psychology Press.

Brasel, B. (1999). *Little white lies: An interview with anti-racist activist Tim Wise.* Retrieved from *http://www.tbwt.com/views/feat/feat1456.asp*

Brooks, R. (1999). *When sorry isn't enough: The controversy over apologies and reparations for human injustice.* New York: New York University Press.

Constable, P. (2001, September 9). Racism meeting reaches accord but delegates remain divided. *Washington Post,* p. A20.

Doosje, B., Branscombe, N. R., Spears, R., & Manstead, A. S. R. (1998). Guilty by association: When one's group has a negative history. *Journal of Personality and Social Psychology, 75,* 872–886.

Estrada-Hollenbach, M., & Heatherton, T. F. (1998). Avoiding and alleviating guilt through prosocial behavior. In J. Bybee (Ed.), *Guilt and children* (pp. 215–231). San Diego, CA: Academic Press.

Frijda, N. H. (1986). *The emotions.* New York: Cambridge University Press.

Frijda, N. H., Kuipers, P., & ter Shure, E. (1989). Relations among emotion, appraisal, and emotional action readiness. *Journal of Personality and Social Psychology, 57*(2), 212–228.

Goodman, D. J. (2001). *Promoting diversity and social justice: Educating people from privileged groups.* Thousand Oaks, CA: Sage.

Hitchcock, J. (1999). *The quest for innocence.* Retrieved from *http://www.euroamerican.org/editorials/the_quest.asp*

Hodges-Aeberhard, J. (1999). Affirmative action in employment: Recent court approaches to a difficult concept. *International Labour Review, 138,* 247.

Hoffman, M. L. (1976). Development of prosocial motivation: Empathy and guilt. In N. Eisenberg (Ed.), *The development of prosocial behavior* (pp. 281–313). New York: Academic Press.

Hoffman, M. L. (1991). Empathy and prosocial activism. In N. Eisenberg, J. Reykowski, & E. Staub (Eds.), *Social and moral values: Individual and societal perspectives* (pp. 65–85). Hillsdale, NJ: Lawrence Erlbaum.

Iyer, A., Leach, C. W., & Crosby, F. J. (2003). White guilt and racial compensation: The benefits and limits of self-focus. *Personality and Social Psychology Bulletin, 29*(1), 117–129.

Japanese premier tells Koreans of his remorse. (2001, October 16). *San Francisco Chronicle,* p. B6.

Kravitz, D. A., Harrison, D. A., Turner, M. E., Levine, E. L., Chaves, W., Brannick, M. T., Denning, D. L., Russell, C. J., & Conrad, M. A. (1997). *Affirmative action: A review of psychological and behavioral research.* Bowling Green, OH: Society for Industrial and Organizational Psychology.

Kristof, K. (2002, April 13). IRS has paid millions in illegal slavery credits; taxes: The agency says the bogus filings have soared and it mistakenly accepted some claims. *Los Angeles Times,* p. A1.

Kugler, K., & Jones, W. H. (1992). On conceptualizing and assessing guilt. *Journal of Personality and Social Psychology, 62*(2), 318–327.

Leach, C. W. (2002). Democracy's dilemma: Explaining racial inequality in egalitarian societies. *Sociological Forum, 17*(4), 681–690.

Leach, C. W., Snider, N., & Iyer, A. (2002). "Poisoning the consciences of the fortunate": The experience of relative advantage and support for social equality. In I. Walker & H. J. Smith (Eds.), *Relative deprivation: Specification, development, and integration* (pp. 136–163). New York: Cambridge University Press.

Lecouteur, A., & Augoustinos, M. (2001). Apologising to the stolen generations: Argument, rhetoric, and identity in public reasoning. *Australian Psychologist, 36*(1), 51–61.

Lipsitz, G. (1998). *The possessive investment in whiteness: How white people profit from identity politics.* Philadelphia: Temple University Press.

McGarty, C., & Bliuc, A. -M. (2004). Refining the "collective" in collective guilt: Past harm, collective guilt, and harm reparation in Australia. In N. R. Branscombe & B. Doosje (Eds.), *Collective guilt: International perspectives.* New York: Cambridge University Press.

McGarty, C., Pedersen, A., Leach, C. W., Mansell, T., Waller, J., & Bliuc, A. -M. (2002). *Collective guilt as a predictor of commitment to apology.* Unpublished manuscript, Australian National University.

McIntosh, P. (1989, July/August). White privilege: Unpacking the invisible knapsack. *Peace and Freedom,* 10–12.

Minow, M. (1998). *Between vengeance and forgiveness: Facing history after genocide and mass violence.* Boston: Beacon Press.

Montada, L., & Schneider, A. (1989). Justice and emotional reactions to the disadvantaged. *Social Justice Research, 3,* 313–344.

Nagata, D. (1990). The Japanese-American internment: Perceptions of moral community, fairness, and redress. *Journal of Social Issues, 40*(6), 133–146.

Niedenthal, P. M., Tangney, J. P., & Gavanski, I. (1994). "If only I weren't" versus "If only I hadn't": Distinguishing shame and guilt in counterfactual thinking. *Journal of Personality and Social Psychology, 67,* 585–595.

O'Connor, L. E., Berry, J. W., Weiss, J., Bush, M., & Sampson, H. (1997). Interpersonal guilt: The development of a new measure. *Journal of Clinical Psychology, 53,* 73–89.

Opotow, S. (1990). Moral exclusion and injustice: An introduction. *Journal of Social Issues, 40,* 1–20.

Ortony, A., Clore, G. L., & Collins, A. (1988). *The cognitive structure of emotions.* Cambridge, UK: Cambridge University Press.

Pedersen, A., Contos, N., Griffiths, B., Bishop, B., & Walker, I. (2000). Attitudes toward Indigenous-Australians in city and country settings. *Australian Psychologist, 35,* 109–117.

Pedersen, A., Iyer, A., & Leach, C.W. (2002). Unpublished data file. Murdoch University, Perth, Western Australia.

Pratkanis, A. R., & Turner, M. E. (1999). The significance of affirmative action for the souls of white folk: Further implications of a helping model. *Journal of Social Issues, 55,* 787–815.

Roseman, I. J., Spindel, M. S., & Jose, P. E. (1990). Appraisals of emotion-eliciting events: Testing a theory of discrete emotions. *Journal of Personality and Social Psychology, 59,* 899–915.

Roseman, I. J., Wiest, C., & Swartz, T. S. (1994). Phenomenology, behaviors, and goals differentiate discrete emotions. *Journal of Personality and Social Psychology, 67,* 206–221.

Salovey, P., Mayer, J. D., & Rosenhan, D. L. (1991). Mood and helping: Mood as a motivator of helping and helping as a regulator of mood. In M. S. Clark (Ed.), *Prosocial behavior* (pp. 215–237). Newbury Park, CA: Sage.

Salovey, P., & Rosenhan, D. L. (1989). Mood states and prosocial behavior. In H. Wagner & A. Manstead (Eds.), *Handbook of psychophysiology* (pp. 371–391). New York: Wiley.

Schmitt, M., Branscombe, N. R., & Brehm, J. (2004). Gender inequality and the intensity of men's collective guilt. In N. R. Branscombe & B. Doosje (Eds.), *Collective guilt: International perspectives.* New York: Cambridge University Press.

Sidanius, J., & Pratto, F. (1999). *Social dominance: An intergroup theory of social hierarchy and oppression.* Cambridge, UK: Cambridge University Press.

Smith, C. A., & Ellsworth, P. C. (1985). Patterns of cognitive appraisal in emotion. *Journal of Personality and Social Psychology, 48,* 813–838.

Smith, E. R. (1993). Social identity and social emotions: Toward a new conceptualization of prejudice. In D. M. Mackie & D. L. Hamilton (Eds.), *Affect, cognition, and stereotyping* (pp. 297–315). San Diego, CA: Academic Press.

Smith, V. E. (2001, August 27). Debating the wages of slavery. *Newsweek,* 20–24.

Steele, S. (1990). *The content of our character.* New York: Harper Perennial.

Swim, J. K., & Miller, D. L. (1999). White guilt: Its antecedents and consequences for attitudes toward affirmative action. *Personality and Social Psychology Bulletin, 25*(4), 500–514.

Tangney, J. P., & Fischer, K. W. (Eds.). (1995). *Self-conscious emotions: The psychology of guilt, shame, embarrassment, and pride.* New York: Guilford.

Tangney, J. P., Miller, R. S., Flicker, L., & Barlow, D. H. (1996). Are shame, guilt, and embarrassment distinct emotions? *Journal of Personality and Social Psychology, 70,* 1256–1269.

Tummala, K. K. (1999). Policy of preference: Lessons from India, the United States, and South Africa. *Public Administration Review, 59,* 495.

Waller, J. C., Mansell, T. K., Koh, K. J., Raja, M., & Pedersen, A. (2001). Unpublished data file. Murdoch University, Perth, Western Australia.

Weiner, B. (1982). The emotional consequences of causal attributions. In M. S. Clark & S. T. Fiske (Eds.), *Affect and cognition: The seventeenth annual Carnegie symposium on cognition* (pp. 185–209). Hillsdale, NJ: Lawrence Erlbaum.

Wierzbicka, A. (1992). Defining emotion concepts. *Cognitive Science, 16,* 539–581.

Zebel, S., Doosje, B., & Spears, R. (2004). It depends on your point of view: Implications of perspective-taking and national identification for Dutch collective guilt. In N. R. Branscombe & B. Doosje (Eds.), *Collective guilt: International perspectives.* New York: Cambridge University Press.

NOTE

1. Some emotion theorists (e.g., Batson, 1987) use the terms "sympathy" and "empathy" interchangeably to address people's feelings of concern for another. Others (e.g., Hoffman, 1976) distinguish between sympathy (feeling for another) and empathy (feeling as another). In our theoretical framework (Leach, Snider, & Iyer, 2002), we conceptualize sympathy as distinct from empathy, focusing on feelings for another.

TWENTY-SIX

White Educators as Allies: Moving from Awareness to Action

Sandra M. Lawrence and Beverly Daniel Tatum

I am 35 years old and I never really started thinking about race too much until now, and that makes me feel uncomfortable. I just think for some reason I didn't know. No one taught us. That's what I tell my students.

—White female teacher

Who teaches white teachers about the meaning of race? What do they need to know? How well prepared are white teachers to understand their own "whiteness" and the meaning it has when interacting with students and parents of color? How cognizant are they of their own racial social-ization and how it may influence their perceptions of the performance potential of all of their students? Educators concerned about the increasing "whiteness" of the teaching force and the increasing racial diversity of the student population have begun to ask these and other ques-tions. Even in schools with very small populations of color, educators are becoming more aware of the need to prepare white students to live in a multiracial society. Yet this is a world with which the current teaching force has limited experience. Most white teachers were raised and educated in predominantly white communities. Their firsthand knowledge of communities of color and their cultures and histories is quite limited. The secondhand information they have received through textbooks, media, and from friends and family has often been distorted by the negative, stereotypical attitudes about people of color that are so pervasive in American culture.

One way to address this deficiency in white teachers' experiences is to provide them with educational courses or programs that involve teaching about race and the impact of racism in American society. But although teacher education programs and school districts alike are strug-gling to address racial issues, the systematic study of the effects of antiracist educational efforts on the attitudes of teachers, either preservice or in-service, is limited. Existing studies involving white teacher education students enrolled in multicultural or ethnic studies courses reveal some positive changes in white students' attitudes about people of color (Adams & Zhou-McGovern, 1994; Baker, 1977; Bennett, 1979; Grant, 1981; Haberman & Post, 1992; Lawrence & Bunche, 1996). However, fewer studies of the effects of in-service antiracist multicultural programs have been conducted and the results of these studies are mixed (Redman, 1977; Sleeter, 1992;

Washington, 1981). Although some teachers do make fundamental changes in their thinking about race or redesign their teaching methods in positive ways as a result of this kind of formal instruction, many participants do not. As Carter and Goodwin (1994) suggested, we still have much to learn about the impact that effective antiracist professional development can have on teacher attitudes and teacher behaviors.

The Professional Development Program We Studied

Given the paucity of formal studies on the effects of antiracist education for teachers and our belief that the professional development program we knew about was fundamentally different from others, we decided to conduct our own study on the effects of antiracist professional development for teachers. Our primary focus in conducting this study was to investigate the ways in which the course influenced white participants' perceptions about race and racism, and how those perceptions are manifested in schools. We were especially interested in whether white teachers' understanding of their own racial identity influenced their thinking and daily classroom practice.

In contrast to the commonly used one-day "flash and dash" in-service workshops, this professional development program extended over a period of seven months. Most of the sessions were three hours in length and took place immediately after school. The classes were scheduled approximately two weeks apart. The course was taught by a biracial team of instructors, one of whom was Beverly Daniel Tatum, an African American woman and coauthor of this reading. Course activities included lectures, films, small and large group discussion, and in-class exercises. Between class meetings, participants were assigned reading material and asked to write reflection papers in response to the readings. The structure of the course experience encouraged ongoing reflection and integration of the course ideas into daily practice. Beginning with the first class meeting, the course content required participants to think about their own racial group membership and its meaning in the context of a race-conscious society.

In fact, helping educators to recognize the personal, cultural, and institutional manifestations of racism and to become more proactive in response to racism within school settings was one of the explicit goals of the course. Topics covered that were specific to this goal included an examination of the concepts of prejudice, racism, white privilege, and internalized oppression; an analysis of racial stereotypes in the media and in curricular materials; an explication of the process of racial identity development for both whites and people of color; and a discussion of the historical connection between scientific racism and common assumptions about the "fixed nature" of the intellectual capacity of students. In addition, participants were asked to chart their own growth through the use of a self-reflective taping exercise (described in Tatum, 1992) and to produce a case study or action plan based on actual school experience.

Because there were a significant number (30%) of participants of color in the course, voices that are often silent in predominantly white schools were frequently heard. The active participation of people of color in the classroom discourse was supported both by the leadership role of the African American facilitator (an uncommon experience in these school contexts) and by the presence of so many of their colleagues of color.[1] All of the participants of color, including the one Latina, seemed to feel comfortable contributing to the dialogue and challenging white participants to look at their own assumptions and positions in the racial order. Though the impact of the course experience on the participants of color is also being investigated (Elliott & Tatum, 1995), we are intentional here in choosing to focus primarily on the effects of the course on white educators.

WHITE RACIAL IDENTITY DEVELOPMENT:
A THEORETICAL FRAMEWORK

As we indicated earlier, the focus of this reading is on the responses of the white participants to the course. In particular, we were guided in our thinking by Janet Helms's (1990,
1995) model of white racial identity development. As explained by Helms (1990, p. 3),
"Racial identity development theory concerns the psychological implications of racial group
membership, that is belief systems that evolve in reaction to perceived differential racial-
group membership."

For whites, the abandonment of individual racism and the recognition of and opposition
to institutional and cultural racism are central components to the development of a positive
white racial identity. In the process, "the person must become aware of her or his Whiteness,
learn to accept Whiteness as an important part of herself or himself, and to internalize a
realistically positive view of what it means to be White" (Helms, 1990, p. 55).

Helms (1995) theorized that white persons experience a developmental process involving
six statuses: contact, disintegration, reintegration, pseudo-independence, immersion/emer-
sion, and autonomy. These developmental statuses are neither rigid nor pure; rather, they
may change as societal situations change, and they often reflect characteristics that are
"blends" (p. 189) of more than one status. Usually, however, one status will be more dominant than another given a certain set of circumstances.

White persons exhibiting dominant "contact status" thinking and behavior tend to be oblivious to institutional racism and often view people of color through a color-blind lens. When
such persons hear that racism is not just a thing of the past but is in fact operating today,
they may experience a range of emotions and confusion about their prior beliefs in the face
of the new racial content. This "disintegration status" signals a "racial moral dilemma" (Helms,
1995, p. 185) of sorts that necessitates a choice between past and prior views. Persons who
exhibit dominant "reintegration" attitudes and behaviors have alleviated their dilemma somewhat by relying on previously learned stereotypes about people of color to explain the racial
inequalities they now witness. Blaming the victims of racial oppression for the mistreatment
they receive is a commonly voiced rationale by "reintegrated" individuals.

When white persons can, more often than not, acknowledge that institutional racism exists
and are able to abandon some of their stereotypes and past beliefs about the racial order,
they are capable of moving toward a nonracist identity. This dominant "pseudo-independent" thinking, however, tends to result in an intellectual commitment to ending racism
rather than an active one. A dominant "immersion/emersion" status is exhibited by an exploration of whiteness in all its many configurations, a search for self-definition as a white person,
and efforts that challenge racism and white superiority. The sixth status, "autonomy," is characterized by a deep understanding of one's white racial self, effective actions that interrupt
racism, and multiracial alliances that work toward a more just society.

Helms (1995) suggested (and we agree) that individuals with more "developmentally sophisticated" (p. 184) statuses in terms of their racial identity development are better prepared to
work effectively in multiracial settings than those with statuses that are less developmentally
sophisticated. Professional development programs that are intended to increase teacher effec-
tiveness with multiracial populations should attend, then, to the impact that these programs
have on the racial identity development of the participants.

The Current Study

Although it was our intention to include all white participants of the course in our study, some either did not complete the course assignments needed for data collection[2] or did not give permission to have their assignments reproduced. In all, 20 of the 28 white participants were included in this study. Of the 20 white educators, there were 14 women and 6 men, who were in their mid-30s to late 40s.

The data we collected included essays and reflection papers participants wrote for the course, as well as pre- and postcourse interviews conducted with four (three women, one man) of the teachers. The interviews were conducted by a white female interviewer, Sandra Lawrence (coauthor of this essay), who had not been involved with the course instruction. The open-ended interviews were approximately 1 and a half to 2 hours in length and focused on each participant's prior racial history, teaching practices, educational philosophy, and course-related experiences.

We coded and categorized the transcribed interviews and the written documents qualitatively using Helms's theoretical framework. Specifically, we evaluated participants' statements about their own behaviors, attitudes, and beliefs and categorized them in terms of the characteristics outlined by Helms as typical of particular statuses. For example, comments reflecting a desire to connect with other white people working against racism were seen as indicative of the immersion status, whereas comments reflecting a color-blind attitude, minimizing the social significance of race, were seen as indicative of contact status thinking. A profile of each individual's racial identity characteristics was constructed, based on the pattern of responses they exhibited.

In addition, we identified themes across the profiles that illustrated the ways in which the course affected participants' thinking, classroom practice, and interpersonal interactions related to race. The profiles and themes, when considered together, provided information about the outcomes of the course in terms of participants' attitudinal and behavioral changes and their movement along a continuum of racial identity development.

Recognizing Privilege: I Never Thought of Myself as White

Many of the participants had grown up in the 1960s and considered themselves "liberal" in their thinking concerning political and social movements for equality. In relation to race, they were not color blind: They acknowledged the differential treatment that whites and people of color receive, and they were concerned about the racial oppression that people of color experience in this country. They were also aware that society in general and the educational system in particular had distorted, repressed, and silenced the voices and experiences of people of color.

But although all participants were aware of racial oppression and the differential treatment that whites and people of color receive, they tended to view this oppression as the result of individuals' acting in racist ways rather than the combination of individual and long-standing institutional racist practices and policies. In addition, they had given little thought to the racial privilege and power that accompanied their own position in the racial order or the possibility of their own complicity in the racist practices they condemned. As Belinda wrote in her first paper, "I had been taught that racism was an individual act of meanness perpetrated against some minority group. I never suspected that it was an intricate system of advantage, of which I was a part." When asked about how they view their racial privilege, many participants, like Pam, were honest about the lack of consideration they had given to their racial positions: "I do admit that I have rarely thought of the position I hold because of my race. I have taken for granted the power and in most cases the security that my whiteness gives me." In reflecting back on the course, other participants explained how their avoidance of whiteness enabled them to perceive racism as external to their lives. Faith, in listening to an interview of herself taped at the beginning of the course, reflected on her precourse thinking about her participation in the racial order: "I realize a certain naïveté and white liberal smugness in my responses but without the depth of understanding of why racism exists and without the acceptance that I, as a white person, take an active role in perpetuating racism."

As exemplified here and throughout their writings, Faith and other teachers seemed to possess what Frankenberg (1993) called a "power-evasive" orientation in regard to their racial privilege and racial dominance, having failed to notice the social power conferred simply by being white. From the perspective of Helms's (1990, 1995) racial identity theory, most participants entered the course in a position characterized as the pseudo-independent status of their white identity development, a status consistent with "white liberal" thinking about race and characterized by avoidance of responsibility for racial inequality and injustice.

It was apparent in both the written documents and the interviews that the course had a profound impact on most of the participants in the study. Although each person's response was unique, there were areas of similarity that we could identify across responses. These three linked dimensions were (1) the knowledge they received about race and racism, (2) the ways in which their learning altered their thinking about themselves as racial beings, and (3) the manner in which their thinking moved them to change some of their behaviors regarding race and racism. The course was also instrumental in helping some of the participants to think about themselves as white persons in a white dominant society and in fostering the development of white antiracist identities.

New Learnings — Initial Movements

All participants related either in writing or during interviews that they learned more about racism as a result of the course. For some, this learning concerned new knowledge, such as definitions of racism and prejudice, the notion of "acting white," information about the cultural and institutional manifestations of racism, and theories of racial identity development. In addition to "new" learning, most participants mentioned that the course gave them a "heightened awareness" of existing knowledge: information they had some prior knowledge of, or thought they knew, but which the course "helped to bring more into consciousness." Anita's comments from the end of the course interview captured this view of learning, which other participants experienced as well:

> I mean I thought that I had a pretty good understanding. I thought I was aware of what was happening, but there are lots of things that I had no conception of that in a million years I would never even imagine! So, [the course] heightened my awareness. That was interesting because I did go [into the course] thinking, OK, this isn't going to be a problem for me because I already know a lot. And I did know a lot, but I certainly did not know as much as I thought I knew.

Participants had some prior knowledge of racist policies and practices within schools and other social institutions. They were aware of the negative impact of a legacy of distortions, stereotypes, and omissions concerning the lives and experiences of people of color, and they saw examples in their daily lives where whites and people of color were treated differently. But they were less aware of the pervasiveness of these occurrences. As a result of the course, Greg can now see the extent of the structural inequalities inherent in some school policies that he didn't see before the course:

> I think in general our education is structured to make white kids successful and we don't do those things that need to be done to make the black kids successful. Some administrators see that the problem is with the kids: they're not as smart, they're not as good. It is not a problem with the school system. But I don't see things that way anymore. I see it that we, our culture, has done things for generations to depress the academic achievement of certain individuals in our society, and those happen to be people of color.

Although relating his new thinking about the institutional practices that result in whites and people of color being treated differently, Greg also acknowledged, through pronouns such as "we" and "our," his membership in the dominant culture, a culture responsible for the inequities he described.

As the course evolved, other participants also began to see their relation to the power structure in important ways. For example, nearly every participant reflected on her or his white privilege after reading Peggy McIntosh's (1989) "White Privilege: Unpacking the Invisible Knapsack," and for many that reflection was instrumental in forcing the white participants to think of themselves as racial beings. Evelyn, a woman who speaks frequently about gender oppression to her middle school students, related the impact this reading had on her image of herself:

> Despite my keen awareness of the white male culture and its dominance and oppression over me as a woman, McIntosh's article put a new slant on privileges I had simply because I was white. I feel guilt associated with my unearned advantages because of my color, but I never closely examined the ease with which I can move within my world — how I do not have to be overly concerned with how I might be seen because of my color. After reading the article, I am more aware of being white.

These teachers, as well as others in the course, experienced a new level of awareness about systems of advantage that benefited them as white persons, and this deepening awareness of their white privilege was, for some, a further movement within pseudo-independent thinking with a direction toward a more positive white racial identity.

SHIFTS IN THINKING

When commenting about the course, teachers referred to their new awareness as something that caused a "shift" in their thinking, so that they viewed the world in relation to racism differently. Leslie described this process as not just intellectual but personal as well:

> Before the course my thinking on racism, a lot of it was like how you learned how to think in schools. Like you think about things because you know they are the right thing to think

about and you don't own them. From this course now, it is more a part of me, it's more than just part of the lens I look out on the world with. It's just the way I look at the world.

Belinda also noticed a change in her perceptions: "All around me I constantly see injustice and racism."

Participants began to notice not just the racist behaviors and practices of others; they also recognized their own racist attitudes and actions. Faith not only recognized how her past and present ways of being are racist, she also saw how her actions maintain the racial order and her dominance as a white person:

Throughout this course I have been coming to terms with my own personal and group responsibility in allowing racism to persist. It is not simply someone else's problem that I can step in and referee, it is my own problem as well. At this point, having confronted my own racism and learned view of superiority, I am teaching myself, through a constant state of processing events and feelings about people, that I can be genuine and truly understanding of the racism confronted by people of color.

The remarks of these teachers are typical of those in the course who began to realize that to be white meant to acknowledge the privilege that accompanied their whiteness. But rather than dwell on their white privilege as the primary defining aspect of their whiteness, they envisioned a more positive, less guilt-inducing definition of their white identity: one that might enable them to become "allies" (Tatum, 1994) in the struggle against racism. This search for a new, more affirming, antiracist white identity is indicative of the immersion/emersion status of Helms's racial identity model.

Changes in Personal and Professional Practices

Although some participants were contemplating the need to take action, others felt ready to interrupt racist practices both in their personal lives and in their teaching. In their personal encounters, they challenged racist jokes and comments made by colleagues and family members and began to question those in authority about policies and procedures they suspected to be racist. Anita, for example, decided to tell the library director of her town that a sign in the children's room that read "Unattended children will be sold as slaves" was offensive.

As the course progressed, participants began to translate learning about their position in the racial order into classroom practices as a way to question the status quo or change "the ways things have always been." Prior to the course, teachers seldom brought up the topic of race with their students, even though they taught in racially mixed classrooms. Although they acknowledged that "kids are hungry to talk about racism," some teachers were afraid to address the topic. They expressed fear about the emotions that students might express and felt inadequate to respond to students who might use racist language or who might become angry if racism was brought out into the open. However, as a result of the course, some teachers became more willing to bring the topic of race into the classroom. They integrated race and race-related topics into classes on social studies, language arts, and mathematics through lessons on stereotyping, black history, and current events.

As a result of being more comfortable addressing the topic of race with students, some teachers altered their course content and made it more "inclusive" of the experiences and histories of people of color. For example, when team-teaching their middle school students the fundamentals of essay writing, Paul and Donald decided to model aspects of effective essay writing by having students read and discuss a newspaper article titled, "Calling the Plays in Black and White" (Jackson, 1989), which dealt with the stereotypical language used by sportscasters and announcers. Through class activities, the teachers were able to illustrate to students how a clear focus, engaging introduction, descriptive examples, and a solid conclusion made for an effective essay. Paul and Donald were also able to use this essay to "start to raise students' awareness of racial stereotyping." They helped students to recognize the harmful implications of announcers' referrals to white players as intelligent strategists and African American players as only physically powerful athletes. These middle school teachers then continued to build several lessons on the article, one of which required students to watch athletic activities on television and critique the announcer's portrayal of black and white athletes. Both Paul and Donald were pleased by the results of their lessons and felt that they had "broken the silence" by bringing issues of racism into the classroom.

Some participants changed their teaching practice in ways that did not involve curriculum. After a class discussion in which teachers acknowledged that they kept their distance from students of color in their classrooms and seldom communicated with parents of color, many teachers reflected on the negative effects of these behaviors. Once they realized how different communication patterns with students advantaged white students and disadvantaged students of color, some decided to step out of this pattern and take more initiative to interact with students and parents of color. Anita, writing for one of her reflection papers near the end of the course, chronicled her interactions with a student of color who was not doing well in her class:

> My thinking throughout this course has prompted me to call Dwight at home one night just to see if he was doing his homework and to let him know that I was thinking about him and wondering if he needed help on the math problems. He was shocked that I called but I could tell that he was pleased to get the special treatment. Dwight has been a different student since that phone call. Things are far from perfect, but in general he's doing much better.

Anita has not stopped with this student, however. She has reached out to other students of color in her classes and feels more comfortable talking with their parents as well. Similarly, Kay and other white teachers also feel more comfortable talking with parents of color than they did prior to the course.

Nearly all participants (85%) reported taking a least one form of action to combat racism (some took four and five different actions) either in personal or professional spheres as a direct result of the course. Although taking action is not necessarily characteristic of any particular status in Helms's theory, it is indicative of persons moving toward more positive racial identities. Some took action as they moved more deeply within a pseudo-independent status of white racial identity; others took action as they became more immersed in defining what their white identities meant to them. Although in most cases there was no dramatic movement from one status to the next, it is important to point out that these participants, unlike the college students we have taught, were already in the second phase of Helms's model of development — developing an antiracist identity — at the beginning of the course. They had been recruited for that reason. Yet even this group found they had things to learn and actions to take in creating a more inclusive learning situation for all their students. Regardless of their racial identity status, all "actions" represented positive moves out of the silence and complicity, which, in the past, have worked in tandem to maintain the cycle of oppression.

The Dynamics of Trust

It is important to reiterate that the white educators participating in this pilot course were recruited because they were viewed as possessing some sensitivity to the needs of students of color and were willing to talk about race. They seemed eager to hear about the experiences of people of color, and they actively sought out newspaper and magazine articles about the effects of racial oppression to share with each other. But that eagerness subsided when the discourse focused on the racial dynamics between themselves and people of color in the room. Most often the source of tension revolved around questions of trust.

For example, a black male participant commented about using his "radar" to assess whether this racially mixed situation would be "safe" for him. When other African Americans nodded their heads and exchanged knowing glances, many of the white people were taken aback that their colleagues would be suspicious of them, assuming that their very presence in the course would warrant the trust of the people of color. An excerpt from Anita's interview captures this puzzlement and the sense of insecurity that this information produced:

> We somehow got on the topic of black people's radars. . . . The African American people in our group got talking about the radar that they feel goes off when they are around white people. And we just started getting into, well, what do you mean, radar? . . . Do you evaluate a person before you even know them?

The idea that white people were not assumed to be trustworthy, unless proved otherwise, was a recurring theme that consistently upset the white participants. This theme was sometimes brought into the discussion when white educators shared stories of their interactions with black parents. During one particular session, a white teacher talked at length about his frustration that a black mother had challenged his placement recommendation for her child. When black participants spoke supportively of the parent's concern, placing it in the context of racist tracking policies, the teacher had difficulty accepting that his recommendation might be seen as part of that pattern.

In general, it seemed that many white participants were unprepared to acknowledge the legacy of racism that followed them into the room. This lack of acknowledgment, and belief that one could be seen only as an individual, was in itself a vestige of their white privilege. Although white participants were troubled by the mistrust between themselves and people of color, participants of color understood it to be business as usual in a white-dominated, race-conscious society. Coming to terms with this reality was an ongoing source of tension for white participants, which for some remained unresolved.

Staying off the Cycle?

Maintaining an opposition to racism in the face of societal pressure to "not notice" the racial order is difficult (Ayvazian, 1995). Our earlier studies (Lawrence & Bunche, 1996; Tatum, 1992, 1994) examining the impact of courses on racism have highlighted the anxiety white undergraduates feel when "stepping off the cycle of oppression." The educators in this study expressed a similar anxiety. Some of them worried about returning to schools where racism, not antiracism, is the norm. They knew they would find little support for continued dialogue about race in their buildings, and they questioned whether they would be able to maintain their commitment without a strong support network.

Creating a new identity, that of educator as an ally, an advocate for students of color, and a much-needed antiracist role model for white students, is a long-term process. It means undoing years of "color and power-evasive" socialization (Frankenberg, 1993). Undoing racism in institutions that have historically perpetuated the racial order is a daunting task. The fact that this professional development effort was institutionally supported offered these participants a glimpse of hope that they might be able to make a difference in their districts. But more needs to be done to keep this hope alive. School systems like these, which have marshaled their professional development efforts into courses such as the one described here, need to create ongoing opportunities for follow-up and establish peer support networks for educators to ensure continued movement from awareness to action.

REFERENCES

Adams, M., & Zhou-McGovern, Y. (1994). *The sociomoral development of undergraduates in a "social diversity" course: Developmental theory, research, and instructional applications.* Paper presented at the American Educational Research Association annual meeting, New Orleans, LA.

Ayvazian, A. (1990, October/November). Being, not doing. *Fellowship*, 15.

Ayvazian, A. (1995, January/February). Interrupting the cycle of oppression: The role of allies as agents of change. *Fellowship*, 6–9.

Baker, G. C. (1977). Multicultural imperatives for curriculum development in teacher education. *Journal of Research and Development in Education, 11*, 70–83.

Bennett, C. T. (1979). The preparation of preservice secondary social studies teachers in multi-ethnic education. *High School Journal, 62*, 232–237.

Carter, R. T., & Goodwin, L. (1994). Racial identity and education. *Review of Research in Education, 20*, 291–336.

Elliott, P., & Tatum, B. D. (1995, February). *Anti-racist professional development: What do black educators have to say about it?* Presentation at the National Association of Multicultural Education, Washington, DC.

Frankenberg, R. (1993). *White women, race matters: The social construction of whiteness.* Minneapolis: University of Minnesota.

Grant, C. A. (1981). Education that is multicultural and teacher education: An examination from the perspectives of preservice students. *Journal of Educational Research, 75*, 95–101.

Haberman, M., & Post, L. (1992). Does direct experience change education students' perceptions of low-income minority children? *Midwestern Educational Researcher, 5*(2), 29–31.

Helms, J. E. (Ed.). (1990). *Black and white racial identity: Theory, research and practice.* Westport, CT: Greenwood Press.

Helms, J. E. (1995). An update of Helms's white and people of color racial identity models. In J. G. Ponterotto, J. M. Casas, & C. M. Alexander (Eds.), *Handbook of multicultural counseling* (pp. 181–197). Thousand Oaks, CA: Sage.

Jackson, D. (1989, January 22). Calling the plays in black and white: Will today's Super Bowl be black brawn vs. white brains? *Boston Sunday Globe*, p. A25.

Lawrence, S. M., & Bunche, T. (1996). Feeling and dealing: Teaching white students about racial privilege. *Teaching and Teacher Education, 12*(5), 531–542.

McIntosh, P. (1989, July/August). White privilege: Unpacking the invisible knapsack. *Peace and Freedom*.

Redman, G. L. (1977). Study of the relationship of teacher empathy for minority persons and in service human relations training. *Journal of Educational Research, 70*, 205–210.

Sleeter, C. E. (1992). *Keepers of the American Dream: A study of staff development and multicultural education*. London: Falmer.

Tatum, B. D. (1992). Talking about race, learning about racism: The application of racial identity development theory in the classroom. *Harvard Educational Review, 62*(1), 1–24.

Tatum, B. D. (1994). Teaching white students about racism: The search for white allies and the restoration of hope. *Teachers College Record, 95*(4), 462–476.

Washington, D. T. (1981). Impact of anti-racism multicultural education training on elementary teachers' attitudes and classroom behavior. *Elementary School Journal, 81,* 186–192.

NOTES

1. The high percentage of people of color in the course was especially significant because most of the educators present work in buildings where there are often only one or two educators of color, if there are any at all.

2. Though teachers attended the course voluntarily, many felt overwhelmed by the time commitment required in terms of after-school meeting time, reading assignments, and written work. Consequently, some participants did not complete enough of the assignments to be included in the study.

TWENTY-SEVEN

The Racing of Capability and Culpability in Desegregated Schools: Discourses of Merit and Responsibility

April Burns

I wonder what you'll name my sin: Complicity? Loyalty? Stupefaction? How can you tell the difference? Is my sin a failure of virtue, or of competence?

— Orleanna Price in *The Poisonwood Bible* (Kingsolver, 1998, p. 356)

It's like America. I like to think we are where we are because we worked hard and we worked ... that *the work is relative to where you are in the social status, whatever*. But, there is also this sinking feeling that you are where you come from and that no matter what the country's standards are, you still have your background as the dominating force of who you are.

— Myra, White suburban honors student

The question of whether the failure of privileged students to challenge practices that support racial or ethnic and economic stratification constitutes a failure of virtue or is actually an indication of how well they have interpreted and taken on the performance demands imposed on them, is the issue I address in this essay. Rather than stating that social status derives from work or effort, Myra says instead that the *work* "is relative to" social status. This reversal of the usual order is important, as it suggests that who you are (racially and economically, in this context) influences the amount and kind of schoolwork you are expected to do. Her experience, understood as a "suspicion," and described here as a "sinking feeling,"[1] is an example of the ways in which privileged youth actively negotiate — sometimes painfully — the contradictions that emerge in the gap between the values of equality and inequitable outcomes, between self-image (as hardworking, deserving, good) and their imagined evaluation by others (as racist, privileged, uncaring), between their desire for connection to students of color and (for many White students) their persistent desire to enforce racialized outcomes in academic success.

ACCOUNTABILITY MEASURES

Racialized (and class-based) differences are not only are exacerbated in schools today but are in fact constituted there (Apple, 2004 [this volume]; Bourdieu & Passeron, 1977; Fine, Burns, Payne, & Torre, in press). Howard Winant, drawing from earlier work with Michael Omi (Omi & Winant, 1994), wrote, "In racial formation theory, racial projects link significations or representations of race on the one hand, with social structural manifestations of racial hierarchy or dominance on the other hand" (Winant, 2001, p. 100). The racial project instantiated as the "minority achievement gap" operates at the intersection of the racial signification of Whiteness as giftedness (Staiger, 1997) and the hierarchical structuring of merit and academic worthiness in public schools today (see Fine, 2004 [this volume]). Concerned with how educators might facilitate critical consciousness around schooling, merit and racial formation in academically successful youth — typically students privileged by race or ethnicity and class — I investigate herein the relationship between discourses of racial and class advantage, academic merit, and sense of social responsibility for racial equality. I document the multiple fractures that exist within the cement of apparent acceptance of social privilege that is assumed to characterize academically successful students, as well as identify some of the ways in which the current social investment in individual and liberal notions of academic merit in public schools tend to elaborate, support, and maintain Whiteness and White privilege in the United States.

More than a decade ago, Michelle Fine, in her expert testimony on the effects of segregation on students in an affluent and predominantly White neighborhood, argued, "The extent to which these students, privileged by social class and race, take for granted their 'entitlement' and perceive no social consequence in having a basically Black high school and basically White high school separated by only a few miles, suggests the inherent superiority and justice of unjust outcomes" (Fine, 1990, p. 114). Fine concluded that these students were "denied the thorough and efficient education that New Jersey law requires, [were] socially miseducated, and deprived of the diverse social and academic experiences available to students at Dwight Morrow High [an integrated public high school]" (p. 114).

Such victories, however, give way to the headache of resegregation between and within public schools (Mickelson, 2001; Oakes, 1985; Wells & Serna, 1996). Although urban schools continue to disproportionately enroll minority youth (and educate them at half the per-pupil funding of suburban districts; see Acosta et al., 2003), inner-ring suburban schools, not yet abandoned by the White middle class, increasingly educate a racially broad range of youth as well (Orfield, 2002). What can privileged students, similar to those reported by Fine only now in ostensibly integrated settings, tell us about the current state of education? Under what circumstances do notions of social responsibility emerge within accepted discourses of individual merit, intelligence, and achievement? I look to a group of integrated "good" suburban schools, actively struggling with the opportunity-achievement gap and attempting to address the segregated experience of students within the school itself, to identify some conditions under which academically successful students challenge rather than legitimate structures of racial or class privilege that they benefit from.

These questions are posed at a particular moment in history in which we are witnessing both the dismantling of public institutions and the ever-increasing reliance on high-stakes accountability measures enforcing arbitrary academic "standards," and fueling the proliferation of status anxieties, especially around education and schooling (Powell & Barber, in press). Although the severest of consequences are suffered by students in the most distressed schools,[2] disproportionately enrolling low-income students and students of color (Darling-Hammond, 2002; Fine & Powell, 2001), there are consequences even for students attending "good" schools in the suburbs and who are doing well academically.

Anthony Elliott (2002) understood the ongoing deregulation of public institutions to be a "privatisation of politics in the broadest sense: of the individual, citizenship and moral responsibility" (p. 12). This privatization is presented as a version of psychic splitting at the societal level. Elliott emphasized the trauma of our globally interconnected and postmodern lives, increasingly characterized by an overwhelming and inescapable sense of relational risk, as well as a felt loss of both tradition and sense of omnipotence. The defensive response to such losses is a reinvestment in psychologically safer modernist projects and identifications at both the individual and societal level, which limits the parameters of moral responsibility for others. The increasing interrogation and challenge to Whiteness as a modernist project (Winant, 2001), though, represents a loss for those identifying as "White" (see Fine & Weis, 1998; Hurtado & Stewart, 1997), or as socially autonomous, facilitating a defensive investment in individualized notions of self, merit, and responsibility. Such investments are apparent in the ways that high-achieving youth in racially desegregated schools tend to narrate their relative privilege — described as the performance of merit as individually earned, and staged by accountability measures (with minority students used as props), and (for White students) further supported by a safety net of human and material resources ensuring their continued success.

This work is embedded within a larger research project investigating youth perspectives on, and experiences of, opportunity, achievement, and racial and class stratification in a consortium of 12 desegregated inner-ring suburban school districts. The Critical Opportunity Gap Project[3] was a 2-year youth participatory research project in which a diverse (by race or ethnicity, social class, and academic history) collective of youth researchers, drawn from urban and suburban schools, collaborated with graduate students and peers to design, analyze, and present research data from their schools. The following analysis is based on data generated from focus groups and interviews with high school students identified by their schools as "high achieving." Privilege is operationalized in terms of academic success, in an attempt to move discussion away from a demographic analysis that locates the production of inequality within bodies and, instead, toward the persistent and troubling processes and structures reproducing racial and class disparities in educational outcomes (Omi & Winant, 1994).

Looking at privilege through racialized outcomes is not the only, nor even necessarily the best, way of analyzing structures of inequality, but it is an important means of investigation. As Michael Apple (this volume) asserted, "We must differentiate between intentions and functions in educational policy and practice. We need to get beneath the rhetorical surface of claims about reforms and examine the *patterns* of differential benefits and losses in the seemingly beneficial educational reforms being proposed." Apple argued that although "intentional explanations are those self-conscious aims that guide our policies and practices," they cannot "guarantee at all ... whose interests they will ultimately serve ... and what identifiable patterns of differential benefits will emerge." Problematizing, then, the most successful students (rather than the least) shifts the analysis to one of accrued benefits while also challenging a deficit model of learning imposed on poor or working-class students and students of color. There are important distinctions to be made between successful students and privileged students. The unsettling fact remains that racial or ethnic positionality, in interaction with social class, tends to structure and overdetermine available opportunities for success in school and beyond (Fine, Bloom, et al., in press).

PRIVILEGE: A STAGED WHISPER

> I think a White student gets a head start whereas someone else started back there and if you run fast enough, you can catch up. If you don't or don't know how, you stay there. Even if the White kid isn't motivated, I still feel, that the whole school experience.... It's different. I thought maybe I'm being paranoid because I thought I'm just ultrasensitive to this but I don't think so. So many other people notice it. Even *White* people that I know.
>
> —Angela, Latina honors student

For all the writing and theorizing on critical consciousness, it is simply not expected from, nor asked of, those individuals in contexts and positions of (relative) privilege. Instead, much social justice work has historically focused on "raising" disadvantaged group members' consciousness, or otherwise ridding the oppressed of their "false consciousness."[4] Despite an explosion of research in critical White studies and antiracist scholarship, little has been written on the potential of Whites (or other dominant groups) to effectively engage in socially conscious action (see Lawrence & Tatum, 2004 [this volume]; Leach, Snider, & Iyer, 2002; Twine, 2004 [this volume] for exceptions) beyond historical expositions (e.g., Brown, 2002; Thompson, 2001). Mostly, writing has focused on the ways in which the relatively advantaged, subtly and explicitly, avoid responsibility for challenging racial and economic oppression, but rarely on the ways in which they recognize, consider, and accept the fact of their privileged position, and develop a moral imperative for social equity. Although this work similarly identifies the ways in which privileged youth come to deny their privilege and avoid responsibility for social justice, I argue as well that such young people are also anxiously aware of their privilege and actively negotiate their position toward a variety of ends — ends that are self-critical as well as self-promoting.

France Winddance Twine (1997) talked about Whiteness as an acquired interpretive frame, "a way of perceiving and responding in social interaction," but understands this frame as a form of identification that is not static, nor necessarily bound to specific bodies (p. 235). As this work shows, young people readily articulate the most salient features of their interpretive frame, or *habitus* (Bourdieu, 1984), even if they do not call it Whiteness *per se*. Zero-sum and vertical notions of success are characteristic of a White interpretive frame — if you didn't fail, then I must have. To the extent, then, that students identify with, and invest in, their track or level, honors status, or class rank (a doctrine of accountability, standards, and hierarchical success) — all at the expense of their larger integrated community — they are also "possessively investing" in Whiteness (Lipsitz, 1998).

There is evidence that high-status students, even those "practicing" a White interpretive frame, are aware of their academic and social privilege, and in fact are ambivalent about the legitimacy of an ideology of individualism and meritocracy in the school settings within which they are succeeding (Brantlinger, 1993; Cookson & Persell, 1985; Kuriloff & Reichert, 2003; Simmons & Rosenberg, 1971). Brantlinger (1993), for example, found that fewer high-status students than low-status students believed that grades were an indication of intelligence (p. 119). Furthermore, high-status students emphasized, to a greater degree than did low-status students, speech and conversation patterns as signs of intelligence (p. 118). Thus, high-status students seem to have some inkling of the arbitrary nature of school standards and the ways in which middle-class and upper-class cultural values are performed as a criterion of intelligence and a prerequisite for school success. Similarly, Flanagan and Tucker (1999) presented data indicating that privileged youth "were least likely to believe that opportunities were equal and that support from the government promotes dependency" (p. 1203). They also found that privileged youth "were more likely to note the situational or structural roots of unemployment, poverty, and homelessness, whereas the least privileged youth tended to hold individuals accountable" (p. 1207).[5]

Shifting from race and class privilege to academic or track privilege, consider a group of student researchers working with Ondrea Reisinger and Alison Cook-Sather (Dunderdale, Tourscher, Yoo, & Reisinger, 2001) who researched and presented student narratives of bias. Within the context of tracking, stories of witnessed bias were narrated mostly by students in the upper tracks.[6] What became clear is that students are aware of, and hold, contradictory and complex understandings of the social and material reward afforded by their upper-tracked position. One student researcher concluded that although "each class must have a different grading standard based on ability," he later questioned such an organic understanding of intelligence, asking, "If the teacher can just assume that the 'A' students will always get A's, then why not assume that 'C' students will always get C's? Perhaps a 'C' student had wonderful ideas and worked very diligently preparing a marvelous paper, and it is returned to him with a C. This destroys the student's self-esteem as well as his will power to do any work" (Yoo in Dunderdale, p. 64).

Student ambivalence suggests that high-status students might also very well be motivated to ignore or protect themselves against the knowledge that the educational system, and especially their own school, is unfair or biased, as it may activate fears about their own worthiness and the veracity of received praise and positive feedback or challenge the legitimacy of the disproportionately fewer resources (both human and material) for lower tracked students (or students in poorer urban schools or districts), as well as highlight unsettling desires for maintaining advantage in a competitive and hierarchical structure of schooling (Berlak & Moyenda, 2001).

According to equity theory (Walster, Berscheid, & Walster, 1976), the sense that one has been overrewarded, relative to their inputs, is associated with distress. Similar to the experience of guilt, distress around one's compensation-to-input ratio is argued to trigger an "equalizing" response. However, in their study of White guilt, social psychologists Iyer et al. (2004 [this volume]) have argued that precisely because guilt is associated with "a narrow concern for restitution," it is not typically the basis for more general efforts to combat inequality, such as affirmative action. Although this project is not about privileged guilt per se,[7] it is concerned with the psychologically "equalizing" practices that alleviate the distressing experience of unearned advantage yet work to maintain such inequality. Therefore, it is necessary to address privileged anxiety, specifically the ways in which individuals enact institutional and national anxieties around merit, privilege, and race (Eng, 2001; Powell & Barber, in press), as well as mobilize such anxieties for social change.

METHOD

I rely primarily on focus group and interview data: seven semistructured focus groups[8] and six interviews were conducted with youth identified by their schools as "high achieving." This sample of academically successful youth was mainly, although not exclusively, White[9] and middle class. Three broad questions were asked in the focus groups, including what students liked about their schools, what they wanted to see changed, and what helped or hindered academic success in their schools. We then described what has been called the minority achievement gap, and we asked participants to explain why students identified as White and Asian Pacific Islander, as well as those families with more money, tended to do the best in school academically. We[10] asked students to discuss the kinds of things, including environments, qualities, people, and structures, help students do well academically in their schools. Across the schools, we heard that teachers and parents play a major supportive role, that students need to be self-confident, and that they "can't be completely apathetic." When the notion of hard work comes up, it is in terms of working hard to earn higher quality teaching in the upper tracks and securing teacher interest and concern.

At times I condense lengthy sections of transcript but only when the intent and context would not significantly change. I have used [...] to indicate where in the transcript dialogue has been removed or to make notations clarifying context and meaning.

PERFORMING SUCCESS: MAKING IT BY MAKING YOURSELF KNOWN

The long acting out of a role, with its appropriate motives, will often induce a man [*sic*] to become what at first he merely sought to appear.

—C. Wright Mills (1975, p. 165)

A connection between the understood quality of upper level courses and perceived student motivation emerges very early across focus groups. From this perspective, "working hard" earns better teachers, highlighting the perception that teacher support is contingent and the responsibility for quality teaching is located within the student. Being in the top tracks becomes then the way to perform or enact one's interest and concern about their education. The perceived contingency of teacher help emerges in a focus group at Andrews High in a racially mixed group. Tobias indicated that he goes for help even when he does not need it in order to secure adult investment in him.

Q: What impact does the teacher, the staff, the building, or the institution, have on [student] achievement?
TOBIAS: Yeah, because if you say, "Am I doing okay?" "How can you help me?" You say, "Hey, I don't really understand this assignment," even if you do, just in September, so your teacher knows, stay after school if he [the teacher] needs it, you know and they'll help you out. Same way in life. If someone doesn't care and just wants to do their thing and go and just fall through the cracks, you can fall through the cracks too. The people who get ahead, the people who are successful in whatever they do are the people who [...] advocate for themselves.

Securing teacher interest and investment is understood as "advocating" for one's self, whether struggling with the material or not. As staying after school is actually for the benefit of the teacher ("stay after school if he needs it") and not for the student, going for help is revealed to be the rationale teachers require in order to "legitimately" treat students preferentially. Indeed, across the consortium, students in advanced placement (AP) or honors courses were significantly more likely than students in regular, basic, or special education classes to report that their teachers were responsive.[11] Tobias's understanding of success in starkly individual terms, his commitment to self-reliance, and the belief that students are on their own if they fail to enroll others in supporting their achievement cannot be understood outside of a national context of punitive accountability measures and privatization or outside of an institutional context in which resources and teacher quality and concern are made differentially available, most obviously through tracking. The distribution of human and material investment in students by race or ethnicity requires a justification that the "staying after school" performance helps provide. Thus, student performances of academic merit (test scores, grades, and class participation) justify, rather than cause, racialized differences in resources and adult investment.

As Nick, an African American honors student at Kane, pointed out, not every student who seeks extra help finds a receptive adult. Kane High is in many ways a typical representation of participating schools across the consortium. This mixed, but predominantly White, suburban school of approximately 1,500 students is located in an upper-middle-class community in a northeastern suburb and is demographically similar to other participating suburban schools. At the time of the project, the student body was roughly 65% White, with a fairly stable 8% to 10% African American population and a growing Latino community currently around 20%. Approximately 70% of White and Asian students in this school are enrolled in AP and honors classes, compared with 35% of African American and Latino students at this school.

> NICK: There's another thing about when you get extra help. I have a strong feeling about this. A lot of times when I've gone for extra help, I've been criticized before I get helped. Once you're criticized ... I know for myself personally, I don't go back. I'm not going back to anybody who's going to sit there and criticize me. Like I've been told, "Nick, you should know this stuff" when I've gone for help. And, that's a big problem with kids. They don't want to be criticized when they go for help.

Although seeking extra help is read as motivation and eagerness in White students, it is interpreted as a need for remediation when students of color ask for help. Such interactions communicate to Nick, and students similarly positioned, that he should avoid asking for help. Tobias, on the other hand, learned that failure is the failure to ask for help and thus originates within the student. Even within de-tracked classrooms, though, the performance of "Whiteness as giftedness" (Staiger, 1997) continues to figure prominently. Continuing at Kane High, Henry (a White middle-class senior) offered an example of favoritism at the intersections of race, gender, and class.

> HENRY: I'm in the economics class now. It's not advanced at all and the teacher knew who I was and I almost feel like he's nicer to me than other students and it's noticeable. [...] He's just—whatever I do, it's almost ... it's a good thing. He gives me quite a lot of compliments. He knew me before hand. And, you can tell the other people notice.

Being advanced in some classes distinguishes Henry in all of his other classes as well, and comes with a set of goods, such as attention, praise, respect, and what he later described as "pretty good treatment." As Staiger (1997) argued in her analysis of a White magnet school within a large urban school, "once labeled gifted, always gifted: The label provides access to high-quality education throughout a student's career and thus amplifies the earlier inequalities in access to education and identification" (see also Perry, 2003).

In Henry's mind, there is an intimate connection between who he is, what classes (track) he "comes from," and the treatment he gets. However, the actual legitimacy of this favored treatment is questioned: It is not assumed to have been earned at all. Instead, there is a level of distress in Henry's description of advantage, as predicted by equity theory (Walster et al., 1976). However, the tension is not so much an internally originating confliction (Mills, 1975; Sampson, 1981) but one borne from the national and institutional tensions between a vocal commitment to equality regardless of race or ethnicity and the whispered commitment to Whiteness as privilege in practice. What effect does it have on Henry's sense of social responsibility or his perceived ability to make change, when whatever he does is considered a "good thing"?

Henry was also upset by the fact that his teacher made his favoritism obvious. He twice asserted that others "noticed" the favoritism. Henry's concern reveals the importance of keeping preferential treatment quiet, not making it obvious or overtly known. The strategy is to perfect a performance of hard work and fairness, while downplaying the expression of favoritism — a staged whisper performed by both teacher and student to which Angela, quoted earlier, referred.

[continuing]

Q: So, what is that like when other kids notice?

HENRY: I don't really mind. It's not that big of a deal anymore. We don't really care. It's assumed . . . it's going through school now. It's not like the biggest deal in the world.

JAKE: I think teachers are always going to play favorites though because it's just human nature. It'd be ideal if they didn't, but if a teacher likes you and you start doing badly in their class, they'll tell you because they want you to do better. They don't like [you] and you're doing badly in their class, they won't care. That's where the lack of motivation comes in and then if you don't go to the advanced classes and you get the worst teachers and it's a cycle.

The more Henry was questioned, the more anxious and defensive he seemed to get. In his defensiveness, he shifted from "I" statements to "we" statements in an effort to distribute responsibility and garner support. Jake responded to this call for help and introduced a universalizing discourse about human nature, thereby dispensing with any critique or the necessity for change. Ultimately, Jake reframed favoritism as earned and deserved, thus psychologically and discursively reestablishing "equity," although unequal outcomes are maintained. This is not a distortion of merit but rather an important way the meaning of deserving is actually created, what Phoenix, Frosh, and Pattman (2003) called a "practical achievement." Merit and deserving — like Whiteness — are not a set of enduring, identifiable, and consistent qualities or characteristics so much as a set of practices, or moral and discursive positions, always in repair, that are taken up and ultimately supported or challenged institutionally and structurally. Later on within this same group at Kane, anxiety around race and merit erupted more explicitly.

Q: What might make a teacher think you wouldn't succeed?

NOAH: You want somebody to say minority, don't you? Like, I really don't think that's the case. If someone works hard, then, it's golden. . . . Unless —

JAKE [interrupting]: You don't make it known.

NOAH: No, I think it is true.

JAKE: Well, if the kid works hard, but they don't make it known to the teacher, then, to me, it's almost like, well, yeah, you're learning and you're bettering yourself, but you're not getting the most you can out of all the work you're doing. I mean, again, I sit next to people that do much more work than me. But, I feel like I get just as much out of the class just by sitting there and paying attention to the class and getting a lot out of the 50 minutes we have in class rather than going home and taking 3 hours of notes. Because, we come to a class and the teacher doesn't see your notes and it's almost like, you're not getting the most out of it.

Noah's comments indicate a sense of being monitored, and of the monitoring of adult expectations, indicating an anxiety around being labeled "racist" and a concern for adult perceptions. Thus, "getting the most" out of one's schooling experience comes to mean the display, or performance, of one's intelligence, specifically in terms of product — as the possession of knowledge rather than the process of acquiring or constructing it. "Making it known" is a crucial aspect of *making it*, both as showing one's success and as creating or constituting the fact of one's intelligence. More than that though, the practice of "making it known" is a stand-in for practices constituting race or Whiteness, because one is actually made known through institutional structures of race and class.

Moreover, being seen as not smart, vis-à-vis one's tracked position, is just as aversive as being seen as a racist or as someone who enjoys unfair advantage. In the following discussion at Douglas High, a deep concern with getting into the top tracks emerged, particularly for White students, underscoring an intense anxiety around being identified with the lower tracks, coded as "minority" in the public imagination. Jennifer, a White student who wanted to add even more AP courses to her school's already broad range of options, explained her experience in a detracked setting, while Omara, an African American student, is asked to respond.

> JENNIFER: In ninth grade we had the challenge projects [...] and all this other stuff to get into honors. And I really was interested in what we were learning; I always really loved world history. And I basically, I would do my homework every day and I knew what was going on, and there are people in my class who kept telling me Europe was a country! And I'm like, O-kay, and I ... it's not like — I don't have anything against them because of that. It's just that I would prefer to be with people who were just as interested in that as I am, and stuff like that. And so as I worked, like I worked harder and harder, but like the first marking period I got really bad grades, and I was like, oh, my God, I'm not going to get into honors social studies, and I'm going to be in the stupid class one year and I'm not going to be able to concentrate. And I was just like really ... it was horrible to put like that much stress on someone.
>
> [group silence]
>
> JENNIFER [to Omara, the only African American in the group]: I was just ... sorry.... No, I ... I'm sorry. I'm sorry. I didn't mean it that way, but like, no, it's like there are a bunch of kids in my class who really didn't try, and they were really like, they would say things that they know ... they knew were wrong, just to like drive people who are working and seeing, and like I don't mean to call them stupid.
>
> OMARA: I know. [SEVERAL PEOPLE TALKING] Like, I have some honors classes, and then I have Regents courses, and then it's like, in this school, we look at Regents courses as being the dumb class, but it's like we're above a lot of other schools. Like my cousin, he lives in the south, they don't have Regents classes. So what are we going to call them, the mentally challenged class? ... [LAUGHTER] No, I'm serious. [...] And that is a barrier. And I think the minority achievement gap is like — a lot of minority kids are in Regents classes, and they're like, okay, I can't be in honors class because I'm in Regents, and in this school it seems like Regents is the bottom level. [...] And that's why a lot of kids are like "I'm not going to go to honors, because I don't want to have that attitude and look down on other people." And I'm not saying that you're looking down on people. I'm saying that is like the *theme* of this school.

Thus, we hear an intimate connection between one's racial identity and one's tracked identity, the base of which is the structure and culture, or "theme," of many suburban schools. Jennifer's fear about ending up in the "stupid class" says a lot about how "regular" Regents classes are viewed; how they are differently valued by students, parents, and teachers; and ultimately who they are reserved for. Jennifer shifted from defining Regent's students as "stupid" to simply as unmotivated and, in fact, as antagonistic toward her (and their) education. This discursive maneuvering from derogation to victim blaming, in the form of righteous indignation, is another way in which equity is psychologically reestablished. In either situation, lower tracked students and students of color are a means of distinguishing White students as intelligent and motivated.

> MYRA: It's just like, you walk around and you see different people and you see people all around you and we're like, we go to a diverse school. But, it's almost like self-congratulatory because you know at the same time you're going to a school with people who are different from you. *It feels like they're there just to make you better.* [emphasis added]

Backstage Moms (and Dads and Bank Accounts) in the Context of Youth Performance of "Smart": Privatization and the Performance of Hyperactivity

Although Leah does not implicate herself explicitly in the following discussion, except perhaps as a member of the community, she does reveal the cache of privatized supports that enable some students to present an academic hyperactivity. Her structural critique of the race- and class-stratified distribution of wealth, coupled with a sense that things might be "a lot different," suggests an emerging sense of moral outrage (Deutsch, 1979; Leach et al., 2002), which becomes clearer further on.

> LEAH: I think financial issues play a huge role, especially in a community like this, like the majority of people who belong to minority groups are of lower income and they don't have the money to get a private tutor for every class your child has, you know, below a 95 in.
>
> Q: Is that common here?
>
> LEAH: Yeah, I mean, my neighbor has a daughter who is a freshman who has a 99 average in biology and she got her a private tutor for that. And, like, so imagine for a kid who doesn't have a 99 average and who doesn't have the money to put into that. And, who, not even money for tutors, but maybe you need to have a job every day after school, so you have less time to study. And, like, even beyond high school, college, you're limited by what college you can go to depending on what you can pay. And, it puts severe limitations especially like in a community where the playing field is so uneven because you're either getting so much because of the money or so little and […] like, if everyone is just working on their own merit, then it would be a lot different than people who can get all this extra help compared to kids who can't.

Leah's description of the excessive measures that families sometimes resort to also points to anxiety related to the extreme performance demands felt by both students and parents, but particularly by White affluent students (Luthar & Becker, 2002). Students are not only expected to present themselves in market terms — as one student reported, "You have to sell yourself" — but are also expected to assert their academic dominance over others as the basis of White identity formation (whether or not they actually consider themselves White). There is a parallel between the national demand put on schools to demonstrate their moral worth and educational quality through largely punitive accountability measures (such as showing rising test scores and grades [Apple, 2004 (this volume)]) and the demand put on individual students — understood as representing their nation, school, and communities — to publicly demonstrate their academic deservedness by distinguishing themselves within a tracked, percentile-based, raced, or classed system of reward.

SOCIAL (IN)SECURITY: "RACING" TOWARD PERFORMANCE DEMANDS

> So I guess when I discovered one day that I was really good at BS-ing my work, I just stopped really trying, but still did well. It just magically happened.
>
> —Eric, high-achieving White student, Douglas High School

Kuriloff and Reichert (2003), researching an elite private school for boys, described a "no sweat" attitude displayed by many of the students, especially the highest achieving ones. In this context, sweat referred to the perspiration of hard work. They found evidence of a school cultural demand for the presentation of one's superior academic standing as achieved without breaking a sweat (Kuriloff & Reichert, 2003; also Cookson & Persell, 1985). But why would anyone want to downplay what has been fairly earned? The desire and demand to show how easy academic success has been achieved is the desire to display "inherent" academic superiority and constitutes a downplaying of one's hard work as well as one's material and privatized supports. One reason for the slippage between the discourse of effort and ability may be the attempt to reduce the sense of relative advantage and account for the perceived arbitrariness of one's success (Leach et al., 2002).

If we refuse to believe that the sweat doesn't exist, both as hard work and as anxiety and concern, then where does it go and how is it managed? The following discussions reveal the "racializing" of sweat (both in terms of hard work and anxiety) to be a means of dealing with (in)security around privilege — the fear of losing advantage as well as the anxiety produced by having access to what others do not.

NO SWEAT: THE RACIALIZATION OF PERSPIRATION

At Douglass High, a school demographically similar to Kane, I spoke with Eric, a White student finishing his junior year. Eric described himself as a wealthy kid whom nobody could "picture without money," who aspired to be friends with everyone. He was doing well in his AP and honors courses but considered himself a "slacker."

APRIL: You said [earlier] that you do enough to get by. Do teachers ever tell you that they know you could do better?

ERIC: Well, some of them, not all of them. Like my history teacher last year, she got mad at me because she knew I could do so much better than I was doing. But then she goes, "Well, you're Eric, and you're going to do fine so...." I have teachers tell me that. I mean, it's very supportive. That's great, thanks. My work habits aren't getting any better, but they tell me I can do well in life.

APRIL: What do you think of that?

ERIC: It makes me happy, but it makes me confused at the same time. I always hear "Work hard," and, you know, I work hard the day before it's due. That's when I work hard. For example, I have a presentation to do tomorrow in American history, and I haven't started that yet. But I did the same thing last time. I got a 97.

APRIL: So what does that tell you?

ERIC: It tells me that the way you present things and the way you do things, like the kind of style or the words you choose or the process you do, like, you know, that means more than the work behind it. It's one of those lessons in life that you don't tell kids, but is really true. You know, you don't want kids to find out the secret so young in life so they'll do what I do, you know.

Eric understands that he is being rewarded for staging a credible justification for his success, but he is less sure about his level of hard work and merit. However, like the public at large, he ultimately comes to equate one with the other, having been led to believe — at least on one level — that he has earned his privilege whereas other students have earned their failure. His privilege is inevitable, secured emotionally and materially by the history of racialized success (and successes thwarted) propping up and legitimating his advantaged position. Still, not all successful students employ a White interpretive frame uncritically, nor do they understand success as zero-sum. In a separate interview with Nick, the African American honors student, we hear the acknowledgment of the power of performance as well as resistance to it.

> APRIL: Well do people — any students, ever consider you privileged in any way?
> NICK: [pause] I don't see it. Maybe because, I guess . . . I don't know, I just, I don't know. It's a really hard question for me to ask [myself] because I'm one of those, I don't know, people that like, just because a test says I scored 90 doesn't mean I'm smart. Like I just [LAUGHS] . . . I really feel that I'm smart in my little own ways, in my own way I'm smart. But I wouldn't — I don't, I don't see people like that. . . . I feel like in this school if you're *in* those smart classes, even though you're not smart [LAUGHS] . . . [then] you *are*.
> Q: Oh, yeah? In what way?
> NICK: Because [the principal] knows your name. . . . [LAUGHS] And you also fit in with the, a big clique of people that, you know, we're all part of APs you know? We often discuss literature and like that. Or like, I'm in those English classes and I can't discuss half the stuff, you know. It's like . . . well for me it's, I don't know. That's enough about the issue. It's stale, it's . . . I think a lot of people, like Tim brought up before, that, you know, a lot of people are in the APs.

Nick struggles with his position vis-à-vis the top classes, as does Omara (quoted earlier), suggesting a Dubosian contradiction (Du Bois, 1935) in his identification with high level (and predominantly White) tracks and his sense of self. Scores do not make you smart, even though they mark you as intelligent ("we discuss literature" and "we're all a part of APs"), and yet he does not feel smart in the same ways ("I can't discuss half the stuff"). He ends by downplaying his position, stating, "a lot of people are in the APs." Echoing Omara, this might be read as resistance to setting himself apart from other students in lower levels or distinguishing himself as "better than." The devaluation of accomplishment is actually downplaying having what others do not have (i.e., access to what is made scarce) and is thus a response to a felt threat to one's integrity. The problem with acting smart is not "acting white" as much as "better than," which is seen as profoundly anti-Black in its divisiveness and countercollective in its individual focus and is thus understood as inherently supportive of White privilege (Carter, forthcoming). For poorer students and students of color, the demand that they publicly perform their academic superiority is understood as jeopardizing collective engagement and threatening community separation, social isolation, and vulnerability. For Nick, doing well is not solely determined by outward measures but subjectively and based in his school experiences: "I know when I'm doing well when I sometimes step out of my comfort zone and nothing bad happens."

The difference between Eric and Nick, then, is the level of security of their position as smart and deserving students. Whereas Nick provided several examples of teachers and administrators challenging his place in upper level courses, Eric was amazed at the "magical" way he manages to maintain his position. Both students narrated considerable ambivalence about their academic success, yet Eric is assured that no matter what, he will do just fine whether he puts forth his best effort or not. On the other hand, Nick worried about paying for college and surviving his senior year. Not only did Nick have a part-time job, he also was forced to take on a heavier course load during his senior year to compensate for his lower tracked courses in middle school in order to get into the college of his choice. Eric, however, was able to complete several unpaid internships even before entering his senior year of high school. Whereas Nick had to type his papers in the school computer lab, Eric relied on his mother to provide administrative assistance with his homework and had a host of technical equipment at his disposal, as well as professional and school contacts to use. Consequently, the amount of sweat that must be expended by students varies significantly by one's racial or ethnic positionality.

Sweating It: The Racialization of Anxiety

Powell and Barber (in press), connecting the dire state of urban education to the exceptionality of suburban education, understood the simultaneous defunding and privatization of public institutions, specifically urban schools, to be a systemic response or defense mechanism to increasing levels of social and individual anxiety around schooling. "In actuality, what appear to be our 'failures' in urban education are extreme and unconscious attempts to protect adults [and youth] from fundamental questions about 'merit' and 'value' of various demographic groups" (Powell & Barber, forthcoming, p. 16). Just as the sweat of hard work is racially distributed, so is the apprehension and unease around notions of academic merit felt by schools (Powell, 1997), with students of color acting as lightning rods for larger social and institutional anxieties.

In the following discussion at Kane, we hear the repression of aspiration as well as the seeding of self-doubt and worry. We also hear the compensatory influence that a single concerned adult can provide. Nick and Angela discussed with Chuck (who is White) their navigation of the college entrance process.

> NICK: I have to say my counselor, maybe because she's also African American, has been like my second mother. [...] My counselor is kind of like, "Nick, I'm keeping you focused. This is what I want you to do. You can do it." She's always hounding me to do stuff.
>
> [...]
>
> ANGELA: I think counselors have actually predetermined who you are and base your whole school experience on that. And, my counselor, I made a point of never going to her. She didn't help me at all. I went in there and I came out ... [crying] ... I got my SAT scores back and she told me I didn't do that bad—I got an 1120—and she said, "Well, you did well for a Hispanic. Your verbal score is better than your math score. Considering that your parents don't know how to speak English." She never met my parents. My parents speak English fine. They speak it amongst themselves. And, [as] we were going through the college process, I told her I wanted to apply to BU, which I don't think is a hard reach. I don't think it's especially difficult to get into. She said, "Well, try shooting a little lower. I don't know if you'll be able to get in there. Think about other colleges."
>
> Q: Did you apply to Boston University?
>
> ANGELA: No, I ended up not applying there. She totally disillusioned me. I mean, I don't know if I could've gone there—now I still don't know. Maybe I could've gotten in.
>
> [...]

CHUCK: Well, the college process, I think in particular, is the biggest thing that you have to do with your counselor. And, my counselor here was just basically ... he just gave me a list of schools, but it wasn't anything really specific. And, I got this college counselor, like another counselor. [...] This was someone we got recommended from families. People that are professional college counselors, that's all they do. It's like ... I never heard of that. I didn't know what was going on. My mom heard about it from another family friend whose daughter used her. [...]

Here we see how much educational outcomes depend on interactions with counselors and school administrators when students lack the financial ability to make up for, much less compete with, structural inequalities. Nick is lucky to have a counselor that has made it her priority to push him as well as support him academically. Angela—who said that as a Latina, she felt she made it into honors and AP courses "by mistake"—was not as fortunate with her counselor. Ultimately, she had no financial net to bounce her back into the elite ranks the way that Chuck did. It makes little difference if Chuck gets helpful advice from his guidance counselor, because he is able to bypass that resource altogether. Angela, who enrolled at a small local college, will probably remain angry with herself and continue to doubt her intelligence and the quality of her education far into the future. What is tragic is that she, and students like her, will carry forward— and transform into her own—the social and institutional anxieties around her academic ability, further tempering her educational aspirations and sense of self-efficacy.

Thus, there are important distinctions to be made between youth who are privileged by race or social class, or both, and academically successful youth, although I am currently defining one group in terms of the other. Young people privileged by race or class, or both, often will be successful even if they do not work hard or are not "naturally bright" or "quick," whereas students of color, and poor or working-class students, have often had to push past heavily monitored educational boundaries to experience some or, in a few cases, much success in school. Even though academic success for less advantaged students will ultimately translate into greater privilege in the future, it does not diminish the relative disadvantage facing people of color and poor students in relation to White and middle-class students (Arnold, 1995).

Still, although successful but less privileged students are more likely to introduce social critique into discussions and bring up racism as opposed to diversity, they also frequently forward very similar arguments as their White and upper-classed peers do. They take up similar positions around student responsibility: the need to make one's academic eagerness known to adults in the school, to take advantage of all available opportunities, and to proudly protect their schools, seeing them as positive places overall that prepare them well for college. Because schools are an integral part of student identity, as well as sources of pride, most students resist critiquing them. For White students, often pessimistic (as well as ambivalent) about the possibility of change, school critique just sounds like derogation. However, for students of color (and some Whites)—many who believe intensely in the possibility and desirability of change— critique is seen as constructive, representing social engagement and community investment.

RESPONSIBILITY FOR CONTEXTS—LESSONS IN POSSIBILITY

When you see any sort of injustice that's going on in the world, there has to be someone who's motivated to change it or else it will never get changed. And if you don't have exposure to anything but your own little White, bright community, then why would you ever be motivated to change anything?

—Leah, White senior at Kane

Because the opportunity-achievement gap is seen primarily as an issue for students of color and their families, rather than an issue of school structures and cultures, the responsibility for addressing structures and practices perpetuating racialized differences in educational outcomes tends to be assigned to students of color, their families, or individual White students holding progressive values. However, without the whole cache of privatized resources available to their peers and against which they must compete, minority students are forced to decide between their own success, requiring silence and complicity, or challenging school power structures and thereby putting their chances of achievement in jeopardy. Individual White students, although not risking their own success when pushing for progressive social change, are nevertheless forced to "assert," over and over again, their commitment to interrupting institutional silence and production of stratification. Yet students do assert their commitments, make their concern and confusion known, and defiantly call for equal opportunity — particularly academically successful students. There are three major areas in which schools can facilitate caring critique and socially responsible action toward racial equality. These areas include the individual support and models provided by adults in schools; the availability of free spaces encouraging critical thought, student leadership, and action; and the inclusion of young people in the power structure and decision-making process in schools.

Adult Supports

In the discussion with Nick about the kinds of things that helped him succeed academically in his school, he mentioned his close relationship with his counselor, also a woman of color. He described her as advocating for him and his inclusion in higher tracks, as pushing him to work hard, and as providing a constant source of encouragement through an educational process that often felt hostile and forbidding. Her support helped Nick challenge the inaccessibility, and accepted superiority, of the upper tracks, providing him a measure of safety to speak from when all his experiences have told him to shut up and be gratefully invisible. Nick told me, "When you are prepared you can stand up for yourself and speak your mind." In more than one school, a strong adult — often a guidance counselor, and more often a woman of color as well — actively and visibly working to make change provided an invaluable resource for students of color. To students of all racial classifications, though, such adults also symbolize possibilities for voicing constructive critique and changing school practices. The concerned counselor, dean, teacher, or school psychologist identified by students as an ally concerned with issues of racial equity was also very much seen as a committed member of the school community. These adults face their own uphill battle when they agree to sponsor controversial student groups, such as gay-straight alliances or groups concerned with racism or racial equity, and when they choose to lead discussion groups, integrate social spaces, or attempt to include ESL students in school functions.

Although these concerned adults are sometimes asked to leave, or leave (without being asked to stay) for settings in which they can hope to be heard and assisted, without others to continue the struggle against racial or ethnic stratification, the loss of their caring dissent is particularly devastating to students. When school administrations do not appear to care about maintaining the engagement of people of color or others willing to pose critique, who forward excitement and optimism for change, they send a strong message to the student body that these folks are not valued and that their revolutionary contributions only put themselves at risk.

Opportunities for Critical Thought, Student Leadership, and Action

Although academically successful students are typically understood to be rule followers (Fine, 1991), concerned with fulfilling institutional or school obligations rather than mounting critique, it is often the very privilege that academic success affords that allows some students the space and security to make social change efforts. This is particularly the case for one young woman, Leah, a White senior. Leah discussed the experiences of witnessing acts of injustice at her school and how it led her to action:

> APRIL: If there is something going on in your school that you don't like [...] whose responsibility do you think it is to change that? [...]
>
> LEAH: Well I think if it's something that's affecting you, then ... unless for some reason like you really feel threatened or you know, like in danger, then it should be to some degree your responsibility. [...] I think if you're someone who witnesses something, then it becomes your responsibility. And I think once it's, once any issue is brought to the attention of, you know, an authority figure who actually can do something, then it's their responsibility to at least address it, like as opposed to the response I got, like, "Oh, you're so smart!" or "Why don't you join the debate team?"

Many more advantaged students, however, choose not to participate in such efforts. When asked about the source of this sense of responsibility, Leah identified her participation in social action groups, both in and outside of school, as supportive environments broadening the range of imagined options and as a catalyst for her critical thinking. In particular, Leah described her summer camp experiences, her family, and her involvement in her school's gay-straight alliance. She described her progressive camp as a "second family" that showed her that "you could not only feel this way about things but we can do something about it and that was like—I mean, I was a little kid but I was like, 'Oh, my God, I can *do* stuff.'"

Leah's comments illustrate the importance of community investment in the notion of young people as active agents of change rather than as passive members. Community and school groups emphasizing the fact that youth can be concerned and capable citizens with valuable insight develop young people who also believe that about themselves. Understanding one's community as family, as Leah does, provides the opportunity to engage in relational risk outlined by Elliott (2002). Furthermore, Leah indicated that her task is not so much to change people's minds as to engage those who do hold progressive beliefs and move them toward taking action for change.

Leah described a time when she did speak out, with a written letter to her principal, questioning the way the school administration chose to respond to the events of 9-11-01. Leah never got a response from the adults in her school that wasn't merely a legitimation of her merits as an outstanding student ("Why don't you join the debate team"), illustrating that even when privileged youth make their minority opinions known, their privilege is not really at risk—just their sense of moral imperative and perceived ability to make change. Leah described how advantaged young people, bolstered by a sense of entitlement, are willing and capable of directing their work efforts toward social equity. In collaboration with her campus gay-straight alliance, Leah helped organize a speak-out and public education event at her school.

> LEAH: [...] So we took control of all 1,300 students ... [LAUGHS] and all the teachers and we began like dividing them up into groups and surrounding myself with miles and miles of paperwork. [...]

What distinguished this event from typical "cultural exchanges" sponsored by many school districts is the push toward political context. The choice of speakers connected the local community (e.g., panel of ESL students in the school, and a district attorney discussing local hate crimes) to the national context (e.g., political cartoonist, and Native American discussant on indigenous people's rights) to international concerns (e.g., participation of a "Muslims Against Terrorism" organization).

Leah informed me that she and several other students had been thinking about organizing such an event for 2 years but "just didn't really know how we could pull it off. Like, we weren't getting support from the administration." That a small group of students were ultimately able to push past the opposition mounted by their school is a feat unto itself, but that it took 2 years to accomplish points to the subtractive power (Valenzuela, 1999) of schools resistant to change. It also locates gaps in social responsibility within the privileging processes of schools themselves.

As Darren, who also participated in the event, pointed out, though, in isolation, the efforts of students and adults are not enough to create change: "There are teachers here that are *really* good teachers and they will sit here and tell you that there are real problems in the school. But at the same time, they can't do stuff alone, you know. And the same thing with the GSA (Gay-Straight Alliance), we can't do things alone, or I can't do things alone. You know, it's going to take people getting together and the school."

INSTITUTIONAL COMMITMENTS TO CHANGE

Privileged engagement with social change efforts must also be supported by institutional commitments to change that are made public and that include young people. Establishing and funding more initiatives addressing the stratifying structures and practices within a school and community, such as the Task Force on Racial Equity mentioned next, build in opportunities for socially responsible action for young people.

> KYLE: [...] I'm on the task force for racial equity for like the superintendent. We're looking at test scores. You have that achievement gap all the way through! But then, like, one of the ways this school is like, quick, fix the problem and prevent racial tension is by saying, well, if a kid wants it, we'll put him in 5 or if a kid wants it, we'll put him in 4. [...] What I see a lot of is they try to avoid creating a problem more than solving a problem. [...] We're not fixing anything. We just look and say, the problem is Black kids and the White kids don't sit together. The problem is the AP classes are a large percentage White. Well, the reason the AP classes are a large percentage White is because when I was in middle school, if I didn't get into a top-level class, or some of my friends didn't, my mom was coming in to raise hell. Where otherwise, there are some kids that don't have that opportunity. [...] And, I just think we're just kind of standing still. We're on a treadmill, but we think we're running up the hill.

Kyle is able to engage in change efforts and look critically — and safely — at stratifying practices and performance demands in his school. Although many student researchers identified the Critical Opportunity Gap Project as a context and structure of possibility, it was one outside of the power structure of the school and district itself. After students research, analyze, and present back their research findings and recommendations, the schools must then carry forward such student and community mandates.

Conclusion

> All identifications are inevitably failed identifications, a continual passing as a coherent and stable social identity. Even the most orthodox of subject positions, finally, are ambivalent and porous.
>
> —Eng (2001, p. 26)

Who do we designate to "sweat" for us when we are not allowed or expected to? This is not a question of scapegoats but rather a question specifically designated people to care. Too often caring is shouldered primarily by students of color and occasionally by one or two White students committed to racial or economic justice, a single guidance counselor, dean, or teacher. Just as our academic expectations of students are primarily race based, so are our expectations for social justice action. Like the student sitting in class who is denied, whether passively or actively, a rigorous education and intellectual engagement because he or she refuses to enact a raced performance of merit, privileged and academically successful students, although allowed critique, are nevertheless denied the opportunity to engage in relational risk, especially when their own status is at stake, because they are assumed to be incapable of, or unwilling, to care.

Students live their context, not automatically nor remotely but interpretively, using the information and resources at their disposal to make sense of and navigate their worlds. And if we ask them to maintain privilege, many of them will. If the very adults understood to be responsible and in charge turn blind eyes and hearts to the experiences of injustice that students actively bring to their attention, they teach them a powerful lesson in priorities and values. If we ask them to suppress and ignore their own discomfort around injustice and their role in it, deny their consistent overreward, we do harm and perpetuate injustice. Too often, schools teach students not to trust themselves but instead to monitor the demands of others, but only those students in positions of power and influence. We teach young people that a performance of equality is not the same as equal opportunity but just as acceptable, and then we blame them for not caring or doing enough. We teach them to isolate themselves and instill in them a fear of relating to others by structuring access to a quality education hierarchically or competitively, and then we accuse them of being self-serving.

Assumptions of concern must be incorporated into the educational process itself, and those fought for spaces, such as student political organizations, that afford and facilitate the acknowledgment and negotiation of power (Torre, 2003), that move discussions beyond blame or guilt, and that value students equally, must be nurtured institutional and financially. Beyond establishing student-directed spaces, supporting caring critique by students and adults, and including students in the very decision-making processes effecting their education, schools must also acknowledge and address evidence of—and outrage about—academic opportunities that are consistently made differentially available by race.

References

Acosta, N., Castillo, J., DeJesus, C., Genoa, E., Jones, M., Kellman, S., Osario, A., Rahman, N., Sheard, L., & Taylor, J. (2003). Urban students tackle research on inequality. *Rethinking Schools, 18*, 31–32.

Amrein, A. L., & Berliner, D. C. (2002). *An analysis of some unintended and negative consequences of high-stakes testing* (EPSL-0211–125-EPRU). Tempe: Educational Policy Studies Laboratory, Arizona State University.

Apple, M. W. (2004). Making White right: Race and the politics of educational reform. In M. Fine, L. Weis, L. P. Pruitt, & A. Burns (Eds.), *Off White: Readings on power, privilege, and resistance* (2nd ed.). New York: Routledge.

Arnold, K. D. (1995). *Lives of promise: What becomes of high school valedictorians.* San Francisco: Jossey-Bass.

Augoustinos, M. (1999). Ideology, false consciousness and psychology. *Theory and Psychology,* 9(3), 295–312.

Berlak, A., & Moyenda, S. (2001). *Taking it personally: Racism in the classroom from kindergarten to college.* Philadelphia: Temple University Press.

Bourdieu, P. (1984). *Distinction: A social critique of the judgement of taste* (R. Nice, Trans.). Cambridge, MA: Harvard University Press.

Bourdieu, P., & Passeron, J. C. (1977). *Reproduction in education, society and culture.* London: Sage.

Brantlinger, E. A. (1993). *The politics of social class in secondary school: Views of affluent and impoverished youth.* New York: Teachers College Press.

Brown, C. S. (2002). *Refusing racism: White allies and the struggle for civil rights.* New York: Teachers College Press.

Carter, P. L. (forthcoming). *Not in the "White" way: Aspirations, achievement and culture among low-income African American and Latino youth.* New York: Oxford University Press.

Cookson, P. W. J., & Persell, C. H. (1985). *Preparing for power: America's elite boarding schools.* New York: Basic Books.

Darling-Hammond, L. (2001). Apartheid in American education: How opportunity is rationed to children of color in the United States. In *Racial profiling and punishing in U.S. public schools* (pp. 39–44). Oakland, CA: Applied Research Center.

Delgado, R. (1996). *The coming race war? And other apocalyptic tales of America after affirmative action and welfare.* New York: New York University Press.

Deutsch, M. (1979). Awakening a sense of injustice. *Theory,* 46–57.

Du Bois, W. E. B. (1935). Does the Negro need separate schools? *Journal of Negro Education,* 4, 328–335.

Dunderdale, K., Tourscher, S., Yoo, R. J., & Reisinger, O. (2001). What's your bias?: Cuts on diversity in a suburban public school. In J. J. Shultz & A. Cook-Sather (Eds.), *In our own words: Students' perspectives on school.* Lanham, MD: Rowman & Littlefield.

Elliott, A. (2002). Identity politics and privitisation: Modern fantasies, postmodern after-effects. In V. Walkerdine (Ed.), *Challenging subjects: Critical psychology for a new millennium* (pp. 11–22). Hampshire, UK: Palgrave.

Eng, D. L. (2001). *Racial castration managing masculinity in Asian America.* Durham, NC: Duke University Press.

Fine, M. (1990). The "public" in public schools: The social construction/constriction of moral community. *Journal of Social Issues,* 46(1), 107–119.

Fine, M. (1991). *Framing dropouts: Notes on the politics of an urban public high school.* Albany: State University of New York Press.

Fine, M. (2004). Witnessing Whiteness. In M. Fine, L. Weis, L. P. Pruitt, & A. Burns (Eds.), *Off White: Readings on power, privilege, and resistance* (2nd ed.). New York: Routledge.

Fine, M., Bloom, J., Burns, A., Chajet, L., Guishard, M., & Torre, M. E. (in press). Dear Zora: A letter to Zora Neale Hurston fifty years after Brown. *Teachers College Record.*

Fine, M., Burns, A., Payne, Y. A., & Torre, M. E. (in press). *Civic lessons: The color and class of betrayal.* New York: Teachers College Press.

Fine, M., & Powell, L. (2001). *Small schools as an anti-racist intervention. Racial profiling and punishment in U.S. public schools* (ARC Research Report Applied Research Center).

Fine, M., & Weis, L. (1998). *The unknown city: Lives of poor and working-class young adults.* Boston: Beacon Press.

Flanagan, C. A., & Tucker, C. J. (1999). Adolescents' explanations for political issues: Concordance with their views of self and society. *Developmental Psychology, 35*(5), 1198–1209.

Hurtado, A., & Stewart, A. J. (1997). Through the looking glass: Implications of studying Whiteness for feminist methods. In M. Fine, L. Weis, L. Powell, & L. M. Wong (Eds.), *Off White: Readings on race, power, and society* (pp. 297–311). New York: Routledge.

Iyer, A., Leach, C. W., & Pedersen, A. (2004). Racial wrongs and restitutions: The role of guilt and other group-based emotions. In M. Fine, L. Weis, L. P. Pruitt, & A. Burns (Eds.), *Off White: Readings on power, privilege, and resistance* (2nd ed.). New York: Routledge.

Jost, J. T. (1995). Negative illusions. *Political Psychology, 16*(2), 397–424.

Kingsolver, B. (1998). *The poisonwood bible.* New York: Harper Perennial.

Kuriloff, P., & Reichert, M. (2003). Boys of class, boys of color: Negotiating the academic and social geography of an elite independent school. *Journal of Social Issues, 59*(4), 751–770.

Lawrence, S. M., & Tatum, B. D. (1997). White educators as allies: Moving from awareness to action. In M. Fine, L. Weis, L. Powell, & L. M. Wong (Eds.), *Off White: Readings on race, power, and society* (pp. 297–311). New York: Routledge.

Leach, C. W., Snider, N., & Iyer, A. (2002). "Poisoning the consciences of the fortunate": The experience of relative advantage and support for social equality. In I. Walker & H. J. Smith (Eds.), *Relative deprivation: Specification, development, and integration* (pp. 136–163). New York: Cambridge University Press.

Lipsitz, G. (1998). *The possessive investment in Whiteness: How White people profit from identity politics.* Philadelphia: Temple University Press.

Luthar, S. S., & Becker, B. E. (2002). Privileged but pressured? A study of affluent youth. *Child Development, 73*(5), 1593–1610.

Marx, K., & Engels, F. (1846). The German ideology. In R. C. Tucker (Ed.), *The Marx-Engels reader* (pp. 146–200). New York: Norton and Company.

Mickelson, R. A. (2001). Subverting Swann: First- and second-generation segregation in the Charlotte-Mecklenburg schools. *American Educational Research Journal, 38*(2), 215–252.

Miliband, R. (1972). Barnave: A case of bourgeois class consciousness. In I. Meszaros (Ed.), *Aspects of history and class consciousness* (pp. 22–48). New York: Herder & Herder.

Mills, C. W. (1975). Situated actions and vocabularies of motive. In A. Lindesmith & S. Anselm (Eds.), *Life as theater: A dramaturgical sourcebook* (pp. 162–170). Chicago: Aldine.

Mizell, L. (2002). *Horace had it right: The stakes are still high for students of color.* Oakland, CA: Applied Research Center.

Oakes, J. (1985). *Keeping track: How schools structure inequality.* New Haven, CT: Yale University Press.

Omi, M., & Winant, H. (1994). *Racial formation in the United States: From the 1960's to the 1990's* (2nd ed.). New York: Routledge.

Orfield, M. (2002). *American metropolitics: The new suburban reality.* Washington, DC: Brookings Institution.

Perry, P. (2003). *Shades of White: White kids and racial identity in high school.* Durham, NC: Duke University Press.

Phoenix, A. Frosh, S. & Pattman, R. (2003). Producing contradictory masculine subject positions. *Journal of Social Issues, 59* (7), 179–193.

Powell, L. (1997). The achievement (k)not: Whiteness and "Black underachievement." In M. Fine, L. Weis, L. Powell, & L. M. Wong (Eds.), *Off White: Readings on race, power, and society* (pp. 3–12). New York: Routledge.

Powell, L., & Barber, M. E. (in press). Savage inequalities indeed: Irrationality and urban school reform. In S. Cytrynbaum & D. A. Noumair (Eds.), *Group relations reader 3*. Jupiter, FL: A. K. Rice Institute.

Sampson, E. E. (1981). Social change and the contexts of justice motivation. In M. J. Lerner & S. C. Lerner (Eds.), *The justice motive in social behavior: Adapting to times of scarcity and change* (pp. 97–124). New York: Plenum Press.

Simmons, R., & Rosenberg, M. (1971, April). Functions of children's perceptions of the stratification system. *American Sociological Review, 36*, 235–249.

Staiger, A. (1997). *"This gifted program is for White students only": Racial formation in a Los Angeles high school.* Paper presented at the American Anthropological Association, Washington, DC.

Torre, M. E. (Forthcoming, 2004). The alchemy of integrated spaces: Youth participation in research collectives of difference. In L. Weis & M. Fine (Eds.), *Beyond Silenced Voices.* Albany, NY: State University of New York Press.

Thompson, B. (2001). *A promise and a way of life: White antiracist activism.* Minneapolis: University of Minnesota Press.

Twine, F. W. (1997). Brown-skinned White girls: Class, culture and the construction of White identity in suburban communities. In R. Frankenberg (Ed.), *Displacing Whiteness: Essays in social and cultural criticism* (pp. 214–243). Durham, NC: Duke University Press.

Twine, F. W. (2004). White antiracism and the transracial transfer of racial literacy in multiracial families. In M. Fine, L. Weis, L. P. Pruitt, & A. Burns (Eds.), *Off White: Readings on power, privilege, and resistance* (2nd ed.). New York: Routledge.

Valenzuela, A. (1999). *Subtractive schooling: U.S.-Mexican youth and the politics of caring.* Albany: State University of New York Press Press.

Walster, E., Berscheid, E., & Walster, G. W. (1976). New directions in equity research. In L. Berkowitz & E. Walster (Eds.), *Advances in experimental social psychology* (Vol. 9, pp. 1–42). New York: Academic Press.

Wells, A. S., & Serna, I. (1996). The politics of culture: Understanding local political resistance to detracking in racially mixed schools. *Harvard Educational Review, 66*(1), 93–118.

Winant, H. (2001). White racial projects. In B. Brander Rasmussen, E. Klinenberg, I. J. Nexica, & M. Wray (Eds.), *The making and unmaking of Whiteness* (pp. 97–112). Durham, NC: Duke University Press.

Notes

This work was made possible by the generous funding of The Spencer Foundation Discipline-Based Studies in Education for Social Justice and Social Development (DBSE) Fellowship, the Leslie Glass Foundation, and funding from The Rockefeller Foundation.

1. Iyer, Leach, and Pedersen (2004 [this volume]) characterized personal guilt as a "sinking feeling."

2. For detailed analysis of the outcomes of high stakes accountability practices, see (Amrein & Berliner, 2002; Darling-Hammond, 2001; Fine & Powell, 2001; Mizell, 2002).

3. The Critical Opportunity Gap Project, Michelle Fine, principal investigator; María Elena Torre, project director; with Janice Bloom, April Burns, Lori Chajet, Monique Guishard,

Yasser Payne, Tiffany Perkins-Munn, and Kersha Smith. Funded by the Rockefeller Foundation with Leslie Glass and Spencer support. A detailed description of the study design can be found in "Youth Researchers Critically Reframe Questions of Educational Justice," by M. E. Torre and M. Fine, 2003, *Harvard Evaluation Exchange*, 9(2), pp. 6, 22. Preliminary analyses can be found in Fine, Bloom, et al. (in press).

4. The Marxist notion of false consciousness (Marx & Engels, 1846) is the idea that subordinated peoples are persuaded or forced — by means of ideology — to accept as natural and inevitable, beliefs, policies, and stereotypes that contribute to their material and psychological oppression (see Augoustinos, 1999, and Jost, 1995, for a social psychological review of the concept). A bourgeoisie or privileged false consciousness is understood as the belief that action undertaken in the interest of privilege is also in the best interest of the oppressed classes (Miliband, 1972). See Delgado (1996) for a discussion of privileged false consciousness.

5. Flanagan and Tucker (1999) noted that their findings were shaped by the fact that they surveyed youth persisting in school, when the most disadvantaged schools in their sample had drop-out rates that exceeded 40%. They explained their findings — that disadvantaged youth tended to hold individuals accountable for class oppression — by suggesting that the least advantaged youth, "may have had to disregard failures of the system and believe intensely in the efficacy of individual effort" (p. 1207) in order to continue their education in settings of profound failure.

6. This is not to say that higher tracked students have a clearer vision of bias, but it suggests that perhaps they were selected on the basis of their school success.

7. See Iyer et al. (2004 [this volume]) for an extensive review of privileged guilt literature.

8. One group was all female, one group was all White; all other groups were mixed by race or ethnicity, gender, and grade.

9. The sample was 63.1% White ($n = 24$), 13.1% African American ($n = 5$), 10.5% Latino ($n = 4$), and 13.1% Other (i.e., Korean, African, Indian) ($n = 5$).

10. Although I conducted all of the interviews, the focus groups were a collaborative effort. María Elena Torre and I conducted five of the seven focus groups; Yasser Payne, Janice Bloom, and Lori Chajet facilitated the other two groups. Facilitator questions are indicated with a "Q" for question.

11. The large-scale survey produced by the larger Critical Opportunity Gap project covered a wide range of questions about students' school experiences, such as sense of equality in their school and the nation, perceptions of opportunity, goals and values, sense of the future, and preparedness for college.

TWENTY-EIGHT

White Antiracism
in Multiracial Families

France Winddance Twine

On September 16, 2000, the *Guardian* published a story titled "Black Women Win Payout for Soldier's Racial Abuse."

> Two black women who were subjected to a barrage of racial abuse at an army base have been awarded thousands of pounds in compensation by a judge. Sue Hunter and her sister Angie DeMeyer suffered racial chants of "nigger" and say that had guns pointed at them when they attended a dance at Oakington Barracks, Cambridgeshire, in August of 1995. The women say their ordeal came at the hands of soldiers of the first battalion of the Chesire regiments, based at the barracks, whose commander in chief is the Prince of Wales. (Dodd, 2000, p. 18)

Kenneth Bragg, the soldier who racially abused Sue Hunter and her sister Angie DeMeyer was dismissed from the army after a court martial in August 1997. He was ordered by the Nottingham Crown Court to pay £7,000 compensation to Angie DeMeyer and £5,000 to Sue Hunter. According to the *Guardian* the catalyst for this incident was Sue Hunter's intervention on behalf of a Black soldier who was being abused by Bragg. Sue Hunter, referred to as Black in the newspaper article, is the daughter of a White working-class woman and a Black U.S. serviceman from Detroit. Sue was raised by her Irish-born mother on a housing estate in the East Midlands of England. Her mother, born in Belfast, met her father, a Black serviceman, in the 1960s when he was stationed at an Air Force base located about 40 miles outside of Leicester. Sue reported that her mother and father had an amicable separation after her mother declined her father's invitation to relocate to the United States after he was discharged from the air force.

In demographic terms Sue is not an anomaly. Although she may represent only a racial fraction of the larger British population, she is an increasing segment of the Black British population. In 1991, half of British-born Black men and a third of British-born Black women had selected a white partner. Thirty-nine percent of children born to Black Caribbean mothers or fathers had a white parent, and in the majority of these cases the mother was the white parent (Modood et al., 1997).[1] Because interracial marriages between Blacks of Caribbean origin and Whites continue to increase in the United Kingdom, these numbers pose significant theoretical and political questions about how racial identities and hierarchies are managed in these families.

Multiethnic families deserve more sustained attention when considering black community formation in Western Europe.

This demographic trend in the United Kingdom raises important theoretical questions about racial formation and the process by which children of Anglo-British and African Caribbean heritage are taught to interpret and negotiate racial hierarchies and resist racism as members of multiracial families. The significant proportion of children of Black Caribbean ancestry born to white parents provides sociologists with a strategic empirical case in Europe to examine how White parents interpret, negotiate, and counter racial hierarchies. Despite this long history of interracial family formation, little analytical attention has been given to the ways that White parents conceptualize and counter racism.[2]

Multiracial families provide an innovative site to theorize about the processes by which white parents teach their children to manage racial hierarchies and resist racism. In this article I draw on empirical research to provide a new conceptual frame that illuminates how White parents challenge racial hierarchies that idealize whiteness by teaching their children of multiracial heritage to resist racism. My analysis of the transference of racial literacy from White parents to children of multiracial heritage provides a conceptual framework that contributes to and builds upon an interdisciplinary body of literature on antiracism/racism and whiteness studies.

In an analysis of the intergenerational transfer of race-related resistance strategies among U.S. Blacks, Janie Victoria Ward (1996) analyzed Black parents' descriptions of their efforts to train their children to resist racism. Ward identified "homespace" as an important site for teaching Black children to resist. She argued, "In the safety of homespace of care, nurturance, refuge, and truth, Black mothers have learned to skillfully weave lessons of critical consciousness into moments of intimacy between a parent and child." White parents and a number of their adult children described daily practices that prepared them to resist racism in ways not unlike those reported by African American parents.

A number of studies have examined the identity struggles of mixed-race children and the racism they face; however, none have attempted to offer a conceptual frame for understanding the transference of cultural knowledge from white parents to their children of African Caribbean heritage in an effort to promote their child's self-esteem and to cultivate their identification with black struggle against racism. The practices of White transracial parents who embrace an antiracist position offer some important insights about what could have not been theorized.[3] My research departs from the mixed-race identity studies in that it places the racial consciousness and antiracist practices of White parents who are members of multiracial families at the center of analysis.

In my analysis of the narrative accounts that white parents provided of their racialized experiences as transracial parents, I discovered a pattern of practices among those parents who reported actively training their children to strongly identify with the struggles of Blacks. In this writing I offer a conceptual framework by examining three practices that White parents employed in their efforts to train their children to resist racism. Combined, the practices I detail constitute a form of what I call *racial literacy*. These projects are not formalized and do not register in conventional sociological accounts of racial formation. However, their practices facilitate the acquisition and transmission of racial logics and the integration into Black-oriented social networks and provide children of African Caribbean ancestry with resources that assist them in counters "everyday racism."[4]

My analytical focus on White parents offers a partial and restricted view of the dynamics in these families. Elsewhere I analyze the gendered aspects of these processes and the racial logics and practices of white parents who are not invested in their children's identification with the

Black British community.[5] I focus on the ways that white parents train their children to resist racism because I am interested in the practices and processes that can be antiracist or counter-racist in intent. I am also devoted to providing empirical cases that illuminate how white parents struggle to translate and invert racial hierarchies. The antiracist struggles of Black communities of African Caribbean origin in Britain may become increasingly dependent on the labor of white parents who could play a pivotal role in training their children to identify with the antiracist struggles of people of African and Caribbean origin.

RESEARCH METHODS

This paper is based on interviews and participant observation conducted between 1995 and 2002. I collected the data over time in four phases. During the first phase in the spring of 1995 I conducted pilot research in London and Leicester. I interviewed 25 white birth mothers of African-descent children in these cities. After analyzing this first set of interviews I found that the mothers described the same social processes. In other words, the racial ideologies, racial logics, and social practices that I identified did not differ dramatically among the women in my pilot interviews.

In 1997 I began the second phase of my research. I recruited 51 white birth mothers into my study and lived in a community in the East Midlands of England for 8 months.[6] I regularly attended social and political events in the Black Caribbean community and slowly became integrated into a small network of university-educated Black Caribbean women of working-class origin who had white sisters-in-law. During the period of 1996 to 1999 I interviewed and reinterviewed 61 white birth mothers including the women in my pilot research. I remained in contact with the women interviewed in my pilot research, and some of these women became part of a core group with which I remained in regular contact and revisited each year.[7] Group members provided me with referrals to other women and to their Black male partners.

The transracial mothers who volunteered to participate in my study were between 28 and 70 years old. Sixty-one percent of those interviewed were between the ages of 30 and 39; 27% were between the ages of 40 and 49; and 12% were older than 50. Irish women represented 12% of the mothers interviewed, with half of this group having been born in Ireland. The women in this study gave birth to their first child between 1959 and 1999. At the time of my first interview their children ranged in age from 3 months to 37 years.[8]

During the third phase of my research I requested permission from the mothers interviewed to contact their Black male partners or spouses and sisters-in-law. I interviewed 15 black men who were the partners or former partners of white mothers. These men were divided into the following categories: (1) second-generation Black men of Caribbean origin born in the United Kingdom, (2) first-generation Caribbean-born Black men who migrated as children to the United Kingdom, or (3) North American Black men of non-Caribbean origin who had been born in the United States and migrated to the United Kingdom as part of the U.S. military. I also interviewed a comparative sample of white men raising children with black women.

RACIAL LITERACY: ANTIRACIST VOCABULARIES

White parents who were training their children to align themselves politically with the Black community reported that they trained their child to describe to them in detail their social interactions that occurred at school. This enabled parents to obtain information so that they could evaluate the racial and cultural climate at their children's schools. The provision of a discursive space to routinely evaluate and discuss their child's experiences with race emerged as a practice that was central to transferring forms of racial literacy.

The first practice that I uncovered and consider to be a central part of antiracist socialization was the provision of conceptual tools at home. Parents described training their children to discuss their school experiences with them on a daily basis. They used their time at home to teach their children how to analyze texts and visual images that they encountered in school texts. White parents also described a number of discursive practices in which they trained their children to discuss and to critically evaluate media and textual representations of Black people.

Taisha is the 21-year-old daughter of Mary Hunte, an Irish woman who immigrated to England at the age of 19 in the late 1950s and later established a family with a Black man from Barbados. The youngest of six children, Taisha was raised by her mother who became a single parent after she divorced Taisha's father in the 1980s. Taisha, a university student, is pursuing a master's degree in social work. Recalling her mother's practices when she was a child, she argued that her mother routinely discussed race and racism with her and thus provided her with a vocabulary for thinking about the political meaning of being of Black, Irish, and British heritage. In her analysis of the why she became strongly identified with the African Caribbean community and shifted from self-identifying as a "mixed-race" woman to a "Black" woman, Taisha cited the alternative history lessons that her mother provided at home.

Periodically breaking down in tears while we sat in the kitchen talking, Taisha described to me the forms of racial abuse she experienced at school and how her mother helped her to cope with it. Taisha described practices that remain beneath the radar of registered antiracist acts in sociological analyses precisely because they are improvised, informal, and in response to the daily experiences of children. These practices are not always part of a formal strategy but over a career of child rearing they may cohere into a strategies that are adopted. In Taisha's analysis of how she learned to resist racism at school and maintained her self-esteem as a woman of Irish and African Caribbean parentage, she argued, "When I used to come home from school and tell her what I'd been through, and she used to talk to me about [racism]." Taisha described her mother's efforts to help her cope. When Taisha shifted her analysis to the content of the curriculum, she identified alternative history lessons and discursive space that her mother offered her at home as enabling her to detect in the school curriculum which discussions of racism and colonialism and Blacks were avoided.

> When you're doing history, all it is on the first and second World Wars. They never tell you that black soldiers fought in the war, or that they were put to the front line to be killed first. They never tell you about colonialism. They tell you about the British Empire, but they never tell you [...] how they achieved it. And I was always lucky in the sense that I knew that history [from my mother] I knew all of the things like slavery ... and not just the negative but the positive things that black people had contributed to world history. There's nothing there for you to relate to [in the British curriculum].

Taisha considered the informal and supplementary education that her white mother provided as crucial because in her analysis of the British curriculum she argued, "Basically I think black kids are made by the educational system to feel ashamed of who they are and their heritage because there's never anything positive. It's always negative."

This supplementary education described by Taisha is a central component of racial socialization because this facilitated Taisha's ability to analyze racism and British colonialism. It is Taisha's belief that her mother provided her with conceptual tools, particularly a vocabulary and concepts necessary to identify and analyze patterns including the contributions of Caribbeans to British culture in the educational curriculum. If we accept Taisha's analysis, we can argue that the conceptual training that she received from her mother constitutes a form of racial literacy that enabled her to identify symbolic and systematic racism in the readings and visual images that she encountered at school and to begin to counter this form of racism (Rampton et al., 1981).

I extend and build on the earlier research of two developmental psychologists, Barbara Tizard and Ann Phoenix (1993), by providing an empirical case that is parent centered and draws on a diverse group of parents who describe their parental practices. Barbara Tizard and Ann Phoenix interviewed 58 adolescents of mixed-race heritage in London. Tizard and Phoenix assigned "scores" to young people for their experiences of racism based on their answers to a series of questions. In analyzing the racial scores they concluded that although they did not find gender or class to be a significant variable, "[The scores] *were* significantly related to the extent of family communication about racism, and the extent to which they believed their parents had advised and influenced their attitudes to racism. They were also significantly related to the centrality of their own colour in their lives, and the extent to which they held politicized views and saw black and white people as having different lives and different tastes" (p. 105).

Tizard and Phoenix (1993) drew on two examples of girls who lived with an Afro-Caribbean and white parent and described their social networks as "neither had any black friends or links with black youth culture, and neither girl had experienced name-calling or discrimination in shops." What is significant about these findings is that the student who scored the highest had a black parent who talked to her frequently about the racism she had encountered in Britain. Tizard and Phoenix only provided two cases to support their argument so we do not learn whether their sample included any White parents who discussed racism with their children.

SUPPLEMENTARY SCHOOLS: SELF-SEGREGATION, SOCIAL ISOLATION, AND SOCIAL WORLDS

In an analysis of the "old" and "new" racisms in Britain, Paul Gilroy (1993, p. 59) argued,

> The school provides a ready image for the nation in microcosm. It is an institution for cultural transmission and therefore a means of integration and assimilation. It hosts two important and related confrontations which have been of great interest to the popular press. The first arising where conflicting cultures have to contend for the attention of the child who may be caught between them, and the second takes shape where the multicultural zealotry of the local authorities who set overall educational policy has had to struggle against the ideologies and politics of heroic, individual teachers who have sought to resist this unwholesome tide of politically motivated zealotry. Mother-tongue teaching, anti-racist and multicultural curricula are all under attack.[9]

The "black voluntary" school movement emerged in Britain in the late 1970s and has been described as "part of a broader political and education ideal that has directly risen from an assessment by Afro-Carribeans of their social position in Britain and of the part that the existing white dominated education plays in its perpetuation" (Chevannes & Reeves, 1987, p. 147). In their analysis of how voluntary or supplementary schools differ from other educational projects, Chevannes and Reeves (1987, p. 148) noted,

The schools have been set up for the benefit of children of Afro-Caribbean descent: they are indeed black schools in aim and composition. The fact that there may be no deliberate colour bar (a white or Asian child may be allowed to enroll or a white volunteer invited to help) has little bearing on the organizer's view that the schools have been set up to provide in a predominantly black environment for the needs of black children. Black children attend because they are deliberately recruited from families where the parents believe in the need for their children to undertake extra study with children from the same racial group and to obtain support from teachers who understand what it is to be black in white society.

The African Caribbean Education Working Group (ACE), which was founded and is staffed almost entirely by African Caribbean women, operates the Saturday School.[10] The primary goal of the school is to foster black childrens' self-esteem (and racial and cultural pride) rather than to pursue a specific curriculum. The supplementary school in Leicestershire is known as "Saturday School" because it is held for 2 hours on Saturday morning during the official school term, and it has been operating since 1981. Children between the ages of 5 and 16 years are welcome to attend.[11] Until 3 years ago the school was free of charge but a nominal fee of 10 British sterling per family has since been charged to cover the costs of the workbooks. Because it receives no permanent funding, the Saturday School depends on annual grants and is operated by a small voluntary organization.

Sending their preteen children to supplementary schools is a practice that differs from the first three practices because it is intended to provide access not only to privileged racial and cultural knowledge but also, more important, to social relationships with black adults and children. I was told that they were concerned not only with the curriculum but also with the cultural experiences and black social networks that their children would access. This is of particular importance for multiracial families residing in predominantly white or middle-class residential communities, or both, where their children do not routinely meet blacks in schools or as neighbors. Families who are raising their children in predominantly or exclusively white middle-class communities argued that it is important for their children to have regular social contact and form social relationships with the less economically privileged black children who reside in working-class communities.

Schools, as well as playgrounds, were described as among the first sites where children were racially abused and experienced social exclusion, rejection, and racism on the basis of their color or ancestry. Tizard and Phoenix (1993) documented several forms of racism that children of mixed-race heritage experience at school where they were treated as the cultural and intellectual inferiors of other racial and ethnic groups.

Mercedes, the daughter of an Australian mother and a Dutch father, is a striking 36-year-old blonde. Born in Brisbane, Australia, she spent her early childhood years in Ghana, where her father taught. When her parents split up, she was taken to Ghana by her father, where she attended her first school and established her first close friendships. Mercedes is one of the white women whom Blacks described as "living in the Black scene" and who has dated Black men most of her life. She works with youth ages 9 to 25, as a youth and community coordinator at the African Caribbean Centre. She described her job responsibilities as "to develop their educational and social skills." As a single mother of a teenage daughter whose beautiful cinnamon-colored skin conceals her Dutch and Australian ancestry, she expressed her concern that her daughter does not strongly identify as Black.

Mercedes left school at the age of 14 without any academic qualifications. Describing her academic experiences she said, "I was bored. I was too clever for them. The lessons were going too slowly." When I asked Mercedes to describe her expectations for her daughter she explained why she was motivated to send her to the local African Caribbean supplementary school for Black children:

> "I sent her to [Saturday School] to educate her. I mean she gets her European culture here [at home] so I would send her to Saturday School, which provides classes which tell her the conditions around being black and black culture and being about Africa and the West Indies and all that. But if I ask her how she identifies, she doesn't see herself as Black."
>
> "She doesn't?"
>
> "No."
>
> "I'm going to ask you to talk more about that."
>
> "And I'm quite upset because I've always said to her, 'Look, you're Black.' She goes, 'Well, I'm not Black because if I say I'm black I'm disrespecting you.' And I thought, 'You have a good point there.' But what I said to her was 'Okay, put it this way. Society sees you as Black. And it's best that you know that because at the end of the day if it came to one or the other it would be Black people that would accept you. The white people don't see you as "mixed with White." ... At the end of the day it's the Black people who will look after you. If push comes to shove, it's the black people. I'm not going to tell you any different. I'd rather you be safe, than be in a position where you're not comfortable.'"

In this exchange between Mercedes and her daughter, we see that Mercedes is trying to socialize her daughter and to train her to locate herself alongside Blacks rather than positioning herself as "mixed." As a white woman who currently works in both predominantly white areas and racially mixed areas, Mercedes concluded that white people will not distinguish between her daughter, who is of mixed parentage, and a black person who has no European parentage. Mercedes argued that in the eyes of the white people with whom she is familiar, her biracial daughter will be perceived as "just a non-white person in their face." In contrast to her mother's perception, Mercedes's daughter is resisting and rejecting this version of the one-drop rule and argues that her mother's racial and cultural relationship to her must be recognized and acknowledged. This is an example of the troubled terrain and competing conceptual maps that white mothers (and fathers) reported encountering as they attempted to cultivate cultural and political allegiances to the Black community among their children of multiracial heritage, while not denying their biological ties to their children.

White mothers such as Mercedes send their children to Saturday School in part because they want their children to affiliate with black children and adults. The desire that their children identify with the Black community often masks the disagreements and struggles that some white parents have if their children strongly identify with them as positive role models. For example, a daughter's identification with her white mother may result in her embracing her mother's European heritage rather than her African Caribbean heritage, which may be interpreted by her white mother as her daughter's identifying with white supremacy, British colonialism, and racism.

Mercedes belongs to a cohort of white mothers who argue that the Black community would be a social and political resource for their children if and when they were in need of support. Mothers such as Mercedes who reported sending their children to Saturday School identified exposure to the Black community as one of their primary motivations. Their hope is that if their children are integrated into black social networks they will be better able to defend themselves against racism.

In an analysis of the 1991 U.K. census data, Tariq Modood and his associates (1997, p. 185) found, "Ethnic minorities are concentrated into the South-East region, and, in particular Greater London. Fewer than one out of ten whites lived in Greater London, but more than half of Caribbeans, African Asians and Bangladeshis lived in this area." Anne Wilson (1981) identified spatial isolation from Blacks and other ethnic groups, rather than isolation from whites, as a problem for the interracial families she interviewed in the late 1980s. This was identified as a serious problem in my conversations with white parents of multiracial children. Although blacks are concentrated in the major urban centers and are not evenly distributed across geographic regions in the United Kingdom, they nevertheless live in closer proximity to non-blacks and are more "exposed" to white English people than their counterparts in the United States.[12]

In my conversations with white transracial parents in interracial families neither spatial isolation nor social exclusion from whites was identified as one of their primary concerns. Instead, mothers such as Mercedes expressed their fear that their children's social isolation from black children could result in their rejection by the Black community and that this could be another potential source of injury to their children's self-esteem and well-being. This was of particular concern for middle-class families that were not restricted financially to residential areas reserved primarily for poor and working-class people. Their desire to increase their children's social exposure to Blacks was motivated by their belief that establishing friendships and social relationships with Blacks would enhance their children's well-being and promote both their cultural identification with Blacks.

In *The First R: How Children Learn Race and Racism*, Debra Van Ausdale and Joe Feagin (2001) provided a penetrating analysis of playgroups involving children between the ages of 3 and 6. Van Ausdale and Feagin offered a vivid portrayal and insightful analysis of how and when the very young acquire and use racial distinctions and concepts. They argued, "Early friendships are often precursors of relationships formed later in children's lives. How and with whom children form relationships at this stage can influence how and with whom they will choose to affiliate with as they grow up. Early friendships inform children on what social groups are suitable for them and what groups they can expect to be included in over time. Some recent research suggests that these early relationships are the foundation for social understanding, intelligence, self-evaluations, social comparisons and social competence" (p. 90).

HOME INTERIORS: AESTHETICS AND ANTIRACIST SYMBOLIC CULTURE

White parents who had been actively involved in antiracist and antifascist political work and "race-awareness" training prior to forming interracial families reported that the visual and material culture of their homes was one way that they tried to counter racist depictions of blacks in the public sphere. This practice is the second practice that I identified as a method of training children to embrace a Black sociopolitical identity. Parents described consumption practices that included selecting and purchasing Black-produced cultural objects to promote Black aesthetics as they designed their home interiors. They collected and displayed visual art, toys, books, music, and decor that idealize Black Africans, Black Caribbeans, and North American Blacks. The interiors in their homes constituted a specific form of socialization that provided children with a symbolic and visual culture that facilitated their identification with Blacks on both sides of the Atlantic.

One fifth of the parents interviewed argued that the selection of Black-produced art, material objects, music, toys, and symbols was important for their children's self-esteem and would facilitate their positive identification with the Black diasporic community. Parents described their careful selection of visual art, music, books, toys, and other cultural objects that would idealize and privilege African, African Caribbean, and African American culture. In particular, the search for visual images and literature that depict African-descent people as the social and cultural equals of the Anglo-British is a repeated theme in the narratives of racial consciousness for those parents who anticipate that their children will have to be prepared to resist racism and will need a heightened sense of self-esteem as Black children.

Claire, a statuesque blonde with brown eyes, is the 35-year-old parent of a teenage son. She and her son reside in a middle-class white professional neighborhood located within walking distance of Leicester University. She is the vice principal of a school located in an inner-city neighborhood that now services a predominantly Muslim and immigrant student population. This same school historically served the African Caribbean community that is concentrated in this inner-city neighborhood. Claire described her efforts, as a single mother, to provide her son, who is now 18, with Black-centered images and books at home.

> I've always attempted to make sure that there are different images on the walls, that there are different books on the shelves. That, you know, there are these representations [of black-ness].... It was very, very difficult to do this at the time [1960s] — it's not so difficult now. I would sort of purposely hunt out books that had black children or Asian children or people of color in them, lots of different situations, and read those things. They were very difficult to find [when he was a child]. There were lots of books about Black Sambo, I think, but nothing positive. And it got easier. But I did feel at one point that home was the only place that [antiracist images] was happening.

And as Claire's comments suggest, she perceived herself as having to actively seek out nonracist images of Blacks. Claire belongs to a subset of university-educated white parents who have worked both within communities of color and who have struggled to educate themselves about racism and antiracism.

Vivian, a 48-year-old mother of a young daughter, belongs to the Letter Box Library,[13] a mail-order book club that provides resources for children of color. Vivian described some of the difficulties of trying to provide pro-black messages for her prepubescent daughter in a national context in which there continues to be aesthetic hierarchies that privilege blonde and blue-eyed girls in British popular culture. She relies on a range of material and social resources.

> I order books from there which show black children and stories about black children.... I mean, that's just an example of trying to look at books and things like that give a positive image and actually show black people ... now she's getting older. I'd like to do more sort of structured things ... perhaps look at things like the history of the Caribbean. I mean, the other very useful input that she goes to an after-school club, which a [black] colleague of mine at work has sort of been instrumental in setting up, where they've done quite a bit with the children on things like African history and so on.

When asked to describe how they decorated their home interiors, White fathers, like mothers who were involved in parenting, described similar antiracist aesthetic projects. Andrew, a 61-year-old trainer and consultant in Equal Opportunities and an antiracist consultant for the Episcopalian Church, is the father of two black sons. He has been married for more than 25 years to Lauren, a nurse who immigrated from Trinidad in the 1960s. Andrew is part of a cohort of white antiracists who became active in race relations and antiracism prior to establishing families with black women. Andrew is a member of the first generation of university students to be trained in the post-World War II era that witnessed the rapid decline of the British overseas empire as its colonies in Africa, the Caribbean, and South Asia and the emergence of an antiracist movement in Britain.

Andrew's son was born in 1976, the year that the National Front received 18% of the vote in the outlying suburbs of Leicester. In the mid-1970s Leicester was a site of intensive organized racism and served as the national headquarters of the National Front party. When the National Front marched through Leicester, Andrew took his infant son with him on antifascist political marches. Andrew served as an elected member of the city council during the period when the National Front narrowly lost its bid for a seat on the city council. He described how he and his wife Lauren decorated the interior of their home to counter the rampant racism in the public sphere during a period when it was still very difficult to obtain books outside of a few specialty bookstores in London that did not present racist images of black people.

> We saw it as important for [our son] to grow up in a world where he saw successful black men. And also that the books and the images and the toys that he had reflected the cultural diversity. There were not many on the market, but they were becoming increasingly available 21 years ago. We had to look for it in those days.... We've made sure that there were images around the house which reflected black success and achievement, which were not stereotypes. It would be very easy to get figures which reflected stereotypical views of black people ... and White views of their beauty and aesthetics and so on, but we wanted [our son] to grow up in that kind of ethos, how black people portray themselves.

White fathers such as Andrew expressed concern about their children's racial self-esteem. They concurred, however, that in the past two decades increased access to antiracist or nonracist children's books depicting brown-skinned children (as well as black and multiethnic families that include African Caribbeans) is one arena in which their options had expanded significantly. They also reported that at the local library their children had more access to multicultural books (many were U.S. produced) that do not recycle racist ideologies and that provide "imaginary possibilities" for black characters. This point was emphasized by a number of black and white parents raising African-descent children as they described their struggles to promote their children's racial literacy. In this case, racial literacy involved their ability to "imagine" possibilities for themselves and to identify with black characters in fictional worlds in addition to being able to "see" the "absence" of black characters in their formal school curriculum.

THE ONE-DROP RULE: A VIEW FROM BRITAIN

The U.S. Bureau of the Census has not historically used a scientific definition when enumerating the number of Blacks in the nation but instead used a cultural one. This rule is known as "the one-drop rule." The one-drop rule refers to the practice of classifying a person as black on the basis of "one drop of black blood." Some courts have called it the "traceable amount rule." No other ethnic population in the United States is defined or counted according to a one-drop rule. According to Floyd James Davis (1991), "Apparently the rule is unique in that it is found only in the United States and not in any other nation in the world" (p. 13). The 2000 U.S. Census changed the criteria by which individuals could self-identify by race (Perlman & Waters, 2001).

In their study of 58 adolescents of mixed-race, Tizard and Phoenix (1993) briefly situated interracial family formation in the British context, which, in contrast to the United States, was never criminalized. Tizard and Phoenix noted,

In Britain there was no legal definitions of a black person, or legal restrictions on mixed marriages. This may have been in part because until the mid-1950s the number of Black people in Britain was very small — never more than 15,000, often less. The few "half-castes" were generally recognized by both black and white people as different from black. But they were stigmatized in Britain as elsewhere, perhaps more so, since they were usually born into the poorest sector of society, whilst in other countries they tended to be part of an intermediate class. (p. 3)

Thus, although the census, state, and federal courts in the United States have generally upheld the one-drop rule, blackness has not been legally defined in England. Consequently in the United Kingdom the social and legal classification of children of mixed ancestry has been characterized by more fluidity (Davis, 1991). Although the absence of the one-drop rule does not diminish the complex forms of racism that children of multiracial heritage face in England, it may nevertheless generate "peculiarly English" dilemmas. This absence of a state-sanctioned legal definition of black-ness in Britain places a burden on parents who, perhaps perceiving their children as "both" or "neither" black or white, nevertheless perceive their children's African Caribbean heritage as a cultural and political resource that can empower them in the face of racism.

The transmission of cultural knowledge that promotes an acquisition of social production of a Black identity among children of multiracial heritage. I am not arguing that white parents are adopting a version of the North American one-drop rule but rather they conceptualize cultural and social inclusions in the Black community as one way to protect them from the harshness of racism. They view a cultural and political identification with Black Britain as a resource that will equip their children to function more effectively in black and non-black communities in England. The trans-racial parents I interviewed were neither motivated by nor invested in a version of the one-drop rule. Their promotion of their children's cultural and political identification with Blacks was framed as either a recognition that their children would not be positioned as white or a direct response to racism. Few parents reported having consistently referred to their children as black or as white but they had struggled with terminology as much as methods of socializing them. Glenda argued that her daughter needed to be defended from racism and that she feared that she would identify with whites and whiteness if she did not provide her with alternatives.

Approximately half of the parents I interviewed reported that the terms that they used to refer to their children had changed during their parental career and that their conceptualizations about race had shifted. Some used to refer to their children as "half-caste" and they now used the term "mixed-race" or Black-European or biracial but only a handful perceived their children as Black, rather than acknowledging that they were of African Caribbean ancestry and could be excluded or discriminated on this basis.

Chelsea is the 45-year-old mother of a daughter whom she is raising alone. She is of middle-class origin, has a university education and a professional job, and has chosen to live in the inner-city community where Blacks and Bangladeshis are dominant on the streets surrounding her. Chelsea has been the sole non-Black member of a number of committees and community organizations that service the Black and South Asian community. During the first meeting she attended with her daughter, when her daughter was 11 years old, she expressed the following concerns:

You know, subconsciously [children] very quickly take in the view that in [British] society that to be white is to be desirable. And occasionally [my daughter] has said to me that she wants to be white.... I think my main fear at the moment is that she will grow up sort of feeling that she's white. And I wouldn't want that. I would want her to embrace her African

heritage, to put it rather grandiosely. I suppose, I feel that I'm not perhaps up to the task —
of enabling her to do that.

Chelsea felt disempowered because she does not want her daughter to identify with her whiteness. Chelsea has cultivated a social network that consists of Black and South Asian women as
well as Black male friends who have white partners. She reported to me that her closest friend
is a black woman of Caribbean origin, whom she has designated to be the guardian of her
daughter in the event of her death. Chelsea organizes her daughter's social activities to maximize
her contact with black children. She pays $10 per week to send her to an after-school club run
by one of her Black male colleagues. This colleague is also someone whose family I became
quite close to after I interviewed his wife for my study. He and his wife became a central part of
my social network prior to my learning of their relationship with Chelsea. She has declined
higher paying jobs because she does not wish to relocate to a predominantly White area where
her daughter might feel socially excluded and isolated as the only girl of color and possibly face
more discrimination.

Parents such as Mercedes and Chelsea struggle to socialize their children to be proud of their
African Caribbean heritage because they are not able to transfer their white status and the privileges that accompany it to their children whose African Caribbean ancestry is visible. In their
view their children are at risk for racial discrimination. Racial and ethnic affiliations are not
taken for granted but are actively negotiated. It is not a belief in the one-drop rule but rather a
recognition that racism and racial hierarchies continue to structure British life and that they
need to prepare their daughters and sons for this reality.

In her research with white women engaged in interracial parenting, Ruth Frankenberg (1993,
p. 128) found that for some interracial couples "the desire to provide contexts in which their
children could identify with their father's Chicano and Black heritages clashed with issues of
class." I found a similar pattern when talking to white mothers and their black partners of
working-class origin who, if their children were being raised in middle-class households,
expressed concern that they would not strongly identify with blacks. For parents such as
Mercedes and Chelsea their decision to live an inner-city community that they termed Black
meant that they did not have to struggle as much as their middle-class counterparts to cultivate
social relationships for their children or to organize Black-centered activities for them. They
lived in an area that would maximize their children's exposure to Blacks of working-class and
middle-class backgrounds. They were less dependent on the Saturday School to fulfill this function because they lived within close proximity to the African Caribbean center.

CONCLUSION

The experiences of White parents' caring for their children of multiracial heritage require a
rethinking of conventional analyses of whiteness, racism, and antiracism. The complex ways
that White parents train their children to manage racial hierarchies and racism provide insights
into forms of invisible labor that has consequences for how racial ideologies and boundaries
are negotiated in the public sphere by members of multiracial families. My analysis of the
intergenerational transfer of racial literacy from white parents to their birth children of second-
generation African Caribbean ancestry enables us to rethink how racial belonging and racism is
negotiated in multiracial families where the boundaries between blackness and whiteness are
complex and permeable. My data also suggest that racialized experiences are actively negotiated by the parents of children who may strongly identify with their white parent but will not be
socially classified or treated as white in public spaces.

White parents of children of African Caribbean heritage constitute a significant population from the perspective of the Black community in Britain. The growth of multiracial families requires a rethinking of how racial boundaries, racial identities, and racial hierarchies are negotiated within multiracial families. For race scholars concerned with antiracism, they provide a strategic case of primary caretakers of children who will be socially classified as black, multiracial, or simply not white. They are exposed to multiple forms of what Frankenberg (1993) termed "rebound racism" as well as what one mother described to me as "my second-hand racism." Little is known about how these white parents transmit racial logics and forms of antiracist knowledge from white birth parents to their children of multiracial heritage.

Accounts of race and racism that can theoretically account for the complex ways that white members of multiracial families respond to racial hierarchies are needed if we are to understand how racial and ethnic boundaries are reproduced and resisted in post colonial societies where these borders are permeable. My analysis of the intergenerational transfer of racial literacy from white parents to their children of second-generation African Caribbean ancestry enables us to rethink how a strong affiliation with the Black community may be conceptualized as a political and cultural resource by white parents. White parents engage in practices that resist racial hierarchies that privilege whites and people of multiracial heritage over blacks in a context in which the boundaries between blackness and whiteness are complex and permeable.

Minkah Makalani analyzed the "deployment of whiteness" by advocates for a distinct biracial identity for people of mixed parentage (PMP) in the United States. Analyzing congressional testimonies on the census and biracial-identity Web sites, Makalani concluded, "Whiteness is deployed as a tool to distance PMP from African Americans politically, socially and culturally" (2003, p. 82). I have provided a European case study of parents who, rather than training their children to deploy their whiteness in ways that distance them from other African-descent people, are teaching them to strongly identify with the political and cultural struggles of black people. My cases, although neither randomly selected nor representative of the majority of White parents, nevertheless offer an example of a racial project that seeks, however varied and improvised, to position their children as the political allies of African-descent people in Britain.

The racial literacy projects that I have detailed among white parents in multiracial families in Britain can be read as one strategy for resisting racial hierarchies that privilege people of African-descent who have one White parent over people of African-descent who have two Black parents. In other words, these projects by White birth parents are one way that white parents negotiate racial and color hierarchies within the Black and non-Black communities that privilege individuals of any known or recognizable European ancestry.

References

Alexander, C. (1996). *The art of being Black: The creation of Black British youth identities.* Oxford: Oxford University Press.

Banton, M. (1955). *The coloured quarter: Negro immigrants in an English city.* London: Jonathan Cape.

Becker, H. S. (1963). *Outsiders: Studies in the sociology of deviance.*

Benson, S. (1981). *Ambiguous ethnicity: Interracial families in London.* Cambridge: Cambridge University Press.

Chevannes, M., & Reeves, F. (1987). The Black voluntary school movement: Definition, context, and prospects. In B. Troyna (Ed.), *Racial inequality in education* (pp. 147–148). London: Tavistock.

Davis, F. J. (1991). *Who is Black? One nation's definition.* University Park: Pennsylvania State University Press.

Dodd, V. (2000, September 16). Black women win payout for soldier's racial abuse. *The Guardian*, p. 18.

Domiguez, V. (1986). *White By Definition: Social Classification in Creole Louisiana*. New Brunswick: Rutgers University Press.

Drake, S. C. (1954). *Value systems, social structures and race relations in the British Isles*. Unpublished doctoral dissertation, University of Chicago.

Essed, P. (1991). *Understanding everyday racism: Towards an interdisciplinary theory*. Thousand Oaks, CA: Sage.

Feagin, J., & Sykes, M. (1992). *Living with racism: The Black middle-class experience*. Boston: Beacon Press.

Frankenberg, R. (1993). *White women, race matters: The social construction of Whiteness*. Minneapolis: University of Minnesota Press.

Gilroy, P. (1993). *Small acts: Thoughts on the politics of Black culture*. New York: Serpent's Books.

Ifekwunigwe, J. (1998). *Scattered belongings: Cultural paradoxes of "race," nation and gender*. London: Routledge.

Lazarre, J. (1996). *Beyond the Whiteness of Whiteness: Memoir of a White Mother of Black Sons*. Durham and London: Duke University Press.

Little, K. (1947). *Negroes in Britain: A study of racial relations in an English society*. London: Kegan Paul, Trench, Traubner and Company.

Luke, C., & Luke, A. (1998). Interracial families: Difference within difference. *Ethnic and Racial Studies, 21*(4), 728–753.

Makalani, M. (2003). Rejecting Blackness and claiming Whiteness: Antiblack Whiteness in the biracial project. In A. W. Doane & E. Bonilla-Silva (Eds.), *White out: The continuing significance of racism*. New York: Routledge.

Massey, D. S., & Denton, N. A. (1993). *American apartheid: Segregation and the making of the underclass*. Cambridge, MA: Harvard University Press.

McBride, J. (1997). *The Color of Water: A Black Man's Tribute to His White Mother*. New York: Riverhead Books.

Modood, T., Berthoud, R., et al. (1997). *Ethnic minorities in Britain: Diversity and disadvantage*. London: Policy Studies Institute.

O'Brien, E. (2001). *Whites Confront Racism: Antiracists and Their Paths to Action*. New York: Rowman & Littlefield.

Olumide, J. (2002). *Raiding the gene pool: The social construction of mixed race*. London: Pluto Press.

Patterson, S. (1963). *Dark strangers: A sociological study of the absorption of a recent West Indian migrant group in Brixton, South London*. Bloomington, IN: Indiana University Press.

Rampton, A., et al. (1981). *West Indian children in our schools: Interim report of the committee of inquiry into the education of children from ethnic minority groups*. London: Her Majesty's Stationery Office.

Reddy, M. T. (1996). *Crossing the Color Line: Race, Parenting and Culture*. New Brunswick: Rutgers University Press.

Roediger, D. ed. (1999). *Black on White: Black Writers on What it Means to Be White*. New York: Schocken Books.

Rosenblatt, P. C., Karis, T., & Powell, R. (1995). *Multiracial couples: Black and White voices*. Thousand Oaks, CA: Sage.

Ruddick, S. (1989). *Maternal thinking: Towards a politics of peace*. Boston: Beacon Press.

Small, S. (1994). *Racialised barriers: The Black experience in the United States and England in the 1980s*. London: Routledge.

Smith, S. (1989). *The politics of "race" and residence: Citizenship, segregation and White supremacy in Britain*. Cambridge, UK: Polity Press.

Solomos, J. (1989). *Race and racism in Britain* (2nd ed.). New York: St. Martin's Press.

Song, M. (2002). *Choosing ethnic identity*. Cambridge, UK: Polity Press.

Thompson. B. (2001). *A promise and a way of life: White anti-racist activism*. Minneapolis: University of Minnesota Press.

Tizard, B., & Phoenix, A. (1993). *Black, White or mixed race? Race and racism in the lives of young people of mixed parentage*. London/New York: Routledge.

Twine, F. W. (1996). Brown-skinned White girls: Class, culture and the construction of White identity in suburban communities. *Gender, Place and Culture: A Journal of Feminist Geography*, 3(2), 205–224.

Twine, F. W. (1996b). Transracial mothering and antiracism: The case of White birth mothers of 'Black' children in Britain. *Feminist Studies*, 25 (3), 729–746.

Twine, F. W. (1999). Bearing Blackness in Britain: The meaning of racial difference for White mothers of African-descent children. *Social Identities: Journal of Race, Culture and Nation*, 5(2), 185–210.

Twine, F. W. (2001). Transgressive women and transracial mothers: White women and critical race theory. *Meridians: Feminism, Race, Transnationalism*, 1(2), 130–153.

Van Ausdale, D., & Feagin, J. R. (2001). *The first R: How children learn race and racism*. Lanham, MD: Rowman & Littlefield.

Ward, J. V. (1996). Raising resisters: The role of truth telling in the psychological development of African American girls. In B. R. Leadbeater & N. Way (Eds.), *Urban girls: Resisting stereotypes, creating identities* (pp. 85–99). New York: New York University Press.

Wellman, D. T. (1993). *Portraits of White Racism*. Oxford: Cambridge University Press.

Wilson, A. (1981). *Mixed race children: A study in identity*. London: Allen and Unwin.

Notes

1. Women like Sue, who until the 2001 census did not have the option of a "mixed race" box and may have appeared on the 1991 UK census as either a "Black Other" or simply an "Other."

2. Between 1954 and 2001 anthropologists, sociologists, and social psychologists on both sides of the Atlantic produced numerous case studies that examined race relations, racism, racial identities and multiracial family formation (For examples see Little (1947), Drake (1954); Patterson (1963); Benson (1981); Wilson (1981); Gilroy (1993); Solomos (1989); Rosenblatt (1995); Tizard & Phoenix (1993); Luke & Luke (1998); and Twine (1991a, 1999b, and 2001).

3. A number of books have theorized about the experiences of mixed-race people. See *Choosing Ethnic Identity* by Miri Song (2002) for an original analysis of how people of multiracial heritage in the United States and Britain manage their ethnic identities. See Jill Olumide's (2002) *Raiding the Gene Pool: The Social Construction of Mixed Race* for a theoretical study that problematizes and examines the experience of mixed-race communities across national contexts. For an example of a work that theorizes mixed-race identity from the experiences of a small sample of women of multiracial heritage in Britain see Jayne Ifekwunigwe (1998), *Scattered Belongings: Cultural Paradoxes of "Race," Nation and Gender*.

4. See Philomena Essed's (1991) *Toward Everyday Racism: Towards an Interdisciplinary Theory* for a groundbreaking conceptualization and analysis of everyday racism.

5. See *Bearing Blackness and Whiteness in Britain: An Ethnography of Racism and Racial Formation at the End of Empire* (Forthcoming from Duke University Press).

6. This raises the question of whether I am getting different results because of the demographic differences between Leicester and London. Leicester, a city located 99 miles north of London by rail, belongs to the East Midlands of Britain. It is one of the largest cities in the region and serves as the transportation hub for the county. In 1991 Leicester had a population of 293,400, including a student population of around 30,000 associated with the city's two universities. Leicester has the distinction of being the local authority with the highest percentage of all ethnic minorities including the largest Asian Indian population in the United Kingdom. Asian Indians constitute 22.3% of the population. However Blacks constitute only 2.4% of the population whereas Pakistanis and Bangladeshis constitute 1.4%.

7. I returned to Leicester every year and revisited the same women.

8. I used four avenues of access to the women I recruited into my study. First, I advertised my research project at the sociology department at Leicester University and received referrals from Black students who had White sisters-in-law or friends who were partnered with Black men. Second, I contacted a local housing association that rents housing to low-income families and asked them if they would advertise my research and provide the names of women willing to talk to me. Third, Black Youth Workers in the department of education at Leicester City Council provided me with a number of referrals to White women, primarily women who were married to Black professional men. Finally, I also used snowball sampling. These four avenues actually provided me with a relatively diverse sample in terms of class background, residential neighborhood, ethnicity, occupation, and place of origin. My sample is a purposive sample. I did not attempt to use a random selection because there was no sampling frame or database that would enable me to randomly identify multiracial families that include a White mother or father. I had learned from earlier research reports in Britain that random sampling would be less likely to generate interviews with people who would necessarily be willing to talk to me about sensitive topics such as interracial sexuality, racialized violence in their families, and racism.

9. In *Racialised Barriers* Stephen Small (1994) provided an analysis of how racialized ideologies circulate among teachers, coaches, trainers, and managers of sports institutions. He noted, "While the state is central to the dissemination of some racialised ideologies, other racialised ideologies are important and are embraced and disseminated by groups outside the formal political arena."

10. In Leicester several of the women who have chaired and administered ACE and who regularly teach at the Saturday School are qualified teachers who earned their degrees in England and are committed community activists. As in other supplementary schools there is no formal syllabus and the focus of the lesson plans varies considerably depending on the interests and areas of specialization of the volunteer teacher who leads that week's session.

11. Six of the 20 students who had attended all year were mixed race. The population of the Saturday School fluctuates between 20 and 40. Aisha cited the retention of the preteens and teenagers as a major problem.

12. See *American Apartheid* by Douglass Massey and Nancy Denton (1993) for an analysis of residential segregation by race and *The Politics of "Race" and Residence* by Susan Smith (1989) for an analysis of the British case.

13. Letterbox Library is based in London and is located at Leroy House, 436 Essex Road, London N1 3AP.

TWENTY-NINE

Whiteness of a Different Color?

Lani Guinier and Gerald Torres

A series in the *New York Times* titled "How Race Is Lived in America" focused on two Cubans, one white and one black. They were best friends as boys in Cuba, but their lives took a disconcerting turn when they each emigrated separately to the United States.[1] Their experience illustrates the difficulty of "living on the hyphen" in this country and the powerful pressures to conform to the black-white imperative of racial management. For Latinos, it also points toward a less visible but potentially more viable path over this racialized terrain — through a pan-ethnic Hispanic/Latino identity that would challenge not just the racial borders themselves but the underlying systems of wealth and power that the racial border patrol currently protects.

Joel Ruiz and Achmed Valdez grew up together in Cuba. Though Joel was black and Achmed white, neither thought much about the difference when they were young. Racism was a feature of prerevolutionary life in Cuba, and it had not been totally stamped out, but it did not seem to determine one's chance there, and it did not stand in the way of friendship between the two boys. Their common identity as Cubans trumped divisions of race.

When Joel and Achmed grew up, they made independent decisions to leave their homeland. Each was apprehended by the U.S. Coast Guard and sent to Guantanamo before being allowed to enter Miami. Joel's experience in Cuba had not prepared him for the way race matters in the United States. In Miami, Joel found a segregated city. Whereas Achmed went initially to Hialeah, the first stop for white Cubans, Joel went to the black ghetto of Liberty City. As the reporter, Mirta Ojito, put it, "This was Miami, and in Miami, as the roughly 7 percent of the area's Cubans who are black quickly learn, skin color easily trumps nationalism."

This point was driven home to Joel one night when a white Cuban American policeman stopped and frisked him. Joel had been celebrating Valentine's Day in a popular Cuban restaurant with his uncle and three women friends. The policeman said to him, "I've been keeping an eye on you for a while. Since you were in the restaurant. I saw you leave and I saw so many blacks in the car, I figured I would check you out." Though the officer used Spanish to communicate with Joel, the actual words drew a racial line between them and denied their common nationality. After that incident, Joel felt trapped. Though he still identified himself as Cuban, whites saw him as black, and blacks saw him as Cuban. "They tell me I'm Hispanic. I tell them to look at my face, my hair, my skin. I'm black, too. I may speak different, but we all come from the same place."

Joel's experience of being named black by white Americans in a way that subordinated his Cuban-ness shows how the black-white boundary in the United States disciplines those who would challenge its impermeability. The white Cuban American police officer disconnected Joel from his national identity and placed him firmly on the black side of America's principal divide, between blackness and whiteness. What Joel's fellow Cubans had already discovered, and what was expressed most clearly by this officer's conduct, is that "whiteness" in the United States is a measure not just of the melanin content in one's skin but of one's social distance from blackness. The Cuban American policeman asserted his own shaky claim to whiteness by harassing Joel for being black. But native-born black people rejected him, too; as a dark-skinned Cuban American, he was too Cuban to be black, and too black to be white. Joel Ruiz, like many other nonblack nonwhite immigrants, found himself precariously balanced on the hyphen of America's racial divide.

The Racial Bribe

The toughest border patrol in this country may be the one that polices the racial boundaries between black and white. And no group has played a more important role, historically, in the way whites have policed these borders than the group known today as Hispanics or Latinos. Whereas dark-skinned Hispanics like Joel have been pushed into the black category, lighter skinned (or richer) Hispanics like Achmed have been offered a chance to become white, so long as they maintain their social distance from blackness. This offer is part of what we call the racial bribe.

The racial bribe is a racial management strategy that invites specific racial or ethnic groups to advance within the existing black-white racial hierarchy by becoming "white." The strategy expands the range of physical characteristics that can fall within the definition of "white," in order to pursue four goals: (1) to defuse the previously marginalized group's oppositional agenda, (2) to offer incentives that discourage the group from affiliating with black people, (3) to secure high status for individual group members within existing hierarchies, and (4) to make the social position of "whiteness" appear more racially or ethnically diverse.

The official U.S. census has been instrumental in managing the racial bribe by assigning the many types of Hispanics to the category of white, although the racial makeup of the various Latino groups was indeterminate by conventional analysis. In 1930, the sociologist Max Handman noted, "The American community has no social technique for handling partly colored races. We have a place for the Negro and a place for the white man: The Mexican is not a Negro, and the white man refuses him equal status."[2] The problem of what to do with the "partly colored races" represented by Mexicans and other Latinos can be seen clearly in the 1930 census. The basic racial categories that year, in the eyes of census officials, were "White," "Negro," and "Other race." But "Mexican" was also included on the census questionnaire in an attempt to keep track of the nation's growing Spanish population.[3] In prior years the majority of Mexicans, who considered themselves white, had answered accordingly on the census. This had so skewed the numbers of Spanish origin as to make that population seem invisible, and this invisibility led to the addition of "Mexican" as a racial category in the 1930 census. Yet, when many Mexicans switched their identification from "White" to "Mexican" in that year's census, the white population appeared to suffer a significant decrease.[4] To protect the numerical supremacy of whites, the Census Bureau never again used "Mexican" under the race category. In future censuses, it subsumed the entire Mexican category directly into the white category, reinforcing the Mexican racial ideology that had long denied the presence of Africans in the Mexican cultural mix. This denial helped retain a numerical advantage among whites. But it was also important to Mexican Americans because, as Professor John G. Mencke put it, "America's racial system recognizes only the dichotomy of white and black, and the mixed blood is invariably classified as black if his ancestry is known."[5]

Despite inconsistencies within the census groupings, the management of relations between Hispanics and whites has always contained the peculiar promise to some Hispanics that they could become white.[6] Implicit in this promise was the assumption that Mexicans would not be treated like black people and locked into a permanent condition of racial inferiority. In California in the early 20th century, it contained the implicit assumption that Mexicans would not be treated like Asians, either. Prior to the large black migration during World War II, the big distinction in California was among whites, Mexicans, and Asians, and virulent anti-Asian racism made Mexicans "whiter."[7]

The promise of assimilation has also been extended to some elite groups among Hispanics, such as Argentines or Chileans, in distinction to other ethnic subgroups, such as Guatemalans, Hondurans, or Panamanians, whose members are the least European and the poorest and as such do not qualify for whiteness.[8] Conventional conceptions of race construct different kinds of relationships among Hispanics themselves and between Hispanics and others, including non-Hispanic whites or non-Hispanic blacks, in order to control access to power within the Hispanic community itself.

The racial bribe is not unique to Hispanics. At various times in U.S. history, a similar offer of racial assimilation has been made to Jewish, Irish, Italian, and other non-Anglo European groups, who were allowed to move out of their ethnic enclaves and assume the mantle of whiteness. In most regions of the United States, the only groups to whom it has not been available is blacks (though in California, as we have noted, Asians were also denied the option of becoming white for most of the 19th and 20th centuries).[9] Although individual light-skinned blacks may be racially ambiguous in certain contexts and wealthier blacks may be granted certain privileges, as a group blacks traditionally have been the anchor of an oppositional identity. This is what the political scientist Jennifer Hochschild called "black exceptionalism" because it defines the "real" racial divide as lying between "blacks and all other Americans, of whatever hue or background."[10] Or as Professor Pedro Noguera concluded, black people function as "the negative referent group."[11] By offering this option of whiteness over time to selected nonblack nonwhites, the racial binary of black and white is preserved and race in the United States is made more manageable for those seeking to hold onto zero-sum power.

But offering the racial bribe to the group known today as Hispanics or Latinos has proved difficult.[12] The groups that make up this general category range from Europeans to Africans to Asians and comprise a variety of racial types, skin colors, and names — think of Pelé from Brazil or Alberto Fujimori from Peru.[13] Moreover, each Latin American nation has both a racialized and an ethnic identity that preceded the entry of its emigrants into this country, and these designations were rarely drawn precisely on the black-white binary. Because Latinos are neither a uniform "race" nor a uniform ethnic group but still occupy a nonwhite political space in this country, they necessarily complicate the task of racial management for those in power. The prominence of non-Europeans inhibits the assimilation of Latinos on the white ethnic model that more easily accommodated Italians, Irish, Jews, and others.

Simon Bolivar himself, at the dawn of the national period in Latin America, understood that the emerging Latin American identity was an amalgam of peoples.[14] Today, each ethnic or national identity has a specific race discourse rooted in both its colonial history and its immigrant experience.[15] Mexicans, Cubans, and Puerto Ricans have had different interactions with the white/Anglo majority in their country of origin, and those interactions have colored immigrants' encounters with the white majority in the United States. Also, critical differences in conceptions of race come into play from one Latin American nation to the next. Although no Latin American country has escaped the use of racial categories to manage and discipline various populations, the techniques employed contrast sharply with those of the United States.[16] Unlike the pressure to reduce race to either black or white, the dominant ideological response within Latin America has been to celebrate, to a lesser or greater extent depending on the country, the idea of the *mestizaje*.[17] The concept of mestizaje does not necessarily produce the kinds of racial categories constructed by the concept of miscegenation in the United States. According to the mestizaje ideology, the mixture of Indians, Europeans, and Africans created a distinctly new type in Latin America, a kind of cultural suspension within which each element continues to exist but with emphasis on two principle types, the Indian and the European.[18]

Once these various national groups moved into American society, they had to come to grips with their own internal racial politics. Their specific discourses on race, molded by local history in Latin America, had to adapt, somehow, to the dominant American racial framework. Among the different accommodations available, three stand out. One entails creating an identity based on cultural nationalism: Cuban culture would be celebrated as distinct from Mexican culture, and so on. Cuban Americans would seek refuge and recognition within their discrete cultural niche along the hyphen. A second alternative is for select groups to accept the offer to become white. This option draws the internal racial divisions within each nationality into bold relief and highlights the color line. This is what has happened in the case of Cuba. Our nation's official antipathy toward Fidel Castro in fact masks a long relationship between Cuban elites and the United States. As a consequence of this relationship, combined with Cold War iconography, Cubans in the United States have enjoyed the status of preferred immigrants among all the major Latin American nationalities. Light-skinned immigrants like Achmed and the Cuban police officer have been offered, and most have accepted, the racial bribe of whiteness.

A third approach is closely linked to the project of political race. Political race is a geographically specific effort to describe the role race plays as an artifact of social and economic conflict in this country. The project of political race names race as a symptom and source of structural flaws; a political race mobilization derives its energy from people of color but does include whites as well.[19] A political race-type mobilization would construct a pan-ethnic Hispanic/Latino political identity that adapts to the structure of America's racial hierarchy but does not reproduce that structure internally. Thus, a third approach sees the possibility of Latinos joining with blacks, and enlisting whites, to name and challenge national, regional, and local racial hierarchies. Were a pan-ethnic Latino political identity to emerge in defiance of the trajectories of other antecedent immigrant groups, Latinos might destabilize — rather than benefit from — the racial bribe. Such a choice would also reveal the ways in which race has been used to hide the injuries of class. Some who suffer class disadvantage are offered the currency of whiteness to lighten the psychological burden of structural economic inequality.

In the context of U.S. ethnic history, each of these approaches has made sense at one time or another.[20] The assimilationist model is predicated on option two: the assumption that national identities can be suppressed only through the imposition of a more encompassing identity, like race, or a new national identity, such as "American."[21] But in the case of groups whose members take pride in a nonwhite identity, assimilation is not as likely as it was for European ethnic groups, for reasons that originate both inside and outside the group itself. Some survey research suggests, for example, that Hispanics, more so than either blacks or whites, agreed that groups should "maintain their distinct culture" rather than "adapt and blend into the larger society"— that is, they favored option one.[22] But for those who reject the racial bribe offered by option two, or to whom such an offer has never been made, the third approach of creating a social space between the individual national identities and the wholesale adoption of a new national identity might make more sense. Were the Hispanic community to occupy this unique social space, this emerging pan-ethnic identity would have the potential to become a site for progressive political mobilization as part of a political race project. As we emphasize below, local communities that construct this new intermediate identity will do so through political, not just electoral, action on the ground.

MEXICAN AMERICANS

The value, indeed necessity, of this intermediate step can be illustrated through the experiences of Mexican Americans. Mexicans in the Southwest came under American jurisdiction at the close of the Mexican American War. For most of the 20th century, when the term "American" was used in the Southwest, it generally referred only to white Europeans, not to Mexicans. The term "Mexican" was likewise associated with racial background, not with the presence or absence of citizenship.[23] Mexicans were subject to the same kinds of Jim Crow laws that were used to discipline blacks. Discrimination was *de jure*.[24]

Though early white settlers brought slaves with them to Texas, the importation of African slaves from Mexico ended early in the state's history because slavery, though legal in Texas, was illegal in Mexico. What Texans imported from Mexico instead of slaves was a system of peonage similar in some ways to medieval serfdom. The workers were "free," but they were tied to the land through a complex economic and semi-kinship system of sharecropping. Disenfranchised poor whites drifted in from other parts of the South and began competing for resources. For a time cultural inhibitions prohibited landowners from treating these white men and women like Mexicans or recently freed slaves.[25] They were seen as both competitors for land ownership and, as laborers, a source of wage inflation because they could not be paid as poorly as blacks or Mexicans.

In this context, an interesting social discourse emerged.[26] Poor whites came to be considered essentially black by virtue of "scientific" eugenic theory. Their economic failures were, in the eyes of bankers and other suppliers, Darwinian proof of their "unfitness," and thus they could be handled by these white elites in the same way as Mexicans and blacks, who were also "inferiors."[27] In the meantime, Mexicans who had become prosperous began stressing their "Spanish" (that is, European) roots and denying their black heritage. Consequently, in the eyes of white power brokers these Mexican elites became, socially, honorary whites.[28]

What this tells us is that there was a point in Texas history at which poor whites, blacks, and Mexicans were structurally situated in essentially the same social position.[29] The forces that prevented an alliance from forming were many, but in some cases poor whites and Mexicans in South Texas and poor whites and blacks in East Texas created coalitions that formed the roots of modern Texas populism.[30]

The ambiguous relationship between blacks and Mexicans sometimes destabilized the political alliance built out of resistance to an oppressive economic regime. Although shared economic deprivations might have strengthened cross-racial alliances, the color line proved a powerful barrier. Although Mexicans were, as a group, clearly viewed by both whites and blacks as nonwhite, there was internal pressure especially from Mexican elites to situate themselves as white.[31] This meant, of course, defining the group against blackness.

We see this strategy in action when Texas, in order to keep its schools segregated and to avoid spending money on any but the traditionally white schools, used the line between blacks and Mexicans to support white privilege. An unreported 1948 federal court decision, *Delgado v.*

Bastrop Independent School District, clearly declared the illegality of segregating Mexican Americans; nevertheless, state education authorities collaborated with local districts to evade the force of that decision.[32] They simply eliminated the existing category of Mexican schools and declared that Mexican Americans had always been Caucasian. Because there is no obligation to distinguish among Caucasian students, the quality of the Mexican schools did not change; the fact that Mexican children were in substandard schools now became just a matter of bad luck, not discrimination. The Mexican children continued to be treated unfairly. They received none of the material privileges or resources given to the white schools. But they received the psychological boost that came from the state telling them they were no longer like black people.

Despite disastrous consequences such as the *Bastrop* case, the racial identity of Mexican Americans was fiercely contested within the Mexican American community. In the early years of the Mexican American variant of the civil rights movement, the operating premise of the elites was that Mexicans are "racially white" and thus Mexican Americans had to be careful about forming alliances with blacks. Although Mexican mobilization clearly emulated black mobilization in the civil rights movement, some Mexican American leaders went to great pains to distinguish themselves from blacks.[33]

The complicity of Mexican Americans in reinforcing the color line did more than support black disenfranchisement. This strategy undermined potential relationships with other similarly situated people. It fueled the nativist impulse within black communities and contributed to political and social isolation from both blacks and whites. To many whites, some Mexicans might have been white, but as a general matter they were colored and, worse, a debased and mongrelized amalgam of races. To many blacks, Mexicans were racialized by their alien status as outside the black-white binary and in some important sense outside the polity.[34] To the extent that this encouraged blacks to see all Hispanic/Latinos as foreign and a threat to their tenuous grip on social resources, it has continuing implications. In Los Angeles, for example, older blacks joined moderate and conservative whites to defeat a progressive Mexican American candidate in the 2001 mayor's race.

As this short sketch of Mexican Americans in Texas suggests, race would be a central issue within the formation of any emerging Hispanic identity in the United States. It could not be avoided, either internally or externally. The key question is how it would be negotiated.

A CHICAGO STORY

The neighborhoods of Pilsen and Little Village in Chicago are, today, primarily Mexican American, with a significant population of Puerto Ricans and other Latinos. Neighborhood activism dates back to the 1950s, when Mexican Americans became the primary leaders of an organization called the Pilsen Neighbors. This group's first act was to establish a buying collective, but then their focus widened to health care, local schools, job training, and the provision of other social services, including bilingual and bicultural programs. Eventually, Mexican American activists, building on this and similar neighborhood organizations in the city, formed the Independent Political Organization (IPO) in an attempt to fashion an electoral strategy that would allow them to challenge the dominance of Chicago's political machine.

In the 20 years between 1960 and 1980 Chicago's population of Mexicans, Puerto Ricans, and other Latin American ethnics grew from 3% to more than 14%. To discipline community activists and prevent this emerging numerical concentration from translating into electoral clout, the leaders of Chicago's political machine split the Mexican American community into discontinuous aldermanic districts. Within districts, activists realized that they could not succeed by simply organizing around their Mexican-ness. As a result, they began to focus on organizing within the Puerto Rican community and forming alliances with the progressive black community.

The Mexican American and Puerto Rican communities had in fact been cooperating since the early 1970s, when they organized the Spanish Coalition for Jobs, as well as a conference called Latino Strategies for the '70s. This conference was crucial because it put citywide solidarity among Latinos squarely on the agenda. The neighborhood leaders who participated in that meeting stressed their belief that the future of the two communities was linked, both by a shared linguistic heritage and by a political opposition to their treatment by City Hall. Because these neighborhood activists were convinced that electoral politics would be the key, much of their activity centered on voter registration.

The critical moment for the coalition came in the 1983 election campaign of Harold Washington, the first black candidate for mayor. Washington premised his campaign on opposition to the machine's domination of city affairs. To prevail, he would have to galvanize and hold all of the disparate aggrieved groups. The Mexican American and Puerto Rican neighborhoods delivered big for Washington. Of the 48,000 votes that separated Washington from his Republican rival, close to 28,000 of them were cast in the four wards that had been drawn by the machine to disaggregate Mexicans and Puerto Ricans and prevent them from mobilizing resistance to an incumbent machine politician.

One of Mayor Washington's pledges was to reform the patronage system. This meant he would have to dismantle the bureaucracy and replace commission members and committee chairs. He had defined his challenge for City Hall specifically in terms of opposition to the machine and its paternalistic politics that had the net effect of neglecting black and Latino neighborhoods. Besides a more efficient bureaucracy, Mayor Washington wanted to get resources to the neighborhoods, especially those that had historically been low on the distribution list.

Although many Mexican and Puerto Rican activists worked for the election of Washington and his progressive vision, the new mayor and his supporters soon learned that winning is different from governing. Washington found his initiatives strangled by the internal politics of the Board of Aldermen, whose majority was still under machine control. To break this lock on the board, Washington's supporters needed a strategy for getting their people elected to these key positions. A legal challenge for fair representation under the Voting Rights Act, if successful, might give the progressive activists the majority they needed.

The plaintiffs, led by the Mexican American Legal Defense and Education Fund (MALDEF), claimed that the minority vote had been diluted through the familiar stratagems of packing, fracturing, and boundary manipulation. Though they lost in district court, the Seventh Circuit Court of Appeals ordered the creation of districts that would guarantee 19 black wards and 4 mixed Mexican and Puerto Rican wards.

There was an irony to the Voting Rights Act decree and the districts that were created in satisfaction of the court order. Although the Mexican and Puerto Rican activists "won" four wards, in many ways these wards built on what the machine politicians had already done to fragment the existing ethnic Mexican communities. Rather than construct a ward primarily to reconnect the detached pieces of the Mexican community, the court joined these fragments to severed remnants of the Puerto Rican neighborhoods. The new wards maintained the basic footprint of the original wards that had split up the Mexican American community in the first place but simply expanded the total Latino population within each district, by reconnecting more Mexican Americans with Puerto Ricans. The irony was that the remedial choices of a federal court — an external government actor — engineered "pan-ethnic" Latino, rather than Mexican or Puerto Rican, election districts. Those choices then helped fabricate a unique political space from the earlier mischief of machine politicians.

The creation of these four wards pursuant to the Voting Rights Act sped up the electoral coalition between Mexicans and Puerto Ricans. The activists now chose to organize around their self-identification as "Latino." Though the official term used by the Census Bureau is "Hispanic," in Chicago the term people use on the street is Latino: "When we call ourselves Latino we name ourselves; it is other people who call us Hispanic."[35] But the point is not the specific terminology; the point is that a powerful coalition emerged between groups that had previously identified primarily with their nation of origin.

This Latino alliance added persistently high unemployment, gang violence, decaying commercial districts, and high drop-out rates to their electoral agenda. These issues went beyond the old patronage litany that promised to fix potholes and clean up vacant lots. Latino activists linked reorganization of the bureaucracy to issues of access to city resources and commercial reinvestment in the community. The progressive politicians who used Latinismo to join the interests of Puerto Ricans and Mexican Americans focused on structural changes that would bring long-term improvements to each community.

Mexicans and Puerto Ricans in Chicago had to confront the contradictions and discomfort within their own communities in order to make Latino politics work. Indeed, these differences should be expected and should not obscure the fundamental point, which is that local political action — built through community institutions of churches, unions, or neighborhood associations — is a precondition to a national pan-ethnic identity. That point is summed up by Henry Trueba: "Latinos, in fact, are creating a new identity on the basis of common cultural values and the increasing advantages of political alliances for action presumed to benefit the diverse Latino ethnic subgroups. In some real sense, political action seems to play an instrumental role in forming a new ethnic identity with new cultural ties and values among Latinos who have been marginalized and isolated."[36]

That was certainly the case in Chicago, where political action anticipated and took advantage of external interventions by government actors to forge the local pan-ethnic coalition. What the experience of Chicago teaches is that we must be wary of generalizations from national data. Political race is created on the ground. It finds a space for organizing that is rooted in ethnicity but expands beyond parochial concerns. Latinos in Chicago had to organize outside conventional racial and ethnic paradigms. As has so often been the case in the black community, intergroup unity came about because the mistreatment these groups suffered was meted out not according to their specific ethnicity but because they were seen as Spanish-speaking foreigners, despite their citizenship. They were shoved into barrios in the same way that blacks were pushed into ghettos. The brutal beating of two Puerto Ricans by the Chicago police in 1965 galvanized not just the Puerto Rican community but all Latinos, because the beating was emblematic of the treatment of barrio residents. A shooting of a young Puerto Rican man in 1966 caused these resentments to boil over into a riot and pushed progressive Puerto Rican and Mexican American political activists together to oppose a hardening urban inequality.[37]

Electoral politics was one strategy for this opposition, but it was not the engine driving pan-Latino mobilization. In a more general sense the real engine was a fear of permanent outsider and subordinate status. What the Mexican American and Puerto Rican activists understood was that prioritizing their sense of their own cultural distinctiveness could only translate into marginality, whereas a consolidation of efforts and interests could translate into real social gains. As one activist put it, "Individually, we are not going anywhere. So respect for differences could represent a way for us to unite. The idea of Latinismo is a very good strategy.... I feel pity for those leaders that stand up in meetings and say 'We must fight and struggle for the rights of the Puerto Ricans, the Mexicans, or the Cubans separately': I feel pity for these leaders because they do not understand Latinismo. They do not know that we basically have the same culture and needs. And the only way to alleviate those problems and gain political respect is to work together as one group." Or as Rosa Clemente, a Puerto Rican youth organizer in New York proclaims, "Being Latino/a is not a cultural identity but rather a political one."

A LOS ANGELES STORY

The story of the Figueroa Corridor Coalition for Economic Justice in L.A. is about the way a working-class community stood up to forces of the government and large land developers, to demand a share of the local prosperity and a seat at the table when decisions affecting their neighborhood were being made. Yet, what makes this story different from hundreds of tales of working-class resistance is that the coalition had to create a form of politics that would negotiate the changing racial makeup of the community from predominantly black to predominantly Latino. In addition to that general change, community leaders had to transform the resistance from a Mexican-inspired effort to a Latino-based initiative that could encompass what had become primarily Central American neighborhoods. A united Latino community was essential to forging a coalition with neighboring Asian and black communities. If this had been strictly a nationalist effort or a class-based effort, it would have failed. Like the protest led by the black ministers in the Pulpit Forum in Greensboro, North Carolina, it had to give cultural resonance to democratic working-class-based resistance.[38] And it found this in churches, unions, and decades-long street-level organizing.

In 1994 Governor Pete Wilson was in a tight race for reelection in California. He found himself trailing Kathleen Brown, sister of former governor Jerry Brown and daughter of the still-beloved governor who built modern California, Edmund G. "Pat" Brown. In a tactical decision with long-term strategic consequences, Governor Wilson tied his hopes for reelection to his fervent advocacy of Proposition 187. This proposition was designed to protect the public coffers by denying medical and educational services to undocumented immigrants and their children. Although his support of Proposition 187 secured his reelection, Governor Wilson's deal — like every deal with the devil — came at a heavy cost, this time to the Republican Party in California.

Although the majority of voters believed that the proposition was aimed at undocumented Mexicans, in practice it hit a much larger target, including Asians and Central Americans. These immigrants eventually became citizens and they registered to vote. And in every election since 1994 they have punished the Republican Party. Democrats controlled the statehouse, both houses of the legislature, and both senate seats. Even arch-conservative Robert Dornan from legendarily conservative Orange County lost his seat to a Latina and then cemented his defeat by challenging her election with an extended complaint about "illegal" voting by immigrants.

By galvanizing the Latino and Asian communities, Proposition 187 laid the foundation for cross-racial coalition building around issues like those that lay at the heart of the Figueroa Corridor Coalition for Economic Justice. The strength these immigrants found in responding to Proposition 187 has been translated into increased labor activity and has led to additional coalitions among Asian, Latino, and African American communities that have a specific political content apart from "rent-seeking" by each faction of the coalition.

In a dramatic example of this political cooperation, the bus riders' strike joined primarily

Latino bus riders with predominantly black bus drivers in an effort to secure better service and fare stabilization. Though originally opposed by environmental groups because the settlement would take money away from the subway system then under construction, the environmentalists were brought around, and part of the settlement resulted in the creation of Environmental Justice Los Angeles (EJLA).

Community activists took the lesson of defeat and used it to organize the communities that were the target of Proposition 187. Central to their organizing was to make common cause with labor and progressive activists across racial lines in order to create a community base that could defend itself and turn its issues into policy. Efforts to drive a wedge between the historically antagonistic black and Latino communities spurred more creative community organizing that dates back to Governor Wilson's 1994 campaign.

Part of this new cooperation comes from the expansion of the Latino community beyond the traditional Mexican American base. Although Latinos of Mexican descent still predominate, there has been a steady influx of people from Guatemala and El Salvador. The civil wars in each country during the past 30 years have greatly accelerated the stream of refugees and immigrants. Like the circumstances in Chicago, where interaction between Puerto Ricans and Mexican Americans led to the articulation of a Latino identity through which to conduct politics, the existing category of Hispanic/Latino in Los Angeles provided a means to mediate the interaction of these new immigrants with established Mexican American communities as well as with immigrant Mexican communities. The coincidence of this migration pattern with the politics of Proposition 187 gave added immediacy to the need to join these disparate groups into a cohesive whole that could develop a new politics of resistance.

Because of organizing across racial lines and creating a meaningful Latino identity, Los Angeles came close to getting its first Latino mayor in more than a hundred years. Yet if Antonio Villaraigosa, a Mexican American, had succeeded in being elected mayor, he would not have been just a Latino mayor; his candidacy was the product of the progressive coalition building that produced the bus riders' strike, EJLA, the Cornfield Park, and the Figueroa Corridor Coalition. But he faced a formidable challenge. He had to unite the various Latino subgroups as well as progressive whites, Asians, and blacks. Having a Spanish surname was not enough; he had to speak directly to the needs of each group in a way that could join them together to a common vision of progressive change.

Electoral politics make identity politics a high-stakes enterprise. By focusing on the descriptive elements of community and reducing a candidacy to those elements, electoral politics feeds interracial competition because it offers the appearance of racial symbols but does not encourage genuine cross-racial political engagement over time. Even the groundwork of groups like Environmental Justice Los Angeles, the Figueroa Corridor Coalition, the Cornfield Coalition, the Community Coalition, and the Organization of Los Angeles Workers did not give Villaraigosa enough of a cross-racial foundation to stand on in the heat of an election.

THE CHALLENGES OF AN ELECTORAL STRATEGY

Although an impressive coalition between progressive younger elements of the Latino and black communities emerged around the candidacy of Villaraigosa, what is important to remember is that this was not just a coalition cobbled together for an election. In Los Angeles and in California generally there has been historic antipathy between the Mexican American and black communities, borne of racism on one side and nativism on the other. Although they might not always stand together behind a single candidate, the groundwork for a more enduring unity was being laid in the labor struggles that united bus drivers and bus riders, that sought to bring "Justice for Janitors" and to translate the hopes and democratic aspirations of working people of all races.

The leadership came from the dishwashers, chambermaids, janitors, and bellhops who spent their days off going "door-to-door canvassing in the barrio neighborhoods of Los Angeles, confronting their neighbors with a forceful warning that unless they vote, they can forget their dreams of a living wage, health insurance protection, and better schools for their children."[39] It was the Latino working-poor and immigrant families of Los Angeles who took the insult and threat of Proposition 187 and turned it into a force for remaking democracy from the street up. When this united Latino effort moved citywide, it had to find a way to include the black community. This proved to be its greatest challenge.

Villaraigosa's candidacy was plagued by conflict, even though he had qualms running as the "Latino" candidate. He ran a campaign that suggested this was not just about Antonio Villaraigosa but about speaking to the needs of the people who lifted him up.[40] Nevertheless, he had to run in an electoral climate in Los Angeles where the black/Latino coalition is fragile.[41]

One reason for this seeming deadlock is the lingering effect of identity politics, in which electoral coalitions are mobilized around ethnic or racial identity, a source of pride and energy that yields high voter turnout but may then exacerbate friction between competing ethnic or racial groups. A second is the residue of Hispanic whiteness. Because the promise of the racial bribe invites some Hispanics to turn their back on their indigenous roots, many blacks do not trust Latinos to fight alongside them over the long haul. Blacks fear that new immigrants will monopolize the good jobs but, more important, will displace them as the racial group with the strongest moral claim on existing resources.[42]

Immigrants bring new energy and pride to progressive struggles. But they also bring their ignorance of the history of U.S. slavery and its enduring legacy.[43] Latinos and other nonwhite groups may need to do more to convince the black leadership and the black community that they share their fate and are willing to join forces directly rather than compete for a small sliver of elite recognition. This is not to say that blacks are innocent bystanders. Indeed there is mutual suspicion, reinforced by black anti-immigrant sentiment. But these sources of intergroup friction could be worked out were there a political party or political space that built on neighborhood organizing efforts and was accountable to local, democratically rooted institutions.

This, then, is the third and perhaps more important explanation for the current instability of black-Latino alliances. It is simply not enough to concentrate on electoral politics in a winner-take-all contest if the goal is to develop and sustain cross-racial coalitions. The chance of electing a person of color does not create the conditions for sustained mobilization beyond election day, even when that person is a racial-group pioneer. Indeed, it would take an extraordinary candidate to produce a vital coalition without the experience of working together in a nonelectoral setting. Even the example of Harold Washington, despite his importance in galvanizing community groups, would have come to nothing if the communities themselves had not begun cross-ethnic and cross-racial organizing decades before.

A preoccupation with electoral politics can distract from the hard work of organizing a base of community participation. Especially if electoral strategies are founded primarily on shared identity without ever anticipating the second or third stages of political race, the potential for long-term cooperation growing out of an understanding of shared interests is less likely. The focus is on winning an election, and the challenges of government are often neglected. The community is disengaged once victory is theirs.

In the long run, a social movement will not evolve to create this intermediate space — that we call political race — if its efforts are constrained by either simple identity politics or liberal interest-group politics. Successful social movements draw on the courage, faith, and commitment of participants, rooted precisely in the fact that their endeavor is about broader themes of social justice and not simply about narrow self-interest. Their energy to continue comes from the struggle to redefine what their identity means — in economic, political, and moral terms.

To remain animated beyond a single electoral victory, the energy of racial identity has to be summoned as a moral force with social justice commitments. Otherwise it just devolves into patronage and the special pleading that typified the Chicago machine. Gerald Torres made this point forcefully in 1994, when, as a minor appointed functionary in the first Clinton administration, he was summoned to a meeting in the Old Executive Office Building. The meeting was called to discuss ways to get out the message about the various good things the administration had done for the Hispanic community. After some discussion, the person leading the meeting suggested that those present construct a list of all the Clinton appointees who are Hispanic. This list, when publicized, would demonstrate the administration's noble intentions and goodwill toward the Hispanic community. The discussion continued until Gerald slammed his hand on the table. He said that if the administration wanted to earn the support of the Hispanic community, it would have to demonstrate that desire through an enumeration of the various *policy initiatives* that have actually improved the lives of significant numbers of the Hispanic population. "Except for my mother," he explained, "no one voted for Bill Clinton so I would have a job."

Yet, policy initiatives to improve the lives of Hispanics alone are also not enough to sustain a social movement. Even when ethnic politics seems to work, as in Chicago, it is critical to keep the racialized position in mind but not as an end in itself. It is a means to diagnose and respond to deeper structural infirmities.

In sociologist Cathy Schneider's description of Brooklyn politics, for example, the progressive content of an organized Puerto Rican community was blunted when activists failed to move beyond the nationalist impulse.[44] Their initial organizing took race into account but then failed to push through the isolating structure of identity-based interest-group politics. Instead of recognizing that the community needed the resources for both poor Jews and Puerto Ricans, activists attempted to oppose the outside attacks by defining their political community narrowly and electorally, thus weakening both the potential impact of their efforts and their capacity to resist.

Though our mostly preliminary assessment of the mayor's race in Los Angeles seems to suggest that real street-level cross-racial and cross-ethnic mobilization is a precondition for building the kind of cooperation that we have characterized as political race, we want to be clear that we are also saying the battle never ends. Even the longevity of coalitions does not eliminate the obligation to continually attend to the roots of cooperation and to be vigilant about challenging the reproduction of both racial categories and racial hierarchies. Democracy, we would argue, is about finding spaces for power *with* the community, not simply power for the candidate.

THE PERSISTENCE OF RACIAL HIERARCHY AND RACIAL PRIVILEGE

We cannot be totally sanguine about the natural possibilities of a transition from a Hispanic/Latino identity to political race because the pressures to conform to the conventional system of racial management are great. As the historian Noel Ignatiev recounts in his book *How the Irish*

Became White: "It was a passage in *Boston's Immigrants* that first drew me to my own question: it recounts the complaints of Boston Irish 'that colored people did not know their place.' How, I wondered, did an Irish immigrant, perhaps fresh off the boat, learn 'the place' of the Negro."[45]

Andrew Hacker takes Ignatiev's discovery to make the claim that the pressures of racial management in the United States will compel Latinos to choose between being white or black. As it stands now, Asians are gradually becoming honorary whites, according to Hacker's view, whereas Latinos are, at minimum, nonwhite and still have a choice to make.[46] It is precisely against this view that we have been writing. We argue, rather, that there is a third way, an intermediate space that draws on the concept of political race. But the social pressures Hacker and other scholars describe cannot be discounted.

Many people today view Asians (a complex pan-ethnic term in itself) as lying on the white end of the racial spectrum.[47] As Hochschild wrote, "Asian Americans frequently resemble whites (so far as we can tell from very scanty survey data)." Although there are important analogs between the Latino and the Asian experience with race in this country, there are also important differences. Nonetheless, as the experiences in the Figueroa Coalition illustrated, a similarity in outlook toward many issues can permit a coalition to be built across Latino and Asian communities. As Hochschild pointed out, "A survey in Los Angeles shows the pattern clearly. Latinos and Asian Americans are consistently more likely to give the response sympathetic to immigrants than are whites and African Americans."[48] This similarity of attitude helps explain the ready affinity between the Asian and Latino communities in response to Proposition 187.

But immigrant issues are not the only ones that unite Asians and Latinos. Even on the question of Asian assimilation, Hacker may be wrong. Hochschild noted, "In every one of the dozens of survey questions on the point [of racial and ethnic separation] Anglos see much less racial discrimination than do African Americans, even though they are more likely to express racial or ethnic stereotypes; Hispanics and Asians typically fall somewhere in between, but closer to blacks in their perceptions."[49]

This reality is reflected in local politics, where Asians have sufficient numbers to form a constituency to which aspirants for political office must respond. In Monterey Park, California, Latinos and Asians joined together to stop the city from declaring English the official language. Out of that struggle a Latino-Asian coalition was formed that propelled Judy Chu into the California State Assembly. Significantly, Chu did this by beating a Latino candidate in a district where Latinos outnumbered Asians by close to 20%. Although her opponent was a respected Latino mayor of a neighboring city, Chu secured the backing of the outgoing assemblywoman, Gloria Romero, as well as progressive, pro-labor Latina Congresswoman Hilda Solis.[50] Chu neither rejected her racial identity nor merely embraced the symbolic nationalism of a candidate-centered campaign. Instead, Chu forged an alliance that used the outsider status of both Asians and Latinos to create a progressive political identity.

Despite the important examples of cross-racial coalition building in California and Chicago, political race — using race as a tool for diagnosis, critique, and mobilization — requires that we exercise constant vigilance in renegotiating the black-white binary. The internal dynamics of race within each national subgroup are complex. And like any historical moment, the contingencies admit of many possible futures. There are, however, reasons to believe that political race may ultimately prevail over the alternative approaches of simple cultural nationalism or cooperation with the racial bribe. The maintenance of a large and cohesive political group means that even the elite, at whom the racial bribe has been historically aimed, would have to reject it as corrosive to the political strength of the Hispanic/Latino population. Division of the potential political base along conventional black-white lines would dissipate the numerical strength that the political elite is counting on. It needs to have the numbers even as its relationship to black-ness continues to evolve. By choosing to become white on the European ethnic model, each of the component groups within the pan-ethnic Hispanic/Latino identity would either have to repress the black content of their own national or familial identity or rewrite the meaning of their culture consistent with the black-white binary that governs race in America. There are political costs to either strategy. Those costs are inconsistent with the national political ambitions of the Hispanic/Latino elite.

This is because the construction of a national platform through the development of a pan-Hispanic/Latino identity requires the maintenance of as large a grouping as possible that can come together across a range of issues. One key is to organize according to interest, within a larger social justice frame, rather than any essential characteristic. Such an approach promises to reduce the fric-tion between the major ethnic groups within the Hispanic/Latino grouping. This is one of the lessons from the coalition between Puerto Ricans, Mexican Americans, other Latin Americans, blacks, and progressive whites in Chicago. From the perspective of the imperatives of liberal interest-group politics, success with that vision would rupture bipolar racial hierarchies and build from a Hispanic/Latino identity into a cross-racial affiliation with blacks and whites.[51]

A related pressure that might prevent groups who in the past would have taken the racial bribe from doing so is fundamentally political. By political we mean a growing awareness of the energy within the Hispanic/Latino community for mobilizing around a social justice agenda that starts with race but does not end there. To succeed as a national strategy, creation of a Hispanic/Latino identity must accommodate the wide "racial" and color variation within each of the component groups without reproducing domestic racial hierarchy. This issue will not be worked out once but must be dealt with self-consciously and locally time after time.

If a third way can be forged from the pressure to develop a Hispanic/Latino identity with racially indeterminate — though nonwhite — content, it will illustrate two foundational ideas of political race. First, this pan-ethnic identity will remind us that political race is not about membership in an externally defined racial group; instead, it is about commitment. Second, it will help teach those outside the community important lessons about building progressive alliances on the ground.

These lessons are reflected in the emerging black-consciousness movement in Brazil described in an earlier essay. Yet we need not look all the way to Brazil to see leadership of color using race to generate progressive alternatives that benefit more than their own careers or their immediate constituents. The Latino leadership who designed and fought for the Texas 10 Percent Plan — to diversify the state's flagship public colleges — could safely have done nothing and most would not have suffered electoral repercussions. They could have saved their rela-tionships with their legislative colleagues for conventional gains for their constituents. Instead, they understood their constituents not just as the people in their districts but as the black, Latino, and poor white rural students who had traditionally been excluded from the flagship campuses.[52]

Those committed to the political race project understand this as well. For example, the progressive coalition that emerged in the aftermath of Proposition 187 has helped move the political debate and the grounds for political action from race to class without pretending that race does not have a role. The coalition has enabled labor to join forces and to link Asians, Mexicans, and black people. It has experienced setbacks as well as victories. But when it succeeds, it is because it continues to work through issues of race internal to the coalition as well as in the larger society. Because whiteness is measured in social distance from blackness, the coalition has had to have leaders who actively oppose the efforts of conservatives to exploit both the racism of Mexicans and the nativism of blacks.[53] By using racial identity and immigrant status to energize a movement for social and economic justice, it moves beyond interest-group pleading to confront the question Hochschild and others have posed—"whether African Americans, other people of color, and like-minded whites can surmount their partly outdated assumptions, mutual mistrust, and substantive disagreements enough to pursue their shared material and philosophical goals."[54]

The lessons from Chicago, Los Angeles, and Texas demonstrate that the political space opened up by the Hispanic/Latino identity may initially be defined externally by government census categories or electoral districts. It may be driven by national elites interested in maximizing their numerical constituency, but it will be occupied by local communities of interest, and its content will not be determined in advance. These communities will then have an impact on the construction of issues that will inform the elite's conception of the meaning of the category.

CONCLUSION

Our discussion of Hispanics/Latinos and others who find themselves on the hyphen of the black-white binary is situated within a peculiar local racial history. But it foreshadows the danger that a multiracial movement that simply succeeds in repopulating a racial hierarchy may nevertheless simultaneously reproduce or fortify the hierarchy itself. The many stories collected in this essay indicate the promise of a cross-racial and democratically committed alliance whose leaders are people of color but who struggle together against hierarchies of power at the right historical time. Some of these stories also illustrate the difficulty of maintaining transformative political commitments in an era of scarcity when the promise is not greater democracy but the acquisition of more material resources for some. Our discussion of Mexican Americans highlights both of these points, but it also illustrates our central claim that race is connected to power and that the Hispanic/Latino identity has within it a promising and powerful role to play in destabilizing the black-white binary.

We take two lessons from interpreting the Hispanic/Latino identity in the United States in light of the pressures to conform to the black-white binary and other conventional racial management techniques.

First, the use of race as a political category gains its legitimacy from its promise to increase the quantum of democracy in society and to resist unfair concentrations of wealth and power. As we have already argued, merely acquiring power for one's self or one's own group without challenging the very nature of that power does not constitute political transformation. We cannot assume that, once confronted and negotiated, the impact of race fades as a fundamental political issue.

Second, the use of political race makes sense only when some of the political efforts aim to change the nature of power away from zero-sum competition for resources. Power constructs the self, and in a hierarchical capitalist society that is not shaped by democratic pressures, it will eventually construct selves in the shapes of winners and losers.

One of the critical issues raised in the context of the emerging Hispanic/Latino identity in the United States is how to value racial difference within the context of political unity. We have not been describing new racial categories. We have not been talking about doing away with race. Instead, we think that the lessons of the development of a Hispanic/Latino identity point to the possibility of using race and politics to create an identity that resists conventional categories and supports democratic renewal. That, we think, is at the heart of the concept of political race.

NOTES

1. Mirta Ojito, "How Race Is Lived in America—Best of Friends, Worlds Apart," *New York Times*, June 5, 2000, at Al.
2. Max Sylvius Handman, "Economic Reasons for the Coming of the Mexican Immigrant," 35 *American Journal of Sociology* 609–610 (January 1930). In an earlier journal article Handman tried to identify the source of the confusion as to race and treatment. "The Mexican presents shades of color ranging from that of the Negro, although with no Negro features, to that of the white." This "problem" was perplexing because, according to Handman, "the temptation of the white group is to push him down into the Negro group, while the efforts of the Mexican will be directed toward raising himself up to the level of the white group." Max Sylvius Handman, "The Mexican Immigrant in Texas," 7 *Southwestern Political and Social Science Quarterly* 27,40 (June 1926).
3. "Spanish origin" is the name that was and has been used by the Census Bureau to classify all Spanish-speaking ethnic groups. Within the historical charts of the 1940 Census, no "Mexican" race category appears under the 1930 section. Bureau of Census, Department of Commerce, *Report of the 1940 United States Census* (1942). 1950 Bureau of the Census: Special Reports at 1A-13.
4. From Bureau of Census, Department of Commerce, Fifteenth Census of the United States: Vol. 2, Population at 25 (1933).
5. "If it is known that an individual is even remotely descended from a black person, he is classified as a Negro.... Although words like mulatto, quadroon and octoroon have been used on occasion in America, in reality they have little or no social significance." John G. Mencke, *Mulattoes and Race Mixture: American Attitudes and Images, 1865–1918* (1979).
6. See Neil Foley, "Becoming Hispanic: Mexican Americans and the Faustian Pact with Whiteness," in *Reflexiones; New Directions in Mexican American Studies* at 64 (Neil Foley, ed., 1998) (debating whether Hispanics are white is a key moment in the definition of the shape of Mexican American political engagement in the struggle for civil rights).
7. Stan Lieberson, *A Piece of the Pie: Blacks and White Immigrants since 1880* (1981). Lieberson argued that Asians were singled out because they represented a threatening combination of economic, political, and social numbers of people with visibly different physical characteristics.
8. See Noel Ignatiev, *How the Irish Became White* (1995) (especially chaps. 6 and Afterword); Neil Foley, *The White Scourge: Mexicans, Blacks, and Poor Whites in Texas Cotton Culture* (1997) (discussing the economic and social structure of the cotton culture of Texas and the accommodation to competition between poor whites, Mexicans, and blacks).
9. Until the Immigration Act of 1917, immigration from Mexico was essentially open, with Mexicans considered white for purposes of eligibility for citizenship. Asians, on the other hand—first Chinese, next Japanese, and later Sikhs—even during periods of legal immigration were denied the opportunity to become citizens. The naturalization bar was then

the basis on which land ownership rights were restricted as well. Mexicans, however, wound up on the white side of this divide until their numbers became so much greater during the 1920s, a fact that prompted the deportations of the 1930s and, along with the influx of southern whites during the same period who also were competing for employment, led to the establishment of clearer lines of segregation of schools, swimming pools, and other public facilities.

10. Jennifer Hochschild, "Madison's Constitution and Identity Politics" at 19–20 (unpublished manuscript, May 18, 2000).

11. Pedro Noguera, "Anything but Black," in *Blackness and Invisibility* (Percy Hintzen and Jean Rahnier, eds., 2002. New York: Routledge, 193–200).

12. See, for example, Tomas Almaguer, *Racial Fault Lines: The Historical Origins of White Supremacy in California* (1994); Carlos Arce et al., "Phenotype and Life Chances among Chicanes," 9 *Hispanic Journal of Behavior Sciences* 19 (1987); Frank D. Bean and Marta Tieda, *The Hispanic Population of the United States* (1987); George Sanchez, *Becoming Mexican-American: Ethnicity, Culture and Identity in Chicago and Los Angeles, 1900–1945* (1993); Ilan Stavans, *The Hispanic Condition: Reflections on Culture and Identity in America* (1995). See also Peter Skerry, *Mexican Americans: The Ambivalent Minority* (1993).

13. The lack of specific ethnic definition (defined in terms of specific national origin) makes "Hispanic American" in some ways the cognate category to "African American" or to "Asian American." See Yen Le Espiritu, *Asian American Pan-ethnicity: Bridging Institutions and Identity* (1992), and Robert Chang, *Disoriented* (1999). "Native Americans" do not fit into this category because they have a specific tribal definition except when spoken of casually or for purposes of popular definition. For example, the 2000 Census form which requires a specific tribal designation if the racial identity "Indian" is selected.

14. Simon Bolivar, *Selected Writings of Bolivar*, vol. 1 at 181 (Vicente Lecuna and Harold A. Bierk, Jr., eds., 1951).

15. The confrontation with race was built into the basic structure of what has come to be described as the Hispanic or Latino community. In most cases, the Latin American situation required the dominant white or European elite to undertake a strategy to manage the complex racial differences within their societies and to come to terms with the widespread miscegenation that was at the core of their national realities. When we use the term *racial* in the context of our discussion of Hispanics, we mean that to varying degrees these national subgroups (Cuban, Mexican, Puerto Rican, and so on) are already in a relationship with the dominant white majority that tracks the characteristics of the relationships that we explored in the context of political race. Some of these racial characteristics are historic; others are phenotypic in origin but have been given a political content that has emerged from and been reinforced by distinctive demographic associations and regional variations. Geoffrey Fox, *Hispanic Nation: Culture, Politics, and the Construction of Identity*.

16. See generally David Montejano, *Anglos and Mexicans in the Making of Texas, 1836–1986* (1987); Foley, "Becoming Hispanic"; Foley, *The White Scourge*; Ignatiev, *How the Irish Became White*.

17. See Edward Lucas White, *El Supremo: A Romance of the Great Dictator of Paraguay* (1916). (In his discussion of the racial policies of Jose Gaspar Rodriguez Francia, we see that Francia wanted to make the process of mixing the races a requirement rather than a mere accidental historical process.)

18. See Walter Mignolo, *Local Histories/Global Designs* (2000); Jose David Saldivar, *Border Matters: Remapping American Cultural Studies* (1997). See also Foley, "Becoming Hispanic" (discussing the resistance among the Mexican American elite to embrace an alliance with blacks in the early struggle for civil rights).

19. See Guinier and Torres, *The Miner's Canary* (Harvard Press 2002) at chapters 1 through 3. The enduring significance of race comes from its association with power throughout the history of the United States. As a result, the black/white binary both codes and frames social, political, and economic interests for people of color as well as whites. It produces and hides structural dysfunction that adversely affects poor and working-class people of all colors. At the same time as the political race project helps make visible these connections between race and class, it builds potential energy for change.

20. See Michael Omi and Howard Winant, *Racial Formation in the United States: From the 1960s to the 1980s* (2d ed. 1994); *Theories of Ethnicity: A Classical Reader* (Werner Sollers, ed., 1996).

21. See, for example, the summary of the process described by Herbert J. Gans in "Symbolic Ethnicity: The Future of Ethnic Groups and Cultures in America," in *Theories of Ethnicity* at 425–459 (Sollors, ed.).

22. See Jennifer Hochschild, "Madison's Constitution" at 15 (identifying survey research that suggests Mexican immigrants, for example, have a "unique psychological relationship to American society").

23. See David Montejano, *Anglos and Mexicans* at xvi n49.

24. See *Hopwood v. Texas*, 78 F.3d 932 (5th Cir. 1996).

25. See Foley, *The White Scourge*: "A close correlation existed between race and tenant status in central Texas, with most blacks and Mexicans occupying the rank of sharecroppers and wage laborers. White sharecroppers were stigmatized in Texas, as elsewhere in the South, as white trash, crackers, and rednecks, but even as marginal whites these sharecroppers came to enjoy for a brief time, the social, psychological, and economical advantages of being white. White tenants who had slipped into sharecropping were able, for example, to negotiate contracts as half tenants' or tenants on the halves." Ibid at 85–86.

26. See Gerald Torres's "Local Knowledge, Local Color: Critical Legal Studies and the Law of Race Relations," 25 University of San Diego Law Review 1043 (1988).

27. See Foley, *The White Scourge* (exploring the different business practices that were driven by underlying racial hierarchies).

28. David Montejano explores this process in his book *Anglos and Mexicans*.

29. Foley, *The White Scourge* at 85–86: "As increasing numbers of Mexicans settled in central Texas as sharecroppers, owners no longer felt the need to rent to whites as half tenants. Rather, owners hired them to make a crop as true sharecroppers, no different in status from Mexicans and Blacks."

30. See Foley, *The White Scourge*; Montejano, *Anglos and Mexicans*.

31. University of Texas historian David Montejano called this "an accommodation between Anglo and Hispano elites."

32. *U.S. v. State of Texas.* 506 F.Supp. 405, 412 (E.D.Tex.1981). PL-Int. Ex. 409, #735. It took this case in 1981 to finally prompt the legislature to actually begin to segregate Mexican schools.

33. "Despite numerous examples of those who rejected whiteness and ... White privilege, many Mexican Americans must nevertheless acknowledge their complicity in maintaining the boundaries around 'blackness' in order to claim the privileges of whiteness. By

embracing whiteness, Mexican Americans have reinforced the color line that has denied people of African descent full participation in American democracy." Foley, "Becoming Hispanic" at 65.

34. See Foley, "Becoming Hispanic." Quoting letter of a black El Pasoan to the editor of the local paper in 1936: "Though once pure Indians," he wrote, "Mexicans had become more mixed than dog food — undoubtedly a conglomeration of Indian with all the races Known to man, with the possible exception of the Eskimos." Ibid. at 15.

35. In the 1970s, the Federal Office of Management and Budget, in consultation with officials of Spam, created the term "Hispanic," which OMB defined as, "A person of Mexican, Puerto Rican, Cuban, or Central American or other Spanish Culture or origin, regardless of race." See 43 C.F.R. 19269 (1978). Thus the term "Hispanic" is the official term. In California, as in Chicago, the preferred pan-ethnic term seems to be "Latino." In Texas the term with the most common usage, when not describing just Mexican Americans, is "Hispanic." Within the Mexican American community, there is both a generational and political split over the use of the term "Chicano." Most progressive political activists within the Mexican American community prefer "Chicano" and its derivative "Chicanismo."

36. Enrique T. Trueba, *Latinos Unidos: From Cultural Diversity to the Politics of Solidarity* at 22 (1999).

37. Felix M. Padilla, *Latino Ethnic Consciousness: The Case of Mexican Americans and Puerto Ricans in Chicago* at 46–51, 58 (1985).

38. See Guinier and Torres, *The Miner's Canary*, chapter 5 at 131–138 (describing an effort to use race to connect to class to forge community through collective, cross-racial mobilization).

39. David Bacon, "Crossing L.A.'s Racial Divide," *In These Times*, June 11, 2001.

40. As Steve Erie, a U.C. San Diego professor who studies Los Angeles politics said of the campaign, "You're going to hear a lot more about equity issues, haves and have-nots and what city government can do for the less fortunate." Matea Gold and Tina Daunt, "L.A. Takes a Turn to the Left With Democrat in Charge," *Los Angeles Times*, June 6, 2001, at 1. UCLA Professor Gary Blasi concurred: "Whoever wins the race [housing issues] are going to be on the agenda." In a similar way Jaime Regalado, executive director of the Pat Brown Institute for Public Affairs at Cal State Los Angeles, asserted that "workers' issues will get a full play ... whoever gets in."

41. Hochschild and Rogers, "Race Relations in a Diversifying Nation," at 20 (concluding that electoral coalitions between blacks and other nonwhite groups have been infrequent, and those that have formed have proved ephemeral and susceptible to disruption).

42. The Hahn coalition successfully exploited blacks' resentment of emerging demographic shifts and their fear of what Latino power might mean. See, for example, Todd Purdum, "Los Angeles Race Bares Racial Division," *New York Times*, June 10, 2001, at 18 NE+.

43. See also Hochschild and Rogers, "Race Relations in a Diversifying Nation" at 13 (describing how new immigrants may not interpret racially inflected encounters as blacks typically would, so their subsequent political response [or lack thereof] may seem weak to American eyes. Black leaders may be more attuned to the racial overtones of incidents than are immigrant leaders).

44. Cathy Schneider, memo to Gerald Torres, May 23,1997:

    I saw this very dearly in ... Brooklyn. For decades the Hasidic Jews and Puerto Ricans competed for public housing and other community resources. The positive conse-

quence for the Puerto Rican community was that it became one of the most organized Puerto Rican communities in the city. Through this organization they took
control of the local area policy board, won several lawsuits around public housing,
helped design a new Latino district, and elect[ed] Nydia Velazquez to the House.
The negative was that when the Republicans in the congress. Governor and Mayoral
offices began major cuts, the activist I interviewed observed "Nationalism still mobi-
lizes — 300 people showed up at the last town hall meeting, but there was no follow
up. Everyone screamed fight, fight, fight. After that, nothing." There was no effort to
organize residents against the privatization of social services, the cuts in basic health
care and welfare, the scarcity of or current assault on low-income housing.

45. Ignatiev, *How the Irish Became White* at 179.
46. Andrew Hacker, *Two Nations: Black and White, Separate, Hostile, Unequal* (1992).
47. Yen Le Espintu, *Asian American Panethnicity, Chang, Disoriented.*
48. Hochschild and Rogers, "Race Relations in a Diversifying Nation" at 13.15.
49. Jennifer Hochschild, "Madison's Constitution" at 18.
50. Aurelio Rojas's "Asian Americans Flex Political," *Bee Capitol Bureau,* May 22, 2001.
51. Hochschild and Rogers, "Race Relations" at 18–19 (noting that "Puerto Ricans [and other nonwhites] do not respond neatly" to a bipolar racial classification but "the notion of being a nonwhite group is a strong one" and, on this basis, there appear to be many areas of public policy consensus between large majorities of Puerto Ricans and blacks).
52. See Guinier and Torres, *The Miner's Canary,* chapter 3 at 67–74 (describing the development of a new college admissions strategy inspired by a Latino-led coalition of people of color that also benefited poor people generally, including rural whites).
53. Where such leadership is absent, the black/white binary often creates a wedge between blacks and Latinos rather than forging a bond. For example, in Providence, RI, Sharmah Kurland, "Brown Power vs. Black Power," 4 (1) *ColorLines* (Spring 2001) wrote that Gwen Andrade, a black political and community activist married to a Puerto Rican city council member, sees signs that many Latinos will respond to racism by more readily aligning with whites. –"In America the further away from black you get, the better,"says Andrade. "That's the perception that's been set up — it's the historical perspective of any group of people that has African roots. If you've got that African heritage that comes out in the skin color, or in the hair, you're fighting even harder to distance yourself from it because of what black means in this country." Ibid. at 20–21.
54. Hochschild and Rogers, "Race Relations" at 19.

Contributors

Michael W. Apple is John Bascom Professor of Curriculum and Instruction and Educational Policy Studies at the University of Wisconsin, Madison. Among his recent books are *Educating the "Right" Way: Markets, Standards, God, and Inequality* (RoutledgeFalmer, 2001) and *The State and the Politics of Knowledge* (RoutledgeFalmer, 2003).

Michael Billig is a professor of social sciences at Loughborough University, United Kingdom. Among his recent books are *Banal Nationalism* (Sage, 1995), *Freudian Repression* (Cambridge University Press, 1999), and *Rock 'n' Roll Jews* (Syracuse University Press, 2001).

Stacy Blake-Beard is an organizational psychologist. She has taught at the University of Michigan, Harvard University, and Simmons College. She is currently an associate professor at the Simmons School of Management and affiliated research faculty in the Center for Gender and Organizations. Dr. Blake-Beard has published widely on mentoring relationships, with a focus on how these relationships may be changing as a result of increasing workforce diversity.

Karen Brodkin is a professor of anthropology at UCLA and author of *Sisters and Wives: The Past and Future of Sexual Equality, Caring By the Hour: Women, Work and Organizing at Duke Medical Center, How Jews Became White Folks and What That Says About Race in America, My Troubles are Going to Have Trouble With Me: Everyday Trials and Triumphs of Women Workers*, as well as two documentary videos, *Fishing in the City* and *Let's Own It!*

April Burns is a doctoral student in social personality psychology at the City University of New York, Graduate Center. Her research focuses broadly on issues of privileged consciousness and social justice motivation.

Dennis Carlson is a professor of curriculum and cultural studies in the Department of Educational Leadership at Miami University, Oxford, Ohio. He is the author of *Making Progress: Education and Culture in New Times* (1997) and *Leaving Safe Harbors: Toward a New Progressivism in American Education and Public Life* (RoutledgeFalmer, 2002).

Sarah Carney is a graduate in social personality psychology at the City University of New York Graduate Center. Her dissertation is on media narratives about cases of failure to protect.

Craig Centrie is an assistant professor of foundations of education at Medaille College, Buffalo, New York. He is also executive director of El Museo Francisco Oller y Diego Rivera, a Latino art gallery in Buffalo, New York.

Faye J. Crosby is a social psychologist. She has taught at Rhode Island College, Yale University, Waterloo University, Smith College, Northwestern University, and for the past 6 years at the University of California, Santa Cruz. She publishes widely and has been the grateful recipient of many professional awards. Crosby's most recent book is *Affirmative Action Is Dead; Long Live Affirmative Action* (Yale University Press, 2004).

Ronald David, MD, Mdiv., is currently the staff chaplain for special ministries at the Children's National Medical Center in Washington, D.C. He continues to serve as adjunct lecturer in the Program for Senior Executives in State and Local Government at Harvard University's John F. Kennedy School of Government.

Maria De Jesus is a Canadian Portuguese Ph.D. candidate in developmental and educational psychology at Boston College. In March 2002, she went to Chiapas and stayed with a Zapatista community in one of the autonomous regions called Takiukum, where she learned more about the indigenous struggle for justice.

Mitchell Duneier is a Distinguished Professor of sociology at CUNY Graduate School and University Center. He is the author of *Sidewalk* (Farrar Straus & Giroux, 1999) and *Slim's Table: Race, Respectability, and Masculinity* (University of Chicago Press, 1994).

Michelle Fine is a Distinguished Professor of psychology at the Graduate Center, City University of New York. Her recent publications include *Working Method: Research and Social Justice* (with Lois Weis, Routledge, 2004), *Speedbumps: A Student Friendly Guide to Qualitative Research* (with Lois Weis, Teachers College Press, 2000), *The Unknown City: The Lives of Poor and Working Class Young Adults* (with Lois Weis, Beacon Press, 1998), and *Becoming Gentlemen* (with Lani Guinier and Jane Balin, Beacon Press, 1997).

Perry Gilmore, a sociolinguist and educational anthropologist, is professor emerita and affiliate faculty of Alaska native languages at the University of Alaska Fairbanks and associate professor of language, reading, and culture at the University of Arizona. She is the author of numerous ethnographic studies and the coeditor of two major ethnographic collections, *Children In and Out of School: Ethnography and Education* and *The Acquisition of Literacy: Ethnographic Perspectives*.

Lani Guinier is the Bennett Boskey Professor of Law at Harvard. Professor Guinier is the author of *Becoming Gentlemen: Women, Law Schools and Institutional Change* (with Michelle Fine and Jane Balin), *Who's Qualified* (with Susan Sturm), *Lift Every Voice: Turning a Civil Rights Set-back Into a New Vision of Social Justice*.

Jennifer Jellison Holme is a research associate on the UCLA-Teachers College, Columbia University. She received her Ed.M. at the Harvard Graduate School of Education and her Ph.D.

in educational policy studies at UCLA. Holme recently published "Buying Homes, Buying Schools: School Choice and the Social Construction of School Quality" in the *Harvard Educational Review* (Summer 2002).

Aída Hurtado is a professor of psychology at the University of California, Santa Cruz. Her most recent publications include *The Color of Privilege: Three Blasphemies on Race and Feminism* (Ann Arbor: University of Michigan Press, 1996), *Voicing Chicana Feminisms: Young Women Speak Out on Sexuality and Identity* (New York: New York University Press, 2003), *Chicana Feminisms: A Critical Reader* (coedited; Durham, NC: Duke University Press, 2003).

Aarti Iyer is a Ph.D. candidate in social psychology at the University of California, Santa Cruz. Her research addresses how people's psychological experiences of intergroup inequality lead to particular political attitudes and actions. Specifically, her work considers how members of structurally advantaged groups come to support, and participate in, strategies to achieve social equality.

James M. Jones is a professor of psychology at the University of Delaware and director of the Minority Fellowship Program at the American Psychological Association. A second edition of his classic book *Prejudice and Racism* has just been published by McGraw-Hill.

Apacuar Larry Kairaiuak is a Yup'ik and a fluent speaker, reader, and writer of Yup'ik language. He earned his B.A. in history from the University of Alaska Fairbanks in 1991. He and his two siblings were the first generation of college graduates from their small village, Chefornik, on the Bering Sea coast. Kairaiuak has worked as a program developer and counselor for the Native Student Services program at the University of Alaska. Currently he is the assistant project director for the Circle of Strength Project Healthy Nations Initiative in San Francisco.

Michael S. Kimmel is a professor of sociology at the State University of New York at Stony Brook. His books include *Manhood: A Cultural History* (1996) and *The Gendered Society* (2nd edition, 2003).

Sandra M. Lawrence is an associate professor of psychology and education at Mount Holyoke College. Some of her recent publications include, "Beyond Race Awareness: White Racial Identity and Multicultural Teaching" in the *Journal of Teacher Education*, and "Research, Writing, and Racial Identity: Cross-Disciplinary Connections for Multicultural Education" in *The Teacher Educator*.

Colin Wayne Leach is an associate professor of social psychology at the University of California, Santa Cruz. His research examines the phenomenology and politics of the status distinctions made in purportedly egalitarian societies like the United States, Western Europe, and Australia. He recently coedited two books, *Immigrant Life in the U.S.: Multi-disciplinary Perspectives* (Routledge, 2004) and *The Social Life of Emotions* (Cambridge, 2004).

Setha Low is a professor of environmental psychology and anthropology at the Graduate Center of the City University of New York and director of the Public Space Research Group. The reading is an edited excerpt from her book *Behind the Gates: Life, Security and the Pursuit of Happiness in Fortress America* (Routledge, 2003).

Helen Lucey is a lecturer in psychosocial studies in the psychology group at the Open University, United Kingdom.

M. Brinton Lykes, Ph.D., is a professor of community-social psychology at the Lynch School of Education at Boston College. She is coeditor of three books, and coauthor, with the Association of Maya Ixil Women — New Dawn, of *Voces e imágenes: Mujeres Mayas Ixiles de Chajul/Voices and images: Maya Ixil women of Chajul* (2000).

Pat Macpherson's publications include *Reflecting on Jane Eyre* and *Reflecting on The Bell Jar* for the Routledge series *Heroines?* With Michelle Fine she has coauthored three articles on adolescent girls, "Over Dinner," "Hungry for an Us," and "Insisting on Innocence." "The Revolution of Little Girls" is part of a work-in-progress on heterosexuality and film.

Matthew Mahler is a graduate student at the State University of New York at Stony Brook. His research interests include gender, masculinity, theory, and bodily practice and its connections to violence.

Cameron McCarthy teaches mass communications theory and cultural studies at the University of Illinois at Urbana-Champaign. Cameron is currently working on a new anthology, *Race, Identity and Representation, 2nd Edition* (RoutledgeFalmer, 2005) addressing the impact of globalization, particularly since 9/11, on racial formation and structuration in modern societies.

June Melody is a writer and trainee psychotherapist.

Jill G. Morawski is a professor of psychology and women's studies at Wesleyan University. She is author of *Practicing Feminisms, Reconstructing Psychology: Notes on a Liminal Science* (University of Michigan, 1994). She currently is studying the cultural politics of reproductive technologies and the history of laboratory practices in 20th-century American psychology.

Anne Pedersen is an applied social psychologist with a particular interest in cultural psychology. Her primary research interests revolve around racism (particularly toward Indigenous-Australians and asylum seekers) and its repercussions. Research interests include gender and health and antiracism strategies, as well as general equity issues.

Amira Proweller is an associate professor of educational foundations in the Department of Education, Policy Studies, and Research at DePaul University. She is the author of *Constructing Female Identities: Meaning-Making in an Upper Middle Class Youth Culture* (State University of New York Press, 1998).

Linda Powell Pruitt is an educator, psychotherapist, and organizational consultant. She is currently senior fellow at the Center for Leadership Development, Dialogue and Inquiry at the Wagner School of Public Service at New York University.

Anita Tijerina Revilla is a Ph.D. candidate at the UCLA, Graduate School of Education and Information Studies within the division of Social Sciences and Comparative Education and a research associate on the UCLA-Teachers College Understanding Race and Education Study. Her areas of expertise include Latina and Latino critical theory and critical race theory, and Chicana queer and feminist studies.

Pearl M. Rosenberg is an associate professor of education at Muhlenberg College in Allentown, Pennsylvania. Her research interests and professional activities include the social and psychological development of teachers; race, culture, class, and gender in education; and the role of the arts in human development.

David M. Smith (January 23, 1935-December 9, 2000), was professor emeritus of anthropology and linguistics at the University of Alaska Fairbanks and affiliate senior researcher at the Bureau of Applied Research in Anthropology at the University of Arizona. A visionary and leader in the fields of applied linguistics and anthropology and education, he left a profound legacy of deep commitment to social justice and educational equity through his research, writing, and teaching. While director of the Center for Urban Ethnography at the University of Pennsylvania, he started and for many years directed the University of Pennsylvania Ethnography and Education Forum.

Abigail J. Stewart is Agnes Inglis Collegiate Professor of psychology and women's studies at the University of Michigan. Dr. Stewart has published more than 100 scholarly articles and several books, focusing on the psychology of women's lives, personality, and adaptation to personal and social changes. Recent books include *Women's Untold Stories: Breaking Silence, Talking Back, Voicing Complexity* (1999, edited jointly with sociologist Mary Romero) and the second edition of *Theorizing Feminism: Parallel Trends in the Humanities and Social Sciences* (2000, coedited with Anne Herrmann).

Beverly Daniel Tatum is the president of Spelman College. She is the author of *Why Are All the Black Kids Sitting Together in the Cafeteria and Other Conversations About Race* and *Assimilation Blues: Black Families in a White Community*.

Gerald Torres is H.O. Head Centennial Professor in real property law at the University of Texas Law School. He has published numerous articles in law journals, contributing to *Critical Race Theory: The Cutting Edge* (Richard Delgado, ed., 1995), *The Politics of Law* (D. Kairys, ed., 1998), and *Borderless Borders: U.S. Latinos, Latin Americans, and the Paradox of Interdependence* (Frank Bonilla, Edwin Melendez, Rebecca Morales, and Maria de los Angeles Torres, eds., 1998).

France Winddance Twine teaches critical race studies and feminist studies at Duke University and the University of California, Santa Barbara. She is the author of *Racism in a Racial Democracy: The Maintenance of White Supremacy in Brazil*. Her forthcoming book, *A White Side of Blackness*, is an ethnography of racism and antiracism among white members of multiracial families in Britain.

Valerie Walkerdine is a professor of psychology in the Cardiff School of Social Sciences, University of Cardiff, United Kingdom, and Foundation Professor of psychology at the University of Western Sydney, Sydney, Australia.

Lois Weis is a professor in the Department of Educational Leadership and Policy at University of Buffalo. Her most recent books include *Silenced Voices and Extraordinary Conversations: Re-Imagining Schools* (with Michelle Fine, Teachers College Press, 2003) and *The Unknown City: The Lives of Poor and Working Class Young Adults* (with Michelle Fine, Beacon Press, 1998). Her new book, *Class Reunion: The Remaking of the American White Working Class*, will be released by Routledge in 2004.

Amy Stuart Wells is a professor of sociology and education at Teachers College, Columbia University. She is the author and editor of numerous books and articles, including the editor of *Where Charter School Policy Fails: The Problems of Accountability and Equity* (2002, Teachers College Press).

Howard Winant is a professor of sociology at the University of California, Santa Barbara. He is the author of *The World Is a Ghetto: Race and Democracy Since World War II* (Basic Books, 2001), as well as *Racial Conditions: Politics, Theory, Comparisons* (University of Minnesota Press, 1994) and *Racial Formation in the United States: From the 1960s to the 1990s* (with Michael Omi, Routledge, 1994).

Index

as site of abuse of multiracial children,
399–402
Scientific method, and impossibility of gender
neutrality, 316
Scientific racism, 18, 363
Scientists, historical conceptions of, 218–220
Second-generation human rights, 332–333, 341
Security guards, in gated communities, 37
Segregation
  in contemporary public schools, 288
  intensified by gated communities, 36
  in private vs. public life, 305
  in residential neighborhoods, 298
Selective system bias, 152–153
Self-focus, guilt as, 346–347
Self-fulfillment, via consumer goods, 104
Self-invention, by women in British labor market,
98
Self-reference, as methodological issue, 220
Self-segregation, in multiracial British families,
399–402
Self-transformation, in modern Britain, 105
Serviceman's Readjustment Act of 1944, 23
Sex, women's entitlement to, 181
Sex and the Single Girl, 175, 179
Sex differences, impossible neutrality of study of,
316
Sexist assumptions, in child neglect cases, 187
Sexual innocence, redefinitions in 1960s films,
177
Sexual politics, 179
Sexual revolution, and changing female roles,
175–184
Shaker Heights, Ohio, desegregated schools in,
285
Situated freedom, 280
Soap operas, suburban resentment echoed in, 164
Social aggression, 326
Social class
  in Britain since 1980, 98–111
  of observer as irrelevant, 219
  overcoming disadvantages of, 213
Social exclusion, of multiracial children, 400
Social graces, 320
Social inequality/difference, 108–109
Social isolation, in multiracial British families,
399–402

Social realities, in child neglect cases, 191
Social responsibility, in child neglect cases,
186–202
Social services, decline in inner city, 170
Social splitting, 35, 39–42, 45
  of self and other in white working-class males,
137
Social supports, and academic achievement, 251
Solidarity, 321
  as mechanism for maintaining white privilege,
320–321
South Africa, 335
  construction of apartheid in, 335
  struggle for just peace in, 332
Southern Europeans, racism against, 17–24
Speech tests, as instrument of racism, 21
Splendor in the Grass, 175
Standard track, 247–249
Standards-based education, 78
Standpoint, issues of, 316
State intervention, vs. color-blind ideology, 289
State-sponsored violence, 331, 334, 339–340
Stereotype vulnerability, 279–280
Stereotyping
  in Alaska Native students case, 279–280
  deep and persistent nature of, 154
Stewart, Abigail J., 315
Street book vendors, 206–214
Structural racial conflicts, 9
Style, relationship to class consciousness, 105–107
Subordinate groups, stigmatization of, 322
Subtextual racial politics, 7, 12
Suburban resentment, 163–173
Suburban schools, incidence of violence in,
117–118
Suburban security, discourse of, 168
Suburbanization, 26–29
  reinforcement of racial prejudice via, 43
Summer Place, A, 180
Sun Belt, location of gated communities in, 37
Superiority, 321
  as mechanism of maintaining privilege,
319–320
Supplementary schools, 399–402
Supreme Court
  outlaw of restrictive covenants by, 27